The Irreducibility of the Human Person

The Irreducibility of the Human Person A Catholic Synthesis

MARK K. SPENCER

 The Catholic University of America Press / Washington, D.C.

Copyright © 2022
The Catholic University of America Press
All rights reserved

Cataloging-in-Publication Data available from the Library of Congress
ISBN 978-0-8132-3520-2

For Mike
and
Dom Chrysostom Maria
in eternal friendship

Liebende, euch, ihr einander Genügten
frag ihr nach uns. Ihr geraft euch. Habt ihr Beweise?
Seht, mir geschiehts, daß meine Hände einander
inne werden oder daß mein gebrauchtes
Gesicht in ihnen sich schont. Das gibt mir ein wenig
Empfindung. Doch wer wagte darum schon zu sein?
Ihr aber, die ihr im Entzücken des andern
zunehmt, bis er euch überwältigt
anfleht: nich *mehr*—; die ihr unter den Händen
euch reichlicher werdet wie Traubenjahre;
die ihr manchmal vergeht, nur weil der andere
ganz uberhand nimmt: euch frag ich nach uns. Ich weiß
ihr berührt euch so selig, weil die Liebkosung verhält,
weil die Stelle nicht schwindet, die ihr, Zärtliche,
zudeckt; weil ihr darunter das reine
Dauern verspürt. So versprecht ihr euch Ewigkeit fast
von der Umarmung.

Rainer Maria Rilke

Contents

Acknowledgments xi / Abbreviations xiii

Introduction. Methodologies for Investigating the Irreducible Human Person   1

Part 1. The Irreducible Powers of the Human Person

1. Subjectivity and the Principles of Hylomorphism   41
2. Bodily Powers and the Principles of Sensible Being   75
3. Intellect and the Principles of Real Being   112
4. Will and the Principles of Freedom   165
5. Affectivity and the Principles of Value   199
6. Soul, Powers, and the Principle of *Energeia*   241

Part 2. A Portrait of Irreducible, Beautiful, Liturgical Persons

7. The Transcendence of the Soul and the Principles of Personhood   291
8. The Multiplicity of the Human Substance and the Principles of *Status*   334
9. The Incarnation of Souls and Persons and the Principle of *Prosopon*   359

Bibliography 391 / Index 427

Acknowledgments

I have been thinking about some of this book's themes since I became interested in philosophy in high school, and I thank everyone who influenced my thinking, especially my mentors at Franciscan University of Steubenville and the University at Buffalo: Richard Cohen, John F. Crosby, David Hershenov, Jorge J. E. Gracia, Stephen Lewis, Regis Martin, Mark Roberts, J. J. Sanford, John White, and Neil Williams. Many ideas in this book were developed in earlier works of mine published in *American Catholic Philosophical Quarterly*, *Angelicum*, *The Heythrop Journal*, *International Philosophical Quarterly*, *Journal of Analytic Theology*, *New Blackfriars*, *Nova et Vetera*, *Proceedings of the American Catholic Philosophical Association*, *Res Philosophica*, *Review of Metaphysics*, *The St. Anselm Journal*, *Studia Neoaristotelica*, *The Thomist*, and *Tópicos*. Where ideas are drawn from papers of mine, acknowledgment appears in a footnote. I thank the editors of these journals for permission to re-present those ideas here. Thanks also to David Lampo, who copyedited this book, and to John Martino (who first encouraged me to write this book), as well as to Theresa Walker, Brian Roach, and the other editors at the Catholic University of America Press.

My deepest gratitude goes to Matthews Grant, Jim Hanink, Mirela Oliva, Mike Sauter, Susanna Spencer, and two anonymous referees who commented on this entire text, and to David Bradshaw, Therese Cory, Tim Pawl, Fr. Philip Neri Reese, and Bill Tullius, who commented on particular chapters. For conversation and correspondence that helped this book, I thank: Billy Abraham, Nieves Gómez Álvarez, Gary Atkinson, Fred Aquino, Tomas Bogardus, John Boyle, Fr. James Brent, Fr. Stephen Brock, Chris

Brown, Monte Brown, Rocco Buttiglione, Martin Cajthaml, Mariano Crespo, John Henry Crosby, Richard Cross, Daniel De Haan, Trent Dougherty, Barb Dugan, Jason Eberl, Maria Fedoryka, Francis Feingold, Lawrence Feingold, Marsha Feingold, John Finley, Tony Flood, Gloria Frost, Paul Gavrilyuk, Marie George, Michael Gorman, Rabbi Mark Gottlieb, Dom Chrysostom Maria Gryniewicz, Christopher Haley, Aaron Harburg, Stephen Hipp, Dick Imgrund, John Joy, Billy Junker, Erika Kidd, Fr. Matthew Kirby, Matthew Levering, Steven Long, Mathew Lu, Rachel Lu, Sarah Maple, Mark McInroy, Kevin McMahon, Rob McNamara, Pater Rupert Meyer, Turner Nevitt, David Oderberg, Mirela Oliva, Seamus O'Neill, Bob Pasnau, Faith Pawl, Sydney Penner, Eric Perl, Joel Potter, Alex Pruss, Alice Ramos, Sam Rocha, Miguel Romero, Mike Rota, Josef Seifert, Dan Sheffler, James Spencer, Jamie Spiering, Eleonore Stump, Josh Taccolini, Adam Taylor, Allison Thornton, Kevin Timpe, Patrick Toner, Joe Trabbic, Michael Waldstein, Susie Waldstein, Christian Washburn, Fr. Alfred Wierzbicki, and Michael Wiitala. Finally, I am deeply grateful to my children, Gemma, Lucy, Felicity, and Thomas, and especially to my wife, Susanna, for their love, support, and patience while I wrote this book, and above all for showing me the irreducibility and beauty of human persons.

Abbreviations

Albert
> *In Sent.*   *Commentarii in Sententiarum*

Aristotle
> *DA*   *De anima*
> *EE*   *Eudemian Ethics*
> *HA*   *History of Animals*
> *Met.*   *Metaphysics*
> *OS*   *On Sleep*
> *PA*   *Parts of Animals*
> *Phys.*   *Physics*
> *Pol.*   *Politics*
> *Post. An.*   *Posterior Analytics*
> *NE*   *Nicomachean Ethics*

Bonaventure
> *In Sent.*   *Commentaria in quatuor libros Sententiarum*
> *RAT*   *Reductione atrium ad theologiam*
> *QDSC*   *Quaestiones disputatae de scientia Christi*

Thomas Cajetan
> *In ST*   *Commentaria in summa theologiae*
> *DNA*   *De nominium analogia*

Abbreviations

John Duns Scotus

Ord.	Ordinatio
QM	Quaestiones super libros metaphysicorum
Rep.	Reportata Parisiensia

Thomas Aquinas

CT	Compendium theologiae
DEE	De ente et essentia
DMC	De motu cordis
DME	De mixtione elementorum
DOO	De operantibus occultis
DP	Quaestiones disputatae de potentia Dei
DPN	De principiis naturae
DSS	De substantiis separatis
DV	Quaestiones disputatae de veritate
In 1 Cor.	Super I Epistolam Beati Pauli ad Corinthios lectura
In Col.	Super Epistolam Beati Pauli ad Colossenses lectura
In DA	Sentencia libri De anima
In DCM	In libros Aristotelis De caelo et mundo exposition
In DDN	In librum Beati Dionysii De divinis nominibus expositio
In De Heb.	Expositio libri Boetii De hebdomadibus
In De Trin.	Super Boetium De Trinitate
In DMR	Sentencia libri De memoria et reminiscencia
In DSS	Sentencia libri De sensu et sensato
In Gal.	Super Epistolam Beati Pauli ad Galatas lectura
In LDC	Super Librum de causis expositio
In Is.	Expositio super Isaiam ad litteram
In Jn.	Super Evangelium Sancti Ioannis lectura
In Met.	Sententia libri Metaphysicae
In NE	Sententia libri Ethicorum
In PH	Expositio libri Peri hermeneias
In Phys.	Commentaria in octo libros Physicorum
In Post. An.	Expositio libri Posteriorum Analyticorum
In Ps.	In psalmos Davidis expositio
In SA	Expositio in Symbolum Apostolorum
In Sent.	Scriptum super Sententiis

QDA	Quaestio disputata de anima
QDSC	Quaestio disputata de spiritualibus creaturis
QDUV	Quaestio disputata de unione Verbi incarnati
QQ	Quaestiones de quolibet
SCG	Summa contra gentiles
ST	Summa theologiae

Francisco Suárez

In DA	Commentaria una cum quaestionibus in libros Aristotelis De anima
DM	Disputationes metaphysicae

Hans Urs von Balthasar

E	Epilogue
GL1	*The Glory of the Lord*, Volume 1: *Seeing the Form*
GL2	*The Glory of the Lord*, Volume 2: *Studies in Theological Style: Clerical Styles*
GL3	*The Glory of the Lord*, Volume 3: *Studies in Theological Style: Lay Styles*
GL4	*The Glory of the Lord*, Volume 4: *The Realm of Metaphysics in Antiquity*
GL5	*The Glory of the Lord*, Volume 5: *The Realm of Metaphysics in the Modern Age*
GL6	*The Glory of the Lord*, Volume 6: *Theology: The Old Covenant*
GL7	*The Glory of the Lord*, Volume 7: *Theology: The New Covenant*
TD1	*Theo-Drama*, Volume 1: *Prolegomena*
TD2	*Theo-Drama*, Volume 2: *The Dramatis Personae: Man in God*
TD3	*Theo-Drama*, Volume 3: *The Dramatis Personae: The Person in Christ*
TD4	*Theo-Drama*, Volume 4: *The Action*
TD5	*Theo-Drama*, Volume 5: *The Last Act*
TL1	*Theo-Logic*, Volume 1: *Truth of the World*
TL2	*Theo-Logic*, Volume 2: *Truth of God*
TL3	*Theo-Logic*, Volume 3: *The Spirit of Truth*

The Irreducibility of the Human Person

Introduction Methodologies for Investigating the Irreducible Human Person

This book is an expression of two convictions. First, we human persons are *irreducible* to anything nonpersonal, and we contain many parts and principles that are irreducible to one another. To *reduce* one thing to another is to hold that the former is *nothing but* the latter, and to judge that the latter is what actually exists (or has value), rather than the former.[1] My first and primary conviction is that I am not *nothing but* an animal, an immaterial thinking thing, a collection of atoms, an isolated individual, a part of society, or anything other than a whole human person. This *first conviction* is summed up in Thomas Aquinas's claim that "'person'"—by which I mean what each of us fundamentally and holistically is— "signifies that which is most perfect," most complete and actual, "in all of nature."[2]

In expressing this conviction, I aim to overcome two problems in the Catholic tradition of philosophical and theological anthropology. The *first problem* is that this tradition tends toward certain reductionisms about human persons, despite its opposition to materialist, dualist, and idealist reductionisms, which say that we are nothing but matter or mind. Latent reductionisms in the Catholic tradition include tendencies to see human persons as only substances or relations, to hold that our acts are ultimately explicable by God's causality, and to hold that we are entirely explainable by principles like essence, existence, substance, accident, form, or matter.

---

1. Jorge J. E. Gracia, *Metaphysics and Its Task: The Search for the Categorial Foundation of Knowledge* (Albany: State University of New York Press, 1999), 166–68.
2. Aquinas, *ST* I, q.29, a.3.

Introduction

In each case, we are reduced to some principle distinct from whole persons. To overcome this first problem, I present in this work a comprehensive philosophical portrait of the human person, which builds on Catholic anthropological traditions, but removes their latent reductionisms.

The *second problem* is a tendency among Catholic philosophers to sunder strands of the anthropological tradition that focus on *experience* (such as phenomenology and personalism) from those that focus on *objective principles* (such as Thomism and Scotism). Members of these schools frequently engage in unnecessary polemics against one another. Describing this second problem, therefore, requires defining a few terms. By "experience," I mean not only subjective or conscious acts and passions but also everything given through acts and passions. By "perception," I mean any experience—sensory, intellectual, affective, or otherwise—in which I directly grasp or am given some being or object, but perceptions are different from those experiences in which I grasp something only by means of directly cognizing something else, such as a sign, concept, proposition, or inference. "The given" indicates anything that appears experientially in any way; this phrase is not restricted, for example, to sense data.[3] Something is *objective* when it can be grasped, defined, or described from a third-person point of view; something is *subjective* when it can only be grasped from a first-person point of view.[4] (I use first-person pronouns when describing experiences. Each reader should check my descriptions against his or her experience.) "Principle" refers to any real cause or explanatory feature of a thing, or to a proposition that explains a thing or is a starting point for reasoning. "Objective principles" are causes or explanatory features that can be defined or described from the third-person point of view, including those posited by scholastics like form and matter.

Philosophers who focus on experience (like phenomenologists) tend to think that we grasp what is irreducible about ourselves by setting aside thoughts about objective principles and focusing on how we are directly given to ourselves. Details on this and other methodologies will be presented later in this introduction and in chapter 1. On such views, to attend to what is directly given *just is* to attend to what fundamentally is. The

---

3. See Sameer Yadav, *The Problem of Perception and The Experience of God* (Minneapolis, Minn.: Fortress Press, 2016), chap. 4, drawing on John McDowell, *Mind and World* (Cambridge, Mass.: Harvard University Press, 1996).

4. John Searle, *Mind, Language, and Society: Philosophy in the Real World* (New York: Basic Books, 1999), 44–45.

given is perceived in itself, such that we directly grasp that the given cannot be *nothing but* something other than itself—that is, we directly grasp its irreducibility to anything other than itself.[5] To turn, via abstraction or inference, from what is directly given to underlying objective principles (as scholasticism does) is to turn away from what is directly given—and so to miss what is irreducible about us. Some experiential philosophers accuse objective-principle views of reducing persons to what can be fitted into a conceptual system, overlooking aspects of persons that cannot be so considered such as subjective interiority. We must use a method that, in the words of Karol Wojtyła (Pope John Paul II), "pauses at the irreducible," at how we are each subjectively, uniquely given to ourselves, in a way that exceeds objective description.[6]

By contrast, Catholic philosophers who focus on objective principles (like scholastics) hold that to understand our irreducibility, we must grasp *what it is to be a person* and *what human nature is*. Doing so requires abstraction and reasoning in an effect-to-cause manner from how we appear in experience to what we fundamentally are in order to appear in that way. We grasp our irreducibility by reasoning about what best explains our acts (especially acts distinctive of persons, like intellectual and volitional acts), and arguing against metaphysics that fail to adequately explain those acts. These philosophers often regard experience-based approaches to be subjectivistic and idealist, denying our reality or caring only for how we appear. They claim that these approaches reach their conclusions through mere appeals to intuitions or idiosyncratic experiences, without explaining those experiences through principles that belong to all persons.[7]

But I argue that these strands of the Catholic tradition actually com-

---

5. On this methodology, see Edmund Husserl, *Logical Investigations*, vol. 1, trans. J. N. Findlay (London: Routledge, 2001), especially 165–72; Max Scheler, "The Theory of the Three Facts," in *Selected Philosophical Essays*, trans. David Lachterman (Evanston, Ill.: Northwestern University Press, 1973), 202–4, 219–23, 231–38; Josef Seifert, *Back to Things in Themselves* (New York: Routledge and Kegan Paul, 1987), 80–86, 236–50; Robert Sokolowski, *Husserlian Meditations: How Words Present Things* (Evanston, Ill.: Northwestern University Press, 1974), 235–70; and Dietrich von Hildebrand, *What Is Philosophy?* (Steubenville, Ohio: Hildebrand Press, 2021), 205–8.

6. Karol Wojtyła, "Subjectivity and the Irreducible in the Human Being," in *Person and Community: Selected Essays*, trans. Theresa Sandok (New York: Peter Lang, 1993), 210–11. Cf. Dietrich von Hildebrand, *Ethics* (Steubenville, Ohio: Hildebrand Press, 2020), 32–35, 56, 195–200; Jean-Luc Marion, *In Excess: Studies of Saturated Phenomena*, trans. Robyn Horner and Vincent Berraud (New York: Fordham University Press, 2004), 1–29.

7. See, for example, Jacques Maritain, *The Degrees of Knowledge*, trans. Gerald B. Phelan (Notre Dame, Ind.: University of Notre Dame Press, 1995), 107–18; Michael Waldstein, "Dietrich von Hildebrand and St. Thomas Aquinas on Goodness and Happiness," *Nova et Vetera* (English edition) 1, no. 2 (2003): 403–64; and Roger Scruton, *Sexual Desire: A Philosophical Investigation* (London: Continuum, 2006), 364–76.

plement one another. Each provides evidence for aspects of our irreducibility that the other does not adequately consider. Each can corroborate the other's claims with evidence that the other does not consider. By opposing one another, these strands of the tradition undermine their own respective goals of defending the irreducibility of the human person. Not only do I argue that each strand can bolster the other, but I contend that recent Catholic tradition has devised a method of reasoning that allows a synthesis of these two strands. This is an *aesthetic method*, on which language about *beauty* is the most apt language for expressing the irreducible holism of every being. Aesthetics uses arguments and concepts as guides for perceiving beings as holistic unities, which are irreducible to anything grasped in partial experiences or through abstract principles. My ultimate conclusion in this book is that, while experiential and objective-principle methods reveal irreducible features of human persons, we fully grasp our irreducibility only in perceiving our holistic *beauty*, that is, in any experience of beauty, we grasp the beautiful object as a whole. Beauty simultaneously awakens our senses and our feelings, and it also appeals to our intellects, inviting deeper causal and explanatory thought about beauty, and it calls us to choose to change our lives in response to it.[8] We can unpack aspects of this experience by describing each of these partial experiences of beauty and the ways in which they fit together, as a phenomenologist would do. We can explain other aspects of this experience by positing objective principles and giving an account of how they fit together, as a scholastic would do. But we only fully grasp the beautiful being in holistic perception, which includes but also exceeds what is grasped through those two partial methods.[9] The beautiful exceeds in its splendor and holism anything that could be captured in concepts, propositions, or objective or phenomenological analysis. What is described by experientially focused and objectively focused philosophers are just aspects or partial manifestations of a single, underlying, beautiful whole.

I argue that the best language the Catholic tradition has to describe our full, holistic irreducibility is the language of beauty and of aesthetics. In making this claim, I build on recent Catholic thinkers who hold that

---

8. Consider Rainer Maria Rilke's poem "Archaïscher Torso Apollos": "denn da is keine Stelle,/die dich nicht sieht. Du mußt dein Leben ändern."

9. Natalie Carnes describes how beauty always involves both aspects of a being fitting together and gratuity, which I call excess; see *Beauty: A Theological Engagement with Gregory of Nyssa* (Eugene, Ore.: Cascade Books, 2014), 43–45.

beauty has a central role in understanding being in general and human persons in particular. While beauty has taken on a central role in Catholic anthropology only over the last century, these approaches are rooted in ancient Greek metaphysics of the *kalon* and medieval Latin metaphysics of the *pulchrum*, *honestum*, and *conveniens*.[10] These approaches include scholastics (like Piotr Jaroszyński), realist phenomenologists (like Dietrich von Hildebrand), nonrealist phenomenologists (like Jean-Luc Marion), nonphenomenological continental philosophers (like William Desmond), and analytic philosophers (like Roger Scruton). Above all, I draw on Hans Urs von Balthasar, who most fully developed the aesthetic method.[11] In inquiring into fundamental things like the nature of being and the Person of Jesus Christ, he proposed a method of seeing these things as beautiful wholes (*Gestalt*), on which we allow beauties to manifest themselves to us and allow their self-manifestation to guide our inquiry into them. We treat what we grasp through other methods as partial manifestations of beautiful wholes. When we perceive beauties holistically, we see how the partial manifestations fit together.

I apply Balthasar's method to the human person, using results from experiential and objective-principle views to build up a holistic portrait of the beautiful human person. This portrait is a guide for perceiving the fully irreducible human person as a whole, since it is only by perception that we can fully grasp our irreducibility. My synthesized portrait is also a metaphysics of the human person. By "metaphysics," I mean, following contemporary usage, a philosophical inquiry into what is fundamental about something, including much of what was covered in traditional philosophy of nature (an inquiry into mobile, sensible being).[12] I do not limit metaphysics to an account (like Thomas Aquinas) of being or the immaterial as such, or (like Bernard Lonergan) of reality as proportioned to reason, or (like Theodore Sider) of the necessary structure of all possible realities.[13]

---

10. On ancient and medieval aesthetic terms, see Oleg Bychkov, *Aesthetic Revelation: Reading Ancient and Medieval Texts after Hans Urs von Balthasar* (Washington, D.C.: The Catholic University of America Press, 2010), part 2.

11. Piotr Jaroszyński, *Beauty and Being: Thomistic Perspectives*, trans. Hugh MacDonald (Toronto: Pontifical Institute of Medieval Studies, 2011); Dietrich von Hildebrand, *Aesthetics*, vol. 1, trans. Brian McNeil (Steubenville, Ohio: Hildebrand Project, 2016); Marion, *In Excess*; Jean-Luc Marion, *In the Self's Place*, trans. Jeffrey Kosky (Stanford, Calif.: Stanford University Press, 2012); William Desmond, *The Gift of Beauty and the Passion of Being* (Eugene, Ore.: Cascade Books, 2018); Scruton, *Sexual Desire*; and Balthasar, *GL1*.

12. E. J. Lowe, *A Survey of Metaphysics* (Oxford: Oxford University Press, 2002), 14.

13. Aquinas, *In De Trin.*, q.6, a.1; *In DMR*, lect. 2; *In I Phys.*, lect. 1; *In I Met.*, lects. 1, 3; *ST* I, q.85, a.1,

Metaphysics, as I conceive it, is open to grasping anything fundamental. My metaphysical portrait synthesizes the findings of metaphysical methods like those just mentioned with other metaphysics, other methods of inquiry into what is fundamental. For example, metaphysics includes Jean-Luc Marion's approach, on which the givenness of phenomena is more fundamental than being.[14] The metaphysics in my portrait of the person aims to fully express and describe what existentialist Miguel de Unamuno calls the "concrete" human person, who exists prior to and in excess of all rational theorizing.[15]

This brings us to the *second guiding conviction* of this book: we can best grasp our irreducibility, the "whole truth about man,"[16] if we synthesize many antireductionistic approaches while removing their reductionistic tendencies. Most of the approaches that I synthesize are found in the broadly Catholic tradition, that is, in thinkers who were in communion with the Catholic Church, or with other sacramental, tradition-based churches. These include varieties of scholasticism like Thomism, Scotism, and Suárezianism; approaches stemming from Greek Fathers like Gregory of Nyssa and medieval Greek thinkers like Gregory Palamas; and contemporary movements like personalism, realist phenomenology, and the *Nouvelle théologie*. I also draw on approaches overlapping with this tradition, including strands of phenomenology, continental philosophy, analytic philosophy, and classical Platonism and Aristotelianism. Each approach reveals irreducible aspects of persons that are overlooked or denied by others; we need to grasp each principle or experience posited by each if we are to not only know that persons are irreducible but to also directly, fully experience ourselves that way. We cannot perceive the full truth about or beauty of the human person if we rely just on our own experience; we must let ourselves be drawn into the experiences portrayed in classic texts.[17]

This book is not primarily addressed to reductionists, that is, to those who affirm that the human person is entirely reducible to something nonpersonal. While at times I give arguments and evidence in support of the

---

ad 2; Bernard Lonergan, *Insight: A Study of Human Understanding* (Toronto: University of Toronto Press, 1992), 418–26; and Theodore Sider, *Four-Dimensionalism: An Ontology of Persistence and Time* (Oxford: Oxford University Press, 2002), introduction.

14. Marion, *Negative Certainties*, 103–14.

15. Miguel de Unamuno, *Tragic Sense of Life*, trans. J. E. Crawford Flitch (New York: Dover, 1954), 1–8.

16. John Paul II, *Redemptor hominis*, Encyclical Letter (March 4, 1979), 12.

17. David Tracy, *The Analogical Imagination: Christian Theology and the Culture of Pluralism* (New York: Crossroad, 1981), chap. 3.

basic claim that we are irreducible to anything nonpersonal, this book is mainly intended for those who already share that conviction. There is plenty of recent literature defending the irreducibility of the human person against reductionistic versions of dualism, materialism, and idealism.[18] There is no need for me to repeat that work; rather, I presuppose and build on it. My goal is to portray the human person on the assumption that we are as irreducible as possible, that each strand of the Catholic tradition reveals ways that we are irreducible, and that all these truths are synthesizable. My portrait is meant to help philosophers in each school see how their theories can be synthesized by providing a systematic framework for relating those schools to one another.

Throughout this book, I also offer new, synthesizing solutions to conflicts in the Catholic tradition, including the *de auxiliis* controversy over how God's grace aids us, conflicts over relations between nature and grace, the debate between new and traditional natural law theorists, the debate in political philosophy between integralists and personalists, debates among phenomenologists as to whether anything transcendent to experience is revealed in experience, the debate over the personhood of the separated soul, and debates between Western and Eastern theologians over the nature of divinization. I use "divinization" to denote the process of human persons coming to participate more deeply in God; this term is meant to be equivalent to terms like "deification" and "*theosis*" that are often used in literature on the topic.[19] My approach is philosophical, based on what can be experienced and known apart from appeal to special divine revelation. It is also a Catholic approach, however, so I sometimes incorporate claims based on revelation; perceiving our irreducibility requires considering how we are created in the image of God, in relation to Christ, and for the sake of liturgy and divinization. But I do not argue for interpretations of revelation; rather, I draw on others' theological work insofar as it helps us perceive the irreducible human person. My use of revelation and theology within a largely philosophical book is related to the twentieth-century "Christian philosophy" controversy over whether philosophy is

---

18. See, for example, David Braine, *The Human Person: Animal and Spirit* (Notre Dame, Ind.: University of Notre Dame Press, 1992); Edward Feser, *Philosophy of Mind* (Oxford: Oneworld, 2005); and James Madden, *Mind, Matter, and Nature: A Thomistic Proposal for the Philosophy of Mind* (Washington, D.C.: The Catholic University of America Press, 2013).

19. For the history of this terminology, see Norman Russell, *The Doctrine of Deification in the Greek Patristic Tradition* (Oxford: Oxford University Press, 2004).

transformed by its contact with Christian revelation.[20] I do not wish to stipulate anything *a priori* as to the relation between philosophy and theology, though I affirm that we can philosophize about what is revealed and that we can do philosophy on purely natural grounds. My philosophical approach also has implicit theological content even from the outset. For example, although "person" originates in Roman legal codes and in the masks of the Greek and Roman theater, it has a history marked by Trinitarian and Christological theology.

What I offer here is one way that traditions can be synthesized, and conflicts overcome. Other syntheses are likely possible. I simply want to show that traditions can be coherently synthesized, and that the resulting metaphysical portrait of the human person guides us to perceive our irreducibility better than each tradition taken on its own. To accomplish this goal, I need to propose a coherent synthesis of different traditions' claims, not consider all possible alternative syntheses or objections to such a synthesis. In my synthesis, I endorse many claims about what we irreducibly are. I argue, for example, that we are naturally both soul and body, but can exist without bodies.[21] I contend that we have self-transcending intellectual, volitional, and affective powers, and that we are open to grasping all being and to being divinized.[22] I show that we are made in the image of God and of the cosmos, that we cannot be adequately objectively defined, and that we are fully grasped only perceptually and aesthetically, especially through our experience of liturgy.[23] I draw on a significant range of theories because I am convinced that they all reveal truths about what we are. If in the spirit of St. Thérèse of Lisieux, "I choose all," where theories of the person and of experience are concerned,[24] it is because, along with Terence, I say that "nothing human is alien to me."

---

20. Jacques Maritain, *An Essay on Christian Philosophy*, trans. Edward Flannery (New York: Philosophical Library, 1955); Edith Stein, *Finite and Eternal Being*, trans. Kurt Reinhardt (Washington, D.C.: ICS Publications, 2002), 22; and Gregory Sadler, *Reason Fulfilled by Revelation: The 1930s Christian Philosophy Debates in France* (Washington, D.C.: The Catholic University of America Press, 2003).

21. See, for example, David Oderberg, *Real Essentialism* (New York: Routledge, 2007), 241–60; Eleonore Stump, "Non-Cartesian Substance Dualism and Materialism Without Reductionism," *Faith and Philosophy* 12, no. 4 (1995): 505–31.

22. Dietrich von Hildebrand, *The Heart: An Analysis of Human and Divine Affectivity* (South Bend, Ind.: St. Augustine's Press, 2007), 21; Norris Clarke, *Person and Being* (Milwaukee, Wisc.: Marquette University Press, 1993), 32–34, 40–41.

23. Jean-Luc Marion, *Negative Certainties*, trans. Stephen Lewis (Chicago: University of Chicago Press, 2015), 37–38; Paul Griffiths, *Decreation: The Last Things of All Creatures* (Waco, Tex.: Baylor University Press, 2014); and Catherine Pickstock, *After Writing: On the Liturgical Consummation of Philosophy* (Oxford: Blackwell, 1998).

24. Thérèse of Lisieux, *The Story of a Soul*, trans. Robert J. Edmondson (Brewster, Mass.: Paraclete Press, 2006), 19.

Introduction   9

In each section, my method is to begin with a description of a basic experience (such as sensing, thinking about essences, making choices, or falling in love) from the Catholic tradition. I then show which of our features, as described by various Catholic metaphysics, it reveals. This requires a discussion not just of the metaphysics of persons but of more general metaphysical principles; hence, I offer metaphysics of items like form, matter, existence, value, relations, and substance in themselves (where "item" designates any being, principle, or feature without indicating its metaphysical status[25]). By moving between experiential and objective-principle approaches, and synthesizing them using the aesthetic method, I build up my portrait of the person. A *precis* of the chapters of this book appears at the end of this introduction, but first I more fully explain my goals and methods, by responding to four possible objections to my thesis.

Methodological Objections and Replies

Objection One. A philosopher who focuses on objective principles might object to the fact that I base my arguments on descriptions of experiences. On the one hand, readers who have had an experience as I describe it likely already agree with that description and so already subscribe to the views about irreducibility that I defend on its basis. On the other hand, readers who have not had those experiences will be unable to follow the argument. Its premises (the description of experience on which it is based) will seem false or arbitrarily asserted, and those readers will have no grounds for accepting the view about our irreducibility that I claim follows from that description. My style of argumentation seems a useless enterprise. It would be better to start with universally applicable, objective, explanatory principles, and reason to an account of our irreducibility on that basis.

Reply to Objection One. Even if I grant that only those who have accepted a description of experience can accept the resulting argument, it does not follow that such an argument is useless. One who has had a certain experience or accepted a description of it has not necessarily considered everything revealed by that experience. It is still worthwhile to consider arguments about what conclusions are supported by one's experience. Furthermore, although by Part Two of this book I argue that our irreducibility

---

25. Daniel Novotný, *Beings of Reason: A Study in the Scholasticism of the Baroque Era* (PhD diss., University at Buffalo, 2008), 9.

can be fully grasped only perceptually, we attain this perception only when guided by the right concepts, principles, and arguments. But not every argument is convincing to every person, and not every philosophical school appeals to every person. It is worthwhile to both make arguments and appeal to the claims of experience-based schools of thought, to lead more people to a fuller appreciation of the whole truth about human persons.

But I need not grant that only those who have already accepted a description of experience can accept arguments based on that description. One function of a phenomenological description, as Dietrich von Hildebrand noted, is to guide people to have the experience it describes for the first time, or to discover it in their own past experience. Such a description is meant to put people in "existential, immediate, intuitive contact" with the given.[26] One must verify descriptions that I give by checking them against one's experience and that of others. The experiences that I present as evidence for our irreducibility are not idiosyncratic or rare; they are ordinary bodily, cognitive, affective, volitional, and perceptual experiences. One can easily verify the descriptions I give, and since I draw my descriptions from other philosophers, one can look to those longer descriptions for more complete evidence.

Furthermore, there are certain irreducible features of the human person that we grasp best (or even only) through certain experiences. These include falling in love with another human person, reflecting on subjective self-awareness, being recollected, sensing our own bodies, and seeing the beauty of ourselves and others. In these experiences, we are directly presented with an irreducible unity of content, which cannot be adequately grasped in any other way. In them, we immediately perceive a way in which reality is, which any subsequent argument will have to take as given, and which cannot be explained away, that is, reduced to something else.

An example of an immediately given, irreducible unity of content is a self-evident (or *per se nota*) proposition, like the principle of noncontradiction. Once one grasps this principle's terms and their interrelations, one just sees that it is true, without needing further proof.[27] (Directly grasping objective principles—that is, experiencing them as directly given—is an experience in which philosophical approaches based on experience of the given and approaches based on objective principles come together.) In this

---

26. Hildebrand, *What Is Philosophy?* 206.
27. Aquinas, *ST* I, q.2, a.1.

book, I contend that some irreducible features of the human person can similarly be just seen directly. For example, in seeing the holistic beauty of a beloved person, one just sees that he or she exceeds any possible objective description of him or her. To give as complete a portrait of irreducible persons as I can, I must consider experiences like these.

The objector might respond that some thinkers do not perceive each purported given; different strands of Catholic tradition take different principles and aspects of reality to be directly given. This is illustrated by a contrast between some scholastic and phenomenological claims.

Many scholastics hold that *being* (*ens*) is the most fundamentally given concept: whatever we grasp, we grasp as a kind of being—that is, as actual, having stable identity and perfection, identical to itself, and so forth. Being given any other concept presupposes that we have been directly given the concept of being. Because they hold that the notion of being is given to the mind in any intellectual act, scholastics like Aquinas also take the principle of noncontradiction, which is an analysis of the immediately given notion of being, to also be self-evidently given as universally applicable. Once we grasp being and its self-identity, we grasp that it cannot simultaneously both be and not be.[28]

Some phenomenologists, like Jean-Luc Marion, deny this. Marion holds that *givenness* is the most fundamentally, directly given notion—that is, whatever we grasp, we grasp as a kind of given. But givenness has a wider extension than being. For example, *nothingness* and *events* are grasped as givens, but not as beings, that is, as stably existing things. Because he holds that givenness is more fundamental than being, Marion denies that the principle of noncontradiction is universally applicable. Just as the fundamental scholastic principle is an analysis of the fundamental scholastic concept, so Marion's fundamental principle is an analysis of the notion of givenness: phenomena first appear by giving themselves away. To *be given* is to simultaneously appear and abandon oneself, to simultaneously be (since we can grasp what is given) and not be (since the given as such only appears in its passing away and always contains more or other than what is grasped); to be given is to lack stable being and conceptualizable identity with oneself. The given appears but does not fall under the principle of noncontradiction.[29]

The objector might conclude that no experience could just show that

---

28. Aquinas, *DV*, q.1, a.1; *ST* I-II, q.94, a.2.
29. Marion, *In Excess*, chap. 1; *Negative Certainties*, 104–10.

an aspect of our irreducibility is directly given, since any experience that purports to do so can be challenged by a tradition that takes something else to be directly given. Different strands of the tradition seem to differ not just in descriptions of experience but in standards of rationality and of philosophical analysis. Reasoning about irreducibility, one might contend, must begin with one tradition's principles and standards of reasoning, not with descriptions of the given or experience.

I respond that my aim in this book is to synthesize the findings and methods of as many strands of Catholic tradition as possible. Given this aim, it would be inadmissible to start with the principles of just one tradition. I can bring them together not by favoring one tradition but by turning to the source of all traditions' claims and the starting point for all reasoning, *experience itself*. Apparently incompatible principles and descriptions of givens can be at least partially reconciled by seeing how each arises out of and reveals experiences. Each theory's claims can be understood, in accord with aesthetic method, as partial manifestations of a holistic *Gestalt*. My working assumption is that each tradition is correct when it claims that something is given; each tradition's givens have a place in a full account of our irreducibility. Each tradition may have misinterpreted the givens that it describes, however, and so each tradition stands in need of correction from other traditions. It may be, for example, that we are directly given the contents contained in the notions of both being and givenness, and so neither can be said to be "nothing but" something else. But the judgments that being, givenness, or the principles governing each of them are universally applicable may be mistaken (I consider these concepts and principles later in the book). By following the aesthetic method, we can see how apparently incompatible claims about what is irreducibly given are actually compatible by seeing the place each can have in a portrait of the whole, beautiful human person. While experiential and objective-principle methods give only partial views of phenomena, since each reaches its views through the lens of their accepted principles, aesthetic method brings those methods and their findings together, subordinating those methods to itself but not subordinating either to the other. One of my guiding principles is that what can be directly perceived in itself must irreducibly be something in itself—that is, its content has an irreducible place in a complete metaphysics, though some judgments as to its place in that metaphysics may be mistaken.

The most fundamental response to this objection is that no account of any aspect of the human person (or of anything else) can begin elsewhere than in experience. We have access to things only through experience: something must be given (i.e., we must directly grasp something) before anything can be explained with principles. For this reason, I contend that the better we understand experience, the better will be our account of what things are. A principle not grounded in what shows itself in experience is nothing but ideology; it might express how we wish things were, but it will not describe or explain reality.[30]

Most strands of Catholic tradition recognize that philosophizing is based in experience. Scholastics often begin reasoning about what we are by considering our acts and their objects, and then reasoning back to underlying, explanatory principles. Claims about principles must be rooted in experience; otherwise, they would be unconnected to reality. Phenomenologists are more explicit about the need to begin thinking about human persons with experience. Our fundamental features, those presupposed by all reasoning about what we are, such as the fact that we are rational, cannot be demonstrated; as American Catholic phenomenologist Robert Sokolowski notes, they must be shown directly.[31] Otherwise, we fall into a regress, seeking to prove everything on the basis of ever-more-fundamental principles, without any ultimate basis for these principles. Moving outside the Catholic tradition, even reductionistic anthropologies begin with scientific or thought-experimental experiences, and reason on that basis.[32] Given that reductionisms tend to use different principles than antireductionisms, the only common basis for disputation between these views is experience. All of this suggests that objective principles posited by any tradition are open to revision in light of better descriptions of experience. We are more likely to grasp more of our irreducible features if we attend to many experiences, as described by many traditions, than we would be likely to grasp if we attended to accounts given in only one tradition. We should look at what as many traditions as possible say is irreducibly given; claims that help us grasp our irreducible features can even be drawn

---

30. Cf. Jean-Luc Marion, *Believing in Order to See: On the Rationality of Revelation and the Irrationality of Some Believers*, trans. Christina Gschwandtner (New York: Fordham University Press, 2017), 15.

31. Robert Sokolowski, *Phenomenology of the Human Person* (Cambridge: Cambridge University Press, 2008), 1.

32. A reductionistic anthropology that does a good job of noting which experiences it draws from (and which experiences its opponents draw from) is Daniel Dennett, *Consciousness Explained* (Boston: Little, Brown, and Company, 1991).

from reductionisms like dualism, idealism, and materialism, each of which focuses our attention on genuine aspects of what is experientially given.

Finally, even if one just cannot correlate my descriptions to one's experience, it is still worthwhile to consider my descriptions of experience, insofar as it is worthwhile to see how various thinkers' claims can be reconciled and synthesized. One might not see how those claims are justified, but one will at least be able to grasp the connections that can be plausibly drawn among different strands of the Catholic tradition.

Objection Two. A philosopher who focuses on experience might object that while my proposed methodology starts with experience, I also propose to paint a portrait of the person using objective principles. One might contend that in the perceptions with which my reasoning starts, we are given holistically and fully, but that in any subsequent reasoning, we necessarily move away from that original fullness, and so away from perceiving our full, concrete irreducibility. The best account of our irreducibility would simply describe how we are directly given, without then turning to objective, abstract principles.[33]

This objection could be motivated by claims made by antireductionists in the broadly Catholic tradition like John Milbank and David Bentley Hart.[34] They criticize "dialectical" methods, which aim at defending a metaphysical account of reality rationally, disinterestedly, and from a purely objective point of view. An example of this approach is scholastic or Aristotelian science, which aims at knowing the definition of some subject (like human persons) and understanding that kind of subject by demonstrating what its universal and necessary properties and causes are.[35] Such an approach purports to explain how we are irreducible to anything nonpersonal in objective, universal terms. By contrast, Milbank and Hart contend that reasoning is always perspectival, enmeshed in particular interests, practices, and traditions, and so we cannot achieve the objective "view from nowhere" required by dialectical methods. Rather, they think that we can best grasp things and their irreducibility aesthetically (or "rhe-

---

33. See, for example, the Thomist William Carlo, *The Ultimate Reducibility of Essence to Existence in Existential Metaphysics* (The Hague: Martinus Nijhoff, 1966), 99–145, and the phenomenologists Martin Heidegger, "The Onto-Theo-Logical Conception of Metaphysics," in *Identity and Difference*, trans. Joan Stambaugh (Chicago: University of Chicago Press, 2002) and Emmanuel Levinas, *Totality and Infinity: An Essay on Exteriority*, trans. Alphonso Lingis (Pittsburgh: Duquesne University Press, 1969), 35–40. See also Marion, *In Excess*, chap. 1.

34. David Bentley Hart, *The Beauty of the Infinite* (Grand Rapids, Mich.: Eerdmans, 2003), 1–8; John Milbank, *Theology and Social Theory: Beyond Secular Reason* (Oxford: Blackwell, 2006), 1, 279.

35. Aristotle, *Post. An.*, I.2.

torically"), that is, from a particular perceptual perspective, with all of the personal limitations and lack of objectivity that involves.

The objector might contend that my aesthetic method points me in this direction: I should realize that beauty is always grasped from a particular, personal point of view, which always has only a partial grasp on it, for beauty is grasped through taste, which presupposes a particular tradition's standards of appreciation. A metaphysics that claims to consider reality objectively and in itself, apart from a perspectival position, fails to grasp how its own conception of rationality (and of the human person) has arisen from, and can only be understood within, a particular perspective. According to this objection, we never grasp reality in itself but rather only rival images of reality. We adjudicate among such images on the basis of their beauty, fittingness, or attractiveness. For example, to counter "postmodern" images of the world on which all differences are conflictual, Milbank and Hart posit an alternative image on which differences are fundamentally peaceful. While they think that we ought to perceive the world in a way guided by the latter image, they hold that there are no reasons to prefer that image to the other—at least, no reasons that are accessible outside of the context of commitment to one image or the other. Rather, one can be persuaded to adopt one image only by seeing it as more beautiful or attractive than others. One might object that my portrait-painting project just develops another image of the human person, so I ought to abandon using "dialectical" or objective-principle methods and just synthesize methods that rely on experience and aesthetics.

Reply to Objection Two. While I agree that reasoning about the human person begins in perception, I contend (as I argue in chapter 3) that everything that we perceive intrinsically tends toward being objectively, conceptually, and propositionally understood and explained. Things give themselves to us as such that they ought to be objectively explained. We do not do justice to the fullness of the perceived given as it gives itself (i.e., we are reductionistic about its content) if we refuse to consider it through objective reasoning. Such a view also fails to do justice to ourselves (i.e., it is reductionistic about our powers): human reasoning aims, in part, at transcending subjective perspectives and attaining a universal viewpoint. For these experiential reasons, it is necessary to include dialectic or objective-principle methods, and their findings, in my portrait of the human person.

Objective methods also aim at facilitating more accurate perception.

While we are able to, by abstraction, judgment, and reasoning, grasp that certain claims about irreducible persons are true, such knowledge does not fully satisfy us. Rather, we use knowledge of objective principles to guide our perception, so as to more accurately and directly perceive given realities. Aquinas describes how we do this intellectually when we use concepts to perceive and contemplate essences in themselves; we also use concepts, propositions, and reasoning in conjunction with our senses to grasp precisely what we are sensing.[36] Aquinas thinks that reasoning follows a Platonic *exitus-reditus* structure: we begin with simple understanding or seeing; we unpack what we see through abstraction, analysis, and argumentation; and then we return to what we saw, with our perception now trained by concepts and reasoning to see accurately.[37] In other words, human reasoning begins aesthetically (i.e., by perceiving self-manifesting wholes), unfolds abstractly in grasping principles that explain what is perceived, and so comes to a more precise aesthetic experience. Similarly, phenomenologists like Max Scheler describe how concepts are "functionalized" in our perceptions, habitually guiding us to a more accurate grasp of objects and to perceive objects as falling into conceptualizable kinds.[38] Czech phenomenologist Erazim Kohák likewise contends that the purpose of philosophy, facilitated by dialectical reasoning, is to "see clearly and articulate faithfully the sense given in experience" and to ground all speculation and analysis in "seeing."[39] Members of the "spiritual senses" tradition (discussed in chapter 6), who hold that we can train our perception to even grasp God, maintain the same view.[40]

This sampling of views shows that the position that abstract thinking guides perception is quite widely held in the Catholic tradition. Abstract, objective, or dialectical approaches are not opposed to perceptual, experiential, or aesthetic approaches; rather, the former arise from and facilitate the latter. Milbank and Hart are correct that purportedly neutral rationality can often conceal unexamined perspectives, assumptions, and biases, and that even standards of rationality differ across traditions. Even our most

---

36. Aquinas, *ST* I, q.86.

37. Aquinas, *ST* I, q.79, a.8; *In De Trin.*, q.6, a.1. Cf. Wayne Hankey, *God in Himself: Aquinas' Doctrine of God as Expounded in the* Summa Theologiae (Oxford: Oxford University Press, 2000), 22–24.

38. Max Scheler, "Ordo Amoris," in *Selected Philosophical Essays*, 103, 118.

39. Erazim Kohák, *The Embers and the Stars: A Philosophical Inquiry into the Moral Sense of Nature* (Chicago: Chicago University Press, 1987), xii.

40. See, for example, John Greco, "Perception as Interpretation," *Proceedings of the American Catholic Philosophical Association* 72 (1999): 229–37; Paul Gavrilyuk and Sarah Coakley, eds., *The Spiritual Senses: Perceiving God in Western Christianity* (Cambridge: Cambridge University Press, 2012).

basic principles can be contested, and we must learn to see how standards of rationality arise from different visions or images of the world. But none of this gives us reason to reject dialectical reasoning. Experience, including rational and aesthetic experience, is fundamentally realist, that is, it aims at and grasps reality, about which we can reason together. Reality itself provides a standard beyond all traditions and images. I do not just want to show a beautiful picture of what we are, relying on its attractiveness to be persuasive. Rather, I want to show what we truly are by giving reasons for my claims. I paint my portrait with the ideas and arguments of realist metaphysics, which are well suited to facilitating perception of ourselves as we truly are. Even my ultimate account of the human person in terms of *beauty* will be a metaphysical account, guided by aesthetic concepts.

Nevertheless, Milbank and Hart's approach reveals features of persons that are not grasped on a purely objective or dialectical approach; the findings of their perspectival method must be synthesized into my portrait of the human person. While I argue that some of our cognitive acts allow us (at least partially) to transcend limited perspectives and grasp realities in themselves, I also contend that there are fundamental, irreducible features of human persons that can only be grasped from particular perspectives. Some aspects of the beauty of each person cannot be grasped from a disinterested, neutral, objective perspective. Rather, they can only be perceived if one has the proper taste for that beauty, for example, with eyes guided by interested love or by cultural practices. My approach deliberately lacks a completely detached, critical objectivity: to fully perceive human persons requires being open in reverent, earnest, loving wonder to all that one can be shown by various thinkers and by one's experiences. Such an approach is still objective in the sense that by it we grasp what is really in persons, though those features of persons cannot be grasped from a neutral or value-free perspective.[41] Each perspective is a partial view of the beautiful, self-manifesting whole that each one of us is. Given my goal of synthesizing many strands of Catholic tradition, it would be illegitimate for me, at the outset, to favor one perspective over another. I must rather begin with all purported experiences of the human person and see whether and how they can be fitted into a coherent portrait.

In my synthesizing, aesthetic method, I build on Balthasar's theolog-

---

41. On neutral versus personal senses of "objectivity," see Servais Pinckaers, *The Sources of Christian Ethics*, trans. Mary Thomas Noble (Washington, D.C.: The Catholic University of America Press, 1995), 65–67.

ical aesthetics, which emphasizes that while argumentation is important, most people are fully convinced of the truth of Christianity only when they experientially encounter the beauty or the total holistic form (*Gestalt*) of Christ. Joseph Ratzinger claims that "being struck and overcome by the beauty of Christ is a more real, more profound knowledge than mere rational deduction."[42] Experiences of beauty can be deeply intellectually convincing, delivering profoundly meaningful, immediately apparent knowledge, though difficult to express in words. In the experience of the holistic, self-manifesting beauty of Christ that Balthasar and Ratzinger describe, we transcend every limited perspective and are experientially taken up into a beautiful whole (*Gestalt*), grasping that reality in itself. I am taken out of myself and my own perspective, and the beautiful reality guides my understanding of itself. We can experience human persons in a similar way: we best grasp our irreducible fullness when we are struck by our beauty, by the holistic, self-manifesting wholes that we are. Scholastic methodology considers us only as explained through principles like act, potency, and causality; phenomenological methodology considers us only as we appear as subjects constituting (i.e., bestowing meaning on) or being constituted by (i.e., receiving our meaning from) objects of intentional acts. But the aesthetic method invites us to consider each perspective as distinct appearances of aspects of one unified, self-manifesting whole.

This book, above all, has a contemplative end, which is to guide us to wonder at and enjoy what we are for its own sake (and on that basis contemplate God, in whose image we are made), for philosophical inquiry ultimately is done to facilitate contemplation (*theoria*). This contemplation can be aided by abstract concepts and theories, so long as we remember that a theory (in the sense of a system of concepts and propositions) is meant to guide us toward *theoria*, to beholding real being in awe-struck wonder, which exceeds all theories. *Theoria* has religious connotations; the term is linked etymologically and conceptually to the *theoros*, one who is sent to participate in (and not just be a spectator at) a religious festival.[43]

---

42. Joseph Ratzinger, "The Feeling of Things, the Contemplation of Beauty," Message to the Communion and Liberation Meeting at Rimini, August 24–30, 2002, http://www.vatican.va/roman_curia/congregations/cfaith/documents/rc_con_cfaith_doc_20020824_ratzinger-cl-rimini_en.html.

43. See Hans-Georg Gadamer, *Truth and Method*, trans. Joel Weinsheimer and Donald G. Marshall (London: Continuum, 2004), 121–22. Cf. Aristotle, *NE*, X.7 and 8; Martin Heidegger, "Science and Reflection," in *The Question Concerning Technology and Other Essays*, trans. William Lovitt (New York: Harper and Row, 1977), 163–66; William McNeill, *The Glance of the Eye: Heidegger, Aristotle, and the Ends of Theory* (Albany: State University of New York Press, 1999), 260–66; Josef Pieper, *In Tune with the World*:

To take up a theory is to be called out of unreflective thinking, into the wondering, celebratory, open stance of a participant in a festival, who beholds the beauty and hidden structure made present in the liturgy that reality is with a reverent, excited, antireductionistic attitude, in pursuit of divinization (*theosis*, that is, become God or a god [*theos*]).[44] Methods like Aristotelian science are ways of experiencing, enjoying, and celebrating reality in all its fine-grained structure; my method must include, but not be reducible to, methods like Aristotelian sciences. The philosopher is the lover of wisdom, the one who has fallen in love with an intimate taste for the deepest reality,[45] even though that taste and those realities cannot be fully expressed in words, concepts, and theories. Defending this experience by argument, while necessary, is secondary to guiding others to have this taste, too.

This book also has an ethical end. Part of perceiving our irreducibility is perceiving the ends to which we are oriented, which include contemplation, virtue, and love and reverence toward each person. While my primary goal is to depict what we are, not to defend particular ethical conclusions, I want to help combat the many current attacks on the dignity of human persons, such as abortion, pornography, consumerism, lack of access to healthcare, racist and misogynistic discrimination, and the degradation of our natural environment. The more we perceive our full irreducibility, the more we will be motivated to overcome these attacks. A true philosophical anthropology aims at guiding us to see ourselves as we fully are, for the sake of a more intense, flourishing life, in both its contemplative and ethical aspects. These ends are facilitated by perceiving our beauty, in which, as Balthasar noted, we, above all, see the worthwhileness of knowing truth, pursuing goodness, and existing itself.[46]

Objection Three. One might object that this book either begs the question regarding our irreducibility or just asserts without argument that we are fully irreducible. Since I begin with experiences that purportedly directly reveal our irreducibility, unpack them, and then return to experience

---

A Theory of Festivity, trans. Richard and Clara Winston (South Bend, Ind.: St. Augustine's Press, 1999), 3–12; and Carnes, *Beauty*, 247–48.

44. *Theos* is linked etymologically to religious festival (*feria*), to contemplation (*theoria*), and to enthusiasm. See J. P. Mallory and D. Q. Adams, *The Oxford Introduction to Proto-Indo-European and the Proto-Indo-European World* (Oxford: Oxford University Press, 2006), 410.

45. On this use of "taste," which differs from the more perspectival use of the term that is employed by the objector, see Aquinas, *ST* II-II, q.45, a.2.

46. Balthasar, *GL1*, 18. Cf. Aristotle, *EE*, VIII.3.1248b17–37, 1249b12–17.

as elucidated by that unpacking, my method seems to assume what I claim to show using it. One might insist that the irreducibility of the person must be argued for, not just asserted as a conviction and then explicated.

Similarly, one might apply Karen Kilby's criticism of Balthasar's aesthetic method to my aesthetic method: a method that purports to just explicate a beautiful unity and that does so by drawing on and synthesizing various strands of the tradition, seems to assume a sort of privileged access to things (in my case, human persons) and a mastery over the tradition that no thinker should claim to have. The account of a phenomenon (for Balthasar, Christ; for me, the human person) that results from this method lacks sufficient argumentation to be compelling. It presents one contestable vision of things as definitively true.[47]

Reply to Objection Three. This objection brings us to a difficulty inherent in investigating human persons: the object into which we are inquiring here is also the subject who is doing the inquiring, and so the object of inquiry is presupposed by any inquiry into it. There *is* a sort of circularity between any method and objects that are presupposed by any exercise of that method. For example, to investigate the structure of the intellectual power and to justify its acts, I must use that power, and so I must presuppose that it can investigate. I must also presuppose a particular conception of reasoning, which will be rooted in a contestable tradition. *A fortiori*, investigating the human person presupposes the very thing under investigation, since it is a human person who performs that investigation. One must have some (at least tacit) conception of what we are and how we can investigate in order to investigate anything. Indeed, this book is in part an expression not just of my conviction that we are irreducible to anything nonpersonal, but also of my own perception of that irreducibility: having seen the irreducible beauty of persons, I explicate my perception so that others can see it, too.

These circularities in my motives and methods are necessary and nonvicious, but they call for caution. My method for investigating the human person is, in part, dictated by the object of that inquiry. Many methodological claims made in this introduction are grounded in findings about the human person reached in later chapters, like the account of the intellect in chapter 3. In a sense, the human person (and other phenomena presup-

---

47. Karen Kilby, *Balthasar: A (Very) Critical Introduction* (Grand Rapids, Mich.: Eerdmans, 2012), 12–14, 111–14, 162–67.

Introduction   21

posed by philosophical inquiry) is self-explicating or self-interpreting, but seeing how requires philosophical reasoning.[48] We can be more sure that we are understanding the human person correctly the more we return to experience and draw on multiple traditions' accounts of those experiences and methods for reasoning about them, allowing those traditions' claims to correct one another.

As Balthasar recognized, no method or starting point can be stipulated in advance, other than an aesthetic or perceptual openness to the whole (*Gestalt*) of the person. Balthasar's fundamental criterion is this: the more a method allows us to see, the more we can be certain of it. We must begin *in mediis rebus*, presupposing only a loving openness to whatever is manifested in persons.[49] The aesthetic method trains us to perceive the fullness of a *Gestalt* by examining how it appears from many angles. In his theological aesthetics, Balthasar examined how the *Gestalt* of Christ appeared in the work of twelve exemplary theologians, in the history of metaphysics, and in scripture.[50] Together, these perspectives build up a "stereoscopic" or "symphonic" approach to the *Gestalt* in question, in which many perspectives are held together. These perspectives are not forced into an abstract or conceptual synthesis but are allowed to stand side-by-side and be seen as multiple, fitting manifestations of one self-manifesting, beautiful whole, even if we cannot immediately see how they harmonize.[51]

Responding to this objection requires that I be clear about what I intend to show in this book. Since my goal is not to prove that we are irreducible to anything nonpersonal, I do not assume something I intend to prove by starting with that conviction. Rather, my goal is to explicate that assumed conviction, and to paint a portrait by which the truth of that conviction can be seen. That conviction guides my inquiry in that it is an

---

48. See Balthasar, the introduction and first part of *GL1*; Jean-Luc Marion, *The Reason of the Gift*, trans. Stephen Lewis (Charlottesville: University of Virginia Press, 2011); Gadamer, *Truth and Method*; and Martin Heidegger, *Being and Time*, trans. Joan Stambaugh (Albany: State University of New York Press, 1996).
49. See Balthasar, *GL1*, part II; *TL1*, 128; *E*, 43.
50. This is the project of *GL2-7*.
51. Hans Urs von Balthasar, *Truth Is Symphonic: Aspects of Christian Pluralism*, trans. Graham Harrison (San Francisco: Ignatius Press, 1987), 9. Cf. William Desmond's "metaxological" approach, on which we work "between" multiple approaches, without reducing them to one another, by seeing being as "overdetermined"—that is, including more than can be grasped or articulated on any particular view but without reducing what is grasped on particular views. See *The Intimate Strangeness of Being: Metaphysics After Dialectic* (Washington, D.C.: The Catholic University of America Press, 2012), 48–49; *The Gift of Beauty and the Passion of Being: On the Threshold between the Aesthetic and the Religious* (Eugene, Ore.: Cascade Books, 2018), chap. 1; and *The Voiding of Being: The Doing and Undoing of Metaphysics in Modernity* (Washington, D.C.: The Catholic University of America Press, 2020), 236.

openness to any way that human persons might manifest themselves; that conviction is an expression of the stance of the *theoros* that I described in responding to Objection Two. While I think that the resulting metaphysical account is true, I do not intend to exhaustively defend that truth; it suffices for my purposes if I show what the human person looks like on one view guided by a conviction that we are completely irreducible. Regardless of whether my account is true, considering it is helpful inasmuch as it shows one view of what human persons would be like if complete nonreductionism were true, and one way that strands of the Catholic tradition can be synthesized. To accomplish these goals, less argumentation is needed than if I were defending irreducibility to those who do not think it is true, or if I were arguing that mine is the only way to show our irreducibility or synthesize traditions. Since I do not make these claims, Kilby's critique does not apply to my account.

Objection Four. Finally, one might object that this attempt at a "big picture" synthesis attempts too much. It could only consider each tradition's claims superficially; it will result in an eclectic or syncretic juxtaposition of idiosyncratically chosen views rather than a true synthesis.

Reply to Objection Four. My goal in this book is a portrait of the human person that provides a framework for relating theories together. No portrait of the whole, concrete human person can be complete; indeed, this is entailed by my views about our irreducibility. I will have succeeded in my goals if my framework allows one to see how anthropologies could be related to each other. I cannot delve into many details of theories; I hope that the defects resulting from glossing over particular details are offset by the benefits of seeing how key aspects of theories can be synthesized into a more nonreductionistic portrait of the person. Given my goal of overcoming unnecessary polemics among Catholic schools of thought, I opt to focus mostly on what each school shows about our irreducibility. While I also show ways in which each school is reductionistic, and so needs to be amended, my focus is not on arguing against false claims. By narrowing my goals, I avoid problematically superficial treatments of each school.

This is not a work in the history of philosophy. I do not argue that my views are the correct interpretation of any specific thinker, for example, of Aquinas. Rather, I rely on others' work in history and interpretation of texts for my systematic goals. I even draw on incorrect interpretations of various thinkers, since these are often true in their account of reality, even if they are poor as interpretations. For example, Thomists have debated how Aquinas thinks we know the real existence of beings. Throughout this book, I consider different interpretations of Aquinas on this matter, drawing on readings by John of St. Thomas, Jacques Maritain, Etienne Gilson, Frederick Wilhelmsen, William Carlo, Cornelio Fabro, Lawrence Dewan, and John Wippel. Given their disagreements, they cannot all be correctly reading Aquinas, but I do not intend to assess which of them is giving the correct interpretation, and so I make no claims in that regard. I am interested only in seeing how each view reveals a genuine experience of knowing existence and elucidates existence itself. Their claims about experience and reality can be synthesized, even if they misinterpret Aquinas.

By using an aesthetic method, I avoid the dangers of syncretism and eclecticism, that is, of building a system that merely juxtaposes views in an *ad hoc* or idiosyncratic way. By returning each school's claims to the experiences that are their sources, and by considering each set of claims as a way in which whole, beautiful human persons manifest themselves, we can see how views actually fit together, that is, how they can be synthesized, not just juxtaposed.

Phenomenological and Scholastic Methodology

I turn now to some details of phenomenological and Thomistic methodologies since they figure prominently at the beginning of my portrait. Other methodologies for inquiring into irreducible human persons will be introduced throughout the book; as I said in responding to Objection Three, methodology can be worked out only in examining the object of inquiry, since the latter guides the former. As we discover new aspects of our object of inquiry, the human person, it will be appropriate to introduce new methodologies. Even here, as I present Thomistic and phenomenological methodology, I begin to give an account of what human persons are.

I could have begun my portrait in many places, but I start in chapter 1 with phenomenological accounts of self-awareness and with some basic Thomistic principles. I begin with Thomism because of its central role in recent antireductionistic Catholic philosophy, and because its metaphysical principles are an excellent foundation for synthesizing further material. I also want to show that it is possible and preferable to synthesize central claims of Thomistic metaphysics with those of a range of other theories, especially those often taken to be at odds with Thomism, such as Scotism, personalism, phenomenology, and Eastern Christian thought. I start with phenomenology, in particular, its account of subjectivity, because it provides some of the best evidence from outside the scholastic tradition for Thomistic (and other scholastic) metaphysical principles.[52] It also focuses our attention on experiences that immediately reveal our irreducibility to anything nonpersonal. I also want to show that it is possible and helpful to incorporate into realist metaphysics accounts of experience drawn from traditions sometimes taken to be at odds with realism.

Phenomenology is a twentieth- and twenty-first-century philosophical movement.[53] It was motivated by opposition to psychologism in logic, the view that logical laws are just psychological laws of thinking, and to versions of empiricism and subjective idealism that held that experienced phenomena are nothing but physical or psychological events. Logical laws, however, are given as objective structures with an essential structure, irreducible to our thoughts about them.[54] This opposition to psychologism can be repeated in every area of experience: even something as fleeting as the content of a daydream has an essential structure in itself, irreducible to its association with or causation by physical or mental events. Any content that directly shows itself in experience can be considered in itself.[55]

Phenomenologists hold that philosophers can and should grasp "things themselves," that is, what directly shows itself in experience with its own structure. To do this, we "bracket" or set out of attention thoughts of what does not directly show itself, including explanatory theories and posited principles. By setting such thoughts aside, we directly perceive and attend to the meaning of what shows itself to us. To directly experience something as meaningful is to experience it as something and as fitting with, harmonizing with, or perfecting one of our acts. For example, if I am looking for trees, and then I see a tree, that tree will appear meaningful insofar as I see it as what I was thinking about, and as harmonizing with and perfecting (or filling in the content of) my thought. The experience of

---

52. See Mark K. Spencer, "Habits, Potencies, and Obedience: Experiential Evidence for Thomistic Hylomorphism," *Proceedings of the American Catholic Philosophical Association* 88 (2014): 165–80; Spencer, *Thomistic Hylomorphism and the Phenomenology of Self-Sensing* (PhD diss., University at Buffalo, 2012).

53. Some ideas in this section were developed in Mark K. Spencer, "The Many Phenomenological Reductions and Catholic Metaphysical Anti-Reductionism," *American Catholic Philosophical Quarterly* 95, no. 3 (2021): 367–88.

54. Edmund Husserl, "Prolegomena to Pure Logic," in *Logical Investigations*, vol. 1.

55. Gaston Bachelard, *The Poetics of Space*, trans. Maria Jolas (New York: Penguin, 2014), 28–34.

meaning is one of things making sense, of having security and a sense of purposefulness in what one grasps. In French phenomenologist Maurice Merleau-Ponty's words, bracketing what does not appear to us allows us to step back from the everyday flow of experience, where phenomena are jumbled together and where we tend not to attend to what shows itself, and to notice each given phenomenon in itself, so as to "reveal the mystery of the world and of reason."[56] This method aims not at abstract explanation but at a wondering, vital, intense contact with each thing that shows itself.[57] As the German Catholic phenomenologist Max Scheler explains it, in applying this method, one ceases to perform certain acts so as to completely attend to what shows itself in other acts. For example, one might stop performing acts of being aware of things' real existence, so as to more intensely attend just to essential, intelligible contents.[58]

While phenomenologists disagree as to what we should bracket (and, based on that disagreement, many phenomenological methods have developed), most agree that we need to bracket our natural, everyday attitude toward the world. In that attitude, we consider ourselves, tacitly and unreflectively, according to some religious, cultural, political, economic, or scientific theory that we have adopted, often through societal influence. For example, we might habitually think of ourselves as children of God, as rationally self-interested consumers, or as organisms explained through sciences like neurology.[59] We assume that objects external to us are there, really existing, without examining how we are aware of them or what it means to exist. We generally fail to attend to how things appear directly as meaningful; that is, we fail to focus on how they appear as something or as perfecting our acts. Rather, we tend to think about things as explained by something that does not directly show itself. For example, we might take things to be best explained through a causal theory, assuming that what is given is explained and given meaning by what does not appear to us, that is, its causes. In other words, we conceive of the given as fitting with causes that do not appear to us but are believed to causally explain what does ap-

---

56. Maurice Merleau-Ponty, *Phenomenology of Perception*, trans. Colin Smith (London: Routledge, 2002), xxiv.
57. Cf. Hildebrand, *What Is Philosophy?* 204; Wojtyła, "Subjectivity and the Irreducible in the Human Being."
58. Scheler, "Idealism and Realism," 288–91, 316–18. Scheler wrongly thinks that Husserl thinks of the reduction as a mental exercise or technique, not a shutting down of certain acts.
59. Cf. Walker Percy, *Lost in the Cosmos: The Last Self-Help Book* (New York: Washington Square Press, 1983), 15–17; Heidegger, *Being and Time*, 156–68.

pear. For example, if I think that what appears to me is entirely explained by its constituting subatomic particles, or by God's causality, I think of it as meaningful in the sense that I think of it as fitting with something that does not directly appear to me. For this reason, in the natural attitude, which includes the attitude taken by those practicing the natural sciences, we are often "alienated" from the sources of meaning. Rather than attending to given things as directly meaningful, we mentally transfer their meaning to things we do not directly grasp. The nonappearing explanatory principles are taken to be the true repositories of meaning, and since we cannot directly grasp those, we experience ourselves as cut off from the true sources of meaning. Since we can always doubt the existence of what does appear to us, the natural attitude, including its religious and scientific versions, always runs the risk of *nihilism*, that is, a view on which there is no meaning, no actual fit or harmony among things.[60]

Perceiving how each item meaningfully appears in its own right—that is, is able to be regarded as something in itself, and as fitting with or perfecting our acts—requires setting aside the natural attitude. This method is called a "reduction," but it is not reductionistic; rather, it is a way of pausing at and noticing what is irreducible in what shows itself.[61] It is an ascetic method of training perception, so that we attend to each aspect of our lives and of the world, with its own irreducible content, renewing a sense that each is meaningful in itself.[62] Views that direct our attention away from what appears, and regard the given as something other than itself—like many causal theories—risk reductionism, seeing the given as nothing but something other than itself.

Later in this introduction, I describe the scholastic method of abstraction, in which we mentally turn from particulars to universals or essences, or from wholes to parts. Most versions of the phenomenological reduction include reasoning in a way similar to abstraction. In abstraction, we set aside—or bracket from attention—consideration of the particular or the whole, so as to grasp the universal, the part, or their essential content as

---

60. Cf. Edmund Husserl, *Ideas Pertaining to a Pure Phenomenology and to a Phenomenological Philosophy*, vol. 1, trans. Fred Kersten (The Hague: Martinus Nijhoff, 1983), 51–57; Scheler, "The Theory of the Three Facts," 202–8; and Friedrich Nietzsche, *Twilight of the Idols*, in *The Portable Nietzsche*, trans. Walter Kaufmann (New York: Penguin, 1977), 484–86.

61. Wojtyła, "Subjectivity and the Irreducible," 210–11.

62. Max Scheler, "Phenomenology and the Theory of Cognition," in *Selected Philosophical Essays*, 138; William Tullius, "Renewal and Tradition: Phenomenology as 'Faith Seeking Understanding' in the Work of Edmund Husserl," *American Catholic Philosophical Quarterly* 89, no. 1 (2015): 1–26.

such.⁶³ Most versions of the phenomenological reduction likewise guide us to focus on the essential content of various kinds of acts or objects.

In each version of the reduction, we find that experience is structured in "layers": experiences or given phenomena belong to different layers when one presupposes another, such that the presupposed or "founding" experience or phenomenon can appear without the "founded" layer, but not vice versa. For example, acts of *judging things to be unified objects* are founded on acts of *perceiving them from various perspectives*; we can perform the latter without the former, but not vice versa.⁶⁴ For another example, the phenomenon of *color* is founded on that of *space*, that is, color can only be given as extended in space, but space can be given without any color, such as in mathematical intuition. Throughout this book, we shall see many examples of founded and founding layers, especially in relations between bodily and spiritual experiences. Phenomenological reductions focus on attending to the most fundamental layers and essential structures of experience.

In the most famous version of the phenomenological reduction, the movement's founder, Edmund Husserl, advocates suspending acts of positing (i.e., actively affirming, at least tacitly) the real existence of things apart from our conscious, intentional (i.e., object-directed) acts. In doing so, we suspend thoughts about how what appears is explained by the natural sciences, by traditional metaphysics, by theology, or by any causal reasoning. Objects are then considered only insofar as they have meaning for or appear to our conscious subjectivity, that is, we come to directly perceive objects of our acts just as intentional objects, having a certain meaning for us insofar as we intend them, say, through sense perception, judgment, feeling, or volition.⁶⁵ I start chapter 1 with Husserl's approach and what is discovered through it.

So as to head off possible misunderstandings of the claims with which I start my portrait of the human person in chapter 1, I here consider some objections that Catholic philosophers have raised to this method.⁶⁶ Some

---

63. Seifert, *Back to Things in Themselves*, 86.
64. Husserl, *Logical Investigations*, vol. 2, 27–28.
65. Husserl, *Ideas Pertaining to a Pure Phenomenology*, vol. 1, part 2.
66. See, for example, Maritain, *Degrees of Knowledge*, 107–19; Jacques Maritain, *Three Reformers: Luther, Descartes, Rousseau* (New York: Charles Scribners' Sons, 1929), 57ff.; Scruton, *Sexual Desire*, 364–66; Roman Ingarden, *On the Motives Which Led Husserl to Transcendental Idealism*, trans. Arnór Hannibalsson (The Hague: Martinus Nijhoff, 1975); Max Scheler, "Idealism and Realism," in *Selected Philosophical Essays*, 317; Hildebrand, *What Is Philosophy?* 205–7; Seifert, *Things in Themselves*, 77–117; and Claude

object that this seems to be just a method for considering how things appear to us, without this method telling us anything about what actually is. Others object that in this method we seem to reflect on past experience of objects, construct new mental objects of awareness (or "beings of reason," to use scholastic terminology), and then describe those. In either case, this could not be a method for grasping actual essences of objects, let alone our own irreducible, real essence; in either case, it seems to be just a method for grasping the contents of our own minds or our own creative constructions. If we start just with what appears or is given to us (as phenomenologists and thinkers like Rene Descartes and Immanuel Kant do), we will never be able to get "out of our heads," so to speak, and bridge the gap to the real world.

In reply, I must first emphasize that one of my primary goals is to show one way in which claims and methods of different strands of Catholic anthropology can be harmonized in a single account. Because I have set myself this goal, I cannot reject any method used in Catholic anthropology outright. Rather, I must harmonize the goals of the phenomenologists with the worries and goals of the objector.

Phenomenology is not purely a method for getting at appearances, nor does it construct mental objects to consider. The purpose of the reduction method is to stop positing objects and attend purely to what appears in actual experience, that is, to directly perceive what shows itself to us in its very being and full meaning. If phenomenologists reject claims of traditional or realist metaphysics, it is because they think those claims obscure ways in which things have being or are given.[67] For example, if I assume that I am only or primarily a substance, I will not be able to attend to how I appear as a pure subject who bestows meaning (including the meaning of the concept "substance") on intentional objects. But if I bracket thoughts

---

Romano, *At the Heart of Reason*, trans. Michael B. Smith and Claude Romano (Evanston, Ill.: Northwestern University Press, 2015), 287–98.

67. See, for example, Husserl, *Ideas Pertaining to a Pure Phenomenology*, vol. 1, 89–98; Stein, *Finite and Eternal Being*, 35–64; Max Scheler, *Formalism in Ethics and Non-Formal Ethics of Values: A New Attempt toward the Foundation of an Ethical Personalism*, trans. Manfred Frings and Roger Funk (Evanston, Ill.: Northwestern University Press, 1973), 389–90; and Heidegger, *Being and Time*, 17–23. There is reason to think that Husserl's own view is closer to realism than realist phenomenologists granted; for example, he grants that content comes to our intentional acts already structured, including in teleological, divinely ordered ways. See Husserl, *Gesammelte Werke Husserliana*, vol. 42 of *Grenzprobleme der Phänomenologie: Analyzsen des Unbewusstseins un der Instinkte, Metaphysik, Späte Ethik: Texte aus dem Nachlass (1908–1937)*, ed. Rochus Sowa and Thomas Vongehr (Dordrecht: Springer, 2014), 336–37, cited in William Tullius, "A Critical Evaluation of Edith Stein's Critique of Husserl's Idealism," presentation at 2015 meeting of the North American Society of Early Phenomenology.

of myself as a substance, and all other explanations of things as real extramental beings, I become directly aware of myself as a subject who performs intentional acts, within which things take on new meanings. I am put in touch with a way that I really show up, and with new sources of a sense of meaningfulness.

Different reductions direct our attention to different aspects of the being of things. Husserl's "transcendental" reduction (which I just described) directs our attention to our consciousness insofar as it is the source of intentional acts, to those acts, and to their objects insofar as they are related to those acts. That reduction trains our perception to grasp what is immanent in conscious acts. (Someone might object that perhaps the method only claims to do this, but actually does something else, or yields no results at all. I respond that one must test the method for oneself, carrying it out to the letter, and see what results it yields, for phenomenological results are meant to be reproducible. For this book, I presuppose that these methods yield the results they claim, and I consider how those results can be synthesized with those of other methods.) Others, like Jean-Luc Marion, bracket acts of explanation, acts of positing things as really distinct from consciousness, acts of considering what shows itself as an intentional object, and acts of considering what shows itself as a being in any sense. This is done to purely perceive the given as such, that is, to perceive just what appears, in its very appearing, which in many cases exceeds any meaning that we, by our acts, could assign to it or grasp in it.[68]

Still others, the realist phenomenologists, bracket only explanatory theorizing about what shows itself in experience, not our acts of positing the real, extramental existence of things. This allows them to directly perceive how real beings and essences give themselves to us. It also allows them to grasp our acts not just as intentional (object-directed) but also as *self-transcending* (i.e., as going beyond subjectivity to grasp what is really other than us as such). Realist phenomenologists describe how self-transcending acts give us awareness of real beings as really existing in themselves, not just as objects of our intentional acts that have the meaning "real existence" when intended in those acts. In this respect, their method resembles that of realist scholastic metaphysicians, like Jacques Maritain, who contend that our sensory and intellectual acts fundamentally grasp real being as such. Realist phenomenologist Josef Seifert has shown how his method guides

68. Marion, *In Excess*, chap. 1.

us to directly grasp principles that are central to scholastic metaphysics, like essence and existence, form and matter.[69] This method also resembles some versions of aesthetic method; some practitioners of the latter, like William Desmond,[70] describe the experience of beauty as an experience of what transcends subjectivity (since the beautiful appears as other than me) and of what transcends objecthood (since the beautiful appears as having a meaning that exceeds its place in my intentional acts, and that exceeds any meaning that I could assign to it—that is, given beauty is always more than an object of my intentional acts). Realist phenomenologists also include several personalists, such as Hildebrand, Seifert, and Wojtyła, who take persons to be the foundational feature of reality.[71] Because of these affinities with other methods, the realist phenomenological method has a distinctive role in joining strands of Catholic anthropology.

The realist phenomenological reduction leads to a distinctive mode of argumentation, which I use at times in this book. In order to focus our attention on one phenomenon and its essential structure, they describe contrasting phenomena as they are directly given. We more precisely perceive one thing by circling around it and contrasting it to other things.[72] In order to focus our attention on a kind of sensory beauty in which divine beauty directly appears through sensory phenomena, for example, Hildebrand contrasts it to phenomena, such as kinds of sensory beauty that symbolize things about God and that express phenomena interior to the soul, like moral virtue. By considering the latter and how they are distinct from the former, we get a better grasp on the former than we would if we just tried to directly grasp it in itself.[73] The goal of this method of argumentation is a direct perception, "intuition," or "insight" into the phenomenon being considered.[74] The legitimacy of making philosophical discoveries by insight will be justified further in chapter 3.

---

69. Josef Seifert, "Essence and Existence: A New Foundation of Classical Metaphysics on the Basis of 'Phenomenological Realism' and a Critical Investigation of 'Existentialist Thomism,'" *Aletheia* 1, nos. 1 and 2 (1977): 17–157, 371–459.

70. Desmond, *The Gift of Beauty and the Passion of Being*, chap. 2.

71. Hildebrand, *What Is Philosophy?* 205–08; Wojtyła, "Subjectivity and the Irreducible"; Seifert, *Things in Themselves*. Cf. Juan Manuel Burgos, *An Introduction to Personalism*, trans. R. T. Allen (Washington, D.C.: The Catholic University of America Press, 2018), 207.

72. This method of argumentation is explained well by Robert Sokolowski in his introduction, "Hildebrand's Defense of the Philosophical Life," in Hildebrand, *What Is Philosophy?* xxiii.

73. Hildebrand, *Aesthetics*, vol. 1, chap. 7.

74. For a brief history of realist phenomenology's use of the method of insight (in Hildebrand and his followers Balduin Schwarz, Fritz Wenisch, and Josef Seifert), see Juan García-Norro and Rogelio Rovira, "A New Look at A Priori Knowledge and Hildebrand's Discovery of Different Kinds of Unities," *American Catholic Philosophical Quarterly* 91, no. 4 (2017): 576.

Despite their differences, each reduction directs us to focus on the very meaning of things themselves. No reduction primarily analyzes mere appearances (though phenomenology can describe how mere appearances, like hallucinations or afterimages, show up). Phenomenology asks how beings appear and whence they have their meanings. Far from sundering us from the world, such that we would need to bridge a gap out to the real world, phenomenology directs our attention precisely to actual features of the world, and to how the world as such shows itself to us.[75]

The objector might point out that Husserl sees his method as building on that of Descartes and Kant, and their setting aside a grasp on the real or noumenal external world. But Descartes thinks that we primarily grasp mental ideas, from which we must reason to the existence of the world, while Kant thinks that we grasp only phenomena, objects insofar as they fall under categories internal to our minds, and that we never grasp noumena, real beings in themselves, apart from mental categories. On those views, there is a gap between consciousness and world. Since Husserl saw his method, like their method, as coming to see all phenomena as given meaning by or in relation to consciousness, it would seem to separate one from the real world as their methods do, making it an unsuitable method for grasping our irreducible reality.

I respond that Husserl drew inspiration from Descartes and Kant insofar as they rightly turned our attention to the "transcendental" question of what the conditions are for anything meaningfully appearing.[76] However, Husserl does not follow them in doubting the existence of the world or our ability to know it; rather, on his method, we bracket naively positing the existence of the world, so as to better see how a meaningful world shows up for us. We thereby grasp precisely how we experience the world. Husserl does not follow Descartes in holding that we primarily grasp ideas and then reason out to the world, or in drawing unwarranted metaphysical conclusions from experiential data. When Descartes grasps that consciousness certainly exists but that objective phenomena are dubitable, he concludes that subjectivity is a substance distinct from purely objective (and dubitable) bodies. This is his dualistic view of human persons.[77] Hus-

---

75. Husserl, *Ideas Pertaining to a Pure Phenomenology*, vol. 1, 100–104. Cf. Heidegger, *Being and Time*, 59–88.
76. Edmund Husserl, *Cartesian Meditations: An Introduction to Phenomenology*, trans. Dorion Cairns (The Hague: Martinus Nijhoff, 1973).
77. Descartes, *Meditations on First Philosophy*, in *Selected Philosophical Writings*. The metaphysician of irreducibility must take seriously skeptical experience: in all acts, even in acts of skepticism, some

serl draws no such conclusion, however; rather, as we shall see further in chapter 1, he shows how we can directly experience ourselves as pure subjectivity or consciousness, in relation to which all other things have meaning. He thereby shows that subjectivity is an irreducible feature of the human person, but the meaning "substance" applies to objects of consciousness, not to subjectivity itself, and so we cannot conclude that we are substances that are pure minds or consciousnesses.[78]

I grant that through both Kant's and Husserl's methods, all objects appear as receiving meaning from our conscious, intentional acts. However, Husserl also describes how in experiencing myself as a subjectivity who gives meaning to objects by my acts, I simultaneously experience myself as a subject among others, each of whom bestows meaning on objects by his or her acts, and with whom I experience a shared, meaningful world, the "life-world" (*Lebenswelt*).[79] Contrary to Descartes and others, consciousness is never given as sundered from the world. Still, I grant to the objector that Husserl describes only one facet of our experience—aspects given as immanent to our intentional acts. Many phenomenologists (including Husserl) so focus on one kind of experience that it alone is taken to reveal what we fundamentally are or what is fundamental to the world. They thus draw reductionistic conclusions from their use of the phenomenological reduction, but these reductionistic tendencies and metaphysical misinterpretations of what is given can be corrected by turning to the findings of other methods. As I said, if something directly appears to us, then it must *be something*; it cannot be plausibly claimed that what we grasp as directly appearing actually lacks the content that directly appears to us. Hence, what Husserl describes as directly appearing must be something, and any metaphysics must take it into account, though these findings must be synthesized with what is discovered by other methods. The aesthetic method gives the metaphysician who aims at a completely nonreductionistic account of the human person—whom I refer to as the *metaphysician of irreducibility*—a standpoint for moving among multiple methods and synthesizing what is directly perceived through each one.

---

irreducible content is directly given, which must have its place in a complete metaphysics. For example, our ability to doubt almost all things reveals our own certain, subjective mode of existence, which in turn reveals our freedom and responsibility in discovering and deciding on the value and meaning of all things.

78. Husserl, *Ideas Pertaining to a Pure Phenomenology*, vol. 1, 100–104, 112–14.

79. Edmund Husserl, *The Crisis of European Sciences and Transcendental Phenomenology*, trans. David Carr (Evanston, Ill.: Northwestern University Press, 1970), 182–86.

Introduction   33

As we shall see further in chapter 1, Catholic phenomenologist and metaphysician Edith Stein showed how some phenomenological methods, like that of the realist phenomenologists, converge with scholastic methods.[80] She describes how we can, using Husserlian phenomenological method (which she calls "the Augustinian way"), discover that subjective experience is structured by principles like act, potency, essence, and existence. But we can also (in what she calls "the Aristotelian way") begin philosophical reflection with real beings transcendent to consciousness, which "force themselves on our attention." By abstracting from our perceptions of these beings their essential structure—that is, by using the scholastic method that I consider below—we arrive at the same principles discovered through phenomenological reduction. Properly understood (and going beyond the limits their practitioners sometimes impose on them) these methods and their findings are open to one another.[81]

Following Stein, I propose to join findings about human persons from the phenomenological and scholastic methods—and so come to see each method's findings as a partial manifestation of the single beauty each one of us is—in at least four ways. First, phenomenological method directly reveals irreducible phenomena—including, if Stein is right, principles posited by scholastics. Insofar as it reveals meaningful, irreducible contents, phenomenology just is a method for doing metaphysics. Second, we can reason about phenomenologically revealed phenomena in a scholastic, effect-to-cause manner, that is, we can reason from how we are directly given to what we must fundamentally be, such that we can appear in those ways. Even the experience of performing phenomenological reductions provides evidence for what we are, such that we can perform those acts.[82] Phenomenology can thereby provide evidence for metaphysics. Third, we can take principles grasped directly through the scholastic method (such as potency, act, or the four causes) and use them to interpret phenomenological findings. Phenomenology thereby provides the metaphysician with examples of previously discovered principles. Fourth, as Erazim Kohák

80. Others who join such methods include John Crosby, Mieczyław Krąpiec, Bernard Lonergan, Erich Przywara, Karl Rahner, Kenneth Schmitz, Robert Spaemann, Hans Urs von Balthasar, and Karol Wojtyła.
81. Stein, *Finite and Eternal Being*, 277, 333. Cf. Sarah Borden Sharkey, *Thine Own Self* (Washington, D.C.: The Catholic University of America Press, 2012), 56–59; Donald Wallenfang, *Human and Divine Being: A Study on the Theological Anthropology of Edith Stein* (Eugene, Ore.: Cascade Books, 2017), chap. 1.
82. Cf. Eugen Fink, *Sixth Cartesian Meditation: The Idea of a Transcendental Theory of Method*, trans. Ronald Bruzina (Bloomington: Indiana University Press, 1995).

emphasizes, we can understand phenomenological bracketing not as a rejection of theory altogether but as a method for rediscovering the experiences that first led to positing theoretical principles, and so return those principles to their foundation in concrete, lived experience.[83]

Having seen how to join the phenomenological and scholastic methods, I turn to some details of scholastic method. Scholasticism has a long history in Catholic anthropology. Drawing on Platonism, Aristotelianism, Stoicism, and the Bible and church fathers, it flourished first in the thirteenth and fourteenth and then again in the sixteenth and seventeenth centuries, before giving rise to a number of movements over the last two centuries. Only a brief consideration of Aquinas's version of scholastic method is necessary to get us started.[84] Natural knowledge begins with sense perception, by which we grasp particular features of beings. I use "feature" and "aspect" for anything distinguishable about a being or phenomenon, without indicating its metaphysical status. From what we sense, we intellectually abstract information about intelligible features of beings. As we have seen, in abstraction, we always fundamentally grasp the notion of being (*ens*) or existing thing, that is, whatever we grasp by the abstractive method, we grasp as a being or an aspect of being. From sensory content, we can abstract information about the kinds of beings we have sensed and so form concepts that apply universally to all members of a given kind, or concepts of the essences of beings as such. We can also abstract information about parts or properties of beings, and we can abstract notions that apply to all beings as such, prescinding from specific kinds of beings. Abstraction leads to the actualization or formation of concepts about beings, but it also involves—in the parallel to phenomenological method mentioned above—bracketing some of their aspects, such as what is particular about them or what it is like to grasp them sensibly.[85] To *actualize* is to bring into existence something that was previously only present *potentially*, that is, able to be present but not, in fact, present. On the basis of concepts, we make judgments or propositions about beings. For example,

---

83. Kohák, *The Embers and the Stars*, 24.
84. This quick account of powers and methodology will be elaborated in the next chapter. It is summarized from Aquinas, *ST* I, q.78, q.84, q.85, a.1; *In De Trin.*, q.5, a.4, q.6, a.1; *DPN*; *QDA*, a.13; *In III DA*, lect. 15. See John Wippel, *The Metaphysical Thought of Thomas Aquinas: From Finite Being to Uncreated Being* (Washington, D.C.: The Catholic University of America Press, 2000), chap. 2.
85. For a model of abstraction that emphasizes actualization, see Therese Scarpelli Cory, "Rethinking Abstractionism: Aquinas' Intellectual Light and Some Arabic Sources," *Journal of the History of Philosophy* 53, no. 4 (2015): 607–46. For a model that emphasizes bracketing, see Robert Pasnau, *Thomas Aquinas on Human Nature* (Cambridge: Cambridge University Press, 2002), 300–301.

Introduction　　35

we analyze concepts into propositional definitions, which express beings' essential content. We also reason from one judgment to another, including from judgments about effects to those about causes. *Cause* refers to any real explanatory principle of a being, which confers existence and explains why a being exists or has some property.

The structure of these cognitive acts yields a method for investigating human persons. We reflect on the objects of our acts and thereby conceptualize those objects and acts. We reason back to our acts' causes, the powers or potencies to perform them, and thus to the structure and causes of our being—that is, to an account of what we fundamentally are. There are regularities in the structure of experience; these are the objective principles that underlie and explain experience. By abstraction from sensory experiences of material things, we grasp what matter in itself is; we can then see how certain acts we perform, like intellectual acts, cannot be explained by matter. We thereby see that these acts do not take place in matter, and so we are irreducible to anything material. By this method, which resembles the contrastive method proposed by the realist phenomenologists, we grasp many aspects of what we irreducibly are.

Unlike the potentially nihilistic causal theories mentioned above, the objective principles discovered by abstraction are not posited as hypotheses, which could explain what is given but do not directly appear. Rather, these principles do partially appear in the structure of experience; they must be explicated for our experience to appear with its full meaning, and for us to fully perceive what appears in experience.[86] Thomistic method aims to "save the appearances" that give themselves experientially, not by a theory that could explain them but by reasoning to the truth about things on the basis of how they appear.[87] Thomistic hylomorphic "theory" explains what is given, not through other features of the observable world or by positing entities that do not appear, as a scientific theory does, but by working out the structure of what is given.

Phenomenological methodology has roots going back to Plato. This methodological strand aims at knowing things by direct, intuitive contact, and often describes what it grasps in affective, metaphorical, or even mythic language. Thomism includes a methodology going back to Aristotle, which aims at knowing things by receiving information into oneself and

---

86. Aquinas, *ST* I, q.85, a.1, ad 2.
87. Aquinas, *In I DCM*, lect. 22; *In II DCM*, lect. 17.

then causally analyzing what is known.[88] The former takes knowledge to be isomorphic with or directly revelatory of being, while the latter takes the "order of knowing" to be the opposite of the "order of being" (i.e., the order of dependence among beings and principles); in other words, what is more knowable to us is less fundamental in reality. Both methods are needed to account for all ways that we are irreducible. Experiential contact with things naturally leads to causal reasoning and reflection, which leads back to contact with reality. Aquinas actually combines the two; he describes both experiences of direct contact with reality, as in accounts of spiritual perception and of knowledge by connaturality, and gives causal accounts of other experiences.[89] The compatibility of the two is seen even better in other scholastics, such as John Duns Scotus, and in modern Thomists who incorporate intuitive contact into their methodology.[90] My aesthetic method also synthesizes both approaches.

This book unfolds in two broad parts, divided into nine chapters. The first part, which includes six chapters, launches my metaphysical portrait of the human person by giving an account of our many irreducible powers, as well as the irreducible principles in us that acts reveal. The second part, which includes three chapters, synthesizes the findings of the first part into a holistic portrait of the irreducible human person. Chapter 1 discovers in subjectivity some basic principles of the human person, including a range of powers. Over the next few chapters, I consider those powers and features of reality that the acts of each power discloses, and I show our irreducibility to matter. In chapter 2, I consider bodily powers and the structure of sensible qualities disclosed by those powers. Chapter 3 discusses the intellect and features of real being discovered by intellectual acts. Chapter 4 considers the will and its freedom, and I introduce the problem of accounting for human action as irreducible to divine action. Chapter 5 considers powers of affectivity and the principles of value that

---

88. On these strands, see, for example, Bernard Lonergan, *Verbum: Word and Idea in Aquinas* (Notre Dame, Ind.: University of Notre Dame Press, 1967), 183–88; Joyce Little, *Toward a Thomistic Methodology* (Lewiston, N.Y.: Edwin Mellen, 1988), 102–3, 305–10, 328; and Jean Leclercq, *The Love of Learning and the Desire for God: A Study of Monastic Culture*, trans. Catharine Misrahi (New York: Fordham University Press, 1961), 263–68, 279–83. See the parallel distinction between descriptive and revisionary metaphysics in analytic philosophy at P. F. Strawson, *Individuals: An Essay in Descriptive Metaphysics* (London: Routledge, 1990), 9–11.

89. *ST* II-II, q.45, a.2.

90. See, for example, Scotus, *Ord.* IV, d.45, q.3; Eleonore Stump, *Wandering in Darkness: Narrative and the Problem of Suffering* (Oxford: Oxford University Press, 2010), 51–61; and Jacques Maritain, *Untrammeled Approaches*, trans. Bernard Doering (Notre Dame, Ind.: University of Notre Dame Press, 1977), 207–42.

they reveal, and in chapter 6, I begin to synthesize the findings of the first five chapters, considering experience more concretely and holistically than in those first chapters. I consider the relation between the soul and its powers, and I introduce the concept of *energeia* from the Greek Fathers.

Having completed my account of our powers, I turn in the second part of the book to a more holistic portrait of the person. In chapter 7, I show how human persons are irreducible to our bodies, able to be constituted just by immaterial souls. In this chapter, I consider the proper definitions for *human nature* and for *personhood*. In chapter 8, I argue that we are irreducible to single substances; rather, human persons include a multiplicity of substances. Finally, in chapter 9, I contend that, although we can survive without matter, we are irreducible to our souls, being meant to exist and act in a wholly incarnated way. Here, I show how what we are fundamentally can best be grasped in terms of *beauty* and in terms of our orientation toward liturgical acts.

Part 1 The Irreducible Powers of the Human Person

Chapter 1 Subjectivity and the Principles
of Hylomorphism

I begin my portrait of the human person with experiences of subjectivity. These reveal key features of the human person in a way that presupposes very little other than the private experience of my self. Following Edith Stein, I show how these basic experiences of ourselves reveal, and provide evidence for, features of the person described by scholastic hylomorphism, the view on which we are composites of unchanging form (*morphē*) and changing matter (*hulē*). Even experiences that often receive a reductionistic, idealist, or dualist interpretation (as experiences of subjectivity often do) are evidence for our irreducibility and for the principles of realist metaphysics.

Experiences of Pure Subjectivity

Husserl's phenomenological reduction, as we saw in the introduction, involves suspending (i.e., ceasing to perform) acts of positing things as really existing apart from our intentional acts, as well as acts of explaining what appears to us by means of what does not appear. Once I suspend those acts, objects that I experience appear just as objects of my intentional acts (such as acts of thinking, perceiving, or valuing). I can then examine exactly how each kind of object shows up for me and in which kind of act it appears. For example, this book in my hands appears through acts of perceiving colors and shapes, categorizing and judging those colors and shapes to fall under the concept "book," moving as I turn it to see its various sides, apperceiving as I synthesize visual and tactile aspects into a single never-fully-grasped object, and so forth. Even my body and contents of my mind appear only through certain acts, such as proprioception, memory, introspection, categorization, and judgment. Suspending my spontaneous, natural positing of the book or my body as real extramental beings allows me to perceive and focus on exactly how each aspect of these objects appears to me.

Each intentional act has the same general structure: it has contents, such as colors, tones, or feelings, and, in virtue of the kind of act it is, it bestows a "sense" or "meaning" on those contents—that is, when we intend some content through a specific sort of act, that content appears as something and as fitting with that act in a specific way. Intentional acts *constitute* meaningful objects. This is not to say that acts cause their objects, or that we willfully impose meaning on contents. Rather, objects appear to have some meaning only through intentional acts, and contents and objects are always meaningful for subjects of intentional acts. To return to my book example: as I rotate it in my hand, I receive a range of colored shapes; this content meaningfully appears as colored shapes within acts of sense perception. But I spontaneously, apperceptively synthesize that content together so that I see these moving shapes as sides of a single object. Through acts of thinking or ideation, I recognize and register this object as a book, that is, as falling under the concept "book." If I evaluate this content, I experience it as enjoyable. In each act, content appears to me with a new meaning, that is, a new sort of object is given to me.

Husserl describes the structure of acts in hylomorphic terms; he claims that hylomorphic concepts "force themselves upon us" when we reflect on the structure of acts and objects. The content of each act appears as *matter* (*hulē*)—that is, as something determinable, able to receive various meanings. The act appears as *form* (*morphē*)—that is, as what determines the content or matter to have a meaning, unifying it and giving it a definite identity.[1] In using these terms, Husserl is drawing on the scholastic tradition; phenomenological analysis helps us understand that tradition by showing an example of its basic notions in our experience. Edith Stein makes it clear, however, that Husserl does not use *form* and *matter* with exactly the same sense that those terms have in scholasticism. In the latter, matter and form are principles of real beings, not conscious acts: matter

---

1. Husserl, *Ideas Pertaining to a Pure Phenomenology*, vol. 1, 203–16.

is that real principle that is determinable, changeable, in potency; form is that which determines matter in a definite way, explaining its unity and identity over time, its actuality. But Stein also contends that the Husserlian and scholastic usages of these terms involve analogous senses of *form* and *matter*—that is, these usages have interrelated though differently applied meanings. It is metaphysically significant that a fundamental analysis of both consciousness and real being reveals a structure of form and matter or act and potency. We can discover these principles of determinable content and an act that determines that content's meaning by reflecting on and abstracting the structure of both conscious acts and real beings. We can also find these principles in consciousness by applying principles abstracted from real beings to conscious acts. Each approach reveals that act and potency are central, pervasive features of being in general and of the human person in particular. In each case, act and potency appear irreducible to each other. These approaches converge in a holistic, aesthetic viewpoint where each is a way of perceiving ourselves from a different angle. In Stein's application of aesthetic method, she draws out yet another understanding of form—the holistic, perceivable whole or *Gestalt* of each being, within which all of its aspects take on meaning.[2]

In the Husserlian reduction, I experience all intentional objects—including my body and the contents of my mind—as having hylomorphic structure and as meaningfully constituted by my intentional acts. But I experience myself as those acts' subject—that is, as an existing consciousness or subjectivity that performs these acts but that is distinguishable from and prior to them, in the sense of being experientially more foundational than these acts. What I experience as *I* varies across experiences; part of the problem of figuring out what persons irreducibly are is the problem of figuring out what I am and what "I" properly picks out. In the experiences under consideration here, experiences had within Husserl's bracketing, I experience my *I* or *self* as pure subjectivity, without definite characteristics in itself aside from being the subject of acts. I *live* in my acts—that is, I experience myself not as entirely distinct from them but as experientially entering into and developing through them, but I also experience myself as irreducible to them and their objects. I can stand back from any object or act and regard it as distinct from me and thereby examine its essence, what it shares with other acts or objects of the same kind. Objects appear

---

2. Stein, *Finite and Eternal Being*, parts 2 and 4, especially 155–80, 204–7, 219–27, 267–71.

as real, physical, substantial, or causally related only within certain acts of thinking or perceiving—that is, these meanings are only bestowed on contents within these acts. But I, this pure subjectivity, am prior to those acts and meanings—hence, insofar as I experience myself in this way, I directly grasp myself as something that cannot be reduced to being an object. This is not a conclusion to which I reason or a hypothesis about myself; rather, when I perform the phenomenological reduction, I am directly aware of myself as pure subjectivity.[3]

As I suggested in the introduction, if we directly perceive some content, then that content must be something in itself, with a place in any complete metaphysics. That content cannot be nothing but something else; if it were, it would not be there to be directly perceived. Given these principles, subjectivity must be an irreducible feature of human persons. It is an aspect of each human person that cannot be grasped, by oneself or others, as an object, where an *object* is something that can be entirely defined, described, or grasped in third-person terms, terms that can be understood entirely from a vantage point exterior to the thing being described, or that is entirely something at which an intentional act can aim. The experience of pure subjectivity excludes any account of the human person on which we are entirely accounted for in objective, third-person definable terms. For example, Husserl argues that such subjectivity excludes any account of human persons on which we are only or fundamentally substances. He understands substances as stable, mathematically describable things, related to others by causality.[4] Others, like some hylomorphists and dualists, understand substances as things that exist in themselves and not as a property of something. Regardless of how substance is defined, if it is understood as definable or graspable entirely from a third-person or objective point of view, then the human person cannot be only a substance in that sense. What is missing from any such anthropology—which includes many forms of substance dualism and hylomorphism—is the fact that we have subjectivity, which can only be grasped and understood from the first-person viewpoint, the point of view interior to the I or self. Likewise, the direct experience of subjectivity excludes any version of materialism on which we are nothing but matter, where matter is entirely described, defined, or grasped in objective, third-person terms, such as mathematical terms.

---

3. Husserl, *Ideas Pertaining to a Pure Phenomenology*, vol. 1, 112–24, 156–57, 190–96.
4. Husserl, *Ideas Pertaining to a Pure Phenomenology*, vol. 1, 356; vol. 2, 36–37, 48.

But the experience of pure subjectivity can also be used to ground reductionist accounts of the human person. Husserl sees pure subjectivity as "transcendental," underlying and providing the condition for the possibility for any experience, to and for which all objects are given as meaningful, but which is never given as an object. On his view, only an account of subjectivity describes who we fundamentally are. Transcendental subjectivity is what unites our minds and bodies (rather than, say, a substantial form or soul), insofar as subjectivity is what performs our bodily and mental acts, and is what has the experiences of "having" a body and a mind.[5] This conclusion, however, is unwarranted by the evidence. Other methods reveal other, immediately given aspects of myself: I should not so focus on the experience of subjectivity, or on Husserlian method, that I conclude that I am only or only fundamentally pure subjectivity. That would be reductionistic. Rather, I must synthesize how I appear from a range of perspectives. Views like hylomorphism (on which, traditionally, we are defined in objectively graspable terms) must be augmented with an account of pure subjectivity, but accounts of pure subjectivity must be augmented with accounts of how we appear as real beings (as on scholastic hylomorphisms).[6] Each view tends to be reductionistic about the human person, but each can be made less reductionistic by incorporating the other's findings. While our bodies and minds are united insofar as I can subjectivity experience myself in each of them, they are also united in other ways. We shall later see, following Stein, how subjectivity is an aspect of the powers of the soul, and how the soul as conceived by hylomorphism and subjectivity as described by Husserl each unite aspects of us in distinct senses.[7]

Some phenomenologists in the Catholic tradition, like Scheler, reductionistically hold that persons are fundamentally just subjectivities (or "spirits") who perform, live in, and are prior to mental or bodily acts.[8] But other phenomenologists in the Catholic tradition add experiential evidence that helps overcome these reductionisms. Michel Henry, for example, used a version of the phenomenological reduction on which we bracket consideration of objects or acts in any way distinct from subjectivity. We

---

5. Edmund Husserl, "Phenomenology and Anthropology," in *Psychological and Transcendental Phenomenology and the Confrontation with Heidegger (1927–1931)*, ed. Thomas Sheehan and Richard Palmer (Dordrecht: Kluwer Academic, 1997), 485–500.

6. Like Scruton, *Sexual Desire*, 10–11, I deny that the "transcendental self" is our "metaphysical core," but contrary to him, I affirm that we do have experiences of pure subjectivity.

7. Stein, *Finite and Eternal Being*, 355–80, 427–64.

8. Scheler, *Formalism in Ethics and Non-Formal Ethics of Values*, 390.

cease to regard contents we receive as intentional objects standing over and against subjectivity. In this reduction, I experience my subjectivity not as prior to my acts; rather, I experience my subjectivity entirely as it lives in each experience, as a constantly changing stream of impressions and affects, a "self-feeling" or "auto-affection." The contents of this conscious stream are meaningful, yet, unlike in the Husserlian reduction, that meaning is not constituted by my acts. Rather, my conscious life now appears entirely given to me. The meaning of my conscious life arises out of another source than subjectivity.[9]

We saw in the introduction how Husserl noted that many aspects of my conscious life receive their meaning from other subjectivities, but he still saw my subjectivity as the unique source of meaning for me; I experience other persons as having meaningful content only through acts by which I intend them, and so there is a sense in which my acts constitute other persons as meaningful for me. Henry, by contrast, describes experiences of my subjectivity receiving its meaning and being from elsewhere: I am not the ultimate source of meaning or being, even for myself. The metaphysician of irreducibility must grasp what, in each of these views, is directly given (and so must be retained in any metaphysics) and what is a reductionistic interpretation of what is directly given. From Husserl, we directly grasp that each of us has pure subjectivity, which is a source of intentional acts that constitute meaningful objects, and which is a unique viewpoint upon the world. From Henry, we must retain that this subjectivity is received from some other source, and so is not what is most fundamental in us. Given the latter, deeper layer of experience, subjectivity cannot be the only transcendental condition for meaningful experience. We must figure out how subjectivity arises from more fundamental principles without claiming that subjectivity is an object.

Phenomenological findings are meant to be corroborated by others' experiential observations. Henry's findings have been taken up and extended by Jean-Luc Marion; in the introduction, I described how Marion brackets

---

9. Michael Henry, *Material Phenomenology*, trans. Scott Davidson (New York: Fordham University Press, 2008), 90–92; Henry, *The Essence of Manifestation*, trans. Girard Etzkorn (The Hague: Martinus Nijhoff, 1973), 459–78, 507–14. Henry reductionistically focuses on his results, wrongly concluding that the only thing that exists is subjectivity and its contents; he concludes that our subjectivity is given to us by a more absolute subjectivity of which ours is a part or aspect, which he identifies with God. See *The Essence of Manifestation*, 306–35, 501–19; Michel Henry, *I Am the Truth: Toward a Philosophy of Christianity*, trans. Susan Emmanuel (Stanford, Calif.: Stanford University Press, 2006), 53–57. While he wrongly interprets his findings in a quasi-pantheist way, his findings support the claim that we receive our being from God, who is innermost in us; see *ST* I, q.8, a.1.

everything but the experience of contents being given to us. In that reduction, I experience my subjectivity (and my ability to constitute objects as meaningful) as *given* to me; I am not fundamentally a *subject* who is the source of acts but a *gifted one (l'adonne)*—that is, one who, even in my subjective acts, experiences myself as a *gift*.[10] Henry's findings are also corroborated independently by Husserl's own assistant, Stein.[11] She describes how, in intentional acts, I experience my subjectivity as finite, vulnerable, and "frail," and not as the ultimate source of the meanings I constitute in my intentional acts. For example, I experience myself as distended over time, incomplete at every moment, and not the source of the ongoing flow of my conscious life from moment to moment; I also experience myself as unable to remember and consciously grasp my origins (since my conception and birth are prior to the beginnings of real conscious life), and as always threatened with the possibility of death. Despite the possibility of anxiety in the face of death, I also find that I can rest securely in this experience of the gift of existence received at each moment.[12] From all this, we can see how the Catholic phenomenological tradition calls our attention to a number of layers of subjectivity, all of which are directly grasped and so must have a place in a full metaphysical portrait of the person, and none of which are the only transcendental condition for experience.

Hylomorphic Principles in Pure Subjectivity

If Stein is correct that phenomenological accounts of subjectivity are evidence for positing act and potency as principles of the human person, then, contrary to objections raised in the introduction, focusing on purely interior experiences (like the Cartesian *cogito*) is not necessarily opposed to realist metaphysics. In this section, I explain further how subjective experience reveals hylomorphic principles.[13]

We have already seen how *meaningfulness* is a fundamental experiential phenomenon, and how when something is directly given as meaningful, it fits with one's acts (say, of understanding) and fulfills one's general

---

10. Jean-Luc Marion, *Reduction and Givenness: Investigations of Husserl, Heidegger, and Phenomenology*, trans. Thomas Carlson (Evanston, Ill.: Northwestern University Press, 1998), 204; Marion, *Being Given*, 27–39; and Marion, *In Excess*, 13–23. Cf. Christina Geschwandtner, *Degrees of Givenness: On Saturation in Jean-Luc Marion* (Bloomington: Indiana University Press, 2014).
11. Ian Leask, *Being Reconfigured* (Newcastle-upon-Tyne: Cambridge Scholars, 2011), 82–91.
12. Stein, *Finite and Eternal Being*, 35–64.
13. This section draws especially on Stein, *Finite and Eternal Being*, 35–60. Cf. Balthasar, *TL1*, 173.

desire for things to make sense, fitting with one's interpretive stance toward the world.[14] For example, when I see a book, it fits with and gives content to my act of understanding the concept "book": the book appears meaningful by corresponding to and fitting with a concept that I already know. When I grasp something as meaningless or as unclear, there is a lack of experienced "fit" between me and it. *Fittingness (convenientia)* is both a hylomorphic principle, discovered through abstraction from real beings, and a phenomenon experienced subjectively, as in the case just described. For things to fit is not for them to be strictly, logically necessary for one another but for them to be better together or to form a coherent whole together, as when two causes bring about an effect more effectively than either apart from the other could do. Fittingness is a modal concept, neither strict necessity (where something must obtain) nor mere logical possibility (where something can obtain), but where it is for the best, or at least for the better, for something to obtain. It is also an aesthetic concept: in order to grasp fit, it must be perceived when things fit, even if we cannot explain or demonstrate *why* they fit.[15] We experience things to be more meaningful the more they fit with other things, which allows them to be more effectively grasped. For example, a fact about the color of a single object is low in meaning: it fits with my perceiving powers, but it does not enable me to effectively grasp other things. The essence of triangularity is highly meaningful: it fits with and allows me to grasp all particular triangles and enables me to better understand many other geometric ideas, too.

We have seen how, on the abstractive method of Thomism, when we grasp anything conceptually, we grasp it as a kind of being. I also always grasp that being comes in different kinds: being in the primary sense is substance (that which exists in itself), and properties or accidents (such as the changeable characteristics of things) have being in a secondary sense, that is, they are modifications of and dependent on substances. In the Husserlian phenomenological reduction, being in the primary sense appears in subjectivity, while other things have being in a secondary sense. My subjectivity's being is given as certain for me—that is, in experiencing my own subjectivity, I grasp with complete certainty that my subjectivity exists, that is, that it has being. Intentional objects are given as beings, but

---

14. Cf. Mirela Oliva, "Hermeneutics and the Meaning of Life," *Epoché* 22, no. 2 (2018): 523–39.
15. Aquinas, *In I DA*, lect. 8, n. 130; *In Col.*, c. 1, lect. 4, n. 41; *ST III*, q.1, a.1; and Gilbert Narcisse, *Les Raisons de Dieu: Argument de Convenance Et Esthétique Théologique Selon Saint Thomas d'Aquin Et Hans Urs von Balthasar* (Fribourg: Editions Universitaires Fribourg Suisse, 1997), 102–104, 164–76.

as not entirely certain for me, since I can bracket their existence. My acts are given as beings whose existence is certain for me but whose being is founded on that of my subjectivity. The two methods yield different senses of being, but these senses are related analogically: in each, one bearer of being is primary, while other things' being is in some sense founded on the primary being. From this comparison, we can draw the conclusion that being is given as having analogically related kinds.

We have also already seen how, according to Stein, act and potency appear in all experiences. For example, we saw how intentional acts are forms or actualities for their content. Stein also notes that whenever I am conscious, I experience myself performing some actual act. In performing the act, I can distinguish between what exists (i.e., the act itself) and its actual being (i.e., the existence of this act); in both, being appears as actuality. However, in reflecting on anything actual, I grasp that I must have previously been able to be in that state—that is, before actually being in it, I was potentially in it. Furthermore, in reflection on my present experience, I grasp myself to be in potential to performing future acts—that is, as having the power to perform further acts. I experience specific kinds of acts (such as perceiving, thinking, and evaluating) as such that I can perform them—that is, I find that I have potentialities or powers for these acts, and these kinds of acts are given as in potential to existing in me. I am not just a bare subject of acts; rather, my subjectivity has a definite, given structure, including potencies to perform specific kinds of acts, and all of this is revealed in subjective experience.[16] We can also come to know these principles of act and potency by reflecting on real beings. We can see that real beings are actually existing and of some kind, that the matter from which they are made was in potency to being that kind of thing, and that beings are in potency to taking on various accidents. If it is in this way that we first grasp act and potency, we can then apply these principles to our subjectivity, seeing our experience as exemplifying them.[17] Whichever method we use, we find that act and potency fit together, making sense in reference to one another, as correlated sides of a single meaningful unity. An actuality is a new degree of "perfection" (i.e., being complete or determinate) beyond the capacity for being perfected that was previously pres-

---

16. In these claims, Stein follows Aquinas's account of reflecting on acts. See *DV*, q.10, a.8; *ST* I, q.87, a.1; *In III DA*, c. 3; Therese Scarpelli Cory, *Aquinas on Human Self-Knowledge* (Cambridge: Cambridge University Press, 2014), 41–60; and Husserl, *Ideas Pertaining to a Pure Phenomenology*, vol. 2, 266–67.

17. Aquinas, *DEE*; *DPN*; *In VII Met.*, lect. 1; *ST* I, q.77, a.1.

ent in the subject.[18] (In later chapters, I consider other senses of *actuality*.)

One might object to the claim that subjectivity can be described as structured or explained by principles like act, potency, being, and fittingness. Scholasticism tends to present these principles as fully explainable in objective, third-person terms. If subjectivity were explainable in terms of these principles, then subjectivity would be reducible to what is objective, but we have seen that subjectivity is directly given as irreducible to what can be grasped in that way. It would seem to follow, then, that subjectivity is not explainable in terms of principles like act, potency, being, and fittingness. Karol Wojtyła argues that phenomenology allows us to "pause" at irreducible subjectivity (or, as he calls it, "lived experience") and grasp that it does not fit into any category of being or principle posited by scholasticism. He argues that the metaphysician should posit a new category, members of which are indefinable and can only be grasped from the first-person point of view.[19] One might further motivate this objection by observing that the following propositions are self-evident: everything in an effect must come from its cause, and that nothing can give what it does not have. Given those propositions, subjectivity cannot arise from purely objective principles, since they lack what is found in their purported effect, namely, subjectivity.

What we need is an account that affirms both the directly given experience of subjectivity and the directly given act-potency structure.[20] I propose that we think of actuality (and other scholastic principles) as having in themselves an aspect that can only be grasped "from the inside," from the subjective or first-person viewpoint. Not all aspects of these principles are grasped through their propositional, objective descriptions. The principle of actuality in itself—that is, what actuality in itself is—has an aspect analogous to subjectivity, understandable only by analogy to my experience of myself. If everything about actuality could be described in purely objective ways, then the objector would be right: these principles could not give rise to, underlie, or explain subjectivity—since nothing can give what it does not have. Since experience shows that act and potency do underlie and explain subjectivity, then those principles must have something like subjectivity in themselves, an interior aspect that cannot

---

18. Cf. Aquinas, *ST* I, q.4, a.1.
19. Wojtyła, "Subjectivity and the Irreducible," 210–11.
20. I first developed this argument in Mark K. Spencer, "Aristotelian Substance and Personalistic Subjectivity," *International Philosophical Quarterly* 55, no. 2 (2015): 145–64.

be grasped in an objective, third-person way. Since, as Stein argued, all actualities are analogous to one another (and to other principles like potency), then there is something analogous to subjectivity—something that cannot be grasped, described, or defined from an exterior, objective point of view—in every act, potency, and being. Contrary to Wojtyła's claim, there is no need to posit a new kind of metaphysical principle to account for subjectivity; rather, as Kenneth Schmitz has argued, we must expand how we understand principles already posited in the Catholic tradition. Categories like substance, actuality, and being should not be understood as static foundations, on the model of impersonal things but rather as open and self-transcending, on the model of spiritual persons.[21]

In addition to act and potency, we find other metaphysical principles in experiences of subjectivity. Each act and content of consciousness gives itself as having both essential and variable aspects. Stein shows this by analyzing an experience of joy, though this analysis could be repeated, *mutatis mutandis*, for any other kind of experience. Each experience of joy has a formal structure. It includes a nature or what it is to be joy, which renders it the kind of experience it is, and which remains the same throughout the experience, allowing me to identify it even as the experience develops, changes in intensity, and varies in relation to other experiences. The nature or essential content of joy as such, which I find in every experience of joy, is distinct from a particular episode of joy's full content, which includes that distinct episode's particular, varying features. The nature of joy gives itself as a meaningful unity that in itself is distinct from each joy. It is distinct in that I can regard it through different intentional acts than those through which I experience a given episode of joy. To experience the latter, I must feel it and allow the joy to arise in me; focusing on thoughts about what joy is destroys the experience of joy in itself. But I can consider the nature of joy through acts of thinking. The nature is also distinct in that its mode of being is different: my particular joys are given as dependent on my subjectivity, while the essence of joy in itself is given as something that exists necessarily or eternally with its exact content.[22] Each experience of joy actualizes my conscious life—that is, it completes or adds to my subjectivity in a definite way. Following the scholastics, Stein calls these actualities that I have in addition to what I fundamentally am, accidents.

---

21. Kenneth Schmitz, "Substance Is Not Enough. Hegel's Slogan: From Substance to Subject," *Proceedings of the American Catholic Philosophical Association* 61 (1987): 52–68.
22. Stein, *Finite and Eternal Being*, 62–76. Cf. Sharkey, *Thine Own Self*, 65–80.

Furthermore, in every experience, some things are given as sharing or participating in others. *Participation* is as central a principle to scholastic metaphysics as act and potency.[23] As a particular feeling of joy changes in intensity, my subjectivity participates in (and so instantiates and receives) what joy is in itself—what Stein calls its "ideal essence" (*Wesenheit*)—to different degrees. By this I mean that when I feel joy, my subjectivity does not essentially become joy in itself (or even this particular joy). Rather, joy becomes present in my subjectivity to some extent, without my subjectivity ceasing to be what it essentially is. "Participation" denotes any instance of a subject having some property, where that property does not essentially characterize that subject, any instance of a property being received by or given to a subject. That a principle can be participated in does not entail that it can be participated in by multiple subjects; rather, some principles can be participated in by only one subject.

These experiences as Stein describes them give reason to hold that we participate not only in accidents but also in *existential actualities*. I experience my subjectivity as both certainly existing and as contingently given to itself. The latter experience reveals that I only participate in existence; *to be* does not characterize what I am. I experience a difference between what this subjectivity is and its status as contingently, giftedly existing. If we then abstract general principles from this experience or apply to this experience the scholastic reasoning that I describe over the next few chapters, we find that there is reason to distinguish the being that I am from my actuality of existing, by participation in which I contingently exist. We shall see in chapter 3 that different scholastics describe experiences that motivate positing various kinds of distinction between being and the act of existence—some claim this is a real distinction, others a conceptual distinction, and still others another kind of distinction. The experience of the contingency and reception of one's subjectivity does not settle the debate among these views. But this experience does reveal an act-potency structure in pure subjectivity: even when I bracket attention to all things other than subjectivity, I experience myself as something capable of existing that receives actual existence at every moment. I can also thereby grasp that there is something that it is to exist as such, in which I also participate. I do

---

23. See Aquinas, *DPN*; *In De Heb.*, lect. 2; *DSS*, c. 3; *ST* I-II, q.52, a.1. Cf. Cornelio Fabro, "The Intensive Hermeneutics of Thomistic Philosophy: The Notion of Participation," in *Selected Works of Cornelio Fabro*, vol. 1, ed. Nathaniel Dreyer (Chillum: IVE Press, 2016), 83; Adrian Pabst, *Metaphysics: The Creation of Hierarchy* (Grand Rapids, Mich.: Eerdmans, 2012), 32–34.

not find the full, perfect content of existence in my own existence; rather, what it is to exist can be shared with others.

As I integrate phenomenological and scholastic findings, we shall see that there is reason to distinguish: my essence (*essentia*) or what I am (in the senses of both what I am in particular and the specific kind of thing I am); my factual existence (*existentia*), that is, the fact that I exist; my act of existence (*esse, actus essendi*), the gift and actuality by participation in which I exist; and me, this concrete existent of a certain essential kind (*ens, res*). My essence is in potency to, receives, and exercises an act of existence; essence is related to *esse* as potency to act. I experience existence "from the inside," no less than I so experience other principles that I have mentioned. To exist is not only a logical fact, the ability to be represented in existentially quantified sentences,[24] nor is it only an objective principle.

I also experience myself participating in *essential actualities*. My humanity, personhood, and subjecthood, like my joy and my existence, are experienced as received by and given to me, not objects whose meaning is entirely constituted by my acts. When I participate in something, it gives (or *communicates*) itself to me, and I to it; I can act and experience in virtue of it, it can act or manifest itself through me, I resemble it (or take on its characteristics), and I am in contact and united with it, in the sense that it is present and active in me. I never experience my subjectivity apart from its participation in some content; nothing ever appears in complete isolation from others. My direct awareness of this is reason to think that any view on which I am just one thing or principle (say, subjectivity, a substance, a bare particular) is reductionistic. I am directly given as *including* multiple principles, such as subjectivity, acts, and potencies, and I am irreducible to any one of these. Similarly, on any scholastic abstractive analysis, nothing ever appears or acts in an entirely isolated way. As Wojtyła observes, reality is structured such that things act together or, in his terms, act with *solidarity*.[25] Even in the pure experience of subjectivity afforded by Henry's reduction, in which I bracket awareness even of intentional acts, I experience myself as receiving contents along with other subjects. Henry gives the example of the purely subjective impressions involved in admir-

---

24. *Contra*, for example, Willard V. Quine, "On What There Is," *The Review of Metaphysics* 2 (1948): 32; Peter van Inwagen, "Being, Existence, and Ontological Commitment," in *Metametaphysics: New Essays on the Foundations of Ontology*, ed. David Chalmers et al. (Oxford: Clarendon, 2009).

25. Karol Wojtyła, *The Acting Person*, trans. Anna-Teresa Tymieniecka (Dordrecht: Riedel, 1979), 268–71, 284–85.

ing an artwork along with another: I do not perceive the other's bodily acts and then reason that he or she too must be admiring the artwork; rather, I directly experience myself admiring the artwork with another.[26] Even the most private experiences involve acting together with other principles or beings; all experiences are *intersubjective*.

This solidarity is even more apparent through the realist phenomenological reduction, which focuses on acts of self-transcendence. As we saw in the introduction, my acts of knowing, choosing, perceiving, and so forth are not just intentional acts that meaningfully constitute objects. Rather, in most such acts, I also transcend (or experientially go beyond) my own subjectivity and make real and experiential contact with other beings. In most acts, I participate in what is genuinely other than me, partially receiving its content into my consciousness, even while experiencing its excess over and otherness than what I grasp about it. A structure of self-transcendence is found in all aspects of our lives and being—that is, each of our features, whether discovered by phenomenological or scholastic method, goes beyond itself to make contact with what exceeds it. For example, potencies transcend themselves in being actualized.

Hylomorphic Principles in Bodily and Psychological Subjectivity

Other experiences of subjectivity reveal further irreducible aspects of human persons. On the Husserlian reduction, I can consider my body as an object distinct from my pure subjectivity, but by bracketing attention to other acts, I can also consider how I live in my bodily acts. In addition to experiencing myself as pure subjectivity, I also can experience myself as a body. By attending to other acts, I can experience myself as other kinds of things as well. I experience myself as affected and given meaning by an external world of beings transcendent to subjectivity, and by an internal world of feelings and drives. When I focus on external acts, I experience myself as a body located in a place, extended in space, and sensing itself "from the inside." When I focus on how my subjectivity lives in spontaneously arising psychological acts, such as feelings, drives, habitual acts, and associations among thoughts, I experience myself as what Husserl calls a *psyche*, a unity of those acts. When I focus on my how my subjectiv-

---

26. Henry, *Material Phenomenology*, 114.

ity lives in *spiritual acts*—that is, acts that are *motivated* or arise only when I self-consciously grasp their meaning, rather than spontaneously arising whether or not I grasp their meaning—I experience myself as a *spirit* or *personality*. I experience my spirit and psyche as having a structure that is experienced as structured in a way analogous to space, in which I can subjectively "move about" by attending to different sorts of conscious and subconscious acts, powers, and dispositions.[27]

My conscious acts thus fall into different kinds or *spheres*. A sphere is a unified "place" where acts take place: some take place "in" my body, and others "in" my psyche or spirit.[28] Each sphere directly presents content to my subjectivity; there is something irreducible in each, which must be retained in any metaphysical portrait of the human person, though further reasoning is needed to discover exactly what each of these spheres is, and how they are related. My body and psyche can appear both purely as objects that I consider through intentional acts, and as ways that my subjectivity lives, such that I experience myself as a bodily or psychological "I." The "I" of pure subjectivity is a more foundational layer of experience than my body, psyche, or personality, however, since those can be bracketed and regarded as objects.[29] As Catholic existentialist Gabriel Marcel notes, experience discloses a distinction between *being* and *having*.[30] To experientially be something is to experience that thing subjectively, "from the inside." To experientially have something is for it to appear as mine, intimately associated with but distinct from what I experience subjectively as me. Experientially, I am a pure subjectivity, and both am and have a body, psyche, and spirit.

Stein further notes that contents received into my consciousness (such as colors and tones) are experienced as caused in me.[31] Even when I bracket all consideration of real beings, I experience some aspects of my

---

27. Stein (*Finite and Eternal Being*, 373) describes our inner world using St. Teresa of Avila's image of the "interior castle," in which by religious experience we enter more deeply into "rooms" within ourselves; see Teresa of Avila, *Interior Castle*, trans. E. Allison Peers (New York: Image, 1989). Or, to use a less domestic, wilder metaphor, but one closer to the feel of much interior experience, see Gerard Manley Hopkins's poem "No worst": "O the mind, mind has mountains; cliffs of fall/Frightful, sheer, no-man-fathomed" (*The Major Works* [Oxford: Oxford University Press, 1986], 167).
28. Scheler, *Formalism in Ethics and Non-Formal Ethics of Values*, 100–104.
29. Husserl, *Ideas Pertaining to a Pure Phenomenology*, vol. 1, 124–27; vol. 2, 98, 114–18, 128–33, 184–86.
30. Gabriel Marcel, *Being and Having*, trans. Katherine Ferrer (Westminster: Dacre Press, 1949), 154–66.
31. Stein, *Finite and Eternal Being*, 55. Interiorly experienced causality is distinct from physical causality, which requires spatial contact; see *ST* I, q.75, a.1, ad 3.

subjective life as giving rise to others. Here, again, Stein sees experiential evidence for Aristotelian scholastic principles. Aristotelians enumerate at least four kinds of causes.[32] Each can be found in subjectivity. That which makes contents in my consciousness is their *efficient* or *making cause*. These contents characterize and actualize my consciousness, and so they are *forms* or *formal causes*, actualities that characterizes some subject, in virtue of which the subject exists in some way and has some content. My subjectivity is a *material cause* for this form, a principle that is in potency to, receives, and comes to be characterized by a form. Finally, the contents received in subjectivity are oriented toward being constituted as meaningful by intentional acts—that is, they aim at something beyond themselves. That at which something aims, its purpose or goal, is its *final cause* or *end*.

Subjectivity and Irreducibility to Matter

I have argued that experiences of subjectivity are sufficient evidence against any version of materialism on which I am nothing but a material thing, where matter is understood in purely objective terms. I cannot be nothing but *corporeal matter*—that is, matter just insofar as it has quantitative or mathematically describable properties (like mass or spatial extension), can make spatial contact with things, and is given as an object of intentional acts of perception, scientific reasoning, and measurement. I now consider some further conclusions regarding our relations to matter that can be drawn from phenomenological findings reviewed so far.

According to some versions of materialism, I am *ontologically reducible* to corporeal matter—that is, I am identical to an aggregate of material things, such as atoms or molecules or neurons.[33] One such version of materialism is *eliminative materialism*, which argues that positing consciousness is a poor explanation for human behavior, and that human behavior can be better explained neurologically.[34] Another version is *mind-brain identity theory*, on which accounts of consciousness are just redescriptions of accounts of brain states.[35] On both of those views, we are nothing but organisms that can be adequately described in third-person terms. Other versions of materialism hold that I am ontologically reducible not to cor-

---

32. Aquinas, *DPN*; *In II Phys.*, lect. 5.
33. Madden, *Mind*, 174.
34. Paul Churchland, *Matter and Consciousness* (Cambridge, Mass.: MIT Press, 1988), 43–49.
35. J. J. C. Smart, "Sensations and Brain Processes," *Philosophical Review* 68, no. 2 (1959): 141–56.

poreal matter but to something else that is purely an object, like an algorithmic pattern. For example, *functionalism* holds that conscious acts are objective patterns of taking in inputs, computationally processing them, and giving outputs, as if our brains were basically moist robots or computers.[36]

Still other versions of materialism hold that I am *causally reducible* to corporeal matter—that is, while I am or include more than just objective matter, everything about me (including subjectivity) is explained or caused by objective matter.[37] On some such views, including *emergentism* (which I consider further below), subjectivity is an ontologically irreducible feature of human persons, but it is entirely caused by objective matter—say, by events in the brain, or interaction between the brain and the world.[38] Other views account for subjectivity by positing a causal origin for it—for example, claiming that it arose from a change in brain structure at some point in human evolution, or from the emergence of acts like phonetic writing or silent reading, which allowed us to step back from being experientially immersed in the world and to develop an interior sense of self.[39]

But regardless of when human persons historically first had the experience of pure subjectivity (and regardless of whether every person has it), when one has this experience, one directly grasps the irreducible content of subjectivity as such, which must be accounted for in itself. Furthermore, we have seen that, given the principle that nothing can give what it does not have, subjectivity cannot arise from a cause that altogether lacks its content. All of these materialisms would require us to deny the experience of irreducible subjectivity, which I directly experience; the direct grasp of the content of irreducible subjectivity could not turn out to be nothing but some other content, and it cannot be explained away ontologically or causally. Anything that *appears*, is *something*, not *nothing* or *nothing but*

---

36. Jerry Fodor, "Materialism," in *Materialism and the Mind-Body Problem*, ed. David Rosenthal (Indianapolis, Ind.: Hackett, 2000), 128–49. I owe that metaphor to Owen Imgrund.

37. Madden, *Mind*, 174–75. On ways that hylomorphism can hold that the phenomenology and intentionality of acts are irreducible to functions or matter, see Martha Nussbaum and Hilary Putnam, "Changing Aristotle's Mind," in *Essays on Aristotle's De Anima*, ed. Amelie Rorty (Oxford: Clarendon, 1992), 49–50.

38. John Searle, *The Rediscovery of the Mind* (Cambridge, Mass.: MIT Press, 1992); Alva Noë, *Action in Perception* (Cambridge, Mass.: MIT Press, 2004).

39. David Abram, *The Spell of the Sensuous: Perception and Language in a More-Than-Human World* (New York: Vintage, 1996), chap. 4; Julian Jaynes, *The Origin of Consciousness in the Breakdown of the Bicameral Mind* (New York: Mariner Books, 2000), pt. 1; and Hubert Dreyfus and Sean Kelly, *All Things Shining: Reading the Western Classics to Find Meaning in a Secular Age* (New York: Free Press, 2011), chaps. 4–5.

something else. It has a place in a metaphysics of irreducibility. Appearing is a kind of being. Because we indubitably can have experiences of pure subjectivity, these materialisms—along with any view that explains us in purely objective terms, such as any mechanistic or naturalistic approach—must be rejected as reductionistic and false. We could not even entertain any of these views unless we could regard our bodies and psyches as examinable objects—that is, we can only entertain these views because we have subjectivities that are given as a more fundamental layer of ourselves than everything objective in us. These materialisms deny the very experience of pure subjectivity that makes possible the intentional acts through which we can even entertain these views.[40]

Many contemporary philosophers have rejected views on which we are nothing but objective matter because each experience we have includes *qualia*, or "what it's like" subjectively to be in that state.[41] It is true that there is a subjective sense to every conscious act, which includes irreducible content that cannot be exhaustively objectively described, but my argument goes further. There is not only a subjective "feel" to each experience: we can stand back from every such "feel" and experience ourselves as the pure subjects of the acts in which those "feels" appear. We are irreducible both to objective matter and to qualia, since both can be objects of intentional acts.

Since we experience ourselves as bodies, and so as at least partly material, a metaphysics of irreducibility must consider what matter is. Since I experience a bodily "I" (i.e., I experience my body "from the inside"), at least some subjective experiences arise out of matter. Since nothing can give what it does not have, matter itself must be subjective in some way. Indeed, we have already seen reason to hold this claim. As Stein argued on experiential grounds, every potentiality and actuality are analogous to each other, and some potentialities and actualities are subjective. Matter has potential and actual aspects, and therefore, matter must have something analogous to subjectivity. An experientially grounded metaphysics of irreducibility should conceive of matter along the lines of *panpsychism* (or *panprotoexperientialism*), the view on which matter is intrinsically sub-

---

40. Percy, *Lost in the Cosmos*, 159–66.
41. David Chalmers, *The Conscious Mind: In Search of a Fundamental Theory* (Oxford: Oxford University Press, 1997), 4ff.; Frank Jackson, "Epiphenomenal Qualia," *Philosophical Quarterly* 32, no. 127 (1982): 127–36; and Joseph Levine, "Materialism and Qualia: The Explanatory Gap," *Pacific Philosophical Quarterly* 64, no. 4 (1983): 354–61.

Principles of Hylomorphism 59

jective or ordered toward subjectivity.[42] (My account so far is consistent with the view that our subjectivity entirely arises out of matter understood as something subjective; later, I argue that it does not entirely arise out of matter in any sense.) Nothing is ever given purely as an object; the materialisms I have mentioned are reductionistic not just about us but about everything, since nothing is reducible to purely objective matter.

Materialist reductionisms about subjectivity are sometimes motivated by a view that a theory is explanatory just inasmuch as it allows prediction (and, thereby, control) of future events, including persons' acts. Subjectivity and *qualia* seem to play little or no role in successful naturalistic predictive theories, and so, it would seem, they can be eliminated or reduced (and, for the same reason, appeal to transcendent causes, considered below, is often eliminated on these views).[43] But this is to so focus on the goals of one act, scientific reasoning, that one fails to remember that this act is an abstraction from (or just one part of) the whole of experience. This approach confuses prediction (which is often useful only in controlled laboratory situations) with grasping what something is and what its ultimate causes are.[44] A metaphysics of irreducibility is concerned with the *question of being*, with grasping what it is for something to be, not just with the question of how to control it. It is a mark of our irreducibility that we are not content until we know a thing intimately and deeply; just being able to predict what something will do is a superficial (albeit useful and important), and so ultimately unsatisfying, approach to things.[45]

Reductionistic materialism is sometimes motivated by a limited experience of *values*, which I will discuss further in chapter 5. Max Scheler describes how most cognitive and volitional acts are motivated and guided by feelings in which we perceive values—that is, intentional acts in which we grasp features of things that give them importance of some kind and that prescribe some response as their due. We must form these feelings vir-

---

42. On a version of panpsychism emphasizing its resemblance to idealism, see Susan Schneider, "Idealism, or Something Near Enough," in *Idealism: New Essays in Metaphysics*, ed. Tyron Goldschmidt and Kenneth Pearce (Oxford: Oxford University Press, 2017), 287–88. On a materialist version of panpsychism, according to which matter must be essentially conscious, because it causes our consciousness, see Galen Strawson, "Realistic Monism: Why Physicalism Entails Panpsychism," *Journal of Consciousness Studies* 13 (2006): 3–31.

43. Daniel Dennett, "Quining Qualia," in *Consciousness in Contemporary Science*, ed. A. J. Marcel and E. Bisiach (Oxford: Clarendon, 1988), 42–77; Colin McGinn, "Can We Solve the Mind-Body Problem?" *Mind* 98, no. 391 (1989): 349–66; and cited in Madden, *Mind*, 143–47, 202.

44. Aristotle, *Post. An.*, II.1–3.89b21–90a35.

45. Karl Rahner, *Spirit in the World*, trans. William Dych (New York: Continuum, 1994), 57, following Heidegger, *Being and Time*, 1–17.

tuously if we are to grasp the world aright, for we are guided by these feelings about importance regardless of whether we realize it. Each person has at least an implicit view as to which values are more important than others, which Scheler, following Augustine, calls an "order of loves" (*ordo amoris*). Scheler makes no direct argument for his claims about the true hierarchy of values; he holds that it is grasped only by virtuously formed feeling, but evidence for his hierarchy includes the facts that higher values are longer lasting, can give greater satisfaction when felt, and lead to more virtuous actions when pursued. The least important value, on Scheler's view, is the value of producing pleasure, followed by values of utility, vital values (such as the importance of strength, health, or life in itself), and values of truth, morality, aesthetics, and, most important, holiness.[46]

Since reasoning is always guided by values, there is (as I argued in the introduction) no completely neutral starting point for inquiry. If one is guided primarily by furthering the value of utility, one will value a theory only insofar as it facilitates making practical predictions about what beings will do. Theories do this when they treat beings as just occupying roles in law-abiding causal chains; most such theories treat beings, including persons, as material mechanisms, having value only as a means to further ends (such as survival). These theories guide us to perceive some aspects of persons, those that are mechanistic and explainable objectively. However, being guided only by values of utility, and so exclusively adopting such theories, blinds us to aspects of persons that appear only when we are guided by higher kinds of value—that is, that directly appear only when we regard persons as important in ways other than their utility.[47]

To fully grasp persons, we must feel, for example, their vitality, beauty, goodness, and holiness (or lack thereof). These feelings guide our attention to features of persons that ground these values and that are not considered in mechanistic materialisms. In normal life, we tend to engage with others in ways guided by these higher values; for this reason, most people are at least implicitly aware of persons' nonmechanistic, nonmaterialistic features, such as subjectivity, freedom, and holistic beauty. When we turn to modes of inquiry that abstract from the full content of experience, like scientific reasoning, we tend to lose sight of those higher values. While

---

46. Scheler, *Formalism in Ethics and Non-Formal Ethics of Values*, 90–97, 105–10; Scheler, "Ordo Amoris," 110–11. Cf. Kohák, *The Embers and the Stars*, 238.

47. Max Scheler, *Ressentiment*, trans. Lewis Coser (Milwaukee, Wisc.: Marquette University Press, 1994), 32–42, 126–43.

being guided by utility values allows us to achieve mathematical precision about some aspects of reality, other values guide us to features of reality, which, while not describable with mathematical precision, are nevertheless directly perceived—and so have a place on a complete metaphysics. More importantly, our experience of those other values allows us to perceive that persons (and other beings) are not merely means to accomplishing our goals but ends that are deserving of understanding, respect, enjoyment, and awe in their own right. It is not always wrong to think about persons as useful means or as objects, but doing so exclusively is reductionistic and wrong.[48]

Phenomenological Evidence for My Real Being

In the Husserlian reduction, things only appear as real (or extramentally existing) within intentional acts like sense perception and judgment; only those acts constitute things as bearing the meaning "real." As pure subjectivity, I am prior to everything "real." Other reductions, however, reveal further aspects of reality. If, following Marion, I bracket consideration of intentionality so as to focus purely on the given, I find that much of what I receive exceeds any meaning I can fully understand or constitute in an object. If, following realist phenomenologists, I just bracket explanatory theories so as to focus on my cognitive, affective, and volitional contact with reality, I find that in my acts, I transcend myself and make contact with beings that exceed any meaning I can assign to them. Through both of those reductions, I discover a sense of the "real" that exceeds what Husserl considers. Husserl considers just the notion of reality insofar as I can fully grasp it and apply it to beings through intentional acts, but these other reductions reveal to me phenomena that exceed that notion of reality.[49] I use the phrase *real being* to designate beings insofar as they exist in a way that exceeds what I can grasp about them.

Stein contends that I experience sensory and intelligible contents being

---

48. The distinction between using and enjoying persons, treating them as a mere means or as an end deserving of respect in themselves, has roots in the work of Augustine, Immanuel Kant, and Scheler, and is developed well in Karol Wojtyła, *Love and Responsibility*, trans. H. T. Willets, (San Francisco: Ignatius Press, 1981), 21–45.

49. Marion does not use the notion of "reality" to describe what exceeds my intentional acts, but I think that the realist phenomenological notion of "reality" fits with his account of those phenomena. See John Crosby's "Introductory Study" in Dietrich von Hildebrand, *The Nature of Love*, trans. John F. Crosby (South Bend, Ind.: St. Augustine's Press, 2009), xxxii–xxxvi.

caused in my consciousness; since this causal process is prior to my experience of those contents, there are aspects of me (such as my causal relations to other beings) that exceed what I directly grasp about myself. Due to these causal relations, I experience myself as a real being causally related to other real beings. I also experience my subjectivity as arising from sources within me, from a subconscious life of powers, motivations, tendencies, moods, and vocation. For example, my subjective ability to perform intentional acts is affected by moods (like feeling awake or sleepy) and bodily events (like aging or pain), which are aspects of the "frailty" of subjectivity already mentioned.[50] Even as pure subjectivity, I am given to myself, constituted in my meaning and being by things internal and external to me, which are prior to my subjectivity. Since my subjectivity arises from deeper layers within me, which I cannot grasp from the point of view of my subjectivity, I am more than pure subjectivity. While my subjectivity is not "real" in Husserl's sense, it is real in the sense given in the last paragraph. As Czech phenomenologist Jan Patočka notes, my subjectivity is given as an appearance of an underlying being.[51] In the introduction, I noted that, on scholastic methodology, I reason in effect-to-cause fashion from how I appear in experience to what I am. We see now that there is phenomenological warrant for such reasoning: my full experience of subjectivity points to my existence as a real being underlying and causing my subjectivity.

Catholic personalist John Crosby further notes that I not only experience myself as pure subjectivity but also as failing or succeeding at living in accord with my vocation, that is, with who I truly am and who I am called to authentically be. I discover this not through a reduction but through discernment and recollection, in which I meditatively recall my attention from distractions and reflect on the course and goals of my life.[52] This requires interaction with others: while I know my own subjectivity best, I am often not in the best position to know who I truly am; rather, others must reveal my authentic self and calling to me. This experience is further evidence that I am a real being in whom subjectivity is just one actuality. I, this whole, real person, am not strictly identical to my subjectivity.

---

50. Stein, *Finite and Eternal Being*, 364–70. Cf. Heidegger, *Being and Time*, 127–30; Levinas, *Totality and Infinity*, 230–36.

51. Jan Patočka, *Plato and Europe*, trans. Petr Lom (Stanford, Calif.: Stanford University Press, 2002), 31.

52. John Crosby, *The Selfhood of the Human Person* (Washington, D.C.: The Catholic University of America Press, 1996), 129. Cf. Dietrich von Hildebrand, *Transformation in Christ* (Manchester, N.H.: Sophia Institute Press, 1990), 105–13.

Hylomorphism in Real Beings

Having seen that phenomenology can discover hylomorphic principles of real being in me, I turn to the other method with which I proposed to begin my portrait of human persons, abstractive scholastic method. In this method, we start with perceptions of real beings and reason from what we perceive about particular beings to general principles that describe beings' fundamental structure. Through abstraction, we note universal features of real, perceived beings; these principles are the underlying, explanatory, and causal structure of real being. Aristotle noted that every real, physical being presents itself as changing and as remaining the same, and as unified and multiple.[53] We experience beings coming into and going out of existence, while something persists through those changes; between their origin and their demise, beings persist and retain their identity over time, yet they also continually change their attributes and matter. Things do not just appear as a constant flux, as the ancient Greek philosopher Heraclitus thought, nor is everything reducible to changeless being grasped in thinking, as the Eleatic philosophers held.

Hylomorphism explains these observations with the following principles. When a physical being comes into existence, matter that existed before and during that event takes on a new, limited actuality (*energeia*) or *form*, which it previously potentially had. *Matter* is the principle of continuity through change, and it is what is structured by form. We observe matter only with some definite identity; this is because matter is always actualized by some form. Every actuality that we observe in material things is a perfection, a kind of completion, irreducible to their matter; matter is always completed or made actual in some way. Other principles phenomenologically described above are also discovered through this abstractive method. Events in which matter receives some form are brought about by *efficient causes*. These are forms in substances other than the one receiving a new form, by which the causing substance communicates or gives formal content that it already has to the caused substance. Forms are also *final causes*: substances act to maintain actualities and to achieve further actualities, which fulfill or fit with their potentialities.

Having grasped these universal principles, we can then allow our con-

---

53. What follows is summarized from Aristotle, *Phys.*, I.7, II.3; Aquinas, *In I&II Phys.*; *DPN*; *DEE*; *ST* I, q.76.

cepts of these principles to guide how we perceive substances. When we do that, substances (including human beings) appear intrinsically unified, not as mere aggregates or arrangements of matter. We observe things taking on, retaining, and losing unifying perfections (or forms): matter takes on the perfection of being a substance (like an organism), and substances take on the perfections that are accidents (like sensible qualities and actions). Based on what we grasp by perception, we can see that form is not added to matter extrinsically, nor is it an *integral part* of a substance—that is, a physical part like my arms, liver, brain, or cells.[54] Rather, form is revealed in our experiences of beings and their integral parts as intrinsically unified. For example, we see organisms, acting, perceiving, and manifesting themselves as unities; even when we observe individual parts (like cells) performing actions, these parts present themselves as intrinsically unified. Furthermore, we grasp the full meaning of these acts and parts only when we grasp how they fit into whole organisms—when we grasp how they receive their identity from the organism's form and are ordered to the organism's end. There must be something in substances beyond those parts that explains that unity, perfection, or completion. Form is not a set of relations among integral parts, nor is it "constituted" by matter in the sense of being a unity caused by an aggregation of matter, as a statue is constituted by a lump of clay.[55] Rather, it is an intrinsic perfection and unity that belongs to and gives identity to all of a substance's matter and to each of its parts, a perfection distinct from and unifying of perfections the matter has apart from form. I am human as a whole, as is each of my parts. Form explains why a substance's matter and parts are unified, and so is ontologically prior to them; it confers unity and identity upon matter rather than arising from matter. Form and matter make up single, unified substances, and we experience this intrinsic unity. Form also appears as a normative or value-laden principle; it confers a "nobility," "excellence," or worth upon substances: when I grasp a substance to be unified in a way typical of its kind, I simultaneously grasp it as having value, deserving treatment according to its kind.[56] The experience of things as unified in these ways is evidence that we include form and that we are therefore causally and ontologically irre-

---

54. *Contra* some contemporary versions of hylomorphism, for example, Kathrin Koslicki, *The Structure of Objects* (Oxford: Oxford University Press, 2008), 171–76. For a summary of inadequate hylomorphisms, see Robert Koons, "Staunch vs. Faint-Hearted Hylomorphism," *Res Philosophica* 91, no. 2 (2014): 151–77.

55. Stump, *Aquinas*, 113, 209–10, 304.

56. Aquinas, *In I Sent.*, d.17, q.1, a.2, ad 3; *SCG* I, c. 28.

ducible to matter in any sense, even matter that is intrinsically subjective.

Like fittingness, form is an aesthetic principle, a self-manifesting perfection and activity of a whole being. Phenomenological descriptions of how a substance as a whole manifests itself can serve as evidence for scholastic claims about form. Using a reduction that aims at perceiving the world as I concretely live in it and on which we bracket explanatory theories as much as possible but always recognize that we cannot stop interpreting and theorizing about the world,[57] Merleau-Ponty describes how we always perceive beings as *Gestalten*. In other words, each being gives itself as a unified whole, not a conglomeration of parts, and as distinct from, but fitting with, the surrounding background. Just as we can recognize the unique *style* (or manner of acting) of an artist like Mozart or Rembrandt in each of his works, so we can recognize a unified style in each substance's activities. Each substance's matter appears organized to express and act with this style. For example, when we know and love a person well, we perceive his or her distinctive style in each action.[58] Further evidence that we perceive this style, and exploration of what style is, will be considered later.

I follow several thinkers in the broadly Thomistic tradition (including John Haldane, David Braine, and John Milbank) in holding that we can reason about styles and *Gestalten* in an effect-to-cause manner.[59] We can ask what we must fundamentally be such that we appear in this way—that is, what abstractable, structuring principles would I have to have in order to appear this way.[60] While our matter and the overall perceivable *Gestalten* that we present to the world continually change, each being's unified style, which is present in all of its acts, requires an explanation: there must be an unchanging, self-manifesting principle that explains it. We can call this structuring principle *form* or *actuality*. Similarly, Stein distinguished a

---

57. Merleau-Ponty, *Phenomenology of Perception*, xviii–xxiv.
58. Maurice Merleau-Ponty, *Structure of Behavior*, trans. Alden Fischer (Pittsburgh: Duquesne University Press, 1983), 4/, 156; Merleau-Ponty, *Phenomenology of Perception*, 70–3, 319, 352–53, 382–83; and Merleau-Ponty, *The Visible and the Invisible*, trans. Alphonso Lingis (Evanston, Ill.: Northwestern University Press, 1969), 139.
59. Mary Rose Barral, "Thomas Aquinas and Merleau-Ponty," *Philosophy Today* 26, no. 3 (1982): 204–16; John Haldane, "Insight, Inference and Intellection," *Proceedings of the American Catholic Philosophical Association* 73 (1999): 42; John Haldane, "The Breakdown of Contemporary Philosophy of Mind," in *Mind, Metaphysics, and Value in the Thomistic and Analytic Traditions*, ed. John Haldane (Notre Dame, Ind.: University of Notre Dame Press, 2002), 57–58; Braine, *The Human Person*, 70–73, 309; John Milbank, "The Soul of Reciprocity Part One: Reciprocity Refused," *Modern Theology* 17, no. 3 (2001): 336–38; John Milbank, "The Soul of Reciprocity Part Two: Reciprocity Regained," *Modern Theology* 17, no. 4 (2001): 490–501; and Joshua Miller, *On whether or not Merleau-Ponty's phenomenology of lived body experience can enrich St. Thomas Aquinas's integral anthropology* (PhD diss., Duquesne University, 2009).
60. I first made this argument in "Habits, Potencies, and Obedience" and in my dissertation.

concrete thing's essence (or form) from its full content unfolding over time (i.e., its *Gestalt*). Given this evidence, form is not a limited, static quality that can be captured in an unchanging idea or concept; rather, as what manifests itself in a being's dynamic style, it is a dynamic, aesthetic activity, a being's tendency to act and manifest itself in a definite way.[61]

Since we (like all substances) act and are given in these holistic, intrinsic ways, any view on which our matter or parts are only extrinsically unified by juxtaposition or coordinated action is reductionistic. Similarly reductionistic is any view on which all changes are extrinsic relations among things, such as *atomism*, on which we are just aggregates of simple, extrinsically related particles.[62] Versions of *four-dimensionalism* on which what exists are temporal parts of beings and where change is just an ordering of these parts are reductionistic for the same reasons.[63] The experience of an intrinsic, unifying *style* in beings is also reason to reject as reductionistic the views known as *emergentism* (discussed above) and *animalism* (on which matter constitutes a substance only when that matter is caught up in a dynamic activity, such as homeostasis).[64] Neither of these explains the experiences that motivate hylomorphism, on which beings exhibit intrinsic unity, perfection, and style, where these attributes are prior to, not results of, particular acts and events in those beings. Since nothing can give what it does not have, these perfections could not emerge from the activity of matter. This is not to deny that the natural sciences can and should formulate descriptive and predictive laws of nature, including laws about relations between material processes and consciousness, nor is it to deny that we could model those relations purely as extrinsic relations among material things or as emergent properties of matter.[65] But such laws and models do not tell us what entities or relations fundamentally are, and they prescind from considering aesthetic *Gestalten*, which are given perceptually. A metaphysics of irreducibility cannot prescind from these considerations; rather, it must posit form, which bestows identity and a style of acting on matter, in a way irreducible to facts about that matter.

61. Cf. Aquinas, *In II DA*, lect. 2; Andrew Woznicki, *Being and Order: The Metaphysics of Thomas Aquinas in Historical Perspective* (New York: Peter Lang, 1990), 13.
62. Eric Olson, *What Are We? A Study in Personal Ontology* (Oxford: Oxford University Press, 2007), 180–210.
63. Lowe, *Metaphysics*, 26, 50–55.
64. See, for example, Peter van Inwagen, *Material Beings* (Ithaca, N.Y.: Cornell University Press, 1990), 81–97.
65. Erik Hoel, "When the Map Is Better than the Territory," *Entropy* 19, no. 5 (2017): doi:10.3390/e19050188.

Metaphysics of Powers

I end this chapter with an initial exploration of our powers, the focus of the next few chapters. On the views of many scholastics, such as Aquinas, a *power* is a potentiality in virtue of which a being can act toward or be affected by objects in some definite way (such as apprehending or having an appetite for them), insofar as those objects have certain features, the power's "formal object" (*ratio formalis quae*).[66] For example, the formal object of sight is color. We do not just see color, but colored beings; color is the aspect under which we see them. Powers also act only under certain conditions (*ratio formalis sub qua*). For example, we see only what is illumined; light is the condition under which we see. Many powers also act through some medium, which joins object to subject. For example, we see through a transparent, illuminable medium.[67]

Some object that since all experiences overlap, any delineation of powers is artificial or arbitrary, not an account of actual, discrete properties in us; hence, any categorization of acts into distinct powers would be reductionistic with respect to other ways these acts could be organized, and with respect to full, concrete experience.[68] I respond that reductionistic artificiality would result only if we denied those overlaps.[69] It is not reductionistic to observe that we intend definite kinds of objects, and then to reason that we have powers to do so. Nor is it reductionistic to focus by abstraction on particular aspects of experience, so long as we do not mistake what we grasp by abstraction for the whole of concrete experience. We need to abstract distinct features of experience in order to train ourselves to perceive all aspects of concrete experience. We need an account that both acknowledges distinct kinds of experiences but also explains how they overlap. Aquinas provides an account that shows how powers are both distinct and overlapping. For example, he says that touch is actually many powers,

---

66. Aquinas, *In II DA*, lect. 5; *ST* I, q.77, a.1. See Matthew Walz, "What Is a Power of the Soul? Aquinas' Answer," *Sapientia* 60, no. 218 (2006): 319–48.

67. Aquinas, *ST* I, q.77, a.3; q.78, a.3; *In II DA*, lect. 14; *In DSS*, lects. 5, 6; Cajetan, *In I ST*, q.77, a.3; Suárez, *In DA*, d.3, q.2; and John of St. Thomas, *Cursus philosophicus thomisticus*, v. 3 (Paris: Vivès, 1883), pt. 3, q.1, a.4, 238–42. Strictly, sight's formal object is "the visible," which includes color illumined from without or within, as in bioluminescence. Light is not only quantifiable and physical but intrinsically ordered to sense. See Bonaventure, *RAT*, 318, on how light under this description is a condition for all sensing.

68. See, for example, G. W. F. Hegel, *Encyclopedia of the Philosophical Sciences in Basic Outline*, trans. William Wallace, §379, www.marxists.org/reference/archive/hegel/ li_hegel.htm.

69. See Husserl, *Ideas Pertaining to a Pure Phenomenology*, vol. 2, 266–67.

considered in terms of formal objects, such as temperature, texture, and moisture, but that touch is also one power substantially—that is, all touch occurs through one organ, since all tactile objects are grasped through their impinging on our flesh.[70] A substance's powers—the ways or styles in which a substance can act—are explained (and therefore, on Aquinas's view, efficiently caused) by its essence, and so by its form or actuality.[71] The form of the human person is a single power to act as a human person, expressed in distinct particular powers, through which the substance transcends and reveals itself.

We have seen that there is good reason to hold that actualities and other principles in us have a subjective aspect, and this applies to our powers, too. For example, the power of sight is the actuality of the eyes, the optic nerve, and parts of the brain.[72] It explains the unity of these organs' matter, physiology, and conscious acts, but we should not hold that objective, measurable, physiological events of retinal and neural stimulation are distinct acts from subjective, conscious seeing. It is not apparent what physiological events, considered in purely objective terms, have to do with the rich experience of vision; if we think of them as entirely distinct acts, their correlation appears mysterious and is the source of often apparently insoluble problems like the mind-body problem (or the hard problem of consciousness), that is, the problem of what the connection is between first-person acts and third-person neural events. Some theists contend that the connection can be explained only by divine power joining two otherwise unlike things.[73] The metaphysician of irreducibility must not deny this mysteriousness but must try to perceive (using aesthetic method) subjective and objective aspects of our powers and acts as distinct manifestations of a single unity. The two should be seen to *fit* together as two "sides" or "aspects" of one actualization of our substance, rather than as mysteriously correlated distinct acts. We should see these two aspects of a single act as rooted in a *power*, which is itself both subjective and objective. Just as matter and form are not distinct things, but correlative aspects of substances, so physical aspects of acts of vision and the subjective aspects of vision are distinct aspects of the single phenomena that are acts of vision.

This unity between the subjective and objective helps us understand

---

70. Aquinas, *In II DA*, lect. 22.
71. Aquinas, *ST* I, q.77, a.6, ad 2.
72. Aquinas, *ST* I, q.76 a.1, ad 1; *In DSS*, lect. 5.
73. Hildebrand, *Aesthetics*, vol. 1, 139–40; Maritain, *Degrees of Knowledge*, 125.

how we can reveal our subjectivity to each other. I do not experience others' subjectivity from within as they experience it. Neither, as Stein notes, do I normally come to know others' subjective states by observing their purely physical, objective states (like their facial features) and then reasoning by analogy that as my subjective and physical states correlate, so do their states correlate, and thus, since they appear in a certain physical state, so they must be having a correlative subjective experience.[74] Rather, I often perceive others' subjective acts directly expressed in their faces, tone of voice, or other physical features: I often directly perceive that another person is sad, happy, angry, or tired.[75] (To fully grasp all our irreducible features, we must consider not only our subjective self-experience but also how we appear to others, for some of our irreducible aspects only appear to others.) I propose that this is possible because conscious and physiological events are not really distinct but are, instead, two aspects of single acts and powers. In perceiving the objective state of their faces or tones of voice, I perceive the same actuality that is their subjective state; it is one act experienced by the other and by me from different "sides." Subjective and objective aspects of persons, acts, and powers are joined in one self-manifesting *Gestalt*. William Desmond links this joining of the subjective and objective to experiences of beauty: in the experience of aging, for example, I feel the beauty of my body passing away from within and others observe this from without. The blossoming of bodily beauty in youth and its loss later in life is neither a purely subjective phenomenon, nor a purely physiological event, but one total event that can be fully grasped only by seeing these two aspects joined in a single, dynamic act or event.[76] We certainly can have rich inner lives, which we never entirely communicate, but we always can express any content from our interior lives, either when we will to do so or when that life spills over into my body and is expressed there without my willing it. This occurs because our subjective acts are not purely private but have an objective "side."

My argument that no subjective experience is entirely private resembles arguments against private language made by Ludwig Wittgenstein and taken up by some analytic Thomists.[77] Some such philosophers argue that

---

74. Edith Stein, *On the Problem of Empathy*, trans. Waltraut Stein (Washington, D.C.: ICS Publications, 1989).

75. Hildebrand, *Aesthetics*, vol. 1, 138–40.

76. Desmond, *The Gift of Beauty and the Passion of Being*, chap. 2.

77. Ludwig Wittgenstein, *Philosophical Investigations*, trans. G. E. M. Anscombe (Malden: Blackwell, 2001), 76; Braine, *Human Person*, chaps. 2, 4; and Scruton, *Sexual Desire*, 45–52, 364–76. Cf. Crosby, *The*

the first-person perspective gives us no knowledge of what we are; we can only discover that from the third-person perspective, by analyzing publicly, objectively accessible rules for successfully using terms like "I" or terms for experiences like "pain," "sense," or "thought." On these views, what we refer to as pains, sensations, or thoughts are or involve third-person observable behaviors, not just private subjective acts. Successful and true knowledge of, for example, the fact that I am in pain involves successful use of the socially determined semantic rules for that statement. No such rules could apply to purely private experiences, and so there can be no knowledge given by those purported experiences.

Wittgensteinian arguments help us see that subjectivity is always oriented to manifestation, and that we always act and experience ourselves in an intersubjective context. But the view presented in those arguments sometimes confuses our ability to speak about something with our ability to grasp or perceive that thing; for that reason, they sometimes are reductionistic about subjectivity, even leading to denials that we have interior subjectivity. Subjectivity, on this view, is just a "publicly identifiable phenomenon" or an interpretation placed on observable behavior.[78] Merleau-Ponty shows what these views overlook or deny: underlying any publicly accessible expression of subjectivity is a "tacit *cogito*," an unexpressed but genuine feeling of myself living and engaging with the world.[79] Prior to all public articulation or interpretation of behavior, I experience subjectivity as an actuality in me; first-person experiences thereby reveal aspects of what I am. To capture the full range of human experience, the metaphysician of irreducibility must affirm both that our subjective and objective aspects are two sides of a single actuality and that there is something about each side that is irreducible to the other. That I experience interior, first-person subjectivity, in a way irreducible to exterior manifestation, does not entail that it is something entirely private. There are at least three ways that we can communicate our subjective states, without reducing them to publicly available objective states.

First, I can refer to aspects of subjectivity in literal, intersubjective-

---

Selfhood of the Human Person, 52–58; Hildebrand, *Aesthetics*, 139–40; and Merleau-Ponty, *The Visible and Invisible*, 133–34.

78. Scruton, *Sexual Desire*, 376; Milbank, *Theology and Social Theory*, 292. By contrast, Peter Geach (*God and the Soul* [London: Routledge, 1969], 19), who is part of the Wittgensteinian and analytic Thomist traditions, holds that we have private experiences but cannot speak about them publicly.

79. Merleau-Ponty, *Phenomenology of Perception*, 468.

ly verifiable ways—as when I tell you that I am in pain, and you can see how my pain is expressed in my bodily behavior. Subjective states manifest themselves in observable behaviors. Furthermore, many aspects of subjectivity arise through interaction with others. For example, Balthasar holds that subjectivity is first awakened by a child's interaction with his or her mother. Sokolowski sees evidence that subjectivity is always open to being communicated to others in the fact that I generally articulate my self-awareness in an internalized conversation—the content of which can be manifested to others.[80] Subjectivity can be communicated and awakened through interaction with others because it is one side of unified powers that fit with the world in simultaneously subjective and objective ways; what might seem to be a purely objective interaction with the world also involves subjectivity.

Second, some aspects of subjectivity cannot be literally communicated, but we can talk about them in phenomenological or nonliteral terms. Some versions of the Wittgensteinian view object to the claim that there is a subjective *what it's like to be me* that others cannot know as I know it. This is because it seems that there is no way to objectively assess claims about these aspects of subjectivity using publicly accessible rules of language. I respond that while you can never know my subjectivity as I know it (since you can never be me), I can still make publicly verifiable claims about the fact that I have subjectivity and that it has a certain structure. I can phenomenologically describe subjectivity, for example, by giving an account of my performance of phenomenological reductions. Since you are a being of the same sort as me, with the same powers, you can verify (or refute) my account by doing the reduction yourself. Since all actualities are analogous to each other, to phenomenologically know the structure of your subjectivity is to grasp an actuality that is analogous to mine.

Furthermore, I sometimes have experiences of what it's like to encounter certain objects, which I cannot describe literally or phenomenologically but only in poetic metaphor. Yet, contrary to many Wittgensteinians, even this sort of speech conveys philosophically relevant content. The experience of grasping things poetically or metaphorically is a key feature of human subjectivity, in which objective features of the world are given. Hildebrand observes that we sometimes experience certain relations between subjective states and objective realities, such as between the feeling of love

---

80. Balthasar, *GL5*, 615–18; Sokolowski, *Phenomenology of the Human Person*, 95, 143.

and a blazing fire, as objectively given.[81] Poetic metaphors, symbols, other literary devices, and devices found in other modes of self-expression such as painting and music do not always just capture someone's impression of reality, but they can reveal genuine features of reality; they can make realities present to us that exceed what we can grasp in literal terms.[82] The successful poet or artist evokes an experience of these images or relations and so puts others in touch with those features of reality. Once again, the subjective and the objective intertwine in reality, such that the former is communicable through the latter.

Finally, we have experiences in which we sympathetically grasp that we are having the same experiences as one another. For example, in sharing in a joyful or sorrowful event or in looking at an artwork together, or when a feeling of panic or ecstasy runs like contagion through a mass of people, we can be sympathetically aware that we are coexperiencing the same thing. Despite not being absolutely certain that we are feeling the same thing, we have reliable experiences (which we can check by talking to one another) that we are having the same feeling simultaneously.[83]

Third, some aspects of subjectivity cannot be articulated in words at all, even poetic words, but they are still oriented to public, objectively graspable self-manifestation. Catholic feminist theologian Tina Beattie, following several strands of psychoanalytic and feminist thinking, describes how I express my flow of bodily events, which I experience subjectively and which is objectively present in me, not in rational words but in expressions like tears, laughter, gasps, or groans.[84] There are aspects of feeling sad that cannot be poetically expressed or sympathetically coexperienced but that express themselves only in tears. This is nevertheless an objective manifestation of one's subjective state, explained by the unity between the subjective and objective on a true metaphysics of powers. A metaphysics of irreducibility guides us to perceive every irreducible feature of the human person, even those of which we cannot speak.

I close this chapter with a key experience that reveals the distinction

---

81. Hildebrand, *Aesthetics*, vol. 1, 164–66.

82. Richard Viladesau, *Theological Aesthetics: God in Imagination, Art, and Beauty* (Oxford: Oxford University Press, 1999), 16–17.

83. Max Scheler, *The Nature of Sympathy*, trans. Peter Heath (Hamden, Conn.: Archon Books, 1970), 167–68; *Formalism in Ethics and Non-Formal Ethics of Values*, 386–402; and "Idealism and Realism," 300–303.

84. Tina Beattie, *Theology after Postmodernity: Divining the Void—A Lacanian Reading of Thomas Aquinas* (Oxford: Oxford University Press, 2013), 292–93.

Principles of Hylomorphism 73

and unity between our subjective and objective sides, and which is another piece of evidence for hylomorphism. Merleau-Ponty describes how when I touch my hands together, my attention slides back and forth between the right hand feeling the left hand, and the left feeling the right. Each hand appears simultaneously as a subject and object of perception. I feel this subjective *self-sensing* to be rooted in the objective physical structure of the hand, and I experience the structure and material parts of that hand as facilitating and being ordered to subjective experience. The subjectively sensing and objectively sensible features of my hands "crisscross" or "intertwine": it is almost as though I experience one hand subjectively feeling the subjective experience of other, for the subjectivity of each hand is manifested through its objective features. That is, as my right hand feels the moving surfaces of my left hand, I am aware, through the moving sensations of my right hand, that my left hand is itself a subject of sensation. Subjective and objective features are two intertwined sides of one aesthetically, holistically self-manifesting *Gestalt*.[85]

If we reason about this phenomenologically described experience in a scholastic, effect-to-cause way, we must ask what I fundamentally am so that I can sense myself in this way. I first have matter that is organized or actualized objectively into integral parts like nerves, muscles, bones, and skin. These structures are organized by and for, and so actualized by and teleologically ordered to, my subjective acts. This whole objective-subjective unity is ordered to manifesting itself objectively, such that it can be the content of my own or another's perception. Husserl showed that acts of perception confer meaning on the content they receive, such that act is to content as form to matter, but Merleau-Ponty adds that the object itself structures or provides form for the sensing subject. In one way, my right hand's act of sensing is like a form for the content of the sensed left hand, rendering the latter meaningful as sensed. In another way, my left hand's perceivable content, received by my right hand, forms or structures my right hand's subjective acts of awareness of that content: when I feel my left hand with my right, I am guided in doing so by the content I receive from the left hand. That is, my right hand's acts of sensing are guided by the contours, textures, and movements of the perceived left hand. What is form or matter in one respect, can be the other in another respect. Furthermore, each hand, with all its aspects, is part of the whole *Gestalt* of

---

85. Merleau-Ponty, *The Visible and the Invisible*, 9, 133–34.

my body with its unifying style, which is itself organized hylomorphically. This experience of my hands' self-sensing thus yields evidence that I am a great network or hierarchy of forms and matters; each form-matter unity is one thing, each form and matter being one sides of a single unified entity. Some aspects of form are objective, others subjective, and yet the two always are a unity. At each level of analysis, we find some matter, something organized, and some form, some principle of organization, which, being distinct from matter, is rightly called *immaterial*.

Aquinas reasons that immateriality or irreducibility to matter is not an all-or-nothing property but comes in degrees. Things have a higher degree of immateriality the more perfect and unified they are. Likewise, things are more immaterial the more they are present to themselves, and, I would add, the more they are self-aware. Having more interior effects, more kinds of self-manifestation or self-expression, and a greater range of exterior effects are also signs of greater immateriality. Similarly, the less one's subjective acts (like cognitions and affects) are restricted to attending to the particular or the here-and-now, the more immaterial one is.[86] Merleau-Ponty's example of self-sensing hands illustrates how a distinction among levels of immateriality is discovered through experience: matter is first organized into objective structures, but then, these structures are further organized around subjective self-awareness; the latter is a more immaterial actuality than the former. And yet the two are not entirely distinct actualities but rather are distinct aspects of a single, unified actuality, related as potency and act. A range of kinds of immateriality is found both among substances and in human powers, for the human person can be experienced and understood as a "microcosm" or "little world," mirroring the range of beings and levels of actuality throughout the cosmos.[87] Fully grasping everything that falls into this hierarchy, and the degrees or levels of irreducibility to matter contained in it, requires that we consider particular powers of the human person so that we can see what is irreducible in each. I begin in chapter 2 with a survey of our vegetative and sensitive powers.

---

86. Aquinas, *SCG* IV, c. 11; *QDSC*, a.3; *In II DA*, lect. 5; *In I Jn.*, lect. 1.
87. Aquinas, *ST* I, q.91, a.1.

Chapter 2 **Bodily Powers and the Principles of Sensible Being**

I now turn (in this chapter and the subsequent three) to particular irreducible powers and principles in us, with the goal of then synthesizing these accounts into a holistic portrait of the whole irreducible person. I begin with a portrait of our vegetative, sensitive, appetitive, and locomotive powers, which we have in common with other animals, and which display the lowest kind of immateriality in us. Along with considering these powers, I elucidate irreducible features of beings that are disclosed through their acts. I draw heavily here on Thomas Aquinas's account of these powers; as I said in the introduction, his work provides a good basis for a metaphysics of irreducibility. As I also said in the introduction, my goal here is not to give full arguments for all my claims but rather to build up a portrait of the human person from the conclusions drawn by philosophers in the Catholic tradition, to guide people to perceive each irreducible aspect in us.

Vital and Vegetative Powers

As on his Aristotelian account of material substances in general (which was considered in chapter 1), Aquinas reasons to the nature of *life* by abstracting concepts of general patterns of action in all living things from our sensory experience of particular living things. To arrive at a general account of life and powers of living things, we must consider both everyday perceptions of the acts of living things and perceptions of those acts gained through empirical scientific observation and experimentation. We can arrive at knowledge of the underlying, irreducible patterns or essences that give rise to what we perceive by either Thomistic or phenomenological method, both of which aim at discerning and describing the unvarying, essential structures found in real objects.

Aquinas contends that living (*vivere*) is a more perfect actuality than existing (*esse*) since by it, one not only is, manifests oneself, and is oriented to a final cause, but one is also able to move or change oneself in manifesting oneself and pursuing one's final cause. This is more perfect than existing, both in the sense of being a further positive characteristic over and above existing and in the sense of being a more complete sort of unity with oneself: the living being is united with itself not only in existing but in acting under its own self-motion. It has more interior activities and effects than nonliving things; it is thus more like the fully interior subjectivity we experience in ourselves than a being that acts only on things external to itself. As a living being (*vivens*), I have a degree of perfection and immateriality beyond what I have as an existing being (*ens*). In scholastic hylomorphism, the form of a living (or "animated") thing—that is, its actuality whereby it has the perfection of being able to move itself—is called a *soul* (*anima*).

On Aquinas's view, nonliving things' motions are caused by other material things coming into spatial contact with them and thereby moving them—that is, actualizing their potentialities to be altered or moved from place to place, by pushing, pulling, reacting, or otherwise exerting force upon them. Thomistic nonliving things do not move themselves. One might object that all things, even subatomic particles and waves of force, move themselves in some sense, but this is consistent with Aquinas's analysis of what a nonliving thing would be; it is just a view on which the set of Thomistic nonliving things is empty. I grant that there is something analogous to life in all actual things, just as there is something analogous to subjective interiority; the hylomorphist ought to endorse a version of *panzoism*, as well as of panpsychism. But as Stein observes, there is still an observable distinction between the kinds of self-forming activities found in beings with vegetative powers and those found in being with more rudimentary forms of self-motion, such that only the former constitutes life in a new, irreducible sense.[1]

---

1. Cf. Stein, *Finite and Eternal Being*, 183–84, 190–203, 238–39. Nevertheless, she grants that self-forming abilities of a sort are found in, for example, crystals.

Natural science and naturalistic philosophy often explain my motions (and those of all living things) mechanistically, as if those motions just involved one thing moving another, without anything moving itself, that is, as if I were not actually alive. As we saw in the last chapter, my interior changes cannot be entirely explained in this way.[2] Rather, I directly experience myself changing myself; my motions appear, both to me and to others, as explained not just by my parts moving each other but also by their place in my holistic unity. Aspects of my acts that can be modelled mechanistically—such as nerves moving muscles or muscles moving bones—are taken up into or actualized by holistic, self-manifesting acts, many of which have subjective aspects. I can fully understand human acts only by grasping them as manifestations of a single style and actuality (or form or soul), and as done in service of the ends of a whole substance—that is, I must grasp them as self-moved manifestations of a whole person.[3]

Actualities, including powers, are irreducible to and distinct from matter and are therefore immaterial, though they are not distinct things from the matter they organize but rather distinct sides of form-matter unities.[4] Powers confer new kinds of unity on their substances; each new kind of unity that a substance has is a new way in which it is irreducible to its material parts, and so a new kind of immateriality. We see the new sorts of unity that powers confer on their substances in the way that powers orient substances and their parts to act as *Gestalten*, fitting themselves as wholes into their environment. We find this holistic orientation of powers even in nonliving things. Merleau-Ponty gives the example of an oil drop: its power to become organized leads it to act as a whole, such that it fits into its environment and forms a sphere, the most basic organized shape. It is thereby perfected in a new, whole way. Aspects of this fit can be described scientifically or mathematically, but all such analyses leave out an account of how substances act as whole, aesthetically perceivable unities whose motions have the identity of belonging to a certain kind of substance. There is fit and so something analogous to intentionality and meaning in all substances,[5] but these phenomena are best seen in prop-

---

2. The hylomorphist also rejects vitalistic explanations, since these still seek to fully explain living actions through a material force, albeit one found only in living things.

3. See, for example, Aquinas, *ST* I, q.76, a.4, ad 3; *SCG* IV, c. 11.

4. Aquinas, *ST* I, q.78, a.3. See Daniel De Haan, "Hylomorphic Animalism, Emergentism, and the Challenge of the New Mechanist Philosophy of Neuroscience," *Scientia et Fides* 5, no. 2 (2017): 9–38.

5. Merleau-Ponty, *Behavior*, 137–45; Merleau-Ponty, *Phenomenology of Perception*, 90, 311ff.

erly living beings, which by their powers actively fit themselves into their environment. As compared to nonliving powers, living powers are greater abilities to fit oneself holistically into one's environment and manifest oneself as a unity—thus revealing their greater immateriality, that is, greater irreducibility to matter.

According to scholasticism, a basic kind of self-motion in us is found in acts of vegetative powers, which allow us to move internal bodily parts, take in and metabolize food, grow, and reproduce. By these powers, I am present to myself such that I act physically on myself. I preserve myself through metabolism and growth, by which I aim at internal effects of taking on new matter to be actualized by my form; in these acts, I manifest myself and my essence (i.e., what I am) in new matter. I preserve my species though reproductive powers, by which I aim at the external effect of a child who expresses my species and some of my characteristics.[6] In exercising these powers, I produce *instruments*, like sperm or eggs. Instruments are beings with their own forms that are adapted by another to participate in it, bring about its effects, and manifest it even when exterior to it.[7] I return to the *reproductive power* in chapter 7.

Even more fundamental than vegetative powers is what John Damascene calls the vital or pulsating powers. Aquinas argues that the soul is equally in each part of the body as its form and end, but it principally acts as efficient cause through the systolic and diastolic movement of the heart, which moves other parts of the body.[8] I contend, however, that this fundamental power of vitality, in which all other bodily movements have their efficient causal source, is not just found in the heart. Given the independence of cellular movements and the ways they efficiently move one another, there are actually many first vital movements.[9] In any case, there is a fundamental vitality or continual, intense movement that underlies all our other powers, a quality that we will find in all our other powers as well.

Because there is a principle of continuity through any material change, and because there is something that is organized even by very low-level

---

6. Aquinas, *ST* I, q.78, a.2; *In II DA*, lect. 5.

7. Aquinas, *ST* I, q.105, 118, 119; *SCG* II, c. 86–89; *In II DA*, lect. 7; and John of St. Thomas, *Cursus philosophicus thomisticus*, v. 2, p.1, q.26, a.2, 446–47.

8. Aquinas, *DMC*; John Damascene, *An Exposition of the Orthodox Faith*, trans. E. W. Watson and L. Pullan, in *Nicene and Post-Nicene Fathers*, vol. 9, ed. Philip Schaff and Henry Wace, chaps. 12, 22, http://newadvent.org/fathers/ 3304.htm. Damascene also described the power to excrete, which, unlike other powers, does not involve taking up or responding to an object but rather eliminating an object; it is either part of the power of nutrition or its own power.

9. I am grateful to Alan Shewmon for discussing this point with me.

actualities (like the actualities of elemental particles), Aquinas reasons that there must be a lowest-level matter, *prime matter*, which is pure potentiality, which can be actualized into any particular quantified (i.e., mathematically describable) substance, and which remains identical through all changes. We do not experience prime matter in itself. Rather, in every experience of our own bodies, we find that there is something potential that is organized and actualized in various ways. Underlying every actual feature of our bodies is something potential that can be actualized in each of those ways. Since nothing can give what it does not have, this pure potentiality cannot account for any actuality it receives. Rather, it receives actuality only when acted on by a power that has sufficient actuality to produce a likeness of itself in that pure potentiality. For the same reason, *corporeal matter* (i.e., matter that has quantitative or mathematical properties) cannot account for the actualities it has beyond its quantitative actualities; it must receive these by being acted on by a power with sufficient actuality to produce those actualities. While by my vegetative powers I efficiently cause new act-potency unities, "drawing out" or "educing" actualities from the potentiality of matter,[10] the matter from which actualities are drawn does not entirely explain the genesis of those actualities. They can be fully explained only by actualities that already exist in their efficient causes. Events of efficient causality, in which matter receives actuality, are another reason to reject emergentism.[11] Like all causality, efficient causality reveals the tendency of beings and actualities to express, give, and transcend themselves.[12]

However, while any batch of matter receives actuality from efficient causes distinct from itself, there is reason to think that even prime matter is not just inert, formable stuff. In painting a portrait in which we are as irreducible as possible, I must favor views in which the account of matter is not reductionistic. Both in observation of material things (using the scholastic method) and in experiences of self-sensing (using the phenomenological method), matter of any sort is given as tending to fit with forms. As the Franciscan scholastic Bonaventure noted, something like desire, a

---

10. Aquinas, *SCG* I, c. 16.
11. Many interpreters of hylomorphism wrongly see it as a kind of emergentism, failing to see how it involves "top-down" causality by form, for example, Richard Cross, "Aquinas and the Mind-Body Problem," in *Mind, Metaphysics, and Value*, 45–47; Brian Leftow, "Souls Dipped in Dust," in *Soul, Body, and Survival: Essays on the Metaphysics of Human Persons*, ed. Kevin Corcoran (Ithaca, N.Y.: Cornell University Press, 2001), 120–21; Stump, "Dualism," 520–23.
12. See Aquinas, *DP*, q.7, a.5, ad 7; *ST* I, q.5, a.4, ad 2; *In I Sent*, d.17, q.2, a.2; *ST* I, q.2, a.3.

movement to fit with another, belongs to matter.[13] Matter is potentiality that tends toward being formed, and when it is acted on, restructured, and actualized by an efficient cause, forms come to be in it. By working with this tendency in matter, an efficient cause draws or educes actualities out of matter. Forms are not extrinsic to matter but come to be in matter, such that they are two sides of beings, the one fulfilling the other's tendencies or desires. In growth and reproduction, forms are drawn out of matter by a substance, which thereby manifests itself in that matter.[14] As the Thomist Etienne Gilson notes, aesthetic or artistic experience grounds this picture of matter and efficient causality: we can perceive matter as what cooperates with the artistry of efficient causes such that it is formed to reach higher levels of perfection. We perceive matter being artistically formed by receiving actualities both when we make artifacts and when matter is formed into organisms.[15]

In reproduction, parent substances aim at efficiently causing a new substance. Their primary aim is not to produce a new form. The new form is caused concomitantly whenever a substance is caused, that is, a new form is brought about as part of the process of bringing about the new substance. Reproductive activity involves disposing or rearranging matter such that it is apt to receive a form, and then giving a likeness of one's form to that disposed matter, such that a substance of similar species to the parents comes to be. But the coming about of a new substance in reproduction is not entirely explained by its parents disposing matter and giving a likeness of their form. The event of reproduction—indeed, any event of efficient causality in the material world—raises at least three metaphysical problems, which must be solved if we are to have a full metaphysical portrait of the irreducible human person. I raise these problems now, and they will be deepened over the next few chapters, but I will not have established enough metaphysically to offer a solution until chapter 6. In solving these problems, we shall see how even our vegetative acts reveal many irreducible features in us.

First, in addition to its substantial form, the offspring has an act of existence. we briefly saw reasons for positing acts of existence in chapter 1;

---

13. Bonaventure, *In III Sent.*, d.5, a.2, a.3, 136–37.
14. Aquinas, *ST* I, q.118, a.1.
15. *In IV DDN*, lect. 2; Etienne Gilson, *Painting and Reality* (New York: Pantheon, 1957), chap. 4. Cf. Pierre-Marie Emonet, *The Dearest Freshness Deep Down Things: An Introduction to the Philosophy of Being*, trans. Robert Barr (New York: Crossroad, 1999), 50–51; and Stein, *Finite and Eternal Being*, 184.

Principles of Sensible Being   81

further reasons will be given in chapter 3. This act, by which a substance is something distinct from its causes and is not nothing at all, is an actuality that transcends essence. That something exists and persists in existing is not explained by its essence, nor by its accidents, nor by the essence or accidents of its efficient cause—that is, being of an essential or accidental kind does not explain why one actually exists, nor do efficient causal actions that aim at a being just insofar as it belongs to some species. Further explanation is needed to explain the offspring's existence.

Second, not only does an offspring's form resemble its parents' particular forms, but the offspring also participates in the species as such. To use terms from Stein that were introduced in chapter 1, the offspring participates in an ideal essence of that species. I share in what it is to be human as such. Normally, an offspring belongs to its parents' species and shares in the content of that species, but sometimes, an offspring is of a distinct species from its parents, as when an evolutionary speciation event occurs. We need to explain how an offspring participates in essences that transcend it, its parents, and their forms, and how an offspring can participate in an essence distinct from that of its parents.

Third, the offspring is directed to a final cause. This orientation is partially explained by its form, powers, and genetics, but Stein observes that beings do not aim at flourishing in such a way that their powers unfold toward that end automatically or of necessity. Rather, what flourishing is for a given species is explanatorily prior to any member of that species' acts of pursuing flourishing. Organisms, Stein contends, are drawn toward a perfect form of their species. There would be no need to look for further explanation of this phenomenon only if organisms were just "programmed" to automatically or necessarily unfold toward a preset final cause, but that is not the case. Stein observes that organisms are causally affected by their end, even though there is no one preset end to which they are moving. She explains this by positing and attributing "drawing" power to an ideal *Gestalt* (or "pure form") of the end of a species. We can intellectually grasp this ideal form of a species' flourishing and, in light of that standard, judge how perfected a particular organism is. But no pure form—no ideal unity of perfections for a given species—exists in the physical world.[16] As with the ideal essence of the species, we need an account how the offspring comes to aim at, participate in, and be drawn by this pure form. We also

16. Stein, *Finite and Eternal Being*, 225–31.

need a metaphysical account of what ideal essences and pure forms are.

Given the transcendence of these principles over matter, eduction alone (i.e., the process of an efficient cause drawing or educing a new form out of matter) cannot entirely account for the coming to be of a new substance. My solution will posit principles in which each substance participates and which transcend the material world. Substances' irreducibility to matter is partly seen in the fact that they intrinsically participate in transcendent principles. We shall also see how all efficient causality requires the cooperation of transcendent agents, including God and immaterial intelligences.[17]

Exterior Sensitive Powers

Our conscious, external sensory powers—seeing, hearing, smelling, tasting, and touching—exhibit a degree of immateriality (i.e., of irreducible unity, self-presence, and holistic action) beyond that of vegetative powers. I first consider how acts and powers of sensing are irreducible features of the human person. Then, I examine our *sensible properties*, which likewise are irreducible features of ours that have a key place in a portrait of the irreducible human person.

Sensing involves sense organs coming into spatial contact with something material (such as in seeing, when the eyes make contact with light, and in hearing, in which the ears make contact with sound waves) such that physical changes take place in the organ.[18] When this occurs in my sense organs, I am affected such that I become aware of objects distinct from myself. Phenomenologically, what it's like to be me just insofar as I am sensing consists of being experientially out among objects, being presented with scents, textures, colors, and so forth, without attending to my act of grasping them, and without grasping these qualities intellectually, that is, without any concepts, words, or propositions entering into my awareness. As Merleau-Ponty says, sensing is "anonymous": in it, I am not aware of myself as an intellectual, freely choosing, language-using subject.

---

17. Aquinas, *ST* I, q.104, a.1; q.115, a.3; q.118, a.1, 2; *DP*, q.3, a.9; *SCG* III, c. 69; *DSS*, n. 58. In Aquinas's view, higher causality occurs when nonmaterial persons, angels or separate substances, act through heavenly bodies, such as the sun. Aquinas's view of the heavenly bodies is empirically false, but his view that a full explanation of efficient causality requires positing transcendent causes could still be true despite his false view of the heavenly bodies.

18. Aquinas argues (*In II DA*, lect. 14) that vision involves no material changes in the eye and that light is not corporeal. These claims are false, but this does not show that Aquinas's analysis of sensation in general; rather, vision is more like other senses than he realized.

Rather, my attention is immersed in particular things in my surroundings. Unlike in thinking, I have no sensory awareness of the world as a whole but only of what Scheler calls my "environment," that is, of particular things around me stimulating my attention. Sensible things stimulate my attention when they are of some importance to my biological life, such that my bodily powers spontaneously fit with them; for example, things might stimulate my attention insofar as they are potential dangers or sources of pleasure.[19] As phenomenologist Emmanuel Levinas puts it, in sensation, I am "immersed in" the world; if I bracket thinking about sensation and just sense, I feel the air on my face, the texture of surfaces under my fingers, the harshness or softness of colors on my eyes, and so forth. I can be aware of these things in a range of ways, from them enjoyably "caressing" me, to experiencing the sheer thereness of the mass of sensible things horrifyingly hemming me in, a mass in which my sensation participates without my consent.[20]

Aquinas gives a metaphysical account of sensation that explains and helps us attend to each irreducible aspect of sensation. Just as in the previous paragraph I summed up phenomenologically distinguishable aspects of sensations, so here I sum up a number of metaphysical claims meant to explain the underlying structure of those sensations. According to Aquinas's account, I sense beings through the power of their accidental actualities, which I receive into my sense organs without literally becoming those beings or becoming really characterized by their actualities. Sensing involves both awareness of what is other than me and union with that other: insofar as I receive (and act by the power of) another's actualities, I am united with that other, without being fully, self-consciously aware of my distinctness from that other. This accounts for how sensation both involves awareness of my surroundings and is anonymous.

Sensation requires some process by which things distinct from me become united to me, such that I can act in virtue of their accidents. Aquinas explains this by positing that accidental sensible qualities (like colors and tones) cause sensible species—that is, appearances or likenesses of themselves—when they are in the right medium. For example, when in

---

19. Merleau-Ponty, *Phenomenology of Perception*, 250–51; Scheler, *Formalism in Ethics and Non-Format Ethics of Values*, 398.
20. Emmanuel Levinas, *Existence and Existents*, trans. Alphonso Lingis (The Hague: Martinus Nijhoff, 1978), 60–65; Levinas, *Totality and Infinity*, 75–76, 145–46; Rahner, *Spirit in the World*, 79, 87–97; Hildebrand, *Aesthetics*, 112–15.

an illumined medium, like illumined air or water, colored beings manifest their color. Through species, a medium becomes actualized not only by *real properties* (i.e., properties that really characterize it, such as its mathematical structure) but also by *intentional properties* (i.e., cognizable information). For example, the appearance of color becomes present in the illumined medium, carried by light. Sensible beings use media and species as instruments to manifest themselves. Sensible species participate in their sources: they have their sensible content by sharing in the content of their source's actualities. However, they have this content without their source's matter: for a being to sensibly manifest itself, it does not give off material parts but simply reproduces its forms in the medium around itself. However, these species have some matter, since they actualize material media. When a medium spatially contacts a sense organ with which it fits, it gives the organ new real properties; for example, light effects physical changes in retinal cells. But it also gives the species it carries to the organ; for example, when light hits my eye, I receive appearances of (and information about) sensible beings. These species actualize the sense power intentionally, such that it participates, through the species' mediation, in their source. By receiving a sensible species, I become aware not of the species but of the being that manifested itself in the species, with which the species unites me by participation. I "am" the things that I sense insofar as I am actualized—that is, made to be actually cognizing—by their forms.[21]

Sensation is not purely passive. By receiving species, and thereby acting in virtue of their sources' forms, I spontaneously move myself to consciously respond to what I have received; as acts indicative of life, some Thomists call these *vital acts*. By receiving species, I first perform intentional acts of perception, whereby I am aware of my surroundings. I then spontaneously perform acts of judgment or interpretation—that is, I spontaneously (and without the involvement of intellectual concepts or self-awareness) distinguish different aspects of sensible objects, such as different colors, tones, or textures.[22] These vital acts reveal how sensory powers involve a new degree

---

21. Aquinas, *ST* I, q.78, a.3; *In II DA*, lects. 5, 12. The close connection between real and intentional changes can be seen, for example, in seeing what others are seeing reflected in their eyes. See John Deeley, "The Immateriality of the Intentional as Such," *New Scholasticism* 42, no. 2 (1968): 293–306.

22. Aquinas, *In II DA*, lect. 13; John of St. Thomas, *Cursus philosophicus thomisticus*, v. 3, p.3, q.5, a.2, 302–3. Cf. Yves Simon, *An Introduction to Metaphysics of Knowledge*, trans. Vukan Kric and Richard Thompson (New York: Fordham University Press, 1934), 93, cited in Daniel De Haan, "Simon and Maritain on the Vocation of *Species in Medio*," in *Redeeming Philosophy: From Metaphysics to Aesthetics*, ed. John Conley (Washington, D.C.: American Maritain Association, 2014), 70.

of immateriality beyond that of vegetative powers: I am present to myself as having an interiority that receives others, and I perform acts that do not have just single objects but rather extend simultaneously to many objects insofar as I grasp *Gestalten* of many accidents.

This metaphysical analysis of the order of acts can be phenomenologically supported. Phenomenologists Brian Treanor and Richard Kearney argue that all of our engagements with the world, down to the simplest acts of touch and bodily motion, are interpretive; while our acts are realist (i.e., they get at how the world actually is), they also involve taking an active stance toward the world and fitting with it in a particular way, mediated by the structure of our bodies, powers, and environment.[23] As in Merleau-Ponty's example of my two hands, through my senses, I intertwine or actively come together with the world in simultaneously subjective and objective ways, such that sensible beings affect me, evoke reactions in me, and are affected by me. Intertwining with the world is an extension of my experience of intertwining with myself in self-sensing, which we saw in the experience of my two hands touching. In sensation, I appear as a piece of the larger sensory "flesh" of the world.[24] In other words, sensible things appear as sensible, active, and responsive, as simultaneously subjective and objective, in mutually affecting ways, just as I do. Sensation often involves both I and my objects changing in response to one another: they give themselves to me, and I respond with active judgments and movements, whereby I interpret them in the sense of taking a particular stance toward sensed things, and then those things respond by giving themselves in new ways.

Merleau-Ponty so focuses on the experience of sensation that he reduces us to being only parts of the sensory world: I am just a piece of the intertwined, subjective-and-objective "flesh" of the world. This is a reductionistic view of persons: there are aspects of persons that are separate from the sensory world, which I present in later parts of this book. Aquinas's metaphysics of participation better explains sensation without this reductionism: in virtue of species that participate in their sources, I share in beings outside me. We mutually affect one another, while all beings involved remain distinct. Just as material media are carriers for species outside me, so neurological mechanisms are the material carrier for

---

23. Brian Treanor and Richard Kearney, "Introduction: Carnal Hermeneutics from Head to Foot," in *Carnal Hermeneutics*, ed. Brian Treanor and Richard Kearney (New York: Fordham University Press, 2015), 1–3.

24. Merleau-Ponty, *The Visible and the Invisible*, 127, 148.

species inside me. In both cases, species inform matter, giving it new unity and identity, unifying perceivers and perceived. Variations in the physical structure of organs lead to variations in how species are received, and so to variations in experience, for anything received is received according to the mode of the recipient. What it's like to be me, just insofar as I am sensing, is partly determined by my ability to be actualized and so by my physical structure; by the way I receive species, I spontaneously interpret my surroundings.[25]

Species is also an aesthetic notion: it connotes that beings are beautiful (*speciosum*) and have intrinsic self-manifesting splendor whereby they appear, announce themselves,[26] and draw others into affinity with this beauty. In sensing, I receive this splendor as my own (intentional) property, and in judgment or interpretation, I take up stances toward this beauty, allowing new aspects of it to appear. In the introduction, I considered the objection that beauty cannot be a feature of reality, since beauty can only be grasped by taste, which is always perspectival. In sensation, however, beings offer themselves to my "taste" or interpretive stance; this real feature of things is grasped only in an interpretive, perspectival way. By receiving and responding to this beauty, sensing beings display their own splendor, their own orientation to holistic self-manifestation. To perceive beauty is to become beautiful in some way, since to perceive anything is to become that thing intentionally and by participation. Each sensible being gives itself as beautiful; beauty, which is intrinsically self-transcending (i.e., goes beyond itself to make contact with what is distinct from itself) and self-manifesting, begets more beauty by drawing others into its participatory, unifying structure.[27]

Participating in another mediates that other and make it present.[28] Beings transcend and give themselves through others. Sensible beings can cause their cognizable content to exist in surrounding media with a sensible, intentional, mediated mode of being (*esse sensibile, esse intentio-*

---

25. Aquinas, *ST* I, q.75, a.2; q.85, a.6.
26. See Gerald Manley Hopkins's poem "As kingfishers catch fire, dragonflies draw flame": "Each mortal thing does one thing and the same:/Deals out that being indoors each one dwells;/Selves—goes its self; *myself* it speaks and spells,/Crying *What I do is me; for that I came*" (*The Major Works*, 129).
27. This view of beauty (*to kalon*) is, for example, in Diotima's speech in Plato's *Symposium* and in *Pol.* VIII.5.1340a15–17. Cf. Mark D. Jordan, "The Evidence of the Transcendentals and the Place of Beauty in Thomas Aquinas," *International Philosophical Quarterly* 29, no. 4 (1989): 393–407; Alice Ramos, "Beauty and the Perfection of Being," *Proceedings of the American Catholic Philosophical Association* 71 (1997): 255–68; and Christopher Scott Sevier, *Aquinas on Beauty* (Lanham, Md.: Lexington Press, 2015).
28. Cf. Maritain, *Degrees of Knowledge*, 416.

nale), distinct from the physical mode of being (*esse naturale*) that they have when they actually characterize beings. That sensible beings have this power shows that they are irreducible to aggregates of quantitative matter. This is because in manifesting themselves, the content of their forms becomes unrestricted to their particular location; it becomes available to any sensing animal in the same medium—that is, their content takes on a new degree of immateriality.[29] Since nothing can cause an actuality it does not have, material beings must have something of this immaterial, sensible mode of being, so that they are able to cause to it in the media around them. Balthasar contends that beings must have this higher degree of immateriality in themselves because they sensibly manifest themselves regardless of whether they are ever actually cognized. He also contends that that content reaches new perfection in actually being sensed, for to be united with a sensing being like me is to have a higher, more permanent mode of being than merely to exist, since I can retain those species in memory.[30] Our powers to sense and to sensibly manifest ourselves are irreducible to corporeal matter.

Problems about Exterior Senses

We can better see how both being sensible and sensing reveal irreducibilities in us by answering three reductionistic views about sensation. The first such view builds on the Aristotelian claim that the human soul "is in a way all things."[31] Each sense grasps not only qualities like color and flavor but also quantities like shape, spatiotemporal extension, motion, and the rest.[32] Transcendental Thomist Karl Rahner argues, following Kant, that space and time are *a priori* conditions of sensibility: we always grasp sensible things as having spatiotemporal location or extension; space and time are the background or "horizon" against which we sense any sensible object. He argues that the soul "is" all things in that, ontologically prior to any grasp of a particular object, the senses preconsciously grasp all of space and time (and so the whole sensible world), and we sense particulars as specifications of this universal grasp.[33] Sensible species fit with me

---

29. Aquinas, *In DSS*, lect. 5.
30. Balthasar, *TL1*, 62–71, 80–84.
31. Aquinas, *ST* I, q.16, a.3; q.80, a.1; Suárez, *In II DA*, lect. 5.
32. Suárez, *In III DA*, lect. 1; Aquinas, *ST* I, q.85, a.6.
33. Rahner, *Spirit in the World*, 102–3. Cf. Immanuel Kant, *Critique of Pure Reason*, trans. Paul Guyer and Allen Wood (Cambridge: Cambridge University Press, 1999), 153–92.

by filling in the content of my *a priori* grasp on all space and time. Self-awareness is more fundamental than awareness of others in that my grasp on my *a priori* structures of consciousness is a more phenomenologically foundational layer of experience than my grasp on external beings.

We saw that in the Husserlian reduction, we grasp objects only as aspects of our own intentional acts. We also saw, however, that focusing only on the results of that reduction leads us to overlook what is revealed by the realist phenomenological reduction: that in knowing real beings, I transcend myself, grasping beings that I have never grasped before, which are distinct from me. That realist experience of receiving new actualities is evidence that Rahner's account is reductionistically idealist. A metaphysics of irreducibility should be wary of claims that restrict our self-transcendence by claiming that actualities we grasp already existed in us in some way, even in a general way that is specified by received content. This is because such a view overlooks or denies certain features of sensing. Space and time are not unvarying features of every sensation, but they would have to be were they *a priori* conditions of sensation. The claim that space and time are not unvarying, *a priori* conditions of all sensation is supported by descriptions of experience from both scholastic and phenomenological traditions. Aquinas describes how we do not grasp space and time in every sensation: for example, in gazing at a whole scene without attending first to one part of it and then another, we experience the whole simultaneously, without sensing time. Time is given only as the measure or ordering of motions—for example, if I look at different parts of the scene, one after another, then I will sense time.[34] Merleau-Ponty notes that space and time are given as features of sensible things, not as originating with me.[35] Jean-Luc Marion observes that space and time are sensed differently in different experiences. In scientific measurement, every point of space and time appears the same as every other, but when I am in love, I sense the world to be organized around my beloved, with things spread out in a space-time laden with value relative to her position.[36]

The ability to take on new perceptions of space and time shows that I do not have a single *a priori* grasp on them. Rather, sensible things, including space and time, have unanticipatable features. These features are

---

34. Aquinas, *In DSS*, lect. 8.
35. Merleau-Ponty, *Phenomenology of Perception*, 496–97.
36. Jean-Luc Marion, *The Erotic Phenomenon*, trans. Stephen Lewis (Chicago: University of Chicago Press, 2008), 29–37.

especially found in the normative content of sensation: sensed qualities call for responses of acting in specific ways guided by what is sensed. The rich, glorious world of sensible qualities, of colors and flavors and tones, with all their pleasing beauty and painful ugliness, exert normative calls, including the call to be wondered at for its own sake. In looking into another's eyes, I see not only qualities spread out spatially, but also a value-laden depth calling for a response.[37] Alphonso Lingis notes that visible objects guide me to look at them in definite ways to fully grasp them; for example, foods and drinks guide me to savor them in certain ways to fully enjoy them.[38] Building on Aristotle and phenomenology, Edward Casey argues that place is given prior to space, where *place* denotes a substance's value-laden surroundings, while *space* is a neutral three-dimensional framework in which beings can be located. We generally sense things as located *in places*—for example, home, the countryside, the office—not as first occupying a neutral spatial continuum. The value of each place must be grasped in itself; no *a priori* grasp on the world can anticipate it, nor does the sensed value of a place just give content to an already existing general grasp on the whole world. Our senses are transformed to perceive objects, spaces, and times differently depending on our surroundings.[39] As we shall see in chapter 9, the senses can even be changed to experience spiritual things, which transcend the spatiotemporal world. If there were *a priori* bounds on sensibility, these experiences of excess would not be possible. Since such experiences occur, our sensing is irreducible to any pregiven *a priori* limits.

Still, Rahner's aprioristic approach gets a crucial point right. There is a fit, attunement, and connaturality (i.e., a similarity of nature by which we harmonize with things) between senses and sensible objects, which is in us by nature. As we saw in Merleau-Ponty's idea of the "flesh" of the world, we are dynamically oriented toward *being in the world* (and *being the world* intentionally), and the world is given as oriented toward being sensed by us. Only because of this pregiven attunement can we sense particular things; it belongs, as phenomenologist Martin Heidegger indicates, to our fundamental way of existing as cognizing beings.[40] But this is a correspondence

---

37. Marion, *In Excess*, 78–79.
38. Alphonso Lingis, *The Imperative* (Bloomington: Indiana University Press, 1998). Cf. Abram, *The Spell of the Sensuous*, chap. 1.
39. Edward Casey, *Getting Back into Place* (Bloomington: Indiana University Press, 2009), 318–22.
40. Heidegger, *Being and Time*, 126–31. Cf. Suárez, *In II DA*, lect. 12; Balthasar, *GL1*, 235–50;

of a *potency* in us with what can actualize it; we do not actually precontain those things, as in Rahner's view, which reduces our *open* attunement to a *limited* pregiven grasp on only certain spheres of things.

In a second reductionistic view, analytic historian of scholasticism Robert Pasnau objects to the claim that sensible species are immaterial. Pasnau argues that species represent objects, such that through them, I know them, but for one thing to represent another, it need not be immaterial. Holding that species must be immaterial confuses their *content*, which is separated from its original matter, with its *ontological status*, which need not be separated from matter to have this content. There is no need to hold that species are immaterial.[41]

Pasnau is correct that representations need not be immaterial. For example, written words represent their referents. Sensible species, however, are not merely representations of their sources. A representation is something that stands for another; in cognition involving representations, such as words, I first grasp the representation, and then my attention is conveyed to what is represented. But a sensible species renders me first aware of its source, not of itself. Species contain content not *as represented* but *by participation*, such that its source becomes present to me. Sensation is *intuitive*, an experience of beings as present to me.[42] Species must be immaterial because they transcend the limitations to one place and time that content has in natural existence, by making that content in itself available anywhere in the medium. Contents of material beings have a mode of existence transcending (and so irreducible to) a corporeal, localized mode of being.

According to a third reductionistic view, also Pasnau's, hylomorphism should include the early modern distinction between primary and secondary properties. Primary properties are quantities (like mass and size) understood as existing in things, while secondary properties are sensible qualities understood as arising subjectively in me when my senses interact with material things. Pasnau argues that there is no need for hylomorphists to hold that sensible qualities exist in things; rather, they just exist in me when I causally interact with things.[43]

Merleau-Ponty, *Phenomenology of Perception*, 252; and Robert Spaemann, *Persons: The Difference between "Someone" and "Something,"* trans. Oliver O'Donovan (Oxford: Oxford University Press, 2006), 43.

41. Pasnau, *Aquinas on Human Nature*, 313–16.

42. Rahner, *Spirit in the World*, 262. However, the object is present as it was when the species left it. Relativistic physics shows that presence is always relative to reference-frames; from its own frame, a sensible object has already moved forward in time when I experience it.

43. Pasnau, *Aquinas on Human Nature*, 184–85.

This view does not cohere with experience, however. It reduces sensible qualities to epiphenomena of purely quantitative, material interactions. Rather, we experience both quantities and qualities as giving themselves through sensible species, and we experience both as attributes of beings. Whereas the proponent of the primary-secondary distinction ascribes the latter only to things' appearance, I contend that both belong to things' appearance, and so we have equally good grounds to ascribe each to reality. The idealist (who holds that apparent features of beings are just features or modifications of subjective experience) is correct that all properties of things are intrinsically oriented (and analogous) to subjectivity,[44] but we must transcend ourselves toward material things and their qualitative and quantitative properties; all of these are given as real, extramental, and causally and intentionally impinging on us.

However, quantities and qualities are given as real properties of beings in different ways. Quantities are given as belonging to bodies as such (since bodies are essentially things with measurable dimensions), while qualities are given as belonging to bodies as interacting with surrounding media. Qualities are not "in" bodies as quantities are, but they are the appearance of bodies and quantities.[45] Quantities give themselves to sense through the mediation of qualities. Because of this mediation, the quantitative world of science and the qualitative *Lebenswelt* are given as aspects of one, real world. By *Lebenswelt*, I mean, as does Husserl, the world as it appears meaningfully in everyday, shared, intersubjective experience, laden with practical, ethical, aesthetic, religious, and cultural values, as distinct from the world as explained by natural science, where what appears is a sign pointing to underlying physical explanations that do not appear. For example, while science explains the sun, as a measurable body of gases undergoing fusion reactions around which the earth revolves, in the *Lebenswelt*, the sun is sensibly given as moving through the sky around the earth, marking times for us, expressing joy or wrath, and bearing meanings that have been expressed in poetry and myth. Both are ways the sun is really given, and only through the *Lebenswelt* (and its qualities) do we access the scientific layer (and its quantities). Each layer is irreducible to the others, but they are also united.[46]

---

44. Cf. Robert Adams, "Idealism Vindicated," in *Persons*, ed. Peter van Inwagen and Dean Zimmerman (Oxford: Oxford University Press, 2007), 35–54; Todd Buras and Trent Dougherty, "Parrying Parity," in *Idealism*.

45. Aquinas, *In DSS*, lects. 6, 10.

46. Husserl, *Crisis*, 4–53, building on Wilhelm Dilthey; Edmund Husserl, "Foundational Investigations of the Phenomenological Origins of the Spatiality of Nature," trans. Fred Kersten, in *Husserl: Shorter*

All of these analyses help us see that sensible qualities are given in beings and that they appear meaningful in themselves. It is reductionistic to hold that sensible qualities are only meaningful in relation to intellectual thought, as the following views hold. On some materialisms, sensory givens are purely quantitative or causal, becoming meaningful only when subsumed under concepts. According to *coherentism*, meaning is only found in coherence among beliefs, and sensation only contributes to meaning indirectly, in prompting us to alter those beliefs. In *intellectualist-idealism*, sensible qualities are conceptually or propositionally structured in themselves.[47] I contend that although qualities are potentially intelligible, their given meaning is not conceptual, propositional, or logically ordered. Rather, they have a perceptual order that guides attention from one perceived object to another and often involves mere juxtaposition, as, for example, in the ordering of colors in paintings, tones in music, or features of a landscape or a street scene. They appear meaningful not in a logical order but in an aesthetic order, especially when they appear beautiful (i.e., when they appear as fitting together and manifesting themselves holistically in a pleasing way). The meaning and irreducibility of sensible qualities, a feature of all material things, including human persons, must be perceived.

Transcendent Sources of *Esse Sensibile*: Transcendentals, Media, God, and the Gods

To fully grasp our irreducibility as sensible beings, we must better understand how material substances are revealed through sensible qualities. Balthasar explains this by reference to properties of being (*passiones entis*). The scholastics held that each being, just insofar as it is a being, has properties, sometimes called "transcendentals." While "being" signifies something as existing, Aquinas holds that each being is also *a thing* (it has an essence), *one* (it is undivided from itself), *something* (it is distinct from others), *true* (it is graspable by minds), and *good* (it can be the object of appetite or will).[48] Each of these properties in a being is really identical to that being, but we distinguish them to unpack the content of what being as

---

Works, ed. Peter McCormick and Frederick Elliston (Brighton: Harvester, 1981), 222–33. Cf. Balthasar, *TL1*, 138–50; Abram, *The Spell of the Sensuous*, 31–44.

47. See, for example, Wilfrid Sellars, Donald Davidson, and John McDowell, summarized in Yadav, *The Problem of Perception and the Experience of God*. For a phenomenological response, see Romano, *At the Heart of Reason*, 403–31.

48. Aquinas, *DV*, q.1, a.1; q.21, a.1.

such is. These concepts arise in our minds whenever we reflect upon any being, even when we do not attend to them. When thinking, we are always at least implicitly aware that each being is of some kind, that it is identical to itself, that we are grasping it, so it is graspable, and that we have an orientation or desire to grasp it, so it is desirable. To claim that something is a transcendental is to claim that it is a way each being is immediately given.

More recent scholastics distinguished other transcendentals; they too must be included in an account of the human person on which we are as irreducible as possible. Many recent scholastics contend that every being is *beautiful* (able to please when cognized) and *acting* (doing or effecting something).[49] In Balthasar's view, truth, goodness, and beauty show that beings are intrinsically, *gratuitously self-communicative*. Beings exhibit *values* (i.e., intrinsic importances that exert a normative call) like truth, goodness, and beauty because they do not remain existing only in themselves; instead, they manifest, give, and communicate or express themselves. We can describe beings as *kenotic*, self-emptying or sacrificing their existence in themselves to offer themselves to others.[50] Another way of describing this orientation of beings to self-manifestation is to describe all beings as *loving*: as Hildebrand says, the experience of beauty can be an experience of beings loving us, giving themselves to us and drawing us into union with them.[51]

Since all beings can be experienced in these ways, sensible beauty too can be experienced, as Russian theologian Vladimir Soloviev says, as love made manifest to the senses.[52] Sensible qualities reveal themselves and their substances because all beings are self-manifesting, self-giving, and loving in the sense just described. However, sensible qualities do not give themselves as primitive properties but as pointing to and founded on something other than themselves.[53] Just as with efficient causality in

---

49. Oliva Blanchette, *Philosophy of Being: A Reconstructive Essay in Metaphysics* (Washington, D.C.: The Catholic University of America Press, 2003), chap. 6; Norris Clarke, "Action as the Self-Revelation of Being," in *Explorations in Metaphysics: Being-God-Person* (Notre Dame, Ind.: University of Notre Dame Press, 1994); and Joseph de Finance, *Être et agir dans la philosophie de Saint Thomas* (Rome: Presses de l'Université Grégorienne, 1965), 241–46.

50. Balthasar, *TL1*, 216; *E*, 59–87.

51. Hildebrand, *Aesthetics*, 451. Cf. Ferdinand Ulrich, *Homo Abyssus: The Drama of the Question of Being*, trans. D. C. Schindler (Washington, D.C.: Humanum Academic Press, 2018), 67.

52. Vladimir Soloviev, *Lectures on Divine Humanity*, trans. Boris Jakim (Hudson, N.Y.: Lindisfarne, 1995), 103, cited in Stephen Finlan, "The Comedy of Divinization in Soloviev," in *Theosis: Deification in Christian Theology*, ed. Stephen Finlan and Vladimir Kharlamov (Cambridge: The Lutterworth Press, 2006), 173.

53. *Contra*, for example, Peter Hacker, *Appearance and Reality: A Philosophical Investigation into Perception and Perceptual Qualities* (Oxford: Blackwell, 1987).

vegetative powers, sensible self-manifestation includes an excess that is not explainable naturalistically, by substances, or by quantities. When not focusing on them (as often happens in everyday life), we experience sensible qualities as prosaic and mundane. But when we attend to them, colors and scents and textures blaze with glorious excesses and depths. They appear as existing to draw us into wonder and enjoyment. They appear as shining forth from (and thereby revealing) that to which they belong. But, as Desmond suggests, they also appear as bestowed upon things, since substances and quantities—with their abstractable and measurable natures—are inadequate to account for the excess of beauty in sensible qualities.[54]

All beauties, including sensible ones, gives themselves as having three aspects, according to Aquinas. Beautiful beings first display the wholeness (*integritas*) of the individual and specific things they are: sensible wholeness, with the parts and properties appropriate to the individual things they are, is grasped by the senses, while intelligible wholeness, with all the perfections due to their kind, is grasped by the intellect. Second, beautiful beings display *harmony* or *proportion* (*consonantia*) among their parts and properties; this can also appear on the sensory or intellectual levels. Finally, beauty shines forth with sensible or intelligible *brightness* or *splendor* (*claritas*).[55] The first two aspects of sensible beauty can be explained by the substantial and quantitative structure of a body, but the last cannot: in seeing splendor, radiant shining-forth, one grasps the excess of beauty over substance and quantity, and thereby the irreducibility of sensible quality to substance and quantity. Artists, perhaps, best see the world in this way, but anyone can experience the vitality of colors, tones, and the very feel of the world on one's skin. Sensation reveals a key feature of what it is to be alive: life is not just self-motion but is given as vitality, a holistic sense of intense life, ardor, strength, and health (or their opposites), like fire in one's heart, which the excess of the sensory world can fan into flame, and in which we are not self-conscious but experientially ecstatically stand outside ourselves.[56]

---

54. Desmond, *The Gift of Beauty and the Passion of Being*, chap. 3.
55. Michael Rubin, "Aquinas on Bodily or Sensible Beauty," *Proceedings of the American Catholic Philosophical Association* 94 (2020): forthcoming; Aquinas, *ST* I, q.38, a.8; II-II, q.145, a.2.
56. Scheler, *Formalism in Ethics and Non-Formal Ethics of Values*, 106–7; Scheler, *Ressentiment*, 126–43. Cf. Roberto Calasso, *Ardor*, trans. Richard Dixon (New York: Farrar, Strauss, and Giroux, 2014), 102; William James, *Some Problems of Philosophy* (Cambridge, Mass.: Harvard University Press, 1979), 32; and Bruce Wilshire, *The Much-at-Once: Music, Science, Ecstasy, the Body* (New York: Fordham University Press, 2016).

Following Hildebrand, we can make sense of why and how sensible qualities are bestowed upon bodies by distinguishing three directly given layers of the experience of sensible qualities being bestowed upon things. First, qualities appear as a "human aspect" of the world—that is, they appear not only as existing in real things, but as existing for perception or when perceived, and as more meaningful to us than the aspects of the world discovered through scientific methods.[57] For example, things look differently from different perspectives: a mountain might look blue from far away and green up close, but each appearance is experienced as how things meaningfully ought to look, as a "message" from object to perceiver. Unlike the more value-neutral scientific layer of reality, sensible qualities appear as having significance for human life (and the lives of other perceiving organisms). For this reason, they appear more real than the former layer, contrary to philosophers like Roger Scruton, who accept the directly given meaningfulness of the sensible *Lebenswelt* but hold that, compared to the scientifically describable layer of reality, it is unreal, "shallow," or "surface-level" because it is related to our concepts and interests.[58] Being oriented to, or partially constituted by, human interests does not make something unreal; rather, we should recognize that the sensible world is given as existing in itself for perception.

We cannot fully perceive these qualities unless we take up the right perspective. British writer Owen Barfield notes that what we sense is in part shaped by individual and societal ideas and imaginings: the dominant myths, images, and worldviews of one's culture shape how one senses.[59] But Barfield wrongly thinks that what really exists are physical particles, interaction with which causes our senses to constitute sensible phenomena. Rather, we can account for sensible qualities as they are given by seeing that sensible qualities really exist in substances but are grasped only if we engage with the world correctly. As the scholastics insist, whatever is received is received according to the manner of the recipient. What qualities I grasp (and what species I receive) are in part dependent on the sensitivity or impairment of my sense organs. They are also partly dependent on the interpretations I spontaneously perform after receiving species. These interpretations—how I grasp the sensory world—are, as Barfield rightly

---

57. Hildebrand, *Aesthetics*, vol. 1, 58–61.
58. Scruton, *Sexual Desire*, 8–13, 57–58.
59. Owen Barfield, *Saving the Appearances: A Study in Idolatry* (Middletown, Conn.: Wesleyan University Press, 1988). For a Thomistic appropriation, see Little, *Methodology*, 449–513.

thought, in part guided by the concepts and imaginings I have received from my culture (i.e., how my culture imagines and carves up the sensory world) and from my past experience.[60] Certain ideas and structures of organs make the sensible world appear more fully as it ought, but qualities always appear in things.

The content of species is also affected by the medium that carries them. Species do not just convey qualities on surfaces of bodies, but also content in the medium. We see mountains differently at a distance and up close because of how air affects light passing to us. Sensible species inform media, but forms exist only according to the capacity of matter to receive them. Qualities in a medium change its actualities, including intentional forms.

Alterations in species' content based on qualities in a medium, or on cognitive or physical conditions in a sensing being, do not necessarily distort how the object appears or lead to a loss of realism in perception. We ought to see mountains as blue from far away, even though what we are seeing here is not the mountain in itself, in isolation from all other things, but the mountain as filtered through a medium. As Hildebrand argues, what we should grasp in sensation is not reality stripped of all interpretation but rather the world as it ought to appear to us. Sensible content is properly experienced as a "message" to us, not only conveying information about sensible beings but also normatively guiding how we should comport ourselves to them.[61] While some structures in our organs and some ideas or images can distort the sensory world, it does not follow that the "human aspect" of the sensory world is less real or normative than the purely physical aspects of the world. Indeed, that this aspect is more real and normative is directly given to us. This is so precisely because it is ordered toward persons, who are of greater perfection than the scientific layer of reality.

This aspect of being a message (or normative guide) for persons is a major part of the excess in sensible experience, which cannot be explained naturalistically but requires some other account of its source. We can grasp this source by turning to the second layer of the experience of sensible qualities being bestowed upon things that Hildebrand distinguishes.

---

60. Abram, *The Spell of the Sensuous*, 68–92.

61. Psychologist James Gibson (*The Ecological Approach to Visual Perception*, [Hillsdale, N.J.: Erlbaum, 1986], 47–58) describes media as having "ambient energy," configurations of electromagnetic and other energy such that they carry information, which normatively motivate animals' acts. For a phenomenological appropriation of this, see Sokolowski, *Phenomenology of the Human Person*, 198–200; for a Thomistic appropriation, see De Haan, "Simon and Maritain on the Vocation of *Species in medio*," 75.

Some qualities manifest a *localized personal presence*—that is, they manifest properties that normally belong to persons. We can, as we have seen, experience sensible beauty's bestowal of peace and evocation of desire as if that beauty were loving us. A lovely pastoral scene at evening presents a "poetic" mood, a "fragrant," romantic presence that seems to "hover" over the scene's sensible qualities, unifying and harmonizing them, and bestowing an intimation of a higher, more perfect world. A clear blue sky presents joy, not as a mere projection of one's cheerfulness (for one can see this "joy" even when one is sad or despairing), but as objectively present in the sky's sensible qualities.[62] Mountains and clouds can appear, for example, playful, solemn, brooding, or threatening—in short, as intrinsically analogous to subjectivity.[63] Sensory beauty can also appear as "inhuman" in the foreignness of nonhuman things, in the cruelty and violence of predatory nature, when we sense a forest at night to be threatening or menacing, or in the glorious impassivity and indifference of vast stretches of ancient rock cliffs or of outer space.[64] Beauty can appear seductive, a mere mask for violence or cruelty, "unmanageable," suddenly breaking upon and overwhelming us in its sublime excess over all that is rationally expressible; it can even appear as both loving and breaking us at the same time.[65]

In each of these experiences we sense the presence of something like a person. This presence appears to us both as existing in sensible things themselves, and as appearing only when we attune ourselves to it, for example, by having the right concepts or mythic images. Like all sensible qualities, these more paradigmatic cases of personal presence in sensible qualities also appears as a "message," that is, a normative guide to how we ought to comport ourselves toward these sensible beings; they call us to feel joy, terror, erotic desire, and so forth. But insofar as every sensible quality is given as for me, something of this personal presence can be found in every quality.

---

62. Hildebrand, *Aesthetics*, vol. 1, 180–85, 253–58, 451.
63. Cf. Abram, *The Spell of the Sensuous*, chaps. 1, 3.
64. Albert Camus, *The Myth of Sisyphus*, trans. Justin O'Brien (New York: Random House, 1955), 11; Desmond, *The Gift of Beauty and the Passion of Being*, chap. 2. See Robinson Jeffers's poem "Birds and Fishes," in which he describes gulls savagely eating minnows and yet the "quality" of this spectacle appears as "the beauty of God."
65. Plato, *Symposium* 210e; *Republic* 509a; Song of Songs 6:4; Proverbs 31:30. Cf. Desmond, *The Gift of Beauty and the Passion of Being*, chap. 2; Annie Dillard, *Pilgrim at Tinker Creek* (New York: Harper & Row, 1974), 264–67; Alphonso Lingis, *Dangerous Emotions* (Berkeley: University of California Press, 2000), chap. 9; and McNeill, *The Glance of the Eye*, 39–47, 115–16. Consider the description of Galadriel as "beautiful beyond enduring, terrible and worshipful" in J. R. R. Tolkien, *The Fellowship of the Ring* (Boston: Houghton Mifflin, 1994), 356.

Hildebrand thinks that mythological gods were posited as causes of these properties: people experienced these personal qualities and posited persons manifesting themselves through sensible qualities and sensory experiences.[66] For example, the overarching power and joy of the sky manifests a kingly deity (like Jupiter or Indra), the charm and grace of a well-formed human body seems to manifest a deity of erotic love and sensuous beauty (like Aphrodite or Rati). While describing such gods involves devising images and concepts, the particular kind of transcendent personal quality embodied in the god first appears in sensory experience alone. Indeed, as we saw from Levinas, in sensation, we immediately experience ourselves "threatened" or "caressed" by the sensory world—the personal qualities, and the persons who present those qualities, are directly given in sensation. Although these transcendent persons can become part of an explanatory theory about sensible qualities, they are not first posited as explanations but are instead directly experienced.

Hildebrand, however, argues that there is no need to posit such beings. Rather, personal aspects of sensible qualities are an expression of the essence of those personal properties in themselves.[67] We have "Platonic" sensory experiences, in which multiple sensible beauties reveal a transcendent beauty appearing in all of them, or in which we perceive the essence of some flavor in itself, and not just the taste of a particular piece of food.[68] Sensible qualities are individual intrinsic formal causes of bodies in which they inhere; they directly belong to and characterize sensible bodies. But they also participate in extrinsic exemplary formal causes, actualities distinct from themselves, in which they participate—what I call "Platonic Forms" and which Stein called "ideal essences"—such as the essence of some flavor as such. On Hildebrand's account, these essences, rather than transcendent persons, manifest themselves in sensible qualities and explain the apparently personal presences we find there.

Aquinas does not describe these experiences, but his metaphysics helps us see why holding that there are transcendent persons present in these personal qualities is a plausible part of the explanation for sensible

---

66. Hildebrand, *Aesthetics*, vol. 1, 181–85. Cf. Michael Martin, *The Submerged Reality: Sophiology and the Turn to a Poetic Metaphysics* (Kettering, Ohio: Angelico Press, 2015), 108, drawing on Goethe, and Martin Heidegger, "Building Dwelling Thinking," in *Poetry, Language, Thought*, trans. Albert Hofstadter (New York: Harper & Row, 1971).

67. Hildebrand, *Aesthetics*, vol. 1, 164–69, 207.

68. Plato, *Phaedrus* 250d; Scheler, *Formalism in Ethics and Non-Formal Ethics of Values*, 12–13.

qualities on a metaphysics of irreducibility.[69] Some features of the sensible world are best explained by the action of transcendent persons. Hildebrand's explanation is reductionistic: it portrays properties that properly belong to persons as able to exist impersonally, as pure essences, apart from actual persons. It is more in keeping with a metaphysical portrait of persons as irreducible that the cosmos be conceived on a personalistic model, in which things are primarily understood by relation to persons and in which *person* is the fundamental metaphysical category, as opposed to a metaphysics on which nonpersonal natural substances or essences are the fundamental category.[70] On Aquinas's view, things have sensible qualities and communicate species in virtue of their elements (fundamental kinds of bodies) receiving the influence of heavenly bodies (sun, moon, planets, and stars).[71] The sun's illumination enables elements to imprint species of themselves on visible media. In doing so, sensible beings imitate and share in the power properly belonging to intellectual beings to express themselves. Since nothing can give what it does not have, the heavenly bodies can mediate this participation only if there are intelligent beings acting through them. Heavenly bodies act as instruments of the self-communicating, conscious beings who govern the cosmos, the intelligences, separate substances, angels, or gods.

Aquinas (and the Catholic tradition) hold that there are such beings not just because of biblical revelation but because beings tend to share in what transcends them, as we saw in vegetative powers. For example, all organisms, including plants, fungi, and bacteria (which Aquinas did not know about), have a limited share in animals' ability to sense, feel, and communicate.[72] Animals have a limited ability to exercise practical wisdom and linguistic conceptualization, which are proper to human persons.[73] We share in intuitive cognition, the ability to immediately, intellectually perceive essences and beings.[74] In the former two cases, the limited

---

69. Aquinas, *DP*, q.5, a.8; *In XII Met.*, lect. 9.
70. Kohák, *The Embers and the Stars*, 128–29.
71. Aquinas (*In III DA*, lect. 1) says there could be more than five senses if there were more than four elements. Since there are more elements ("elements" includes all fundamental physical kinds), there are more senses, for example, some organisms sense electromagnetic fields or echolocate, and we impose intentional forms on radio waves.
72. Peter Wohlleben, *The Hidden Life of Trees: What They Feel, How They Communicate—Discoveries from a Secret World*, trans. Jane Billinghurst (Vancouver: Greystone, 2016). For Thomistic appropriation, see Nicanor Austriaco, "Plants Too Have Sensitive Souls," presentation at 2019 Annual Meeting of the American Catholic Philosophical Association.
73. Aquinas, *In DMR*, lect. 1.
74. Aquinas, *SCG* II, c. 91; *ST* I, q.79, a.2; q.85, a.1.

ability points to the existence of higher lifeforms in whom the ability is perfect. Following the same pattern, our self-transcending ability points to the existence of purely intellectual beings, in whose activity we share. We must reject many of Aquinas's medieval views, such as that heavenly bodies are perfect substances, but since we need an explanation for the personal quality of sensible experience, we should retain his view that material things have sensible qualities by participating in powers of transcendent persons.[75] Every sensible quality, as a unique message, manifests a unique personal presence. In this way, a hierarchy of gods, each of whom is a unique mode of unity, goodness, and transcendence, appears (and is not just posited) in sensory experience. On the scholastic and Platonic traditions, these gods do not know the sensible world through species received from the world, because of their superiority over the world. Rather, on Aquinas's view, they intuit sensible things through creative ideas received from God and from other intelligences, the ideas God has of what he creates. For this reason, the gods' relation to the sensory world is also creative; each one stamps the whole world with his own character, but this character also shows up in particular effects, which we can perceive.[76]

These participations ground the experience of material things being identical to spiritual phenomena. Barfield describes ancient Greek experiences of *pneuma* as a phenomenon including what we now distinguish as *spirit*, *breath*, and *wind*. These unities are given because sensible beings just are participations in and revelations of transcendent causes, and so are intrinsically meaningful.[77] How material beings and transcendent causes interact will be discussed further in chapter 6.

In a third layer, Hildebrand describes sensible qualities as "messages from God."[78] In the second layer, qualities display multiple, irreducible

---

75. C. S. Lewis, *The Discarded Image: An Introduction to Medieval and Renaissance Literature* (Cambridge: Cambridge University Press, 1964), 102–21; Michael Ward, *Planet Narnia: The Seven Heavens in the Imagination of C. S. Lewis* (Oxford: Oxford University Press, 2008), 30–39, 75–76, 229–30.

76. Aquinas, *In LDC*, lects. 3, 14; *DOO*; *ST* I, q.15, a.3. See also the ancient Platonic philosopher Proclus, *The Elements of Theology*, props. 113–65, trans. E. R. Dodds (Oxford: Clarendon, 1992), 101–145. Cf. *ST* I, q.55, a.2. The Platonic tradition, summed up in Proclus, distinguishes *gods*, each a unique character of unity and goodness, from *intelligences*, each a distinct mind. The scholastic tradition, summed up in Aquinas, tends to include both of these kinds of transcendent persons in the category of *angels*. The experiences considered here reveal that there are transcendent persons, but do not give grounds to decide between the Platonist or Christian versions of the view.

77. Barfield, *Poetic Diction: A Study in Meaning* (Middletown, Conn.: Wesleyan University Press, 1973), 80–81. Cf. Abram, *The Spell of the Sensuous*, chap. 7. One notion of the divine, *deus*, expresses a similar unity of material and spiritual aspects: the shining of the sky and a divine being. See Mallory and Adams, *The Oxford Introduction to Proto-Indo-European*, 408–9.

78. Hildebrand, *Aesthetics*, vol. 1, 58–64, 90–91, 112–20, 330–35; *What Is Philosophy?* 205–18.

modes of transcendence; we experience multiple transcendent persons.[79] But in some cases, we perceive an absolute call to reverence, wonder, and worship, that is, a call that is of complete importance, which places an incontrovertible normative demand for a response upon us. Furthermore, we can reason from the finite and partial beauties and perfections we sense to an infinite beauty and perfection in which they participate. We can also perceive the glory of the sensible world giving itself as absolute and unified, and in each individual beauty, we can encounter unfathomable depth. An absolute importance appears belonging to the world as a whole.[80] Because of the absoluteness of the call we experience in each of these cases, it is proper to call this unified depth of beauty that shines forth in all particular beauties "God." The reverence called for by each individual beauty refers us to this absolute beauty, which calls for absolute reverence. To just give reverence to finite beauties is the reductionism of idolatry, the failure to respond to beauty as it gives itself, with this reference to infinite depth, by just stopping at the finite beauty.[81]

Augustine describes a related experience when he says that sensible phenomena are not God, yet they confess that God made them and allow us to perceive in the sensible world the invisible things of God; all things express a praise or exaltation of absolute beauty, that is, of God.[82] Another related experience is described by Stein, following phenomenologist Hedwig Conrad-Martius. Flowers are given as oriented to expressing a plenitude and beauty that exceeds what is necessary for individual or species survival. Vegetative powers transcend themselves toward sensible expression in a way that guides their substance's natural formation. Stein explains this by describing how God's absolute creative power appears in them.[83]

The Sophiological tradition in theology, as developed by Russian theologian Sergius Bulgakov, offers a helpful metaphysical model for describing this experience. Whether we reason from the existence of particular beauties to beauty itself in which they participate, or we perceive this absolute depth of beauty shining through all things, we discover God, who is absolute beauty. In this model, the unified, absolute depth of beauty perceived in the world is divine beauty, God's beauty rendered external

---

79. See, for example, Dreyfuss and Kelly, *All Things Shining*; Roberto Calasso, *The Marriage of Cadmus and Harmony*, trans. Tim Parks, (New York: Knopf, 1993).
80. On these experiences, see Plato, *Symposium*, *Republic*, and *Phaedrus*.
81. Cf. Marion, *In Excess*, chap. 3.
82. Augustine, *Confessions*, X.6.
83. Stein, *Finite and Eternal Being*, 266–67, citing Conrad-Martius, *Der "Seele" der Pflanze*, 78–80.

to himself, his self-manifestation in a creaturely way. Beauty is God's self-manifestation or wisdom (*Sophia*), the way in which God wisely shows himself in all things. The sensible world contains and is animated by this divine beauty or *Sophia*, the wise divine presence in all things, and that is fundamentally why the sensible world includes personal properties and makes us aware of God.[84]

Aspects of sensible qualities are bestowed on bodies by God, intelligences, and media, all directed to us. These qualities are instruments of transcendent causes and of sensible beings, and so reveal both. A sensible quality is both an inhering accident and a participation in media, gods, and God; accidents are beings that intrinsically reveal both themselves and the beings in which they inhere and participate. A body is a being that manifests itself sensibly by participating in higher beings and a being that has an intrinsic substantial and quantitative structure.[85] Reality is a network of things existing in themselves and by participation; we discover this, in part, through the excesses in sensory experience. Even qualities that appear in things only when we perceive them still are given as belonging to those things, for things reach out beyond themselves and take on properties through participation in others. For all these reasons, we sensible persons must be partly understood in terms of how we are sensed by others and how we participate in media, God, and the gods.[86]

Interior Sensitive Powers

I continue my portrait of irreducible features of human persons by offering a description, again drawn mostly from Aquinas's descriptions, of our interior senses, which receive effects from exterior senses and exhibit further degrees of immateriality and irreducibility. I experience the sensory world as a unified *Gestalt*, in which everything given in exterior senses is intertwined—what is properly or *per se* grasped through one sense seems to be grasped in a way (*per accidens*) through other senses. For example,

---

84. Sergius Bulgakov, *The Bride of the Lamb*, trans. Boris Jakim (Grand Rapids, Mich.: Eerdmans, 2002), 33–103. Cf. Martin, *The Submerged Reality*; Wisdom 7:26.

85. E. I. Watkin, *A Philosophy of Form* (New York: Sheed and Ward, 1935), 17–18; Cory, *Aquinas on Human Self-Knowledge*, 101–13.

86. Emergentists might object that sensations can be produced by brain stimulation and conclude that sensation is just an emergent property of the brain. However, no quantitative matter suffices to explain *esse sensibile*. While brain stimulation may reliably be followed by sensations, this is because stimulating (like other efficient causation) already participates in transcendent causes, such that, though them, the resulting sensory experiences display the excess found in sensation.

my vision and touch intertwine so that I see when something is rough or sticky; my vision and hearing intertwine so that I see when a glass makes a sound as it breaks; the forms received into each eye or ear are merged; I grasp sensible features of things that are common to many senses, like movement or stillness, and so forth. Within this *Gestalt* experience, I judge that objects of different senses are distinct—for example, colors are distinct from flavors. I cannot intertwine or distinguish objects of different exterior senses through those senses, so there must be another power by which I do this. This is the *common sense*, by which I also grasp my exterior sensory acts, thereby sensing my own life. We have seen that the sense of touch is substantially one, a grasp of what impinges on my body. The common sense is identical to touch in this sense: it is the sensing power of my whole body, a proprioceptive and kinesthetic sense of my body as stimulated by sensible beings.[87] Exterior senses manifest, participate in, and are instruments of this power of holistic sensation. Since I grasp particulars by it, it is an actuality of my body (especially my brain), but it is more immaterial than exterior senses. Although it cannot function unless its material cause, the brain, is structured and functioning well, it prescinds more from localization to a particular here-and-now than do exterior senses, for by it I grasp not just particular objects but whole unified scenes.[88]

Merleau-Ponty, along with enactive and action-based philosophers of perception like Alva Noë, notes that perception involves not just sensory organs and brain but the whole body, including bones and muscles, in interaction with the environment.[89] I always have a tacit sense of my body and its position in the world, my body-schema, and a general sense of how I feel in my body—for example, if I feel awkward or "at home" in my body.[90] The unity among my senses and the self-sensing described in chapter 1 are rooted in the body as a whole sensory system (i.e., in the common sense). Perception involves movements and stimuli felt through-

---

87. Aquinas, *In II DA*, lect. 13; *In III DA*, lect. 2, 3; *ST* I, q.78, a.4. Cf. Abram, *The Spell of the Sensuous*, 123–31; Merleau-Ponty, *The Visible and the Invisible*, chap. 4.

88. Aquinas, *In II DA*, lect. 3.

89. Merleau-Ponty, *Phenomenology of Perception*, 244–46, 262–64, 270–72, 298–302; Noë, *Action in Perception*; James Gibson, *The Senses Considered as Perceptual Systems* (Boston: Houghton Mifflin, 1966); and Sokolowski, *Phenomenology of the Human Person*, 198–200.

90. Hildebrand, *Aesthetics*, vol. 2, 188–89. On how the notion of "common sense" as a feeling of life has been developed (e.g., by Vico, Kant, Oetinger, and Gadamer) into a sense of one's life with others in community, see Mirela Oliva, "The Challenge of the Thomistic *Sensus Communis*: A Hermeneutic View," in *Thomas Aquinas: Teacher of Humanity*, ed. John Hittinger (Newcastle-upon-Tyne: Cambridge Scholars, 2015), 255–70. Compare to the account in chapter 1 of the feeling of life described by Henry and Stein.

out my whole body, which prompt my body to take up new perspectives on things, moving eyes and limbs to focus on objects. I "live" colors and tones, that is, I move with them since they not only give me content but also evoke and call for affective and locomotive responses. To sense is always to be aware of sensory contents as they impinge on and enter into communion with my body, which I only sense insofar as contents impinge on it.

After receiving species into my common sense, I interpret and express what I have received; cognitive activity follows a pattern of receptivity and activity, neither reducible to the other.[91] Sensory interpretations or judgments include distinguishing sensible qualities, focusing on certain qualities, and using previous experiences as a lens through which to view currently sensed qualities. On the basis of received species and my interpretations, I internally produce images (or "phantasms") of *Gestalten*, by means of which I can picture things with my power of *imagination*. While species are not merely representations of beings, they are representations. In such cases, however, I do not consider the representing species; rather, I use the species as a means to consider that which it represents. How I picture things affects how I later interpret sensations.[92] I can picture spontaneously (as in dreams, daydreams, and reveries)[93] or deliberately and creatively. In exterior sensation, qualities appear as real and distinct from me; by imagination, I can consider them as mere appearances. Imagination liberates species' content from rootedness in real sources, so that they can be used as instruments for intellectual creativity. In this liberation, we see the transcendence and greater immateriality of internal sense over external. But imagination also allows me to be deceived, even self-deceived, if I fail to attend to fact that images have their source in real beings, which act on me.[94]

Phantasms (with their content from received species) are stored in the power of *memory*; by means of these stored forms and imagination, what they represent can be remembered. I can attend to remembering as a current act or as presenting something past; this reveals another degree of immateriality, inasmuch as I can prescind from my particular now. Phantasms actualize the body (especially the brain), and they change with

---

91. Maritain, *Degrees of Knowledge*, 126.
92. Cf. Abram, *The Spell of the Sensuous*, 58.
93. Aquinas, *ST* I, q.84, a.8, ad 2; Bachelard, *The Poetics of Space*.
94. Aquinas, *In III DA*, lects. 5, 6; *ST* I, q.78, a.4.

bodily material changes since actualities are received in matter only insofar as that matter is disposed to receive them. Phantasms' "storage" is a disposition of the brain (and the whole body) to be actualized in a certain way, so that by those phantasms, I consider what they represent. Bodily changes, including deterioration of the brain, change the content of memories. We are often mistaken about memories insofar as they purport to present something past; for example, we can doubt that a genuine memory is genuine, or falsely believe that a phantasm presents a genuine memory. We can also forget and suppress memories; the storing of phantasms is not a passive storing of all information we receive but involves interpretation: we actively (albeit often without self-conscious deliberation) organize, synthesize, suppress, and eliminate phantasms. This hylomorphic account of internal sensation supports contemporary psychological findings about memory's unreliability, and about how remembering is not just recall of stored information but a reactualization (and so a partial alteration) of what was received.[95] Since sensation and memory are dispositions of the whole body, external sensations can spontaneously activate stored phantasms, as when a chance smell or taste brings back a flood of memories, or when liturgy and narrative (which I consider further in later chapters) are used to remember accurately.[96]

Through the *cogitative power*, we sense particular objects as having aspects or "particular intentions," that is, particular graspable content (*rationes*) such as being harmful or beneficial, as able to be acted toward in some way, or as an instance of some kind. I grasp how sensible beings normatively call me to act in certain ways; this grasp is sensory, not involving concepts or propositions—that is, it is experienced in how my body is attuned to sensible beings. In being guided in this way, I experience myself as an animal.[97] Repeated experiences of one being or of a kind of being build up cognitive patterns: we note resemblances among beings, group them into categories (though this does not involve a universal concept—a grasp on their essence itself—since that requires the intellect), and experience them through the lens of earlier experiences. This gives practical experience (*experimentum*) of how to deal with beings of different kinds.[98]

---

95. See, for example, Yadin Dudai and Micah Edelson, "Personal memory: Is it personal, is it memory?" *Memory Studies* 9, no. 3 (2016): 275–83.
96. Aquinas, *In DMR*, lects. 3, 5.
97. See Alasdair MacIntyre, *Dependent Rational Animals: Why Human Beings Need the Virtues* (Chicago: Open Court, 1999), chaps. 5, 6.
98. Aquinas, *In II DA*, lect. 13; *In II Post An.*, lect. 20; *ST* I, q.78, a.4. See Daniel De Haan, "Perception

What it's like to be me at the sensory level involves this continually developing experience. I experience the world not just through newly received species but through species as incorporated into and modified by previously received species. Cogitative experience is a habitual or customary framework that allows species to be constituted as meaningful insofar as they fit with phantasms I already have. That can block me from grasping new aspects of things, however, insofar as I am habituated only to expect to experience certain aspects of things. However, this power crucially joins the acts of other powers in the synthesis (which often occurs passively, that is, without my actively, self-consciously brining ideas together) of conceptual meanings I have in my intellect with content received through the senses, such that I identify what I sense *as* falling under some intellectually grasped universal kind, or I spontaneously associate ideas and images.[99] Human persons rarely engage in purely sensory activity; normally, the intellect (to be considered in chapter 3) is involved, such that I think of sensible things as falling under concepts. Furthermore, while we (and other animals) sometimes experience the splendor of beauty just through the exterior senses, the full experiences of beauty described above require interior sensory powers, too.[100] Experiencing the transcendence and personal quality of sensible qualities, or the unities described by Barfield, requires the synthesizing work of common sense, imagination, and cogitative power, generally under intellectual influence.

Appetitive and Locomotive Powers

I am also moved to respond affectively to sensed beings. I directly sense only aspects of beings; for example, if I receive the species of only one side of the desk in front of me, I only directly see that side. I do thereby see the real desk itself, and internal senses apperceptively fill in expectations about and implicit awareness of the other sides in my meaningful constitution of

---

and the *Vis Cogitativa*," *American Catholic Philosophical Quarterly* 88, no. 3 (2014): 397–437. Excessive focus on cogitative experience underlies *resemblance nominalism*, a metaphysics on which only particulars exist and universal words just denote classes of things that resemble one another, not intellectually grasped shared essences; see Lowe, *A Survey of Metaphysics*, 352–57.

99. Aquinas, *ST* I-II, q.50, a.3, ad 3. When cognitive scientists (e.g., George Lakoff and Mark Johnson, *Philosophy in the Flesh: The Embodied Mind and Its Challenge to Western Thought* [New York: Basic Books, 1999], 3) say that most thinking is unconscious, this is true of cogitative thinking, not intellectual thinking. Cf. Edmund Husserl, *Analyses Concerning Passive and Active Synthesis*, trans. Anthony Steinbock (Dordrecht: Kluwer, 2001).

100. Aristotle, *HA*, VIII.9.618a18.

the object *the desk*.[101] But appetites, like loving and hating, intend (i.e., are about and aim at) real beings in their entirety. I cannot have a feeling about some being unless I first know it, but I do not have feelings just about those aspects of beings that I have sensed, but in most cases have feelings about whole beings.[102] I love my whole desk, not just the sides I can currently see.

While both sensitive and appetitive acts are unities of objective physiological events and subjective experiences, Aquinas holds that appetites involve material changes more essentially than sensing does. Physical perturbations in sense organs, like eyes being dazzled by intense light, or ears pained by harsh noises, are unnecessary (and detrimental) for sensory acts. But bodily changes are integral to feelings, in which my whole body takes a stance toward an object.[103] I do not directly feel, for example, adrenaline in fear or oxytocin in attraction, but I do feel that bodily responses are occurring, and that my whole body is the subject performing an appetitive act.[104] Feeling directly reveals how my whole body takes on intentional, subjective and objective relations to (and fits with) other material beings. This bodily intentionality is a crucial experience for realist metaphysics: in it, I directly experience contact with real beings.

But Aquinas contrasts cognitive and appetitive acts too sharply; his account is reductionistic of the full experience of sensation. His own account guides us to see how sensation also essentially involves experiencing changes in my whole body. All senses are rooted in the common sense, by which I grasp what impinges on my body, experiencing physical impacts on my sense organs. This also always involves appetitive responses of pleasure or pain, love (or attraction) or hatred (or aversion).[105] In sensation and in the appetitive responses it engenders, I experience contact with real beings impinging on my body. We primarily experience sensible things as whole bodies, irreducible to particular parts, powers, or acts; what it is like to be me sensing always involves intertwined sensory and appetitive intentionality. Once again, we see this best in the experience of beauty, that is, the experience of what pleases just when perceived. The pleasure involved in grasping beauty arises immediately upon the beautiful object impinging

---

101. Cf. Husserl, *Ideas Pertaining to a Pure Phenomenology*, vol. 1, 86–92.
102. Aquinas, *ST* I, q.80, a.1; I-II, q.22, a.2.
103. Aquinas, *ST* I-II, q.22, a.2, ad 3. Aquinas's example is that anger involves heating of blood.
104. Merleau-Ponty (*Phenomenology of Perception*, 190–98) describes how in sexual attraction, I do not have a feeling that is then communicated to my body, but the desired person draws my whole body into a stance of felt response.
105. Aquinas, *In III DA*, lect. 18; *ST* II-II, q.153, a.2.

on my senses, since common sense, the basis of all senses, and appetite are just two sides of the one sensorium that is my body.

Appetites also influence cognition; for example, love causes us to experience ourselves ecstatically outside ourselves, and it guides our attention toward the beloved, such that we grasp the beloved more deeply and completely than we would without love. Love—an affection or affinity for anything perceived as good—always guides sensation, insofar as sensible objects are goods that fulfill my sensitive powers.[106] Appetites are also ways of cognitively grasping things insofar as appetite conforms itself to, and renders us connatural with, its object.[107] Scheler describes how sensible values evoke felt responses in us through which we grasp those values; for example, there are fearful, enjoyable, and angering properties in beings, which we grasp by being appetitively moved by them.[108] Some such value-properties (like the danger of some substances) are explainable by the natural properties of those substances, but others (like the delightfulness of the sensory qualities of a beautiful human body) exceed what can be so explained; like *esse sensibile*, they too reveal transcendent personal causes.

There are too many irreducible kinds of sensation, appetite, and their objects to consider them all. In every sense, we are directly given contents that are irreducible features of reality, given my general principle that any content that is directly given cannot be nothing but another content. Likewise, what it is like to feel each kind of appetite is an irreducible content, and each appetite reveals irreducible, valuable features of objects. Although I cannot give a complete taxonomy, it is helpful to briefly consider a framework for thinking about kinds of appetites, insofar as such a framework guides us to perceive the many irreducible kinds of appetites.

Aquinas distinguishes two basic appetitive powers. *Concupiscible appetite* responds to cognized beings as good or bad for us. It allows feelings of love, hatred, desire, aversion, delight or pleasure, and sadness or pain. *Irascible appetite* responds to beings as goods or evils that are difficult to attain or avoid. It allows feelings of hope, fear, daring, anger, despair, and (as Francis de Sales adds) victory or triumph.[109] As Plato argues in his account of spiritedness (*thumos*), which parallels the scholastic irascible appetite, that this power motivates us to pursue what is difficult because it

---

106. Aquinas, *ST* I-II, q.28, a.2, 3, 6.
107. Aquinas, *ST* I-II, q.15, a.1.
108. Cf. Scheler, *Formalism in Ethics and Non-Formal Ethics of Values*, 66–70.
109. Aquinas, *ST* I, q.80, a.2; I-II, q.23, a.1; Francis de Sales, *Treatise on the Love of God*, trans. Henry Benedict de Mackey (Rockford: Tan, 1997), 22–23.

is high and noble, that is, because it calls us to greater self-transcendence and appears beautiful, worth pursuing for its own sake.[110] Further feelings are irreducible species of these basic kinds; for example, distress, perplexity, pity, and envy are kinds of sadness, while wonder, stupor, and anxiety are kinds of fear.[111] Other feelings arise from combinations of, causal relations among, or habituations of these feelings: for example, we feel pleasure arising from wonder, from remembering past sadnesses, and from current sadness inasmuch as it leads us to pleasantly think of the good we lack.[112] Habitual feelings arise from inborn temperaments to respond to beings in certain ways, from repeatedly acting in some way, and from infusion from God. Just as habituation of interior senses alters how I receive species and sense myself, so virtuous or vicious habituation of appetites leads me to attend to certain things and avoid others.[113] We are developing beings, always changing in relation to others. Genuine habituation requires guidance by intellect and will, and so will be considered further in later chapters.

A taxonomy of feelings not only helps us map out all of our irreducible powers; it is also helpful because properly exercising and understanding feeling is necessary to do nonreductionistic metaphysics. As Thomas Hibbs has noted, realist metaphysics is a practice that requires virtuously developed feelings that attune or fit us with reality.[114] A *proper metaphysical attitude* requires the right combination of feelings to attune us to the full splendor of beings: love, with its ecstatic openness to and entering into each beloved; enjoyment, including feeling secure and festive; reverence and humility; wonder and amazement, which involve fear at ignorance, awareness of one's limits, desire for knowledge, and awe at beauty; and anxiety and hope, which aim at future things that we cannot fully envision, and thereby open our attention to the unforeseen and unexpected.[115]

Appetitive acts efficiently cause locomotive acts, movements of bodily parts like my limbs; again, these would be inexplicable as human motions were they just discrete body parts, such as nerves or muscles, moving oth-

---

110. *Phaedrus* 253d–254e; Plato, *Republic* 439e–441c.
111. Aquinas, *ST* I-II, q.35, a.8; q.41, a.4.
112. Aquinas, *ST* I-II, q.32, a.4, 7; q.49, a.2. See Spencer, "Habits, Potencies, and Obedience."
113. Aquinas, *ST* I-II, q.51.
114. Thomas Hibbs, *Aquinas, Ethics, and Philosophy of Religion: Metaphysics and Practice* (Bloomington: Indiana University Press, 2007).
115. Aquinas, *ST* I-II, q.32, a.8; q.41, a.4; II-II, q.17, a.2, ad 1; *In I Met.*, lect. 3; Heidegger, *Being and Time*, 172–78; Gabriel Marcel, *Homo Viator: Introduction to the Metaphysics of Hope*, trans. Emma Craufurd and Paul Seaton (South Bend, Ind.: St. Augustine Press, 2010), 23–61; Viladesau, *Theological Aesthetics*, 135–37; and Dietrich and Alice von Hildebrand, *The Art of Living* (Steubenville, Ohio: Hildebrand Press, 2017), chap. 1.

ers. Rather, they are given human identity by appetitive and locomotive acts, which flow from and are ordered to the actuality of the whole human person. As we saw when considering action-based theories of perception, sensory, appetitive, and locomotive powers and acts are intertwined. Sensing causes feelings, and these both directly reveal aspects of objects and lead me to attend to aspects of what I sense; I locomotively move myself to better sense, and the cycle begins again. This mobile sensation gives me a further awareness of interacting, as a unified body, with real beings, whose content is not up to me but that I must receive.[116] This experience is further evidence that I have a form conferring this unity. This unity is further seen in how sensitive, appetitive, and locomotive powers raise vegetative powers to higher, more unified and interior modes of being, for example, in making the power of respiration into the power of *voice*.[117]

Appetites reveal still higher levels of immateriality in me. Once again, something is immaterial insofar as it prescinds from limitation to particular places and times. Some Thomists (like Jacek Woroniecki) and phenomenologists (like Hildebrand) have noted that some appetites, like certain cases of pain or arousal, arise because of physiological changes and not as a response to an experience of sensation. Others, like most of those considered so far, which Woroniecki calls "sensual emotions" and Hildebrand "psychic feelings," are caused by sensation. The former are restricted to a particular point in the body, while the latter involve transcendence over my body insofar as they intend objects beyond me; hence, the latter are more immaterial than the former.[118] But those appetites also display a range of degrees of immateriality, insofar as they put me in intentional contact with objects that transcend my current place and time. Some (like sadness) are about present things, others (like hope) are about future things, and still others (such as great joy) transcend time altogether.[119]

Transcendence over time (or the experience of eternity) in great joy is explained by a distinction made by Aristotle. Some human acts are "motions" or "processes" (*kineseis*): they have distinct stages at different times and aim at achieving an actuality distinct from themselves (e.g., desiring aims at an actual desired thing; reasoning aims at actual knowledge of a

---

116. Aquinas, *In III DA*, lects. 15, 16.
117. Aquinas, *In II DA*, lect. 18; *In III DA*, lect. 18.
118. Hildebrand, *The Heart*, 22–27; Piotr Mazur et al., *Jacek Woroniecki* (Krakow: Ignatianum University Press, 2019), 61.
119. Aquinas, *ST* I, q.10, a.1, 3; I, q.31, a.2; I-II, q.25, a.4.

conclusion; cooking aims at a finished meal). Other acts are "activities" or "acts in which one is completely "at work" (*energeiai*): they are always complete, each moment of the act is essentially the same as every other, and each is done for its own sake, aiming at nothing beyond itself and its object (e.g., contemplative seeing or feeling joy or pleasure).[120] Time is the dimension or measure of motions. We grasp time in the internally perceived flow of experience: normally, each moment is given as retaining elements of past moments, and protensionally, expectantly tending toward future ones.[121] We also grasp time in sensing successions of physical states. Both experiences of time occur through the common sense. For something to be given in time, it must be given as having successive "befores" and "afters," that is, distinguishable stages.

But activities like contemplation and joy (at least in their pure state) are experienced as pure "now's," without successive, qualitatively distinguishable stages; hence, feeling pleasure is experienced as transcending time.[122] They take place in time insofar as other motions take place in me while I experience them, and insofar as they are never entirely unchanging. But in itself, joy or pleasure gives an intimation and participation in what is more perfect or complete than time. In moments of great joy, we feel, to some extent, time being stilled, and, for a moment, sharing in eternity, the activity of perfect life. This reveals sensory powers' immateriality and transcendence over corporeal matter, since corporeal matter as such is always moving. It also helps confirm my claim that space and time are not *a priori* conditions for sensation, since this sensory activity can transcend space and time.

The range of bodily powers in the human person considered in this chapter revealed irreducible features in us, especially our irreducibility to matter, and relations to beings that transcend the material world. But all of the acts and objects considered in this chapter are material. To see our complete irreducibility to matter, we must find powers in us that are not located in matter at all: our spiritual powers. I now turn to the first of them, the intellect.

---

120. Aristotle, *Met.*, VI.6.1048b18–35. I give further senses of *energeia* in chapter 6.
121. Augustine, *Confessions*, XI.20; Edmund Husserl, *On the Phenomenology of the Consciousness of Internal Time*, trans. John Barnett Brough (Dordrecht: Kluwer, 1991). See the discussion of the stream of auto-affection from Henry in chapter 1.
122. Aquinas, *In IV Phys.*, lect. 17.

Chapter 3   Intellect and the Principles of Real Being

In chapters 3 through 6, I consider *spiritual powers*, powers distinctive of persons, whose acts are not just causally engendered but arise only when motivated by the self-conscious grasp of some meaning, that is, a grasp of a meaning in which I am aware not only of the meaning, but also of myself grasping it. I begin with intellect. While sensible qualities are meaningful in that they fit with our sense powers, we cannot attend to that meaning self-consciously by sense, and we grasp sensible objects in a way entangled with sensing the medium and ourselves. We self-consciously grasp beings in themselves by intellect, distinct from the medium and their material impact on us. Senses grasp particulars as restricted to a spatiotemporal position; intellect grasps what beings are, abstracted from particularization and location in space or time.[1]

I first consider intellectual acts including illumination, abstraction, conceptualization, and intuition. I focus on how intellect grasps real being and its irreducible features, including beauty, the essence-*esse* structure, and relations to Platonic Forms. I consider whether we have a natural desire to see God, a question that over the last century has been closely connected to the question of how human nature and divine grace are related. Finally, I consider human practical and productive reasoning, focusing on theories of how we discover the natural law.

1. Aquinas, *ST* I, q.79, a.4–7; I, q.84, a.7; *In III DA*, lects. 7, 8.

Illumination, Abstraction, and Obediential Potencies

Intellectual activity begins with an experience the scholastic tradition calls *illumination*. When I first encounter a being of a kind I have never encountered, I do not know what it is, but I experience its sensible features as able to be understood: I grasp that I could investigate it and discover what it is.[2] In sensory experience as described in chapter 2, nothing was grasped as actually intelligible (as having a meaning that can be self-consciously grasped and articulated) but only as potentially intelligible (able to be rendered actually intelligible). In being moved to figure out what a sensible thing is, my phantasms are rendered actually intelligible. Given that phantasms in me can become actually intelligible, there must be a power in me that explains this actualization. Aristotelian tradition calls this the *agent* (*or making*) *intellect*. The experience of sensed content being rendered intelligible resembles the experience of light illuminating things and rendering them visible, so it is called *illumination*.[3] (Because I experience myself rendering content intelligible, I reject as reductionistic Averroistic and Avicennian views, on which either the whole intellect or the agent intellect are one in all human persons.) Unlike physical light, this illumination adds no content to what I grasp, but it makes sensible things able to be understood. This experience reveals how the intellect transcends the senses and is open to the new: I do not just grasp given objects, but I exhibit wonder and desire for the truth, including about beings I do not yet know.[4] In this section and the next, I describe two kinds of illumination.

In this first experience of illumination, phantasms are rendered intelligible in the sense of being rendered conceptualizable. After illumination—that is, after I become aware that a sensed being has a meaning that can be self-consciously grasped and articulated—I draw out or "abstract" that meaning and so self-consciously and conceptually grasp it. Upon sensing, I almost automatically begin to inquire into, discover, and articulate what kind of things the beings I sense are, and just like colors being illuminated, their essences begin to appear to me, though confusedly at first. For example, upon seeing a dog, I begin to articulate to myself what a dog is,

---

2. Lonergan, *Insight*, 555.
3. Aquinas, *In III DA*, lect. 10; *ST* I, q.79, a.3, 4.
4. Bernard Lonergan, "The Natural Desire to See God," in *Collection: Papers by Bernard Lonergan, S.J.* (New York: Herder and Herder, 1967), 90, cited in Lawrence Feingold, *The Natural Desire to See God According to St. Thomas and His Interpreters* (Naples, Fla.: Sapientia Press, 2010), 403.

as revealed through this dog's sensory qualities—my focus shifts from this dog to what this dog reveals about what a dog is. I thereby receive and am actualized by content not about this dog but about what it is to be a dog as such.[5] This unified content is grasped as belonging equally to dogs thousands of years in the past or future, to this dog and to dogs around the world, and to merely possible dogs. To grasp a being's essence is to grasp what it is, which justifies judgments as to how the being is to be defined.

By abstraction, I grasp kinds of beings either by forming *universals* (which I understand as applying to each being of that kind) or just by grasping their essential content, not as universal or particular but as a *nature absolutely considered*; for example, I can grasp "dog-ness" insofar as it belongs to each particular dog, or in itself and not as belonging to many dogs. By abstraction, I can also grasp mathematical quantities, such as geometric figures or numbers, and features of beings insofar as they are beings, such as transcendentals.[6] In each case, I grasp an actuality whose content is unrestricted to the here-and-now. Prescinding from the here-and-now is, as Sokolowski points out, an intersubjective act: I aim at grasping the truth about beings as it would be grasped by anyone; to conceptualize is to enter a standpoint from which I can converse with anyone about what I grasp.[7] Abstract thinking is a form of living with others. It is linguistic, not in the sense that it always involves a particular language like English or Latin, but in that it articulates and expresses what is grasped. Like any actuality, concepts are oriented to being expressed to others and to building on one another, a notion I build on in chapter 5, when I discuss the centrality of conversation to human personhood.

Illumination and abstraction draw from phantasms *intelligible species*, which (in a way similar to how *sensible species* function) actualize my intellect, contain an essence's content, and mediate my knowledge of that essence. A *concept* is an articulation of a species' content. Species and concepts do not just represent essential content but participate in it, not just as it is in the individual but as universal or absolutely considered. While material things like spoken or written words can represent essences, intellectual participation in essences cannot take place in something material. This is because corporeal matter is quantified and localized in space and time. Even though matter participates in what transcends quantity and

---

5. Aquinas, *ST* I, q.84, a.6, 7; I, q.85, a.13; *DEE*.
6. Aquinas, *ST* I, q.85, a.1, ad 2.
7. Sokolowski, *Phenomenology of the Human Person*, 179–80.

localization, matter always restricts the content of what it participates to particular places and times. Material cognitive powers, as we saw, grasp their objects through physical contact effected by a medium. If intelligible species and concepts actualized a material organ (like the brain), they could mediate participation and cognition of content only restricted to particular places and times, but I intellectually grasp and participate in actualities unrestricted in these ways, and so the intellect cannot be in a material organ.[8]

Many Thomists understand abstraction as selective attention. In the view of the seventeenth-century Thomist Thomas Cajetan, abstraction occurs when we intellectually "see" an illuminated phantasm manifesting its content and we form a concept to match that content.[9] Bernard Lonergan understands it as insight into a being's form through sensory examples.[10] Eleonore Stump and Robert Pasnau understand it to be selectively attending to phantasms' intelligible features while setting aside particular features.[11] But Therese Cory explains an aspect of abstraction missing from these accounts. In illumination, the agent intellect confers on phantasms not only the power to cause intelligible species but also a new mode of being, *esse intelligibile*, whereby their content is rendered actually intelligible, that is, entirely immaterial, graspable in a self-conscious, meaningful manner, separated from particular places and times.[12] Since nothing can give what it does not have, the agent intellect must have that mode of being; it must be a continual activity of manifesting and conferring the intelligible mode of being so that it can, at any time, give rise to acts of understanding.[13] Like any actuality, it is disposed to confer a likeness of itself on other things. Phantasms come to exist in the self-conscious mode of the intellect; this change in mode of being allows the insight or attention that Cajetan, Lonergan, Stump, and Pasnau describe. Without this change in mode of being, there would be no explanation for how this insight or attention occurs.

---

8. Aquinas, *ST* I, q.84, a.2.

9. Cajetan, *In I ST*, q.79 a.3, nn. 9–10. Cf. Daniel Heider, "Abstraction, Intentionality, and Moderate Realism," in *Hircocervi and Other Metaphysical Wonders: Essays in Honor of John Doyle*, ed. Victor Salas (Milwaukee, Wisc.: Marquette University Press, 2013), 177–211.

10. Lonergan, *Insight*, 456–59.

11. Pasnau, *Human Nature*, 300–301; Eleonore Stump, *Aquinas* (London: Routledge, 2005), 264–65.

12. Cory, "Rethinking Abstractionism," 607–46; "Knowing as Being? A Metaphysical Reading of the Identity of Intellect and Intelligible in Aquinas," *American Catholic Philosophical Quarterly* 91, no. 3 (2017): 333–51. See Aquinas, *In LDC*, lect. 13.

13. Aristotle, *DA*, III.5.430a16–19.

According to this view, senses can receive an intelligible mode of being that transcends their natural, sensible mode of being. Understanding this receptivity requires introducing a key scholastic metaphysical idea, *obedience*. My powers are *natural potencies*; they are caused by my essence, not by principles extrinsic to me, and are ways that I can be moved by my own effort.[14] Some, like agent intellect, are active potencies; by them, I move myself toward ends that I can achieve by my own effort. Others, like exterior senses, are passive potencies, which are moved by active potencies outside me. Natural active and passive potencies fit with or *are proportioned to* one another. A necessary condition for two natural potencies fitting or being proportioned is having the same degree of immateriality.

But on the scholastic metaphysics that I am incorporating into my portrait to account for the experience of abstraction, my powers are also *obediential potencies*: they can be elevated by beings that are more immaterial than they are in order to perform acts that exceed what can be done with them by our own effort, and that exceed what is proportioned to them. In scholasticism, *obediential potency* originally denoted a creaturely potency actualizable only by God—such as our ability to receive grace or direct participation in God's life. For example, the intellect naturally grasps what can be abstracted from the senses, but God can give an additional "light" to the intellect, the gift of faith, whereby we can grasp and assent to his supernatural revelation.[15]

There is also a broader sense of obedience and obediential potency in scholasticism, which I develop here, on which a power can be elevated to a new mode of being by causes other than God.[16] Obediential potencies are natural in that they are in us from our origins as aspects of our powers. They are not natural potencies, however, for by them, we perform acts not entirely through our own effort or through something proportioned to them but through a principle greater than them.

If our powers in themselves are obedient and can only be fully explained through principles that they obey, then we are irreducible to what we naturally are. We have seen evidence that our powers are obedient: our bodies share in transcendent powers to have *esse sensibile* and our senses share in intelligible being through illumination. When a power is obedientially elevated, it receives a new way of acting under its formal ob-

---

14. Aquinas, *DEE*, c. 1.
15. Aquinas, *ST* II-II, q.1, a.4.
16. Cf. Suárez, *DM*, d.16, s.2, nn. 17–18; *DM*, d.43, s.4, n. 17; and Feingold, *Natural Desire*, 107.

ject. Interior senses, as natural potencies informing matter, only naturally have effects that are actualities of matter, but when they obey the intellect, they share in *esse intelligibile*, by which they cause intelligible species in the intellect—an effect that exceeds what is proportioned to their natural degree of immateriality. While material things are naturally restricted to the here-and-now and to causing through spatial contact, they can, under obedience, share in a more unrestricted, nonlocalized mode of being.[17] In their natural mode of being and acting, our senses are like those of other animals, but they also share in and are obedientially directed to intellectual activity.

Aesthetic Cognition

Conceptual cognition results from the sort of illumination already described. In it, I "become" a cognized being insofar as my intellect accidentally receives its essence's actuality, is adequated or fitted to it, and so participates in and conceptually expresses it. But we have another experience of illumination—another way that we grasp beings as meaningful, in themselves, and as distinct from us—which some call *aesthetic cognition* or *poetic intuition*.[18]

In a holistic experience involving senses, intellect, will, and appetites, we originally experience each being that we encounter as beautiful. We often just think about material beings as they appear through the first act of conceptualization—for example, as belonging to some kind or as usable in some way. But even if we do not consciously attend to it, beings always first appear holistically, as sensible, meaningful, pleasurable or awe-inducing, motivating us to freely affirm or endorse their existence. The splendor of beautiful beings described in chapter 2 strikes not only our senses and appetites but also our powers to intellectually grasp and spiritually respond and take joy as well. As Lublin Thomist Piotr Jaroszyński explains, sensible contents are not actually intelligible in a conceptualizable way, but they are actually intelligible in an aesthetic way.[19] Servais Pinckaers calls this orig-

---

17. See Aquinas, *ST* I, q.81, a.3; *CT* I, c. 104; John of St. Thomas, *Cursus philosophicus thomisticus*, v. 3, p.3, q.10, a.2, 451–58; Feingold, *Natural Desire*, 101–65; and Spencer, "Habits, Potencies, and Obedience."

18. Jaroszyński, *Beauty and Being*, 171–88; Piotr Jaroszyński, *Metaphysics and Art*, trans. Hugh McDonald (New York: Peter Lang, 2002), 50–53; Mieczyslaw Krąpiec, *Metaphysics: An Outline of the History of Being*, trans. Theresa Sandok (New York: Peter Lang, 1991), 179–89; and Jacques Maritain, *Creative Intuition in Poetry and Art* (New York: Pantheon, 1953), chaps. 3, 4, and 7. Some themes here were developed in Spencer, "Beauty, First and Last of All the Transcendentals," *The Thomist* 82, no. 2 (2018): 157–87.

19. Jaroszyński, *Metaphysics and Art*, 50–53.

inal, holistic, intuitive *Gestalt*-experience "fontal knowledge"—the knowledge from which all subsequent acting, knowing, and judging spring.[20] Jacques Maritain describes it as an experience of being "inspired" by a beautiful being, receiving its holistic self-expression or "spirit," its excess over what fits with my powers, which leads me to perceive new, unexpected meaning. A being must first show itself to my intellect before I can bestow my intellect's mode of being on it and conceptualize its essence. If it did not first manifest itself to me in its distinctness and reality, I would never grasp it as it is in itself. Hildebrand describes this experience as spiritually "going with" beings, aligning one's experience to their holistic self-manifestation and actively receiving their full content.[21] What a beautiful being expresses exceeds my conceptualizing power; when I grasp a being as beautiful, I directly grasp that I could never adequately express what I grasp in concepts or words.

The principle of obedience explains this experience. The intellect is naturally oriented to abstract and conceptualize species and thereby understand beings; in conceptualization, the active powers of the agent intellect and illuminated phantasm fit with the passive power of the "possible intellect," the power to receive and self-consciously grasp intelligible content. I can abstract and conceptualize under my own power, so long as I receive phantasms. By this act, I discover an irreducible feature of any being, its essence. Aesthetic cognition is like the intellect's natural act in that it can happen automatically when I am before any being, but, experientially, it lacks fit between active and passive potencies. I explain this by positing that the active power of the self-manifesting being exceeds my possible intellect—that is, there is an immaterial principle in each being that transcends us. In experiencing holistic beauty, I obey the beautiful being such that I am ecstatically taken out of myself to see the world anew, guided by the being. In abstractive illumination, the agent intellect bestows on phantasms the obediential ability to cause conceptualizable species in the possible intellect. In aesthetic illumination, the agent intellect just opens the possible intellect to receive the self-manifestation of beautiful beings, as mediated through the phantasm, without conceptualization. Maritain calls the agent intellect insofar as it opens me to this sort of act "preconscious" or "spiritually unconscious": since it is not conceptually articulated,

---

20. Pinckaers, *The Sources of Christian Ethics*, 50–52.
21. Hildebrand, *What Is Philosophy?* 20–22. Cf. Merleau-Ponty, *The Visible and the Invisible*, 125–26, 153–55, 180.

it lacks the clear and distinct consciousness of conceptual thinking, yet it profoundly affects and illuminates all our other acts. (Unconscious features of human life often have deep effect on the structure of conscious acts, as we have seen in how conscious subjectivity arises out of other structures in the person.)[22] Each intellectual act can be elucidated through distinct phenomenological methods. For example, Husserl's reduction reveals our ability to conceptualize intelligible objects (i.e., subsume them under concepts and so constitute them as meaningful). Marion's reduction reveals our ability to receive givenness, which exceeds the content of any concept but is still intelligible, and which I call beauty.

Given this account of these two irreducible intellectual acts, we can draw the conclusion that the intellect has a fundamentally obediential and open character. My mind can not only grasp any being; it can also be reconfigured by new principles, such as beauty. My natural acts of abstraction and conceptualization normally follow and are conditioned by obediential acts of perceiving beauty. Beings first manifest themselves holistically, and then I conceptualize aspects of that self-manifestation, though I generally attend more to the latter act than the former. Although I receive their content, I can control when I form and use concepts. But I cannot control when visions of beauty will cut through my normal conceptual way of considering things and overwhelm me with their glory: I receive beauty as a gift. In experiences of beauty, we experience intellectual activity as a form of life, both as self-motion and as vitality and intensity.

Marion describes *saturated phenomena*, given phenomena that correspond to but exceed (and so do not fit with) a concept already in the mind. For example, a painting's dazzling beauty can be experienced as exceeding any conceptual framework (say, from art history or philosophical aesthetics) that can be used to think about it.[23] Experiences of beauties as saturated phenomena are obediential acts of aesthetic cognition subsequent to concept-formation—for example, I first understand a painting to have certain symbolic elements or to express certain ideas, and then suddenly, having those concepts in mind, I am struck by its excessive beauty, which corresponds to yet exceeds what is captured in those concepts. However, I also experience poetic intuition as an obediential act prior to concept-

---

22. Maritain, *Intuition*, chap. 3 distinguishes "spiritual" unconsciousness from bodily or "Freudian" unconsciousness of drives and repressed images and desires, though the two affect one another.

23. Jean-Luc Marion, *Being Given: Toward a Phenomenology of Givenness*, trans. Jeffrey Kosky, (Stanford, Calif.: Stanford University Press, 2002), 39–51; Marion, *In Excess*, chap. 3

formation, when, without any concepts in mind, I am struck by a being's radiant, holistic self-manifestation. Both are intellectual experiences of the given's excess over any expression of it (and so are actualizations of the intellect as obediential potency). Both still move me to express them, however, since all actualities tend to self-expression. By abstraction, I can form concepts of beauty, though they will never adequately define, express, or explain its full content. I can also express these experiences in artworks, such as poetry: a successful poem evokes in the hearer or reader the intuition of beauty that was its inspiring source.

For this reason, phenomenologist Gaston Bachelard describes poetry as "instant metaphysics": it can directly put us in touch with features of being that exceed conceptual explanation, though poems always lack the explanatory clarity of conceptual thought.[24] A successful artwork is "inspired." In my synthesis, artistic inspiration happens (as Maritain proposed) through the agent intellect unconsciously opening us to receive the full self-manifestation of beings' beauty.[25] This involves the intellect obedientially raising sensory powers so that we perform one act through intellect and sense joined together. That which inspires us is a sensory object that, as we saw in chapter 2, has its excessive features partly by participation in transcendent persons, which, following Plato, we can call inspiring "muses."[26] The creative artist is a "seer" who perceives and then expresses how transcendent persons manifest themselves in sensible qualities and who thereby makes those persons further present in the sensible qualities of an artwork. As Russian personalist and Sophiologist Nicolas Berdyaev says, creativity is an act of "theurgy," of making the divine present.[27] As we have seen, the world as given is personalistic. For this reason, a complete metaphysical portrait must include not only philosophical explanations but also contents that can be expressed only in mythic or other images (as seen in many Platonic dialogues). For example, the structure of material substances should not be described just in scholastic language of act or form and potency or matter. Rather, aspects of this structure can be

---

24. Bachelard, *The Poetics of Space*, introduction; Gaston Bachelard, *Intuition of the Instant*, trans. Eileen Rizo-Patron (Evanston, Ill.: Northwestern University Press, 2013), 58–59.
25. Maritain, *Creative Intuition*, chaps. 3, 7.
26. Plato, *Ion* 533d–e.
27. Hildebrand, *Aesthetics*, vol. 2, 12; Nicholas Berdyaev, *Freedom and the Spirit*, trans. Oliver Fielding Clarke (New York: Charles Scribner's Sons, 1935), 241–43; Berdyaev, *The Meaning of the Creative Act*, trans. Donald Lowrie (New York: Collier, 1962), 229–32. Cf. Gregory Shaw, *Theurgy and the Soul: The Neoplatonism of Iamblichus* (University Park: Pennsylvania State University Press, 1995).

grasped only though images since they include a beauty that exceeds the scholastic explanation—for example, in the image of Venus, understood as pure beautiful form, arising from the material chaos of seafoam, which expresses an event that takes place in every eduction of form from matter.[28]

Instead of discussing beauty as excessive, some aestheticians (like Kant) speak of *sublimity*, a quality of beings insofar as they appear unlimited, exceeding what fits with my powers, which overwhelms or even terrifies me, even while it pleases. These aestheticians see beauty as a nonconceptual appearance that is formed or limited and fits with my powers.[29] I use beauty in a broader sense to pick out anything radiantly, perceptibly self-manifesting, including both Kantian beauty and sublimity. Some broadly Catholic metaphysicians of irreducibility argue that notions of sublimity and saturation introduce an element of violence, chaos, and meaninglessness into an account of being, contrary to a view on which God makes all things fittingly and with an orientation to peaceful harmony.[30] Sublimities seem ultimately unintelligible, unable to fit with me and be at peace with me, but I contend that beautiful beings (including beautiful persons) are given as exceeding any meaning I can assign, and they can sensibly appear threatening, numinous, seductive, violent, or horrifying; they can overwhelm us and place absolute demands on us. Yet despite this, beauties also appear meaningful and satisfying; even the most overwhelming givens raise us, in obedience, toward grasping them. As William Desmond observes, beauty simultaneously violently strikes us and bestows peace.[31] As I have said, a metaphysics of irreducibility must have a place even for apparently chaotic or violent features of beauty—in short, for anything directly given.

Because of these experiences, I contend that beauty in different senses is the first and last transcendental we grasp. Even before understanding a being as being, we are struck by its beauty, its excessive self-manifestation, though no concept of beauty is formed at that stage. In our initial encounter with any being, it can appear terrible and overwhelming, even in its beauty. After unpacking the content of the being rationally (including in

---

28. Sebastian Goth, "Venus Anadyomene," in *Venus as Muse: From Lucretius to Michel Serres*, ed. Hanjo Berressem et al. (Leiden: Brill, 2015), 15–40.
29. Immanuel Kant, *Critique of Judgment*, trans. Werner Pluhar (Indianapolis, Ind.: Hackett, 1987), 97–100.
30. For example, Hart, *The Beauty of the Infinite*, 45ff.
31. Desmond, *The Gift of Beauty and the Passion of Being*, chap. 4. Violent beauty's ability to raise us obedientially and convey grace is depicted well in the stories of Flannery O'Connor.

transcendental concepts like beauty), we can experience the beautiful being's fit with us and those concepts. At this stage, we can experience the being as giving us pleasure, a sense of meaningfulness, even at times a deep peace. But we can then also be struck anew by its excess over those concepts: what was merely pleasurable or peace-bestowing can become sublime once again (though it can continue to bestow sense of pleasure or peace even in its sublimity).[32] The original sublime experience both tends toward rational unpacking (as Kant says) and exceeds any rational analysis (as Marion says). Beauty is the origin and end of all knowing.

By effect-to-cause reasoning, we must posit for these experiences a transcendent, immaterial, self-manifesting cause in beings (including in ourselves as beautiful), which our intellects can obey. One principle posited by the Catholic tradition that fits this description is the act of existence (*esse*), the actuality by which each being exists, and which is an actuality over and above its conceptualizable essence. In Aquinas's view, beings have *esse* through their forms. Aquinas calls form a "light" participating in divine light and a "ray" of divine beauty: each being, by its form and *esse*, manifests itself as participating in higher, intelligible, divine realities, and, I add, as actually intelligible (though only potentially conceptualizable).[33] The agent intellect opens the possible intellect to direct contact with phantasms, which participate in a being's self-manifesting form and *esse*, such that the latter's light illuminates the intellect, and the being thereby manifests itself holistically and as beautiful.[34]

A full causal explanation of aesthetic cognition requires an account not only of its cause in cognized beings but also of the metaphysical status of the act itself. Aquinas distinguishes *real relations* from *relations of reason*. In the former, there is a real foundation, an actuality added to the related being, by which it is related to another. In the latter, the relation does not involve an added actuality.[35] "Being a father" is a real relation, for it is

---

32. On how sublime beauty gives rise to terror, see Rilke's first Duino Elegy: "Denn das Schöne ist nichts/als des Schrecklichen Anfang, den wir noch grade ertragen,/und wir bewundern es so, weil es gelassen verschmäht,/uns zu zerstören." How what was seen as terrible can come to be seen as beautiful is depicted well in H. P. Lovecraft's story "The Shadow over Innsmouth."

33. Aquinas, *In IV DDN*, lect. 5; cf. *SCG* III, c. 97. Cf. Jordan, "Evidence," 393–407; Ramos, "Beauty and the Perfection of Being," 255–68; Eric Gill, *Beauty Looks After Herself* (Freeport, N.Y.: Books for Libraries Press, 1933), 25.

34. On distinctions and connections between interior beauty of form (*species*) and exterior sensory beauty (*decor*), see Aquinas, *In Is.*, c. 53.

35. Aquinas, *ST* I, q.13, a.7. Cf. Mark Henninger, *Relations: Medieval Theories 1250–1325* (Oxford: Oxford University Press, 1989), 7.

founded in my acts whereby I brought about children; "being read about" is a rational relation, for I do not take on a new actuality when someone reads about me. In receiving species, I am really related to the being I cognize, since I take on a new accident, a species, by which I am related to (and dependent on) that being. The cognized being is rationally related to me, since it is not actualized further by being cognized. I propose, following suggestions by Norris Clarke and others going back to the Baroque Jesuits, that in aesthetic cognition, my intellect is related to a being in a third way, an *intentional relation*.[36] In aesthetic cognition, my intellect does not receive a new actuality, like a species; I just have a new experience through the being's presence to my intellect, mediated by the phantasm. John Duns Scotus contends that as long as a knower has the form of a being actually in mind (here, in the phantasm) and is in that being's presence, that knower grasps the being.[37] I contend that one can gain an experience without changing in being or in actuality, a claim I shall develop further below.

Against Intellectual Idealism

For intellectual acts to grasp beings in themselves, we require a receptive potency without its own content, which can be actualized by and participate in any intelligible content, at least any receivable from phantasms. The scholastic tradition calls this power the *possible intellect*. That it lacks its own content is a reason to hold that intellectual activity is not in a material organ, for organs contribute content to cognitive acts; if the intellect were in a material organ, I would be restricted by its content in what I could know.[38]

The nature of intellectual acts constitutes stronger evidence for the falsehood of emergentism than the nature of sensory acts, for intellectual acts are not in a material organ, though they do presuppose and are accompanied by sensory acts. Thinking normally involves considering some sensed object, picturing examples, or imagining words.[39] Sokolow-

---

36. Clarke, "A New Look at the Immutability of God," in *Explorations in Metaphysics*, 183–210. Cf. Pedro da Fonseca, *In libros metaphysicrum Aristotelis Stagirita*, c. 8, q.5, s.4–5 (Frankfurt: Schanuuertteri, 1599), v. 2, 382–86; Suárez, *DM*, d.30, s.9, nn. 35–44; s.14, nn. 21–29; Kenneth Schmitz, *The Gift: Creation* (Milwaukee, Wisc.: Marquette University Press, 1982), 95; G. E. Moore, "The Refutation of Idealism," *Mind* 12 (1903): 433–53; and Mark K. Spencer, "The Flexibility of Divine Simplicity: Aquinas, Scotus, Palamas," *International Philosophical Quarterly* 57, no. 2 (2017): 116.

37. Scotus, *Rep.*, 1A.39–40.1–3, n. 70. Cf. Aquinas, *ST* I, q.8, a.2; q.14, a.5, 6.

38. Aquinas, *ST* I, q.75, a.2; q.79, a.2; I-II, q.3, a.8.

39. Aquinas, *ST* I, q.79, a.4, ad 3.

ski notes that thinking about individuals involves reference to universals (I think of someone as, for example, a teacher or a mother) and thinking about universals involves applying them to individuals (in thinking about what it is to be a teacher or a mother, I consider individuals who fall under these concepts).[40] That thinking is dependent on sense in these ways does not entail that it emerges from or depends for its existence on anything material. That we can predict what someone is thinking about based on neural activity (or other bodily signs) merely shows that intellect and sense are connected, but it does not show the nature of that connection. Features of intellect already considered show that it first raises sense to share its mode of being, rather than (as emergentism has it) being caused by sense in a "bottom-up" way.[41]

But while we must avoid causally reducing intellect to matter, we must also avoid "idealist" or "transcendentalist" reductionisms regarding intellect, such as that found in members of the transcendental Thomist tradition like Rahner. He argues that the agent intellect is a "preapprehension" (*Vorgriff*) or *a priori* grasp on all the possibilities of being. On his view, when I think about any finite being, I see its finitude by comparing it to all of being, which I understand *a priori*, though in an anticipatory way, not as a distinct object. I thereby see how that being is a determination of the universal notion of being; all finite beings are grasping against the background or "horizon" of being as such. My recognition that each being I perceive is finite drives me to seek to know further beings and so tend toward knowing the absolute being; hence, all knowing involves, as a transcendental condition, a preapprehension of God, though not a grasping of God as a distinct object. I am not aware of my *a priori* preapprehension of being apart from acts of grasping finite beings, but it is a condition for the possibility of such acts.[42] This position is not idealist in the sense of holding that everything is actually precontained in or constituted by our intellects,[43] but it is idealist in that it holds that every being is always already in some way grasped by our intellects, and so it implies that to be is to be apprehended (in some sense) by me. In this view, all finite beings, including human persons, are in some sense reducible to their place in our

---

40. Sokolowski, *Phenomenology of the Human Person*, 134–35.
41. Cf. Madden, *Mind, Matter, and Nature*, 203–9.
42. Rahner, *Spirit in the World*, 142–45, building on Heidegger, *Being and Time*; Kant, *Critique of Pure Reason*. Cf. Viladesau, *Theological Aesthetics*, 120–23.
43. Francis Fiorenza, introduction, in Rahner, *Spirit in the World*, xlii.

minds. A metaphysician of irreducibility, however, should reject any view in which beings are precontained in our intellects: we grasp our irreducibility in part by grasping our intellectual openness to what is new and to what exceeds all that we have previously grasped. I am irreducible to any content that can be contained in any mind. Having rejected the view that we preapprehend universal being, we need an explanation for how we are open to grasping any being. I propose that this is explained by the agent intellect, which is not an act of actually understanding or preapprehending any being or being as such, but a continual act of giving intelligible being to sensible things, enabling my possible intellect to fit with beings.

Aquinas provides a further account of what is involved in bestowing *esse intelligibile*. To be present to oneself and self-conscious, as my intellectual acts are, is to be immaterial.[44] Since powers and acts belong to subjects, there must be something wholly immaterial in me, to which my immaterial intellect belongs. This thing, my soul, must exist in itself, so that it can have its own powers and acts. Since powers are dependent on and caused by their subjects,[45] the agent intellect is dependent on and caused by my soul. The agent intellect gives *esse intelligibile*—a mode of being by which something is self-present, fully meaningful, and immaterial—to phantasms. Given all of this, my soul must have this mode of being too: for my soul, to be (*esse*) is to manifest intelligibility, to be self-present, and to be open to understanding and being present to others. This is the way in which the soul is actual. Aquinas says that the soul *is* understanding (*intelligere*), acquaintance (*notitia*), and habitual self-understanding.[46] Although I actually understand only when actualized by others, my soul's essence and *esse* are intrinsically oriented to understanding.

Given that it has this intellectual mode of being, I propose that the soul is the root of our subjectivity, which (as we saw in chapter 1) we grasp through Husserl's phenomenological reduction. However, scholastic method shows that the soul is also the body's form, and its *esse* is also the body's. That the soul is both subjectivity and the form of the body is revealed in that I subjectively experience both intellectual and bodily acts.[47] Furthermore, as Hildebrand says, even those aspects of the body that I

---

44. Aquinas, *In LDC*, lect. 15.
45. Aquinas, *ST* I, q.77, a.5.
46. Aquinas, *QDSC*, a.11, ad 8, 14; *QQ*, 7, q.1, a.4; *DV*, q.10, a.8; *In LDC*, lect. 18. See Cory, *Aquinas on Human Self-Knowledge*, 127–31. Cf. Hegel, *Encyclopedia*, §383.
47. Aquinas, *ST* I, q.76, a.1.

cannot experience subjectively (or from within, or from the first-person point of view), such as many internal organs, are experientially given to me as "mine": I (and others) naturally judge them to be part of me.[48] My soul, which is identical (in some sense) to subjectivity, actualizes all of my body.[49] This is a further reason to reject Rahner's view: my intellect cannot have an actual preapprehension of all being, for it is naturally oriented just toward material being, especially that of my body.

The Natural Desire To See God

My rejection of Rahner's idealist or transcendentalist view prompts a consideration of the problem of the natural desire to see God. Since Aquinas's time, but especially during the twentieth century, theologians have debated whether we have a natural desire to see God in himself[50]—that is, whether our natures are of themselves ordered to the beatific vision, an intellectual intuiting of God unmediated by creatures (including any species or concept). Most agree that we have a natural desire to know God inasmuch as our intellects are oriented to reason to the existence of a first cause of creatures, which we can achieve by our own efforts. But this is not a grasp of God as he is in himself. A natural desire is not just an openness but a positive orientation toward something, a connaturality or natural fit with it.[51] The debate has been both over what Aquinas held (which is not my concern) and over what is true (which is my concern); I do not intend to describe this debate in detail but just show how each side reveals our irreducibility. My full solution to the problem must wait until chapter 7.

Seeking a nonreductionistic account of human persons, members of the twentieth-century *Nouvelle théologie* movement, such as Balthasar and Henri de Lubac, argued that if the intellect is open to all being (and the will to all good), then it includes an innate, unconditional longing for the highest being. On de Lubac's view, this desire was given by God as intrinsic to human nature; for Rahner, it is a supernatural gift added to each human nature.[52] This position is motivated by many experiences. We are "restless

---

48. Hildebrand, *Nature of Love*, 180–81.
49. Aquinas, *QDA*, a.1; *SCG* II, c. 68.
50. On this debate's history see Feingold, *Natural Desire*; Kevin Keiser, *The Natural Desire to See God as an Innate Appetite of the Intellect and Its Implications for the Moral Life and the Relationship between the Natural and Supernatural Orders* (PhD diss., Pontifical University of St. Thomas, 2018).
51. Aquinas, *ST* I-II, q.26, a.1, ad 3.
52. Henri de Lubac, *Surnaturel: Etudes Historiques* (Paris: Aubier, 1946); *The Mystery of the Supernatural*, trans. Rosemary Sheed (New York: Crossroad, 1998); Hans Urs von Balthasar, *The Theology of Karl*

until we rest in God," as evidenced by converts experiencing Christ as what they were always seeking; we furthermore feel solidarity with all persons in being oriented to what transcends us.[53] As many in this movement, following Maurice Blondel, have argued, all natural knowing and willing are incomplete.[54] From finite beings and goods, we reason analogically to absolute being and good, which alone could fulfill us—but we cannot grasp absolute being, and so cannot grasp the foundation for the meaning of any being, unless it reveals itself. The natural trajectory of the intellect and will are intrinsically oriented to and given meaning by the supernatural, by God's personal self-revelation.

While I endorse aspects of a version of this position (similar to but not the same as Rahner's view) in chapter 8, de Lubac's version of this view is reductionistic. Some might object that the claim that we have a natural desire for God in himself is inconsistent with the many persons who have no desire regarding God, others who want to never see God, and still others who convert to multiple religions over their lives, experiencing each one as fulfilling their deepest longings. But the *Nouvelle théologie* position can accommodate these facts: that we are naturally oriented to an end does not entail that we must pursue that end. We can come to consciously hate an end for which we have natural desire, though we will then experience ourselves as in some way thwarted since we have opposed ourselves to what alone can fulfill us.

On the *Nouvelle théologie* view, grace, a share in the divine life that allows belief in what God has revealed and allows us to love with God's own love, is just what most fits with human nature, a gift given to human nature from its origin, rather than a free gift over and above human nature. Traditional Thomists have criticized this view for excluding the key Chris-

---

Barth, trans. Edward Oakes (San Francisco: Ignatius, 1992), part 3; Rahner, "Concerning the Relationship between Nature and Grace," in *Theological Investigations*, vol. 1, trans. Cornelius Ernst (Baltimore: Helicon Press, 1961). Similarly, Scotus (*Ord.* IV, d.43, q.2) holds that our natures are oriented to God in Himself, though this desire only becomes conscious through grace; Lonergan (*Insight*, 416, 664–69) thinks that we have an unrestricted desire to know, and hence are open to God; and Keiser (*The Natural Desire to See God*) says that the natural desire to see God is the essential potency of the intellect to be actualized by any intelligible actuality, especially by the most intelligible, God, though it is naturally oriented to acts intending beings through the senses, and requires grace to fulfill its essential potency.

53. Augustine, *Confessions* I.1. Cf. Hildebrand, *Metaphysik der Gemeinschaft: Untersuchungen über Wesen und Wert der Gemeinschaft*, vol. 4 of *Gesammelte Werke* (Regensburg: Verlag Josef Habbel, 1975), 152–54.

54. Maurice Blondel, *Action (1893): Essay on a Critique of Life and a Science of Practice*, trans. Oliva Blanchette (Notre Dame, Ind.: University of Notre Dame Press, 1984), pts. 4, 5; Milbank, *Theology and Social Theory*, 210–28; and Montague Brown, *Reason, Revelation, and Metaphysics* (Washington, D.C.: The Catholic University of America Press, 2020).

tian claim that supernatural grace and revelation are freely gratuitous. This criticism reveals the reductionism about human persons in the *Nouvelle théologie* view, on which our intellect lacks openness to new kinds of acts beyond those to which we are naturally disposed; this is a reductionism similar to that of Rahner, in which we grasp beings only on the basis of our preapprehension of the horizon of being as such. De Lubac's view reduces the intellect to having only its originally given structure, but we saw that in aesthetic cognition, the intellect is obedientially open to new kinds of acts and objects that exceed what is proportionate to it. If the fundamental orientation of our intellects were a natural desire to see God in himself, then no intellectual act could be performed apart from this desire, that is, no intellectual act could be given as exceeding what is proportionate to our intellects. If that theory were right, we could not grasp the sublime or the saturated—but we do grasp them. Creatures could only be really grasped as meaningful insofar as they were grasped as related to (or revealed by) God in himself.

One might object that all creatures just are participations in God, and so grasping them in light of a desire to see God in himself just is grasping them in themselves. But while creatures intrinsically participate in God, beings are also given as existing and meaningfully graspable in themselves. It is possible to experience creatures as meaningful, without any sense of our desire for meaning being thwarted, apart from any consideration of God in himself. A metaphysics of irreducibility must include the real though limited meaning and value of creatures (including us) in themselves. The insistence of the traditional Thomist view on natures and intellects having ends apart from grace safeguards this. In chapter 1, I argued that materialism reduced all other values to that of utility. *Nouvelle théologie* risks a similar reductionism, considering things to be valuable only as directed to God (or being as such), but we grasp natural, limited, yet genuine values and meanings in mundane things, apart from their being ordered to facilitating seeing God or specifying an understanding of being. Not every value reduces to holiness or eternal value; some things are important or meaningful in a merely earthly way.[55] These things also have value in relation to God, and that value is more important than their earthly value, but they are given as having earthly value, and this, along with our ability to grasp it, must be included in any nonreductionistic

---

55. Hildebrand, *Aesthetics*, vol. 1, 238, 256–59, 399–400.

view. "Natural" or "intrinsic" features of beings, including ourselves, could not be grasped if we properly understood things only in relation to God in himself, as de Lubac's view holds. The claim that we have a natural, innate, unconditional desire to see God in himself must be rejected.

A more nonreductionistic account is found in traditional Thomism, on which the desire to see God in himself exceeds our natural intellectual potency, which is naturally oriented to grasping beings on the basis of sense. We only positively desire to see God in himself supernaturally, with the aid of grace, God's free gift of participating in his life and activities, which actualizes an obediential potency in us. This obediential potency is not just an openness to God doing anything logically possible to us but a specific openness of the intellect, the power that acts under the formal object of being, to grasp actualities that exceed our natural ability. We naturally desire to see God in himself only in that our natures are constituted such that, once we understand the idea of seeing him, a conditional desire arises: we would wish to see God if that were possible. While we are only perfectly fulfilled by seeing God, we have no innate longing for this, since it exceeds our nature, and because we are open to receiving what is new.[56]

However, this view must take into account the genuine experiences to which the *Nouvelle théologie* (and transcendental Thomism) appeal. Our hearts are restless because of intellect's formal object, being, is open to specification in ever-new ways, and because our intellects are not just passively open but have a dynamic, searching, wondering openness to the new. We naturally search for what we do not yet know or desire; we have solidarity with one another in this search. This restlessness is truly satisfied only by directly seeing God in himself, but this does not make it originally a positive desire for God. It is true that finite being does not fully explain itself or ground its own meaning; its full meaning can only be seen if he who is being itself reveals it, but it does not follow that we have an innate desire for (or preapprehension of) that ultimate meaning, or that we can grasp no meaning apart from it. Rather, we grasp finite, partially but genuinely satisfying meanings that are proportioned to us, even apart from God's revelation.

---

56. Feingold, *Natural Desire*; Steven Long, *Natura Pura: On the Recovery of Nature in the Doctrine of Grace* (New York: Fordham University Press, 2010).

Analogies of Being

Every intellectual act is open to grasping real being or that there is something. Understanding intellectual acts requires considering further what being is. In the view of most Thomists, "being" is not a simple universal like "dog" or "red," which apply univocally (i.e., in the same sense) to all their referents and pick out the same essential or accidental content in each of their instances. Rather, "being" is an analogous notion, applied in proportionate ways to its subjects: being belongs to (and the term "being" is said of) things insofar as they are related to *esse*. *Esse* and relations to *esse* are not the same in each instance; rather, the relations of different beings to their *esse* are proportionate or analogous to one another. Few issues in Thomistic scholarship are more controverted than the question of how Aquinas understood the analogy of being. I do not wade into that controversy here, nor assert that my view was shared by Aquinas. Rather, I present a view of analogy only insofar as it guides us to better perceive our irreducibility. Here, I consider only the *analogy of proportionality*; I mention the *analogy of attribution* in chapter 7.[57]

The same sort of analogy involved in applying the notion of *being* is found in applying the notion of *seeing*. Inasmuch as they directly grasp objects, both eyes and minds see. We use the same word in "the mind sees" and the "the eye sees," and each predicate has the same nominal content—that is, the word can be defined in the same way. But we do not grasp what seeing is in each case by grasping that nominal content; rather, intellectual and bodily seeing must each be grasped in themselves. They are not instances of one, univocal sort of seeing, nor are they entirely distinct or equivocal sorts of seeing. To grasp what seeing as such is, we must grasp an analogy between these kinds of seeing: as the eye's act is to its object, so the mind's act is to its object. While the mind has a more perfect grasp on its object than does the eye, this does not make the intellect's act alone true seeing. Both are, in themselves, true kinds of seeing. No complete account of seeing as such can be given apart from its analogates. They are two hierarchically related kinds of seeing, which we must grasp both in themselves and in their relation to one another, to grasp the one analogous concept seeing.

---

57. See Aquinas, *In I Sent.*, d.19, q.5, a.2, ad 1; *DP*, q.7, a.2; *DEE*; *DV*, q.10, a.11, ad 10; Thomas Cajetan, *De nominium analogia*, in *Opuscula omnia* (Lyon: Apud haeredes Iacobi Iuntae, 1558), c. 3; Maritain, *Degrees of Knowledge*, 226–27; Joshua Hochschild, *The Semantics of Analogy: Rereading Cajetan's De Nominium Analogia* (Notre Dame, Ind.: University of Notre Dame Press, 2010).

Some in the Greek Orthodox tradition, such as Christos Yannaras, have objected that, in Thomism, analogy amounts to having different quantifiable "amounts" of some content, while on Yannaras's view, Thomistic analogy does not allow us to grasp contents that are both irreducibly distinct from and intrinsically related to each other, as the Thomists think. Rather, this analogy reduces to a univocal sameness of content, parceled out in different amounts in each instance. Such a view would not allow for irreducibly different ways of being but reduces all ways of beings to one univocal way. On a more charitable reading, however, Thomism understands analogy in much the same way as Yannaras. As we have seen, beings for Aquinas consist of not only proportioned principles that could be had in different "amounts" but also intrinsically include qualitative splendor, which can be grasped only by perception. In a better view of analogy, as explained by Yannaras, analogy of proportionality is rightly understood to be "qualitative" or "iconic": one being's content is grasped through other beings. In grasping similarities among kinds of seeing, we simultaneously grasp dissimilarities; perceiving each analogate allows us to better perceive the other in its uniqueness. An icon of Christ or of a saint shows the otherness and unique identity of the portrayed person; through the relations among aspects of the icon, we perceive those in the portrayed person. The icon allows us to enter into relationship with that person; it allows us to *see* what would otherwise remain unseen in that other. Things are made present through others: iconicity and analogicity are aspects of any participation relation.[58]

We saw this iconic relationship in chapter 2, in seeing how sensible qualities reveal transcendent persons. We also saw that beauty includes both quantitative aspects (like proportion) and qualitative, irreducibly perceivable aspects (like splendor).[59] Analogies among beings considered as icons, as described by Yannaras, likewise includes both aspects. For another example of iconicity, we saw in chapter 1 that all actualities are analogous to subjectivity: like an icon, my subjectivity reveals other actualities as similar to and other than itself.

---

58. Christos Yannaras, *Person and Eros*, trans. Norman Russell (Brookline, Mass.: Holy Cross Orthodox Press, 2007), 194, 210–20, building on Plato, *Timaeus* 29b; Theodore the Studite, *On the Holy Icons*, trans. Catherine Roth (Crestwood, N.Y.: St. Vladimir's Seminary Press, 1981). Cf. Hildebrand, *Aesthetics*, vol. 1, 164–66; Desmond, *The Gift of Beauty and the Passion of Being*, chap. 3; Marion, *In Excess*, chap. 5; and Jacob Holsinger Sherman, *Partakers of the Divine: Contemplation and the Practice of Philosophy* (Minneapolis, Minn.: Fortress Press, 2014), chap. 4.

59. Cf. Desmond, *The Gift of Beauty and the Passion of Being*, chap. 4.

Just as with seeing, in grasping one being as being (or as actual), I grasp its similarity and difference to, and revelation of, others. Because beings relate to *esse* in irreducibly unique but proportionate ways (since each being has its *esse* in virtue of its form or essence, the content of which is different in each being), *being* is analogous. We can nominally say that being is "what is related to *esse*," "what is not nothing," or "what is outside of causes." But being in itself (*ens commune*) is analogically one, grasped only in its analogates. Beings' differing ways of participating in *esse* is revealed by their degrees of immateriality; for example, a human *is more perfectly a being* than a rock because he or she is more perfectly immaterial (i.e., more perfectly self-present and transcending of particular places and times). But beings are analogically related to one another in other ways, too. Some beings are analogically related in an axiological hierarchy; for example, a saint is a higher being than a libertine. Some are analogically related not hierarchically but as having incommensurable modes of being; for example, two human subjectivities have qualitatively distinct modes of being, revealed in what it is like to be each one, but neither is given as "higher" or "better" than the other. Grasping being as such requires grasping all these analogies. To grasp being *a priori*—as Rahner thinks we do—would require grasping *a priori* each being in every way it is a being, and in all its relations to other beings, but the analogical concept of being is too rich for us to ever fully grasp, let alone grasp it prior to experiencing each being.

This rich, analogical notion of being applies only to beings that participate in *esse*, and are thereby outside their causes and outside nothingness, not to God. In finite, participatory beings, that which exists and its existence are in some way distinct. We can reason, however, in an effect-to-cause manner, from the existence of beings in this contingent, participatory, relational sense, back to a first cause, that is, a being that explains the existence of participatory being but does not itself require an explanation. That cause, which we call God, cannot have a participatory relation to actually existing (*esse*), since that relation would, in turn, require an explanation. Rather, God must be identical to his *esse*: God must be, not just share in, the full content of what it is for him to exist. (We have seen experiential evidence for this claim: God was revealed as the absolute depth of beauty underlying all finite beauties.) God is a being in a distinct sense from all others. The analogy between creaturely beings and the divine being is not an analogy between two proportions between being and *esse* but rather a comparison between participatory being and that which is being essentially. Each creature iconically reveals every other being, the analogical notion of being as such (*ens commune*), and the self-subsistent being who grounds the existence of all other beings.[60]

A natural end of the intellect is to know God as first cause (not in himself), which includes knowing God as iconically revealed in creatures. The intellect is naturally perfected religiously, that is, by giving God his due, including by apprehending him in each being insofar as it participates in him.[61] We can grasp each being as a sacrament or icon of God (and of every other being). The *esse* of a being, when present to the intellect, whether mediated by species (in natural, abstractive cognition) or just by a phantasm (in obediential, aesthetic cognition), causes my intellect to correspond to and grasp the being's content.[62] Because of my soul's orientation to the body, my intellect is ordered to grasping being in material beings. But in grasping any being, I grasp an analogate that iconically points me to all others. In grasping one being as being—that is, as icon of others and of being as such—I experience my intellect's dynamic orientation and openness to grasping any being (and, hence, its irreducibility to matter). This openness is not based on a preapprehension of being as such; that would limit in advance what content I could grasp, trapping me in the structure of my own mind. Rather, it is a genuine, wondering, seeking openness to any analogate of the concept of being, each of which adds new content to my concept of being. Any intellectual grasp of a single being includes taking on a perspective on what it means to exist as such.[63] Because of these orientations in the intellect, the end of this power is a major part of our end as whole persons. Whatever else we discover our end to be, part of our end is to grasp the meaning of being and of God.

Conceptualization, Platonic Experience, and Creating Beings of Reason

After receiving intelligible species, I move myself to understand the content of the beings in which they participate by articulating to myself concepts

---

60. Aquinas, *ST* I, q.2, a.3.
61. Aquinas, *ST* I-II, q.81.
62. Aquinas, *ST* I, q.16, a.1, ad 3. Cf. Lawrence Dewan, "Is Truth a Transcendental for St. Thomas Aquinas?" *Nova et Vetera* (English edition) 2, no. 1 (2004): 13.
63. Heidegger, *Being and Time*, 10ff.

(or interior words), which express that content insofar as I understand it.[64] I am thereby more fully aware of the understood being and of myself as distinct beings. Insofar as I articulate what I understand, I am reflexively aware of myself as the subject of understanding.[65] However, my attention is then primarily focused not on myself but on some object. Scholastics like Francisco Suárez distinguish "that which is formally conceived" (*conceptus formalis*), that in me by which I understand something (such as a concept), from "that which is objectively conceived" (*conceptus obiectivus*), my intentional object.[66] The former is like a lens through which I intend the latter. I can objectively grasp both real beings and nonreal things, such as fictional objects. In either case, I experience a distinction between that by which (*quo*) I grasp the object, and the object itself, which appears as that which (*quod*) I grasp, even if it does not exist apart from my grasping or constituting it.[67]

We abstract the content of universals, natures absolutely considered, and fictional objects from sensible beings. After abstraction, each of these items appears as an object in its own right, constituted by and dependent on my intentional, intellectual acts. In forming universal concepts, we grasp the content of some essence as able to be predicated of or found in multiple subjects. In natures absolutely considered, we consider the pure content of an essence in itself (such as the pure content of what it is to be a triangle or a lion), abstracting from content having to do with universality, individuality, or being.[68] But sometimes (as Hildebrand describes), I experience a concept's content to be objective in a further sense, as existing in its own right and not just as constituted by my intentional, abstractive acts.[69] When I first grasped what it is to be a triangle, I considered the figures my geometry teacher drew and abstracted conceptual content from them. But then I gained insight into triangularity itself. I realized that no triangle drawn in the three-dimensional world is a genuine (i.e., plane or two-dimensional) triangle. Drawn triangles are only three-dimensional images of or approximations to the perfect triangle, the reality of triangularity itself, which can be present to my mind by direct, intuitive insight.

---

64. Aquinas, *ST* I, q.85, a.2, ad 3; *In I PH*, lect. 2.
65. Aquinas, *ST* I, q.87, a.3; Maritain, *Degrees of Knowledge*, 412–19.
66. Suárez, *DM*, d.2, s.1, n. 1.
67. Suárez, *DM*, d.54, s.2, n. 4.
68. On concepts of aspects of other concepts, such as universality and individuality, which scholastics call "second intentions," see Suárez, *DM*, d.54, s.2, n. 16.
69. Hildebrand, *What Is Philosophy?* 106–8.

In chapter 1, I discussed how (on Stein's description) I grasp my limited properties as sharing in "ideal essences," which are given as transcending, but present in, these limited instances. We experience ideal essences of mathematical ideas (like triangularity), transcendentals (like beauty itself), contents of consciousness (like the essence of joy), and sensible qualities (like redness or the taste of cherries in itself)—any case where I am given a necessary unity of contents, which is never perfectly instantiated in the material world. By contrast, my grasp of the essences of material substances, such as what it is to be a lion or a star, is always more focused on contents as grasped through abstraction. I grasp no necessary unity of contents that all and only lions or stars have, but only a constellation of properties shared by most lions or stars, which Hildebrand calls a "morphic unity."[70] Yet even here, I can grasp that there must be a necessary content of being a lion or being a star that is shared among all members of those kinds, though I have no insight into that necessary content. In each case, this content is given as transcending its instances, and as existing in some sense in its own right.

Realist phenomenologists like Stein and Hildebrand contended that these experiences reveal that ideal essences exist mind-independently; in making this claim, they sought the truth behind Platonists' claims that there exist transcendent Forms. Aquinas says that Platonists held that such Forms exist because they thought that, for our minds to truly grasp reality, there must be isomorphism between what we understand and what exists; given the experience I described, transcendent Forms must exist. We grasp a universal's content as universal, necessary, eternal, and immutable, but essences in material things are individual, contingent, and destructible. For our knowledge to be true, it must correspond to reality: there must be real universals or Forms. Aquinas rightly rejects this line of reasoning, however: for our understanding to be true, it need only be grounded in reality in some way; there need not be isomorphism between mind and reality. We can explain how the mind truly grasps reality by explaining where mentally grasped necessary content arises causally: it is drawn from forms in sensible beings, and thence from God and his ideas. There is no need to posit distinct Forms or ideal essences to explain how our thinking truly grasps the content of reality.[71]

---

70. Hildebrand, *What Is Philosophy?* chap. 4. Cf. Aquinas, *In SA*.
71. Aquinas, *In I Met.*, lects. 14–17; *In VII Met.*, lects. 13–16; *QQ* VII, q.4, a.3; *ST* I, q.84, a.1. See Turner

Were a need to maintain strict isomorphism between mind and reality the only reason to hold that transcendent Forms actually exist, then these arguments would be compelling, but phenomenological method, which puts us in contact with what directly shows itself, gives further reasons to hold that these "Platonic" Forms do exist. This is evidence that Thomism is reductionistic about what substances, including us, fully are. As the examples show, we are directly given clear, perfect insight into ideal essences, like triangularity itself. There is not enough content in imperfect, material instances of triangles to account for the content given in such an insight. Were all our cognition drawn from abstraction, we could grasp only content present in sensible things. At most, abstraction could give us an imperfect, uncertain (though practically usable) concept of triangularity. Since we do grasp essences perfectly and with certainty, and since what is directly given must be something in itself, these directly given essences, whose content exceeds all their instances, must be something transcending their instances.[72]

Aquinas is correct that we can reason from abstracted essences, back to the finite, individualized forms in material beings that cause them, and thence to God and his ideas, which cause individualized forms. But the realist phenomenologist is correct that we also directly grasp ideal essences that transcend their instances, and so exist in themselves in some sense. Ideal essences are not universal concepts or words—that is, concepts or words that are said of many particulars. Universals in that sense (like natures absolutely considered) are constituted by intentional acts in which essential contents are drawn from (and so seen as applying to) many particulars. Ideal essences are also not substances; they are not given as concrete beings that have accidents or that act or engage in efficient causation. If by *being* (*ens*) we primarily mean substances and secondarily their concrete accidents, then ideal essences prescind from being, but they could still be beings in another sense (as will be worked out in later chapters). Ideal essences are, furthermore, not divine ideas or attributes. Whatever is in God is infinite and transcends creatures, yet ideal essences appear as finite, discrete contents, and as belonging to creatures. I experience ideal essences when (for example) after reflecting on many just or beautiful sen-

---

Nevitt, "What Has Aquinas Got Against Platonic Forms?" *Proceedings of the Society for Medieval Logic and Metaphysics* 15 (2018): 67–79.

72. Stein, *Finite*, 97–120; Josef Seifert, introduction to the 1991 edition, in Hildebrand, *What Is Philosophy?* 227–35.

sible things, I gain an insight into participable, creaturely justice or beauty in itself.[73] Following the ancient Platonists, I posit the existence of both individualized "Aristotelian" forms in beings (for each being has its own unity, identity, and essence) and "Platonic" Forms that give essential content and unity to whole kinds of beings, and in which individual beings participate.[74] Neither are complete, substantial beings in their own right; each appear as principles of beings that explain features of beings. Concrete beings, including human persons, are both irreducibly unified as individuals and intrinsically participate in essential contents that transcend them. None of these features can be reduced to one another; fully grasping what a substance is requires grasping each form.

"Platonic" experience reveals further irreducible features of our intellects. Most Thomists hold that almost all intellectual knowledge is drawn from the senses; some claim that concepts are never grasped on their own but only insofar as they provide formal identity for sensory acts, apart from which intellectual acts are never performed or experienced.[75] This is all true of natural intellectual acts, by which I know material substances in themselves. Insight into Platonic Forms, however, shows that we receive content otherwise than through the senses. The ideal essence or Platonic Form must act on our mind in some way, so as to causally account for the presence of its content in our minds, which exceeds all content found in sensible instances of that Form. The Form must raise our minds up to know what transcends material substances, allowing us to know material substances in and through something other than those substances that is, through a Form in which they participate.[76] This is another instance of *obediential* cognition.

Insight into Platonic Forms raises us above our limited viewpoint, in which our knowledge is drawn only from the senses and conditioned by the content of our bodies and by our cultural, local, traditionary imaginings, beliefs, and biases. Insight into Forms allows us to approach a much

---

73. See, for example, Plato, *Republic*, *Symposium*, and *Phaedrus*. Every Platonic experience is an "aesthetic" experience in which a form reveals itself to me. Cf. Stein, *Finite*, 105.

74. Cf. Lloyd Gerson, *Aristotle and Other Platonists* (Ithaca, N.Y.: Cornell University Press, 2006); Eric Perl, *Thinking Being: Introduction to Metaphysics in the Classical Tradition* (Leiden: Brill, 2014), chap. 5; and Shaw, *Theurgy and the Soul*, 27.

75. For example, Adrian Reimers, *The Soul of the Person: A Contemporary Philosophical Psychology* (Washington, D.C.: The Catholic University of America Press, 2014), 147, 168; John Deeley, *Semiotic Animal: A Postmodern Definition of "Human Being" Transcending Patriarchy and Feminism* (South Bend, Ind.: St. Augustine's Press, 2010); Percy, *Lost in the Cosmos*; and Braine, *The Human Person*, chaps.13–15.

76. On the distinction between knowing a substance in itself and in another, see *ST* I, q.14, a.5.

more universal, less perspectival view on the world, an ideal "view from nowhere."[77] Nevertheless, since our knowledge always involves bodily experience, we never fully attain such an idealized experience—nor, given the bodily sorts of beings we are, should we want to do so. It is important to recognize, however, that we can at least participate in such a viewpoint. The tension between our natural and obediential intellectual acts underlies the tension between rhetorical and dialectical approaches to metaphysics, discussed in the introduction.

The Franciscan scholastic tradition offers a helpful metaphysical model that helps explain the difference between these intellectual acts. Following Augustine, Bonaventure contends that we both abstract intelligible species from phantasms by the agent intellect and receive (or "cointuit") immutable truths infused into our intellects.[78] We require the latter for complete certainty about essences. Abstracting species from phantasms is, at times, an occasion for something transcendent to reveal itself to us. Bonaventure explains this as divine illumination, an act of God specially infusing knowledge into our minds, beyond the participation in divine light that is involved in every act of human illumination.[79] I suggest that insight into Forms need not involve illumination by God. Rather, it only requires some transcendent source acting upon us. A solution to the problem of what illumines our minds, such that we grasp the content of Forms with certainty, will have to wait until chapter 6.

Just as essential contents of essences of being can be given as existing in their own right, so also fictional beings like Frodo Baggins or Elizabeth Bennett (and, more broadly, beings of reason, unities of content we create by thinking) can appear as existing in their own right.[80] They appear in an interpersonal "space," accessible to anyone who grasps the signs that refer to them, such as the words in a story. In reading a story, characters that seem real are given to me; I do not entirely constitute them. Even characters' creators sometimes report discovering who they are or experi-

---

77. Cf. Thomas Nagel, *The View from Nowhere* (Oxford: Oxford University Press, 1986).

78. Bonaventure, *QDSC*, 22–27; Augustine, *De magistro*. I grant to Duns Scotus, who rejects illumination on the grounds that we do not need it to achieve certainty (*Ord.* I, d.3, p.1, q.4), that we sometimes achieve certainty by our own effort, for example, by formulating self-evident propositions. But that gives us no reason to reject the experiential evidence for the experience of illumination by Forms. This is all *contra* Lonergan (*Verbum*, 186–87, 194), who holds we cannot know by both abstraction and illumination.

79. Aquinas, *ST* I, q.105, a.3.

80. Cf. Daniel Novotný, *Ens rationis from Suárez to Caramuel: A Study in the Scholasticism of the Baroque Era* (New York: Fordham University Press, 2013).

encing them acting on one another, rather than inventing them at will.[81] They appear as a unity of content given in itself, and so as irreducible to anything else.[82]

John of St. Thomas contends that signs come into existence as relations to existing referents. If the referent of a sign ceases to exist, however, the sign retains the power to manifest the referent's content: for example, I grasp the content of dodos when I read the word "dodo," even though no dodos exist anymore.[83] We can combine concepts drawn from sensible things, as we do when inventing fictional beings, and the resulting, combined concepts manifest content. But concepts participate not only in forms in sensible beings but also in Platonic Forms. I propose that by combining concepts, we bring Platonic Forms into new conjunctions, so that characters and other beings of reason come to exist in a way like Platonic Forms. Signs, like words in books, put us in touch with these combinations of Forms. This explains why we experience fictional characters as existing in their own right, in their own "space."

Acts involving beings of reason reveal how intellectual activity is creative, self-expressive, and interpersonal. These traits were already present in concept-formation, since I "make" my concepts, not in the sense that I invent their content (unless I am biased or deceiving myself), but in that knowledge expressed in concepts "nonidentically repeats" or "recreates" the content of reality in a personal way, with my own *style* and focuses.[84] Concept-formation is an imitation and sharing in the self-manifesting power of transcendent persons and Forms, the creative power of God, and the procession of the Word, God the Father's perfect manifestation of the content of his knowledge in God the Son.[85] But beyond concept-formation, in making beings of reason I self-consciously constitute a new actuality; this artistic sort of intellectual making is not just an imitation and repetition of God's creative act but a creative act, an original "subcreation" of my own, that is, a creation of my own, but done through materials furnished by God.[86] Beings of reason are a shared "social reality" that

---

81. Stein, *Finite*, 164–65.
82. Cf. Roman Ingarden, *The Literary Work of Art*, trans. George Grabowicz (Evanston, Ill.: Northwestern University Press, 1973).
83. John of St. Thomas, *Cursus philosophicus thomisticus*, v. 1, p.1, q.21, a.1, 559–65.
84. Catherine Pickstock, *Repetition and Identity* (Oxford: Oxford University Press, 2013), building on Søren Kierkegaard and Gilles Deleuze; Balthasar, *TL2*, 249–52, following Paul Claudel.
85. Cf. Milbank, *Theology and Social Theory*, 218–20, building on Blondel, *Action*, 386.
86. J. R. R. Tolkien, "On Fairy Stories," in *Tales from the Perilous Realm* (New York: HarperCollins,

transcends the artifacts (like books) that call attention to them.[87] They are partially constitutive of the cultural traditions by which our acts are formed. In grasping beings of reason, my intellect is obediently formed by other intellects and our shared cultural "space."[88]

Formal Distinctions and the Danger of Rationalism

In further intellectual acts, we join concepts into propositions, judge propositions to truly (or falsely) express how attributes belong to subjects, and join propositions into chains of reasoning.[89] Intellectual activity naturally begins with perceiving (*intellectus*) intelligible content, proceeds through reasoning (*ratio*) about it, and aims at contemplating (*intellectus*) beings as explained through reasoning.[90] But we also consider concepts and propositions in themselves and as logically related, disengaging our attention from beings. While (as we saw in the introduction) abstract consideration of concepts risks idealist reductionism, it also reveals irreducible features of beings, including of us, that are not otherwise given. Since concepts and propositions are grounded in real essences, examining their structures can reveal the structure of those essences, as Scotus and Stein found.[91] Once again, the intuitive methods of the Franciscan scholastics and realist phenomenological methods converge.

When I think abstractly about an essence, like the human essence, I distinguish intelligible contents in it, reflected in predicates that are said of it. For example, to be human is to be rational, mammal, animal, living, substantial, a being, and a thinkable object. Earlier categories on this list are contained in and specify (or make more determinate) latter, more general items; through this framework of categories, our essence is grasped. For this list to be accurate, these contents must actually be in our essence. We must consider how these contents exist in me and how they are irreducible to one another.

2008), 351. Cf. Marion Montgomery, *Making: The Proper Habit of Our Being* (South Bend, Ind.: St. Augustine, 2000), 119.

87. John Searle, *The Construction of Social Reality* (New York: Free Press, 1995).
88. See Reimers, *The Soul of the Person*, 282.
89. Aquinas, *In I Post An.*, lect. 1; *ST* I, q.85, a.5.
90. Cf. Aquinas, *ST* II-II, q.180, a.3.
91. Stein, *Finite*, 205–7; Scotus, *Ord.* I, d.2, p.2, q.1–4; I, d.8, p.1, q.4, nn. 177, 192–99; I, d.13, q.un., n. 72; II, d.3, p.1, q.1, 4, 6; and Stephen Dumont, "Duns Scotus' Parisian Question on the Formal Distinction," *Vivarium* 43, no. 1 (2005): 7–62. See Richard Cross, *Duns Scotus on God* (Aldershot: Ashgate, 2005), 105–11.

On the one hand, they cannot be really separated—for example, my *being animal* and *being alive* cannot exist apart from one another—and so these contents cannot be *really distinct*. For two things to be really distinct is for them to be really separable beings, or to have distinct essences, or to be opposites in some way, as two relations can be opposed to each other.[92] I am just one being, and so I have but one actual essence, and so these contents cannot be distinct beings or essences. Furthermore, each content characterizes all of me: I am entirely rational, animal, an organism, a substance, and so these contents cannot be separated from me or from each other. These contents are also not relations that are opposites of one another. For all these reasons, they are not really distinct.

On the other hand, they cannot be *rationally distinct*, that is, distinct only in my thinking, different ways that I can consider my essence's content. Scotus notes that each content gives rise to distinct effects. Although I am entirely rational and animal, I act in one way as rational, and in another as mere animal. If these contents were distinct only in my thinking, they could not ground really distinct acts. Furthermore, each content unifies me with other things in distinct ways. For example, all humans are one in species, and all animals are one in genus. Members of these groups share a *common nature*, not as a stuff overlapping each member or in which each member inheres but rather a unity of intelligible content given in our essences.[93] Once I grasp common natures, I experience solidarity with others, a sense of having common experiences or content, and of shared responsibility for each other.[94] As in "Platonist" experience, I grasp that I share in unities with other beings. Through distinct contents, my essence participates in distinct Forms, such as the distinctly given Forms of rationality and animality; there are distinct participation relations in my essence, prior to my thinking about it.

Scotus calls these intelligible contents "formalities" and Stein calls them "empty forms." They are distinct within essences prior to our thinking about them (and so they are not rationally distinct) and yet the formalities in an essence are all one actuality at one level of immateriality (and so they are not really distinct). Scotus proposes that they are *formally*

---

92. Aquinas, *ST* I, q.28, a.3; Suárez, *DM*, d.7.
93. Peter Abelard, *Logica 'Ingredientibus,'* in *Beiträge zur Geschichte der Philosophie des Mittelalters*, vol. 21, Heft 1, ed. Bernhard Geyer (Münster: Verlag der Aschendorffschen Verlagsbuchhandlung, 1919), 10–16.
94. Balthasar, *TD4*, 99; Scheler, *The Nature of Sympathy*, chap. 5.

distinct, a kind of distinction that is other than a real and rational distinction. Formalities are not parts or principles, do not compose an essence, and are not explanatorily prior to essence. An essence does not participate in its formalities (or vice versa), nor are they related as act and potency. How they are related is revealed in the abstract thinking in which they are given: they *contain* one another; they are related as empty, indeterminate content *filled* by more determinate content, as intentional acts are filled by content from the world.[95] For example, animality, which does not contain the content *rationality* (or its absence), is filled, specified, or rendered more determinate by the content of rationality. As Marcel contends, the empty-filled relation is given as a distinct kind of relation in beings, irreducible to act-potency or participating-participated relations.[96]

Thomists object that all distinctions are either real (i.e., prior to thinking) or rational (i.e., based on thinking), and that positing formalities, like positing Platonic Forms, is based on an exaggerated need for mind-world isomorphism.[97] But, as with Platonic Forms, formalities are not posited just for this reason but directly appear, and so cannot be reduced to aspects of essences just as rationally considered. Furthermore, nothing in Aquinas's account of essence excludes the formal distinction; indeed, he does not consider the possibility of this kind of distinction, either to reject or accept it. Incorporating it into a broadly Thomistic metaphysics makes that metaphysics more precise. Aquinas grants that two things can be really identical in one respect, but not in another; for example, the road from Athens to Thebes is really identical to the road from Thebes to Athens substantially, but the two differ relationally, since these relations are opposites of one another.[98] We can see how two items can be really identical to a substance, without holding that they are really identical to each other, by holding that laws of logic, like the law of transitivity of identity, apply primarily to formalities, not to beings or essences as such. As analytic Thomist Peter Geach says, identity is relative to kinds.[99] In my terms, two formalities can be identical in being (i.e., they can be aspects of a single being) but not identical in every respect or in the strictest sense (i.e., not

---

95. Cf. Husserl, *Logical Investigations*, vol. 2, Investigation Six.
96. Gabriel Marcel, *Philosophy of Existentialism* (New York: Citadel, 1984), 9–46.
97. Edward Feser, *Scholastic Metaphysics: A Contemporary Introduction* (Heusenstamm: Editiones Scholasticae, 2014), 83–85.
98. Aquinas, *In III Phys.*, lect. 5.
99. Peter Geach, "Identity," *Review of Metaphysics* 21, no. 1 (1967): 3–12. See Spencer, "The Flexibility of Divine Simplicity," 123–39.

identical in their intelligible content, such that logical laws like the law of transitivity of identity applies).

The formal distinction elucidates other aspects of actualities. For example, my soul is both my subjectivity and the form of my body, but the content of subjectivity and form differ. These are formally distinct aspects of my soul, which is really identical (or one actuality) with both, but the two are distinct aspects of my soul in itself. As a form, my soul is really identical to a relation to my body, of which it is the form. Scotus calls a relation that is not an accident but is intrinsically identical to its foundation and necessary for that foundation to exist, a *transcendental relation*.[100] The soul is a transcendental relation to the body, but this is just one aspect of it, formally distinct from subjectivity. These aspects of my soul ground distinct acts of mine, yet because they are one in being, they determine (or fill the content of) one another. Because it is really (but not formally) identical to the formality of being a substantial form, my subjectivity is directed to my body; because it is really identical to the formality of subjectivity, my form gives subjectivity to my body so that I can experience my body from the first-person perspective. These relations among formalities are analogous to the relation of "circumincession" (*perichoresis*) that Trinitarian theology posits as obtaining among the Trinitarian Persons, according to which each Person is essentially in and makes himself manifest through the others, and gives content to the others.[101] Another example of circumincessive transcendental relations is found in my powers: each is a single actuality that is really identical to natural and obediential potencies—that is, to multiple transcendental relations—each of which affects the others.

The formal distinction also helps us understand being and how the principles of being exist. The notion of being considered so far is grasped analogically and is quite rich in content. But in abstract consideration of essence, we are given another notion of being: the empty, determinable formality of being not nothing or being possibly existing, which is filled, determined, or specified by nearly every other formality.[102] This formality

---

100. Scotus, *Ord.* II, d.1, q.4.
101. Balthasar, *GL1*, 127–32; *GL4*, 21; *TL2*, 151; Aquinas, *ST* I, q.42, a.5.
102. Even more empty are *supertranscendental* formalities like *object* and *thinkable*, which are found equally in real being and beings of reason, and even in *nothing* and *impossible objects* insofar as they are intentional objects. See Suárez, *DM*, d.3, s.2, n. 4; Miguel Viñas, *Philosophia Scholastica* (Genoa: Antonii Casamarae, 1709), 160–62; Sylvester Mauro, *Opus theologicum* (Rome: Nicolai Angeli Tinassii, 1687), vol. 1, 182–87; John P. Doyle, *On the Borders of Being and Knowing: Late Scholastic Theory of Supertranscendental Being*, ed. Victor M. Salas (Leuven: Leuven University Press, 2012), 178–84, 229–41; Jan Aertsen, *Medieval*

is found in the same sense in every essence; this is a univocal sense of being, representable by predicates like "is a being" and by the existential quantifier. "I am a being" can mean that I have an act of existence, whereby I am something concrete, transcend my essence, and am iconic of and analogical to every other being; or it can mean that I have an essence that is not nothing.[103]

Several metaphysicians of irreducibility have accused Scotus of forgetting actual being and instead grasping being just as this formality, leading to the thin conceptions of being, typical of modern metaphysics, in which being lacks intrinsic normative and aesthetic properties.[104] But the *formality of being* is directly given in essences; denying that it is there is reductionistic of essences. Still, abstract reasoning does tend toward a rationalism that is disconnected from contact with real beings and that confuses the structure of abstract conceptual systems with reality—that is, it tends toward an "idealist" reduction of the world to the contents of one's mind or of one's philosophical system.[105] While I posit formalities to avoid reductionism about what is given in abstract thinking, I also posit *analogical being* (which Scotus himself recognized) in the sense described above to avoid reducing the world to an abstract structure.

Levinas offers an important critique of this rationalist tendency: when I know another through concepts, I reduce (or "totalize") that other to an aspect of myself, such as to the content of concepts by which I think about that other. In forming a concept of another, I risk taking that other to just be an element of an abstract, graspable system, and taking myself to have thereby mastered and so be able to control that other.[106] By contrast, I relate nonreductionistically to others by *transcendence*, acts in which I am aware that others remain separate and distinct from my relations to them. Levinas thinks that we enter into transcendence only when we see another person's face or hear another expressing him or herself, find that we cannot predict or comprehend what the other will say or do, and find ourselves ethically called to respond and so be responsible for the other.[107] In finding

---

Philosophy as Transcendental Thought: From Philip the Chancellor (ca. 1225) to Francisco Suárez (Leiden: Brill, 2012), 610; and Mark K. Spencer, "Transcendental Order in Suárez," *Studia Neoaristotelica* 10 (2013): 175–76

103. Cf. Schmitz, *The Gift of Creation*, 98–101.
104. For example, Milbank, *Theology and Social Theory*, preface.
105. Yannaras, *Person and Eros*, 212–27; Balthasar, *TL2*, 29–35.
106. Levinas, *Totality and Infinity*, 24–26, 161–62.
107. Levinas, *Totality and Infinity*, 41–42, 194–97.

myself called to responsible, ethical service, I relate to the other as other than me, no longer risking reductionistically regarding that other to be summed up in what I know about him or her.[108] I thereby am aware that others stand *beyond being* in the sense of what is constitutable by my intentional acts, that is, beyond the content of formalities.[109] I need conceptual knowledge to effectively serve others, since I must grasp their needs, but knowledge must be subordinated to responsibility and to the excessive, irreducibly normative features of reality, to minimize the risk of totalizing, rationalistic reductionism.[110] Since thinking is interpersonal, I only ever think about others insofar as I am first responding to them. Rationalism overlooks the fundamentally responsive—and responsible—structure of thinking and instead tries to master or "totalize" others. Our relations to others are irreducible to cognition; beings, including human persons, are irreducible to their conceptualizable features. To grasp reality truly, it is not enough that my mind corresponds to it; I must enter a responsive, dialogical drama with others, in which I am called and held responsible.[111]

It is reductionistic to think, however (as Levinas sometimes suggests), that all knowing is totalizing. Some acts of knowing, like aesthetic cognition, are self-transcending.[112] Other persons call not just for ethical service but for a variety of responses, including the response of knowing them. As Hildebrand describes, any act of knowledge can be self-transcending, not regarding the other as reducible to what I capture about it. In self-transcending knowing, the other "fecundates" me (just as occurs in some vegetative and sensitive acts). It gives meaning to me (via species), in what Marion calls "counter-intentionality," in which I find myself constituted meaningfully by the other. This fecundation elicits from me an intentional relation by which I both "conceive" of the other and grasp the other's excess over all that I grasp about it.[113] In the experience of reality "fecundating" us, we experience what Marcel calls a "nuptial bond" with being:

---

108. Emmanuel Levinas, *Otherwise than Being or Beyond Essence*, trans. Alphonso Lingis (Pittsburgh: Duquesne University Press, 1998), 136–40.
109. Cf. Fink, *Sixth Meditation*, 143–44.
110. Levinas, *Totality and Infinity*, 50, 244–47, 304–7.
111. Balthasar, TL1, 179–267; TL2, 267–68; Jean-Luc Marion, *God Without Being: Hors-Texte*, trans. Thomas Carlson (Chicago: University of Chicago Press, 1995), chap. 1; and Marion, *In Excess*, chap. 5.
112. Attempts to express aesthetic cognitions can be totalizing, reducing the original experience to limited expressions. See Emmanuel Levinas, "Reality and Its Shadow," in *Collected Philosophical Papers*, trans. Alphonso Lingis (Pittsburgh: Duquesne University Press, 1998), 1–14.
113. Hildebrand, *What Is Philosophy?* 160–61, 184–85; Jean-Luc Marion, *Prolegomena to Charity*, trans. Stephen Lewis (New York: Fordham University Press, 2002), chap. 4.

for knowledge to be nontotalizing requires fidelity to what shows itself to us, which leads us to creatively bear witness to what we have seen.[114] Even the most abstract knowledge grows out of this "nuptial bond." So long as we retain this context for abstract knowledge, we should not reject what is grasped through it.

Judgment, Narrative, and Grasping Real Existence

Another nontotalizing intellectual act is grasping real existence. Catholic thinkers have proposed a range of accounts of the act by which we do this; here, I survey some of them, focusing on the irreducible features of persons that each account reveals, and seeking to thereby reconcile aspects of each account with each other.

Thomists Etienne Gilson, Bernard Lonergan, and Joseph Owens hold that we intellectually grasp existence through judgments, like "This book is brown" or "This man is a doctor." By contrast, in Husserl's view (seen in chapter 1), judgments constitute sensory content as having meanings, like the meaning "really existing"; judgments are not a grasp on real extramental existence in itself, but only on real extramental existence as grasped and contained in my intentional act.

I contend that Gilson and Husserl are each describing distinct acts, the latter tacitly presupposing the former. Husserlian judgment is performed when I already have concepts and propositions in mind and use them as a "lens" through which I intend objects. Gilsonian judgment is performed when I first formulate a proposition and judge it to be true; I am then not bestowing meaning on objects, but rather conforming my mind to beings as they really exist and meaningfully give themselves. In affirming the "is" of a judgment, I fit with and grasp the "is" (or *esse*) of a real being.[115] In Gilsonian judgment, I do not receive intelligible species of existence or articulate a concept of existence. Real existence remains transcendent to intellectual acts; it is not a content that I can receive—I cannot take the other's reality into myself—and so it cannot be totalized. When I affirm something true about a being, its *esse*, mediated by species and concepts, conforms me to itself, leading me to join subject and predicate correctly,

---

114. Marcel, *Homo Viator*, 91–127.
115. Etienne Gilson, *Being and Some Philosophers* (Toronto: Pontifical Institute of Medieval Studies, 1952), 190–202; Lonergan, *Insight*, 457; and Joseph Owens, "Aquinas on Knowing Existence," *Review of Metaphysics* 29, no. 4 (1976): 670–90.

and so affirm its real structure. To make a false judgment is to fail to respond to this normative call of real being as it gives itself.

We saw in chapter 1 that Stein held that we can discover the difference between essence and existence just by reflecting on contents of subjectivity and seeing that their necessary structure differs from their contingent existence. We can more precisely discover how essence and existence are related, and how each is an irreducible feature of beings (including us), by reasoning from judgments to their causes. Aquinas contends that essences can be grasped as possibly existing, without knowing whether any bearers of those essences exist. He concludes that existence is an actuality added to essences to render them really, extramentally existing.[116] The late thirteenth-century scholastic Henry of Ghent (whose work was used by the fifteenth-century Thomist John Capreolus) invites us to see these as two levels of perfection or completeness in a being: a thing is complete in the order of essence (*esse essentiae*) when it has everything that makes it a certain kind of being; it is complete in the order of existence (*esse existentiae*) when that essence is actualized (or made real) by an act of existence.[117] *Esse* actualizes essence, unifying its formal, material, and accidental contents, such that they are one really existing being. This is reflected in judgment: "is" must be added to subject and predicate to unify them in an actual proposition. But *esse* (like any actuality) is also educed from potency (i.e., essence as had by a being through form). Since every being is of some kind, every being has a limited *esse* through its form.[118] A substance's *esse* manifests its essence but is mediated by the *esse* of each of its accidents, which also manifest themselves. Gilsonian judgments manifest my contact with and conformity to the *esse* of both substances and accidents, giving me awareness of the other being as other (unlike Husserlian judgments, which can lead me to regard a being's meaning as entirely captured in a proposition). When I receive species from a substance, the *esse* of that substance and the *esse* of its accidents leave "traces" in me, impressions that (unlike species) I cannot conceptualize but that guide my mind to conform itself to the being as really existing. A trace, as Levinas describes it, is an impression that a being leaves in me prior to my being aware of it, whereby

---

116. Aquinas, *DEE*; *DP*, q.7 a.2; *ST* I, q.3, a.3, 4.

117. Henry of Ghent, *Quodlibet I*, v. 5 of *Opera omnia*, ed. Raymond Macken (Leuven: Leuven University Press, 1979), q.9; John Capreolus, *Defensiones theologiae divi Thomae Aquinatis* (Turin: Alfred Cattier, 1900), v.1, I, d.8, q.1, a.1, 1–2, 301–12.

118. Aquinas, *In I Sent.*, d.19, q.5, a.2; d.38, q.1, a.3; *In III Sent.*, d.6, q.2, a.2; *In IV Met.*, lect. 2; *In V Met.*, lect. 2.

I am led to respond to the being, and which exceeds what can be captured in a concept.[119]

Hildebrand objects that all judgments just articulate facts rather than being ways of making contact with beings as really existing. He distinguishes acts of *taking cognizance*, in which I grasp beings by receiving content from them, from *responses* to received knowledge. Judgment is a *theoretical response*, as are affirmation, conviction, or doubt. He thinks that no response involves grasping anything beyond what was grasped in taking cognizance. Rather, responses "complete" the object, adding to them my "word" of affirmation or rejection and bestowing on them the value or disvalue of that word.[120]

As we saw in chapter 1, scholasticism distinguishes between powers on the basis of both formal objects and how powers are directed to objects. Both taking cognizance and theoretical response are intentional acts that intend their objects under the same formal object, being—that is, both kinds of acts aim at their objects insofar as they are beings. But these two kinds of acts have distinct directions of intentionality: taking cognizance is receptive, with intentionality going from the object to the subject, while theoretical responses are responsive. Just as the common sense is a single power that unfolds itself in distinct powers of external senses, so the power of intellect unfolds itself in further powers, such as to conceptualize and to theoretically respond. What is irreducibly distinct in these acts is best explained by positing multiple intellectual powers in us, each irreducible to the others.[121]

But while Hildebrand is correct that judgment is responsive and not in itself a grasping of new content, Gilson's, Hildebrand's, and Levinas's claims can be partly synthesized by observing that I do not grasp the trace that *esse* leaves in me until I articulate a judgment about how the being exists. Responses, including affirmation and doubt, often reveal new knowledge; for example, I often discover what I believe about a being only in noting the attitudes that arise in me in relation to it. I even grasp my own existence by judgment. Although I am aware of my existence in pure subjectivity, that is only a grasp of the fact that there is some actuality in me, not

---

119. Emmanuel Levinas, "God and Philosophy," in *Collected Papers*, 162–70; Emmanuel Levinas, *Entre Nous: On the Thinking-of-the-Other*, trans. Michael Smith and Barbara Harshav (New York: Columbia University Press, 1998), 216.

120. Hildebrand, *What Is Philosophy?* 17–18; *Ethics*, 179–88.

121. This argument was first developed in Mark K. Spencer, "The Many Powers of the Human Soul: Von Hildebrand's Contribution to Scholastic Philosophical Anthropology," *American Catholic Philosophical Quarterly* 91, no. 4 (2017): 719–35.

Principles of Real Being   149

a grasp of my full, substantial, unifying *esse*. Lublin Thomist Mieczysław Krąpiec observes that when I judge that I am, I grasp my own *esse*, which unifies in me what I can experience subjectively and what I cannot.[122] I know my substantial, unified existence not by introspection but by being reflexively aware of my acts, receiving thereby a trace of my own *esse*, and then responding to that trace with a judgment—the same way that I am aware of others' existence. I know my existence only in first acting toward others. My judgment that I exist, like all actualities, tends to manifest itself: I declare, to myself and to others, that I exist. Declaring myself, as Sokolowski describes, exceeds my subjective consciousness of myself; to declare that I exist is not just to reveal my subjective consciousness but to affirm that I exist as a unified, real, complete, rational, agential substance.[123] Balthasar notes that all beings give or manifest themselves, but persons do so by saying themselves, again revealing our share in the Word.[124]

I can join judgments into arguments, and into narratives, too. The narrative of my life can be understood in two ways. First, it is the whole course of my life, as shaped by my free choices and the events I undergo. By my every act, especially my free acts, I shape the course of my life, and thereby bring into existence the irreducible shape of my life, with its unique value. These features of my life will be discussed further in later chapters.[125] Second, it is the way in which I consciously, intellectually articulate who I am over time, and so grasp the meaning of my life—how its aspects fit together and fit with other things. My *esse* calls me to declare myself anew at each moment. Since I continually take on new acts and accidents, I can make ever-new judgments about what and who I am, each of which reveals my existence.

Every judgment includes content about my whole life history. While intellectual acts do not emerge from matter, intellectual content is largely drawn from phantasms. Each phantasm includes, to some degree, my whole experience of my body, which is affected by my conscious and unconscious bodily memories, drives, and tendencies. The content of my concepts and judgments about any being, including myself, is affected by my whole bodily situation. Economic, technological, cultural, and other

---

122. Mieczysław Krąpiec, *I-Man: An Outline of Philosophical Anthropology*, trans. Marie Lescoe et al. (New Britain, Conn.: Mariel Publications, 1983), 95–99.
123. Sokolowski, *Phenomenology of the Human Person*, 14–20. Cf. Hildebrand, *Aesthetics*, vol. 1, 108.
124. Balthasar, *E*, 77–83.
125. John Martin Fischer, "Stories and the Meaning of Life," *Philosophic Exchange* 39, no. 1, https://digitalcommons.brockport.edu/phil_ex/vol39/iss1/4. I am grateful to Mirela Oliva for helping me understand these two senses of narrative.

material conditions, including the sort of land and community in which I live, are the basis from which I abstract. They deeply affect the narrative and meaning of my life (and the narrative or history of communities as well). Intellectual ideas, in turn, provide identity to material features of human life and shape the course of material conditions. We should reject as reductionistic views of human life and history in which only material conditions or only ideas cause events and their meaning. Given our hylomorphic structure, both play a decisive, intertwined, causal role.[126]

We are naturally intellectually called not just to grasp information about beings but to tell their stories. This is a creative response: by adding my affirmative word to beings, including to myself, I aim to make them what they ought to be. Judgments and narratives are *performative*: they bring about new actualities, new ways in which a being is completed by our responses to them, by articulating them.[127] They also reveal how intellectual activity is linguistically structured: I think according to syntactic and grammatical rules, through which aspects of the world appears to me.[128] The syntactic structure of natural languages affects my intellectual activity, since my concepts draw from everything contained in my senses, including my language's syntax. Intellectual activity is intersubjective, articulated with and for others, irreducible to what occurs just in me.[129]

Existence as Radical Extramentality and as "Not Nothing"

Other Thomists proposed other views of *esse* and of how we know it.[130] Most Baroque Thomists, like John of St. Thomas, understood *esse* as a

---

126. Christopher Dawson, *Progress and Religion: An Historical Inquiry* (Washington, D.C.: The Catholic University of America Press, 2001), 47–80. We should accept some claims of otherwise reductionistic thinkers, like Marx, Freud, and Nietzsche, that emphasize the role of material conditions in shaping thought's content.

127. John Searle, *Speech Acts: An Essay in the Philosophy of Language* (Cambridge: Cambridge University Press, 1970).

128. For an account of how syntactic patterns in works of literature from a number of languages and cultures reveal and reflect aspects of reality, see Erich Auerbach, *Mimesis: The Representative of Reality in Western Literatures*, trans. Willard R. Trask (Princeton, N.J.: Princeton University Press, 2003).

129. Sokolowski, *Phenomenology of the Human Person*; Aquinas, *In I PH*, lect. 2; Nicanor Austriaco, "Defending Adam after Darwin," *American Catholic Philosophical Quarterly* 92, no. 2 (2018): 350; Marie George, "Aquinas's Teachings on Concepts and Words in His Commentary on John contra Nicanor Austriaco, OP," *American Catholic Philosophical Quarterly* 94, no. 3 (2020): 357–78.

130. John Knasas, *Being and Some 20th Century Thomists* (New York: Fordham University Press, 2003); Little, *Toward a Thomistic Methodology*, pt. 1; and Gerard McCool, *The Neo-Thomists* (Milwaukee, Wisc.: Marquette University Press, 1994).

principle whereby beings and essential contents are not nothing and are outside their causes. *Esse* in this sense adds to essence the conceptualizable fact of existing extramentally.[131]

Existential Thomists, by contrast, sought to more strongly defend realism after the advent of various forms of idealism, such as that of Hegel, who sought to reduce all things to elements of a single, absolute idea.[132] Gilson and his followers challenged the earlier "thin" conception of *esse*, arguing that *esse* is not just a conceptualizable *fact* (*ratio*) but the highest perfection and actuality in a being, whereby it concretely exists and has the transcendentals. Some existential Thomists like Gerard Phelan, William Carlo, and Norris Clarke, argued for a "thick" conception of *esse* and a "thin" conception of essence: *esse* is all the perfection in a being, and what we grasp as essence is just an *esse*'s limitation, not a distinct principle.[133] By contrast, John Wippel argues that essence in comparison to *esse* is nonactual but not entirely nothing; essence is a "relative nonbeing," a potentiality by which a being participates in actuality to some degree.[134]

Another existential Thomist, Frederick Wilhelmsen, denies that *esse* can be grasped in propositions or judgments, which, as Gilson's student Joseph Owens says, grasp existence only at a given time.[135] In Wilhelmsen's view, essence is everything in a being that is conceptualizable, analyzable, causally related to others, and able to be considered statically and as present to us. *Esse* is the synthesis of everything in a being as being, whereby it actually is. This synthesis cannot be grasped as statically present, nor as a dynamic series of what unfolds over a series of "nows"; either of those would reduce it to essence. *Esse*, on this view, is that by which a being exists in a radically extramental way. It cannot be grasped in itself, even in affirmative judgment, for what we affirm to exist is a being (*ens*), not its actuality (*esse*); we can only approximate a grasp on *esse* through an ongoing process of reasoning from claim to claim about *esse* without ever precisely grasping it. Any reasoning that approximates grasping *esse* must be paradoxical; Wilhelmsen claims, for example, that *esse* is not identical to

---

131. John of St. Thomas, *Cursus philosophicus thomisticus*, v. 2, p.1, q.7, a.4, 115–25.

132. Hegel, *Encyclopedia*, §12, §384, §573.

133. Clarke, *Person and Being*; Gerard Phelan, "The Being of Creatures," *Proceedings of the American Catholic Philosophical Association* 31 (1957): 118–127; Phelan, "The Esse of Accidents," *New Scholasticism* 43, no. 1 (1969): 143–48; and Carlo, *Ultimate Reducibility*, 99–145. Cf. Matthew Schaeffer, "Thick-*Esse*/Thin-Essence in Thomistic Personalism," *American Catholic Philosophical Quarterly* 89, no. 2 (2015): 223–51.

134. Wippel, *The Metaphysical Thought of Thomas Aquinas*, 177–83.

135. Owens, "Knowing Existence," 683.

essence (since it is not conceptualizable and essence is) nor distinct from essence (since it is essence's actuality), and that *esse* neither exists (since it is that whereby a being exists) nor does not exist (since it is not nothing).[136] Similarly, Ferdinand Ulrich portrays *esse* as God's highest gift, "fullness given away," continually, kenotically, lovingly pouring itself out in essence, both complete and "nothing" (because nonsubsistent), only giving itself in beings, in obedience to God. Full awareness of existence, insofar as this is possible, requires obedience on our part to this kenotic self-gift in beings, with a matching pouring out of self in creative reasoning.[137]

In what follows, I elucidate what irreducible features of persons each of these views reveals. Wilhelmsen and Ulrich correctly perceive how actual existence concretely unifies everything in a being and is irreducible to anything we can conceptually grasp or express. They (like other antiidealists we have encountered, such as Levinas, Balthasar, and Marion) rightly resist idealist reductionisms, whether Hegelian, Husserlian, Heideggerian, or any other sort; indeed, they resist what is false in a strand of philosophy going back to Parmenides's claim that being and thinking entirely correlate or are identical. This claim is true only in the sense that each being can in some respect be captured in thought; full existence, however, transcends thought.[138]

Centuries before Wilhelmsen, Suárez recognized the paradoxical results that follow from one Thomistic view of *esse* as a principle of being. But unlike Wilhelmsen, he rejected those paradoxes, and so rejected that view. He argued that each being is identical to its actual existing (*esse*): beings exist through themselves, not through a distinct principle. If *esse* were a distinct actuality in beings, it would exist, and so *ex hypothesi* would require an *esse* whereby it exists, leading to an infinite regress; if it does not exist, then it does not explain a being's existence.[139] With Suárez (and against Wilhelmsen), I affirm that actual existence is nonparadoxical, but (with Aquinas), I affirm that *esse* is a principle and (with Wilhelmsen) that it renders beings radically extramental. Synthesizing these various aspects of these views requires more experientially motivated distinctions.

---

136. Frederick Wilhelmsen, *The Paradoxical Structure of Existence* (New Brunswick, N.J.: Transaction, 2014), 44–61.

137. Ulrich, *Homo Abyssus*, 23–30, 165, 341–47.

138. Compare the contemporary, anti-Parmenidean view known as "speculative realism" in Quentin Meillassoux, *After Finitude: An Essay on the Necessity of Contingency*, trans. Ray Brassier (London: Continuum, 2010).

139. Suárez, *DM*, d.31, s. 6, nn. 1–13. Cf. José Pereira, *Suárez* (Milwaukee, Wisc.: Marquette University Press, 2007), 101ff.

Principles of Real Being 153

Ulrich observes that, ordinarily, we are aware of beings, not their existence in itself, which gives itself only in beings.[140] But beings manifest themselves as only contingently existing and so only as sharing in existence—hence, as we have seen, *esse* is distinct from beings in some way. If Suárez were correct, and beings existed through themselves, not through a principle of *esse*, then they would not appear as only partially manifesting the fullness of creaturely being. As beings give themselves as sharing in Platonic Forms through their essences, so by their particular *esse*, they give themselves as participating in the fullness of what it is to exist in a creaturely sense, that is, in being itself (*esse commune*).[141] As with Forms, this fullness of creaturely being is limited and contingent; it must be explained by participation in the fullness of existence as such, that is, God, who is *esse subsistens*.

To explain how both *esse* and *esse commune* exist, without falling into paradox or infinite regress, we must distinguish multiple *kinds* of being and existence. Scholastically influenced analytic metaphysician Kris McDaniel argues that there are distinct, analogically related senses of "exists" (and of the existential quantifier) for different items.[142] I propose that we can quantify over both *ens* and *esse*, but the existential quantifier has a distinct meaning when applied to each. In McDaniel's view, a univocal quantifier, applicable to any item, is derived from the quantifiers for each irreducible kind of item.[143] In synthesis with the scholastic tradition, this can be interpreted as meaning that each item, including *esse*, includes the formality of being not nothing, but only concrete beings exist in the richer sense of sharing in *esse*. If by "exists," we mean the "thick" sense of concreteness, radical extramentality, beauty, and so forth, then *esse* and other principles do not exist: only beings do, and Wilhelmsen's apparent paradoxes apply to that sense of "exists." But if by "exists," we mean "not nothing," then *esse*, *esse commune*, and other principles do exist; they are explanatory aspects

---

140. Cf. Ulrich, *Homo Abyssus*, 28–30; D. C. Schindler, "What's the Difference? On the Metaphysics of Participation in a Christian Context," *The St. Anselm Journal* 3, no. 1 (2005): 19–20.

141. Aquinas, *In V DDN*, lect. 2. Cf. Wippel, *Metaphysical Thought*, 114–15, 123: *Ens commune*, or being considered universally, is the analogical unity of everything participating in *esse commune*. Cf. Martin Heidegger, *Introduction to Metaphysics*, trans. Gregory Fried and Richard Polt (New Haven, Conn.: Yale University Press, 2014).

142. Kris McDaniel, *The Fragmentation of Being* (Oxford: Oxford University Press, 2017), 37, 144–47.

143. I affirm Scotus's (*Ord.* I, d.3, p.1, q.1–3) view that we form a univocal conception of being, but it picks out just the formality of being not nothing. That we can form this concept does not entail that there is anything actually the same between any two beings in their mode of existence. Cf. Josef Seifert, *Essere e persona: Verso una fondazione fenomenologica di una metafisica classica e personalistica* (Rome: Vita e pensiero, 1989), 297–302.

of what exists in the fullest sense. *Esse* is not what manifests itself, but what explains self-manifestation. *Esse* is never fully grasped in a concept, as we grasp essences or formalities. In judgment (as Gilson said), I grasp its self-manifestation; in reasoning (as Wilhelmsen said), I grasp its synthesizing, unifying, radically extramental excess over thinking. However, while *esse* can never be fully captured in a concept, we can (as John of St. Thomas said) form a concept of *esse*, as should be clear from the fact that I have been discussing *esse* conceptually for the last few pages. This concept is formed by separating the notion of existing from judgments: its function is not to capture content but to point at what exceeds it and facilitate our self-transcendence toward real being.

The Mysterious Distinction between Essence and Existence

On this metaphysics of *esse*, essences limit being itself and the full "power of being" (i.e., the activity of self-gift and self-manifestation) to the *esse* and power of a particular being.[144] But while Carlo is correct that creaturely essence is a limitation on *esse*, and while Wippel is correct that, compared to the kind of being that *esse* or beings have, essence is potency and "relative non-being," essence is not only these things. It is a distinct principle and kind of completeness in beings—an irreducible feature of beings that is not nothing in its own way, by which beings participate in what transcends them. As personalist Josef Seifert argues, essences not only limit but also *delimit* a being—that is, give it definite content of some kind. To have definite content is not *ipso facto* to be limited, as the case of God shows; God has definite essential content (he is, for example, perfectly good, beautiful, loving, and so forth), but he is not limited. Limitation on *esse* is a negative function of essence, while delimitation of content is a positive function.[145]

Scholastics have long debated how essence and *esse* are distinct. German-Polish Catholic metaphysician Erich Przywara describes intellectual experiences that guide us to perceive well what is irreducible in each principle. Full attention to either essence or existence opens us up to "mystery,"

---

144. Aquinas, *SCG* I, c. 28; *In LDC*, lect. 4. Cf. Cornelio Fabro, *Participation et causalité selon S. Thomas d'Aquin* (Paris: Editions Béatrice-Nauwelaerts, 1961), 195; John Wippel, "Thomas Aquinas and the Axiom that Unreceived Act Is Unlimited," in *Metaphysical Themes in Thomas Aquinas*, vol. 2 (Washington, D.C.: The Catholic University of America Press, 2007), 150–51.

145. Seifert, *Essence and Existence*, 42ff., 77ff., 401.

a sense for a fullness of meaning that exceeds us and that can be deepened ever further, understood in the following ways.[146]

On the one hand, if we intellectually consider the concrete existence of a being, our minds are led to its abstract essence, since the unfolding existence of a being is delimited and given by its essence and form: to consider that a being exists and to consider its self-manifestation require a consideration of what it is. This leads us to the experience of its Platonic Form (*eidos*), in which the content of an essence is given as exceeding its finite existence in the particular being I am considering. Essence is given both within concrete existence but also beyond it; essence is prior to *esse* insofar as it delimits it, giving it content. Reality is not just composed of dynamic existences, a Heraclitean flux in which things can only be fleetingly grasped *a posteriori*; it has a stable, abstractable structure, which exceeds what we can grasp about it.

On the other hand, if we intellectually consider essences, our minds are led to their concrete, contingent existence. The necessities found in essence are enmeshed in actual existence, which exceeds them. Concrete existence is delimited by essence, but also exceeds it; *esse* is prior to essence as act to potency. This priority of existence over essence is given not only when we intellectually grasp the contingency and givenness of beings but also (as Seifert says) when we feel gratitude or wonder that things exist (or despair at my own existence, if I loathe my life).[147] Reality is not just a static, Parmenidean system of essences: it dynamically exists.

The orders of essence and existence are not just two levels of completion (as Henry of Ghent said) or two items in beings. They are also two ways in which beings transcend themselves by sharing in what exceeds them, in what exceeds our intellectual acts, and in what our intellects must obey. Balthasar describes how, in these two orders, beings have a "mysterious" two-fold "perspectival" depth. To focus entirely on essence or entirely on existence is reductionistic.[148] Essence and existence appear distinct, yet deeply intertwined; we find ourselves "suspended" "in between" (*metaxu*) them.[149] They are not really distinct as two beings are. They are not merely

---

146. The next two paragraphs are based on Erich Przywara, *Analogia Entis: Metaphysics: Original Structure and Universal Rhythm*, trans. John Betz and David Bentley Hart (Grand Rapids, Mich.: Eerdmans, 2014), especially 182–91.
147. Seifert, *Essence and Existence*, 385–94.
148. Balthasar, *TL1*, 192–206.
149. Milbank, *Suspended Middle*, 30–32; Desmond, *The Intimate Strangeness of Being*, 36–37, 48–49; and Desmond, *The Voiding of Being*, 235–37.

rationally distinct, since they are two principles in the very structure of beings. Nor are they formally distinct, since they are not two necessary contents in beings or essences. This distinction is *sui generis*, exceeding what can be rationally grasped; by perceiving this, we grasp the full irreducibility of both our essence and our existence. Given its openness to excessive fullness of meaning, Rahner is right to call the intellect a "faculty for mystery."[150] Yet we are not only mysterious; we also have clearly, rationally definable features.

Intuitive Cognition and Contemplation

Some scholastics furthermore describe another intellectual experience of beings as really existing, the *intuition of being*. Considering this experience requires us to consider irreducibility as individuals. As Jorge Gracia explains, an individual is, unlike a universal, something noninstantiable, something that does not have instances.[151] Aquinas holds that we cannot directly intellectually grasp material individuals in themselves, since we abstract essences from matter and so from individuality (since matter is a principle of individuation, something that renders a being unable to have instances, as we shall see in chapter 7).[152] We can intellectually know material individuals like actions or artifacts as things to be done or made, since this knowledge is not abstracted from beings, but is prior to what it considers.[153] We can also indirectly intellectually grasp material individuals by reflection on phantasms. Once I form a concept, I grasp (by my intellect and cogitative power working together) how its content is instantiated in the being represented in a phantasm, a being that itself cannot have instances of itself. To self-consciously grasp my intellectual acts is to self-consciously grasp my act of considering and receiving content from this individual phantasm. On these bases, I form concepts of individuals.[154]

Aquinas, however, does not consider intuition, which Maritain describes as an experience of certainty at the reality or thereness of what is, and which Franciscans like Scotus and William of Ockham describe

---

150. Rahner, "The Concept of Mystery in Catholic Theology," in *Theological Investigations*, vol. 4, trans. Kevin Smyth (Baltimore: Helicon Press, 1966), 43, cited in Peter Joseph Fritz, *Karl Rahner's Theological Aesthetics* (Washington, D.C.: The Catholic University of America Press, 2014), 166.
151. Jorge J. E. Gracia, *Individuality: An Essay on the Foundations of Metaphysics* (Albany: State University of New York Press, 1988), 43–56.
152. Aquinas, *ST* I, q.86, a.1.
153. Aquinas, *ST* I, q.57, a.2.
154. Aquinas, *ST* I, q.86, a.1.

as nonpropositional, nonconceptual awareness of a being's existence.[155] In it, the intellect receives no actuality or content, but I am aware of a really existing individual being as present to me. Like aesthetic cognition, it is a pure intentional relation in which the active intellect, without internal change to its actuality, "touches" or is "terminated" by (i.e., intentionally aims at) an object.[156] How this occurs, metaphysically, is explored further in later chapters, but we have already seen how Scotus contends that as long as a knower has the form of a being actually in mind and is in that being's presence, that knower intentionally aims at and is aware of the being. In reflecting on intuition, I form concepts of individuals. Ockham objects that if we can form concepts through intuition without receiving intelligible species, then it is unnecessary to ever posit species, but this overlooks the different experiential characters of different intellectual acts. In abstractive acts, I receive content from beings; in intuition, I reach out to and intellectually touch the being's presence. The former's receptivity warrants positing species. By overlooking kinds of intellectual acts, both Aquinas and Ockham are reductionistic about the full range of acts that we can perform through our intellects.

Aesthetic cognition and intuition are direct grasps on beings in their self-manifesting presence. Unlike concepts formed by abstraction, which aim to designate essences adequately and proportionately, in such a way that their meaning can be precisely defined, concepts formed through these acts evoke beings' self-manifesting presence. These concepts play a significant role in poetic, narrative, and other artistic acts; their content is not precisely definable or analyzable but is best expressed in myth, metaphor, and other imagery. But these concepts are no less essential to a complete realist metaphysics than abstract concepts; they draw attention to participatory and other relations that are irreducible to beings' essences.[157] Both acts are also connected to different kinds of contemplation (*theoria*), the activity (*energeia*, as opposed to a process [*kinesis*] like reasoning) of intellectually beholding a being with wonder or awe.[158]

---

155. Maritain, *The Peasant of the Garonne*, trans. Michael Cuddihy and Elizabeth Hughes (New York: Holt Reinhardt, 1966), 132–35; Scotus, *Ord.* IV, d.45, q.3; and William of Ockham, *Reportatio*, v. 7 of *Opera theologica* (St. Bonaventure: Franciscan Institute, 1984), II q.14, 316–21.

156. See John of St. Thomas, *Cursus philosophicus*, v. 1, pt. 2, q.23, a.1, 2, 631–42; John of St. Thomas, *Cursus theologicus*, v. 1 (Cologne: Wilhelm Metternich, 1711) I, q.14, d.18, a.1, 397; q.14, d.19, a.4, 431. Directly grasping objects, without any process or actualization, is further evidence against views, like functionalism, on which cognition is reduced to acts representable computationally.

157. Cf. Maritain, *Creative Intuition*, chap. 4; Kohák, *The Embers and the Stars*, 53–54.

158. Cf. Aristotle, *NE*, X.7–8; Aquinas, *ST* II-II, q.180; and Watkin, *A Philosophy of Form*, 215–23.

First, I can *speculatively contemplate* a holistic beauty after I have analyzed its features conceptually and propositionally. This contemplation is mediated by species and concepts, which unite me to the contemplated being. I can speculatively contemplate beings guided by any transcendental, such as truth or goodness, though I do so most holistically through the notion of beauty, the last transcendental grasped by abstraction, the splendor of the other transcendentals considered together.[159] By participating in beauty, my intellect becomes beautiful—that is, proportioned, complete, splendid, and oriented to further pleasing self-manifestation. Speculative contemplation is a natural act; as the act that consummates the processes of conceptualization, judgment, and reasoning, it is the natural end of the intellect, and so a key feature of the human end. Speculative contemplation can also be done with my intellect's obediential potency when I experience beauty as a saturated phenomenon exceeding my concepts.

Second, I can *intuitively contemplate* a being as it manifests itself prior to all concepts, either as beautiful in aesthetic cognition or as existing in intuition. This is a disinterested, self-transcending contemplation; I receive from the being nothing that renders me beautiful. It is a pure beholding of the radiant, self-manifesting presence of beings. Since this sort of contemplation involves attending to what is directly given, it is the act that allows engagement in many versions of phenomenological reduction. We can experience this contemplation as the delightful presence of beings to my intellect, as intelligible but without abstract meaning. While we sometimes intuit beings as calling for abstract understanding, we also sometimes experience abstract thinking as opposed to this contemplation: sometimes, it seems like a deeper grasp on reality to just behold beings' radiant self-manifestation, and perhaps evoke it in poetry, myth, or song, rather than to try to understand it scientifically or philosophically.[160]

But just as with sensing beauty (as discussed in chapter 2), not all intuitions or contemplations are positive, delightful acts. What is purely *there* can appear strange, unintelligible, even if "intimately" so, as thereness surrounds and sustains me; William Desmond describes this as the "idiocy" of being (from the Greek *idios* or *idiotes*, picking out what is private, in-

---

159. Jacques Maritain, *Art and Scholasticism*, trans. J. F. Scanlan (New York: Charles Scribner's Sons, 1930), 172.

160. Cf. Calasso, *The Marriage of Cadmus and Harmony*, 241: "The first enemy of the aesthetic was meaning"; Archibald MacLeish's poem *Ars Poetica*: "A poem should not mean/But be"; and Angelus Silesius' line "Die Rose ist ohne Warum."

dividual, unshared, and uniquely one's own), its irreducibility to what is determinate. More negatively, intuiting the sheer existence of beings can be an uncanny, horrifying, or disgusting experience, as Levinas and Jean-Paul Sartre describe. I can be suddenly seized with fear at beings' *thereness*, which can appear dark and menacing, hemming me in, even if I fear no particular danger; each being's presence can appear to be "in the way" of the others, restricting others' ability to act freely. I perceive beings as absurd or arbitrary, as not needing to be as they are—that is, as contingent. This claustrophobic feeling of being trapped by meaningless (i.e., not fitting with one's powers or with anything else) existence can induce disgust or nausea at existence, a longing to escape, either by ceasing to be—or by moving beyond mere being to properties that justify being and normatively call for responses to it, like goodness and value.[161]

Desmond reductionistically sees these negative experiences as subjective recoiling before the gift of being. Erazim Kohák similarly objects that these negative experiences arose in modernity when human persons became alienated from nature, due to adopting false scientific views and a mechanized lifestyle.[162] Judgments that existence is only absurd are false because they fail to fit with other experiences, but regardless of their origin, these are ways that things directly appear; hence, they are certainly real in some way. Existence (including our own) can directly appear as absurd or meaningless: these must be features of reality in some sense. In intuition, positive and negative features are given as real, not as projections of my attitudes or beliefs. Different attitudes are needed for either to give itself, but being could not give itself in both ways if it lacked the power to do so. Being has both aspects; I explain how they fit together in chapter 6.

Practical Intellect, Productive Intellect, and Natural Law

In addition to theoretical or speculative thinking (in which we grasp beings as they are), we engage in logical thinking (reflecting on and formulating the structure of reasoning), practical thinking (directing what we

---

161. Desmond, *The Gift of Beauty and the Passion of Being*, chap. 2; Desmond, *The Voiding of Being*, 203–7; Emmanuel Levinas, *On Escape*, trans. Bettina Bergo (Stanford, Calif.: Stanford University Press, 2003), 63–71; Levinas, *Existence and Existents*, 17–23, 65; and Jean-Paul Sartre, *Nausea*, trans. Lloyd Alexander (New York: New Directions, 1964).
162. Kohák, *The Embers and the Stars*, 3–13.

will or ought to do), and productive or poetic thinking (creatively directing what we will or ought to make).[163] Investigating practical and productive thinking turns us to the will and freedom, the topics of chapter 4.

In practical reasoning, I grasp ends that can or must be sought and deliberate about the means to achieve them, and I reason about which ends and means are moral. To act morally well, as a good human person acts, is to act in accord with intellect's nature, which aims at the truth. To act immorally is to use intellect (or other powers) contrary to its natural ordering.[164] The best reasoning here is once again aesthetic: to grasp the natural ordering of our powers is to grasp what harmonizes or fits beautifully with them. To act well is, as Aristotle says, to pursue this beauty (*kalon*).[165] Fully grasping the irreducibilities revealed by practical intellect is aided by considering the contemporary debate between new and traditional natural law theories over how we practically reason, the source of moral normativity (i.e., the source of obligation to act in certain ways), and our ultimate end.[166] I hope that my use of each side to build my portrait of persons allows a synthesis between aspects of each.

On new natural law theory, deliberation starts with a first-person awareness of goods as things that I can pursue.[167] Certain *basic goods*, such as health, knowledge, aesthetic enjoyment, and harmony with self, others, and God, appear as ends that are worth pursuing for their own sake, and as naturally fulfilling to me. When I deliberate, I implicitly describe proposed actions to myself propositionally (for example, I implicitly say "I could eat this pizza" or "I could change careers"). Basic goods appear as the ultimate ends of proposed actions. In grasping this, I grasp a principle of natural law: these goods are to be pursued and their opposites avoided. When I subjectively propose a course of action, the ends of any such course exert normative force on me, that is, I am morally claimed to pursue these goods, which I directly grasp not as objects to be speculatively examined,

---

163. Aquinas, *ST* I, q.79, a.11; *In I NE*, lect. 1.
164. Aquinas, *ST* I-II, q.1, a.1.
165. Aristotle, *NE*, I.7.1098a8-18; III.7.1115b11-13; III.8.1117a8; IV.1.1120a23-30.
166. See Aquinas, *ST* I-II, q.90; q.91, a.2; q.94.
167. I sum up this theory based upon the following sources: Sherif Girgis, "Subjectivity without Subjectivism," in *Subjectivity: Ancient and Modern*, ed. R. J. Snell and Steven McGuire (Lanham, Md.: Lexington Books, 2016), 63–88; Germain Grisez, "Sketch of A Future Metaphysics," *New Scholasticism* 38, no. 3 (1964): 310–40; Germain Grisez, "The First Principle of Practical Reason," *Natural Law Forum* 10, no. 1 (1965): 168–201; John Finnis, Germain Grisez, and Joseph Boyle, "Practical Principles, Moral Truth, and Ultimate Ends," *American Journal of Jurisprudence* 32 (1987): 99–151; Martin Rhonheimer, *The Perspective of the Acting Person* (Washington, D.C.: The Catholic University of America Press, 2008); and Christopher Tollefsen, "First- and Third-Person Standpoints in the New Natural Law Theory," in *Subjectivity*, 95–114.

nor as aspects of what my nature is, but as ends that intrinsically ought to be pursued. Natural law's normative force comes from God having set up my nature with these ends, but natural law's content must be discovered anew by each person for him or herself. I know the object of my act, the kind of act I propose to do, better than anyone else, because I best grasp goods as I pursue and intend them, which are partly defined as goods by my intentions and practical reasoning. In practical reasoning, I creatively and autonomously produce the content of the natural law and give it to myself, even while obeying these goods' normative force. Again, thinking is irreducibly both creative and obedient; we must act through both tendencies to be flourishing persons.

From the subjective practical perspective, my ultimate end appears as an aggregate of basic goods, with many ways to achieve each good; for example, I can achieve the good of knowledge by knowing about paleontology or film theory, and I can achieve the good of aesthetic enjoyment through opera or origami. There are many irreducibly unique ways in which human persons can be fulfilled. Reasoning is, again, creative and open-ended; goods appear as open-ended projects for me to creatively achieve. We saw in chapter 2 that all human persons are oriented to a "pure" or Platonic Form of human flourishing. The experience of practical reasoning reveals that this is an open-ended constellation of goods, not a single determinate form that is the same for all persons.

But new natural law theory overemphasizes the subjective aspects of practical reason and is thereby reductionistic about its interconnections with theoretical reason, which are emphasized by traditional natural law theory.[168] On this view, all reasoning begins by speculatively grasping transcendentals, including goodness. In grasping goodness as a property of every being such that it is to be pursued, we grasp the first principle of natural law: good is to be pursued and its opposite, evil, avoided. I also speculatively grasp my powers' natural orientations to specific goods, such

---

168. I sum up this theory based upon the following sources, prescinding from variations among them: Lawrence Feingold, "Heavenly Beatitude According to Thomas Aquinas," address at Fellowship of Catholic Scholars Conference, September 27, 2014; Steven Jensen, *Good and Evil Actions: A Journey Through St. Thomas Aquinas* (Washington, D.C.: The Catholic University of America Press, 2010); Steven Jensen, *Knowing the Natural Law: From Precepts and Inclinations to Deriving Oughts* (Washington, D.C.: The Catholic University of America Press, 2015); Kevin Keiser, "The Moral Act in St. Thomas," *The Thomist* 74, no. 2 (2010): 237–82; Robert Koons and Matthew O'Brien, "Objects of Intention," *American Catholic Philosophical Quarterly* 86, no. 4 (2012): 655–703; Steven Long, *The Teleological Grammar of the Moral Act* (Naples, Fla.: Sapientia Press, 2007), 1–38; and Steven Long, "Fundamental Errors of the New Natural Law Theory," *National Catholic Bioethics Quarterly* 13, no. 1 (2013): 105–31.

as the reproductive power's orientation to producing children or the vocal power's orientation to manifesting being. Bringing together the first principle and my grasp of my powers' ends or goods, I grasp that those ends are to be pursued and their opposites avoided.

My acts also have *objects* or kinds in themselves, apart from my intentions, with essences whereby they tend to some end; such an end is not the effect that always or likely results from acts of that sort but rather what such an act aims at by its nature if not impeded by external circumstances. To choose an act is to choose its object and ends, regardless of whether I understand them fully. I do not necessarily know best what I propose to do in its entirety; someone who understands my act's object might understand what I am doing better than I do. Stealing aims at others losing their property and lying aims at another believing a falsehood, even if I propose or intend these acts under different descriptions. Consideration of human acts from all perspectives reveals that they (like the whole human person) are irreducible to how they subjectively or objectively appear. Furthermore, practical reasoning (like all subjectivity) is oriented to the body, and human acts are oriented to being embodied in physical act-types. Aiming subjectively at an end involves subjective awareness of my bodily powers' teleologies. Acts also have a social "grammar": to act well, I must know the meaning that act-types have in my society, which is not entirely up to me. Given reason's orientation toward the body, an act that violates my body's teleology is immoral, as is an act that violates a socially given meaning, except when social practices violate our nature.

Contrary to new natural law theory, we can reason from speculatively discovered features of beings, which are normatively structured, to prescriptive principles of natural law: the teleology of powers and act-objects prescribes what I can morally do. Normative force is found both in goods given subjectively as open-ended projects to be pursued and in our natural teleology; each source of normativity is irreducible to the other, and recognizing both reveals how we both are subjective and have a given nature. New natural law theorists contend that basic goods are incommensurable, which is how goods appear from view of subjectivity and practical reason, wherein they are given as open-ended and pursued for their own sake. But once we grasp, with the traditional theory, that these goods also fulfill our powers, and once we experience subjectivity as oriented to our various powers, we see how these goods can be hierarchically compared. Goods that fulfill lower powers (such as health) are subordinated to those that fulfill higher ones (such as interpersonal relationships) since the former powers are teleologically ordered to the latter; hence, for example, it is permissible to sacrifice the former good (as in fasting) for the sake of one's relation to God. But since each basic good is an end in itself, we cannot morally exercise a power in a way that thwarts the achievement of its end. I am not always required to exercise the power of speech and pursue its good of manifesting being, but I ought not exercise the power in a way that thwarts that end—that is, I ought never lie. Furthermore, there are sources of normative force not considered by either theory, as we shall see over the next two chapters; as Amy Richards points out (similarly to Levinas), we are not just first-person agents or third-person observers: we also act in "second-person" ways, responsive to others for their own sake.[169]

Since I am one being with one form, I have one end. New natural law theory shows that basic goods are *parts* of that end, not means to it; I cannot completely flourish if I lack a basic good. But the hierarchy of powers shows that some goods—like contemplating being and God—are more central to my end than others. Human flourishing is an order, not an aggregate, of goods. As a rational being, I am oriented to grasp universals, which pertain to many particulars, and to act on the basis of that knowledge. Given my nature, more than particular goods (like health), I am oriented to *common or universal goods* (like political peace, justice, and contemplation of God), which can simultaneously fulfill and be shared by multiple persons. I flourish more as a member of a community achieving and communicating sharable goods than I flourish as a private individual achieving nonshareable goods. (I consider common goods further in chapter 7.)

Finally, grasping the full irreducibility of our intellect requires understanding productive reasoning. We saw that judgment and narration aim at giving new forms to beings; similarly, practical and productive reasoning give new *intentional forms* to acts and artifacts, which do not have just a physical structure but a *moral* one, a form and meaning given by their relation to reason. Scholastics and phenomenologists sometimes call artifacts *moral substances*.[170] They have their own structure and teleology,

---

169. Richards, "Response to Christopher Tollefsen," in *Subjectivity*, 120–21. Cf. Stump, *Wandering in Darkness*, chaps. 3, 4.

170. Matthew Minerd, "Beyond Non-Being," *American Catholic Philosophical Quarterly* 91, no. 3 (2017): 353–79; Hildebrand, *Metaphysik der Gemeinschaft*, 20, 99–105.

which normatively guide how to produce them (intentional forms will be considered further in chapter 5). Others can grasp intentional forms and so discover agents' or makers' intentions. Acts that produce these forms further show our irreducibility to matter: we not only educe natural forms from matter (say, in reproduction), but we creatively give new forms to matter, which arise through its obedience to our reason. Intellect is not merely open to grasping any being but can creatively invent an open-ended number of new kinds of acts and beings. Creative production of intentional forms generally occurs not by purely planning them intellectually, however, but by interacting with matter, conforming ourselves to its structure or "grammar," by trying out different arrangements of matter, and thereby both discovering and inventing what is to be done or made.[171] Productive and practical reasoning embody beings of reason in the material world and thereby give others access to them. In working out how to embody beings of reason, we alter them; the fictional character I devise in my head, for example, will differ from the character that results from engagement with the matter of words in actual writing, and it is the latter's content that takes its place in our shared "spiritual space" as something like a new Platonic Form. Practical and productive reasoning are carried out in concert with the will, to which I now turn.

---

171. Gilson, *Painting and Reality*, chap. 1.

Chapter 4 Will and the Principles
of Freedom

I now turn to the power of will, which, like the intellect, belongs to the soul, not the body. Reasoning from experience, Aquinas gives a criterion for determining whether a power belongs to soul or body: it belongs to the bodily soul-matter composite, rather than the soul alone, if and only if bodily changes are essential to its act.[1] Acts of will do not essentially involve bodily changes, and so are in the soul alone. I begin this chapter with Aquinas's account of will and expand on it using accounts of experience. I consider how the will can act on our bodies, which introduces irreducible features of matter, and I raise the problem of how God interacts with our free wills, which introduces irreducible features of our freedom.

Will as Intellectual Appetite

On Aquinas's view, based on reasoning from acts of choice to their underlying causes, the will is an *intellectual appetite*. Just as sensitive appetites are movements toward or away from a sensed being, so acts of will are movements toward or away from a rationally grasped being. Will is fundamentally a power to love or to have affinities for known goods, and all appetitive acts like will are voluntary, that is, their principles are within their agent.[2] While sensitive appetites arise automatically after sensing, acts of will are free, which means that they are performed through a pow-

1. Aquinas, *ST* I, q.77, a.6, ad 2; q.78, a.1; *QDA*, a.19.
2. Aquinas, *ST* I-II, q.6, a.1, 2.

er by which one can choose from among multiple contrary acts (i.e., one could have chosen differently than one did) and by which one acts without being compelled by another: one self-consciously determines one's act.[3] The will's formal object involves goodness: I can will to pursue anything grasped as a good, that is, as loveable or desirable.[4] Only the fullness of goodness, God, could bring to rest the will's activity of moving toward goods.[5] But just as we do not have an innate natural intellectual desire for God as such, neither do we automatically and naturally will to pursue God. Rather, willing is naturally oriented towards goods and toward our end of flourishing or satisfying every natural desire in an open-ended way. While God is goodness, and all goods participate in God for their goodness, to will a good under the description "good" is not necessarily to will it under the description "participating in God." Free action is not reducible to nonfree movement, which tends toward a delimited end. Were we to automatically desire a delimited end, like God, we would not be free in the minimal sense defined above. Human freedom's irreducibility to other kinds of movements is safeguarded in part by the possibility of not moving ourselves toward true satisfaction, that is, by the possibility of wrongdoing, disorder, and sin. While Aquinas thinks that we pursue goods only inasmuch as we find them conducive to complete satisfaction of desire, certain experiences (considered below) show otherwise.[6]

Acts of intellect and will are both rooted in subjectivity and are free in that they are open to contrary acts.[7] They are mutually affecting in many ways. I know both sorts of acts reflexively in performing them, and I can also reflexively will to will. Their immediate, reflexive self-presence is evidence for their immateriality. I perform acts of will after intellectually grasping goods, and my thinking can unfold as I will it (though thinking also arises unbidden), as in theoretical responses like belief and doubt. I can specify how I conceive of happiness (as union with God, the aggregate of all basic goods, pleasure, or something else) explicitly by reasoning about happiness and choosing to adopt beliefs about it, or implicitly when

---

3. Aquinas, *SCG* II, c. 48; III, c. 112; *ST* I, q.82, a.2; Albert the Great, *De homine*, v. 27.2 of *Opera omnia* (Aschendorff: Monasterii Westfalorum, 2008), 3.4.1, 519–21. See Jamie Spiering, "What Is Freedom?" *American Catholic Philosophical Quarterly* 89, no. 1 (2015): 31–32.

4. Aquinas, *ST* I, q.82, a.3, 4. See Tobias Hoffman, "Freedom Beyond Practical Reason: Duns Scotus on Will-Dependent Relations," *British Journal for the History of Philosophy* 21, no. 6 (2013): 1,081.

5. Aquinas, *ST* I, q.105, a.4; I-II, q.9, a.6.

6. Aquinas, *ST* I, q.82, a.1.

7. Aquinas, *ST* I-II, q.17, a.1, ad 2; Eleonore Stump, "Aquinas' Account of Freedom," *The Monist* 80, no. 4 (1997): 583–85.

repeated acts of willing certain goods habituate me to regard happiness as having to do with those goods.[8]

Aquinas outlines a sequence of acts by which intellect and will cooperate in human acts.[9] I intellectually *apprehend* goods as means or parts of happiness. By will, I *intend* them as ends, affirming that they should exist and determining myself to pursue them. I then intellectually *deliberate* and *practically reason* about means to achieve them, including by consulting others; on that basis, I intellectually *counsel* myself as to what to do. When I *judge* that some act is to be done, its object becomes a final cause for my will and a formal cause by which my will's act is directed and specified, though I efficiently cause will's act by will.[10] By will, I *choose* means to my ends, *consent* to intellect's judgment, and *use* other powers to carry out my choices, specified by reason's *command*. Throughout this process, I am called by *conscience* to moral responsibility, to will in accord with what reason grasps as the moral law. Scholars debate whether Aquinas's account is *libertarian* (or *voluntarist*), a view on which I could have done otherwise than I do even given the intellect's specification, or *compatibilist* (or *intellectualist*), a view on which my will is open to alternative possibilities but its acts are determined by my intellect. I make no claim about which is the correct interpretation, but I defend libertarianism, partly using Thomistic principles.[11]

Just as we directly grasp that we have subjectivity irreducible to matter, so we directly grasp our freedom and openness to any good. Since (as we have seen) open or spiritual powers cannot be in material organs, the will is not in an organ, and its acts cannot be reduced to or entirely caused by material processes. Furthermore, I directly experience others as free. Just as *esse* leaves traces that leads me to judge that beings exist, so recognizing persons directly leads me to judge that they are free, such that I should not coerce or use them but rather treat them as freely determining their actions. Activities like making laws, giving advice, praising, and blaming presuppose this experience of freedom in self and others.[12]

---

8. Aquinas, *ST* I-II, q.1, a.7; q.2, a.8; q.5, a.8.
9. On the following sequence of acts, see: Aquinas, *ST* I, q.82, a.4; I-II, q.9, a.1, 3; q.10, a.2; q.12, a.1, 2; q.13, a.1; q.14; q.16, a.1, 4; q.17, a.1; q.19, a.3, 5, 6; *DV*, q.17, a.1.
10. On ways in which we subjectively grasp these modes of causality when we exercise freedom, see Seifert, *Essere e persona*, 358–63.
11. See Tobias Hoffmann and Cyrille Michon, "Aquinas on Free Will and Intellectual Determinism," *Philosopher's Imprint* 17, no. 10 (2017): 1–36.
12. Aquinas, *ST* I, q.83, a.1.

Volitional Causality of Bodily Acts and Quantum-Mechanical Matter

Despite how it is directly given in the experiences just described, some hold that free willing is merely apparent and is reducible to (i.e., is nothing but) material processes. On the basis of scientific experiences, they hold that the material world is deterministic or causally closed, where each physical event is entirely caused and sufficiently explained by previous physical events. If this were so, then, even if they existed, immaterial acts and intentions could never affect the course of physical events.[13] Yet when I see you (for example) mowing the lawn or reading a book, I directly grasp that these activities occur because of your intention. My direct grasp of you as a person with intentions informs my perception such that I perceive your intentions in your activities, as part of the explanation for why your activities occur. Belief in causal closure is contrary to how reality is directly given, as affected by intentions that initiate new causal chains. We must synthesize what is given in scientific experience and in perception rather than explain one entirely through the other.

When scientists set up a controlled experiment or observation in order to discover the law-like ways in which physical events are related, it is sometimes helpful for them to assume determinism or causal closure. This allows the scientist to focus strictly on necessary features of events, without needing to worry about the more contingent conditions of the events, but it must be remembered that systems appear causally closed only because of prior intentions in setting up the experiment or observation. Those intentions involve abstraction from the full givenness of concrete reality, in which no physical system is actually causally closed. Erazim Kohák shows how we can see that scientific assumptions involve abstraction through a version of phenomenological bracketing: we set out of attention not only theoretical concepts but also those artifacts—especially scientific instruments—through which experience can be mediated. This bracketing reveals the full scope of concrete experience.[14] Once we realize that all measurement involves abstraction, we are less likely to reduce reality to its measurable aspects.

---

13. Madden, *Mind, Matter, and Nature*, 69–80; E. J. Lowe, *Personal Agency: The Metaphysics of Mind and Action* (Oxford: Oxford University Press, 2008), 180; and Stewart Goetz and Charles Taliaferro, *Naturalism* (Grand Rapids, Mich.: Eerdmans, 2008), 35–38.

14. Kohák, *The Embers and the Stars*, 24.

This helps us understand what is actually happening in experiments that seem to explain apparent free willing through neurological events. In a frequently reproduced experiment first performed by Benjamin Libet,[15] subjects are told to push a button whenever they choose, while their brain activity is monitored. In most cases, a buildup of neural energy, which leads to pushing the button, occurs prior to the subject consciously choosing to do so. Some conclude that our actions are caused by unconscious neural processes, conscious choice being epiphenomenal. Given all of concrete experience, this is not a legitimate conclusion. Neural events appear to determine bodily acts only given the scientist's and subject's prior intentions in setting up the experiment, which are not observed in the experiment, and which explain why the subject's brain is primed to produce the action of pushing a button. In other words, positing determinism presupposes prior free acts.

Fully grasping how the will is irreducible to material powers (and thereby grasping further how human persons are irreducible to matter) requires understanding how the will interacts with bodily powers. Unlike bodily natural potencies, which just aim at one kind of good, the will is open to any good. However, what we actually will as good is affected by bodily orientations to goods, since we will what we have intellectually grasped, and the intellect's content is abstracted from the content of bodily powers. That bodily limitations do not eliminate freedom is evidenced by the open-endedness of freedom, revealed in the ever-increasing range of kinds of artifacts and social arrangements that we invent, and by the fact that we only will when motivated by self-consciously grasped meaning. Contemporary Thomist Daniel De Haan argues that the will does not efficiently act on bodily organs, such as the brain; rather volitional acts interact with bodily acts by formal and final causality. Acts of will (and intellect) nonmechanistically coordinate and actualize bodily acts so that they have intentional meaning. I see your physical acts of mowing the lawn, reading a book, or setting up an experiment as intentional because you have ordered them by your intellectual and volitional acts. On this model, intellectual and volitional acts are forms and ends of bodily acts, and so the two form an observable unity.[16]

---

15. See Henrik Walter, "Contributions of Neuroscience to the Free Will Debate: From Random Movement to Intelligible Action," in Robert Kane, ed., *The Oxford Handbook of Free Will* (Oxford: Oxford University Press, 2011), 515–29.

16. Daniel De Haan, "The Interaction of Noetic and Psychosomatic Operations in a Thomist Hylomorphic Personalism," *Scientia et Fides* 6, no. 2 (2018): 1–29.

I contend, however, that this does not completely account for the experience of willing, in which, Hildebrand notes, we self-consciously initiate new causal chains of bodily acts.[17] By willing, I act on my body such that it performs acts that would not have occurred had I not so willed. We indeed experience our intellectual and volitional acts being unified with our bodily acts by formal and final causality, but we also experience ourselves efficiently causing changes in our bodies: my volitions alter my body's matter, so that it moves in new ways. My will acts on my bodily organs, not just on acts in them.

Antidualists at least since the time of Aquinas have argued that bodies and immaterial minds cannot interact because they cannot make contact; immaterial things have no parts or surfaces by which they can touch bodies, but touching or contact is required for two things to interact. This *interaction problem* is overcome by an experientially motivated hylomorphic distinction between two kinds of contact: things make contact not just spatially but also as actuality contacts potentiality; different kinds of contact allow different kinds of interaction.[18] More recently, some have argued that since in every physical event energy is conserved, nothing from outside the material world could act on matter since that would require introducing new energy.[19] Overcoming this *conservation of energy problem*, and fully overcoming the interaction problem, requires a more precise account of matter.[20]

To overcome these problems, I turn to quantum mechanics, which has revealed many features of matter. I consider it only insofar as one of its interpretations allows a synthesis of what is given in scientific and everyday experiences, showing how immaterial will can act efficiently on bodily matter. According to quantum mechanics, physical systems continually

---

17. Hildebrand, *Ethics*, 307–11.
18. Aquinas, *ST* I, q.75, a.1, ad 3.
19. See Madden, *Mind, Matter, and Nature*, chap. 3.
20. Much of the following is adapted from Mark K. Spencer, "Quantum Randomness, Hylomorphism, and Classical Theism," *Journal of Analytic Theology* 4 (2016): 147–70. Regarding my summary of quantum mechanics, including its relation to hylomorphism, see Roger Penrose, *The Road to Reality: A Complete Guide to the Laws of the Universe* (New York: Knopf, 2005), 423–524, 585–91; Antoine Suárez, "Free Will and Nonlocality at Detection as Basic Principles of Quantum Physics," in *Is Science Compatible with Free Will? Exploring Free Will and Consciousness in the Light of Quantum Physics and Neuroscience*, ed. Peter Adams and Antoine Suárez (Dordrecht: Springer, 2013), 63–79; Wolfgang Smith, *The Quantum Enigma: Finding the Hidden Key* (San Rafael, Calif.: Sophia Perennis, 2005); Philippus Soccorsi, *Quaestiones scientificae cum philosophia coniunctae de physica quantica* (Rome: Gregorian and Biblical Press, 1956), 116–21, 262–73; and Robert Koons, "Hylomorphic Escalation: A Hylomorphic Interpretation of Quantum Thermodynamics and Chemistry," *American Catholic Philosophical Quarterly* 92, no. 1 (2018): 159–78.

change over time in a mathematically describable way, such that they do not take on new definite states for properties like position or momentum; through their continual changes, they do not, for example, become located in definite places. Rather, through these changes, physical systems take on a spread of states for each property, with a distinct probability for being found in each of various values for each property. For example, they take on a distinct probability of being found in various places and a distinct probability for having various momenta. These probabilities are deterministically related to the system's previous probabilistic states. This change can be represented as a "wave" radiating through a multidimensional "space," the points of which represent different probabilities for being found in various states for a given property. Sometimes, however, such as when they are observed, systems "collapse" or "are reduced" to a definite state of some property, only probabilistically related to the system's previous states. Nothing about those previous states sufficiently explains why the system takes on one definite state rather than another—for example, why it is found in one place rather than another. For some pairs of properties, such as position and momentum, the more definite a state that one property takes on, the more the other appears as a spread of probabilistically weighted states.

Like most scientifically posited features of matter, none of the states just described are directly given in experience; rather, what is directly given are measurements or experimental results, which are regarded as signs of explanatory principles, like the states just described. Insofar as they are confirmed by good observation and experimentation, scientifically posited features of matter can be taken to be genuine aspects of reality. These quantum-mechanical features of matter, however, have received several ontological interpretations. Some interpretations are reductionistic about what is given in these experiences. For example, in the Copenhagen interpretation, probability states are just useful features of our understanding of measurements, not features of reality. This reduces intellectual activity to just producing models or representations of reality, without grasping reality in itself. In the pilot wave interpretation, material reality is deterministic but appears probabilistic. Like the deterministic interpretation of Libet's experiment, this is reductionistic of our directly given freedom, since free action on the physical world would be impossible if the latter's changes are entirely deterministic, that is, entirely explained by prior physical states of the world. In the many-worlds interpretation, in every collapse event, every possible state comes about, such that a distinct world comes into being stemming from each collapse event. This is reductionistic of features of reality that are directly given as unique, and of the experience (to be examined below) of choices being decisive—if every possible state of the world is real, then no state is unique and no choice decisive.

Given my goal of painting a portrait of human persons as entirely irreducible and that it is beyond the scope of this book to adequately assess scientific theories, it makes sense for me to adopt an interpretation of quantum mechanics on which (unlike those mentioned in the last paragraph) probabilistically weighted states and unique, contingent state-collapse events are actual features of reality. One piece of evidence for this interpretation is that probability states are sometimes observed to interfere with one another, similar to how other sorts of waves interfere with one another, indicating that systems are actually simultaneously in multiple, probabilistically weighted states for a single property, such that those states can actually interfere with each other—that is, that probability states are real properties, not just aspects of our models.

In scientific observations, matter is given (albeit indirectly) as randomly collapsing to a particular state, but never simultaneously in definite states for pairs of properties like position and momentum. In perception, however, persons are given (directly) as changing freely, not randomly or deterministically, and as simultaneously in definite position and momentum states. A materialist might argue that what actually exists are probabilistic systems, which appear definite in everyday perception only because of how the probabilities of many particles equal out in large systems.[21] This reductionistically views us as nothing but aggregates of quantum systems. On the other hand, a hylomorphist might argue that what actually exists are everyday substances with definite properties, while quantum mechanics describes only abstracted, quantifiable aspects of those substances' matter.[22] But this is reductionistic about what is given in scientific experience, which is distinct from what is given in everyday perception, not merely an abstracted aspect of the latter, as evidenced by the interference just mentioned and by other observable quantum effects.

21. Richard Feynman, *Six Easy Pieces: Essentials of Physics as Explained by Its Most Brilliant Teacher* (Reading, Mass.: Addison-Wesley, 1995), 47–67.
22. Charles de Koninck, *The Philosophy of Sir Arthur Eddington* and *The Cosmos*, in *The Writings of Charles de Koninck*, vol. 1, trans. Ralph McInerny (Notre Dame, Ind.: University of Notre Dame Press, 2008), 143–46 and 271, respectively.

We have seen that matter is, at different levels, pure potentiality, and what is quantified, localized, and spatially extended. In Aquinas's view, the matter underlying substances is prime matter, pure potentiality for particular actualities, which persists through substantial changes and never exists except as actualized by substantial form. On this view, all nonessential properties of material things, including quantities, are actualities belonging to composites of prime matter and substantial form. By contrast, on Francisco Suárez's view, prime matter is first quantitatively structured, and this *quantified matter* (rather than pure prime matter) is actualized by substantial form and persists through substantial change.[23] Matter has properties explanatorily and ontologically prior to substantial form, though this quantified matter never actually exists apart from substantial form.

Quantum-mechanical experience is a reason to prefer something like Suárez's account to Aquinas's. In a modern revision of Suárez's view, matter first receives spreads of states, that is, probabilistically weighted states of properties, which deterministically change of themselves. Suárez holds that among nonsubstantial forms, only qualities (such as powers) can efficiently cause.[24] But scientific experience shows that probabilistic quantities efficiently cause subsequent quantities. Probabilistically quantified matter is actualized by substantial form, which confers on it a definite kind, powers, and end. Were all quantities accidental actualities ontologically posterior to substantial form (Aquinas's view), they would all be definite, since form gives definiteness to matter. Matter has real properties that are probabilistic spreads, however, and so are nondefinite; these are explained by quantitative principles existing in matter prior to form. Suárez (like Aquinas and most other scholastics) divides all creaturely beings into ten basic kinds or *categories*: they include substance and nine categories of accidents (actualities that modify substances with definite content and presuppose substantial form), including quantity. In that account, only definite quantities are accidents, but probabilistic quantities, which inhere in matter ontologically prior to substantial form, are neither substantial nor accidental actualities (because they are prior to substance), nor forms at all (because they are nondefinite). Like forms or actualities, they give characteristics to an underlying potentiality that retains continuity through their changes, but like potentialities, they are indefinite. Scientific experience

---

23. Suárez, *DM*, d.13, s.3, nn. 13–16; s.14, nn. 15–16.
24. Suárez, *DM*, d.18, s.4, n. 3

merits positing a new kind of metaphysical principle, irreducible to those classically distinguished.

These probabilistic quantitative principles do not explain "collapse" events in which matter takes on definite states. As we have seen, collapses are not sufficiently explained by prior, probabilistic, quantitative properties, but it is self-evident that every actuality must have some sufficient cause—that is, every actuality that comes to exist does so through some other actuality. Since no prior feature of matter suffices to explain collapse events, they must have an immaterial cause. I propose that all substantial forms, which are immaterial, give substances a power to select among their matter's states and confer definite quantitative forms on that matter. Matter presents a range of probabilistically weighted states (say, of position and momentum) to a substance. Each substance, by its form, "selects" among those states and actualizes or efficiently causes some of them, that is, makes some of them definite. It does so in a way that abides by and is limited by matter's quantities' probability weightings. Through these selections, collapse events occur, and substances take on the definite position and momentum states that appear in everyday perception, but without eliminating probabilistic, quantitative properties. These actually remain in any substance's matter and appear in scientific experience. Energy is quantified matter; forms "steer" energy by bringing about collapse events, without creating or destroying energy. Quantified and prime matter should not be pictured as amorphous "stuff" or as composed of discrete "things." Rather, it is just what remains in abstraction from form, with the properties (including some wave-like and particle-like properties) described through the methods of philosophical abstraction and mathematical physics.

I can freely, efficiently act on my body's material parts and direct what my matter does because of my power to confer definite states on matter. By rapidly bringing about many quantum collapse events, my substance, by my form, steers my body to definite positions and momentums, such that it acts according to my will, without this requiring creation of new energy.[25] My free willing is affected by physical systems, since which actions are possible for me is limited by my matter's probabilistically weighted properties, but it is irreducible to an aggregate of quantum events. As in De

---

25. Contrast to the view of John Eccles, *How the Self Controls Its Brain* (Berlin: Springer, 1994), 148–60, on which choices merely raise the probability of bodily states coming about.

Haan's view, my will gives formal identity and final direction to bodily acts, but as in Hildebrand's view, it initiates new causal chains and acts directly on my body's matter. In my proposal, all substances' forms "select" definite states for their matter, and so have something analogous to freedom (just as, as we saw, all substances have something analogous to subjectivity and life). The analogy runs the other way, too: free willing is like (and involves) the spontaneous state-selection exhibited in nonpersonal substances. In nonpersons, however, causality is not, strictly speaking, free since it happens in pursuit of goods specified by the substances' nature.

This account supports a metaphysics on which the physical world includes genuinely contingent events. Phenomenologist Claude Romano describes how we directly perceive contingent events as undetermined by any intelligible decisions, even divine ones. Contingency both is required for us to be free—since we could not freely act upon a deterministic world—and accounts for our experience of being vulnerable before physical things.[26] The uncanniness, horror, and absurdity of existence mentioned in chapter 3 are partly explained by the fact that willing contends against contingent events in quantified matter that cannot be fully controlled or comprehended. That material substances are, in part, unintelligibly contingent is supported by the experience of some beauties in the material world—like the wistful beauty of the fragility and ephemerality of organisms, the apparent contingency of the records of evolutionary events, and what Japanese aesthetics calls the *wabi-sabi*, the beauty of impermanent, imperfect, rustic, shadowed things—can be perceived only when guided by the view that material things are radically contingent.[27] These given features of reality are explained in my view in that energy has been steered over the history of the universe by myriad numbers of free acts (and acts with a quality analogous to freedom) on quantified matter by substances. I return to the problem of accounting for the contingency of the world when I introduce the problem of divine causality below.

---

26. Claude Romano, *There Is: The Event and the Finitude of Appearing*, trans. Michael Smith (New York: Fordham University Press, 2015), 23–25.

27. Leonard Koren, *Wabi-Sabi for Artists, Designers, Poets, and Philosophers* (Point Reyes, Calif.: Imperfect Publishing, 2008); Jun'ichiro Tanizaki, *In Praise of Shadows*, trans. Thomas Harper and Edward Seidensticker (New Haven, Conn.: Leete's Island Books, 1977); and Stephen Jay Gould, *Wonderful Life: The Burgess Shale and the Nature of History* (New York: Norton, 1989), 288–89.

Cognitive Experience through the Will and the Will's Two Affectiones

I now examine how the will is irreducible to other spiritual powers, like intellect. I consider three cognitive aspects of willing that are evidence for this irreducibility. We can consider acts of will, including their cognitive aspects, in at least two ways. First, as Aquinas says, acts of will are present to intellectual acts, and I thereby intellectually grasp the structure of acts of will as they occur. Second, Scheler introduces a distinct phenomenological reduction, the "Dionysian reduction," in which I bracket (i.e., stop performing) intellectual acts and just experience the striving of my will (and appetitive and vital drives).[28] Since will arises from subjectivity, I can directly experience will's acts without considering them intellectually.

A first cognitive aspect of willing is described by Aquinas. Willing to attain a good is a sort of experience (*quasi experientiam*) of that good insofar as by my will I "consent" to or affirm the good by resting in (*complacet*) it and feeling my attunement or fit with it.[29] Since all goods are analogically related, to consent to one good is implicitly to feel my attunement with (and so to grasp) all goods as goods.[30] For the will's attunement with a good to be a reliable experience of that good in itself, it must develop in virtue. Unlike intellect, will does not receive forms from beings; it receives only *habitus* such as moral virtues and vices like courage, temperance, cowardice, or lust.[31] *Habitus* are stable, active dispositions to act freely in certain ways. They are infused by God or acquired by habituation or repeated action. As actualities by which I act, they are efficient causes of my free acts, but they do not impose necessity on my acts, nor are they mere mechanical or rote habits; rather they strengthen my ability to quickly and freely pursue a good.[32] Virtues are the health and beauty of the soul, making powers fit with one another and with their proper goods.[33] They

---

28. Max Scheler, *The Constitution of the Human Being*, trans. John Cutting (Milwaukee, Wisc.: Marquette University Press, 2008), 99–100, 401–6; Scheler, *Man's Place in Nature*, 65–68.
29. Aquinas, *ST* I, q.15, a.1.
30. Balthasar, *GL1*, 235–41.
31. See Keiser, *The Natural Desire to See God*.
32. Aquinas, *ST* I, q.49, a.1, 3; Mathew Lu, "*Hexis* within Aristotelian Virtue Ethics," *Proceedings of the American Catholic Philosophical Association* 88 (2015): 197–206; and Mazur et al., *Jacek Woroniecki*, 178.
33. Aquinas, *ST* I, q.55, a.2; Scotus, *Ord*. I, d.17, p.1, q.2, n. 62. Cf. Mary Beth Ingham, "Symphonic Grandeur: Moral Beauty and the Judgement of Harmony in John Duns Scotus," in *Beauty and the Good: Recovering the Classical Tradition from Plato to Duns Scotus*, ed. Alice Ramos (Washington, D.C.: The Catholic University of America Press, 2020), 319–46.

are "connatural" with certain goods—that is, they are of like nature with them, insofar as they fit with them—and thereby incline my will toward those goods. By experiencing this inclination and fit, I "consent" to those goods and know them by "connaturality" or "sympathy." By temperance, for example, I am inclined toward pleasures as I ought to be, and I thereby have a feel for which goods I ought to pursue.[34] Vices render my will less connatural with goods and so less capable of perceiving them in this way. We can intellectually form concepts and judgments on the basis of this felt affinity. However, as with intuitive acts considered in chapter 3, content grasped in acts like this exceeds what we can adequately express in concepts; we best express and call attention to this felt content of these acts by metaphors, myths, and poetic imagery.

We have seen how beauty first impacts multiple powers at once. Beauty is the self-manifestation of being, and as such, it is the radiant appearance of what is true (or intelligible) and good (or loveable). Volitional experience of connaturality with the good is an experience of beauty, as it calls for pursuit, union, admiration, even worship. Experiencing beauty places a normative claim on my will; although I can approach it disinterestedly, I ought not just impassively contemplate it. Rather, an encounter with beauty draws me into dramatic interaction with it. My will must be attuned by virtue to beauties if I am to be drawn into this drama.[35]

In the second cognitive aspect of willing, Scheler describes how in willed striving we experience things resisting our efforts. This is not a sensory or intellectual grasp of properties like pressure or solidity but a grasp of things as withstanding (or presenting difficulties to) my efforts to act upon them, an encounter with the real existence of beings. More than intellectual intuition does, the experience of resistance reveals the sheer otherness of beings, as items with their own forces and efforts, distinct from and often contrary to mine.[36] Once again, matter is not something whose content can be pictured or fully positive grasped; it must be encountered in other ways. Scheler's reduction, by which this is grasped, is named for Nietzsche's "Dionysius," the sphere of experiences in which I try to set aside limiting, content-bestowing form and just experience my

---

34. Aquinas, ST I, q.45, a.2; Aristotle, NE, III.4.1113a30ff; and Maritain, *Creative Intuition in Poetry and Art*, chap. 4.
35. Aristotle, NE, II.9.1109b20–23; X.4.1174b15–35; Balthasar, TD5, 68–75; TL1, 17–32; E, 63–71.
36. Max Scheler, "Idealism," in *Selected Philosophical Essays*, 317–22. Cf. Nicolai Hartmann, *Zum Problem der Realitätsgegebenheit* (Berlin: Pan-Verlagsgesellschaf, 1931); Kohák, *The Embers and the Stars*, 230.

vitality, as in experiences of intoxication, dreams, rhythmic music, ecstatic rituals, mass gatherings, or the "sympathy" or shared feeling mentioned in chapter 1.[37] By matter, I am one with all other material substances, a unity I can feel when I bracket form and meaning bestowing intellectual acts (a sphere of experience that Nietzsche names "Apollo"). But since I always act as formed matter, even within this reduction, other material things always resist my individual efforts. Heidegger and Levinas further describe two distinct kinds of resistance.

Heidegger describes how matter directly appears not just as quantified or as a bearer of tactile properties like hardness or roughness but as a force for changing (seen in the constant change of quantitative properties it undergoes) and for enduring (seen in its persistence through changes). This force is experienced in how matter itself, rather than its sensible or intelligible qualities, resists our efforts.[38] While by hylomorphic, effect-to-cause reasoning, I can conclude that there is a principle of matter underlying change, it is through its felt resistance to willing (or through Dionysian immersion in bodily experiences) that I directly grasp matter's distinctness from anything intelligible like form and grasp its essence as forcefulness. Matter is not just potentiality or desire for form but is also what resists form, requiring expenditure of effort or exertion of power to be formed. Given how it appears, matter has its own proper, irreducible being.[39] Given this experience, any theory in which material substances are nothing but forms is reductionistic. Robert Pasnau and Christos Yannaras have independently argued that substances are just bundles of actualities; what was traditionally called "matter" is just quantitative and qualitative forms.[40] But experiences of resistance show that matter is irreducible to definite, potentially intelligible forms.[41] Since matter's resistance is given as nondefinite, nonquantitative, and nonintelligible, it should be ascribed either directly to prime matter or to another nondefinite property that is in matter prior to substantial form.

Levinas describes the moral resistance of other persons to my will;

---

37. Friedrich Nietzsche, *The Birth of Tragedy*, trans. Francis Golffing (New York: Doubleday, 1956). The Dionysian layer of experience is depicted well in the stories of H. P. Lovecraft.

38. Martin Heidegger, *Aristotle's Metaphysics Q 1–3*, trans. Walter Brogan and Peter Warnek (Bloomington: Indiana University Press, 1995), 75–77. Cf. C. S. Pierce, *Collected Papers*, vol. 1 (Cambridge, Mass.: Harvard University Press, 1965), 149, quoted in Reimers, *Soul*, 42.

39. Suárez, *DM*, d.31, s.11.

40. Pasnau, *Thomas Aquinas on Human Nature*, 131–40; Yannaras, *Person and Eros*, 87–89, citing Gregory of Nyssa, *In Hexaemeron explicatio apologetica*, in PG, v. 44 (Paris: J.-P. Migne, 1863), 69c.

41. Milbank, *Beyond Secular Order*, 265.

willing, like thinking, is always experienced intersubjectively. By willing, I often strive selfishly to attain goods for myself and my community, but when I encounter other persons, they resist my will by morally demanding that I serve them, not use them for my projects. This moral resistance invests my will with responsibility, troubling its complacency and making it beholden to others. I experience the other as other, and my responsibility to him or her, through this resistance to my willing. I do not first intellectually grasp that this other is a person, and then conclude that I must be responsible; rather, I first experience myself called to responsibility in the face of the other, and only then, perhaps, theorize about what it is to be a person. This grasp of the otherness of others and our responsibility through will helps overcome the intellect's totalizing tendency.[42]

This account is phenomenological evidence for a metaphysical distinction that Scotus makes about the will. My will is not just oriented to pursue goods for myself like happiness (*affectio commodi*) but is also oriented to and desires goodness as such (*affectio iustitiae*). This distinction is necessary to safeguard freedom: if I only had the *affectio commodi*, I would always will what I rationally judged most conducive to my happiness.[43] I would not be free in the sense of actually being able to do otherwise than what I did; I would only be free in having a power open to alternative possibilities. Having multiple ends (like having multiple basic goods in the New Natural Law view) gives my will the lack of determination necessary for full freedom. In the encounter with another, I feel myself set free to responsibly pursue goodness as such, or to choose to resist this responsibility.

I propose the following explanation of these orientations in the will. My will, like practical rationality, is naturally oriented and proportioned to my happiness, the full actualization of my natural potencies; by nature, I feel only the *affectio commodi*. My will, however, is obedientially open to other ends (so long as they fall under the formal object *goodness*), which exceed what is naturally proportioned to it, including goodness as such, apart from reference to my happiness. The obediential potency to will goodness as such is the *affectio iustitiae*, and it is actualized in encounter-

---

42. Levinas, *Totality and Infinity*, 84–87, 216–19; David Walsh, *Politics of the Person as the Politics of Being* (Notre Dame, Ind.: University of Notre Dame Press, 2016), 20. For the claim that versions of a view like this are found in Fichte and Hegel, see Roger Scruton, "Confessions of a Skeptical Francophile," *Philosophy* 87 (2012): 477–95.

43. Scotus, *Ord.* II, d.6, q.2. I make no claim as to whether other scholastics, such as Aquinas, posit anything like the *affectio iustitiae*. Cf. Seifert, *Essere e persona*, 277.

ing other persons.[44] Fully self-determining freedom requires this *affectio*; full freedom does not belong to will's natural potency but is received when my will is invested by the moral call of another person, which renders me able to respond in a way that transcends my desire for happiness. Similarly, on Aquinas's view, charitable acts (acts performed out of friendship with God, with his love) and willing to achieve union with God require that our obediential potency be actualized by grace and infused virtues—that is, this willing presupposes encountering another person, God, who gives these gifts.[45]

Just as natural and obediential potencies of my intellect are normally both actualized from the first moment that I think, so both volitional potencies are normally actualized from the first moment that I will. Balthasar describes how in experiencing love displayed on their mother's faces, children are opened to experiencing beings as gifts.[46] This aesthetic experience includes the moral experience of the mother's face's call to responsible freedom and its resistance to the child's self-aggrandizing, self-fulfilling freedom—once again, the full experience of beauty brings one into a dramatic, responsible relation to the beautiful being. The other, the person addressed as "Thou," is encountered not just as someone knowable but as someone who frees my will from being limited to always referring goods to myself and limits freedom by investing it with responsibility. Nonpersonal things can call me to responsibility—for example, natural beauty calls me to admire it for its own sake—but persons first actualize my responsible freedom. However, with the awakening of freedom unrestricted to what is proportioned to my nature, I can also choose worse evils than I could if I chose everything for the sake of happiness. I can be spiteful, inflicting pain though I know it will lead to no one's happiness, if I make that my good, saying, with Milton's Satan, "evil, be thou my good."[47] I can choose among ends and willfully take something other than God as my end, though it would be evil for me to do so.

Scotus notes another, related irreducible feature of will.[48] The practical

---

44. In Scotus's view, both *affectiones* are natural. Calling *affectio iustitiae* "obediential" does not entail that it is supernatural but recognizes that it arises only through encountering others who exceed what is proportionate to my powers.

45. Aquinas, *ST* I-II, q.110; II-II, q.17, a.2; q.23, a.1, 2. See Mark K. Spencer, "Ethical Subjectivity in Levinas and Thomas Aquinas," *The Heythrop Journal* 53, no. 1 (2012): 137–47.

46. Balthasar, *GL5*, 615–18.

47. John Milton, *Paradise Lost and Paradise Regained* (New York: New American Library, 2001), 4.110.

48. Scotus, *Ord.* II, d.6, q.1; d.38, q.un.; III, d.26, q.un. Cf. Tobias Hoffmann, "Freedom Beyond Practical Reason," 1,071–90.

intellect acts as a "combining power" (*vis collativa*), ordering means and ends in plans. Likewise, willing also orders goods, and not just as determined by thinking and planning. I sometimes *will* that some means bring about an end, even when I *know* that it will not happen or that my willing cannot affect whether it happens. For example, I might will superstitiously that an event come about through the use of charms, even though I know that they have no causal power. I might choose to pray that I have done well on a test, even though the event, being past, cannot be now affected by my willing. Or I might will something other than God as my end, even if I know God is my proper end. Sometimes I will to order goods not in a means-end fashion; for example, I will to attain God not as a means to happiness but as a superior good that, when attained, will overflow into the inferior good of my happiness. (One good *overflows* into another when the former efficiently causes the latter as a participation in itself.) By willing, I actively order my life, and determine the importance that goods have for me.[49] I do not create goods' importance; often, I must discover the importance that things actually have, to which I ought to conform myself. But goods have importance that makes a difference to me only if I freely will their importance; no intellectual discovery of a good's importance compels me to conform myself to it. These experiences reveal that my willing is not fully free if its acts' content is sufficiently determined by anything other than me as acting through my will, even by my intellect. Indeed, I can freely choose when to stop reasoning and take a given conclusion of practical reasoning as my final cause for willing and acting.[50] I remain open to alternative possibilities not just given prior conditions but even in the moment of acting. Even while acting, I retain the power to do otherwise, though I cannot simultaneously perform contradictory acts of will.[51]

In a third cognitive act of the will, I grasp myself in willing in a way similar to self-sensing, described in chapter 1. Scheler describes how willing includes direct awareness of my power to act, including an awareness of my ability to freely and effectively use my body. Merleau-Ponty describes how I experience something as a possible object of choice only if it is given as attainable by my bodily powers; I do not experience myself

---

49. On how freedom can act "symbolically," fitting things together, or "diabolically," setting things at variance with each other, see D. C. Schindler, *Freedom from Reality: The Diabolical Character of Modern Liberty* (Notre Dame, Ind.: University of Notre Dame Press, 2019), 151–92.
50. See Sacred Congregation of Studies, *24 Thomistic Theses* (Rome, 1914), thesis 21.
51. Scotus, *Ord.* I, d.38, 39, q.1–5, nn. 16–17.

as freely able to lift certain weights or scale certain heights. In willing, I feel myself as alive, capable of vital exertion.[52] When I have moral virtues or bodily abilities like dancing or playing an instrument, in which bodily powers obey will and intellect, this vital experience is stronger and more pleasant.[53] When I am less virtuous or physically able, but I wish that I were, my body feels like a prison, since its powers resist my will.[54] This resistance also occurs when the body is broken down by aging, suffering, or fatigue; in each case, I feel my freedom betrayed by the loss of my self-sensed power to act.[55] This is more than just not being able to implement willing in my body: it is an experience of a breakdown in willing itself, since will, like intellect, draws from and is directed to the body. As with thinking, I experience willing as both transcending and lived in the body.

The Problem of Divine Causality

Freely willing involves meaningfully actualizing and determining myself; to be free is to be "lord of one's acts" ("*dominus sui actus*").[56] Wojtyła notes that willed efficacy is an experience of self-consciously creating oneself, at least partially causing the narrative of one's life.[57] Free creaturely persons are given to themselves, but they must also, as Bulgakov notes, freely accept themselves and affirm (or "posit") their own existence.[58] A metaphysics of irreducibility must include an account of how the will causes itself to act, without being a self-caused cause (which is logically impossible) or an uncaused cause creating my acts *ex nihilo* (which would reduce me to God). This brings us to the problem of divine causality (anticipated above).[59] This problem has had a long history in Catholic anthropology and theology, beginning with the medieval debate over how God is causally involved in our free acts, and reaching a climax in the sixteenth- and seventeenth-century *de auxiliis* debates between Dominicans and Jesuits over how grace aids our free acts to move toward our supernatural end.

---

52. Scheler, *Formalism in Ethics and Non-Formal Ethics of Values*, 232–34; Merleau-Ponty, *Perception*, 512–15, 527–28. Cf. Michel Henry, *Philosophy and Phenomenology of the Body*, trans. Girard Etzkorn (The Hague: Martinus Nijhoff, 1975), 33, 52–55, 77–81, 106.
53. Aquinas, *ST* I, q.81, a.3, ad 2.
54. *Phaedo* 83a.
55. Levinas, *Totality and Infinity*, 163–69, 222–40.
56. Aquinas, *SCG* III, c. 155.
57. Wojtyła, *The Acting Person*, 66.
58. Bulgakov, *Bride of the Lamb*, 30, building on Fichte and Schelling.
59. Some of the ideas in this section are from Mark K. Spencer, "Divine Causality and Created Freedom," *Nova et Vetera* (English edition) 14, no. 3 (2016): 375–419.

In this section, I raise the problem; further aspects of the problem will be raised in chapters 5 and 6, and a solution given in chapter 6.

According to many scholastic views, including those of Scotus and of Aquinas as interpreted by the Dominican tradition, both I and God cause my free acts.[60] God, as the primary cause of being, is the source of my acts' being, though this does not exclude my genuine, though secondary, causality. Scotists and Thomists reject both *occasionalism* (which reduces all causality to God's causality) and *mere conservationism* (on which God conserves creatures in being, but they alone cause their acts) and favor instead *concurrentism* (on which God both conserves creatures in being and concurs with their acts—that is, acts with them). In most versions of concurrentism, God permits, but does not cause, the sinfulness of my sinful acts, but he directly causes all acts' positively existing features. Concurrentists contend that were positive features of acts not caused by God, they would exist contingently without receiving existence from God; this is impossible, however, as it would require a source of existence other than God, a position some identified with *Manicheanism*. Since an act is an actuality greater than that of the power by which it is done, no power can be reduced to act by itself but must have actuality added to it, and all actuality must ultimately come from God. Some concurrentists held that God directly causes creatures to act. Others held that God directly causes creatures' acts simultaneous with their causing them but that he does not cause their causing of those acts. Still others held that God augments creatures' power or premoves them to act, by which they cause their own act in a way determined by God's decree or determination.[61]

Contingent reality gives itself as participating in one absolute source, identical to the transcendentals as such. Arguments for the existence of God from contingent things, like Aquinas's five ways, are icons pointing to perceptual awareness of God as the pure actuality who is the necessary source of all actuality and who shines through all things.[62] A pure

---

60. Aquinas, *ST* I, q.105, a.4; I-II, q.9, a.6; q.79, a.1, 2; Gloria Frost, "Scotus on How God Causes the Created Will's Volitions," in *Interpreting Duns Scotus: Critical Essays*, ed. Giorgio Pini (Cambridge: Cambridge University Press, 2021). Cf. Reginald Garrigou-Lagrange, *Predestination*, trans. Bede Rose (St. Louis: Herder, 1946), 256–65, 293–94, 319–23.

61. See Alfred Freddoso, "God's General Concurrence with Secondary Causes," *American Catholic Philosophical Quarterly* 68, no. 2 (1994): 132–35; Gloria Frost, "Peter Olivi's Rejection of God's Concurrence with Created Causes," *British Journal for the History of Philosophy* 22, no. 4 (2014): 656–57; and texts cited in chapter 6.

62. On what follows, see the arguments and the unpacking of their conclusions in Aquinas, *ST* I, q.2–11.

actuality is *simple*—that is, lacks parts and passive potentialities, is not made out of anything, and does not participate in anything—since those properties imply lack of actuality. It is *eternal*, that is, it simultaneously, perfectly possesses all its life and activities. In this actuality, everything is really identical—one in actuality and being—with everything else. Lacking the imperfection of passive potentiality, God is also impassible—that is, he cannot be actualized, made more perfect or complete, by receiving anything from outside of himself. All of this can be directly perceived in the absolute beauty that appears through contingent reality, and it can be concluded from effect-to-cause arguments that explain contingent reality. Views like *open theism* and *process theology*, in which God develops in time, or *Manicheanism*, in which there are multiple ultimate sources of being, must be rejected because they conflict with the full range of experience, which reveals one absolute source of all things.

Many scholastics reason that, being impassible, God cannot receive knowledge about creatures but can only know them by knowing his acts of causing them. Were God not a cause of my free acts, it seems he could not know them, nor could he providentially and omnipotently guide the history of the world. While many events are contingent or random in relation to their creaturely causes, they are also entirely ordered and caused by God. On this view, even though God causes my free acts, I am still free, in the sense that I move myself to act through a power that is open to alternatives and undetermined to any act by itself or by any condition prior to my acts. As Matthews Grant argues, God's causing of my act is ontologically and explanatorily simultaneous with, not prior to, my causing of my act.[63]

I object that were this view true, I would not be able to determine myself such that it would be entirely up to me what I do, nor would I be able to do otherwise than I do given all of my act's conditions. On concurrentism, were God to decree or cause a different act, I would perform a different act. Most versions of concurrentism are not good explanations for experiences of freely acting, three of which I now consider.

First, I experience my acts as under judgment by a transcendent source; in experiencing myself to be called to responsibility, I feel my acts to be categorically judged as to whether they are good or evil. Once again,

---

63. W. Matthews Grant, "Can a Libertarian Hold that Our Free Acts Are Caused by God?" *Faith and Philosophy* 27, no. 1 (2010): 22–44; Grant, "Aquinas on How God Causes the Act of Sin without Causing Sin Itself," *The Thomist* 73, no. 3 (2009): 455–96; and W. Matthews Grant, *Free Will and God's Universal Causality: The Dual Sources Account* (London: Bloomsbury, 2019).

the encounter with persons (and beauties more generally) brings me into a dramatic relationship with others, in which I am required to respond. Finite beauties convey my attention to what is absolutely beautiful, and I thereby find myself categorically called to act in certain ways. Beauty, if fully perceived, does not allow me to be Hegel's "beautiful soul," who refuses to act out of a desire to maintain purity.[64] Rather, it requires me to act and then face my acts' moral consequences. I then feel myself to be guilty or justified before what is absolutely beautiful, holy, good, and just.[65] This is an experience of divine providence, and it underlies claims that God judges, punishes, and rewards us for our free acts. But were the aforementioned versions of concurrentism true, God would be unjust in judging, punishing, or rewarding me for my acts, given that I can only act as God decrees. Were God to permit me to do evil, it would be unjust for him to punish me, since he could have caused me to do otherwise, and I could not have done otherwise unless he had caused me to do so. God is not obliged to cause me to do well, but if he causes me to act sinfully, or permits me to act sinfully where that permission is sufficient for my acting sinfully, then he cannot also justly punish me for my sins, since I could not genuinely have done otherwise. It belongs to the very notion of unjust punishment that the one punished have been led to wrongdoing in any sense by the judge or that the judge have permitted the wrong when it was entirely in his power to prevent it. The same can be said, *mutatis mutandis*, regarding rewards for good acts. The experience of being under judgment before the absolutely holy and just one is incompatible with a view on which God entirely causes me to do what I freely do. For this reason, the metaphysician of irreducibility must reject, as unjust, views like those held by many scholastics on which God predestines or chooses, even just by permission, certain persons to receive punishment prior to any consideration of the demerits of their actions.[66] This is not to deny the experience, continually described in the Bible, of being elected by God to receive graces or vocations apart from any connection to one's merits.[67] I just defend the view that God cannot justly reward or punish our acts if God's decrees or acts are sufficient for them to occur.

64. G. W. F. Hegel, *The Phenomenology of Mind*, trans. J. B. Baillie (New York: Harper & Row, 1967), 675–76.
65. Cf. Rudolf Otto, *The Idea of the Holy*, trans. John Harvey (Oxford: Oxford University Press, 1958).
66. Garrigou-Lagrange, *Predestination*.
67. Roberto Calasso, *The Book of All Books*, trans. Tim Parks (New York: Farrar, Strauss and Giroux, 2021), 25.

Second, I experience myself as a gift given to myself, and as able to give myself as a gift to others, including to God. For a gift to be fully given, as Kenneth Schmitz argues, building on Marcel, it must be received, but reception cannot be caused by the giver, or else the purported gift-giving would actually be compulsion or exchange. In giving, the giver risks that gift not be received. As a self-conscious being, I am not merely passive to God's gifts but can actively receive or reject them; while God is not passively affected as pure actuality by my reception of his gift in the sense of taking on new perfections when I receive it, he is affected and vulnerable as giver, insofar as he risks the rejection of his gifts.[68] Were my reception of God's gifts decreed by God, God would not truly be a giver, but that is contrary to how God appears in experience, as when he appears as the shining, giving fullness of beauty. Likewise, it belongs to the notion of gift that its being given not be caused by the recipient. C. S. Lewis rightly says that I experience my will as mine, so that I can freely put it at God's disposal, as a self-gift.[69] Were God to decree that I give myself back to him, that would be appropriation. For me to be able to give myself back to God, the gifts God has given me must be at my disposal, not his. Gift-giving requires separation between giver and recipient, such that although we are created, we do not purely exist by dependence on God.[70] I can also experience myself as appropriated by God, as in being called to a vocation, but this is a distinct experience from giving myself to him. Likewise, one can experience one's acts to be controlled (or "possessed") by a transcendent person, but that, too, is a distinct experience from responsible action and self-gift.[71] Concurrentism cannot account for the experience of giving myself as a gift on my own initiative; it reduces my self-giving to appropriation by God and would render our experience of God as giver illusory. While I experience the ability to give myself as a gift from God, I experience its exercise as up to me. Similarly, I experience myself and others as freely able to follow or violate laws and advice, including those given by God. Were concurrentism true, God's giving of laws and advice would be pointless or just play-acting, since they could not be followed unless God caused us to follow them. Even worse, our dignity as self-conscious, free persons would

---

68. Schmitz, *The Gift*, 44–87, 93. Cf. Marcel, *Homo Viator*, 7–22.

69. C. S. Lewis, *The Four Loves* (London: Fontana Books, 1960) 117–18. Cf. Russell, *The Doctrine of Deification in the Greek Patristic Tradition*, 215–16.

70. Levinas, *Totality and Infinity*, 58. Cf. Ulrich, *Homo Abyssus*, xlvii.

71. Calasso, *The Marriage of Cadmus and Harmony*, 94–95.

be a humiliating illusion since our free acts would ultimately be decreed by God. "Humiliation" is here to be understood not as a proper religious sense of dependence and submission before God but as the absurd condition of seeming to have the dignity of self-possession but not really having it.[72]

Third, I experience myself as able to creatively invent new artifacts, artworks, or styles of acting, in which I reveal myself on my own initiative through content I have made up. This differs experientially from receiving content from another. As Russian theologian Georges Florovksy noted, I experience myself and other human persons as the primary shapers of history.[73] Similarly. Rahner describes how I can irrevocably commit myself to a course of action or a moral stance that shapes all my acts.[74] Were God the concurring cause of the content of all these free acts, what is given in them would again be deceptive. I would seem to contribute content to reality on my own initiative, but really, I could not have done otherwise than I do. There would be no human creativity or what Tolkien called (as we saw in chapter 3) "subcreation"; rather, all apparent creativity would actually be, contrary to experience, just discovering what God has decreed. This is not to deny that creativity involves something like discovery: the author discovers who his or her characters are, the sculptor discovers the sculpture in the block of stone and creates just by removing pieces of the block, the engineer discovers the perfect form for a machine by discovering how its function best fits with nature.[75] Creativity requires obedience, but in each of these cases, there is also the experience of adding something new to the world. Concurrentism reduces the world to something like God's play or novel rather than something serious and fully real, in which we shape history as God's partners.

Baroque Jesuit scholastics like Luis de Molina and Francisco Suárez moved toward a view in which creaturely freedom is genuinely self-determining. In their view, God orients me toward the good and gives existence to any free act of mine, but I alone determine which acts I perform, by cooperating or not with the God-given general orientation to goodness.[76]

---

72. See arguments from Sartre, Nietzsche, and Robert Browning in Schmitz, *The Gift*.

73. Paul Gavrilyuk, *Georges Florovsky and the Russian Religious Renaissance* (Oxford: Oxford University Press, 2014), 82.

74. Karl Rahner, "Theology of Freedom," in *Theological Investigations*, vol. 6, trans. Karl-H. and Boniface Kruger (New York: Seabury, 1974), 185; Crosby, *The Selfhood of the Human Person*, 91.

75. Aristotle, *Met.*, IX.6.1048a20–30; Antoine de Saint-Exupéry, *Wind, Sand and Stars*, trans. Lewis Galantiére (Orlando, Fla.: Harcourt, 1992), 41–43.

76. Luis de Molina, *Liberi arbitrii cum gratiae donis, divina praescientia, providentia, praedestinatione, et reprobatione concordia* (Antwerp: Ex officina typographica Ioachimi Trognaesii, 1595), 7–8, 109–10;

However, this view still does not capture freedom as experientially given. First, we experience many evil acts and acts that are the bearers of merely earthly values to not reveal God, but on this view, God directly causes each act and so should be revealed in them. Second, another feature of this view is that there are "conditionals of freedom" that God eternally knows, according to which for each situation there is something that I would freely do were I in that situation.[77] But if I am free, then there is no particular thing that I would do were I in some situation, which God could know prior to my acting. If we are free as we experience ourselves to be, then there are no true conditionals of freedom. The solution to this problem of reconciling our will's free causality with God's being the ultimate source of all created being must wait until chapter six, after further aspects of this problem have emerged. I turn now to a fuller discussion of the will's self-determination.

The Temporality of the Will, Epektasis, and the Human End

Henri Bergson linked experiences of freedom to those of time, which is given in two ways.[78] First, moments of quantitatively measurable time are given in experiences of mathematical or scientific abstraction and representation as points on a continuum, which can be considered from a perspective external to the present, a "view from nowhere." Temporal moments in this sense are qualitatively identical and only mathematically related, with nothing distinguishing past, present, and future. Second, qualitative "duration" is the interior sense of time's flow, similar to the time-consciousness described in chapter 2 and the stream of auto-affection in chapter 1. Each durational moment has a qualitatively distinct character: some are significant, others boring; some stretches of time move quickly, others slowly. Duration moves toward the future and is open to what is new. In what Bergson calls "intuition" or "sympathy" (a sort of knowledge by connaturality), I grasp moments' qualitative character by living in them.

Suárez, *DM*, d.24, s.1, nn. 6–19; s.2, nn. 7–15; s.4, nn. 3–8, 15, 21; and Francisco Suárez, *De concursu, motione, et auxilio Dei*, in *Opera omnia*, v. 11 (Paris: Vivès, 1858), 38, 42, 143–44, 183.

77. Molina, *Concordia*, 202–8; Suárez, *DM*, d.22, s.4, nn. 38–39; Francisco Suárez, *De scientia Dei futurorum contingentium*, in *Opera omnia*, v. 11, 369–73.

78. Henri Bergson, *Time and Free Will*, trans. L. Pogson (Mineola: Dover, 2001); "An Introduction to Metaphysics," in *The Creative Mind*, trans. T. E. Hulme (Mineola: Dover, 2010). Cf. J. M. E. McTaggart, "The Unreality of Time," *Mind* 17, no. 68 (1908): 457–73.

I thereby experience my ability to freely do new things at each moment. To act and create myself is to do more than I intended; there is an excess to action, and so all creative acting involves giving or sacrificing myself, so as to open up this newness.[79] Some reductionistically see duration as a good sense of time and measurable time a fallen sense, but each discloses genuine, good features of time and human experience: quantitative time allows for intellectual understanding and technological control, with all the benefits that can bring, while qualitative time allows for deeper insight into the ways that time is ordered toward persons.[80]

Even when engaged in continuous activities (*energeiai*), rather than processes (*kineseis*), like feeling pleasure or contemplating, I feel the opening up of new free possibilities, including the possibility of deepening the quality of these activities. In scholastic terms, by activities I share in *aeviternity*, a mode of temporality involving not quantifiable processes but whole activities succeeding one another, and in *eternity*, having one's whole life simultaneously.[81] We saw in chapter 3 that our natural and supernatural ends involve contemplating God, which involves participating in eternity, but we are not only intellectual but also volitional beings: our wills must be fulfilled—actualized in creative, self-determining, durational or future-oriented acts—for us to be fulfilled. Fulfillment must involve bringing all our powers to full performance.[82] Our intellectual acts are oriented to being manifested in creative, self-determined, free acts; in grasping the one, unchanging God, we grasp goodness itself, which ever overflows abundantly. Given the durational, open-ended structure of willing and acting, we could not be fulfilled unless, while contemplating, we were also open to new moments and creative acts. Our end must include ongoing creative willing, but since it is part of our end, that ongoing creative willing cannot be a process that is a means to an end. But creative willing is not always a process: it can be done for its own sake, as in liturgical action (to which I return throughout part 2 of this book).

The end required by the experienced structure of our will is captured in Gregory of Nyssa's notion of *epektasis*, in which one continually contemplates and participates in God's eternal, restful activity (which involves no

---

79. Milbank, *Theology and Social Theory*, 210–19, building on Blondel, *Action* (1893).
80. Griffiths, *Decreation*, chaps. 15, 16; Jacques Maritain, *Bergsonian Philosophy and Thomism*, trans. Mabelle Andison (New York: Philosophical Library, 1955), 155.
81. Aquinas, *ST* I, q.10.
82. Pinckaers, The *Sources of Christian Ethics*, 12.

processes, becoming, or striving), but in which this contemplation continually deepens, becoming qualitatively more intense, penetrating ever further into the incomprehensible mystery that is God.[83] At each moment, one's felt and willed desire for God is heightened and simultaneously fulfilled, without weariness. I add that this involves creatively performing ever-new, freely self-determined acts. Such an end gives rest to the intellect's restless search for knowledge, but in attaining a vision of God (or, to a limited extent, in any contemplation of beauty), there is born in us a more intense but restful longing for ever-deepening union with that good, even though it is already securely possessed. Restful longing is deepened and fulfilled just in contemplation and enjoyment, not requiring striving or a process to be fulfilled. This ever-deepening desire is motivated not by unfulfilled lack and need but by respect, reverence, and awe for the beautiful being one contemplates, which impel ever-deeper union with that beauty.[84] As aesthetician Byung-Chul Han describes it, the most profound beauties do not just bestow satisfying peace on us but also wound us (and even, as we have seen, terrify us), opening us in vulnerability to deeper exposure to beauty, and veil themselves, inviting (or seducing) us to awe-struck penetration beyond those veils, and so to deeper perception and enjoyment of beauty; through these features, great beauties give ever-deepening satisfaction.[85]

This account allows a further *rapprochement* between new and traditional natural law theories. Seeing God fulfills intellect's natural tendency, as traditional natural law affirms, but this fulfillment, as an intellectual act, is oriented to manifestation in free action, which is needed for our entire fulfillment. This free action requires taking responsibility for and bestowing goods and gifts upon other persons. While traditional natural law is correct that contemplation has a central place in our end, a complete account of our end must involve many goods, as new natural theory contends. A helpful model for our end is Albert's and Bonaventure's notion of

---

83. Gregory of Nyssa, *Contra Eunomium*, in PG, v. 45 (Paris: J.-P. Migne, 1863), 339–40. Cf. Balthasar, *TL2*, 99; Griffiths, *Decreation*, chap. 6; Liviu Petcu, "The Doctrine of Epektasis," *Revista Portuguesa de Filosofia* 73, no. 3 (2017): 771–82; and Christopher Brown, *St. Thomas on God and Perfect Human Happiness: Philosophical Problems, Thomistic Solutions* (Washington, D.C.: The Catholic University of America Press, 2021), chap. 2, objects that different persons will have union with God to different degrees based on merits, and that such merits cannot be increased after death—but on the *epektasis* view, we can deepen union beyond what we merited, which would be unjust. In response, we could reject this view of merit, or respond that each person's original "level" of union will continually intensify but that different people will eternally have different "levels" of union—say, participations in different divine formalities.

84. Carnes, *Beauty*, 101–2, 166; Brandon Dahm, "Distinguishing Desire and Parts of Happiness: A Response to Grisez," *American Catholic Philosophical Quarterly* 89, no. 1 (2015): 97–114.

85. Byung-Chul Han, *Saving Beauty*, trans. Daniel Steuer (Cambridge: Polity, 2018), 27–45, 67–81.

affective cognition, a union of speculative and practical intellect, such that one enjoys God both intellectually and with affection and will.[86]

Obedience and Creativity in the Will

Nicolas Berdyaev contends that to be free is to be fundamentally self-determining, self-creative, and self-perfecting; this is a more fundamentally and continually given layer of freedom than being able to choose among alternatives. We can choose among alternatives only because we can determine ourselves. To be free is also to be able to act for truth and goodness; this aspect of freedom is more perfect than the others, but we can only achieve it through self-determination and choice among alternatives. To regard ourselves as free only inasmuch as we can act for truth and goodness is to be, in Berdyaev's terms, *enslaved* by truth and goodness rather than freely responding to their call. It is in our power to follow this call, to reject it and assert our own power, or to abdicate self-determining freedom and live in slavery to, for example, biological nature, an idea of God, society, or the lure of sex, allowing these to control our actions rather than freely determining ourselves to obey.[87] Freedom is called to responsibility but, to be fulfilled in its nature, it must respond by conscious self-determination.

Being self-determining allows us to reject those calls, engaging in wrongdoing (refusing obedience to legitimate calls of natural powers and values) and sin (refusing obedience to God). We experience ourselves as radically fallen, disordered, and concupiscent, tending to slavery in Berdyaev's sense, yet even these tendencies, especially their expression in overreaching or wanting more than we should (*pleonexia*), perversely reveal our orientation to self-transcendence and the will's creative openness. Fulfillment requires renunciation of desires, even the sacrifice of one's will to God in the sense of continually offering it to God, but it cannot involve enslavement, refusal to act as a self-determining person.

By creatively, freely taking up what is given in my nature, environment, community, history, and relation to God, I create, as Berdyaev and Hildebrand say, a *personality*, an unrepeatable, unique *Gestalt* of characteristics or "style" by which I possess myself and freely, authentically engage with

---

86. Albert, *In I Sent.*, d.1, a.4, 18–9; Bonaventure, *In I Sent.*, proem., q.3, 13.
87. Berdyaev, *Freedom and the Spirit*, 121–31; Nicholas Berdyaev, *Slavery and Freedom*, trans. R. M. French (New York: Charles Scribner's Sons, 1944). Cf. Balthasar, *TD2*, 207–43.

others.⁸⁸ We find ourselves both normatively called by given values and natural law, and called to authenticity, to be "true to ourselves," freely developing personalities and responding to calls in a way that fits with the unique person each of us is and wills to be. Discovering and harmonizing these calls is a key feature of moral life; it is reductionistic to only focus on one of these calls. While my obediential potencies can be actualized without my freely allowing it, I must freely accept this actualization to live authentically, without enslavement to those I obey.⁸⁹ I ought to accept and conform myself to what is given in obedience, but I must determine the importance, meaning, and value they have for me; it is reductionistic of this experience to regard us purely as determined by that which I obey. That I give importance to things reveals my intrinsic importance or dignity, since nothing can give what it does not have.⁹⁰ Because of this dignity, it is wrong and enslaving to objectify or commodify persons: any practice that renders a person a mere object of use by another (or by oneself), a mere means to something whose value is given only by persons and so is less than the value of persons, is wrong, as occurs in making or viewing pornography (which treats persons as means to sexual pleasure) or in kinds of employment that treat persons and their labor as mere means to the value of some product.

V. Bradley Lewis worries that on views like Berdyaev's, everyone would have a right to determine the value of things in any way they see fit.⁹¹ Indeed, Berdyaev holds that natural causality and teleology are deterministic, automatic tendencies; that act-potency metaphysics entails that lower actualities (like ours) are entirely determined by higher ones (like God); and that freedom and personhood are opposed to anything graspable by metaphysical reasoning, which is all intrinsically enslaving, and so to be resisted. In making these claims, he overlooks the analogies to freedom in nature, and he fails to see that natural tendencies have their highest expression in freedom. Freedom is called, not necessarily enslaved, by natural tendencies. Nature does not in itself pose a threat to freedom; views that oppose the two, as Berdyaev's does, are reductionistic of both. But

---

88. Berdyaev, *Slavery and Freedom*, 22–31; Hildebrand, *Liturgy and Personality* (Steubenville, Ohio: Hildebrand Project, 2016), 13–19. Cf. Jacek Woroniecki's distinction (*Woroniecki*, 43–44) between *personality*, a self-guided formation of powers, and *personalence*, perfected personality oriented to the true good.
89. Cf. Berdyaev, *The Meaning of the Creative Act*, 115–18. Some might worry that this excludes cognitively disabled persons from authenticity; this will be addressed in chapter 8.
90. J. David Velleman, "A Right of Self-Termination?" *Ethics* 109, no. 3 (1999): 606–28.
91. V. Bradley Lewis, "Personalism and Common Good," in *Subjectivity*, 189–91.

we should not (like Lewis) hold that this reductionism follows necessarily from holding that we creatively develop ourselves. Our wills are both obediential and creative, not only natural and dependent but also free and self-determining. In receiving being from God, we are constituted by him as autonomous and self-creative, called to freely conform ourselves to his life but also able to reject this. Dependency and autonomy are formally distinct transcendental relations in the will, which must be developed together in virtue.[92] I am called to add my own affirmation to gifts I am first given, and I must do so to have a fulfilled, irreducible personality. Lublin Thomist Andrew Woznicki sees in this movement the will's intersubjective, temporal character: I first receive calls and autonomy, then I give my creative response; then I must *wait* for a response from others, to which I must again respond.[93]

We must also avoid *Pelagianism*, according to which we can, by natural willing, determine ourselves in any way. To will higher goods than those to which we are naturally, intellectually ordered—and to turn away from selfish, sinful notions of happiness, rectifying the will's ordering once it is disordered—requires obediential reception of grace or assistance from God. Like the view that we have a natural intellectual desire for God in himself, Pelagianism reduces us to what we are by nature, not recognizing our openness to obediential supplementation by transcendent principles. Although Pelagianism rightly emphasizes our ability for self-determination, it presents too pure and sunny a picture of the will to match the full range of experience.[94]

The will is vulnerable, influenced and beset by bodily tendencies, conscious and unconscious, and by influences and judgments from the world and God. While dependency and vulnerability imply that we are limited in actuality, embracing dependency and obedience can lead to higher values, like holiness; as we saw in chapter 3, inferiority in actuality does not necessarily imply inferiority in value. Authentic self-creation requires not self-assertion, which enslaves one to one's own will, but self-transcendence in pursuit of goodness, which requires self-renunciation. However, virtues

92. See Georges Florovsky, "Creation and Creaturehood," in *Creation and Redemption*, vol. 3 of *The Collected Works of Georges Florovsky* (Belmont, Mass.: Norland, 1976), 46–49; Blondel, *Action (1893)*, 14; Wojtyła, *The Acting Person*, 69–70; and MacIntyre, *Dependent*, 1–10, 119–28.

93. Andrew Woznicki, *Metaphysical Animal: Divine and Human in Man* (New York: Peter Lang, 1996), 183–86.

94. See Peter Brown, *Augustine of Hippo: A Biography* (Berkeley: University of California Press, 2000), 346–53, 383–99.

emphasizing dependence and self-renunciation, like piety and gratitude, require authentic, self-determined responses in order to not become enslaving. As Hildebrand recognized, I can be so focused on responding to others that I fail to develop my personality and a legitimate sense of what is of concern to me (*Eigenleben*).[95] Virtue requires an interplay between dependence and autonomy, self-renunciation and self-determination.

The Will and Our Lack of Stable Identity

The experience of freedom is also, as Sartre showed, an experience of a lack of a stable identity.[96] Motivated by atheism, Sartre goes too far in this claim, reducing us to our freedom and claiming that I lack any given nature or teleological orientation.[97] Rather, I have a given identity (for example, my body, nature, and past) whereby I exist "in-itself." I can never entirely identify myself with anything existing "in-itself," however, for I also exist "for-itself," as one who must freely live in accord with or refuse those givens. I can detach myself from all given realities; my freedom allows me to "nihilate," to withdraw from what is given, as when I question or doubt it, and then act toward it as I will. To be free is to have concern for what I will be, by deciding on and aiming at a stable identity in which I coincide with what I value most.[98] I am irreducible to and transcend what I am actually at any moment, since I must freely choose at every moment. Inasmuch as they take on new actualities, all creatures are irreducible to what they are at a given moment, but unfree creatures are actualized by beings extrinsic to them, while a free person is a self-determining cause (*causa sui*).[99]

Since I must transcend what I am at any moment, I always lack a completely stable identity, and my will has an infinitude and absoluteness in its orientation to self-transcendence. All of this again requires that my end be *epektatic*. My will is structured such that I must continually choose and affirm what I shall be; even in seeing God, I shall not be identical to him,

---

95. Dietrich von Hildebrand, *The Nature of Love*, trans. John F. Crosby (South Bend, Ind.: St. Augustine's Press, 2009), 204–5.

96. See Stephen Wang, *Aquinas and Sartre: On Freedom, Personal Identity, and the Possibility of Happiness* (Washington, D.C.: The Catholic University of America Press, 2009), especially 89–90. Cf. Ulrich, *Homo Abyssus*, 323.

97. Cf. Burgos, *An Introduction to Personalism*, 220.

98. Jean Paul Sartre, *Being and Nothingness*, trans. Hazel Barnes (New York: Washington Square Press, 1984), 60–63, 138–40, 560–82.

99. Aristotle, *Met.*, I.2.982b25–27.

and I shall desire to participate more deeply in him. While the lack of stable identity can be a source of restlessness in this life, it is consistent with resting in God and deepening an identity received from him, without ever ceasing to receive this identity. This ceaseless excess of willing is grand and noble, yet it also allows vices like haughtiness, pride, and an extreme focus on autonomy. Our will's lack of stable identity is also poor and vulnerable, yet this is the basis for virtues like obedience, humility, and piety. Furthermore, as Levinas describes, my creative quest for an identity is challenged when I encounter the command that other persons' dignity and suffering places on me to serve them. This call also requires epektatic, unshirkable moral action; even in perfect happiness, we shall be oriented to endlessly bestow goods on others, even if they have no suffering to alleviate.[100]

Sartre observes that since I must freely determine myself, and my freedom is given to me (i.e., I did not choose to exist as a free person), freedom gives me a responsibility to choose for myself; as we saw earlier from Bulgakov, persons must be able to posit themselves.[101] Even apart from the calls of persons, values, natural law, and grace, freedom makes normative demands on me. Just as every intellectual act involves an implicit perspective on being as such, so, as Albert Camus notes, every volitional act is an implicit answer to the question of the value of my life and of the whole world, the question of whether life is worth living.[102] To evade this question and just passively receive my value from others is to act in what Berdyaev called enslavement and Sartre called "bad faith."[103] To be authentically moral requires that I will for myself whatever I will, but contrary to those like Kant who hold that this means I am a pure end in myself, and that I must give myself my moral law and never receive it from others, experience reveals that I receive my value and the moral law obediently.[104] We are both rooted in a given order to which we are called to conform ourselves and alienated from anything given, in the very structure of free willing. Affirming radical, existential freedom does not imply that freedom is opposed to the body, to the inclinations of my nature for the good, or to being formed in that inclination by *habitus* like virtues. Rather, it is to say

---

100. Cf. Marion, *In Excess*, chap. 5.
101. Sartre, *Being and Nothingness*, 707–8.
102. Camus, *The Myth of Sisyphus*, 3.
103. Sartre, *Being and Nothingness*, 87ff.
104. Immanuel Kant, *Grounding for the Metaphysics of Morals*, trans. James Ellington (Indianapolis, Ind.: Hackett, 1993), chap. 2; Charles Taylor, *The Ethics of Authenticity* (Cambridge, Mass.: Harvard University Press, 1991) 25–29.

that freedom is both oriented to and affected by my body and nature, and must take up and obey those givens anew at every moment; we have, in Servais Pinckaers's terms, both "freedom for excellence," oriented to and fulfilled by genuine goodness, and "freedom of indifference," open to any self-determination.[105] Any ethics or politics that denies one of these aspects of freedom does not prescribe a flourishing life. Trying to overcome alienation and our intrinsic lack of complete rootedness by giving a complete identity to persons—say, as citizens of a nation—is enslaving and, as such, reductionistic. As Søren Kierkegaard saw, we must assume both our finitude and our infinitude, in relation to God; to reject either or both, or to reconcile them without obedience to God, is to despair, to view oneself reductionistically.[106]

A Metaphysics of Free Actuality

Some intellectualists argue that since the will is an intellectual appetite, reasons completely explain why we choose one thing over another. Otherwise, our choices would be arbitrary and not free at all. Every actualization must have a sufficient reason or prior explanation; nothing can reduce itself (or another) from potency to act except by a prior equal or greater actuality, since nothing can give what it does not have. Any actuality in an effect must be drawn from an actuality in a cause. Furthermore, some insist that an act is free or rationally self-determined only to the extent that it aims at one's genuine good and flourishing, that is, insofar as one's act is caused by correct reasons.[107]

But while our reasons motivate action, they cannot be sufficient or determining causes of or reasons for our acts. My experience of free action is not of acting spontaneously or randomly, nor of doing only what reason dictates; rather, in free acts, I contribute meaningful content such that I meaningfully and sufficiently determine what I do; my *election* adds to my reasons a meaningful explanation why I choose some good, but this meaning is grasped in performing the act of will, which is (as we saw) a power with cognitive aspects. This experienced, meaningful aspect of

---

105. Pinckaers, *The Sources of Christian Ethics*, 335–36. Cf. Nikolaos Loudovikos, *Analogical Identities: The Creation of the Christian Self* (Turnhout: Brepols, 2019), 9–10.

106. Søren Kierkegaard, *The Sickness unto Death*, trans. Howard V. and Edna H. Hong (Princeton, N.J.: Princeton University Press, 1983).

107. See, for example, David Bentley Hart, *That All Shall Be Saved* (New Haven, Conn.: Yale University Press, 2019), Fourth Meditation.

Principles of Freedom 197

willing is neither deterministic (as it would be if reasons or grasped goods sufficiently explained my acts) nor a random selection. This contribution by will of a sufficient condition for free acts is "mysterious" or "dark" to intellectual explanation, but it is entirely meaningful to the agent who performs the act.[108] I grant that for me to freely reduce myself from potency to act toward any good, I must already have an actuality that is equal to or greater in actuality to my act, on the basis of which I act. But unlike other actualities, it cannot be a fully determinate perfection, such that it would fully specify the content of my acts.

To explain this, I propose that an aspect of the soul's mode of being is *free actuality*, by which the will actualizes and determines itself, and which has two aspects. First, my will naturally aims at happiness and obedientially at other ends. These acts of aiming at an end are given to my will, not self-determined. Through them, I can reduce myself from potency to act with regard to any particular act undertaken in pursuit of that end. Those given acts of aiming at an end provide the "surplus" (*superabundans sufficiens*) of actuality that allows me to determine myself to any act I choose in that pursuit, reducing my will from potency to act in a way undetermined by anything other than myself.[109] More fundamental than my "gnomic" power to choose (to use terminology introduced by Maximus the Confessor) is my "natural" will or open directedness, in my soul's very being, toward ends and the total good of my being.[110] Second, the lack of determination in this free actuality is provided by the fact that my acts of intending ends are participations in God's infinite freedom. Just as this is a distinct kind of actuality, so also is it a distinct kind of participation. In being free, I do not take on the definite characteristics of infinite freedom, that is, I do not automatically will what God wills. Rather, to participate in God's freedom is to share in his openness to any act. To share in God in this way is to be separated from him, that is, enabled to act on my own.[111] For this reason, I can be free—creatively self-determining "in good faith"—even when I do not pursue my genuine good.

My natural free actuality is finite, restricted with respect to those acts

---

108. Mazur et al., *Jacek Woroniecki*, 60–61; Calasso, *Ardor*, 61–62; and Nicolas Berdyaev, *Spirit and Reality*, trans. George Reavey (New York: Scribner's, 1939), 33, 115.
109. Scotus, *Ord.* I, d.3, q.2, n. 520; *QM*, bk.9, q.15, 683; *Rep.* II, d.26, q.un. (Vivès 23:125–33).
110. Loudovikos, *Analogical Identities*, 69–70.
111. Levinas (*Totality and Infinity*, 58–59) sees separation and being created as free as not involving participation, but that is a reductionistic view of participation: being free just involves a unique kind of participation.

it allows me to perform, since I have it by being ordered to a specific end, happiness proportioned to my nature. By being so ordered, I can pursue any good intellectually graspable as conducive to happiness. This gives me the dignity described above, which I have not purely as an end in myself but as oriented to a dignifying end. I do not, just by having free actuality, have the actuality or value of any act that it allows me to perform. Just as *intelligere* in the soul together with apprehended actualities in phantasms allow me to perform any particular intellectual act, so free actuality in the soul together with apprehended goods allow me to perform new free acts and add value to myself, shaping the course and value of my life. Actualizing my will's obediential potencies adds both orientations to new ends, and further free actuality, whereby I can reduce myself to act toward those ends. For example, I can respond to grace only by a free actuality that is an aspect of grace. I freely act only on the basis of given free actualities, but these never determine my acts; they are the surplus actuality that allows new self-determinations. Since freedom has this self-determining structure, God cannot ensure by giving grace that any given person will reach union with him. We can act against fulfillment or act freely without perfect knowledge, and so hell, continual separation from God, remains a definite possibility for human persons, though so does salvation for all. But all of this discussion of dignity requires a more focused discussion of the irreducibility of our value, and it is to that which I now turn.

Chapter 5 Affectivity and the Principles of Value

Jorge J. E. Gracia describes how most reductionisms make an *ontological* claim (that the reduced thing is replaceable by, nothing but, or entirely explained by that to which it is reduced) and an *axiological* claim (that the thing being reduced is of less value than that to which it is reduced).[1] So far, I have focused mostly on ontological irreducibility. Now, I must investigate value in itself, which will reveal our irreducible value and the irreducibility of value as such. I begin by considering how acts are motivated; this will unveil a new principle of being, *modes of importance*, including values. I also describe, following the personalists, an irreducible power of the soul, *spiritual affectivity* or *heart*, which has to do with value.[2]

Motivations by Subjective Satisfaction, Objective Goods, and Values

We are motivated in several irreducible ways. By motivation in the present context, I mean something that draws us to act in some way insofar as it gives itself as important in some way. I consider the experience of each mode of motivation and importance as they have been described by phenomenologists and then consider whether these experiences can be causally explained by metaphysical principles posited by scholastics. If no scholastically posited principle explains or fits with an experience of

---
1. Gracia, *Metaphysics and Its Task*, 166–68.
2. Burgos, *An Introduction to Personalism*, 225–26.

motivation, I propose ways that the scholastic metaphysical framework can be expanded to do so. While for the sake of metaphysical and phenomenological precision I consider each motivation in itself, each is rarely experienced in isolation from the others. To hold that we usually do or ought to have one motivation purely, apart from others (as Kant, for example, holds) is reductionistic. Utilitarianism, egoistic eudaimonism, and any view in which we are reduced to consumers, desire-maximizers, or self-interested rational agents are reductionistic of the full range of ways we are motivated, insofar as they hold that we always act for our own sakes or for pleasure. I first consider three modes of motivation that Hildebrand describes.[3]

First, I can be motivated by what is *subjectively satisfying*—that is, I pursue a good because I prefer it or see it as conducive to feeling pleasure or satisfaction, regardless of whether I *ought* to find it satisfying or whether it fulfills my nature. *Being subjectively satisfying* is a mode of importance that I confer on objects by my desires, feelings, wishes, choices, or beliefs; after conferring this importance, I can freely pursue satisfying goods to achieve happiness, conceived egoistically or in community with others. We saw in chapter 3 how (for example, in making artifacts) I confer intentional forms on beings, whereby they take on new meanings; I similarly confer this mode of importance. We saw in chapter 4 that I must have importance in myself if I can confer it on others; an instance of that conferral is experienced here.

Second, I can be motivated to pursue something because it is an *objective good for a person*: it fulfills a need, it is a particular or common end to which a person is naturally or obedientially ordered, or it adds perfection to a person (or, at least, I believe it meets one of these conditions). Natural law reasoning is concerned with these goods; I feel normative force in grasping them, and they engender desires or appetites. Some objective goods, those the scholastic tradition calls "beautiful goods" (*bona honesta*), fulfill a person only when pursued for their own sake; for example, God as common good of all creatures fulfills us when loved for his own sake and loved more than ourselves, and when our happiness is subordinated to and overflows from him.[4] To be motivated by objective goods for a person is not to be motivated purely egoistically or altruistically, but to be motivated

---

3. The following paragraphs draw upon Hildebrand, *Ethics*, chap. 3.
4. Aquinas, *ST* I-II, q.2, a.8; q.3, a.1; q.90, a.2; II-II, q.3.

to realize goods wherever they are found. Still, if I love God as objectively good, my pursuit of him essentially includes a reference to the happiness of myself or of others in my motivational state.

Third, some goods motivate by having *value* or *importance in themselves*: they give themselves as being such that they ought to exist even if no one knows or values them, and as worth responding to for their own sake or for the sake of something else that has importance in itself (regardless of whether they fulfill any power, teleological orientation, or preference). We can freely order our acts toward values without considering or being motivated by their relation to anyone's happiness.[5] To experience something as valuable is to experience it categorically or unconditionally calling for a response. Value is a source of normative force beyond goods discussed by natural law theories. We are confronted by many kinds of normative force: we are bound cognitively to logical standards, aesthetically to standards of appreciation, and morally such that violation would render us guilty or blameworthy. In each case, the value appears as radiantly self-manifesting—that is, as a kind of beauty. Examples of value include the beauty of Haydn's *Emperor Quartet*, which calls for aesthetic admiration; the nobility of Socrates's death, which calls for emulation; the justice of the possible situation of equality among races, which calls for realization; and the holiness of God, which, apart from any reference to his benefiting us, calls for worship. (By holiness, I mean the combination of bliss, vitality, beauty, justice, glory, might, uncanny and awe-inspiring numinousness, and tremendous and fascinating mystery whereby a being is wholly set apart from others.[6]) Whereas natural law ethics is rooted in our orientation to objective goods, value ethics adds that we find ourselves called to transcend our pursuit of fulfillment so as to respond to what presents itself as a categorical norm.

However, the deepest happiness results from responding to values. For example, appreciating beauty in itself requires allowing it to confer joy upon us.[7] Valuable objects are not sought such that they overflow

---

5. There are antecedents for value-motivation in the mystical tradition, for example, in the "dark night of the soul," which involves self-transcendence toward God while setting aside one's own fulfillment. See, for example, John of the Cross, *The Sayings of Light and Love*, in *Collected Works of St. John of the Cross*, trans. Kieran Kavanaugh and Otilio Rodriguez (Washington, D.C.: ICS Publications, 1991), 86–87, n. 20.

6. Scheler, *Formalism in Ethics and Non-Formal Ethics of Values*, 93–94; Otto, *The Idea of the Holy*, 12–24.

7. Hildebrand, *The Nature of Love*, chap. 5. Romano Guardini (*The Lord*, trans. Elinor Castendyk Briefs [South Bend, Ind.: Gateway, 1954], 90) objects that taking oneself to be motivated purely by value,

into our happiness; rather, the happiness received from them is either part of the response that is due to them or is evoked by the value without our willing it. We can be motivated by value in at least two irreducible ways. First, I can be motivated purely by value. Acting on this motivation, I avoid totalizing the valuable object, since I respond to it for its own sake, rather than trying to comprehend or control it, or subordinate it to my projects. Second, I can be motivated simultaneously by value and by the happiness I expect to receive from it.[8] I am in such a case fulfilled not by focusing on my happiness, nor by ignoring my happiness, but by transcending myself and my concerns for my own happiness in giving myself over to a response to the value.[9] This second value-motivation often involves being motivated by a combination of value and objective goodness. Most importantly, love for a particular person joins these motivations in what Hildebrand calls a "super value-response."[10] Sometimes, I first love another person entirely for her sake, but then a special affinity for her arises in my heart and she becomes an objective good for me, one who is fulfilling to me precisely because I first recognized her value. Love involves being concerned for the good of another (*intentio benevolentiae*) as other, not as a part of myself or as "another self," and intending some form of union with that other. This *intentio unionis* manifests itself as a desire that is a need for the other when I am not fully united with her; as in the account of *epektasis* considered in chapter 4, it ceases to be a need but increases and intensifies when union is achieved.[11]

Love motivated by super value-response requires perceiving the beloved as an unrepeatable person who embodies a unique value, a beauty entirely her own (*Gesamtschönheit*).[12] The gaze of love perceives the other to be unique and unrepeatable. This is not to say that I could define what makes my beloved unique, nor is it to say that I could, in a thought-experimental situation in which there is a qualitatively identical duplicate of her, distinguish the two. Rather, when perceiving this person as person, I positively perceive that she is unrepeatable and unique. I grasp that

---

without thought of reward, is rooted in pride. While this is a danger, it does not necessarily follow, especially motivation by value involves receiving happiness from the valuable object as a gift.

8. Dietrich von Hildebrand, *Moralia*, vol. 9 of *Gesammelte Werke* (Regensburg: Verlag Josef Habbel, 1980), 316, drawing on Josef Seifert, *Was ist und was motiviert eine sittliche Handlung?* (Regensburg: Pustet, 1976).
9. Hildebrand, *The Nature of Love*, chap. 9.
10. Hildebrand, *The Nature of Love*, 118–19, 147–79.
11. Hildebrand, *The Nature of Love*, 76, 144–45, 163–69. Cf. Aquinas, *ST* II-II, q.27, a.2.
12. Hildebrand, *The Nature of Love*, 22–23. Cf. Aristotle, *EE*, VIII.3.1248b17–37, 1249b12–17.

as valuable, she transcends anything connatural or teleologically proportioned to me, though as an objective good for me, she is connatural to me and the end of one of my inclinations. The experience of loving another person—and hence relationships like friendship or marriage—are crucial for grasping persons' irreducibility, and these relationships are also the highest expression of our grasp of persons' irreducibility. If I have not loved others in these ways, I cannot fully grasp how persons are irreducible to anything nonpersonal. By abstraction from experiences like these, I grasp the irreducibility of all human persons.

Motivations by Interior Fullness and by Persons

Other philosophers describe further irreducible modes of motivation. We can be motivated by an interior sense of abundance or fullness found in willing. We saw in chapter 4 that particular free choices are made on the basis of an interior abundance of free actuality. I can feel this interior excess in interior joy or vital strength. This motivation can take negative forms: I can act out an interior fullness of vital strength with a will to power and self-aggrandizement. I can be motivated by a will to power or *libido dominandi*, a longing to exert my power upon the weak, as if they were my prey. But I can also be so motivated because I experience life as tragically fated and I desire to overcome this fate by affirming everything that occurs, regardless of its goodness or evil.[13] This motivation can also take positive forms: I can be motivated to act not because of anything about others but just to pour out upon them an interior surplus of bliss, to give myself out of my interior spiritual abundance.[14] We receive this bliss, for example, by responding to holiness and by thereby becoming holy; such a response quiets restless desire, which gives one interior peace and bliss, which motivates further action. This interior welling-up of a desire to act is based not in need but in a selfless longing to pour out one's bliss on others, similar to the epektatic desires described in chapter 4.[15] We are motivated

---

13. Gilles Deleuze, *Nietzsche and Philosophy*, trans. Hugh Tomlinson (New York: Columbia University Press, 1985), interpreting Friedrich Nietzsche, *On the Genealogy of Morality*, trans. Maudemarie Clark and Alan Swensen (Indianapolis, Ind.: Hackett, 1998), First Treatise.

14. Jacques Maritain, *The Person and the Common Good*, trans. John Fitzgerald (Notre Dame, Ind.: University of Notre Dame Press, 1994), chap. 3; Scheler, *Formalism in Ethics and Non-Formal Ethics of Values*, 346.

15. Consider Plato's claim in the *Republic* that once one achieves vision of the Form of the Good, one returns to order the earthly city, or St. Thérèse of Lisieux's statement that she would spend her heaven doing good on earth.

not just by *eros* of seeking perfection (i.e., objective goods) but also by *agape*, an inner impulsion to bestow goods on others not because of their value but because goodness just gives itself—as the Trinitarian Persons give themselves to one another and bestow goods on creation.[16]

Levinas objects that interior fullness often just motivates pursuit of subjective satisfaction (which he calls "enjoyment") and preserving one's own flourishing even to the detriment of others. Reposing in and acting out of interior fullness, even a fullness based in the bliss of holiness or the joy of a close relationship, is called into question when I encounter the face of a suffering person. I then realize that I have focused too much on my happiness and too little on caring for others. I realize that in affirming all beings, I have affirmed those that bring evil and suffering. I must recognize the dangers of such affirmation and the need to set it aside with regard to beings (like immoral acts and unjust situations) that ought not exist. Once I recognize this, an ethical desire (which I call "motivation by persons") arises in me to serve the other neither with reference to my fulfillment nor because I see unique value in the other, but purely out of an infinite desire to altruistically do good and to transcend myself.[17]

Motivation by persons is another experience of the durational, open-ended future: at every moment, there is the possibility of ever-new ethical action. It is also a new experience of dependency and the past: I can have this motivation only by being called by others, and I have always, as it were, "arrived" too late to do all that could have done for others. In being called to serve the other, I perceive the infinite call of God, of absolute moral goodness, in the face of the other.[18] For this reason, experiencing this motivation is indispensable for perceiving persons' irreducibility. To be a person is to bear the trace of God's call to infinite service to others, a call that motivates by being perceived. Correctly theorizing about what irreducible persons are requires abstracting from these experiences.

Experiences of being motivated by values and persons reveal how, as the realist phenomenologists claim, we transcend ourselves and make contact with what is other than us.[19] Theories that take us to be ordered only to objective goods, like some natural law theories, reductionistically fail

---

16. Frederick Wilhelmsen, *The Metaphysics of Love* (New York: Sheed and Ward, 1962), 80–81, building on José Ortega y Gasset and Xavier Zubiri.

17. Levinas, *Totality and Infinity*, 33–35.

18. Emmanuel Levinas, *Difficult Freedom: Essays on Judaism*, trans. Seán Hand (Baltimore: The Johns Hopkins University Press, 1997), 159, 275.

19. Hildebrand, *The Nature of Love*, 29–40; Hildebrand, *Ethics*, 26–32, 203.

to recognize other ways in which we are motivated, not allowing for true self-transcendence. An ethics based in all motivations must grapple with adjudicating among sources of normativity, including objective goods, values, persons, and interior fullness. Such an ethic must adjudicate among responses called for by the fact that many beings simultaneously bear values and disvalues or can both bear values and be contrary to our objective good. Methods like scholastic casuistry or Jewish *halakha*, which weigh precedents, interpretations, and arguments within a nonrelativist framework, would be integral to such an ethics.

Aquinas argues that having a single nature, we have a single end. Were there not a single, definite end, deliberation could never begin, because we begin deliberation with the end at least implicitly in mind, and then reason to the best means to it.[20] But these experiences reveal that such claims are correct only about acts motivated by objective goods and subjective satisfaction. Given that we always naturally act in a means-end fashion (or by considering an end and its overflow), but that motivation by value and persons do not always so operate, then the latter must involve more than natural potencies.[21] These motivations must actualize obediential potencies to act in ways that exceed what is proportionate to our nature. We do not always act by starting with our ultimate end and reasoning to the best means to it; rather, we sometimes act in a way motivated by the sudden call of a value or person, or by spontaneously wishing to pour out interior fullness. What unifies these acts, and allows deliberation among these motivations, is the formal object of goodness. This should be understood analogically as whatever is given as choiceworthy or important, including what is regarded as desirable or valuable. As we saw in chapter 4, I can even regard what is evil as good or important, and so it can motivate my willing. Views, like those of Aquinas or Hildebrand, on which we only will what is positively importance, at least in the sense of what is pleasurable, misdescribe, and so are reductionistic about, acts like those done out of spite. Those cases of serious wrongdoing motivate the view that the formal object of will should be regarded as goodness in the sense of what is important in any way. Once the obediential potencies of our wills and intellects are actualized, we deliberate not just about how to reach our end but also about which are the sorts of goodness to which we should respond.

20. Aquinas, *ST* I-II, q.1, a.6.
21. See Seifert's distinction (*Essere e persona*, 353) between our end-directed "entelechial" acts and our pure responses to importance, which are "transentelechial."

Value as Principle of Being

In experiences of motivation, persons are given as transcending all that can be intended about them by intellect or will. Intellect intends beings insofar as their essence or existence manifest themselves; will intends beings insofar as they can be dealt with by acts achievable by our own self-determination. But beyond these features, things, especially persons, appear as important in themselves. On this basis, personalists Dietrich von Hildebrand, Josef Seifert, and John Crosby posit *value* as an irreducible principle of being in addition to substantial and accidental *esse*, that is, essence, form, and matter. Aquinas showed that each being, as being, has the transcendental property of being *good* (*bonum*).[22] By calling each being *good*, Aquinas meant that it has perfection—completion as a being of some kind—and, by that perfection, gives of itself and can serve as a final cause of desire, appetite, or will.[23] But some beings also give themselves as worthy of existing and of a due response, regardless of whether they fulfill appetite or will. Each being as being is good, but to be valuable—to not just be perfected but to be worthy of being perfected—is a further kind of importance. Since this further kind of importance is a judgment upon the worthiness of the ontological layer of being, it needs to be explained by a principle beyond those that explain beings as beings or as goods. This principle is *value*.[24]

My portrait of the person synthesizes personalist claims about value with Thomistic claims about goodness. Considered *ontologically* or as beings, my acts actualize my potencies, give me intelligible content, render me more immaterial and self-present, and give me new accidental unity. If morally good, they have a due relation to right reason, and they increase my goodness or completion as the kind of being I am; if morally evil, then they lack these features to some extent. Considered in terms of being or actuality, evil is a privation or lack of a perfection that ought to be in a being. Evil acts (like murder or adultery) include many ontological actualities or perfections, such as physical movements, in addition to privations of relations to right reason. In addition to the ontological features of acts being given, we also experience acts *axiologically*, as such that they ought

---

22. *DV*, q.21, a.5. Cf. Ulrich, *Homo Abyssus*, 484–85.
23. Aquinas, *ST* I, q.5.
24. John Crosby, "The Idea of Value and the Reform of the Traditional Metaphysics of *Bonum*," *Aletheia* 1, no. 2 (1977): 268–85; Hildebrand, *The Nature of Love*, 82.

or ought not to be—that is, as such that their ontological perfections are worthy or unworthy of existing and of receiving some response. Although an act of murder includes many positively existing movements, they ought not to have been performed; it would be better had these beings never existed: they have *disvalue* or *negative importance*.[25]

That value (and disvalue) are distinct principles of being is also revealed in *axiological unities*, which we perceive when a being appears as such that it ought or ought not to exist. When I grasp the evil of murder, I do not just grasp a privation (though this account of evil is correct ontologically); the act also presents itself as such that it ought not be.[26] Ontologically, a human substance with his or her acts has accidental *unity of order*, a unity among distinct beings insofar as they are together directed to some good or function. Unities of order are reducible to (i.e., "nothing but") the beings in them.[27] But human persons with their acts also appear as *unities of value*: each of us has the value of dignity and unique beauty, and when we perform good acts, we have the value of moral nobility. Regarded axiologically rather than ontologically, a person appears unified with his or her acts in a distinct and deeper way, insofar as the whole unity displays this nobility. Likewise, things that are ontologically not unities of order, but *aggregates* or *heaps*, like a pile of stones, are unified insofar as they have values or disvalues like beauty or ugliness. This is not a unity of what the heap is or of the constitutive stones' ordering to some good, but a *unity of importance*.[28] Similarly, evil acts and situations appear unified insofar as they have disvalue. I can, as we saw earlier with the example of spite, choose these acts knowing that they are evil, directing my free acts to realize the disvalue as if it were a good.

It is an axiom of scholastic metaphysics that things act insofar as they exist (*agere sequitur esse*). One can discover things that irreducibly exist in their own right by discovering things that act. Axiological unities give themselves to perception and call for responses—that is, they act as uni-

---

25. Hildebrand, *Aesthetics*, vol. 1, 192.
26. Crosby, "The Idea of Value and the Reform of the Traditional Metaphysics of *Bonum*," 268–69, 300. For a debate over the metaphysics of evil, see Patrick Lee, "The Goodness of Creation, Evil, and Christian Teaching," *The Thomist* 64, no. 2 (2000): 239–70; John Crosby, "Is All Evil Really Only Privation?" *Proceedings of the American Catholic Philosophical Association* 75 (2001): 197–210; Patrick Lee, "Evil as Such is a Privation," *American Catholic Philosophical Quarterly* 81, no. 3 (2007): 469–88; and John Crosby, "Doubts about the Privation Theory That Will Not Go Away," *American Catholic Philosophical Quarterly* 81, no. 3 (2007): 489–505.
27. Suárez, *DM*, d.42, s.3, n. 15; d.51, s.2, n. 10.
28. Hildebrand, *Aesthetics*, vol. 1, 279.

ties. Hence, they exist. But this existing unity requires an explanation—and so a principle, value, is posited. This raises a further aspect of the problem of divine causality. In chapter 6, I explain how to reconcile the claims that that disvalue is a principle, that the privation theory is the correct ontological account of evil, that all being and value come ultimately from God, and that no disvalue comes from God (and neither is it caused by a Manichean evil god).

Value as Constituting a Level of Being

Josef Seifert distinguishes three analogically related, irreducible *levels of unity and being* that we perceive in the structure of each concrete being.[29] Being gives itself as having a dynamic structure, "unfolding" (to use Stein's word) meaningfully in a range of levels that give themselves to us, some of which found, explain, and give rise to and manifest themselves through others; the structure of being is like an ongoing, transcendental event.[30] By developing this distinction of levels, I better show the irreducibility of value to other principles of being, and better show the relations among various irreducible features of persons.

The first level of being and unity includes principles and aspects of beings that have *intelligible unity* and an internal structure of formalities, such as beings' essences and relations of order among beings. In us, the first level is the *human essence*, considered apart from *esse* and other principles. This level also includes relations of participation in Platonic Forms. A deficiency in the first level of being is found in phenomena that lack of intelligible order, *chaotic beings*, such as heaps and aggregates.[31]

The second level includes principles and aspects of being that have *real or existential unity* and an act-potency structure. This level includes and presupposes the intelligible unity of the first level of being but adds something to it—and so distinct principles must be posited to explain this level. In human persons, the second level includes our unities of essence and

---

29. What follows is developed from Joseph Seifert, "Die Verschiedenen Bedeutungen von 'Sein,'" in *Warheit, Wert und Sein: Festgabe fur Dietrich von Hildebrand zum 80. Geburtstag*, ed. Balduin Schwartz (Regensburg: Habbel, 1972), 301–32, summarized at Crosby, "The Idea of Value and the Reform of the Traditional Metaphysics of *Bonum*," 296–97.

30. Stein, *Finite and Eternal Being*, 331–33. Cf. Ulrich, *Homo Abyssus*, 162–65; Przywara, *Analogia Entis*, 182–91; Balthasar, *TD5*, 68–95; and Thomas Gricoski, *Being Unfolded: Edith Stein on the Meaning of Being* (Washington, D.C.: The Catholic University of America Press, 2020).

31. Cf. Hildebrand, *What Is Philosophy?* 92–94.

esse, relations of participation in *esse commune*, form, matter, substance, and accident. At the first level, an essence is an intelligible unity of formalities; at the second level, it is an actuality in itself and is in potency to *esse*. Only beings as real engage in efficient causality, while principles and beings at the first and third levels just exert formal and final causality.

Seifert's account of the first two levels of being can be understood as a development of Aquinas's distinction of four senses of *being*.[32] Before turning to Seifert's third, axiological level of being, I consider Aquinas's four senses of *being*; this will ground an integration of personalist claims about value with scholastic metaphysics.

In a first sense, being is what is expressed in true judgments; anything conjoinable with "is" or "are," including privations, is a being in this sense, grasped as an intelligible (or propositionally expressible or existentially quantifiable) unity or unity of formalities—that is, an aspect of Seifert's first level of being. In a second sense, a being is a member of one of the ten categories, the most fundamental kinds of actual things with limited, definable essences. Substance (what exists in itself) is the first category; the other nine are categories of accidents, beings that are apt to exist in another, ways that a substance can be modified or gain additional content. Quantities modify substance through its matter, qualities through its form, relations in orienting it to something extrinsic, and the remaining six categories (*actio, passio, ubi, quando, situs, habitus*) include ways in which substance is modified by extrinsic causes and measures.[33] A being in this sense is anything that has an essence that is actualizable by *esse*; this being belongs to Seifert's second level. In a third sense, being is primarily actuality and, secondarily, potentiality. Accidents, for example, are not just essences that are members of categories and that add content to substances but actualizations of substances. As beings in the former, second sense, they are subordinate to substance; as beings in the latter, third sense, they are more perfect than (and are perfective of) substance. God is an actuality (and so a being in this third sense) but is not a member of a category (and so is not a being in the second sense), since he is not limited or definable. Whereas substance is the primary sort of being in the second sense, persons (especially God) are the primary sort of beings in this third sense, since they are most actual.[34] Being in this sense also belongs to Seifert's

---

32. Aquinas, *DEE*, c. 1; *In VI Met.*, lect. 4; *In VII Met.*, lect. 1.
33. Aquinas, *In III Phys.*, lect. 5; *In V Met.*, lect. 9.
34. Seifert, *Essere e persona*, 320–28, 344–48.

second level. In a fourth sense, on Aquinas's view, being is accidental unity (i.e., a unity of order of a substance with its accidents); they belong to Seifert's first and second levels.

Seifert also posits a third level of being, which includes principles and beings insofar as they have *axiological unity*. Just as the second level takes the first into an act-potency structure, so this third level takes the first two levels into a value-laden structure. We grasp beings at the first two levels when we intellectually intuit, conceptualize, or judge them; we grasp beings at this third level when we perceive or feel their worthiness to exist or their call for a due response. We grasp human persons at this level when we grasp their holistic dignity or unique beauty and the call to reverence, respect, service, or love that they express; as we have seen, these experiences disclose irreducible features of persons, which are explained by positing principles like values in beings and Platonic Forms of those values, such as finite justice or beauty themselves, in which beings participate. Values are fully and directly given only when their motivating power is felt; they do not appear as intellectually graspable actualities (unlike essences, *esse*, or accidents), though I can abstract a concept of value from the feeling of being motivated by value. Since they give characteristics to beings, values are analogous to formal causes, but since they confer importance (not ontological actuality), their causality is *sui generis*. Unlike actualities, values do not correspond to and fulfill potentialities; rather, their correlate is being as ontologically perfected and transcendentally good, which they render important or worthy of existing in itself (rather than just existing as able to be desired or willed).[35]

Some values give themselves as intelligibly related to and embodied in their bearers. For example, by grasping what an act of justice ontologically and essentially is—an act that gives to each their due—we perceive why it has the moral value of nobility whereby it ought to exist and calls for a response of admiration, praise, and emulation. "Justice" refers to a value at the third level and to a definable relation among acts, persons, and right reason at the second; the two are related in a *sui generis* way analogous to formal causality.

Other values transcend their bearers. For example, in artworks like Beethoven's symphonies or in natural landscapes like Yosemite Valley,

---

35. Crosby, "The Idea of Value and the Reform of the Traditional Metaphysics of *Bonum*," 306–13; Hildebrand, *The Nature of Love*, 79–82.

nonpersonal beings like sounds and rocks bear a value of beauty that greatly transcends them. "Beauty" refers at least to transcendental properties and categorical relations among beings by which they are pleasing to behold (at the first and second level) and to a value (at the third level). Transcendent beauties whose beauty outstrips their bearers appear as a "message from God," a case of the personal presence described in chapter 2. The more we understand about their being at the first and second levels, such as acoustic or geological properties, the *less* intelligible it is how such mundane beings could ground so spectacular a beauty. This value, which Hildebrand calls "beauty of the second power," just appears "on" its bearers, similar to how a statue stands on a pedestal: the ontological foundation just allows a value to appear.[36] The unique beauty of all persons (including the physical beauty of some persons) is a case of this beauty of the second power. What is ontologically less significant can thereby bear a very high value. Likewise, what is ontologically great (for example, immaterial thoughts of scientific discoveries) can bear a value far lower than the value of holiness that belongs to a single charitable action. Ontological and axiological hierarchies, as we have seen, do not correspond in all respects.[37] Values do not always supervene on or emerge from their bearers; they give themselves a distinct kind of unity and mode of being beyond the essential and the ontological. This is evidence for the irreducibility of value and the level of being it engenders.

Communities, Artifacts, and Gestalten Constituted by Value

We have seen that one piece of evidence that value is an irreducible principle is that it explains new unities, such that it acts analogously to formal and final causes. These unities include artifacts and communities. To fully grasp our own irreducibility, we must understand how we participate in such unities through the unifying power of value.[38] We saw in chapter 3 how we conceive intentional forms and then impose them on substances, giving them new purposes and meanings beyond those given by their

---

36. Hildebrand, *Aesthetics*, vol. 1, 211–14.
37. Hildebrand, *Aesthetics*, vol. 1, 208.
38. Some of this section's content is from Mark K. Spencer, "The Metaphysics of Justice: The Category of Artifacts and Free Cooperative Causality," *The Heythrop Journal* 61, no. 2 (2020): 241–52; Spencer, "Beauty and Being in von Hildebrand and the Aristotelian Tradition," *Review of Metaphysics* 73, no. 2 (2019): 311–34.

substantial and accidental essence and *esse*. At the second level of being, artifacts resulting from these intentional forms are accidental unities of order. A 1936 Alfa Romeo, for example, consists of many substances and accidents ordered to a single end by an imposed intentional form. But the car also gives itself to perception as a single *Gestalt*, unified by values like elegance and beauty, calling for a response of admiration and fast driving.[39] This axiological unity presupposes intentional forms and unities of order at the first and second levels. But we fail to fully perceive the axiological unity and its value if we reductionistically "explain away" artifacts by holding that they are "nothing but" arrangements of natural substances and accidents. That view fails to do justice to what appears in everyday experience. Concrete beings, including persons, are irreducible to their second level.

Hans-Georg Gadamer describes a paradigm case of a community, the conversation, which reveals the structure of third-level unities and their irreducible role in human life.[40] This axiological analysis of conversations builds on the intellectual, ontological account that I gave in chapter 3. When we converse well, the conversation takes shape as a unified form or *Gestalt*, with its own style, similar to how each substance has its own style. The whole that is a *Gestalt* has its style and meaning through the unifying power of a value. A conversation's unity is irreducible to any party's understanding of or contribution to it; a conversation is ordered toward a goal, like shared understanding or aesthetic display of wit, but this orientation emerges spontaneously over the course of the conversation and is not necessarily specified by any party's explicit decision. To be a good conversationalist requires that one not entirely control a conversation but surrender to the style that emerges when the participants aim not just at producing their own speech acts but allow those acts to be unified spontaneously. A good conversation has a unity that, as it were, "descends" upon the participants and draws them up into a new structure. This structure instantiates a kind of importance: a value draws the acts of the parties to the conversation and reorients them by the style it confers. The value acts as a final and formal cause in bringing about the *Gestalt* with its style. We can explain the structure of a conversation through the values that guide and unify it.

---

39. Cf. Hildebrand, *Metaphysik der Gemeinschaft*, 20, 99–105; *Aesthetics*, vol. 2, 5–9, 155–57.
40. Gadamer, *Truth and Method*, 383–89.

Other axiological unities include states of affairs, events, artifacts, human communities, natural communities like ecosystems, and aesthetic unities like landscapes. In each case, a value guides the *Gestalt*'s constituents such that they act together and give themselves to each other, the value, and to shared action, so that the *Gestalt* with its style emerges. For example, a landscape is a unified whole when unified by aesthetic values like beauty or picturesqueness, such that its parts contribute to that value and take on its style. Because a *Gestalt* is formally and finally dependent on and unified by a value, it is irreducible to its constituent substances and accidents. It bears value in its own right, and gives itself to perception as axiologically unified, not as an aggregate, unity of order, or other accidental unity.

Phenomenologically considered experiences of causally acting on (and being acted on by) values and *Gestalten*, do not fit scholastic models of causality; they are evidence for a distinct kind of causality having to do with values and *Gestalten*, which is further evidence that value is an irreducible principle and that human persons can be fully grasped as irreducible only if we perceive their value. In a first mode of causality posited by scholastics, some of my acts and effects are caused *per se*—that is, I directly cause my acts and I direct them toward definite effects. I *per se* cause my acts of, for example, breathing, seeing, speaking, and thinking. Human persons also cause aspects of *Gestalten* by *per se* causality. For example, an artisan deliberately organizes an artifact's parts in relation to some function, or a ruler gives laws to members of a community. In a second mode of causality posited by scholastics, effects are caused *per accidens*—that is, when substances' lines of *per se* causality intersect, a chance, unintended event occurs. For example, I might *per se* cause myself to walk through a forest, while the *per se* causality of gravitational interactions causes a rock to fall from a cliff; when the two causal lines intersect, the rock falls on me—an effect at which neither cause aimed *per se*, but rather that came about through their chance intersection. Some *Gestalten*, such as some large events in which many people participate, seem to gain their structure by chance.[41]

But at times we cause and engage with *Gestalten* neither through *per se* causality nor by their coming about by chance. Rather, we allow their unity

---

41. Aquinas, *In II Phys.*, lect. 8; *DPN*, 39–41; *ST* I-II, q.90, a.1; *In VIII NE*, lects. 9–10; *De regno* I, c. 3. I owe the example of a rock falling to J. J. Sanford.

and style to emerge spontaneously, as in a conversation. The conversation is experienced as giving meaning and direction to its constitutive speech acts, as its style comes to be presented through them. The whole *Gestalt* acts with that style. Communities, when acting as unities, are experienced as the subjects of rights, duties, collective guilt and merit, and acts of sin and repentance.[42] They develop over time in a spontaneous but intelligible way, as in the history of customs, languages, fashions, and of laws based on precedent, such as English common law. These unities exhibit what F. A. Hayek called "spontaneous order," in which order arises through the confluence of many substances' activities.[43] No individual person aims *per se* at creating the definite structure of natural languages or of a nation's organic customs, but their coming about is not purely *per accidens*, since each party aims at the coming about of some language or body of customs. When a game is played, players adapt themselves to its rules, but no player dictates the game's structure; rather, they all allow the game's *Gestalt* to (in Gadamer's phrase) "come to presentation" through them.[44] An artist does not *per se* plan a form for an artwork and then impose it on matter; rather (as Gilson shows), an artwork arises from the artist working with, responding to, and cooperating with matter and its causality.[45] In each case, the acts of many substances allow the arising of a new *Gestalt* under the unifying, *sui generis*, quasi-formal causality of a value. This *Gestalt* requires some ontological basis but is not wholly present in any of its constituent substances, on which it confers meaning. Just as sensible qualities reveal a Platonic Form transcending the material world, so *Gestalten* disclose the presence of a transcendent, unifying value—a principle transcending the constituent substances in the *Gestalt* that accounts for the excess of the *Gestalt* over its participants. Often, as in sensible qualities, this principle includes a transcendent, personal, divine presence—the "spirit" of a conversation, game, nation, or artwork.[46] This new mode of causality, which I call *per communionem* causality, causality through a communion of substantial and axiological causes, will be explained further in chapter 6.

Some ontological items (such as forms, activities, substances, and es-

---

42. Max Scheler, *On the Eternal in Man*, trans. Bernard Noble (New York: Harper, 1960), 416–17.
43. F. A. Hayek, "The Results of Human Action but Not of Human Design," in *Studies in Philosophy, Politics, and Economics* (Chicago: University of Chicago Press, 1967), 96–105.
44. Gadamer, *Truth and Method*, 101–21.
45. Gilson, *Painting and Reality*, chap. 1.
46. Cf. Walter Wink, *Unmasking the Powers: The Invisible Forces That Determine Human Existence* (Minneapolis, Minn.: Fortress Press, 1986).

sences) wholly exist at each moment at which they exist; others (such as *kineseis*) exist one stage at a time, being unified by their order. But values unify items with stages existing at distinct times into a *single axiologically constituted Gestalt*. These include four-dimensionally-extended events like battles, historical periods, and human lives, another irreducible feature of human persons. They also include occasional events that periodically recur, being both the same unity with the same values each time but also displaying various differences, such as Christmas and Easter, times of day like morning and evening, or artworks that can be performed multiple times like symphonies or songs. Values and *Gestalten* come to presentation through what happens at various times but also transcend those times and can be grasped in themselves; I can grasp a symphony or battle in itself as a unity, a saturated phenomenon.[47]

All of this is evidence that *Gestalten* are in a category of being distinct from those at the first two levels of being. Aristotle, for example, distinguishes four basic ways that a being can exist, which are representative of the categories of beings at the first two levels, each of which can be distinguished from *Gestalten*.[48] First, *Gestalten* are not substantial natures (such as "human" or "animal"), which are predicable of substances but not present in them: no axiologically unified *Gestalt* is a nature of a substance or predicable of it; *Gestalten* are distinct sorts of unities from substances. Second, *Gestalten* are not accidental natures (such as "blackness" or "musicality"), which are present in substances but not predicable of them. No *Gestalt* is the nature of an accident; rather, *Gestalten* transcend all that belongs to particular substances. Third, they are not accidents (such as "black" or "musical"), which are present in and predicable of particular substances, nor are they a new kind of accident inhering in multiple substances.[49] *Gestalten* do not inhere in or modify their constituents; rather, they come to presentation through them and bestow new meaning on them. Fourth, they are not substances, but have substances as their constituents. A community does not depend on any particular substances, and it can survive when all its original members have died, though it appears through the members it has at any given time. *Gestalten* are related to their

---

47. Hildebrand, *Aesthetics*, vol. 1, 296–303; Gadamer, *Truth and Method*, 119–25; and Marion, *In Excess*, chap. 2. Cf. Stein, *Finite and Eternal Being*, 122, 206.
48. Aristotle, *Categories*, c. 2.
49. *Contra* Norris Clarke, "System: A New Category of Being," *The Creative Retrieval of St. Thomas Aquinas* (New York: Fordham University Press, 2009), 44–47.

constituent substances and accidents as empty or meaning-bestowing form to filling content. Values and *Gestalten* cannot efficaciously act except through their constituent substances' efficient causality, but they give new meaning to substances and draw substances to new goals, acting by formal and final causality.

Gestalten are grasped by interpretation, which is not a single act but a weaving together of affective, intellectual, volitional, and perceptual acts. I affectively grasp a value, and then (in a way similar to knowledge by connaturality) allow this mode of importance to guide my perception to the meaning of the *Gestalt* it constitutes, such that that meaning comes to presentation through my cognitive acts. My attention moves among the aspects of the *Gestalt*, and I attempt to articulate in language (or in another bodily mode of expression) what I perceive in it. I thereby build up my interpretation as a *Gestalt* of ideas, judgments, and perception that fit with and articulate the structure of the *Gestalt* that I am interpreting. Building an interpretation involves acts of both conceptualization and poetic evocation that direct others' attention to the *Gestalt* being interpreted. To interpret a text, for example, is not to abstract a form from it but to allow the meaning bestowed on the text to come to presentation in my thinking, as I work through the various parts of the text, guided by my feeling of its values. Since each *Gestalt* is a saturated phenomenon, its total meaning will always exceed what my interpretation grasps. *Gestalten* appear against a background or "horizon," such as the "background" of a tradition. To see *Gestalten* against correct backgrounds, I need a holistic "taste" for them, an aesthetically cognitive feel or savor for the community, artifact, or artwork in its proper, traditional context.[50] I "tacitly" (rather than directly) grasp a *Gestalt*'s meaning by living with it in the proper context, integrating it in interpretation with other *Gestalten* that appear against that background.[51] In living with a community or artifact so as to grasp its meaning, I allow it (and its value) to modify how I comport myself, in my linguistic and other bodily acts, toward the world, but I also modify it insofar as my acts of interpretation add to or change its meaning. My creative perspective, the "word" that I add to things in affirming them, is an irreducible aspect of reality. The self-manifesting beauty of things, especially of dynamic *Gestalten*, draws me into interaction with the "drama" of the *Gestalt* as I interpre-

---

50. Margaret Hughes, "Does Taste Matter for Thomists?" *The Thomist* 81, no. 1 (2017): 107–23.
51. Michael Polanyi, *The Tacit Dimension* (Chicago: University of Chicago Press, 2009).

tively engage with it. Once again, engagement with the beautiful renders me beautiful, at least in how I perceive and creatively act (and sometimes morally or religiously as well): beauty always gives birth to more beauty.[52] But this mutually transforming interpretive stance is still a realist, not a relativist, perspective on *Gestalten*. In interpreting a *Gestalt*, I let it give itself to me, even as I creatively engage with it; there is, as Gadamer says, a "merging" of our "horizons," of the *Gestalt* being interpreted and the *Gestalt* that is my interpretation, a joining together of our perspectives on the world.[53]

Interpretable *Gestalten*, like ecosystems, appear even in the natural world (by which I mean the community of nonpersonal material substances); for example, the sensible qualities of a plant or animal unify into what Hildebrand calls an *aesthetic essence*, a beautiful appearance typical of a given being's kind. Trees, hills, buildings, and their sensible qualities take on the aesthetic unity of a landscape. These are unities of appearances insofar as they bear an aesthetic value, a "style" or "atmosphere" that gives them meaning and makes them appear as being how they ought to be.[54] A further way that I am irreducible to my ontological level is that my body has an aesthetic essence, and I am in (and given new, irreducible meaning and ways of existing and acting in the world by) natural *Gestalten* like landscapes and ecosystems and human *Gestalten* like political communities and culinary cultures.

Some might object that my metaphysics has excessively multiplied items. But this is not a problem given my goal to portray the person as irreducible. My metaphysics is not meant to be parsimonious but to guide perception to each given feature of reality in itself and to awaken wonder at them all. Focusing on aesthetic experience, as I do, invites an excessive metaphysics: with an eye for beauty, every being and event, down to the slightest rustling of a leaf in the breeze, displays unique unity, content, and principles. Parsimonious metaphysics must account for these features of the world, but they do so either by implausibly denying that these features are given, or they smuggle back into their metaphysics many items that they claim to reduce—for example, by saying that they emerge from, supervene on, or are connotations of other features of the world. But if one thing emerges from another, then it is something and not nothing but that

52. Balthasar, *TD1*, 16–17; Hildebrand, *Aesthetics*, vol. 2, chap. 35; Plato, *Symposium*, 206b–207c.
53. Gadamer, *Truth and Method*, 438ff.
54. Hildebrand, *Aesthetics*, vol. 1, 189–90, 204–5, 308–12.

other thing—that is, it must, in itself, have a place in one's metaphysics. Each feature given in experience decorates or ornaments the world, augmenting reality and conveying our attention to yet other given features of reality; everything exists and comes to presentation through excessive ornamentation, like the curlicues and flourishes of Rococo art.[55]

Spiritual Affectivity

We must now consider the acts by which we grasp values. We saw in chapter 4 that, in Aquinas's view, the will is primarily a power to love; it is a power whereby we respond, in a way involving a felt affinity for various goods (including nonmaterial ones like God). In many free choices, I feel love, joy, or other feelings, in a way that is active, not passive, as in the felt aspect of willing good to another.[56] Following the personalists, I call this sphere of experience *spiritual affectivity*. Aquinas contends that spiritual affects lack passion (i.e., undergoing being moved by their object). A first reason for this claim is experiential: spiritual affects lack the feeling involved in the body being moved by other bodies—say, in being moved to anger or sexual arousal—though they involve greater delight and satisfaction. A second reason is Aquinas's view that passion, lacking complete self-presence, is a sign of materiality, imperfection, and ignobility.[57] He affirms a Platonic principle: we can do everything by higher powers that we can do by lower powers, but in a more excellent or noble way—that is, an ontologically and axiologically higher way.[58] But though self-presence is one sign that a power is immaterial and ontologically more perfect than material powers, it does not follow that an immaterial, self-present power cannot involve being moved. That *being moved* belongs to bodily passions does not *ipso facto* make that characteristic ontologically lower or axiologically ignoble, nor does it follow that being moved does not belong to spiritual affectivity. Hildebrand, Stein, and Scheler hold that we have spiritual feelings that involve being moved by objects, not just spiritual feelings in active willing.[59]

---

55. Gadamer, *Truth and Method*, 151–52.
56. Aquinas, *ST* I, q.20, a.1; q.82, a.5, ad 1; I-II, q.22, a.3; 2.26, a.3; q.31, a.3-4; III, q.46, a.8.
57. Aquinas, *ST* I-II, q.22, a.3, ad 1; q.31, a.5.
58. Aquinas, *QDA*, a.18; *In LDC*, lects. 16, 17. Cf. Scotus, *Ord.* IV, d.45, q.2, II ad 2; Suárez, *In DA*, d.9, q.3, n. 3.
59. This and following sections are synthesized from: Scheler, *Formalism in Ethics and Non-Formal Ethics of Values*, chap. 2; Scheler, "*Ordo Amoris*"; Stein, *Finite and Eternal Being*, chap. 7, §9; and Hildebrand,

Being moved by beauty, falling in love, prideful hatred, reverence and adoration, contrition for sin, anxiety and distraction are not just bodily affects (though they are normally accompanied by them) but acts of the soul. This is because, although they involve being moved by their objects, they are meaningful, intentional, self-conscious acts, and some have immaterial beings, being as such, or being's properties as their objects. They are motivated by modes of importance; they arise only upon grasping their objects' meanings and are not merely caused in us, without our having to grasp their objects' meaning, as many bodily passions are. While less tumultuous than bodily feelings, they are more ardent, an intensification of our feeling of vitality.

We grasp these feelings' intrinsic meaningfulness not just through interior experience of them but also by *qualitative analogies* or *correspondences* that are directly perceived as features of reality. For example, the feelings of being in love and of vitality give themselves as analogous to *fire*. We perceive something irreducible and meaningful about these feelings by perceiving their mysterious connection to fire, their burning intensity. In grasping these correspondences, we once again grasp how concrete beings reveal Platonic Forms (such as Forms of feelings and their connections to other Platonic Forms, like that of fire) and transcendent personal presences.[60]

Using the scholastic principle of distinguishing powers on the basis of formal objects and direction of acts, it is reasonable to distinguish the power of will from a power for the sort of spiritual affectivity that involves receptivity or being moved, which I shall call the *heart* or just *spiritual affectivity*. While both will and spiritual affectivity have an affective aspect, and both are motivated by modes of importance or goodness, they intend their objects in distinct ways. Volitional acts aim at objects in an active, self-determined way; even acts of will that are given to us, like our natural intention of happiness as our end, are also active. Spiritual affects intend their objects in a receptive way, insofar as those objects' importance is felt.[61] This distinction of powers guides us to perceive what is irreducible in both volitional and affective acts.

Ethics, chap. 17. Cf. Leclercq, *The Love of Learning*, 266–77, on similar views in Augustine and Bernard of Clairvaux.

60. Hildebrand, *Aesthetics*, vol. 1, 166; Calasso, *Ardor*, 102; Bachelard, *Intuition of the Instant*, 62; and Aquinas, *ST* I-II, q.28, a.5.

61. Hildebrand, *Ethics*, 215–16.

The Thomistic and personalist distinctions among powers can also be synthesized. In chapter 3, I posited multiple powers unfolding from the power of intellect. In chapter 2, I said that the external senses unfold from the common sense. Furthermore, all of our powers unfold from the unified power of the subjective soul. I propose that the unified spiritual, subjective power of the soul is a power for intending beauty, the holistic self-manifestation of beings. This power unfolds first into the intellect (the power for intending being as intelligible) and a power for intending beings as good or important; this latter power then unfolds into the powers of will and heart. This account captures the unity among good-intending acts noted by the scholastics, and it guides us to perceive with the personalists what is irreducible in acts of will and heart. Distinguishing powers is helpful only insofar as it guides us to perceive irreducible ways in which we act, experience, and are open to the world. It would be reductionistic of our unity as acting, experiencing persons to think of these powers as little agents in the soul. Rather, they are ways in which we are oriented to act; they are related, overlap, and unfold from each other in many ways, all of which must be perceived to grasp our irreducibility.

To be moved to spiritual affect is not ignoble or inferior to the active will; rather, being moved is fully meaningful and among our most valuable acts. Moral virtue requires not just being motivated to will excellently but being disposed to be moved well. If I am virtuous, I must be disposed to receive affects (like being moved by beauty or a moral act's nobility) as gifts that reshape who I am and make me more capable of willing aright. The person who merely wills rightly, but is not appropriately moved—say, the one who upon encountering a suffering person chooses to perform compassionate acts but is not moved to feel compassion for that person—is not yet fully virtuous. Such a person's powers are not in full harmony with one another, nor does such a person give each valuable object its full due. Innocent suffering deserves being moved to compassion, just as beauty is due feelings of admiration and my wife calls for feelings of love from me. There is a fit or normative correspondence between certain modes of importance and feelings, such that the latter is part of the most meaningful and just response to the former. To act without these feelings is, while not bad, to fail to fully act as a complete, irreducible human person, and to fail to give oneself to that which calls for self-gift. But there is also reciprocity between will and affectivity: feeling motivates willing, and I must will to sanction feeling for it to fully take effect in me (or disavow it if I judge it an improper feeling, so that it does not take effect in me).[62]

Value-Perception, Preference, and Kinds of Values

Experience reveals that the heart unfolds into further powers. First, there is the power for *value-perception* and perception of other kinds of importance. Value-perception is an intuitive act, resembling aesthetic cognition, but with a felt, nonintellectual character. When I grasp values, I cannot entirely intellectually define them or articulate why their bearers have them, but I self-consciously, meaningfully grasp their call for a due response. I feel the call of (and do not just perceive, conceptualize, or make a judgment about) a painting or mountain's beauty, an athlete's vital prowess, a saint's holiness. These feelings are meaningfully object-directed, as opposed to nonintentional bodily feelings (such as hunger, tiredness, or intoxication) or intentional sensible feelings that are just automatically caused by their objects (rather than being motivated by grasping their meaning) and that essentially involve bodily changes. For example, I feel spiritual fear at an object's terrifying aspects when I grasp the object as fearful and experience fear as part of the correct response to it, such that I can, if I sanction the feeling, make a due response of flight. By contrast, when I feel sensory fear, I am immediately, without fully realizing what is happening or the meaningful correspondence between feeling and object, impelled to flee. Normally, though, when I feel fear, I feel the two kinds of fear together.

Whereas grasping objective goods for me shows me why it is good for me to be thankful, to praise God, or to sacrifice my life for another, only in feeling values do I feel called to whole-heartedly give myself to another or to unreservedly throw myself into wonder, praise, or gratitude, transcending myself without considering its benefit to me.[63] As we have seen, responding to this call produces an even deeper fulfillment than achieving objective goods does; in grasping values, I feel gratitude for the immense privilege it is to be a self-transcending person. Feeling this privilege reveals my axiological irreducibility, that is, the irreducibility of the importance of being me to anything else that can be grasped about me.[64]

---

62. Hildebrand, *Ethics*, 335–57.
63. Cf. Crosby, "The Idea of Value and the Reform of the Traditional Metaphysics of *Bonum*," 298–99.
64. Cf. Dietrich and Alice von Hildebrand, *The Art of Living*, chap. 8.

In value-perception, we also perform acts of what Scheler calls "preference" and "placing after." To prefer a value in this sense is not to subjectively gravitate to it or choose it but to feel that it is greater, deeper, or more choiceworthy than another value; conversely, to place one value after another is to feel that it is inferior, shallower, or less choice worthy than the other. In chapter 1, I described Scheler's hierarchy of values, with pleasure as the lowest level, followed by values of utility, vitality, aesthetics, morality, truth, and holiness as the highest, that is, the value most worthy of existing and to which we most are called to make a due response.[65] Each value makes a categorical claim on us, but categorical normative force comes in kinds.

Hildebrand expands Scheler's distinction of kinds of value and shows that not all values fall into a strict hierarchy.[66] Since we can bear each kind of value, we should briefly consider several of them, so that we perceive more irreducible aspects of ourselves. Most importantly, Hildebrand considers the value (described above) of the beauty of persons as such (*Gesamtschönheit*), which, like holiness, is an absolute value calling for awe and reverence, and that sets its bearer apart from all others. Hildebrand also adds to Scheler's taxonomy *ontological values*, the importance that belongs to real beings as really existing or as members of kinds, such as the value of being human or of being an animal; *technical intellectual values* like the value of cleverness, genius, and giftedness; *technical artistic values* like the value of brilliance, importance, and viability of an artwork; and other *technical values*, belonging to functioning powers as such, like the value of strength of will.

Hildebrand also distinguishes a range of aesthetic values. Some, like beauty of the second power, appear as messages from God—that is, to feel them is to feel the presence of the eternal and absolutely significant, which categorically demands admiration in a way similar to the call of moral

---

65. Hildebrand denies that pleasure is a value (*Ethics*, 42), but he is wrong to do so. Pleasure generally motivates as subjectively satisfying, yet one can also grasp the (low-level) importance that it has in itself, for example, in trying to bring it about for others, as one whom Scheler calls a *bon vivant*—a person whose calling in life is to make life enjoyable for others—does, or in taking oneself to be obligated to pursue pleasure, for example, with a lover. Things at any level of the hierarchy can have utility value in the sense of *indirect importance*—importance insofar as they are a means to a thing having the kind of value belonging to that level of the hierarchy. But some things, like money, have a pure value of being useful. Cf. Hildebrand, *Ethics*, 65–70.

66. This paragraph and the next few are drawn from Hildebrand, *Ethics*, chaps. 10–12; Hildebrand, *Aesthetics*, vol. 1, chaps. 10–12, 17–19; vol. 2, 399–419, 535–53; and Dietrich and Alice von Hildebrand, *Graven Images: Substitutes for True Morality* (Steubenville, Ohio: Hildebrand Press, 2019), 55–76.

value. These aesthetic values (along with moral, religious, and some intellectual values) are appearances within the temporal, creaturely order of what transcends that order and demands a response that will have everlasting worth.[67] Other aesthetic values, like the value of the poetic (mentioned in chapter 2), given in feelings like nostalgia, intimates both something eternal and something *earthly*, which is not of everlasting significance yet still calls for a response for its own sake. Still other aesthetic values are given as lacking any eternal significance, yet they retain importance in themselves (and can display a transcendent, localized personal presence), including the values of elegance, gracefulness (as in the gracefulness of a ballet), and comedy, which call for various sorts of aesthetic appreciation. Responses to these earthly values (which include both the aesthetic values just mentioned and many of the technical values mentioned above) do not, as it were, reach into eternity and take on everlasting weight, but they are not evils, disvalues, or the subjectively satisfying. Even though values of eternal significance are preferable to earthly ones, the latter still call for a due response. It is not wrong to give such a response, though often such values must be set aside for the sake of higher ones, and full human perfection often requires renouncing goods that bear such values. Something like these earthly values is found in other odd axiological features of reality that we have considered, such as seductive aspects of beauty (in chapter 2), uncanny and horrifying aspects of being (in chapter 3), and the aesthetic value of contingency (in chapter 4).

These distinctions add further aspects to the problem of divine causality. First, if God directly caused all values, then value-perception would be misleading, for what seemed to be earthly values would actually be as much from God as eternal values. Second, were God the cause of all beings distinct from himself, God would have to be the source of bearers of disvalue that thereby ought not to exist, which is contrary to his goodness. Third, while God does not owe creation to anything—since no value is to be preferred to his holiness, and so no other value must be instantiated—given that he has created beings with values, it seems that God owes responses to various values. We need a metaphysics on which God is not the direct cause of all values or any disvalues and can make responses to values without being ontologically dependent on them. But we must wait for the next chapter for a solution.

67. Cf. Kohák, *The Embers and the Stars*, 83.

Personal Value-Essences and Conscience

Acts of preference that are properly ordered by virtue reveal an objective value-hierarchy. Tendencies to focus on our own subjective satisfaction can blind or distort our value-perception, such that we perceive a value that is objectively more important to be less important, or such that we fail to perceive a particular value at all. This, in turn, can lead us to fail to perceive features of reality which those values guide us to perceive (as we saw in chapter 1 in considering how focusing on utility values motivates adopting materialist views). Each person tends to perceive values as falling onto a hierarchy, determined by his or her own desires and focuses; each person has his or her own value-hierarchy or order of loves (*ordo amoris*). Values call each person to conform his or her own personal *ordo amoris* to the objective value-hierarchy. But this does not entail that everyone must prefer values in exactly the same way. As Scheler saw, while no value calls us to violate another (or, I add, to violate an ordering to an objective good), and while all values are ways that beings are important in themselves and not just to someone, some values call for responses only from certain persons or groups.[68] For example, I experience myself (and others experience me) as the only one equipped to fully perceive and respond to certain values in particular persons, such as the unique beauty of my wife or close friends. Some values are messages to particular persons at particular times, as in the "call of the hour," or "*kairos*" described by Hildebrand, which addresses itself to persons uniquely equipped to proclaim some truth, condemn some error, or respond to a crisis at a particular moment in history.[69]

By experiencing these unique calls, persons are revealed to have a "personal value-essence," a vocation to respond to certain values. Since my acts other than value-perception are guided by my value-perception, I have an entirely unique viewpoint on the world through my personal value-essence.[70] Grasping who a person is requires grasping, in an affective act that Stein calls "empathy," his or her personal value-essence. In empathy, persons are given as irreducible to instances of a species. In our most spiritual, transcendentally open powers, we each uniquely feel and interpret the

---

68. Scheler, *Formalism in Ethics and Non-Formal Ethics of Values*, 489–93; Scheler, "Ordo Amoris," 103.
69. Dietrich von Hildebrand, *Trojan Horse in the City of God* (Chicago: Franciscan Herald Press, 1967), 61–68.
70. Cf. G. W. Leibniz, "The Principles of Philosophy, or, the Monadology," in *Philosophical Essays*, trans. Roger Ariew and Daniel Garber (Indianapolis, Ind.: Hackett, 1989), n. 57.

world, and this is disclosed in empathy.[71] The artist like Giotto or Debussy who discovers a new kind of beauty, the saint like St. Francis or St. Thérèse who discovers a new way of being holy, responds to values in a new way; such a person may also be called to make these values available, for the first time, to be felt by others.

Since every person is called to prefer values in accord with the objective value-hierarchy, each person is called to be a saint. A saint is one who prefers holiness to all other values, and so becomes holy, that is, willingly participates in God's absolute value of being just, numinous, awe-inspiring, set apart from all others, and so forth. A saint participates in this value over and above the participation in holiness and absolute value that belongs to the beauty of persons as such. Willingly received and sanctioned holiness most perfectly completes that absolute value of personal beauty that persons as such have. Being a saint requires renouncing all that impedes holiness and orienting all of one's acts to God.

But while all are called to prefer holiness, some are called to focus on lower values. Scheler distinguishes exemplars of persons who are called to focus on values for which they, by their personal value-essence, have a special calling. For example, the *bon vivant*, the one skilled at entertaining, at comedy, or at festivity is called to focus on providing pleasure to people, and the artistic genius is called to focus on sensory aesthetic values. Only some people are called to be saints in the sense focusing in a distinctive way on holiness, a sort of "genius" for holiness in the way that an artist is a genius about aesthetic values.[72] I only create for myself an authentic style and personality if I creatively and obediently live out my personal value-essence, responding to the objective call of what transcends me, demanding a response for its own sake from me in particular.

As we saw in chapter 1, felt value-perception guides intellectual and volitional acts; prior to being a willing being (*ens volens*) or thinking being (*ens cogitans*), I am a loving being (*ens amans*).[73] Since my feeling of values, in accord with my personal value-essence, affects what I can know and will, there are facets of reality that I alone can fully perceive, which I am called to reveal to others. Discovering my personal value-essence requires a stance of love, an openness to the call of any value. In chapter 4, I

---

71. Stein, *Finite and Eternal Being*, 207; Edith Stein, *On the Problem of Empathy*, trans. Waltraut Stein (Washington, D.C.: ICS Publications, 2016), 109.
72. Scheler, *Formalism in Ethics and Non-Formal Ethics of Values*, 585.
73. Scheler, "*Ordo Amoris*," 110–11.

described how the will implicitly consents to and affirms all beings, even those that bring suffering. But spiritually affective love modifies this stance of the will: it is an openness to all values, and a rejection of disvalues and of beings that ought not exist (such as sinful acts). Hatred, by contrast, is a stance of being closed to values.[74] Basic stances like love, hatred, bliss, and despair largely determine which other acts are available to me. Affectivity, no less than intelligibility and freedom, belongs not just to a particular power but to the subjectivity and substance of the soul, such that it affects all my powers.

These personal experiences reveal that while broad kinds of values—vital, aesthetic, holiness, and so forth—fall into a hierarchy, many values within each family have no objective hierarchical arrangement. Earthly aesthetic values—such as the elegant, comical, or cool—call for distinct responses, but there is no given objective fact of the matter as to which is preferable to the others. Likewise, each person has a unique beauty, but these do not fall into an objective hierarchy, though I may be called to focus on one person's value (say, my wife's) more than that of others. In chapter 3, we saw that beings can be analogically related without being hierarchically related; the same is true of some values. Holding that each being and value has a definite place in a single hierarchy is a reductionism that leads to immoral habits and acts. Many forms of racism are motivated by the view that the value of each person or group occupies a strict place on a hierarchy, higher or lower than each other person or group.

These particularized experiences of value are related to the experience of *conscience*. I apply general principles to sensed particulars in many areas; *conscience* names this application in practical matters.[75] I do this before acting, when I find myself bound by general ethical principles, and after acting, when I judge my act in light of principles, and accuse or confirm myself. These acts are ideally exercised with the virtue of prudence or practical wisdom (*phronesis*), though I can exercise conscience in an erroneous, ill-formed, or vicious manner. Through habituation and learning about precedent, I become adept at applying principles to particular cases. John Henry Newman notes that, similarly, scientists, historians, geographers, biographers, and others must also have a knack for applying principles to particular matters, which he calls the *illative sense*.[76] This sense is a

---

74. Scheler, *Formalism in Ethics and Non-Formal Ethics of Values*, 90–98, 488.
75. Aquinas, *DV*, q.17, a.1.
76. John Henry Newman, *An Essay in Aid of a Grammar of Assent* (New York: Image, 1955), 270–83.

habitual conjoining of intellect and cogitative power with respect to some particular kind of object.

In exercising natural conscience, I grasp particulars' objective goodness for me. This is an experience of *autonomy*, of being ruled by oneself, by adopting a set of moral rules, such as the natural law. But in being called by value, I am *heteronomously* ruled by a distinct source of normativity, value, which calls me to obedience. I am not reducible to an autonomous being; I am also called and bound by other persons, values, and the communities in which I come to exist. In a sense, I belong to others. I can be called to respond to or instantiate some value that addresses itself to me personally; much as I experience transcendent personal presences through my senses, I can likewise experience a particular personal call to act in some way, an experience that the Platonic and Christian traditions explain as the prompting of an angel or *daimon*.[77]

But I can also experience an absolute command to act in some way, a message from God experienced in some calls of moral value or the natural law; when this happens, I feel my acts to be (as described in chapter 4) under absolute judgment.[78] We are not only autonomous or heteronomous but *theonomous*, ruled by God. In the call of conscience, as John Crosby describes it, I experience myself irreducibly as one who must act and absolutely commit myself.[79] In the experiences of conscience and of personal value-essences, we perceive the uniqueness of each human person (including ourselves), a uniqueness that can be fully described only in normative terms (as one who ought to do certain acts), and that can only be fully felt by spiritual affectivity, not intellect. These experiences also reveal that we have irreducible universal and individual aspects: we are instances of kinds and are called by universal norms, but also receive individual calls. Ethics like situation ethics or particularist virtue ethics that recognize only individual norms, or that seek to deconstruct all universal calls as mere masks for power, are reductionistic about the former.[80] Ethics that recognize only universal norms are reductionistic about the latter.

---

77. Cf. Plato, *Apology*.
78. Scheler, *Formalism in Ethics and Non-Formal Ethics of Values*, 318–28; Hildebrand, *Ethics*, 182–83, 481–84.
79. Crosby, *The Selfhood of the Human Person*, 214–15.
80. Cf. Desmond, *The Gift of Beauty and the Passion of Being*, chap. 3.

Being Affected, Affective Response, and Quiescence or Gelassenheit

Another kind of spiritual affection is *being affected* by value—for example, falling in love (not just perceiving another's unique beauty), being moved to sorrow for sin (not just feeling its disvalue), or being struck with joy by a beautiful mountain (not just perceiving its beauty). This is the spiritually affective act most like sensory passion, but unlike passion, it is a self-conscious, meaningfully motivated, intentional, self-transcending act. I am affected by value only on the basis of a prior value-perception. Here, I experience feeling as a gift, evoked by a valuable object. As Hildebrand puts it, I experience its "word" or "message" in me (and sometimes I experience this "word" as coming from God or another transcendent person). Given the distinct ways in which these acts occur, it makes sense to posit, as unfoldings of the power of the heart, distinct powers for these acts and for value-perception.

Karol Wojtyła distinguishes actively performed acts (such as acts of will) from passively received events that happen in me (such as passions). Both actualize my potencies, but when I perform the former, I experience my dynamism and efficacy, whereas when the latter happens in me, I experience another's dynamism and efficacy in me. Wojtyła holds that it is primarily through the former that a person is revealed.[81] But the experience of being affected shows that our relations to the world cannot be reduced to these two modes. In being affected, I experience the efficacy or word of a value in me, yet the feeling evoked in me by that word, though not a freely willed act, reveals who I am and issues out of my personal powers even more than a freely willed act. If I want to know a person (including myself), I must observe how they are moved by value to feel love, joy, fear, anger, and so forth; one's responsiveness or impassivity shows one's true depths, character, virtue or vice, and personal value-essence.

Yet another kind of spiritual affection is *affective response*.[82] Some values require a theoretical response: for example, the value of truth calls for intellectual assent to beliefs about its bearers. Others call for a volitional response: values of justice, for example, call for acts of instantiating them. But most values call for an affective response as their due, such as vener-

---

81. Wojtyła, *The Acting Person*, 68.
82. See Hildebrand, *Ethics*, chap. 17.

ation, admiration, reverence, or love. I cannot directly will to have these feelings; rather, they well up in me when I am properly disposed and am in the presence of a value. The jaded or hard-hearted person, even if not blind to perceiving value, cannot be affected or make these due responses. I can dispose myself to respond well to value by willing to place myself in the presence of values and to do what virtuous persons would do in their presence, but these acts do not guarantee that I will be affected appropriately or be moved to a due response. Full virtue requires the disposition to be "melted" and moved by things as they demand.[83] While these are responses, they arise as gifts from objects in cooperation with my disposition to respond. For example, a beautiful landscape should, upon perceiving the call of its beauty, affect me and call forth a response of deeply felt wonder in me; the liturgy should evoke reverence and adoration. A response is a self-transcending self-gift to the valuable object for its own sake; an offering of my feeling (and of myself) to the object is a "word" or "message" that confirms and completes the value. This is not a physical alteration of the object, nor an intentional completion of it (as in intellectual judgment), but rather a new kind of intentional form added to the object by affective affirmation.

The experiences of being affected and affective response call our attention to a key distinction that Hildebrand makes between two irreducible kinds of self-awareness. First, I can be "frontally self-conscious": I attend to my acts as intentional objects, about which I have thoughts, feelings, and so forth. Second, I can be "laterally self-conscious": I "live" or "enact" my acts, and so am reflexively self-conscious of them, conscious of them from "within" them, in subjectively performing of them, without regarding them as intentionally distinct objects.[84] Authentically being affected and duly responding works best if I have lateral consciousness of my feelings. To be frontally conscious of them—that is, to consider them as objects— risks weakening or destroying the possibility of transcending myself in a felt due response; for example, when I am before some beautiful scene in nature or before God in worship, my attention should be directed to them alone, rather than focused on my feelings.[85]

---

83. Cf. John Henry Newman, *Discussion and Arguments on Various Subjects* (London: Longmans, Green, and Co., 1907), 293. Aquinas sees "melting," an experienced "softening" of feeling toward the beloved, as an effect of love (*ST* I-II, q.28, a.5), but he does not see being affected as a perfection in itself.

84. Hildebrand, *Aesthetics*, vol. 1, 20–22.

85. Paul Griffiths (*Decreation*) argues that in our ultimate end there is nothing that it is like to be me: in my best state, I do not attend to my acts, but am ecstatically rapt in God and other persons. While this

However, given the self-determining structure of freedom, for this response to be fully authentic and personal, I must, by an act of will, sanction or allow the feeling to well up in me, adding my free consent to that affective response. I can have two kinds of freely willed stance toward spiritual feelings. The first is an explicit, self-determined "yes," freely affirming them on the basis of the gift they are; the feeling gives my will the ability and strength to affirm it, similar to how I can only respond to God's grace in virtue of the actuality of grace. But this way of sanctioning feelings is frontally self-consciousness, and so risks destroying the experience of authentically being affected. For example, Blondel describes the attitude of *aestheticism* in which one is open to (and a "connoisseur" of) any experience, even religious ones, but without ever committing to making an authentic response of self-gift to any object. Aesthetes focus on their experience, regarding it frontally so as to savor it, rather than whole-heartedly giving themselves to valuable objects in a due response. This ironic, detached stance leads to boredom and jadedness, to considering all experiences as games, or to regarding one's experiences as the only genuine bearers of value.[86] Such a worldview is always reductionistic; it fails to be open to what gives itself, as it gives itself, since most experience is not of experience, but of what is given in experience.

In a second freely willed stance toward feelings, the will is radically open: one does not explicitly and frontally affirm or reject anything but rather wills to allow oneself to be affected. Analytic Thomist Eleonore Stump describes how, prior to receiving God's grace, the will can be "quiescent," neither rejecting grace nor actively accepting or seeking it. This is not a morally good or evil state but a state of openness and availability, in which God can give gifts without violating one's will.[87] I can be quiescent not just toward grace but in willing to let myself be affected in general without anticipating or willing how I shall be affected. I can will this openness by will's natural potency, for I can naturally reason that if there are causes beyond what is naturally available, then it would be good for me to sometimes be affected by them. This belief can prompt me to cultivate openness or quiescence of will.

---

is reductionistic—there is irreducible value in frontally attending to many of my acts, so we can expect to continue to do so in our ultimate end—we often should not frontally attend to acts like being affected; in those acts, I should be ecstatically rapt in their objects.

86. Blondel, *Action* (1893), 16–33. Cf. Hildebrand, *Aesthetics*, vol. 1, 231, 247–52.
87. Stump, *Aquinas*, 401–404.

Heidegger, building on medieval theologian Meister Eckhart, calls this stance "letting things be," or "releasement" (*Gelassenheit*). In this stance, I do not think about what beings or acts are, nor do I consider concepts that apply to them. Rather, I open myself to beings' holistic self-manifestation, waiting for a "word" from them, not in anticipation or restlessness but restfully letting things give themselves and festively celebrating anything that appears.[88] This experience anticipates epektatic rest; it is an ongoing stance of potentially ever-deepening receptivity. If I adopt this stance, I allow value to give itself to me, to affect me, and to elicit a due response from me, without frontal self-consciousness; I allow the union of will and affectivity needed for a fully personal, free response to values, while retaining lateral self-consciousness. As Ulrich describes it, this stance is eminently creative: I freely "determine" all things, including myself, "in the sense of letting them be."[89] In this stance, I affirm and so eminently participate in God's creativity, since here I, in a sense, will all things to be, and so share in creating them, rather than just creating particular acts, artifacts, or beings of reason. In Hildebrand's terms, I add to all values and valuable beings "completing words" of due affective response and of free affirmation. However, *Gelassenheit* can also be an evasion of value, a refusal to commit to any definite response or an affirmation even of disvalues; the moral quality of an attitude of *Gelassenheit* is determined by the virtue or vice, and the stance of love or hatred, that motivates it.

Balthasar calls this stance *indifferencia, Gelassenheit, apatheia,* and *disponabilité*. In order to receive one's mission or vocation in life, or to receive any call (even the relatively mundane call that a role gives to an actor), one must be humble, permeable, poor in spirit, lacking prior willed attachment to any plan or creature, having a stance not of grasping particular goods but being open in hope to whatever valuable object will bless one's life.[90] This transcendentally open stance is the root of the greatest union between obedience and creativity in us. In this self-transcending openness, I permit values and valuable beings to act in me, not as enslaving myself to them but in continually freely receiving and allowing their activity to form my personality. For example, I can receive from God habits like the gifts of the

---

88. Martin Heidegger, *Country Path Conversations*, trans. Bret Davis (Bloomington: Indiana University Press, 2010), 77–89, 103–4.

89. Ulrich, *Homo Abyssus*, 363. Cf. Deleuze, *Nietzsche and Philosophy*.

90. Balthasar, GL5, 102, 628–33; TD1, 285–91, 645ff.; TD2, 59–62. Cf. Marcel, *The Philosophy of Existentialism*, 38; Caitlin Smith-Gilson, *The Metaphysical Presuppositions of Being-in-the-World: A Confrontation between St. Thomas Aquinas and Martin Heidegger* (New York: Continuum, 2010), 185.

Holy Spirit (such as wisdom and fear of the Lord [Is. 11:2]), whereby I am disposed to be moved by him. By these gifts, I perform acts, the beatitudes (acts like being meek, such that one inherits the whole earth [Mt. 5:3–10]), and achieve effects, fruits of the Spirit (like joy and peace [Gal. 5:22–23]), which result from God moving me, exceeding what I can achieve by my own power, which leads to divinization, sharing in God's own life.[91] Just by assuming this hopeful stance, I open the cosmos to receiving any value without affirming anything disvaluable about beings.[92]

Obedience, Participation, and Intentional Relations in Spiritual Affectivity

Some spiritual affections are natural, others obediential. Recall that natural potencies and acts fit with (or are proportioned to) their objects, while obediential potencies are ways we are open to being actualized by what exceeds our nature and exceeds what fits with us. Some spiritual affections arise when one thinks about or wills subjectively satisfying or objective goods; these modes of importance naturally fit with our powers, so these feelings are actualizations of the natural potency of our hearts. Other spiritual feelings are aroused by an objective good that exceeds our nature, such as God in himself; these actualize the heart's obediential potency.

Values also do not proportionately fit with powers. Intending values is like a natural act in that we seem predisposed to perceive, prefer, and focus on values. For example, we seem predisposed to grasp values as belonging to other persons or to an Absolute Being; we seem oriented to grasp something as holy and something as having the unique value of persons.[93] But just as (as we saw in chapters 2 and 3) no beings are contained *a priori* in the senses or intellect, so our apparent *a priori* openness to values does not mean that values proportionately fit with those powers. Rather, as experience shows, given values always exceed our feelings. For this reason, the openness to values found in these predispositions is an obediential openness. I become aware of these predispositions only when I encounter value, which elevates my heart to feel what exceeds my nature. We saw in chapter

---

91. Aquinas, *ST* I-II, q.68, a.1; q.69, a.1; q.70, a.1, 2; *In Gal.*, c. 5, lect. 6. Cf. Russell, *The Doctrine of Deification in the Greek Patristic Tradition*, 237.
92. Cf. Thomas Merton, *No Man Is an Island* (New York: Image Books, 1955), 31.
93. Scheler, *Formalism in Ethics and Non-Formal Ethics of Values*, 386–402; Scheler, *On the Eternal in Man*, 312–15.

3 how aesthetic cognition, though obediential, is generally part of the first awakening of the intellect, and how it involves the impact of beauty on multiple powers at once. This includes spiritual affectivity: in encountering the self-manifestation of being, I also encounter value, which actualizes the obediential potency of my affectivity. Full awakening of subjectivity requires receiving a call to full self-transcendence, to what is beyond ontological being. This call is experienced, for example, in another's face.

Experiences of value-feeling are best explained by distinguishing two kinds of obediential potencies. The first is any potency to receive actualities at the second level of being that exceed in perfection and immateriality what is proportionate to our nature, such as obediential potency to receive actual and sanctifying grace, supernatural participations in God's life and membership in the Church insofar as it is a unity of order. The second is any potency to participate in items at the third level of being, like values, which exceed the first and second levels of being and so exceed human nature and powers.

We saw that the ontological and axiological hierarchies do not always match; this is because we experience several different kinds of perfection. At the second level, a being is more perfect the more active and actual it is; being passively actualized is a sign of imperfection at this level. But at the third level, receptivity, vulnerability, and a tendency to communion with others are perfections, as we saw with being affected. Receptivity at this level does not involve passively received actualizations but is an open welcoming of beings, persons, or values. It is a stance taken by a person (like an action) but is also oriented entirely to receiving others (like a passion); as a new kind of receptivity, it is irreducible to ontological actions or passions. A person (like a divine person) who was ontologically impassible could still have this kind of receptivity or vulnerability.[94]

Value-perception, being affected, and due responses are intentional relations to and participations in values. As participations in items at the third level of being, these acts do not ontologically actualize me, but after performing such acts, I often perform cognitive and appetitive acts (like thinking about a perceived value or feeling a sensory appetite that corresponds to my spiritual affection) that ontologically actualize me. These subsequent acts are guided by the perceived value. In spiritual affection it-

---

94. Norris Clarke, "Person, Being, and St. Thomas," *Communio* 19, no. 4 (1992): 611–14; Schmitz, *The Gift of Creation*, 93; and Balthasar, *TD5*, 66–99.

self, however, I just become axiologically better. In abstractive cognition, I "become" the object of my cognition by participation when I am actualized by its species—that is, I take the object's content into my intellect. But to feel the value of, say, justice is not to receive justice's content or any species; it is not to become just but to feel and receive the value's call (though this presupposes that I have intellectually or sensibly perceived the valuable being). This is a *sui generis* intentional act and participation relation.[95]

Value-perception, being affected, and due response can be performed apart from one another in a few ways. I can perceive value without being affected; for example, when helping a person in distress, I might notice the beauty of nature around me and recognize that it calls for admiration without being moved by it, since I am rightly responding to a higher value. I can also perceive value but refuse to allow myself to be affected by it, as when I am distracted by pursuit of subjective satisfaction. I can even thereby become blind to value, such that nothing appears worth responding to for itself, or such that I can only perceive certain lower values, not higher ones.[96] I can also be affected by value without making a due response. For example, I might be moved to joy by beauty, but due to jadedness or cynicism be closed to admiring it, taking all being affected to be sentimentality, indulgence in feeling for its own sake. Finally, I can misperceive value, be affected wrongly, or make undue responses. When I feel values, my spiritual affectivity participates in and perceives values' Platonic Forms, such as justice or beauty itself. If I sense objects, form phantasms, or form intelligible species wrongly, or my vices affect the content of what I cognize, then I might participate in and so perceive a Platonic Form of value that does not correspond to the values actually in the beings before me.

Value, Secularity, and the State of Pure Nature

To grasp a thing's nature and the powers that directly proceed from it is to grasp what is necessary for being a thing of that kind. It is logically impossible that a thing exist without its nature; it is logically possible and conceivable that a thing exist without any particular property beyond its nature. Since value-perception is an obediential act, a human person

---

95. Dietrich von Hildebrand, "The Modes of Participation in Value," *International Philosophical Quarterly* 1, no. 1 (1961): 58–84.

96. For a taxonomy of ways in which I can become blind to value, and how these explain many false moralities and modern trends, see Hildebrand, *Graven Images*.

could exist who never feels or is motivated by value. This could happen through culpable value-blindness or be neurologically caused (since receiving phantasms, which occurs in the brain, is a necessary condition for value-perception). Reflecting on obediential acts like value-perception is an opportunity to consider what properties irreducibly belong to us by nature. It is worthwhile, in pursuit of figuring that out, to consider whether it could have been the case that no human person ever cognized value or had any other obediential potency actualized. In chapter 1, I mentioned Scheler's view that value-cognition is our first experience of a being. This is normally true, but it is not necessary for being a human person—that is, one can coherently conceive of a human person who never perceives value. Perceiving value is only our first fully self-conscious experience; sense-perceptions are temporally and efficiently causally prior to value-cognition.

Scholasticism explored what is possible for human nature by considering "states" (*status*) in which persons with human nature could have existed.[97] Considering possible states helps us grasp how we, in our actual state, are irreducible to (and include more than) what is natural in us, and it helps us grasp the many irreducible possibilities available to human persons. One state that scholastics considered is the possible *state of pure nature*, though no one has actually existed in this state. In that state, one would exist with all human natural potencies but without obediential potencies being actualized. One would lack supernatural gifts from God like grace and actual ordering to divine union, one would be mortal, and one's senses and reason would not be in harmony, just as in our current *fallen state*. But those lacks would not be punishments for original sin, which would not have been committed, since original sin presupposes an *original state of grace*. Rather those lacks would just have resulted from the disparate natural tendencies of our matter and powers. Our bodily and spiritually powers naturally pull in contrary directions, since they are naturally fulfilled by disparate goods; this, in part, leads to concupiscence and wrongdoing. Given my account of obediential potency, in a state of pure nature, one would also lack aesthetic cognition, intuition of being, affection for goodness in itself, and value-feeling.

---

97. Francisco Suárez, *De statibus humanae naturae*, in *Opera omnia*, v. 7 (Paris: Vivès, 1859); Feingold, *The Natural Desire to See God*; Long, *Natura Pura*, chap. 1; and Mark K. Spencer, "Grace, Natura Pura, and the Metaphysics of *Status*: Personalism and Thomism on the Historicity of the Human Person and the Genealogy of Modernity," *Proceedings of the American Catholic Philosophical Association* 91 (2017): 127–43.

A controversy over whether such a state is possible was part of the debate over the natural desire to see God considered in chapter 3. Those like the *Nouvelle* theologians who argued that we have a natural desire to see God in himself, rejected the possibility of such a graceless state; on their view, human persons are essentially ordered to sharing in God's life, and so could not exist without such an ordering. Any mortal, disharmonious, concupiscential state is a fallen state. They also argued that positing this state as a possibility led to the modern, secular, naturalistic view in which we are naturally self-contained and not ordered to God or other transcendent realities, a view they regarded as reductionistic of persons.[98] I shall not assess this as a historical claim about the genealogy of modern secularism. Rather, I partially concede it as a conceptual claim: the state of pure nature would be a "secular" state in that, although we would be naturally ordered by and to God as our first cause and natural end, we would do everything through knowledge drawn from creatures and for the sake of ends attainable by our own effort. In chapter 3, I contended that given a correct view of the irreducible openness of our intellects, we must deny that we have an unconditional natural desire to see God in himself. For this reason, and because I affirm the obediential character of various acts of intellect, will, and affectivity, I contend that we could have existed in such a state.

We could have reasoned, willed, and felt in a way that just aims at our own natural happiness, but we, in fact, do more than this. To deny the possibility of existing in a state of pure nature is experientially indefensible: it is to deny (as phenomenologist Emmanuel Falque notes) the naturalistic, self-moved character of much ordinary experience and its correspondence to what is strictly proportionate to our powers.[99] It is also to deny the gratuitous excess of other experiences and our radical openness to the new. Such experiences are safeguarded by positing the possibility of our nature existing without being ordered to what exceeds it and by positing an irreducible nature in us ordered to proportioned goods.

Given how at least some obediential potencies are normally actualized from the first moment of one's experience, however, it is very unlikely—

---

98. de Lubac, *The Mystery of the Supernatural*, 60–64, 90–94; Hans Urs von Balthasar, *A Theological Anthropology* (New York: Sheed and Ward, 1967), 84; John Milbank, *The Suspended Middle: Henri de Lubac and the Debate Concerning the Supernatural* (Grand Rapids, Mich.: Eerdmans, 2005), 35–37; and Yannaras, *Person and Eros*, 96–104.

99. Cf. Emmanuel Falque, *The Metamorphosis of Finitude*, trans. George Hughes (New York: Fordham University Press, 2012), 15–19, 158–59.

but not metaphysically impossible—that the entire population of human persons could ever have existed in a complete state of pure nature. When the scholastics discuss the state of pure nature, they only mean a state in which we are not given grace, not a state in which other obediential potencies are actualized. That sort of state is more clearly possible—and its possibility must be affirmed, at the risk of denying the experience (and fact) of the gratuity of grace, the transcendence of God, who *must* act only for the sake of the highest value and good, his own holiness, and at the risk of denying, again, the radical openness of human spiritual powers. However, it is highly unlikely that it could occur, given divine goodness and love.

I furthermore contend that some experiences frequently had in the modern, secular world have revealed irreducible features of persons not previously understood as well as they are now understood. Just as philosophical movements like phenomenology have highlighted features of self-consciousness to a new degree, and just as scientific movements like quantum mechanics have revealed features of reality that cannot be captured by a purely Aristotelian metaphysics, so political movements like liberalism and ethical movements like the ethics of authenticity have highlighted irreducible features of freedom. Just as phenomenological bracketing focuses our attention on features of experience otherwise easily overlooked, so secular movements bracket, say, religious aspects of human life and so focus our attention on irreducible aspects of ourselves. Those movements have revealed, for example, ways in which human flourishing is dependent on self-determination, and on creation and discovery of an interior identity, distinct to some extent from the identity received from nature or communities. Some members of these movements hold the false, reductionistic view that freedom and personal identity are absolute goods, or that we are nothing but our psychological or self-created identities. Holding that flourishing requires open, self-creative freedom, or that human persons have an interior identity of irreducible value, however, do not entail that these things are of absolute value, or that we are reducible to them. Rather, self-determinative, nonenslaved freedom and a robust sense of one's interior identity are necessary conditions for flourishing—but we can only fully determine ourselves through obedient reception of given natures, values, and *Gestalten*. We would not properly grasp "secular" features of persons if we took them to be only deviations from correct ordered natures. That is how they are taken by the *Nouvelle* theologians or by critics of modernity like Alasdair MacIntyre, who sees in modern views of the self only a reduction of persons to a content-less, emotional, irrational, therapeutic, pure "I."[100] While that is a risk of secular views, this does not negate the fact that in modernity, we are directly presented with features of persons that are actually given and were not previously appreciated. A metaphysics of irreducibility should include discoveries made in every age and by every school of thought, while synthesizing them and rejecting their reductionistic tendencies.

Charles Taylor has argued that in premodern societies, human persons experienced themselves to be "porous," open to affectively charged religious and other normative influences (like the influence of God, spirits, gods, demons, holy objects, and so forth), and so they experienced the physical world to be "enchanted," intrinsically including these influences. We contemporary persons, by contrast, experience the world to be "disenchanted," exerting purely physical or psychological (i.e., nonnormative) influences, and we experience ourselves to be "buffered," able to distance ourselves from influences by freely taking up stances toward them. When he calls modern experience "secular," Taylor means that we experience ourselves as always having many options regarding religions and worldviews, and as always able to change our positions on them.[101]

My interest here is not in whether these are accurate historical claims. Many contemporary persons experience themselves as porous and the world as enchanted; many premodern persons could distance themselves from influences, like through a focus on law or by turning myths into rationalistic systems.[102] Rather, Taylor's distinction is important as a phenomenological account of two ways that human persons can relate to the world, each of which discloses something irreducible about our powers. Affectivity (like sensation) is, for the most part, a "porous" power, while the will is a "buffering" power. In the former, as Desmond describes it, I experience, especially in experiences of beauty, a receptivity to being (*pas-*

---

100. Alasdair MacIntyre, *After Virtue* (Notre Dame, Ind.: University of Notre Dame Press, 1984), 30–35.

101. Charles Taylor, *A Secular Age* (Cambridge, Mass.: Harvard University Press, 2007), 37–41.

102. See Jason Josephson-Storm, *The Myth of Disenchantment* (Chicago: University of Chicago Press, 2017). Believing in enchantment, which is frequently found in a secular age, is not the same as feeling its influence in a porous way. The language of enchantment and disenchantment is from Max Weber, "Science as a Vocation," in *From Max Weber: Essays on Sociology*, ed. H. H. Gerth and C. Wright Mills (New York: Routledge, 2009), 129–56. Weber also notes how, with the eclipse of monotheism in the modern world, many people experience the modern world as "re-enchanted," full of many sources of transcendence. I offered a metaphysics of the "enchanted" features of reality in chapter 2.

sio essendi) that is more fundamental than, and presupposed by, any striving to determine myself or create beauty (*conatus essendi*).[103] When the will is quiescent, we experience axiological influence more fully, and we experience the world to be "enchanted," for example, having many directly given sources of transcendence and many holy and demonic aspects. By contrast, when one habitually frontally sanctions or disavows any feeling, then one experiences those influences less powerfully and experiences the world more "secularly."

Freedom's self-determining structure is an irreducibly "secular" core in us. Buffered freedom reveals our transcendence over all that would enslave our actions, but our porous affectivity makes us irreducibly "religious" and oriented to enchantment; it gives us a sense of creatureliness, rootedness, piety, and being at home in a particular land and in *Gestalt* forms like cultural practices, traditions, and rituals, influenced by natural beings and transcendent persons.[104] An ethics or politics fulfilling to irreducible persons must aim at conserving rootedness in tradition, land, nature, and liturgy, not in a manner that enslaves persons to a place or a tradition but fosters free openness to those elements of life. Any ethics or politics that allows us to freely remake ourselves or plan society entirely as we will is reductionistic of these rooted features of persons. This is so whether it allows this by treating us purely as individuals (as in some versions of *libertarianism* or *individualism*), by prescription by a centralized authority or by treating us as parts of mass society (as in some versions of *collectivism* or *totalitarianism*), or in a way allowed by spontaneous transactions or by treating us purely as consumers or maximizers of self-interest (as in some versions of *liberalism*). But the will's alienation from and transcendence over anything given must also be retained in any ethics or politics. Contrary to some *conservative* or *traditionalist* politics, we are not reducible to our place in a given order—say, in a culture, race, or class. Fulfilling all aspects of persons requires both a cosmopolitan orientation that transcends particular times and places, aiming at freely and creatively bringing about goodness and value, and rootedness in meaning-bestowing *Gestalt*-communities.

Our secular condition also helps us understand the relation between will and intellect. In Aquinas's somewhat porous view, we will to assent

---

103. Desmond, *The Gift of Beauty and the Passion of Being*, introduction and chap. 1.
104. Roger Scruton, *How to Think Seriously About the Planet: The Case for an Environmental Conservatism* (Oxford: Oxford University Press, 2012), chap. 7.

to beliefs or to what is not demonstratively known, but we immediately grasp and assent to self-evident propositions like first principles (like the law of noncontradiction or the first principle of the natural law) without needing to will these assents. We have natural dispositions to assent to principles, such as *synderesis*, which disposes us to grasp and assent to first principles of natural law.[105] According to some Thomistic views, when we practically reason, applying universal principles to particular situations in a practical syllogism, the conclusion just is a volitional choice.[106] But secular or buffered experiences show that dispositions to assent to principles can be overridden, revealing irreducible aspects of freedom that are hidden on an enchanted or porous view. We experience ourselves as able to both reject the conclusion of a practical syllogism and convert to various competing worldviews, including paraconsistent logic (suspending belief in the law of noncontradiction), antimoral worldviews (suspending belief in first principles of natural law), or deconstructionist accounts of meaning (where, given the deferral of grasping any meaning, no proposition appears self-evident). Blondel describes how we choose to affirm that *there is something*, at least implicitly, in choosing to continue acting and living, rather than affirming that *there is nothing*, which we could affirm, given the transitoriness and ambiguity of many experiences.[107] These experiences all reveal that free election accompanies any intellectual act, even if it is just (as in many porous experiences) quiescence to what intellect is disposed to grasp. The buffered or secular view, in which we experience ourselves as able to choose alternative beliefs, shows us how we are freely open to all of being, though we are normatively called to freely sanction and open ourselves to what is only given in many enchanted, religious, or porous acts.

---

105. Aquinas, *ST* I, q.79, a.6, 7; I-II, q.51, a.3; II-II, q.2 a.1.
106. See, for example, Thomas Osborne, *Human Action in Thomas Aquinas, John Duns Scotus, and William of Ockham* (Washington, D.C.: The Catholic University of America Press, 2014), 68–70.
107. Blondel, *Action (1893)*, 51–54.

Chapter 6 Soul, Powers, and the Principle of *Energeia*

As I begin to synthesize the last few chapters, I need to consider how powers relate to the soul, distinguish additional powers in the soul (including for social acts, spiritual perception, and memory), and offer a solution to the problem of divine causality. Most importantly, in this chapter, I work out a more complete metaphysics of our activities, self-manifestations, and nature, drawing on notions of *energeiai* and *ousiai* from the Greek Fathers, especially Gregory Palamas. This will set the stage for the fuller portrait of the human person that will be presented in the second part of this book.

Relations of Powers to the Soul

Over the last three chapters, I have examined transcendentally open intellectual, volitional, and affective powers in our souls. Scholastics have debated how the soul and powers relate and are distinguished. Aquinas argued for a real distinction between soul and powers (and among powers): powers are proper accidents (*propria*)—that is, properties efficiently caused by our essence as soon as it exists. Evidence that powers are really distinct from the soul is found in experiences of different kinds of acts impeding one another (as when feeling distracts from thinking) or aiding one another (as when feeling guides thinking). That acts can interact in these ways is explained by positing distinct principles for each kind of act; were there only one principle for all these acts, they could not simultaneously occur or interact.¹ Scotus, by contrast, argued that powers are distinct formalities in the soul. This view is motivated by the experience of my acts as directly mine. Were they actualizations of powers distinct from my substance, even acts like beatific vision would not be immediately my perfections (i.e., perfections of this substance) but would rather belong to me only through the mediation of beings distinct from me.² Evidence for this view is found in the presence of the mode of being of each power in the soul in itself; as we have seen, for the soul to cause spiritual powers, their mode of being must be in the soul itself, and so the soul is really identical to (and has as formalities) subjectivity, intelligibility, free actuality, and affectivity. I reject William of Ockham's view that powers are really and formally identical to the soul.³ This fails to explain the experiential evidence just mentioned for distinctions among them.

We can see what each view gets right by considering more experiences (as described by phenomenologists and others) and then reasoning about what principles would fit with those experiences. Drawing on experiences of subjectivity like those described in chapter 1, Scheler describes how we experience ourselves as subjectivities entering or "flowing" into each act. Stein describes how we experience our subjective life as a single power differentiated in a plurality of directions: receptive, active, retentive, and so forth.⁴ (The phenomenological metaphor of "flowing" resembles the scholastic metaphor of "overflow" explained in earlier chapters.) Scotus's view fits with the experience of oneself as a single subject entering into acts. Subjectivity, freedom, intelligibility, and affectivity are formalities in the soul, and each affects and enters into all our powers; each formality affects the other formalities through circumincession. But this experience is consistent with Aquinas's view that powers are also actualities distinct from the soul and its formalities, which the soul uses as instruments to perform acts that fundamentally belong to and actualize the soul. In acting, my soul's subjectivity flows into these powers. Since acts are efficiently caused by the soul, I not only can use more than one power at a time such that their acts impede or aid one another but I can also perform single acts that belong to more than one power at the same time.

---

1. Aquinas, *In I Sent.*, d.17, q.1, a.2, ad 2; *ST* I, q.77, a.1; *DEE*, c. 5.
2. Scotus, *Ord.* II, d16, q.un., n. 15–19.
3. William of Ockham, *Quaestiones in librum secundum Sententiarum*, v. 5 of *Opera theologica* (St. Bonaventure: Franciscan Institute, 1981), q.20, 435.
4. Scheler, *Formalism in Ethics and Non-Formal Ethics of Values*, 386–402; Stein, *Finite and Eternal Being*, 435.

Before proceeding further, a few scholastic terms must be defined more precisely. *Powers* (or *natural powers*) are potencies open to any act done under some formal object, regardless of whether such an act moves its substance toward its end. *Dispositions* are orientations of powers to acts that move their subject toward or away from their end. *Habits* (*habitus*) are stable dispositions directed by reason.[5] *Basic powers*, as defined by analytic Thomists following Elizabeth Anscombe, are abilities to directly perform acts, as opposed to abilities to perform acts by doing something else.[6] I do not have a basic power to produce a book, since I do this by consciously doing more basic things, like thinking, planning, and typing. I have a basic power to raise my arm, since I self-consciously raise my arm just by doing it, though this act includes my nerves firing and muscles contracting as this act's material causes. To gain new basic powers is to take on a new mode of existing or fitting with the world.[7] People who are just learning to play a musical instrument must deliberatively move their fingers; the latter are their basic actions, and they play the instrument by moving their fingers. But master musicians directly play an instrument: *playing the instrument* is their basic action, and their fingers' motions are just material causes within that basic action. Similar experiences are found in any skilled practice, such as athletic ability, dance, reading, writing, and speaking a language. Many acquirable basic powers actually meet the definition just given for natural powers; hence, we have powers that use multiple, more fundamental natural powers. For example, affective cognition (mentioned above) joins acts of intellect and affectivity in a single act of grasping content through feeling. Unlike moral virtues and vices, these powers are not new dispositions or habits, since acts like reading or playing an instrument are neutral with respect to our end: they do not make us better or worse as human substances or persons.[8]

Social Acts

One power that joins together a few more fundamental powers is *a power for second-person acts* (mentioned in chapter 3), which are essentially re-

5. See Spencer, "Habits, Potencies, and Obedience."
6. See Koons and O'Brien, "Objects of Intention," 662, following G. E. M. Anscombe, *Intention* (Cambridge, Mass.: Harvard University Press, 2000).
7. Cf. Merleau-Ponty, *Phenomenology of Perception*, 164–66.
8. *Contra*, for example, Scotus, *Ord.* III, d.33, q.un. n. 19, ad 3; Suárez, *DM*, d.39, s.2, n. 37; d.44, s.2, n. 1–4; d.53, s.2, n. 3.

sponsive to other persons.⁹ Hildebrand, building on realist phenomenologist Adolf Reinach, distinguishes a power in the soul for "social acts," such as promising, telling, commanding, and forgiving.¹⁰ When I promise or command, I determine myself to have a stance toward another, but my act is only complete if the addressee receives this act in the proper way, which I cannot cause—for example, responding to my command or accepting my promise. While most human acts have an intersubjective aspect, social acts essentially take another person as their objects; *directedness to another* is part of their formal object. That they have this distinct formal object is evidence that they belong to a distinct power, though one that includes the will. The ability to promise or tell something is not a disposition (since I can do these acts well or badly) nor an obediential potency (since I can perform these acts by my efforts alone). This ability fits the definition for a natural power.

Responsiveness to others' social acts is itself a social act. We saw in chapter 4 that, as Balthasar described, our minds are often first opened by seeing love on our mothers' faces—that is, opened by a social act, an act that takes another essentially as its object. But such an act also actualizes intellect and will. For example, to promise is to intellectually grasp and will to manifest a relation to another while willingly determining myself to be related to that other. Social acts involve the formal objects of intellect, will, and often affectivity but add the formal object of reference to other persons. Social acts involve a new power that joins these more fundamental powers.

To speak, Aquinas says, is to refer a mental concept to someone, to manifest intellectual content by an act of will. However, Aquinas argues that human persons' wills are not "rules of truth"—that is, to grasp what someone wills is not *ipso facto* to grasp the truth about him or her. For this reason, he holds that learning what another wills does not perfect my intellect, while grasping universal truths does. I only perfect others intellectually by helping them to grasp universal truth about beings for themselves.¹¹ This describes intellectual perfection at the second level of being, where intellect is perfected by grasping higher actualities and more universal concepts and causes, up to grasping God, the first cause.

---

9. Stump, *Wandering in Darkness*; Andrew Pinsent, *The Second-Person Perspective in Aquinas' Ethics* (London: Routledge, 2013).

10. Hildebrand, *Ethics*, 216–17; Adolf Reinach, "The A Priori Foundations of Civil Law," trans. John Crosby, *Aletheia* 3 (1983): 1–142. Cf. John MacMurray, *Persons in Relation* (New York: Harpers and Brothers, 1961), 69–74.

11. Aquinas, *ST* I, q.107, a.1–2; q.117, a.1. Cf. Plato, *Meno*.

However, getting to know other persons and their *ordo amoris* or the deepest desires of their hearts is often experienced as more satisfying and perfecting than abstract cognition.[12] We experience this deeper perfection, as Marion describes, when longing for love; if I do not know myself to be loved or capable of loving, then abstract knowledge is worthless to me.[13] Martin Buber describes how I can relate to another as a "Thou," a unique person addressed for his or her own sake rather than a bearer of universalizable properties, an examined object, or a conveyor of knowledge; I can also relate to another as a fellow member of a "we," an experienced coacting community.[14] While in speaking about others we focus on concepts that apply to them, in speaking to or with others, we focus on the others themselves, and employ concepts only to guide our focus on them or to evoke responses from them. Speaking well with others involves receptively welcoming all the other reveals about him or herself through social and other second-person acts. These social acts perfect us at the third level of being, drawing us into *Gestalt* communities with others, like the conversation as described in chapter 5.

As we have seen, each power of the soul has as its formal object either being, a principle of being, or a transcendental property of being. One might think that the power for social acts cannot be a power of the soul because its formal object, *directedness to other persons*, seems to fit none of these conditions. But this is a transcendental, one that Balthasar found to be implicitly described in the Old Testament: relating to another as other requires righteousness in fidelity (*sedaka*), a refusal to reduce the other to a totalizable object and a bestowing of favor, kindness, and hospitable openness that makes space for the other.[15] Indeed, all beings, especially (but not only) persons, give themselves to such an attitude as items with which we can enter into relationship, that can give us space for our unfolding and fulfillment, and that we can give space to for theirs. Through relating to another, I become open to the world in a new and unique way, guided by that other being or person, and such that, reciprocally, that other becomes open to the world in a new way guided by contact with me. While in its ontological being, no being is changed by being sensed or known, at a higher level, it is thereby perfected: when a being's content is received by sense or

---

12. On "desires of the heart," see Stump, *Wandering in Darkness*, 431.
13. Marion, *The Erotic Phenomenon*, 16–29.
14. Martin Buber, *I and Thou*, trans. Walter Kaufmann (New York: Touchstone, 1970).
15. Balthasar, *GL6*, 138–65.

intellect, it comes to exist in a higher way than its natural mode of being, such that it relates to the world in ways it could not on its own. As persons, we can, by intertwining and participation, give to other beings new ways of being open to the world, and we can receive new ways of being open to the world from them.[16] When I contemplate beings, they are perfected if I relate to them in this social way. Furthermore, I can be entirely fulfilled only if I am perceived and related to by others. I am irreducible to my natural being; rather, I include how I appear to others and the unique way I allow them to relate to the world when they relate to me. That the power for social acts aims at its objects via this transcendental, which I call the *hospitality* of being, shows it to be a distinct, irreducible power.

Spiritual Perception

The power for social acts presupposes that we can perceive persons as persons. Such perception requires not only that we intellectually grasp that other as a person but also that we perceive (by will) the other's moral resistance to our acts and (by affectivity) the other's unique beauty. This perception points to a broader power for *spiritual perception* or *spiritual senses*, a power that joins intellect, will, and affectivity.[17] To spiritually perceive is to have direct, intuitive acquaintance with a spiritual or immaterial reality rather than reasoning from claims about physical, sensible things to claims about these realities.[18]

Some acts of spiritual perception, considered in earlier chapters, are acts of intellectual, affective, volitional, or sensory powers; they do not require positing an additional power of spiritual perception. For example, we sense the "human aspect" of the world and angels' or God's personal presence; we can intellectually perceive essences, *esse*, and divine activity; and by intellect, will, or affectivity, we can cognize aesthetically, intuit being, know by connaturality, and perceive value. In some perceptions, spiritual realities (such as God or Platonic Forms) are perceived "sacramentally"

---

16. Balthasar, *TL1*, 62–79.
17. Philip of the Trinity, *Summa theologiae mysticae* (Lyon: Borde, Arnaud, and Rigaud, 1656), 179.
18. What follows is from Balthasar, *GL1*, 356–418; William Alston, *Perceiving God: The Epistemology of Religious Experience* (Ithaca, N.Y.: Cornell University Press, 1991); Greco, "Perception as Interpretation"; Gavrilyuk and Coakley, *The Spiritual Senses*; Mark McInroy, *Balthasar on the Spiritual Senses* (Oxford: Oxford University Press, 2014); Yadav, *The Problem of Perception and the Experience of God*; and Mark K. Spencer, "The Phenomenology and Metaphysics of Spiritual Perception," *New Blackfriars* 97, no. 1072 (2016): 677–92.

through the mediation of physical beings that participate in them—that is, physical beings efficaciously serve to make these higher realities present.[19] Some intellectual perceptions arise obedientially, such as experiences of prophecy and mystical knowledge, when God infuses species and "lights" (cognition-enabling conditions) into our intellects whereby we perceive him preternaturally—that is, exceeding what is naturally possible for us and requiring a special divine gift, but without involving a supernatural, graced participation in his life in itself. God can also act on our intellects so that we perceive him directly, without mediation by concepts or species, in the beatific vision.[20]

But other acts of spiritual perception are not explicable as acts of just intellect, affectivity, will, or sense. These require positing new powers in the soul. The Christian and other traditions have described such acts as resembling bodily sensation. I have mentioned the principles that whatever is found in lower powers is found in higher powers in a more excellent way, and that some higher acts are qualitatively analogous or correspond to material things, such that the latter reveal things about the former. If qualities analogous to those found in bodily acts are found in certain spiritual acts, such that the latter have a character distinct from acts of already distinguished powers, then there is reason to posit a new power of spiritual perception for these acts. The scholastic tradition described spiritually perceptive acts corresponding to each bodily sense. We feel God's loving penetration (*illapsus*) into the soul in a way experientially like taste and touch, even to the extent that the experience is analogous to sexual experiences, and the perceived union with God is called "divine union" or "spiritual marriage." We taste the sweetness of his mercy; exercising the gift of the Holy Spirit of wisdom (*sapientia*) is like taste (*sapor*), an intimate entering into who God is, such that we gain knowledge of him and his ways by experienced direct contact. We touch his power, and even when we cannot see or grasp him clearly, the experience of being joined to him by faith can be like a tactile experience. We see God through the gift of understanding (*intellectus*) and, ultimately, in the beatific vision. We smell the fragrance or intimations of his holiness and that of his saints, and even those who lack the gift of wisdom (or tasting God) can nevertheless spiritually smell or gain intimations of what wisdom reveals about God. Further experi-

19. Aquinas, *ST* III, q.60.
20. Aquinas, *In II Sent.*, d.23, q.2, a.1; *DV*, q.18, a.1; *ST* I, q.56, a.3; q.89, a.1; II-II, q.173. Cf. Albert Farges, *Mystical Phenomena*, trans. S. P. Jacques (New York: Benzinger, 1926), 72.

ences of God from the dark night of the soul to hearing interior words of knowledge and wisdom are also described in sensory terms.[21]

If, as I think, these descriptions are phenomenological, not merely metaphorical, then properties analogous to sensible qualities are found in immaterial things; having sensible qualities or qualities analogous to them is thus a transcendental. Through this experience, we can grasp that the whole analysis of sensible beauty in chapter 2 applies analogously to all beings. Spiritual perception grasps objects under this distinct, transcendental formal object, and so warrants positing a new power or set of powers in the soul. But this power need not be natural to us; experiences of spiritual perception often include experiences of receiving this power, and in receiving it, my soul's obediential openness is actualized. The soul's powers are intertwined with our sensing bodies; hence, our spiritual powers take on characteristics analogous to our bodies' sensory modalities and qualitative character. Our souls are to open to all being but in a specifically human way. Had we other bodily senses, like echolocation or awareness of magnetic fields (as other animals do), we might have had spiritual senses that grasped spiritual realities in ways analogous to those senses.[22]

Experiences of social acts and spiritual perception are evidence that we can act through more than one natural power simultaneously and support synthesizing Thomistic and Scotistic theories of powers. I turn now to another piece of evidence for these claims, that of acts taking place at varying levels of "depth" within me.

Surface and Depth: Attention, Memory, Superactual Attitudes, and Moods

Our acts are best explained by positing a few levels within them; doing this helps us avoid reducing our acts to just some of their aspects. First, human acts are actualizations of powers: our potentiality to perform an act and our actual performance of it are two states of a single power. Second, they are actualizations of the soul. Acts of seeing and pumping blood actualize

---

21. Aquinas, *ST* II-II, q.8, a.7; q.45, a.2; *In I Cor.*, c. 12, v. 17; *In Ps.*, 33[34].9; *ST* II-II, q.8, a.7; q.45, a.2; *In I Cor.*, 12:17; Salmanticenses, *Cursus theologicus*, in *De beatitudine*, v. 5 (Paris: Victor Palmé, 1878), 206; and Boyd Taylor Coolman's essays on Alexander of Hales and Thomas Gallus in Gavrilyuk and Coakley, *Spiritual Senses*.

22. For some empirical evidence that humans can sense magnetic fields, see Connie X. Wang et al., "Transduction of the Geomagnetic Field as Evidenced from Alpha-band Activity in the Human Brain," *eNeuro* 6, no. 2 (2019), https://doi.org/10.1523/ENEURO.0483-18.2019.

not only powers but the subsistent organs—eyes and hearts—actualized by those powers. Likewise, acts of thinking or willing actualize my soul, in which my spiritual powers inhere. In chapter 7, I consider further levels: our acts belong to and modify substances, supposits, and persons. Here, I consider further ways that acts relate to soul and powers, given in experiences of *superficiality* and *depth*.[23] Some thinkers have used "surface" and "depth" to distinguish what actually and holistically appears, such as beauty in the full sense, from purported underlying characteristics used to explain away surface beauty, as when philosophers try to explain beauty away as nothing but a manifestation of unconscious acts, or economic conditions, or the will to power.[24] I endorse the claim that surface beauty is irreducible to such characteristics, but here, by "surface" acts, I mean superficial acts.

Sometimes, I act distractedly, unable to fix my attention on any one object. In this state, I self-consciously and meaningfully perform acts of thinking, willing, and feeling. Yet all these acts are fleeting, and I cannot fully attend to their meanings; nothing fits them together into a meaningful sequence of acts, a single *Gestalt*. At other times, I am distracted such that I attend only to what is less valuable or more superficial, when greater values call my attention. By contrast, I can also be recollected or wakeful, freely attending to each object with the attention it deserves, a state the Greek tradition calls watchfulness or stillness (*hesychia*).[25] I am then motivated both by the importance of objects and by an interior abundance of actuality, acting out of what Hildebrand calls my depth or "free center." I become recollected by voluntarily withdrawing my attention into myself so that I can then give each object appropriate attention, or by being moved by a value, especially the highest value, that of God. Recollection is necessary for self-transcending love or contemplation, for a healthy subjectivity or sense for what concerns me and my good, and to overcome enslavement and develop a full personality.[26] But recollection alone does not achieve these goals; I can be recollected and yet enslaved to myself, to my will to power.

23. Dietrich von Hildebrand, *Sittlichkeit und ethische Werterkenntnis* (Paris: Vallendar-Schönstatt, 1982), 89–111.
24. Desmond, The *Gift of Beauty and the Passion of Being*, chaps. 2, 4; Hart, The *Beauty of the Infinite*; and Scruton, *Sexual Desire*.
25. See, for example, Hesychios the Priest, "On Watchfulness and Holiness," in *The Philokalia*, vol. 1, ed. Nikodimos of the Holy Mountain and Makarios of Corinth, trans. G. E. H. Palmer et al. (New York: Farrar, Straus and Giroux, 1979), 162–198.
26. Hildebrand, *Transformation in Christ*, 105–13; Crosby, *Selfhood*, 100–102.

Acts actualize my powers regardless of whether I am recollected or distracted. I here propose a metaphysics, building on the Franciscan scholastic tradition, that causally accounts for this experience. In addition to formalities already posited in the soul, I posit in our souls an orientation to acts of attention. The Franciscan scholastic Peter John Olivi posited attention as a cognitive activity that goes out from a subject and actively grasps an object.[27] As an act of a formality, not a power, attention is a directing of my subjectivity toward the actualizations of my powers. We have already seen that acts of multiple powers can be joined into single acts; likewise, acts can be actualized by further acts. When I perform an act with a power, such as intellect or will, I can further actualize that intellectual act with an act of attention, such that I attend to it deeply or with recollection; if I fail to do this, I am distracted from that act and perform it superficially. Through attention, my subjectivity participates to varying degrees in my powers' actualizations. Scotus's metaphysics of powers explains acts that directly actualize formalities of the soul; Aquinas's metaphysics explains acts that actualize powers and so can be unified with other acts, or attended to with greater or less superficiality.

Another act that I explain as actualizing a formality is *memory*. On Aquinas's view, we have both sensory and intellectual memory. By the latter, I retain intelligible species and concepts so that I can recall their content later, though this requires turning to the correct phantasm; if the latter has been forgotten or lost through neurological decay, I will not be able to remember the content of the corresponding concepts.[28] But Marion, building on Augustine, contrasts this memory of particular concepts to a deeper act of attentionally uniting and retaining all my acts.[29] As Stein describes it, this is a deep sense of myself that affects and unites all my other acts. This is not an intellectual act whereby I grasp what I essentially am but rather a feeling or perception of myself that accompanies and underlies my other acts.[30] Aquinas partially accounts for this experience with his notion of habitual self-cognition, which is a disposition to grasp itself that is intrinsic to the soul.[31] This uniting and self-grasping is not merely a habit, however, but a continual experience of myself and my acts

---

27. See Robert Pasnau, *Theories of Cognition in the Later Middle Ages* (Cambridge: Cambridge University Press, 1997), 131–34, 168–81.
28. *ST* I, q.79, a.6.
29. Marion, *In the Self's Place*, 69–81, building on Augustine, *On the Trinity*, X; *Confessions*, X.
30. Stein, *Finite and Eternal Being*, 454–56.
31. Aquinas, *DV*, q.10, a.8.

as united; it is a spiritual analogue of the body's common sense, which roots all the other sensory powers. As formalities in the soul, rather than distinct powers, abilities to remember and to attend are not distinguished by having distinct formal objects; rather, they are ways in which I can unite and actualize powers' acts.

By this memory, I am aware of time (including Bergsonian duration and a sense of the now, which includes retention of the past and a protension of the future) in a more meaningful and self-conscious way than how I grasp time (and myself) through the common sense. By memory, I unite all the acts that have befallen me in an overall sense of myself; I have an inchoate sense of things toward which I can transcend myself, such as happiness or God. By memory and attention, I am also aware of what is absent from me.[32] By intellect and sense, I grasp what is absent through what is present, as when I grasp what is pictured in a photograph (though it is not present) or when I apperceive the unseen sides of a physical object as I move around it (though they are not directly given to me). But by this deeper memory, I am aware of the absent as absent (not as an intentional object), as an ever-present background or periphery to what is present, as when my thoughts are colored by what I have forgotten or by what I am not currently attending to, when I am aware that I have forgotten something, or when retention of the past or anticipation of the future colors my experience of the present.

Like memory, moods and habits also form a background to our acts. I can form virtues and vices that dispose my powers to be actualized in certain ways. These include natural acquired virtues, which orient me to objective goods, and obediential acquired virtues, which orient me to values. Acquired virtues are genuine virtues, since they direct us to a genuine, natural end, even though, unlike infused virtues, they do not direct us to our highest end, God in himself.[33] I can also form habits that transform my whole outlook on the world. Hildebrand distinguishes the potential to perform acts, occurrent acts themselves, dispositions (including virtues and vices) to perform definite acts, and "superactual" attitudes—lasting attitudes, beliefs, or dispositions that color all of my acts. For example,

---

32. Sokolowski, *Phenomenology*, chap. 9; John Panteleimon Manoussakis, "The Time of the Body," in *On Time*, ed. Marina Marren (Newcastle-upon-Tyne: Cambridge Scholars, 2016), 32–43.

33. Brandon Dahm, "The Acquired Virtues are Real Virtues," *Faith and Philosophy* 32, no. 4 (2015): 453–70, against Eleonore Stump, "The Non-Aristotelian Character of Aquinas' Ethics," *Faith and Philosophy* 28, no. 1 (2011): 29–43; and Andrew Pinsent, *Second-Person Perspective*.

my every act can have a tonality of reverence or faith, love or hatred, lust or pride. These attitudes actualize my soul, such that my acts of attention and memory (and thereby all my other acts) take on a particular character. Forming virtues and vices involves forming superactual attitudes; Hildebrand speaks of actions proceeding from a reverent or prideful "center."[34] Some particular acts (like falling in love) that touch me deeply, give rise to a superactual attitude, such that the whole world is then experienced in a way colored by that love. Others (like a momentary infatuation) are superficial, that is, they do not give rise to such an attitude.[35] A moral or religious conversion is, in part, a change in superactual attitudes, a change in how formalities of attention and memory are actualized and directed, which colors all other acts. Stein speaks of persons "changing natures" when they have conversions or other shifts in character, as when, through a religious conversion, a person who was vain and petty becomes reverent and charitable.[36] While such a convert is still essentially the same human person, his or her nature has changed in that formalities belonging essentially to the soul are actualized in a new way. My superactual attitudes form the *Gestalt* of my character or personality; as person and human substance, I can survive a change in this *Gestalt*, but there is a metaphysical and phenomenological sense of *who I am* that does not survive such a change. This is not only a change in accidents but also a change in that character by which my soul is directly actualized, and with which I subjectively identify myself and with which others socially identify me.

In addition to long-lasting superactual attitudes, particular moods directly actualize my soul whenever they affect all my powers' acts. Unlike spiritual affects and sensitive appetites, which intend distinct objects, moods are feelings that lack a distinct object but open me to reality in distinct ways and give an affective tonality to other acts.[37] Like attention, objectless acts such as moods actualize and give further content to powers' acts. Unlike nonintentional bodily feelings like drunkenness and hunger, moods are not merely caused but are meaningful, self-conscious acts—and

---

34. Hildebrand, *Ethics*, 314–15, 387–88. One attitude is a basic moral tenor, a tendency toward certain values or disvalues (Scheler, *Formalism in Ethics and Non-Formal Ethics of Values*, 112); others include my *ordo amoris* and my love or hated in the sense of being open or closed to values in general.

35. Hildebrand, *The Nature of Love*, 33–34, 292. Superactual attitudes are an aspect of the "unconscious" layer of experience to which I alluded earlier. Further inquiry into this layer could help with understanding mental and spiritual illness (which are different than personal sin) in the context of a holistic portrait of the person.

36. Stein, *Finite and Eternal Being*, 75.

37. Hildebrand, *The Heart*, 39.

hence are spiritual acts rooted in the soul. They include the moods mentioned in chapter 1, anxiety (whereby, on Heidegger's description, I am aware of the nothingness underlying all finite beings) and security (whereby, on Stein's description, I feel able to rest confidently in the support of being). Other moods include boredom, in which (as Marion describes it) I am indifferent to and dissatisfied with not only all beings, but with being and existence themselves; surplus pleasure or enjoyment (*jouissance*), in which (as Luce Irigaray describes it) I feel pleasure and welcome others to enter into intimacy with me; and experiences of oneness with all things, in which (as mystics in the Catholic and Buddhist traditions describe it) the experience of distinction between subject and object is lost.[38] Indeed, in each mood (as in self-sensing), one experiences oneself and the world holistically, without a fully experienced distinction between oneself as subject and other things as objects. Each mood directs or actualizes my acts. For example, one who knows beings while anxious grasps those beings' finitude and insufficiency for providing fulfillment, since they appear against a background of nothingness.

This exploration of acts helps us better understand our end. Aquinas holds that our ultimate fulfillment is an intellectual act. In his view, the intellect is the noblest (or most valuable) power because it attains its objects so that they are united to us. The will, by contrast, aims at objects distinct from itself, either as desiring them (and so they have not yet been attained) or as delighting in them (and so they have already been attained). We unite with God by the intellect, and all other powers' acts just prepare for this most unitive act or are consequences of it. Scotus, by contrast, holds that our highest happiness is an act of will, which he thinks is our noblest power, because it is better to love God than to know him; because the will aims at things in themselves, not just at things in us; and because intellect's object is contained in the will's as one good among many.[39]

But we have seen that (contrary to Aquinas) we directly grasp objects by our wills and so are united to them through will, and (contrary to Scotus) by our intellects, we grasp objects in themselves by aesthetic cogni-

---

38. Marion, *God Without Being*, 115–19; Luce Irigaray, *Speculum of the Other Woman*, trans. Gillian Gill (Ithaca, N.Y.: Cornell University Press, 1985), 229; Saunak Samajdar, "Intimacy, Hospitality and Jouissance," *Michigan Feminist Studies* 20 (2006–2007), http://hdl.handle.net/2027/spo.ark5583.0020.004; and William Johnston, *The Still Point* (New York: Fordham University Press, 1970). Compare "oceanic" or "cosmic" experiences described in Pierre Hadot, *The Present Alone Is Our Happiness*, trans. Marc Djaballah (Stanford, Calif.: Stanford University Press, 2009), 8–9.

39. Aquinas, *In IV Sent.*, d.49, q.1, a.1, qc.2; ST I-II, q.3, a.4; Scotus, *Ord.*, d.49, p.1, q.4, 342ff.

tion. Acts of will and intellect also unfold into one another: in the epektatic state, we simultaneously contemplate God, desire to contemplate him more deeply, and that desire is satisfied. If all of that is correct, then neither is absolutely prior to the other. Furthermore, happiness also involves affectivity, including value-response: we seek God not merely as objective good and not just motivated by seeking our happiness. Rather, we only attain full happiness in responding to the unique beauty God has in his personal holiness, by pouring ourselves out in ecstatic praise entirely for his sake. Most importantly, all these acts are joined and further actualized in spiritual perception (which is needed to fully grasp God, and beauty, in all aspects), in attention, and in memory. Each power's acts are ordered to being conjoined with others. As Scotus argued, the acts that ultimately fulfill us must fully engage and actualize the soul itself. Our ultimate flourishing cannot consist chiefly in the act of just one power; rather, it is a single act of all the powers and formalities of the soul coordinated together. Anything less than such a conjoined act would reduce our fulfillment to the fulfillment of just particular powers. A metaphysics of irreducibility rejects both *intellectualism*, on which the intellect is nobler than other powers and we are primarily fulfilled through its acts, and *voluntarism*, on which the will is nobler and we are primarily fulfilled through its acts. Rather, we are transcendentally open through each power of the soul, but fundamentally through the soul itself. We are completely fulfilled in the union of these powers' acts. No power is nobler than another *simpliciter*; rather, each is nobler than others in certain respects, and the value of all powers is united in that of the soul.

The Problem of Divine Causality Reviewed

I have now considered enough material to begin working out a solution to the problem of divine causality. This solution is necessary to reject "theological" reductionism, by which our acts are causally reducible to God's acts or we are reducible to what is ontologically or axiologically higher than us. As Aquinas says, we are the midpoint, "border," or "horizon" between corporeality and incorporeality, participating in each but reducible to neither.[40]

We have already considered the following aspects of the problem of

---

40. Aquinas, *QDA*, a.1; *DP*, q.3, a.9; *SCG* II, c. 68, 80; *ST* I, q.77, a.2; *In LDC*, lect. 9.

divine causality. First, human reproduction (and, to some extent, any event of efficient causality) raises the problems of the origin of the child's *esse* and of the child's participation in Platonic Forms of humanity and of the human end. Second, how Platonic Forms exist and illumine our minds needs explanation. Third, uncanny, horrifying, and earthly values need explanation since they do not deliver a "message" from God, and so it is implausible to hold that they were produced by God. Fourth, the existence of disvalues needs explanation, since although all being comes ultimately from God and the privation theory of evil is true ontologically, nevertheless disvalues have positive reality at the third level of being. Fifth, the content of my free acts cannot be caused by God; such a causal explanation fails to fit with experiences of self-gift, creativity, cooperation with others (as opposed to acting by *per se* or *per accidens* causality), and finding myself under judgment. The metaphysician of irreducibility must reject any concurrentism on which God sufficiently specifies or determines (rather than just permits) the content of my free acts, on which there is some fact of the matter as to what I would do prior to my free acting, or on which God entirely plans history or determines the truth-value of all propositions.[41]

This problem also extends beyond human acts. As we have seen, all substances "select" among their matter's quantum states and all substances cooperate in forming *Gestalten*, and these acts, too, must be explained. Each substance gives itself as, by its form, sacramentally reflecting, participating in, and making present God, but each substance also gives itself as having causal independence, quasi-free action, and an earthly (or nonsacramental) value of its own. Natural substances give themselves, as we have seen, as radically extramental, real in the sense of being irreducible to any being's experience of them, even the experience of a divine mind. We encounter this in what Quentin Meillassoux calls the experience of the "great outdoors": wild, natural things stand outside of all relations to minds and carry on their own real actions, which are of importance in themselves.[42] For example, in scientific experiences of evidence for cosmological, geological, and biological evolution, substances are given as cooperating and developing by their own contingent efforts. There is a saturated excess to each self-revealing, finite beauty in itself, apart from its revelation of God:

---

41. *Contra Scotus, Ord.* I, d.38-39, q.1-5, nn. 23-24, v. 6, 428-29.
42. Meillassoux, *After Finitude*, 7. Cf. Graham Harman, *Guerilla Metaphysics: Phenomenology and the Carpentry of Things* (Chicago: Open Court, 2005).

natural beings appear both as an *ontophany*, a revealing or illumining of their being (and of being as such), and as a *theophany*, a revealing of or illumination by God (and other transcendent persons)—and the former is not entirely reducible to or revealing of the latter.[43]

Were we to conceive of natural beings' activities as ultimately and entirely orchestrated by God, we would become blind to their independent causality and to their earthly value, which are features of beings that are directly given. The metaphysician who seeks a portrait of the human person as irreducible must recognize the irreducibility of nonpersonal beings, too, especially since their mode of irreducibility is included in ours insofar as we have a material, animal body. Furthermore, since we freely shape material things when we make artifacts, they must be open to receiving content from us, rather than being entirely specified by God. Finally, if God gives causality to natural substances without directing its course, allowing them to exercise something like creativity and self-gift, this shows greater generosity and love on his part than he would show were he to determine all events, and so is more in keeping with his nature as absolute goodness and beauty.

Yet creatures are certainly dependent on God for their existence, essence, and other principles. Events in which ontologically lower items take on higher actualities, as occurs in both natural evolution and free action, are not sufficiently explained by emergence from lower actualities. All actuality must ultimately come from pure actuality (i.e., from God), and no actuality can be caused except in virtue of an equal or greater actuality, for nothing can give a perfection that it does not have in some way. Furthermore, not only do we perceive God in all things, but when guided by the value of holiness, we perceive him to be providential, giving meaning to all events, even chance events and free acts, a meaning that exceeds any given to them by creaturely causes.

These problems about divine causality are also related to the problem of how a simple God can freely act (like the problem, presented above, of how an ontologically impassible God can come to know creaturely events without causing them). Free acts, it would seem, are actualities or contents that would have been different had their agent chosen differently. But if God is simple, then it would seem that he could not freely act, since that

---

43. Cf. Fritz, *Karl Rahner's Theological Aesthetics*, 11.

Principle of *Energeia* 257

would *per impossibile* require variation in his actuality.⁴⁴ We need a metaphysics in which God is both pure actuality *and* has additional, contingent free acts.

The Palamite Distinction between Energeia and Ousia

In order to solve these problems, I now turn to a more complete account of what acts and actualities are. Aristotle's term *energeia*, which can be translated "actuality," "activity," or "being at work," picks out instances of a being giving and manifesting itself and bringing about effects.⁴⁵ So far, I have introduced two senses of this notion. First, an *energeia* is an activity in which one is "completely at work," in which (in contrast to processes [*kineseis*]) each moment of the activity is like every other, and which is done for its own sake, not for some further goal. Contemplating, perceiving, and feeling pleasure are activities (*energeiai*) in this sense. Second, an *energeia* is an actuality or perfection at the second level of being, a way that a being is ontologically at work, actively manifesting itself. Form, *esse*, processes, and activities (*energeiai* in the first sense) are all *energeiai* in this second sense. Aside from God's pure actuality, all *energeiai* in this sense are actualizations of a potentiality (*dunamis*), making perfect a prior possibility for perfection or completion.

I now introduce a third sense of *energeia*; for the rest of this book, I use the untranslated Greek word *energeia* with this sense, reserving "activity" for the first sense and "actuality" for the second.⁴⁶ *Energeia* in the third sense is a further layer of being beyond the three already proposed; it is any manifestation, self-gift, or self-diffusion of a being, considered holistically. Every actuality involves and is included in an *energeia*, but *energeiai* are more than just actualizations of potencies. (What "including" is, metaphysically, will be worked out over the rest of this chapter and the next one.) Taking on *energeiai*, unlike activities or actualities, does not necessarily involve taking on distinct principles or accidents; rather, *having energeiai*—that is, manifesting oneself—belongs to the structure of being as such. We saw in chapter 2 that acting, at least in the sense of giving or

---

44. See Mark K. Spencer, "The Flexibility of Divine Simplicity" and (with W. Matthews Grant) "Activity, Identity, and God: A Tension in Aquinas and His Interpreters," *Studia Neoaristotelica* 12 (2015): 5–61.
45. See Joe Sachs' translation of Aristotle's *Metaphysics* (Santa Fe, N.M.: Green Lion Press, 1999), xxiv.
46. This term is often transliterated as "energy," but this has misleading materialist or spiritualistic connotations, so I leave the term in Greek.

manifesting oneself, is a transcendental property of being; I explain that property by positing *energeiai* in the structure of being. Perceiving beings as irreducible and holistic requires perceiving them as acting in themselves and as wholes, not just acting through others, even if those others are principles, parts, or accidents in them. Positing *energeiai* guides us to perceive how beings in themselves are manifested in particular acts.

For example, as an actuality at the second level of being, an act of conceptual thinking is an accident inhering in and actualizing my soul, in which I participate, with its own essence and *esse*, which gives me a certain degree of immateriality and perfection, and a new way of being—that is, a new way of comporting myself toward the world, beyond how I comport myself just as a human substance. But this analysis in terms of principles does not fully capture what my act of thinking fully is or how I directly and concretely experience it: when I think, I, this whole person who I am, directly manifest myself and enter into my act. While most of my acts add to me principles or accidents, all of my acts are events that belong to the very structure of my being. My acts manifest the being I intrinsically am, and so are modes of that being, ways that that being comports itself toward the world; they do not just add new modes of being to me. Beings both take on new principles and "encompass" or "include" those principles within themselves as they "flow" or "enter into" being at work and self-manifestation.

We have seen that some acts, such as the intuition of being, are purely intentional relations, not involving taking on new perfections, real relations, or accidents. These acts add no ontological perfection (like a species) to me, but they change me experientially. By this sheer awareness of the presence of some being to me, I manifest myself and enter into an experience. This unique sort of change must be accounted for metaphysically in some way. I propose that we understand these acts as pure *energeiai*, without a distinct actuality included in them. They are purely manifestations of the being that I intrinsically am or ways that I am "at work." I just enter into an *energeia* without taking on a new ontological actuality—that is, I am not, by these acts, more perfected, complete, or immaterial at the second level of being. However, these *energeiai* are done through a power. Hence, my powers are not only natural or obediential potencies for actualities but also are ways that I am intrinsically oriented to manifest myself and be at work.

This account of *energeiai* is drawn from the Greek Fathers, especially the fourteenth-century theologian Gregory Palamas.[47] As with Aquinas, I consider his work just to draw out principles and distinctions that help us perceive our irreducibility and to synthesize this strand of broadly Catholic tradition with others. I hope that my remarks here help overcome debates between Aquinas and Palamas, and between Western and Eastern theology in general.[48] Just as I contend that Thomistic metaphysics can and should be augmented by Scotus's metaphysics, so I contend that they both can be augmented with Palamas's notion of *energeia*. I do not argue that these thinkers are entirely reconcilable, nor do I try to remain true to all that any of them says; my goal, as always, is just to offer a portrait of the person by which all aspects of our irreducibility are perceived.

While Palamas does use effect-to-cause reasoning, he focuses more on direct spiritual perceptions of God's presence and activities. For example, in deep prayer, people report directly perceiving God's presence, his illumining of their minds and flooding their hearts with joy, and even sometimes a visible light, which Palamas identifies with the light of the Transfiguration (Lk 9:29), and which is experienced as a divine activity. But we also perceive God to be transcendent over every experience of him, and to include aspects of unknowability and "darkness." Palamism draws on principles posited in the broadly Catholic tradition to account for both the directly perceivable self-manifestation of beings, especially God, and their transcendence and hiddenness.[49] We perceive beings to act and manifest themselves, but out of what they fundamentally are, which we never grasp in itself, apart from its manifestations.

---

47. My discussion of Palamas is from *The Triads*, III.i.23-III.ii.11, trans. Nicholas Gendle (Mahwah, N.J.: Paulist Press, 1983), 80-107; "Topics of Natural and Theological Science and on the Moral and Aesthetic Life: 150 Texts," in *The Philokalia*, vol. 4, ed. G. E. H. Palmer et al. (London: Faber and Faber, 1995), 378-417; and *Dialogue between an Orthodox and a Barlaamite*, trans. Rein Ferwerda (Binghamton: Episteme, 1999). Palamas owes a lot to Maximus the Confessor, *On Difficulties in the Church Fathers: The Ambigua*, vol. 1, trans. Nicholas Constas (Cambridge, Mass.: Harvard University Press, 2014), chap. 7. See David Bradshaw, *Aristotle East and West* (Cambridge: Cambridge University Press, 2007), chaps. 9, 10; John Demetracopoulos, "Palamas Transformed," in *Greeks, Latins, and Intellectual History 1204-1500*, ed. Martin Hinterberger and Chris Schabel (Leuven: Peeters, 2011), 263-372; and Yannaras, *Person and Eros*, 57-70.

48. For Palamite objections to Thomism, see Bradshaw, *Aristotle East and West*, and Yannaras, *Person and Eros*; for Thomistic objections to Palamas, see Dionysius Petavius, *Opus de theologicis dogmatibus* (Venice: Ex Typographia Remondiniana, 1757), 95-102; Balthasar, *TL3*, 128-30; and John Milbank, "Christianity and Platonism in East and West," in *Divine Essence and Divine Energies*, eds. C. Athanasopouls and C. Schneider (Cambridge: Clarke, 2013), 158-209.

49. See statements (Heinrich Denzinger, *Enchiridion symbolorum: A Compendium of Creeds, Definitions, and Declarations of the Catholic Church*, ed. Peter Hünermann [San Francisco: Ignatius Press, 2012]) of the Third Council of Constantinople that each *ousia* in Christ has its own *energeia*, and the Second Council of Nicaea, at which the depiction of divine persons in terms of their *energeia* was prescribed.

Up until now, I have called the principle by which each being is of some kind its *essence*. Essences in the sense considered up until now include aspects that we directly grasp by conceptualization or definition; for example, the human essence is grasped as rational and animal. Every way that something manifests itself is an *energeia*, but for there to be manifestation, there must be something that manifests itself and underlies manifestations (or else we fall into a regress of manifestations rooted in ever-deeper manifestations); both belong to the intrinsic, transcendental structure of a being. That which underlies manifestations is a being's *ousia*, often translated as "substance," "essence," "being," or "nature," but I leave it untranslated to indicate that an *ousia* in the sense of what underlies manifestation is just one aspect of essence. Essences also include *energeiai*—such as the formalities grasped in acts of defining, which manifest what that being fundamentally is, and which are present in all of that being's acts. These formalities are, to use Hildebrand's terms, "messages" or "words" about that being conveyed in its acts; Maximus and Palamas call them *logoi*. God has *logoi* for all kinds and instances of possible beings; each being and kind reveals something unique about God, and these *logoi* are contents manifested in God's particular acts. God's *logoi* are all included in his one *Logos*, the Son.[50]

In this view, the human essence includes formalities of rationality, animality, body, and soul; our essence makes itself known in these ways, but our essence also has an ineffable, hidden core that exceeds and underlies them. This *ousia* explains the mysterious excess of each being over all that can be grasped about it. *Ousia* manifests and gives itself in *energeia* but without being manifested and given *as ousia*. It is a core of each being where it is alone with itself, whereby (in Xavier Zubiri's terms) a being acts and exists as a being "in its own right" (*de suyo*), exceeding all that can be grasped about it.[51] It underlies my essence and *esse* in the Thomistic sense; it is the core of my *form*, whence comes my essence, and is thence given to me.[52]

In memory, I feel myself as a being in my own right; this experience brings me close to my *ousia*, but even here I do not directly grasp what I

---

50. Maximus, *The Ambigua*, vol. 1, 95–111.

51. Xavier Zubiri, *On Essence*, trans. A. Robert Caponigri (Washington, D.C.: The Catholic University of America Press, 1980), chap. 9; *Dynamic Structure of Reality*, trans. Nelson Orringer (Champaign: University of Illinois Press, 2003), 102, 121. Cf. Harman, *Guerilla Metaphysics*, 226–27.

52. Aristotle, *Met.*, VII.3.1028b33–1029a7, VII.17.1041b5–11.

fundamentally am. Even experiences of pure subjectivity are experiences of *energeiai*, of my manifestation of myself to myself, though there I experience the core of who I am "flowing" or "entering into" my activities such that I become present through them. But my experience is always first directed outwards, and I am brought to consciousness by contact with and reception from others. I am always to some extent separated or alienated from myself, beholden to some extent to others (especially God) for my self-awareness. I must transcend myself toward the core of who I am; it is always somewhat absent from my experience, but it is also a subconscious background underlying all my experiences. There is an irreducible duality between my conscious, empirical self and the underlying core of who I am.[53] In experiences of deep recollection or contemplation, I experience myself acting out of that depth of myself.[54] (Our ultimate fulfillment would have to involve ever-deepening contemplative acting out of this core self.) Likewise, in experiencing a beloved person, I aim at grasping his or her *ousia*—at grasping who he or she is most fundamentally—but I am always aware that the core of who he or she is transcends all that I could grasp. Only God, who is causally more inward to things than they are to themselves, completely grasps *ousiai*—that is, because God is the ultimate cause of my essence, because causes are always present in their effects, and because my essence is an expression of a divine *Logos*, God is intimately present to and directly grasps my essence.[55] But this is not to say that my "true self" is something entirely in God, or that this earthly substance is not truly me, as on the view of Plotinus or of some in the Indian and Sophiological traditions; I am given as distinct from, though participating in, the self (*Atman*) that is God.[56]

But I am not reducible to my *ousia*, to what I fundamentally am. My *energeiai* are also aspects of my being, though they do not all belong to me essentially or necessarily; many are contingent and free. In some views, like that of Leibniz or Stein, "what" I am includes all of my acts and changes, such that when God wills me to be what I am, he wills all these things.[57]

53. For ways in which the Indian philosophical tradition highlighted this feature of human persons well, see Calasso, *Ardor*, 119–22.
54. Thomas Merton, *New Seeds of Contemplation* (New York: New Directions, 1961), 1–10.
55. Augustine, *Confessions* III.6.11.
56. See Bulgakov, *Bride of the Lamb*, 112–14 and many of the Upanishads in *A Sourcebook in Indian Philosophy*, eds. Sarvepalli Radhakrishnan and Charles A. Moore (Princeton, N.J.: Princeton University Press, 2014).
57. G. W. Leibniz, "Discourse on Metaphysics," in *Philosophical Essays*, trans. Roger Ariew and Daniel Garber (Indianapolis: Hackett, 1989), n. 8; Stein, *Finite and Eternal Being*, 75.

But the experiential basis for the *ousia-energeia* distinction excludes any such view: I am an active, self-manifesting, self-determining, variable, beautiful *who*, not merely a *what* that could be grasped without personal contact with my *energeiai*.

Some object that if every being has an *ousia* or hidden core that never manifests itself as such, then no being, even God, could ever fully give itself to another, since its *ousia* would never be given.[58] We have seen that accounting for the possibility of full self-gift is needed to solve the problem of divine causality. But the Palamite *ousia-energeia* distinction does not entail that no being can fully give itself; it actually makes sense of how a being can give itself without ceasing to be itself. *Ousia* and *energeiai* are not distinct parts or principles but rather are aspects of the intrinsic structure of each being. ("Intrinsic" here does not mean what necessarily belongs to a being, but what is one in being with it, which on the proposed view includes necessary and contingent features of beings.) When a being manifests itself in an *energeia*, as it does every time it acts or has a property, the being is holistically giving itself, but since it does not give itself in such a way that it ceases to be, there must be another aspect of it that is retained. Beings both wholly give themselves and entirely remain themselves; this experientially given distinction is captured in the metaphysical distinction between *ousia* and *energeia*.

This is a *sui generis* distinction within the structure of each being; it does not fit the model of other distinctions. First, aspects of a being that are conceptually or formally distinct belong to that being necessarily, but many of a being's self-manifestations are changeable and contingent. So, although they belong to the structure of the being as such, they cannot just be conceptually or formally distinct from the other aspects of that being. Grasping beings holistically requires perceiving that beings as such (and not just insofar as they take on accidents) enter into contingent acts and self-manifestations. The intrinsic yet contingent aspect of acts is not captured on a strict act-potency or substance-accident metaphysics.

Second, really distinct things are either distinct beings with their own essence and *esse*, or opposed relations, or distinct like actuality and potentiality, with differing levels of perfection, completion, or immateriality. But *energeiai* are one in being with their subject, not relations that are opposites of some other relation in a being, and not related to *ousia* as act

---

58. See, for example, Milbank, "Christianity and Platonism in East and West."

to potency. No being, no matter how ontologically actual, perfect, or simple, could be without *energeiai*; all beings, as beings, are at work and self-giving. Rather, *ousia* is that out of which manifestation arises, and *energeia* is manifestation. So, although they are variable and contingent features of beings, *ousia* and *energeiai* are not really distinct, not distinct in being. We have already seen, in considering the Scotist formal distinction, that multiple items can be one in being with each other, without being one in every respect or one in the strict, logical sense.

The distinction between *ousia* and *energeia* also captures well aspects of the perception of beings' beauty. When beings act, what they are shines forth; every act of a being (and of principles like value) is an event of holistic self-manifestation, an opportunity for perceiving its holistic beauty.[59] When we perceive a being as beautiful, we see it as having depths that shine forth excessively in its activities and can confer beauty and splendor on others, though they remain depths behind all of the being's splendor.[60] We human persons (like all beings) are not fundamentally just composites of form and matter, substance and accident, essence and *esse*, or being and value; more fundamentally than all of these, we are holistic, self-manifesting beauties. As such, we include principles but are irreducible to them—that is, the content of these principles captures much, but not all, of what we are and do. The unique beauty of persons, which is glimpsed through love and aesthetic cognition, which calls for reverence, love, and wonder, and which grounds a full account of human dignity, is explained by *ousia* and *energeia*: out of our depths, we give ourselves as calling for this response.

Seeing how the Western scholastic account of being is open to being synthesized with the Palamite account is aided by considering another item in scholastic metaphysics, *modes*. On Aquinas's view, while immanent activities (activities that actualize a being and do not aim at effects in another, such as contemplating) are qualities belonging to a subject, transitive actions (processes that have their effect in another, such as teaching or cooking) are accidental actualizations belonging not to their agent (not to the teacher or cook) but to the patient (the student or food). When I teach, I actualize or perfect my students, not myself; I already have the perfection (knowledge) that I give to my students. Actions and passions

---

59. See Hildebrand, *Aesthetics*, vol. 1, 95.
60. See Spencer, "Beauty and the Intellectual Virtues in Aristotle."

(which constitute two categories on Aquinas's view) are really one accidental being in the patient, but considered from two different angles, one with reference to the agent and the other with reference to the patient.[61] Later Thomists, like John of St. Thomas, however, noted that something comes to be in the agent when acting on another, even if not an actualization or increase in perfection and immateriality. When I teach, I differ from how I previously was in that now I relate to the other as having brought about a change in that other, and I undergo a change in experience. To account for this change, scholastics posit *modes*, ways of being terminated or limited in or by another, as a point is the terminus of a line but not distinct from the line. Through a mode, I am directed toward the world in a definite way (for example, as performing actions that aim at, or are terminated or completed, in these students). Modes are not acts but a distinct kind of metaphysical item.

Having my acts terminated in or completed by another is a way of manifesting myself; hence, modes involve *energeiai*. Modes and *energeiai* are not equivalent notions—modes, but not *energeiai*, are distinct from their bearers; modes explain why beings are terminated or aim at another but do not fully explain the manifestation that occurs when the being is completed in this way. To explain that, the mode must be seen as included in a more holistic structure, a self-manifesting *energeia*. The positing of modes, however, shows that scholastic metaphysics already includes the possibility of a feature of a being that is not an actuality or potentiality but is still something. Accounting for beings' limits requires positing items that do not fit an act-potency analysis; hence, there is space in scholasticism for items beyond that analysis, including, I propose, *energeiai*.

The members of the minor Aristotelian categories are modes, as we just saw with the category *actio*. The same thing can be seen with the other minor categories. To be in a place (*ubi*) or at a time (*quando*) is to be terminated or limited by my spatial or temporal surroundings; to be in a position (*situs*) like sitting or standing is to be terminated by my internal spatial arrangement. Since I have powers that are transcendentally open, I engage with the world in an open-ended way: just as there is no limit to what I can intellectually cognize, so there is no limit to how I can engage with the world. When I use an artifact, like a tool or a piece of clothing, this open-ended tendency for engaging with the world is terminated or

---

61. Aquinas, *In III Phys.*, lect. 5, nn. 319–22.

directed in a definite, limited way; I am intelligently oriented toward the world in different ways when I take up, for example, a pencil or a shovel. Modes of being so directed are members of the category *habitus*. In each category, I am manifested by how my open-ended tendency to relate to things around me is terminated or limited and directed by those things.[62] Because of my accidents, I have a vast number of *energeiai*: every relation, similarity, or difference of size or color with respect to another is a way I am manifested, and so is an *energeia*. But while at the second level of being, we must posit a vast number of distinct accidents in me, at the level of *energeiai*, all of these self-manifestations are all one in being with me.

Sun-Energeia, Per Communionem Causality, and the Covenantal Structure of Reality

Another motivation for distinguishing *energeiai* and *ousiai* is the experience of sharing in others' activities. When I act, something distinct from me—say, accidents, Platonic Forms, *esse*—is at work in me, and I share in its activity: as we have seen, beings are oriented to solidarity with others. Beings and their self-manifestations are oriented to join in *Gestalten*. Most importantly, we can experience acting with God, as in exercising gifts of the Holy Spirit or in the examples of spiritual perception that Palamas describes. *Energieai* explain these experiences. Not only do we "flow" into our acts, and not only can acts of multiple powers in me "flow" or be joined into single acts, but multiple being's acts "flow" together, such that they join into single instances of coacting without confusion among the different beings' acts.

Beings participate in one another's *energeiai*, without participating in one another's *ousiai*; beings share in others' acts only inasmuch as they give themselves. This is an experientially given kind of participation distinct from that described by the Thomists. In Thomistic participation, one being participates in another when the former has a property in virtue of the latter primarily having it. Different Thomists distinguish different sorts of participation, each of which appears in experience.[63] Cornelio

---

62. Aquinas, *In III Phys.*, lect. 5; John of St. Thomas, *Cursus philosophicus*, v. 1, p.2, q.19, a.1, 540. See Mark K. Spencer, "The Category of *Habitus*," *The Thomist* 79, no. 1 (2015): 113–54; Spencer, "The Personhood of the Separated Soul," *Nova et Vetera* (English edition) 12, no. 3 (2014): 891. Cf. Pasnau, *Metaphysical Themes*, chap. 13.

63. Wippel, *The Metaphysical Thought of Thomas Aquinas*, 124–31.

Fabro distinguishes *logical participation* (in which species participate in genera, which we have seen is actually a relation among formalities and Platonic Forms), *real participation* (in which matter participates in form or substance in accidents), and *transcendental participation* (in which a subject participates by likeness in a higher perfection, such as in *esse*). Fabro contends that these modes of participation explain the limitations in finite beings: perfections are limited by being participated in and received by some subject.[64] But Louis-Bertrand Geiger argues that these modes of participation do not fully explain creatures' limitations. He posits a more fundamental kind of participation: *participation by similitude or formal hierarchy*, in which essences immediately, rather than by reception, imitate God and have content that was originally in God to a limited degree.[65]

In any version, Thomistic participation is a transitive relation: for example, I exist by participating in my *esse*, through which I participate in *esse commune*, and thence in God's subsistent *esse*. I can participate in God in multiple ways because God (like any being) has multiple formalities and *energeiai*, in which I share.[66] In this Thomistic sense, I participate in others' *ousiai* (including God's), through their *energeiai*. Palamite participation, on the other hand, is nontransitive. We not only participate in other things by resembling them or taking on content originally in them (as in Thomistic views) but we also take on others' characteristics in their own manner. I can share in another's acts or *energeiai*, that is, I can act with another's style and through that other's powers. I can take on the characteristic activity of another, and two beings can jointly perform *energeiai*, which Palamas and other Greek Fathers call *sun-energeia*. To participate in the *ousia* of another by Palamite participation, however, would be to share in the other's *ousia* in that other's own way—that is, it would be to be identical to that thing and have its nature, which is impossible. In each being, we must distinguish that which is imparticipable (*ousia*) and that which is participable (*energeia*).[67]

Sun-energeia explains *Gestalten*, which transcend the accidents and substances in them, and give new meaning to those beings. When a group produces a *Gestalt* like a conversation, each person *per se* causes accidents like speech-acts and sensible species. These acts are also *energeiai*, mani-

---

64. Cornelio Fabro, *La nozione metafisica di partecipazione secondo S. Tommaso d'Aquin* (Turin: Società edittice internazionale, 1950), 317–18.

65. Louis-Bertrand Geiger, *La participation dans la philosophie de S. Thomas d'Aquin* (Paris: Vrin, 1942).

66. *Contra* Little, *Toward a Thomistic Methodology.*

67. Cf. Proclus, *Elements of Theology*, props. 23–24; Eric Perl, *Theophany*, 23.

festations of their being and of their accidents. As such, they are disposed to join with each other and with *energeiai* of transcendent items like values. Beings act not only by direct (*per se*) and chance (*per accidens*) causality but also by what I called in chapter 5 *per communionem* causality, which I explain as the intrinsic orientation of *energeiai* to join together. We not only act toward one another as subjects and objects; we can also participate in each other's activities. By this causality, we produce *Gestalten*, such as communities.[68] Because they are rooted in *ousia* and participate in others' *energeiai*, our *energeiai* include more content that we intend, and by them new unities—conversations, communities, traditions, and so forth—spontaneously arise without our intending them. Orientation to communion and spontaneous emergence of meaningful forms through cooperation belong to the structure of being as such. I follow Jesuit theologian Donald Keefe, who argues that the biblical notion of *covenant*, in which beings and persons fully commit themselves to one another and genuinely join together, is transcendental: to be is to be oriented to entering covenants arising by cooperative activity and self-gift.[69]

One example of covenant or *sun-energeia* is promising, a social act. When I promise, I *per se* cause mental and speech acts directed to, say, my wife. If she accepts my promise, she shares in my self-manifestation by allowing herself to be bound to me and my promise. We are both bound now within a covenant constituted by our participation in one another's activities, such that each takes on something of the other's *style* of relating to the world. Another example of *energeia*'s tendency to intertwine and bring about communities is "emotional infection." Multiple people jointly attending to something, like an object of grief or joy, experience themselves feeling in common; this can happen with large groups, during a liturgy, festival, concert, or patriotic celebration, when moods like euphoria or fear move through a crowd. I can affectively identify myself with another, and sympathetically coexperience another's subjectivity, such that I almost think I am that person.[70] Another example is a friendship centered

---

68. See Spencer, "Divine Causality and Created Freedom," 961.

69. Donald Keefe, *Covenantal Theology: The Eucharistic Order of History* (Lanham, Md.: University Press of America, 1991). Cf. all of Balthasar, *GL6*; *TD2*, 200–203, 251–54, 296–302; and Little, *Methodology*. I do not follow him in holding that the New Covenant in Christ is the only substantial reality. See Mark K. Spencer, "Covenantal Metaphysics and Cosmological Metaphysics: An Aesthetic Critique and an Aesthetic Synthesis," *The Saint Anselm Journal* 15, no. 2 (2020): 19–38.

70. Scheler, *The Nature of Sympathy*, 8–37, 167–68; *Formalism in Ethics and Non-Formal Ethics of Values*, 386–402; and *On the Eternal in Man*, 312–15; "Idealism and Realism," 300–303.

around objective goods or values, in which I experience living, thinking, perceiving, and acting virtuously with my friend. I experience my subjective identity to be bound up in our mutual self-gift to one another and to the shared good or value, such that we become "at work" together in a shared communion or *Gestalt*.[71]

As we have seen, Balthasar describes how the way we manifest ourselves provides a receptive, hospitable "space" for others' freedom to act.[72] My unique vocation or personal value-essence gives me a unique way of relating to others, including a unique way of helping others' vocations develop. When I follow my vocation, my free acts are a space in which others can participate, such that they act more freely and effectively. For example, the master artist helps disciples discover their style, which is developed in cooperation with the master and a tradition. By sharing in the master's *energeia* (and those of earlier artists in the tradition) and by together performing acts of creativity which neither directs completely *per se*, disciples are rendered better able to manifest their personal style.

Similarly, the founder of a religious order facilitates others' freedom by allowing them to participate in his or her charism; I can better respond to God and serve others as the unique person I am by sharing in the style and mission of, say, St. Francis or St. Teresa—not by copying their acts but by allowing their style of acting to inform mine. We can also take on others' suffering, making that suffering fruitful in our own life, *coinhering* in one another.[73] These experiences are furthered in praying with patron saints (or other transcendent or human persons) for particular sorts of intercession; this includes an experience of particular domains of reality being connected with the personal style of a saint, and of my own acts in that domain being joined with the saint's acts. In such experiences, we experience our membership in a single ecclesial *Gestalt* or body.[74]

Again, designating a political representative is a covenant between citizens and that representative, such that the latter shares in, makes present, and directs the activities of the former.[75] Government, as the institution by which a people pursue natural common goods and values, can only have legitimacy with such representation. My acts and my representative's acts

---

71. Aristotle, *NE*, IX.9.1170b4–19.
72. Balthasar, *TD3*, 271–76.
73. Galatians 6:2; Charles Williams, *Descent into Hell* (Grand Rapids, Mich.: Eerdmans, 1966).
74. See David Vincent Meconi, *The One Christ: St. Augustine's Theology of Deification*, (Washington, D.C.: The Catholic University of America Press, 2018), 208.
75. Balthasar, *GL3*, 400–415, 435–509, building on Charles Péguy.

intertwine, such that my representative's acts are in a sense mine; through this *sun-energeia*, a whole community can become better or worse, and incur merit or guilt: the acts of the whole community or its representative give meaning to each citizen and his or her acts, regardless of his or her personal moral state. My acts have particular meanings because I am a citizen of a particular country, state, or city; I can even inherit guilt or merit of a sort because of the communities in which I share, and whole social structures or *Gestalten* can become virtuous or vicious, insofar as they are oriented to justice or injustice: communities as such can be oriented toward goods like holiness or evils like racism.[76] A political order rooted in all aspects of the irreducible human person will avoid rule purely by *per se* acts of lawmaking and command, or purely by spontaneous cooperation and *per communionem* causality. Rather, the good representative will know which situations call for *per se* direction and which call for allowing spontaneous, *per communionem* causality, for both are needed to reach our full flourishing.

Something like this kind of *sun-energeia*, in which we and our representatives coinhere, helps explain the state of original sin in which the whole human race finds itself through the misdeeds of one representative member of our species, and the possibility of redemption by one representative member of our species. We shall see in chapter 7 how human persons are made in the image of God; as such, we represent God in the world, our way of manifesting ourselves intrinsically participating in his, with all the responsibility that entails.[77] Each of these examples is a way that our acts or *energeiai* are open to being joined in by others, such that a new meaningful structure emerges that no party entirely determines; this is possible because of the orientation of *energeiai* to joining, supplementing one another, and forming communions.

Since being always diffuses itself, *energeiai* bring about works (*erga*). A work is distinct (even if only as a being of reason) from the *energeia* that produced it, and it manifests its *energeia*'s content. Artworks, for example, are produced through joining the *energeiai* of an artist, some matter, and a value, such that they together produce a new *Gestalt*, a new meaningful unity that includes many beings and principles. Yet many artworks persist after the artist ceases working (or even dies), and this shows another aspect

---

76. Cf. John Paul II, *Reconciliatio et Paenitentia*, Post-Synodal Exhortation, December 2, 1984.
77. Khaled Anatolios, *Deification through the Cross: An Eastern Christian Theology of Salvation* (Grand Rapids, Mich.: Eerdmans, 2020), 304.

of *sun-energeia*: *Gestalten* constituted by cooperative activity can continue even after the initial cooperation has ended. An artwork continues (in David Walsh's term) to "radiate" the content of the shared activity.[78] Through the artwork, later viewers can participate in, live with, and interpret the artist's *energeiai* and style. By artifacts like writing and artwork, we can manifest ourselves at distant times and places.[79] Through *sun-energeia*, a person (including God) can imprint his or her style on the *energeia* of other beings (such as icons), which then serve as that person's "glory," a perceivable display, revelation, or "sacrament" of that person's beauty, which augments that person's being inasmuch as it adds *energeia* to reality, and which calls for honor and reverence.[80]

Divinization, Grace, and Energeiai

The highest case of *sun-energeia* is divinization, in which God by his *energeiai* is present in me, and we act together covenantally, giving ourselves to one another and to the *Gestalt* of our covenant, such that I become God by participation. This can occur, for example, in receiving sacraments, exercising gifts of the Holy Spirit, in having Christ's eternal resurrection life actualizing me, and in the beatific vision. Recognizing how we act jointly helps resolve a debate between Palamites and Thomists over whether we are divinized by created or uncreated grace. Palamites hold that no creature can divinize us—that is, no finite being can render us fitting and connatural with the infinite God. Rather, sharing in divine life requires that we join together with and act through God's uncreated, variable *energeiai* that are present to us. Thomists hold that the Son and Holy Spirit are sent on missions to bring about our divinization, and that the whole Trinity dwells in us when we are divinized; in this way, rather than by *energeia*, God is present to us. A mission of a divine person is a way that his procession from other divine persons is terminated by creatures when he is sent to them; for example, when the Son is sent to me, the act by which the Father begets the Son also aims at me, such that I become adopted as a

---

78. Walsh, *Politics*, 176. Cf. Loudovikos, *Identities*, 379.
79. Cf. Aquinas, *In I PH*, lect. 2.
80. Aquinas, *ST* II-II, q.132; Francisco J. Romero Carrasquillo, "The Role of *Gloria* in Aquinas' Philosophy of Religion," *Acta Philosophica* 23 (2014): 311–32; Theodore the Studite, *On the Holy Icons*; and Gadamer, *Truth and Method*, 134–38, *contra* Plato, *Republic*, for whom a picture like an icon is always a mere copy and diminution of the manifested being. I owe several of these points to Mark McInroy.

son of God, a son within the Son.[81] However, Thomists also hold that divinization requires our obediential potencies to be actualized such that we participate in divine life, and since this actualization begins to be in us at a particular time, it is a created accident. Such accidents include sanctifying grace (an actualization of the soul, whereby we share in divine life and sonship) and the light of glory (a participation in God's glory, whereby we are directly aware of him in heaven). God himself causes our supernatural fulfillment, but this involves our participation in him, and this participation relation is created, since it is an effect and an attribute of us.[82]

Using the notion of *sun-energeia*, these views can be synthesized. In divinization, God's *energeiai* and the divine persons become present in us, such that we are rendered connatural with God. Their presence actualizes an obediential potency in us so that a new participation in God's *energeiai* comes to be in us. In being divinized, I act in virtue of God's activities in me, but this also produces a new participation relation in me. This participation, which Thomists call *grace*, is a creature, since it is the *work* (*ergon*) of divine *energeiai*, not identical to it. But it presupposes that I share in, and act jointly with, God's *energeia*. Divinization is a covenant to which both created and uncreated *energeiai* contribute.

The debate on divinization is also about our ultimate end. Thomists contend that the only thing that can perfectly satisfy our restless longing for understanding is to see God in himself, the first cause and ultimate explanation for all things—that is, to see God's essence, not just his manifestations. Palamites contend that we can never experience God's *ousia* in itself, only his *energeiai*, the ways he manifests himself. We only know that God has *ousia*; we do not know *ousia* directly, for even in divine union, I shall only grasp divine *energeiai*. This fits with my epektatic account of our end: however deeply we penetrate into God, we will still have infinitely more to discover and love, more *energeiai* in which to share and with which to act, always having apophatic ignorance and awe before the mystery and holiness of the divine *ousia*, toward which we transcend ourselves.

Thomists and Palamites understand *essence* in different senses. The Thomistic divine essence is God's being or *esse* with which everything in him is really identical, that is, one in ontological being. The Palamite divine essence is his *ousia*. To see God in the Palamite sense would be to

---

81. Aquinas, *ST* I, q.43.
82. Aquinas, *ST* I-II, q.5, a.6, ad 2; q.110, a.2.

be him by nature, which is impossible, but this still allows seeing God's essence in the Thomistic sense: in the beatific vision, God acts as a form for our minds—that is, our intellects act through his being or *energeiai*, without any mediating accidents, such that we directly experience his being.[83] Since on the Palamite view to grasp a being's *energeiai* is to grasp that being in itself, and since in God all things are simply one in being, to grasp God's *energeiai* directly just is to grasp his essence in the Thomistic sense.

Still, since Thomistic participation is transitive, on that sense of participation, to participate in the divine *energeiai* just is to participate in his *ousia*, though not in such a way as to see or become it by nature. The Catholic tradition, however, does describe experiences that attain to God's *ousia* in a sense. Apophatic awe is a sort of perceptual experience.[84] Nicholas of Cusa describes "learned ignorance" in which one contemplates God's incomprehensibility, his inability to be encompassed by our acts.[85] Stein, following John of the Cross, describes "nocturnal" experiences in which one lacks all positive experience, but thereby is more fully united to the depths of God.[86] Marion describes experiences of praise in which one does not grasp God, but rather speaks to him, exalting his utmost depths in speech, thought, and affection.[87] (An analogous praise and apophaticism can rightly be given to any being, for I cannot comprehend any being's *ousia*.) Maritain, also building on John of the Cross, argues that in love, the beloved and the lover are intentionally in one another: love aims at (and so is an experience of) the whole of the other and loses itself ecstatically in the other.[88]

In all these experiences, my intentional acts aim at all of God, and charity, the love that God himself is, unites with all of God, including his *ousia*, though not by grasping or comprehending it in itself. Similarly, God's "grasp" of my *ousia* should be understood as occurring by a divine act analogous to our acts of love, not our acts of knowledge; as beings who exist "in our own right," we are radically outside all minds, including God's. Loving union can be experienced to the point that it is no longer an intentional or object-directed act, and experienced distinction between

---

83. Aquinas, *ST* I, q.12.
84. Maximus, *The Ambigua*, 270–71.
85. Nicholas of Cusa, *On Learned Ignorance*, trans. Jasper Hopkins (Minneapolis, Minn.: Benning, 1981). Cf. Balthasar, *GL5*, 230–38.
86. Stein, *The Science of the Cross*, trans. Josephine Koeppel (Washington, D.C.: ICS Publications, 2003), 23ff.
87. Marion, *In Excess*, chap. 6.
88. Maritain, *Degrees of Knowledge*, 392–408.

myself and God ceases.[89] Because we can unite with God in his entirety in these ways, our ultimate epektatic, beatific state is restful. Although in that state we will participate in God's *energeiai* in ever-deepening, never-comprehending ways, this will be a continual, satisfied happiness in God, always a union with his being.

A Solution to the Problem of Divine Causality

God has all properties that belong to being as such, including *ousia* and *energeiai*. This is consistent with his simplicity: the claim that God is simple is an entailment from the claim that God is ontologically pure actuality; the claim means that God lacks distinction of potentiality, participation, or parts, and, since he is the first cause of all things, there is no principle prior to God such that he would be made out of it or participate in it. Whatever is consistent with actuality or being as such exists in God. Since he is free, God's acts must be variable—that is, he must be capable of doing otherwise than he does—without these acts adding an accident or actualization to him. That would involve an increase in his degree of being, and a composition of parts or principles in him, which is impossible, since he is pure actuality. As the being who is freedom and intelligence itself, God's *energeiai* include acts of understanding and willing—that is, these are among the ways God manifests himself. Like our pure intentional relations, God's *energeiai* are purely a manifestation of himself and an experience he has.

Many concurrentists reason that since God is immutable, then he is the same whether or not he creates. Hence, God can only have relations of reason to creatures, not real relations, since the latter implies change or coming to be, and ontological dependence, which God cannot have. Divine activities that intend creatures (such as willing or knowing them) involve real change only in creatures and add only a relation of reason to God. But some Baroque Jesuit scholastics, such as Suárez and Pedro da Fonseca, held that this is an inadequate account, for God must experience creatures. While this cannot involve ontological dependence on creatures (say, by receiving species), experiences cannot consist in mere relations of reason, if these are understood as involving no difference in their foundation. In

---

89. William Johnston, *The Still Point*; Thomas Merton, *Zen and the Birds of Appetite* (New York: New Directions, 1968). For phenomenological support, see Michel Henry, cited in chapter 1.

intending creatures, God is intentionally and experientially different than he would have been had he created other beings or not created at all.[90] He is intentionally and experientially related to creatures, without this involving ontological change.

We have seen that we perform acts involving pure intentional relations, such as intuitions of being, without ontological change. We do this when we have the act's intended object's form or species in our minds and the object is present to our intellects. Given those conditions, my intellect "touches" or is "terminated" by the object such that I experience it without new ontological actualization. While this involves no change at the second level of being—no becoming more perfected or actualized—it does involve my performing an *energeia*, my subjectivity "flowing" out to the object such that I experience it. As pure actuality in which all beings participate, God always has the forms of all possible beings in his mind. My proposal is that, when present to a being, God knows it by intellectual *energeiai*, regardless of whether he causes it or not, without any ontological change in him.[91] This intentional, experiential relation (just like pure intentional relations in us) is an *energeia*, a directing and "termination" of his being in creatures. As *energeiai* of the one pure actuality that God is, variable divine acts do not presuppose or actualize a prior potentiality. God just directs the pure actuality and being that he is toward a certain object; since all such objects have less actuality than him, and since all actualities are precontained in him, this involves no augmentation to his being.[92]

We have seen the objection that God could not know our acts unless he caused them, since he cannot receive content from creatures. My proposal that God's knowledge consists of pure intentional relations and *energeiai* is a solution to that problem, and it resembles aspects of mere conservationism (mentioned in chapter 4), which was held by some Franciscan thinkers, including Peter Auriol and Peter John Olivi, though I do not endorse all aspects of this view.[93] According to this view, God conserves substances and their powers in being and allows them to exercise them without caus-

---

90. Pedro da Fonseca, *In libros metaphysicorum*, VII, c. 8, q.5, s.4–5, 382–86; Suárez, *DM*, d.30, s.9, nn. 35–44.

91. Cf. Michael Torre, *God's Permission of Sin* (Fribourg: Studia Friburgensia, 2009), 110–13, 319; Clarke, "A New Look at the Immutability of God," 194–96.

92. Cf. Cajetan on "free perfections" that God adds to himself when he freely acts: *In I ST*, q.19, a.2–3.

93. Peter Auriol, *Commentariorum in secundum librum Sententiarum*, v. 2, d.38, q.1 (Rome: Zannetti, 1595), 302–4; Peter John Olivi, *Quaestiones in secundum librum Sententiarum*, v. 3, q.116 (Quaracchi: Collegii S. Bonaventura, 1926), 333–47; both cited in Frost, "Peter Olivi's Rejection of God's Concurrence with Created Causes."

ing their acts. Many concurrentists object that this view violates the logic of essentially ordered causality. Causes are essentially ordered when one depends on another to cause its proper effect. For example, for a tool to move, a hand moves it, and the hand is in turn moved by a will. Each subordinate cause must receive its actuality from a higher actuality, and the first cause in the series is the primary cause of all subsequent actualities and events of secondary causation. Concurrentists argue that all causality and actuality can and must be essentially traced back to the first actuality, God, who is thereby the primary cause of all actualities, essential and existential, including of free creaturely acts. They contend that were mere conservationism true, and creatures were just given powers that they could then actualize, then the resulting actualities could not be essentially traced back to an ultimate cause and so would exist without explanation.

Scotus, while not a mere conservationist, shows how to maintain the mere conservationist claim that creaturely acts are not directly caused by God, without violating the concurrentist principle about essentially ordered causes. One being can cause another in an essentially ordered way by directly causing it, by directly moving another to cause it, or (as Scotus argued, adding to what other concurrentists recognized) the primary cause can give to the secondary cause its "total causality."[94] God is the primary cause of all that exists—all being ultimately comes from him—but he causes some things, including our free acts, by giving actuality and causality to us. I propose that he does this by giving us the free actuality described in chapter 4, the orientation to our end, participation in infinite freedom, and surplus of actuality sufficient for us to reduce ourselves from potency to act with regard to any willable object. Some Thomist concurrentists, like Domingo Bañez, hold that God must give us a distinct actuality (a "physical premotion") for each act that we perform, in virtue of which we move ourselves to act; this is so for acts done naturally and for acts done by grace.[95] But I contend that such a view is inconsistent with our freedom: God instead gives (or "premoves" us to) a surplus of free actuality (or "total causality") in virtue of which we can reduce ourselves to act as we wish, without God also having to reduce us to act.

---

94. Scotus, *Ord.* II, d.34–37, q.5, n. XI7. See Frost, "Scotus on How God Causes the Created Will's Volitions."

95. Domingo Bañez, *Scholastica commentaria in primam partem*, q.105, a.4 (Salamanaca: S. Stephanum, 1585), 515; Garrigou-Lagrange, *Predestination*, 256–65, 293–4, 319–23. See Spencer, "Divine Causality and Created Freedom."

Concurrentists also object that were God not the direct, *per se* cause of all created actualities, he would not be able to providentially guide the universe, and the perfection of the universe could only come about *per accidens* or by chance, contrary to divine wisdom and goodness. Rather, God must directly perfect the universe, which requires him to *per se* decree all creaturely events.[96] But while I agree with concurrentists that all actuality is ultimately traced back to God, this objection fails because there is another sort of causality: *per communionem* causality. The perfection of the universe comes about by both *per se* and *per communionem* causality, such as through covenantal *sun-energeia* between God and creatures, through *sun-energeia* among creatures, and through God allowing creatures to specify their acts independently of him. It is not purely the result of God's design but also the result of creatures being allowed to contribute to that perfection in ways not decreed by God. (God's uncontrolling openness to our free acts is what otherwise reductionistic theologies like open theism get right.[97])

While this explains how created persons can cause free acts without God directly causing their content, we still need an explanation as to how nonpersonal creatures can cause their acts in a quasi-free way. We also still need an explanation as to how creatures come to participate in Platonic Forms of various sorts. We need to grasp this not just to understand the irreducibility of nonpersonal creatures but especially to grasp the irreducibility of our own nonfree acts, especially those in which we exercise efficient causation.

On most Thomistic views, in eternally knowing himself, God knows how he is participable—that is, he eternally knows his *logoi* (or ideas), the exemplars or types of all possible creatures, including every possible creaturely act, and he knows every way that he could respond to any creaturely action.[98] I contend that God wills, in this creative way, by contingent and free *energeiai*, that the content of certain *logoi* be constituted as Platonic Forms. Divine ideas or *logoi* are uncreated content as such, imitable formalities in God with his infinite mode of being; Platonic Forms are created finite essential content as such, the limited, participable expressions of di-

---

96. Cf. Aquinas, *ST* I, q.47, a.1.
97. Thomas Jay Oord, *The Uncontrolling Love of God: An Open and Relational Account of Providence* (Downers Grove, Ill.: IVP Academic, 2015).
98. Gregory Doolan, *Aquinas on the Divine Ideas as Exemplar Causes* (Washington, D.C.: The Catholic University of America Press, 2008), 243; Balthasar, *TD2*, 278.

vine ideas that are principles for concrete beings and their acts. In constituting Platonic Forms, God wills that his beauty and wisdom (*Sophia*) be, as it were, externalized, made available to creation.[99]

Some object that Platonic Forms cannot be caused since they are necessary and abstract, not contingent and concrete entities, which are what enter into efficient causal relations. Were they created, they would be the term of an efficient causal relation, and so would be concrete, and their content would be contingent.[100] But none of this follows. First, the necessity of their content is ensured by their reflecting and participating in divine *logoi*. The intelligible world of the Platonic Forms is an everlasting, unchanging effect of God's will, unlike his *logoi*, which are necessary formalities in him, *energeiai* emanating from his *ousia*.[101] Second, while Platonic Forms are works (*erga*) resulting from divine *energeiai*, they are not caused in the way that concrete beings are. Rather, God performs multiple kinds of causal activities. By *creation*, he *per se* brings into existence concrete beings, participants in *esse*, out of nothing. By *con-creation*, he brings into existence principles of being, which exist only with reference to concrete beings, rather than existing concretely or by directly sharing in *esse*.[102] Platonic Forms are not concrete substances with *esse* but principles of kinds of being, existing in themselves only in being not-nothing and an effect of divine will. They only exist in being orientated to providing content to concrete substances (including illumination to our minds). Contrary to Plato's own views, Platonic Forms are not what is "really real"; rather, they are only principles for concrete beings, which are what primarily exist. This is a realist, not an idealist, account of Platonic Forms. God causes Platonic Forms by *con-creation*, as an aspect of his causing concrete beings. While there are *logoi* for all possible beings and kinds of beings, we need posit Platonic Forms only for some kinds of actually existing beings.

Platonic Forms mediate essential content from God to creatures. They are a "repository" of surplus actuality and content available to creatures. Since this content is available within the created order, and since all creatures are what they are by participating in this content, creatures can draw essential content and actuality from Platonic Forms, whereas no creature

---

99. Cf. Bulgakov, *Bride of the Lamb*, 17, 55.
100. Peter van Inwagen, "God and Other Uncreated Things," in *Metaphysics and God*, ed. Kevin Timpe (New York: Routledge, 2009), 3–20.
101. Cf. Gavrilyuk, *Georges Florovsky and the Russian Religious Renaissance*, 154.
102. Cf. Aquinas, *ST* I, q.45, a.4, 8.

can act through God's power except on God's *per se* initiative. This allows creatures to act independently of God's *per se* causality, though all actuality and content comes ultimately from God. God need not *per se* specify the content of particular creaturely acts or effects, though he could do so. We have seen that created substances always act with Platonic Forms. When creatures have sensible qualities, cause an offspring with an essence, are directed to an end, or cooperate to bring about a *Gestalt*, they do so by sharing in Platonic Forms and their *energeiai*. When we think, the objects of our thought participate in those Forms, which can illumine our minds, allowing insight into their content. By making Platonic Forms, God covenantally commits himself to allow his *energeiai* to be shared in whenever a creature acts by participation in those Forms.

God also gives to each substance a surplus of actuality, like our free actuality, by which it actualizes itself in acts specific to its kind.[103] A surplus of actuality is not a potentiality: our *free actuality* is not actualized by particular acts but is a directedness to an end and a participation in infinite freedom in virtue of which we can reduce ourselves from potency to act for any act directed to that end. Likewise, all creatures can specify their acts and effects, and they can reduce themselves to act on the basis of their God-given directedness to their end, without God determining when they act or what they do. We are not only free beings but animals with probabilistic quantum matter; one aspect of our acts' irreducibility to divine action is the way that our forms specify our nonfree acts independently from God. I do not deny that, as many Thomists contend, God's *per se* primary causality is consistent with *per accidens* secondary causality, such that events that are contingent, random, or a matter of chance in relation to their creaturely causes could also be directly caused and specified by God. But there is ample evidence that God does not directly or *per se* cause all events in the material world. As we have seen, creatures bear earthly values that do not give themselves as caused by God. Nonpersonal creatures have an analogue of freedom in the way they actualize their matter, and in how they give themselves to one another and to value when they act through *per communionem* causality, such that they constitute *Gestalten* like landscapes and ecosystems. Most importantly, unless material substances could act in a way independent of God's causal determination, unless they were in themselves open to purely creaturely causal determination, we could

---

103. Cf. Blondel, *Action* (1893), 318–25.

not freely act on and specify their properties, but we experience ourselves doing this. For these reasons, God gives a surplus of actuality to each creature, by which it can act in a self-directed way not also specified *per se* by God.

A significant example of an event in which a creature draws on this surplus is evolutionary speciation through natural selection. In a speciation event, members of one species have offspring belonging to a new species with a more perfect essential actuality than their own actuality. This is not purely a matter of chance.[104] Rather, I suggest that the cooperation and pressures that drive natural selection are an example of *per communionem* causality and *sun-energeia* among creatures in an ecosystem, a natural *Gestalt* community, and among parts of substances, like their genetic material. This allows later biological species to descend from earlier ones, such that the development of one species into another happens, at least partially, through changes to matter of members of parent species.[105] The significance of this account of evolution for understanding our irreducibility will be made clearer in chapter 8.

Some Thomists have objected to the theory of evolution in that it implies that ontologically imperfect beings cause more perfect ones, which seems impossible.[106] Other Thomists have contended that there are only two essential species of nonhuman organisms, plants and animals, and all evolutionary change is just accidental changes within those species, developing toward the more perfect interiority, knowledge, and love found in human persons.[107]

I propose that while parent organisms are more ontologically imperfect than offspring of a descendent species in their individual actuality, all organisms share in and can act in virtue of the surplus of actuality and perfection found in Platonic Forms. By drawing on that surplus, in which they always already participate, more imperfect substances can produce more perfect ones. What appear to be merely accidental changes (like rearrangements of matter such as genetic mutations) are actually changes involving participation in and *sun-energeia* with Platonic Forms; considered holistically, seemingly accidental changes are actually acts of substantial

---

104. Cf. Peter van Inwagen, "The Place of Chance in a World Sustained by God," in *God, Knowledge, and Mystery* (Ithaca, N.Y.: Cornell University Press, 1995), 42–65.

105. On interpretations of evolutionary theory, see Stephen Jay Gould, *The Structure of Evolutionary Theory* (Cambridge, Mass.: Belknap Press, 2002).

106. Michael Chaberek, *Aquinas and Evolution* (The Chartwell Press, 2020), 51ff.

107. de Koninck, *Cosmos*, in *The Writings of Charles de Koninck*, vol. 1, 258ff.

production. Due to their participation in Platonic Forms, efficient causes can bring about new kinds of participation in those Forms, and all efficient causation brings about the effect's participation in the Form of the effect's species and that species's end. Creaturely efficient causation, including our own, is irreducible to observable features; it also involves drawing on and participation in the excess of the Platonic Forms.

Some might object that on my proposal, all possible kinds of life seem to be specified by God in advance, when he constitutes Platonic Forms, but that this is contrary to the experience of entirely new things coming to be. I grant that since God necessarily and eternally has *logoi* of all possible creatures and creaturely kinds, no content new in every respect can come to be, but it does not follow that when a new creaturely kind comes to be, God bestows or designs its content or that its content is drawn from a "preexisting" Platonic Form. When lizards evolved into snakes, for example, lizard parents' reproductive acts need not have drawn the content of snake nature from an already existing, "predesigned" Platonic Form of snake nature, and need not have involved God bestowing the content of snake nature.[108] Rather, lizard parents could have brought about snake nature in their offspring just by their reproductive acts and by events of mutation and natural selection, where the content of that nature did not previously exist in the created order.

We saw in chapter 3 that human persons make new Platonic Forms, as when we invent fictional characters; likewise, nonpersonal beings can produce new Platonic Forms just by acting together. This metaphysics can affirm that the arising of new species is as it appears, a contingent event, but new species' actuality must still be drawn from some higher actuality, some form, since every actuality must arise in virtue of an equal or greater actuality. One explanation would draw on the resemblance, on my metaphysics, of Platonic Forms to items proposed in early medieval thought like "seminal reasons," new forms latent in nature, and the "world soul" (*anima mundi*), the unifying, quasi-animating principle of the natural world.[109] One way of understanding the idea of a "world-soul" is as a Platonic Form of finite life, a surplus of actuality in which every living thing participates. By disposing matter in the right ways and acting in virtue of that Form of life, organisms cause their offspring to participate in a higher

---

108. I owe this example to Fr. Nicanor Austriaco, OP.
109. Marie-Dominique Chenu, *Nature, Man, and Society in the Twelfth Century*, trans. Jerome Taylor and Lester Little (Chicago: University of Chicago Press, 1957), 69.

way in that Platonic Form, thereby educing a new substantial form in the offspring, and a new Platonic Form for its species. That there is a single ultimate source of meaning and being, God, does not exclude the spontaneous emergence of meaning and being from free or evolving creatures.[110] For organisms to bring about new forms in this way requires that matter can be disposed to have properties ontologically prior to receiving form, the metaphysics of which will be explained in chapter 7.[111] On this view, God has covenantally committed himself to allow new species to share in his *energeiai* and *logoi* through the mediation of a Platonic Form when they arise.

Another possible explanation is that transcendent persons like angels bestow forms and bring about speciation events, with God committing himself to actualizing whatever they specify.[112] (God can also cause speciation events, but the purpose of this argument is to show how they can be caused by creatures alone.) The Sophiological tradition proposes that a transcendent person or quasi-personal agent just is the world-soul or Form of life, a continual self-transcending power in the cosmos for bringing about greater, more fecund life, which that tradition calls *Sophia* or *Natura naturans*, a creature making present creative divine *energeiai*. As on my account of Platonic Forms, this *Sophia* is the externalization of the content of divine beauty or wisdom. On this account, this agent contains and communicates divine content and superior actuality to new species but brings about the natural history of the world without that history being entirely specified by God.[113]

While this account of creatures acting through surplus actualities shows how essential content need not be determined by God, it still seems that God must give *esse*, the supreme actuality, to each act. Yet we have seen that many acts ought not to be because of their disvalues, and so it would be morally wrong for God to actualize them. God, as subsistent *esse*, is the ultimate source of all creaturely *esse* in all its modes (necessary, contingent, and free) and hence the primary cause of all creatures' existence,

---

110. *Contra* deconstructionist reductionisms, like that of Anne O'Byrne, *Natality and Finitude* (Bloomington: Indiana University Press, 2010), 122–23.
111. Cf. de Koninck, *Cosmos*, 278–83.
112. De Koninck, *Cosmos*, 285–86; J. R. R. Tolkien, "Ainulindalë," in *The Silmarillion* (New York: Del Rey, 1999). *Contra* Charles Winckelmans de Cléty, *The World of Persons* (New York: Sheed and Ward, 1967), 409–10, it would be reductionistic of organisms' powers to hold that all evolutionary events must happen through transcendent persons' acts, especially since some evolutionary events appear to occur just through organisms' causality.
113. Bulgakov, *Bride of the Lamb*, 79–103, 176–77; Martin, *The Submerged Reality*.

including of creaturely free acts, But I contend that God need not directly bestow *esse* on each being. Rather, just as God first con-created Platonic Forms, so He also first con-creates the fullness of creaturely existence, *esse commune*, which is a principle of concrete beings. God covenantally commits himself to allow creatures to participate in *esse commune* and thereby in his subsistent *esse* (so that he is present to them and able to know them). By this participation, creatures exist in a radically extramental way, as beings and agents independent and separate from God. They can, by participation in *esse commune*, bestow that same participation on other beings and thereby bring about particular *esse*, without God having to specially intend to bestow *esse* upon them. God conserves beings by making *esse commune* available to them.[114] Since participation in *esse commune* allows us to bestow *esse*, we can cause evil acts, which ought not be, without God causing them, except in Scotus's third sense of essentially ordered causality as described above.

Creatures also share in Platonic Forms of values, by participation in which they have individual values and bestow them on others. These are Forms of a sort distinct from those of essential actualities; they are modes of importance as such. All individual substantial forms correspond to Platonic Forms. Substantial forms are principles that are "divine in things"[115]: they make God's *energeiai* sacramentally present, and (in the words of Thales of Miletus) make it that "all things are full of gods," participations in divine activity.[116] As we saw in chapter 5, however, only some values appear as messages from God (such as holiness, beauty of the second power, and moral values), exerting a call that is absolute and has eternal significance; unlike all substantial forms, only some values are principles that are something divine in things and make God sacramentally present. Other values are merely earthly values (such as aesthetic values like elegance, the wabi-sabi, and the "inhuman" forms of beauty), categorically calling for a response but without eternal significance. On my proposed metaphysics, only the former have Platonic Forms and are thereby direct participations in divine *energeiai*. Once values exist in concrete beings, then they are aspects of those beings' *energeiai*, and through those *energeiai*, beings can

---

114. Cf. John Beaudoin, "The World's Continuance," *International Journal for Philosophy of Religion* 61, no. 2 (2007): 83–98.

115. Aquinas, *In I Phys.*, lect. 15. Cf. Lawrence Dewan, *St. Thomas and Form as Something Divine in Things* (Milwaukee, Wisc.: Marquette University Press, 2007).

116. Aristotle, *DA*, 411a7-8; *PA*, 645a20.

Principle of *Energeia* 283

modify those values' content, specifying the content of earthly values and disvalues, for which there is no Platonic Form and no direct participation in divine *energeiai*. No creature can produce values or disvalues *ex nihilo*; they produce them by modifying the values in which they participate, which ultimately come from God. While earthly values and disvalues can at times lead to enslaving moral and cultural systems, value as such is not an arbitrary force imposed upon us to motivate us. Rather, it is fundamentally the way that we are most perfectly drawn into communion with God and other beings, a perceivable aspect of their *energeiai*. As we partly saw in chapter 2, beings have value through their self-emptying (*kenosis*), their pouring themselves out in self-giving, self-manifesting, self-expressing, and unifying *energeiai*.[117]

The earthly value of elegance, for example, is a redirecting, through human free acts, of the God-given value of beauty. We can still reason in an effect-to-cause manner from elegance back to the beauty of which it is a modification, and thence to God, but elegance, unlike beauty, does not allow direct perception of God's presence and activity in things. Disvalues, like evil, ugliness, and banality are a redirection of values' *energeiai* in a perverse way. Earthly values and disvalues can also come about through acts of transcendent persons, like angels and demons; some disvalues display the presence of an evil transcendent person.[118] God in no way, either by causal or permissive decree, specifies anything evil, but he permits creatures to specify evil (and good) acts because he does not control what creatures freely do. Disvalues arise only when a being ontologically lacks some actuality it ought to have—hence, at the second level of being, the privation theory of evil is true. However, beings act and manifest themselves (i.e., have *energeiai*) when they have such a privation, and the content of such *energeiai* are disvalues. While evil is ontologically a privation, evil is not nothing since it appears and is experienced. At the third level of being and at the level of *energeiai*, evil and other disvalues have positive reality: they are redirections of the good *energeiai* of values, in ways specified by creatures, and are genuine manifestations (i.e., contents of *energeiai*) of those creatures. All value and being originate with God but can take on new content as specified by creatures. Given that *energeiai* are the beauty of a being in the sense of its splendid self-manifestation, disvalues can be

117. *Contra* Loudovikos, *Identities*, 39, following Nietzsche.
118. Jean-Luc Marion, *Prolegomena to Charity*, trans. Stephen Lewis (New York: Fordham University Press, 2002), chap. 1.

seen as a sort of "negative beauty," a perverse (yet often seductively attractive) appearance of the being. This shows us yet further how fundamental beauty is: all phenomena—no matter how evil or ugly at the three levels of being—are, at the level of *energeiai*, a form of beauty.[119] With this solution to the problem of divine causality, together with the earlier arguments against materialism, we can see how we and our acts are irreducible both to what is below and to what is above us.

Theological Reflections

This account can be furthered in light of Christian theology. In addition to his covenants with all creation, God forms special covenants with human persons. The subsistent human soul, being immaterial and so not made out of anything, and yet as something caused along with the body, since it is the form of a particular body, can come to be only *ex nihilo*—that is, by divine creation.[120] But any successful human act of reproduction, whether through sexual intercourse or through laboratory techniques like *in vitro* fertilization or cloning, results in a human person—that is, certain free human acts are necessarily followed by the coming into being of a human soul. We need an account of how this can be, without claiming that human persons can efficiently cause human souls.

God has covenantally bound himself to create human souls (and, thereby, persons) whenever fitting material conditions obtain. Unlike with nonpersonal beings, God directly creates each human form and wills its content. This does not imply that our souls preexist our bodies (since my soul is the form of *this* body), only that each soul's content is uniquely specified by God when it comes into being. Human sexual intercourse makes God sacramentally present in a way unlike other physical acts. All other acts just "reach up" to Platonic Forms and "pull down" content, making God and his *energeiai* mediately present. Sexual intercourse is an invocation of God to directly create a new human soul, anticipating how the sacraments of grace, like the Eucharist, make his supernatural life present through physical acts.[121]

God's covenantal self-commitments reveal, as Balthasar says, a humiliation on his part, a lowering (*kenosis*) of himself such that he acts within

---

119. Cf. Balthasar, "Transcendentality and *Gestalt*," *Communio* 11, no. 1 (1984): 4–12.
120. Aquinas, *ST* I, q.75, a.5, 6; q.76, a.2.
121. Balthasar, *TL2*, 59–63, following Matthias Scheeben.

the laws of the creation he has made.[122] God's motivation can be understood by analogy to the overflowing bliss, the longing to bestow goods on others, described in chapter 5. Balthasar traces through Western literature the theme of the *holy fool* (e.g., in Parsifal, Don Quixote, and Prince Mishkin) who ridiculously but with childlike merriness lavishes love on others without concern for himself and without desire to have power or control over them.[123] This wild, merry, festive stance, which in a fallen world is misunderstood and leads to the heartbreak and redemption of the cross, displays how God deals with us. The purely sacrificed person, seen above all on the cross, reveals the fullness of self-giving beauty; in what might appear supremely ugly from a purely sensory perspective, we find the true glory of being and of God.[124] Likewise, we, who are made in his image (as we shall see in chapter 7), are called to act in this way; to have grace, to share in God's supernatural life, is primarily to be able to love with this overflowing, self-lowering love (*agape, caritas*). Ontologically, this is a humiliating turning from the perfect to the imperfect, but at the level of *energeiai*, it is an aspect of the fundamental structure of being and beauty, which lavishly pours itself out in what is lower, always tending toward what is sensory and finite, raising it to participation in what is higher.

The history of the universe, humanity, and each human life is not a drama scripted by God, a narrative he writes, or a machine he designs; rather, he makes us (and all creatures) his partners so that we make a genuine contribution to it. God does not ontologically need the world, but as one who delights in lavishing gifts, creates the world as a gift to us and a gift among the divine persons.[125] As we saw in chapter 4, this involves separation of a sort between us and God: he gives us "space" to respond to him as we choose. Insofar as they participate in *esse* and divine beauty, creatures do not add being to God but exist only by sharing his being; insofar as they are distinct beings and beauties with their own *ousia* and *energeia*, creatures are separate from God and add to reality over and above God's reality. But while on the metaphysics I propose God does not cause all history, my metaphysics allows that he does intervene in it, especially in the Incarnation and by allowing participation in his life. This involves his direct *per se* causality, unmediated by Platonic Forms. God also has providence over

122. Balthasar, *TD2*, 369–72.
123. Balthasar, *GL5*, 141–205.
124. Carnes, *Beauty*, 87, 168–69, 185–86..
125. Balthasar, *TD5*, 506ff.

all things, that is, all things are contained within and given a surplus of meaning by the covenantal *Gestalt* he effects between himself and creation: all substances receive a surplus of meaning insofar as he reveals himself through them. God gives all things a place in his overall plan for creation: he knows all that exists, intervenes according to his plans, and guides all things towards their ultimate consummation. We should be "abandoned" to divine providence in trusting God's plans and hoping for ultimate fulfillment and the revelation of God in all things, being poor in spirit, lacking narcissism in openness to his every call. But a metaphysics of irreducibility is opposed to *quietism*, on which we just allow God to act without realizing we make genuine contributions—a danger that lurks behind concurrentism. God is providential in a way that allows creatures to add their own contributions to creation and to the covenantal *Gestalt* involving God and creatures. God acts providentially in a way that risks creatures not abiding by his covenant: while he cannot be thwarted or harmed ontologically, he is vulnerable in his *energeiai*. While the world is God's loving gift to his creatures, it is not a mere game or loving recreation that God plays with his creatures; it is a morally serious place, where we must make choices that have decisive, fully meaningful outcomes undetermined by God.

Reality has a *Christological* or *Incarnational* structure. Christ, who unites in his person (or *hypostasis*) created and uncreated *ousiai* and *energeiai*, is a pattern for creation and the fulfillment of that pattern. By taking created nature into a divine person, He makes available to all creatures the possibility of sharing his divine life, and to persons the possibility of knowing and loving as God does. A metaphysics of irreducibility opposes every form of *Docetism*, on which any creature is a mere appearance, an epiphenomenon of God's acts or plans. It opposes every form of *nihilism* that would drain meaning from the world such that it resides only in God or in any other single being like the human self.[126] God's supreme self-revelation comes in a bodily death and resurrection, showing the concrete, material world to be fully real, indispensably important, and totally serious. The *Logos* has assumed humanity, animality, materiality, and historicity, without annulling their reality and otherness from his divinity, making them potential vehicles for sharing in him.[127] Aside from his human nature,

---

126. Loudovikos, *Analogical Identities*, 1–11.

127. *Contra* Maximus, as interpreted in Jordan Daniel Wood, "Creation is Incarnation," *Modern Theology* 34, no. 1 (2018): 82–102, this is not to say that the *Logos* is somehow incarnate in all beings. God not only relates to the world Christologically but also in the other ways we have seen.

creatures share in God and make him manifest through *sun-energeia*, not hypostatic union—though it is that union that makes supernatural *sun-energeia* possible.

Reality also has a *Mariological* structure: as Mary consented to allow God to be at work in her in every aspect of her life, but also contributed to that work in her flesh, thereby manifesting both beauty and wisdom (*Sophia*) as they are found in God and as they are found externalized in creatures, so each creature is called to bring its *energeiai* into obedient and creative cooperation with God's. And reality has an *ecclesial* structure. By covenantal cooperation between God and creatures, *Gestalten* emerge, including the universe as a whole and the Church, the community of those who share in his supernatural *energeiai*. Though God cannot be a part of anything ontologically, he can, by *sun-energeiai*, enter these *Gestalten*. By drawing beings into the Church, God exercises his greatest providence. As we saw in chapter 4, understanding, loving, and willing have a "combining power," ordering what falls under them. God's *energeiai* likewise gather creatures to take on their ultimate form and meaning. Our ultimate end must involve joining with others in a covenantal community.

Part 2 A Portrait of Irreducible, Beautiful, Liturgical Persons

Chapter 7 The Transcendence of the Soul and the Principles of Personhood

In this second part of the book, I synthesize the last six chapters into a unified portrait of the human person, considering especially the interrelations between soul and body and between our personhood, the three levels of being, *ousia*, and *energeiai*. In this chapter, I argue that we are irreducible to our bodies—that is, that we can exist constituted just by a soul. I consider debates about the separated soul (the soul after death and prior to the resurrection), individuation, the definition of human nature, the image of God in us, and what persons as such are and how principles are included in persons. In chapter 8, I argue that we are irreducible to single substances; rather, we include many substances. I consider debates over what sex is, over when embodied life begins and ends, and over how we have variable *status*, such as states of pure nature and grace. Finally, in chapter 9, I argue that we are irreducible to our spiritual souls, which, with spiritual acts, are meant to be embodied. I show how beauty is our central aspect, introducing a final metaphysical notion, the *face* or *prosopon*, and giving a culminating account of our end as involving liturgical activity.

The Immortality of the Human Soul

If something is a subject of acts, then it exists such that it can act in its own right—that is, it is *subsistent*.[1] Action follows being: what something is, is

---

1. Many claims in sections on the separated soul are from Spencer, "The Personhood of the Separated Soul," 863–912; "What is it Like to be an Embodied Person? What is it Like to be a Separated Soul?"

revealed by what it does. The last four chapters have given ample evidence that many of our acts do not essentially involve the body because they are self-conscious, meaningfully motivated, self-transcending acts that prescind from material conditions. Rather, they actualize the soul, and so human souls are subsistent subjects of acts. The soul has an act of existence (*esse*) in its own right. Experientially, my spiritual acts are paradigmatically mine; my subjectivity is more closely associated with acts of the soul than with bodily acts, which (as described in chapter 1) can more easily be regarded as objects I have. The soul and its *esse* are paradigmatically mine: in agreement with Aquinas, I contend that my soul's *esse* just is *my esse*. My act of existence belongs primarily to my soul and only thence is given (or "communicated") to my body.[2] All material substances' *esse* and *ousia* belong primarily to their forms and thence are given to their matter, but nonspiritual forms have these principles only in a state of communicating them to matter, not in themselves. By contrast, human souls have these principles in themselves, such that they act in their own right.

Being subsistent and immaterial, the human soul is immortal.[3] Beings are corrupted when they receive properties incompatible with their natures; for example, if properties like disease or injury sufficiently disrupt our body's natural structure and homeostasis, then the body cannot maintain its actuality and it dies. The soul's powers, however, are transcendentally open: we can think of any being, will any good, feel any mode of importance, and socially relate to any person. No property our souls can receive is incompatible with its nature. Furthermore, to be corrupted, a thing must be composed of spatially separable pieces of matter. Since the soul is not so composed, it cannot become corrupted so long as God conserves it, that is, allows it to participate in *esse commune*.[4]

Aquinas also argues that we have a natural intellectual desire for immortality: upon grasping the notion of perpetual existence (as only intellectual beings can), our natures are constituted such that we automatically desire it. Natural desires (i.e., desires or orientations to an end that a being has through its nature) cannot be in vain; teleological ordering only comes to be through fitting with reality, and so these desires can be directed only

---

Angelicum 93 (2016): 219–46; and "The Separated Soul," in *Disability in Medieval Christian Philosophy and Theology*, ed. Scott Williams (New York: Routledge, 2020), 235–57.

2. Aquinas, *ST* I, q.76, a.1, ad 5.
3. Aquinas, *ST* I, q.75, a.6; *SCG* II, c. 79–81.
4. Cf. Aquinas, *ST* I, q.104, a.3.

to attainable objects. If we have a natural desire for perpetual existence, then it must be something we can attain.

Yet some people seem to desire not to be immortal, worrying that perpetual existence would be boring, tedious, or oppressive. Or they think that if one believes oneself to be immortal, one will lose a sense of the urgency of ethical calls, since one might assume that one can always respond to it later, or one might believe that one can evade having to respond once one is in a pleasurable afterlife.[5] Furthermore, it is difficult to distinguish natural desires from acquired desires and wishful thinking.[6] For these reasons, I don't think we should posit a natural intellectual desire for immortality in us, although since our souls are naturally immortal, we have a natural, but nonintellectual, desire for immortality, in the sense of being naturally oriented to that state. One might respond that claims to not desire immortality are actually cases of people failing to really understand perpetual existence or to know what they really want. It would be disingenuous to deny people's experience when it does not fit with our preferred metaphysical system, however, and it may be question-begging to argue in this way.

Rather, a better experiential argument for immortality begins with the experience of being directly called to infinite moral goodness and creativity. So long as this call has been given at least once, it requires an explanation. As Kant observed, fulfilling this call requires immortality, for no finite amount of time would be sufficient to fulfill it.[7] Marion likewise contends that the call directly given in saturated phenomena, like others' faces or events, is experienced as a call for an infinite response: I have never done enough to ethically respond to others or to adequately understand events.[8] Far from leading to evasion of these calls, only everlasting life would be adequate to fulfill them. If this is right, then the afterlife cannot consist only of pleasure or self-fulfillment; rather, our ultimate state must be a life of ever-increasing responsibility and goodness, not necessarily involving difficulty or overcoming suffering, but always creatively communicating goodness to others.[9]

---

5. Bernard Williams, "The Makropulos Case: Reflections on the Tedium of Immortality," in *Problems of the Self* (Cambridge: Cambridge University Press, 1973), 82–100.

6. Cf. Scotus, *Ord.* IV, d.43, q.2.

7. Immanuel Kant, *Critique of Practical Reason*, trans. Mary Gregor (Cambridge: Cambridge University Press, 2015), pt. 1, bk. 2, chap. 2, s. 4.

8. Marion, *In Excess*, 33–34, 123–27.

9. See Luke 19:17.

Turning from the immortality of the soul to its connection to the body, we must consider how some in the Catholic tradition, like Karl Rahner, have argued that human persons are necessarily embodied, and so at death, the soul would immediately receive a new body, rather than ever existing in a disembodied state.[10] Those who hold this view erroneously think that all of our experiences are experiences of embodiment, and so no human conscious life can occur without the body. They fail to consider experiences given as transcending the body, such as insights into Platonic Forms. (That we have experiences transcending—and so not requiring—the body should not be taken to devalue the body or to show it is opposed to the soul; these are just different sorts of experience we have.) This view also fails to do justice to our experiences regarding death. I experience myself as tending toward death, presaged in bodily suffering as tending toward sundering from the body.[11] In perceiving another's death, the other is given as no longer present and able to passively suffer in a body. For God to immediately replace our bodies with new ones at death would render these experiences deceptive. It fits better with these experiences to hold that, after death, the soul exists and acts apart from matter.[12]

This conclusion raises the further problem of whether my separated soul will be me, this person, a subject of debate in analytic Thomism. On one side of this debate are corruptionists, who hold that despite the human soul's immortality, the human person goes out of existence at death and comes back into existence at the resurrection.[13] On the other side are survivalists, who hold that the person survives death constituted by or identical to the soul.[14]

---

10. Karl Rahner, *Foundations of Christian Faith*, trans. William Dych (New York: Crossroad, 1999), 266–78. Cf. Peter van Inwagen, "The Possibility of Resurrection," *International Journal for Philosophy of Religion* 9, no. 2 (1978): 114–21.

11. Heidegger, *Being and Time*, 231–33; Emmanuel Levinas, *Time and the Other*, trans. Richard Cohen (Pittsburgh: Duquesne University Press, 1987), 70–71; Panayiotis Nellas, *Deification in Christ: Orthodox Perspectives on the Nature of the Human Person*, trans. Norman Russell (Crestwood: St. Vladimir's Seminary Press, 1987), 64–65; and Balthasar, *TD4*, 121–37.

12. Matthew Levering, *Mary's Bodily Assumption* (Notre Dame, Ind.: University of Notre Dame Press, 2016), chap. 3.

13. See, for example, Patrick Toner, "St. Thomas Aquinas on Death and the Separated Soul," *Pacific Philosophical Quarterly* 91, no. 4 (2010): 587–99; Christina Van Dyke, "Not Properly a Person: The Rational Soul and Thomistic Substance Dualism," *Faith and Philosophy* 26, no. 2 (2009): 186–204; and Turner Nevitt, "Aquinas on the Death of Christ: A New Argument for Corruptionism," *American Catholic Philosophical Quarterly* 90, no. 1 (2016): 77–99. I do not consider the debate over which position Aquinas held, though I think he was a corruptionist; see Aquinas, *In IV Sent.*, d.43, q.1, a.1, qq.1, ad 2; *DP*, q.9, a.2, ad 14; *QDA*, a.1; *SCG* IV, c. 80-1; *ST* I, q.29, a.1, ad 5; III, q.50, a.4; *In 1 Cor.*, c. 15, lect. 2. Cf. John of St. Thomas, *Cursus philosophicus*, v. 2, q.7 a.3, 114.

14. See, for example, Christopher Brown, "Souls, Ships, and Substances: A Reply to Toner," *American*

Corruptionism is defended on the grounds that we are essentially animals, since we engage, by nature, in sensory and other animal activities, which occur in material organs and so essentially require matter. Animals and their natures are essentially, not accidentally, composites of form and matter. My soul can preserve my formal identity and existence, and powers, acts, and habits that do not require matter (such as intellect, will, and heart), but it cannot be me, since it lacks an essential part of what I am, matter. Corruptionists also contend that only their view explains the experience of death as a great evil and the resurrection as an immense good; were survivalism true, I would not need to be resurrected to live again after death, for I would never have ceased to live. In the resurrection of the body, according to Christian doctrine, the matter of those who have died will be raised by God and rejoined to their souls. While the resurrection is not necessary for the fulfillment of the soul's powers in themselves—given that the soul can, by itself, grasp and love God—the resurrection is supremely fitting for us.

Properties of Persons as Such

I argue for survivalism below, but first, I confront the question, which is starkly raised by the debate over the separated soul, of what it is to be a person, the central question of this book. In my introduction, I said, following Aquinas, that "person" designates "that which is most perfect in all of nature." To be *perfectum* is to be "thoroughly made" (*per factum*).[15] It is to be as complete as possible, entirely irreducible to what is other than itself. All my analyses of principles and acts so far have operated at some level of abstraction from our full concrete reality, but now I consider who we are concretely and fully as persons. While I experientially am a subjectivity, substance, and being, each of these is just an abstractable aspect of or formality in me. By contrast, *person* designates me most concretely and holistically. I first consider three marks that many scholastics ascribed to persons as such.

First, persons have eminent dignity and nobility (or beauty).[16] As spir-

---

Catholic Philosophical Quarterly 81, no. 4 (2007): 655–68; Jason Eberl, "Do Humans Persist between Death and Resurrection?" in *Metaphysics and God*, 188–205; Oderberg, *Real Essentialism*, chap. 10; and Stump, *Aquinas*, 50–54.

15. Aquinas, *ST* I, q.4, a.1.
16. Alexander of Hales, *Glossa in IV Libros Sententiarum* (Quaracchi: Collegium S. Bonaventura,

itual beings high on the ontological hierarchy, persons have transcendental goodness (i.e., are proper objects of love and respect) to a high degree. We are naturally and obedientially ordered to contemplating God and to ethical action. Things must be treated in accord with their end, and so we ought to be treated with the care necessary to facilitate movement toward this lofty, eternal end. We have also seen that since we rationally and freely confer importance on other beings, we must have importance in ourselves. These sources of dignity stem from our human nature, by which we are all equal.[17] But, as John Crosby describes following Romano Guardini, love and value-perception reveal each person to have unique beauty or holiness, the highest kind of value, which calls for a distinct respect, ethical care, reverence, and love for each person. Love grasps another not as a contingently unique combination of universalizable properties but as irreplaceable.[18] As persons, we are radically unique and incommensurable, each with our own sort of dignity, irreducible to nature and the dignity it gives.

Second, persons are singular and one through themselves. (*Persona* is analyzed by some scholastics as *per se una*.) They are not one through a distinct principle, to which personal unity would be causally reducible.[19] Persons are not just substances in the sense of individualized natures, natures plus some principle that renders it this instance of that kind of nature and that renders it unable to have instances of its own. Nor are they just subsistent beings, things that exist in themselves, regardless of whether they have a complete nature. Rather, they are *supposits*, primary subjects of acts and of *esse* with complete natures. Persons are intellectual supposits, complete and unified in themselves not only substantially but also in that they can self-consciously possess and govern themselves. Persons are distinct from their natures; they are *res naturae* and *hypostases*, that is, what underlies, bears, has, or carries a nature. I am not just what I am, but a who that bears a nature, a "self-sustaining whole" who encompasses and per-

---

1957), I, q.23, a.9, 225–26; Bonaventure, *In III Sent.*, d.5, a.2, q.3, 136–37; Aquinas, *In I Sent.*, d.10, q.1, a.5; d.25, q.1, a.1, ad 8; *ST* I, q.29, a.3, ad 2.

17. Stephen Brock, "Is Uniqueness at the Root of Personal Dignity? John Crosby and Thomas Aquinas," *The Thomist* 69, no. 2 (2005): 173–201; Charles de Koninck, *On the Primacy of the Common Good: Against the Personalists*, trans. Sean Collins, reprinted in *The Aquinas Review* 4 (1997): 60.

18. Romano Guardini, *The World and the Person*, trans. Stella Lange (Chicago: Regnery, 1965), 215–16; Crosby, *The Selfhood of the Human Person*, 51. Cf. John Crosby, "A Neglected Source of the Dignity of Persons," in *Personalist Papers* (Washington, D.C.: The Catholic University of America Press, 2004), 3–32.

19. Aquinas, *ST* I, q.29, a.2; Bonaventure, *In III Sent.*, d.5, a.2, q.3, 136–37; Albert, *In III Sent.*, d.5, a.15, 115.

forms my acts.[20] As Robert Spaemann notes, I do not just passively bear my individual nature; rather, as the Roman jurists had it, to be a *persona* is to exist in one's own right (*sui iuris*), by which I understand that I have rule and rights over myself, able to freely choose whether to endorse the nature that I bear and live as it calls me to live.[21]

Third, persons are incommunicable. To be communicated is to be given to another, to be not complete or existing in oneself, but only through or by reference to another. Scholastics distinguish three kinds of communicability.[22] First, parts are communicated to wholes, having identity and existence only in relation to the latter. Integral parts like organs, logical parts (or formalities) like genera, and metaphysical parts like form alone cannot be persons. Second, universals are communicated to particulars, being what is apt to be said of or applied to many, so no universal is a person. Third, natures can be assumed by others, at least by the Trinitarian Persons; Christ's human nature, though an individuated form-matter composite and a bearer of powers and acts, belongs not to itself but to another, the Son. This case (even if it were only possible, not actual) shows that individual, subsistent natures alone are communicable and so are not persons.

Personalists distinguish further sorts of incommunicability.[23] Incommunicability is not just a metaphysical fact but is experienced: I experience myself as belonging to myself, as spiritually self-present.[24] While many aspects of me are explained by my parts and principles, in order to have those parts and principles, I must be (in some sense) prior to them and so not explained by them in every respect. I have my essence, existence, and value; each of these is, in me, unique. Although I cannot be entirely possessed by another, I show myself as incommunicable, and others grasp this through love and value-perception. To be incommunicable, with unique value, is to have a unique style or way that my unique beauty manifests itself out of my depths, which can only be grasped by having a spiritual "taste" for (or interpretive attunement to) it.[25]

20. Stein, *Finite and Eternal Being*, 207–13, 356–59.
21. Spaemann, *Persons*, 19–23, 73. Cf. Krąpiec, *Metaphysics*, 131–32.
22. Aquinas, *In III Sent.*, d.5, q.2, a.1, ad 2; Albert, *In I Sent.*, d.23, a.6, ad 2, v. 25:599; Bonaventure, *In III Sent.*, d.5, a.2, q.3, 136–37.
23. Crosby, *The Selfhood of the Human Person*, chap. 2; Guardini, *The World and the Person*, 118; Maritain, *The Degrees of Knowledge*, 462–63; *The Person and the Common Good*, 41; Wojtyła, *Acting Person*, 105–8; and Balthasar, *TD2*, 207–13.
24. Hildebrand, *The Nature of Love*, chap. 8.
25. Balthasar, *GL3*, 374–77 on Gerard Manley Hopkins on the incommunicable "taste" of the self

My incommunicability calls me to freely govern and recollect myself, and so live up to my personhood. Unlike nonpersonal beings, which are metaphysically incommunicable but just automatically manifest their natures whenever they act, I must freely appropriate my nature and then act out of it. Persons are not merely natural, self-contained substances but are also like artifacts; they are *Gestalten* partly resulting from free self-determination, with lives having a narrative structure, and who reach beyond themselves to include and coexist with others.[26] That I must shape my life as a *Gestalt* also opens me to the possibility of failing to live up to my personhood by not governing or determining myself, instead letting my natural tendencies have free rein. Contrary to Berdyaev (as described in chapter 4), nature and personhood are not opposed in themselves, but they are opposed if I fail to govern and properly take up the calls of my nature.[27] For example, sin rooted in concupiscence (i.e., in allowing our sensory nature to move toward its ends without being directed by spiritual acts to our true end) is a failure to live as an incommunicable person. Yet persons are not reducible to self-determined *Gestalten*; even if I fail to determine myself, I remain a person, since personhood is prior to anything I possess. Personhood is a new level of unity beyond Seifert's three levels and that of *energeia* and *ousia*, which unites all my aspects.

Proposals for Definitions and Formal Constituents of Persons

"Person" is from the Greek *prosopon* and the Latin *persona*.[28] These words indicated theatrical masks or roles; *persona* was also used in jurisprudence to indicate one who is *sui iuris*, or not ownable by another. While notions of dramatic role and juridical subject reveal key features of persons, including that persons and their beauty are not static but dynamic, narrative, or event-like, person cannot be fully defined by particular attributes, like roles. For this same reason, personhood cannot be constituted entirely by

---

and its "inscape" and "instress," the beauty of the indescribable but contemplatable way that beings are "en-selfed."

26. Cf. José Ortega y Gasset, *What Is Philosophy?* trans. Mildred Adams (New York: Norton, 1960), 206–52.

27. Cf. Loudovikos, *Analogical Identities*, 354.

28. There are cognate concepts in other languages, which pick out distinctive features of persons, like the Sanskrit *purusa*, the enduring, self-sacrificing self; see Radhakrishnan and Moore, *A Sourcebook in Indian Philosophy*.

consciousness, as in the view of John Locke, who holds that personal identity is explained by continuity of memory or consciousness.[29] While I can experientially identify myself with subjectivity, and while subjectivity is a formality in my soul's substance, it is not the only such formality. There are aspects of me, of this person, that are "mine" but not subjectively accessible, such as internal organs. More importantly, there is a true core of myself, *ousia*, which underlies empirical subjectivity (which is so often a mask for that core) but is not reducible to it. I am not reducible to or defined by my consciousness, or by conscious phenomena like my personality.

More accurate is Boethius's definition of *persona* as "individual substance of a rational nature."[30] Yet individual here cannot mean just a noninstantiable instance of a nature since, as we have seen, they are communicable. Rather, it must mean an incommunicable supposit, but even with this sense, this definition still mentions only abstract formalities of persons; it is not an account of concrete personhood in itself. Similarly problematic and abstract is Scotus's explanation of personhood by a negation: a person is an individualized intellectual nature not assumed by another.[31] Personhood adds to nature not just a negation but positive, perceivable uniqueness. Hence, other scholastics explain personhood through a positive principle or formal constituent added to an individualized nature.[32] Cajetan argues that there is a "mode" (in the sense explained in chapter 6) that completes an individualized nature, rendering it incommunicable, entirely its own, and not assumable by another.[33] Modes, however, add no intrinsic content. Rather, they just complete a being, while personhood adds positive, perceivable uniqueness and unrepeatability: persons are not just incommunicable but are so with their own unique style. Hence, modes cannot explain personhood—though, in full a portrait of the irreducible person, we should still posit such a mode, since it explains why my essence is incommunicably mine.

---

29. John Locke, *An Essay Concerning Human Understanding*, vol. 2 (New York: Penguin, 1997), chap. 27.

30. Boethius, *Contra Eutychen*, c. 3-4, available at http://individual.utoronto.ca/ pking/resources/ boethius/ Contra_Eutychen.txt.

31. Scotus, *Ord.*, d.23, q.un. Cf. Thomist Othmar Schweitzer, *Person und hypostatische Union bei Thomas von Aquin* (Freiburg: Universitätsverlag, 1957), 114-17.

32. Stephen Hipp, *The Doctrine of Personal Subsistence: Historical and Systemic Synthesis* (Fribourg: Studia Friburgensia, 2012).

33. Cajetan, *In III ST*, v. 11, q.4, a.2, nn. 10-12, 76-77. See Spencer, "Personhood," 890-91. Earlier views rooting personhood in modes, like a mode of subsistence, are found in Rusticus the Deacon and Leontius of Byzantium; see Scott Williams, "Persons in Patristic and Medieval Christian Theology," in *Persons: A History*, ed. Antonia LoLordo (Oxford: Oxford University Press, 2019), 52-86.

Since personhood is a new level of unity, being, and perfection beyond that of essence, other scholastics, such as the neo-Thomist Louis Billot, explain it through *esse*, since *esse* renders an essence actually, concretely, extramentally existing, with all the transcendentals.[34] Persons are real, concrete beings, exceeding all that can be conceived about them. Full incommunicability and self-possession require that one exist by one's own proper *esse*, rather than by the *esse* of another, as Christ's human nature does, existing by divine, not human, *esse*.[35] A supposit's *esse* unifies and actualizes not only its substantial essence but also its accidents' essences and acts of existence, so that (as seen in chapters 2 and 3) accidents manifest the supposit. Having my proper *esse* renders me a supposit, a complete, incommunicable being in the order of existence. While *esse* is an actuality in me, I as an individualized essence also just share in *esse* when I receive and exercise it. By receiving *esse*, I am rendered incommunicable in that I cannot then be a part of or assumed by another, and in that this *esse* is now mine and cannot belong to another.

But this explanation in terms of *esse* and suppositality is still not a complete explanation of personhood. *Esse* gives no unique content, and it does not complete me in every respect, since beyond *esse*, at the third level of being, I share in values and *Gestalten*. I also am a unique, self-manifesting beauty, and so am irreducible to being constituted by distinct principles like value or *esse*. Personalist Juan Manuel Burgos, following Julián Marías, rightly says that persons are not just rational supposits but an entirely new way of being, having a level of completion exceeding what belongs to supposits.[36] One of the fundamental experiences of my completeness and unity as a person is of being self-possessed and existing in my own right, not merely through another, such as through a principle like *esse*. I possess, and so am in a sense prior to, everything that is mine, including my principles. I not only receive and participate in principles like *esse*, but as a person, I "include" them as aspects of who I inwardly am. Persons "encompass" or "include" what is distinct at various levels of being. I propose that principles belong to personhood in a way analogous to how formalities are included in essences, as determinations of its mode of being

---

34. Louis Billot, *De verbo incarnato* (Rome: Propaganda Fide, 1895), 69–75.
35. Aquinas, *ST* III, q.2, a.2, ad 2.
36. Burgos, *An Introduction to Personalism*, 204; Julián Marías, *Antropología metafísica* (Madrid: Alianza, 1970), 41.

that are not really distinct from it. For all these reasons, the explanation for personhood cannot be any principle distinct from me.[37]

Considering one last proposed definition of persons will help us grasp what we actually, fully are. Richard of St. Victor defines persons as "incommunicable existents of an intellectual nature."[38] While this includes more of what is central to personhood than the Boethian definition, there are three problems with this definition. First, being an existent is not the core of personhood as such, since personhood is prior to *esse*, by which we are existents.

Second, while it is preferable to call persons intellectual rather than rational (as on the Boethian definition), this is still inadequate for defining personhood. Reason is our ability to engage in discursive thinking, while intellect is our ability to grasp anything under the formal object of being, whether discursively or intuitively. There could be persons who think purely intuitively, not rationally, as Aquinas envisions angels or intelligences, and so intellectuality is more fundamental to personhood than rationality.[39] It seems plausible to define persons by intellect, since intellect grasps under the formal object of being, which has generally been taken to be the most fundamental transcendental, and so intellect seems to be the most fundamental spiritual power. But experiences of aesthetic cognition and of the many modalities of spiritual perception showed us that beauty is grasped more fundamentally than being. We have also seen ways in which will and affectivity are more fundamental than intellect. Hence, it would be better to define persons as "of a spiritual nature," not of an intellectual one. Other beings are analogous to persons insofar as they can be addressed as "Thou" in social acts, are complete supposits, manifest divine activities, and have intrinsic value (including beauty and even holiness of a sort, calling for love and respect), but only spiritual beings have the transcendental openness to all others that makes them the most perfect or complete beings.[40]

Third, there is a problem with giving a definition of personhood at all.

---

37. Cf. Balthasar, *TD3*, 208–12. Personhood also cannot be explained through a mode that completes beings over and above *esse* (see Suárez, *DM*, d.34, s.4, nn. 20, 23) since this would again explanatorily reduce personhood to a principle distinct from persons.
38. Richard of St. Victor, *De Trinitate*, in PL, v. 196 (Paris: J.-P. Migne, 1855), bk. 4, c. 23–24, 945–47.
39. Aquinas, *ST* I, q.58, a.3.
40. Compare and contrast to Kohák, *The Embers and the Stars*, 128–30, 206–14, who sees all beings as persons (for the reasons I give for seeing all beings as analogous to persons) but also grants that human and transcendent persons alone have spiritual openness to truth, goodness, beauty, and holiness.

A definition should pick out what something fundamentally is, but since personhood transcends essence, strictly speaking, there is no "what" to persons as such, and so no definition of "person" in terms of genus and specific difference, though a list of necessary and sufficient conditions for personhood could be given. Any definition, however, would always describe personhood in terms of aspects grasped at some level of abstraction, and so would always be an inadequate account of personhood as such. At best, a definition or account of personhood can function iconically, guiding our perception and attention to the full, holistic, concrete reality of persons. The Boethian and Victorine definitions fulfill this iconic task fairly well, but better accounts can be given. To think that personhood can be adequately defined is always depersonalizing: as David Walsh notes, following Levinas, persons call for responsibility prior to definition, and give themselves as beyond all universals and transcendentals, including being.[41]

The "Including Relation" in Persons

Since personhood cannot be explained or defined by anything abstractable, grasping persons as such can occur only aesthetically, that is, by perception. The function of the concept "person" is to iconically guide perception of a concrete, holistic reality. Persons can be grasped only by perceiving their unique, holistic self-manifestation: a person is fundamentally a beauty. This is not the beauty that is a transcendental property of ontological being, however, but rather an intrinsically self-manifesting unity, which includes but is irreducible to ontological being and its properties; my view is consistent with Walsh's claim that persons are prior to transcendentals like beauty.[42] Persons are not reducible to generic, analogical, transcendental beauty; rather, as the Sophiological tradition puts is, the beauty of the world, which members of that tradition like Bulgakov identify with God's created or externalized wisdom (*Sophia*), is a tendency toward being concretized in *hypostases*.[43] The language of the Platonic tradition (discussed in chapter 2) is helpful here. Proclus speaks of the gods (*henads*) as each a unique way of being one and good, each bestowing its unique mode of goodness on the world; they are not merely one and good

---

41. Walsh, *Politics of the Person*, 36–50.
42. David Walsh, *The Priority of the Person: Political, Philosophical, and Historical Discoveries* (Notre Dame, Ind.: University of Notre Dame Press, 2020), chap. 1.
43. Bulgakov, *Bride of the Lamb*, 79–103, 176–77.

by participation.⁴⁴ Such language, on my view, is appropriate for all persons: each person is an entirely unique hypostasization of beauty, irreducible to anything included in it, including participation relations. However, persons are partially explained by the principles that they include, and so we must consider what the *including* relation is.

Some philosophers, such as Stein, describe persons as "bearing" or "carrying" their aspects and principles—this is to be the foundation or substratum for something distinct that accrues to one.⁴⁵ Considered abstractly as supposit or individualized essence, I "bear" *esse*, accidents, and values; as actualizing them, these principles are not extrinsic to the supposit or individualized essence, but they are distinct from them. But considered holistically as person, these principles are not distinct from me. Rather, I include them in a way internal to the holistic *Gestalt* that I am as person. As I proposed above, this is similar to how essences include formalities, although much of what I include (such as most of my accidents, values, and *energeiai*) are contingent and variable, unlike formalities in an essence. Personhood adds to suppositality complete self-possession, having all my principles and aspects entirely in my own right as mine, and it adds unique self-giving, self-manifesting, self-expressing beauty.⁴⁶ The more I possess myself, the more I can transcend and give myself to others, sharing my world and allowing others to participate in my activities.⁴⁷

The structure of personhood is distinctly revealed in the experience of *world-openness*. Scheler argues that animals' (including our) surroundings are given to nontranscendentally open powers like senses as *environment* (*Umwelt*), that is, animals are stimulated to be aware of things in their surroundings only insofar as they are relevant to the animal's biological life, for example, as potential food, mate, predator, or shelter.⁴⁸ These powers are open enough to allow animals (including us, insofar as we act just as animals) to communicate, teach their offspring, remember, plan, and experience some beauty, playfulness, and something like religious awe.⁴⁹ But

---

44. Proclus, *The Elements of Theology*, props. 113–65. Cf. Edward P. Butler, "Bhakti and Henadology," *Journal of Dharma Studies* 1 (2018): 147–61.
45. Stein, *Finite and Eternal Being*, 207–13.
46. Cf. Balthasar, *TD*2, 285–92, 387–94; Hildebrand, *The Nature of Love*, chap. 9.
47. Hildebrand, *The Nature of Love*, chap. 9. Cf. Wojtyła, *Acting Person*, 181.
48. Max Scheler, *Man's Place in Nature*, trans. Hans Meyerhoff (New York: Farrar Straus & Giroux, 1962), 35–55, building on the biologist Jakob von Uexküll. Cf. Crosby, *The Selfhood of the Human Person*, 165–67; Josef Pieper, *Leisure the Basis of Culture*, trans. Alexander Dru (New York: New American Library, 1963), chap. 2; and Heidegger, *Being and Time*, 62–67.
49. Donovan Schaefer, "Do Animals Have Religion? Interdisciplinary Perspectives on Religion and Embodiment," *Anthrozoös* 25 (2012): 173–89.

they are still only limitedly open to their surroundings; this is explained in scholasticism by the claim that sensory powers operate under a formal object that is not a property of being as such. Persons, by contrast, are aware of their surroundings as *world*: we can disengage ourselves from any particular viewpoint on things, including a biological one, and relate to things as they are in themselves. By spiritual, transcendentally open, and self-transcending powers, persons are "in a way all things" (*quodammodo omnia, ta onta pōs estin*), at least in that we have obediential potencies for grasping anything in any way. (In Aristotle and Aquinas, these phrases are said of the soul.[50] Since persons are primary subjects of action and power, this phrase more fundamentally applies to persons than souls.) Existentialist Karl Jaspers calls the relation of a person to his or her world "encompassing," a free openness to what gives itself.[51] Persons encompass—or, in my terms, include—what is other than themselves, without reducing its otherness to themselves, that is, without being idealist or totalizing.

Existential Thomist William Carlo offers an image that is helpful for understanding this including relation. In his view, each being just is its *esse*; a being's essence is its "amount" of *esse*. On views (like mine) where essence and *esse* are distinct, *esse* is like (Carlo says) a fluid poured into a container; on his view, *esse* is like a fluid congealed into a distinct shape, without needing a container. An *esse* is "reshaped" through accidents, which are thus "included" in *esse*; each *esse* can be "congealed" into ever-new shapes. While I reject this account of *esse*, the image is useful for understanding persons on my view: we take on different "shapes" by internally including new acts and principles, and we can "flow" together with other "fluids" (in *sun-energeiai* and solidarity, including every intentional and self-transcending act) without ceasing to be the persons we are, and without reducing others to ourselves.[52]

Eric Olson and David Hershenov have objected to hylomorphism on the grounds that it introduces a "too many thinkers" problem, an ambiguity about who thinks my thoughts. My soul, my substantial soul-matter composite, and the person that I am can all be said to be the subject of my thoughts, that is, that in which my thoughts inhere. Since these are not strictly identical, it seems that multiple things think my thoughts, which is

---

50. Aristotle, *DA*, III.8.431b21; *ST* I, q.16, a.3.
51. Karl Jaspers, *Philosophy of Existence*, trans. Richard Grabau (Philadelphia: University of Pennsylvania Press, 1971), 17–29.
52. Carlo, *The Ultimate Reducibility*, 99–145. Cf. Yannaras, *Person and Eros*, 52–53.

implausible. Furthermore, if the composite or the person thinks thoughts only in virtue of the soul and its powers, then it seems that I do not properly think my own thoughts but think them only by sharing in another's thinking. The problem can be repeated, *mutatis mutandis*, for other activities, such as willing, feeling, and even existing.[53]

My view of personhood solves this problem. Strictly speaking, *I* am just a person, who includes all his aspects, acts, and principles, such that they belong primarily and properly only to the person who I am. That our activities are explained by principles and abstractable aspects included in us does not negate the fact that all these items belong primarily to us as persons, who subsist and act through ourselves. To identify myself, my "I," with subjectivity, powers, a body, a soul, a composite substance, an individualized nature, a supposit, or an existing being is not to identify myself with these things in the strictest sense. It is to make a claim about what I experience myself as or to consider myself at some level of abstraction. There is only one thinker in me (and one will-er, feeler, exist-er, and so on for all other acts in me), this person who I am.

Just as a great painting appears beautiful even when we just consider its subject matter, how its colors are arranged, or the values it instantiates, so persons appear beautiful even when we just grasp their sensible, intelligible, essential, ontological, or axiological features by themselves. But a painting appears most beautiful when we are struck by its fullness, seeing its features as manifestations of a unity that includes them without annulling their distinctness, and seeing its interconnections with other things, such as how it alludes to other paintings, symbolizes beings, or reveals the beauty of its subject and of God. Likewise, persons appear in their full beauty not when we focus on a particular way of grasping them but when we allow them to manifest all their principles, relations, and activities, as aspects of a single, nontotalizing beauty.

---

53. David Hershenov, "Shoemaker's Problem of Too Many Thinkers," *Proceedings of the American Catholic Philosophical Association* 80 (2007): 225–36; Hershenov, "Soulless Organisms? Hylomorphism vs. Animalism," *American Catholic Philosophical Quarterly* 85, no. 3 (2011): 474–76; and Olson, *What Are We?* 172–76. Cf. Sydney Shoemaker, "Self, Body, and Coincidence," *Supplement to the Proceedings of the Aristotelian Society* 73, no. 1 (1999): 287–306.

Intrinsic Relationality and the Image of God in Us

We saw in chapter 3 how essences and beings are really identical to "transcendental relations."[54] Persons are also identical to transcendental relations. Aquinas argues that my relation to God of being created is accidental to my individualized essence, since it does not belong to the content of that essence, as such, which is to be this rational animal.[55] But, as John of St. Thomas argues, this relation is intrinsic to me as a being.[56] Since all my relations are included in me as person, and since I could not be this person unless I were created by God, this relation is intrinsic and necessary to me as person. I could not exist unless I were related to God by this *being created* relation; it is not ontologically posterior to me, as it would be were it only an accident. It is constitutive of who I fundamentally am, and so is a transcendental relation really identical to me.

David Schindler argues further that to be a created person is not just to be from (*esse ab*) God, but to exist in (*esse in*) oneself and to be oriented toward (*esse ad*) others through action, receptivity, and self-transcendence.[57] A person not only includes many principles distinct from him or herself as such but as person has aspects (or "poles") really identical to personhood, including three relations, understood as follows. We are fundamentally gifts given to ourselves, intrinsically related to God as receptive and as ordered to him as our highest good.[58] We are intrinsically related to ourselves, but never fully experientially coinciding with or grasping ourselves.[59] We are oriented to others, to be grasped as beauties by them and to join with them in *sun-energeia*; our fundamental way of existing is one of being with (*Mitsein*) others, always having some positive or negative concern or care for others.[60]

Some have argued that human persons are fundamentally relational

---

54. Points in this section were developed in Mark K. Spencer, "Created Persons are Subsistent Relations: A Scholastic-Phenomenological Synthesis," *Proceedings of the American Catholic Philosophical Association* 89 (2015): 225–43; Spencer, "Perceiving the Image of God in the Whole Human Person," *The Saint Anselm Journal* 13, no. 2 (2018): 1–18.

55. Aquinas, *DV*, q.21, a.1, ad 1; *ST* I, q.45, a.3, ad 3.

56. John of St. Thomas, *Cursus theologici in primam partem divi Thomae*, v. 2 (Lugundi: Petrus Prost, 1642), d.18, q.44, a.2, nn.19–22.

57. David L. Schindler, "Norris Clarke on Person, Being, and St. Thomas," *Communio* 20 (1993): 580–92; Schindler, *Heart of the World, Center of the Church* (Grand Rapids, Mich.: Eerdmans, 1996), 275–311. Cf. Emmanuel Mounier, *Personalism*, trans. Philip Mairet (London: Routledge, 1952), 33–50; de Finance, *Être et agir*, 241–46; Macmurray, *Persons in Relation*; and Buber, *I and Thou*.

58. Schmitz, *The Gift*, 47–57.

59. Kierkegaard, *The Sickness unto Death*, pt. 1, chap. 1.

60. Heidegger, *Being and Time*, 111–18.

rather than subsistent. I contend, however, that we are subsistent relations, really identical to (and having as formalities within personhood as such) both subsistence and transcendental relations. We thereby analogically image the Trinitarian Persons, who are really identical to relations subsisting in the divine nature (for example, the Son is really identical to the "being begotten" relation and to the divine nature). As the Trinitarian Persons are distinct while being open to and present in one another (and as Christ includes in his person two natures, without blending or confusion, according to the Council of Chalcedon), so are we intrinsically open to and include others.[61] We have, as Nikolaos Loudovikos has it, an identity analogous to the consubstantiality of the divine persons, which can be deepened by deepening our relations with human persons and our participation in the circulation of self-giving love in the Trinity.[62]

But although I shall argue that we are not reducible to relations, we must not be reductionistic of our relational aspects either, either by seeing them as secondary to our subsistent aspects or by emphasizing one relation over another—for example, by seeing persons as more present in self-directed relations than in receptive ones (*passio essendi*).[63] We have seen how many of our aspects (like essence and existence) are relational, and how we are "suspended" and "in between" (*metaxu*) various aspects of being, reducible to none of them, pointing beyond ourselves to ultimate and absolute beauty.[64] Balthasar argues that if I prescind from all relations, I cannot fully grasp who I am and my life's meaning; my nonrelational content, like the content of my essence or my autonomous self-determinations, is contingent, and so in itself is unexplained and not ultimately meaningful. My life also does not appear entirely meaningful just through my relations to other human persons. For example, being affirmed or heteronomously given meaning by other human persons cannot give ultimate meaning to my life, though it is a necessary condition for a clear sense of my personhood and my value. Such affirmation is contingent and transitory, unable to definitively reveal to me the meaning of my life. I can only grasp my meaning by theonomously receiving a mission or vocation from God, paralleling how the Son and Spirit are sent by the Father.[65]

61. Aquinas, *ST* I, q.42, a.5; q.28, a.2.
62. Loudovikos, *Analogical Identities*, 243–70.
63. Desmond, *The Gift of Beauty and the Passion of Being*, introduction and chap.1.
64. Przywara, *Analogia Entis*, 159–60, 182–85. Cf. Milbank, *The Suspended Middle*, 30–32; Desmond, *The Intimate Strangeness of Being*, 36–37, 48–49.
65. Balthasar, *TD3*, 203–12.

These intrinsic relations to God reveal how we are made according to the image (*eichon, imago, selem*) of God.⁶⁶ We have seen how our relationality can be understood by comparison to the Trinitarian Persons and to Christ, who is the image of the invisible God.⁶⁷ We share in Christ's imaging of God in the relational structure outlined by Schindler, being from God and oriented to God, like the Son. Drawing on what we saw earlier from Bulgakov, we image God because just as the divine Persons are hypostases of divine beauty and wisdom (*Sophia*), so we are creaturely hypostasizations of God's externalized beauty. But we image God in other ways, too.

Aquinas, following Augustine, describes an image of God that is in us, not identical to us as persons, which flows from our essence as the end of our coming-to-be.⁶⁸ An image shows the accidents, essence, or mode of being of what it images—for example, a coin shows a ruler's accidental appearance; one dog shows the essence and mode of being of all other dogs and so images all other dogs.⁶⁹ We image God by sharing in and revealing his spiritual mode of being.⁷⁰ We image God in our souls' substantial intelligence, freedom, immortality, goodness, and beauty, and in our powers and acts of memory, intellect, and will. From memory's self-grasp proceeds articulated knowledge, a word, about oneself and about God, which brings forth love for self and God. This images the Trinitarian processions of the Son or Word (*Logos*) from the Father and the Spirit (or the breath of divine love) from both.⁷¹ Just as (according to Przywara) my sense of self is heightened as my attention moves between awareness of my essence and of my existence, transcending each as my attention moves toward God, so this image of God in me can be deepened: the more I know and love God, the more I image him and the more my being refers to him. The structure of our powers shows our openness to divinization, to becoming, as we saw in chapter 6, adopted as words within the Word and sons within the Son.⁷²

---

66. Genesis 1:25–27.
67. Colossians 1:15, 3:10.
68. Aquinas, *ST* I, q.93 pr.
69. Aquinas, *In I Sent.*, d.3, q.3, a.1, ad 5; d.28, q.2, a.1, ad 3; *In II Sent.*, d.16, q.un., a.1; *ST* I, q.35, a.1, a.2, ad 3; q. 93, a.1, ad 2, a.2, a.6, ad 1.
70. Aquinas, *In II Sent.*, d.16, q.un., a.2; d.17, q.1, a.1, ad 2; *ST* I, q.93, a.2; *DV*, q.10, a.1, ad 5; *DP*, q.9, a.5; *CT* I, q.75.
71. Aquinas, *ST* I, q.93, a.5, following Gregory of Nyssa, *De hominis opficio*, in PG, v. 44 (Paris: J.-P. Migne, 1863), c. 16; John Damascene, *On the Orthodox Faith* II, c. 11, 12, 30; Hilary of Poitiers, *De Trinitate* V, c. 8; and Augustine, *Trinity* 9.4.4, 28.
72. Henry, *I Am the Truth*, 114, building on Meister Eckhart.

The image of God in me stands in obediential potency to God's grace and *energeiai*: the more I participate in his life, the more I image and reveal him. I first find the image of God in me by reflecting on myself, but as an image (i.e., a participation in the *energeiai* of its exemplar), it refers me toward its exemplar, and so to participating in it more.[73] Human persons, more than nonpersonal beings, which are divine in their forms, are meant to be gods.[74]

However, while our imaging of God is rooted in our spiritual powers and participation in the infinite God, this image is finite in us. As Levinas recognized, we perceive others' imaging of God when we perceive their limitations, finitude, vulnerability, and suffering. These features call for ethical concern and thereby mediate and image God's call to goodness. Furthermore, in our finitude and humiliation, we image Christ who has entered, in self-humiliation, into our finitude. In Christ, we see how there is a metamorphosis, not a removal, of finitude, such that finitude is revealed as the definitive site of God's loving self-manifestation—and so as the site of the definitive, never to be transcended, revelation of what it is to fully be.[75] I present further ways in which we image God, including in our bodies and in our relations to other persons, here and in chapter 9.

Intrinsic Relations to Creatures

We are transcendentally related not only to God but also to creatures. We have seen how each being is iconically, symbolically, and analogically related to all others, and how human persons are "microcosms": we image, and so are related to, the macrocosm of the universe, including nonliving, vegetative, sensitive, and intelligent beings. While arguments can be given for this claim (for example, reasoning from our resemblance to each aspect of the hierarchy of being to the claim that we image the whole cosmos), it is fundamentally a perceptual claim. We can perceive ourselves sharing in the beauty of the cosmos and in the actions of transcendent persons that bring about that beauty.[76] Images are meant to be perceived, so that through them their exemplar can be perceived. By being a microcosm, I

---

73. Aquinas, *In I Sent.*, d.28, q.2, a.1, a.2; *ST* III, q.60, a.2.
74. Cf. Nietzsche, *Thus Spake Zarathustra*, in *The Portable Nietzsche*, trans. Walter Kaufman (New York: Penguin, 1977), 198; Schmitz, *The Gift*, 137–38.
75. Nellas, *Deification in Christ*, 35–38; Falque, *The Metamorphosis of Finitude*, 77.
76. Cf. Mircea Eliade, *The Sacred and the Profane: The Nature of Religion*, trans. Willard R. Trask (Orlando, Fla.: Harcourt, 1987), 165.

intrinsically resemble and so am related to each other creature, and so my full meaning and value as this person is dependent on, and only given in the context of, the meaning and value of all other things. Perceiving our irreducibility requires perceiving that of all other things.[77] Like the image of God, the microcosmic image can be developed. As Renaissance philosopher Giovanni Pico della Mirandola recognized, following the Platonic tradition, each of us determines freely (including by obedience to God's grace or other influences) which portions of the macrocosm we reflect in our acts, whether we shall come to reveal what is bestial and below us, or what is divine and above us.[78]

It would be reductionistic to focus on just the image of God or the microcosm relation to the exclusion of the other.[79] To focus on the latter, Gregory of Nyssa cautions, can obscure how our infinite value is rooted in our relation to God, leading us to see our value as entirely bound up with that of the world.[80] The two images must be perceived in relation to one another. In *Genesis*, the claim that we image God is linked to the divine command to have dominion over all nonpersonal creatures—that is, the image of God is linked to our relation to creatures. One way we image God is in our spiritual powers; hence, understanding our relation to—and dominion over—creatures requires understanding those powers' structure. They are oriented, above all, to self-transcendence, responding to importance, ever-greater contemplation, ethical service, creativity, and love. Our dominion must be an orientation to intend all beings through spiritual powers, to ethically care for them and respond to their value, and to join with them in *sun-energeiai*. If that is correct, then our dominion is not a right to use or control them however we please. It requires balancing when we direct them to ends we specify by *per se* causality, when we allow them by *Gelassenheit* to develop on their own, and when we enter cooperative communities with them by *per communionem* causality. While

---

77. Consider Walt Whitman's lines in "Song of Myself," n. 31: "I find I incorporate gneiss, coal, long-threaded moss, fruits, grains, esculent roots,/And am stucco'd with quadrupeds and birds all over," where each of those natural beings is itself irreducible: "a leaf of grass is no less than the journey-work of the stars."

78. Giovanni Pico della Mirandola, *Oration on the Dignity of Man*, trans. Elizabeth Forbes, in *Renaissance Philosophy of Man*, ed. Ernst Cassirer et al. (Chicago: University of Chicago Press, 1948). Cf. Carnes, *Beauty*, 199.

79. Balthasar, *TL2*, 165–72; John Paul II, *Man and Woman He Created Them: A Theology of the Body*, trans. Michael Waldstein (Boston: Pauline Books and Media, 2006), 180, 203–4.

80. Gregory of Nyssa, *De hominis opficio*, in PG, c. 16–17. Cf. Nellas, *Deification in Christ*, 30, building on Maximus and Simeon the New Theologian.

nonpersonal creatures exist for our sake as possible objects of spiritual powers, they do not exist for our sake in every respect: rather, each has its own ends, values, and relations to God, many of which have nothing to do with us, as we perceive, for example, in the beautiful indifference of nature to us.[81] In grasping our intrinsic relations to the cosmos, we better see how we image God. God does not control the world in all respects but allows it to unfold on its own, sharing in and sacramentally revealing his *energeiai* in ever-new ways. We image God as his vicars or priests, ministering to the world, allowing things' sacramentality to better appear, taking up beings' forms and values through contemplative perception, and sacrificially offering the gift of creation back to God.[82] This *priesthood* is what is most distinctive about human persons: we are the animals who contemplatively grasp the intelligibility, goodness, holiness, and, above all, the beauty of beings, draw these properties into ourselves, and sacrifice or offer it all back to God.[83] More will be said below on how this is done.

We also image the cosmos, as we image God, in our finitude. Insofar as they are radically contingent, all creatures image each other. In Heidegger's words, we are "thrown" into the world; we are originally unstably put into existence, into participation in *esse commune*, without our consent.[84] As Balthasar said, we lack fully meaningful connections to other creatures; in relation to *esse commune* in itself (apart from relations to God's subsistent *esse*) all creatures appear as ephemeral and transitory. This is manifested in aesthetic values like the wabi-sabi, uncanniness, and even the violence and horror of the natural world. In being identical to a contingent, "thrown" relation to finite being itself and to all other creatures, we appear as both one with all things and as lacking stable identity—a feature of us emphasized by some schools of analytic and Buddhist metaphysics, which claim that we have no stable, enduring self.[85] These schools capture genuine features of persons, though they so focus on one formality in us that they reductionistically overlook all others. Human persons are intrinsically related to and reveal by their beauty both the abyss of the self-giving, loving beauty of God and the abyss of the contingent, uncanny, self-revealing and

---

81. *Contra* those who see all of natural evolution as just aiming at human persons, such as Pierre Teilhard de Chardin, *The Phenomenon of Man*, trans. Julian Huxley (New York: Harper and Row, 1965).
82. Cf. Berdyaev, *Creative Act*, 56–68; Jean-Louis Chrétien, *The Ark of Speech*, trans. Andrew Brown (New York: Routledge, 2004).
83. Kohák, *The Embers and the Stars*, 83.
84. Heidegger, *Being and Time*, 127.
85. Derek Parfit, *Reasons and Persons* (Oxford: Oxford University Press, 1986).

self-concealing mystery of contingent, finite being as such. Our ultimate epektatic state must perfect both relations.[86]

Solitude, Subsistence, Givenness, and Liturgy

I am not reducible to relations; I also subsist in myself. Although I receive myself from God and world, I then have myself as my own. Scotus calls the person "the furthest solitude" (*ultima solitudo*).[87] Nothing is more incommunicable and self-possessed, given over to him or herself, than a person. While I am intrinsically related to others, I am also alone with myself, in two ways. First, I experience my subjectivity and vocation "intimately," alone before God.[88] In experiencing myself grasped and called by God, I come closest to grasping my *ousia*, the core of who I am, my true self. For me to fully perceive others' beauty, I must be aware that there is this intimate sphere out of which they manifest themselves, to which I have no direct access. Second, I experience myself just as my own, separated even from relations to God. While I become self-aware only through actualization by things external to me, I am then aware, reflectively or in a laterally self-conscious way, of my private self and of what concerns me most intimately. I cannot be reduced to my God-given vocation or relations; I also include aspects that are just my own. These solitary depths in me are often masked from me, for example by *Gestalten* like institutions, or by subjective self-conceptions.[89] Self-discovery risks enslavement to self, but grasping and acting out of this private, solitary sense of self is required to make a full self-gift.

Our relationality and solitude reveal further why persons and personhood must be perceived and cannot be strictly defined. Gregory of Nyssa argues that since God is incomprehensible, we who image him are incomprehensible, too. While we can partially explain or define the image of God in us, say, in terms of spiritual powers, we image God fundamentally by relation to him, so the image in its fullness is incomprehensible. Since

---

86. Contrast to views that reductionistically oppose these, for example, Fritz, *Karl Rahner's Theological Aesthetics*, 255–56.
87. Scotus, *Ord.* III, d.1, q.1, n. 17.
88. Scheler, *Formalism in Ethics and Non-Formal Ethics of Values*, 562–72; John Paul II, *Man and Woman He Created Them*, 146–56; and Balthasar, *TD1*, 252–54.
89. Thomas Merton, "Marxism and Monastic Perspectives," in *The Asian Journal of Thomas Merton* (New York: New Directions, 1975), 326–43; Merton, *The New Man* (New York: Farrar, Straus and Giroux, 1961), 71–100; and Merton, *Zen*, 84–87.

this image is a transcendental relation really identical to each person, no person is fully comprehensible.[90] We must perceive our beauty and how it reveals the absolute beauty that is God. This is why a full account of persons requires portrait-painting, guiding perception of each person's incomprehensible beauty.

Marion similarly argues that I fundamentally experience myself not as pure subjectivity or stable being but as a "gifted one" (*l'adonné*). In encountering saturated phenomena—anything whose meaning exceeds that which I can intentionally constitute, and which instead gives me meaning by "counter-intentionality"—I experience myself as having received myself prior to that experience, receiving even my ability to respond to this gift of myself (or to ignore it, or to experience myself in solitude prescinding from it). This experience of receiving myself entirely as a gift reveals a deeper relation to God than efficient causality, signification, participation, or analogy. Insofar as I am a being, God efficiently causes me. In one sense of the term "being" (described in chapter 3), I have being in myself related to God's being by the analogy of proportionality. In another sense of "being," only God properly speaking has being, and I have being just as signifying, participating in, and being caused by his being—that is, I only have being by the analogy of attribution. Insofar as I have graspable spiritual powers that image him in a definable way, I signify him. Insofar as I share in Platonic Forms and in his life, I participate in him.

But just as I as person include but also exceed all these relations, so also my relation to God as whole person must include but also exceed those relations. To *be given* is to be caused as gift by the giver and to reveal and participate in the giver insofar as one shares in the giver's act of giving, but it is simultaneously to be separated from the giver insofar as the gift is truly given. By this holistic *being given* relation, more fundamentally than by anything "visible" (directly cognizable and definable) in me, I am an icon of the "invisible" God, a perceivable or aesthetic structure that makes present and perceivable the absolute beauty that in itself is entirely transcendent to creatures.[91]

As we saw earlier, drawing on the Sophiological tradition, I am a unique (and so, separate) hypostasization of divine beauty; as the Trinitarian Persons are positively distinct from one another, so created persons

---

90. Gregory of Nyssa, *De opficio hominis*, c. 11; Nellas, *Deification in Christ*, 22.
91. Marion, *Negative Certainties*, 44. Cf. Theodore the Studite, *On the Holy Icons*.

are positively distinct. Distinction from others is not a mere negation of being another (*aliquid*) but a positive feature of beings and persons: to be, and especially to be a person, is to be a member of a multitude (*multitudo transcendens*).[92] To be a person is to bear what is one's own and to be able to bear what is other than personhood, such as nature; it is to be distinct from but open to others, where this distinction is a positive kind of self-transcendence, not a competition with or a limitation by others.[93]

Marion describes persons as analogous to *confessio* or prayer: I declare in my structure the God who continually gives me to myself, and my creaturely (and sinful) inadequacy before him. To be given to myself by absolute beauty is to both be called to ever greater beauty and to be under continual judgment by that beauty, and so under a call to responsibility in becoming beautiful. As person, I am thus oriented to liturgy. Indeed, I am a liturgy, a ritually, repeatedly, religiously performed activity of receiving myself from God and making a return to him by receiving from him again.[94] As Khaled Anatolios says, we are "doxological" beings, intrinsically oriented to praise God by being his glory, his radiant manifestation in the world.[95]

Our ultimate structure is revealed in that of the Mass or Divine Liturgy, in which we receive gifts only to offer them back to God. Through acts of creative obedience, we elevate gifts to new modes of existence (for example, in bread and wine being rendered holy, an actualization of obediential potencies, in the offertory, even prior to consecration and transubstantiation). In receiving the Eucharist that divinizes us as whole persons, we respond by receiving more: not only the body, but also the blood.[96] I can make no adequate return to God for all that he has given me, or, more fundamentally, for the beauty he is, apart from his gifts to me; the correct

---

92. Aquinas, *ST* I, q.30, a.3, ad 2; *DV*, q.1, a.1. On ways that the scholastic tradition has seen the image of God in loving relations among persons or relations among beautiful beings, see Richard of St. Victor, *De Trinitate*, 949–61; Gilles Emery, *The Trinitarian Theology of St. Thomas Aquinas*, trans. Francesca Aran Murphy (Oxford: Oxford University Press, 2010), chap. 2.

93. Anatolios, *Deification Through the Cross*, 240–60, 409, building on Matthias Scheeben, *The Mysteries of Christianity*, trans. Cyril Vollert (New York: Crossroad, 2006), 61–71, and Dumitru Staniloae, *The Experience of God*, vol. 1, trans. Ioan Ionita and Robert Barringer (Brookline, Mass.: Holy Cross Orthodox Press, 1994), 256–75.

94. Marion, *In the Self's Place*, chaps. 1, 2, 284–88.

95. Anatolios, *Deification Through the Cross*, 264–71, 409, *contra* those for whom sacrifice is always a diminution or destruction of that which is sacrificed, or always implies limitation by or rivalry with others, for example, René Girard, *Things Hidden Since the Foundation of the World*, trans. Stephen Barr and Michael Metteer (Stanford, Calif.: Stanford University Press, 1987).

96. Consider the priest's praying, at Mass, of Psalm 116:12–13 between receiving the Eucharistic body and blood.

response is to make the structure of *confessio* that I am deliberately the structure of my life, to make my life fundamentally an act of *gratitude* in response to God's graciousness. My ultimate state must be one in which all my spiritual acts are part of an ever-deepening liturgical activity performed by my whole person; I am an endless sacrifice or offering to God. In this, too, I image God, the absolute goodness and absolute beauty who is a continual self-gift and self-sacrifice, in His Trinitarian relations, in creation, and in redeeming and divinizing us. Here, again, we see that our ultimate state must include ethical service to others: to offer myself to God is to be conformed to his self-giving life, and so be immediately turned toward others.[97]

As *l'adonne* and *confessio* (including dynamic principles like form, *esse*, and *energeiai*), I am an event, not just a delimited stable object. We persons are not just beings that have a life, but we include our growth, development, and narrative internally. I am given to myself in conception and birth prior to subjectively grasping anything. I tend toward an event, death, that exceeds what can be grasped or envisioned. I am temporally distended as I receive each moment from the irrecuperable past and move into the unforeseeable future, which allows both for the monotony and loss of self in the life of sin, and for the ever-greater reception and confession of liturgical life.[98] But I am not reducible to only an event or to being a gifted one. Following the scholastics, John Milbank has challenged Marion, arguing that being must be prior to givenness: a thing must first be. God is first a being and then gives himself; we receive ourselves as beings, and then give ourselves.[99] Similarly, Catherine Pickstock argues that what is given to us (as revealed in the structure of the liturgy) is being.[100] We must not, like Jacques Derrida, reductionistically deny that gifts can really be given, since they would be known by giver and receiver, and then be drawn into an economy of exchange and cease to be a pure gift.[101] We are really given to ourselves and called to make a return, but in our receiving and giving with God, in accord with the metaphysics of the holy fool from chapter 6,

---

97. Plato, *Republic*, 540b; Levinas, *Otherwise Than Being or Beyond Essence*, 148–49.
98. Marion, *Negative Certainties*, chap. 5; Marion, *In the Self's Place*, 85, 212–29. Cf. Griffiths, *Decreation*.
99. John Milbank, "Can a Gift Be Given? Prolegomena to a Future Trinitarian Metaphysics," *Modern Theology* 11, no. 1 (1995): 119–61.
100. Pickstock, *After Writing*, 240–52. Cf. Philip Rolnick (*Person, Grace, and God* [Grand Rapids, Mich.: Eerdmans, 2007], chap. 5), for whom person and gift are mutually constitutive.
101. Jacques Derrida, *Given Time*, vol. 1, *Counterfeit Money*, trans. Peggy Kamuf (Chicago: University of Chicago Press, 1992), 13–14.

there is no economic proportionality between what is given and received but rather a wild, beautiful, festive, carnivalesque gift-giving. More fundamental than exchange and its justice is mercy, the giving of unanticipatable, beautiful gifts, including the gift each person is: I am fundamentally one allowed to be and to mercifully give to others by the God who is not just a giver but Mercy itself.[102]

Milbank's and Marion's views can be synthesized if we recognize that each of them actually reveals a distinct formality in personhood, each of which beautifully interpenetrates the others. Persons are given by God, but they are also beings and gifts, separate from God but oriented to make liturgical return to him. Furthermore, the position of Milbank and Pickstock does not go far enough in elucidating our nonrelational aspects. Given earlier points about solitude, secular experiences, and pure nature, we each have an entirely nonrelational formality. Our return to God must include something of our own if we are to be God's partners, and not just his humiliated, even if happy, subjects; this requires that we be mercifully given to ourselves such that we are (as Levinas says) separate from him and have something of our own to give.[103]

The Personhood of the Separated Soul

Having proposed a vision of personhood as such, I return to the problem of whether separated souls are (or constitute) persons. I defend survivalism, on which I, this person, survive death constituted by my soul and its properties and principles. Evidence for this view includes acts typical of persons that do not require the body, such as social acts like mental prayer in which I intend my thoughts to be known by another, reception of infused species via illumination by Forms or God, and intuiting beings' existence without requiring new information from bodily senses.[104] (While some scholastics, like the Franciscan Matthew of Aquasparta, held that the soul could draw new species from material things without senses, there is no experiential evidence for that.[105]) Since these personal acts do not

---

102. Aquinas, *ST* I, q.21, a.3, 4.
103. *Contra* objections of Sartre and Nietzsche reviewed in Schmitz, *The Gift*, 44–82, 130.
104. Aquinas, *ST* I, q.55; q.89, a.1–4; *QDA*, a.18, 20; *QQ* III, q.9, a.1; *DV*, q.19, a.2; *SCG* II, c. 81; Bernard of Trilia, *Quaestiones de cognition animae separatae a corpore*, ed. Stuart Martin (Toronto: Pontifical Institute of Medieval Studies, 1965), a.1, ad 5, 46–47; a.2, ad 14, 82–3.
105. Matthew of Aquasparta, *Quaestiones disputatae de anima separata, de anima beata, de ieiunio et de legibus* (Quaracchi: Collegium S. Bonaventura, 1959), a.4, 62–71.

require the body, they could continue in the separated soul. Hence, the separated soul retains *energeiai* typical of human persons. *Energeiai* proceed from *ousiai*: thus, if human *energeiai* are present in the separated soul, so must human *ousia*—and if my *ousia* and most distinctive *energeiai* are present, it is reasonable to think that I would be present. Furthermore, *esse* fits with and actualizes individualized natures. Were an individual human nature not present in the separated soul, human *esse* could not be present there—but it is. Therefore, the human essence must be present there, and so the human being and person will be present there.

Were the person not present in the separated state, the soul's *energeiai* would be performed by no one (since there would be no one—no person—there), which is incoherent. The separated soul is not a "semi-person" or "incomplete person," having all the marks of personhood except incommunicability and having only an "inadequate" exercise of *esse*.[106] "Person" denotes something irreducibly complete; personhood cannot be present partially. My separated soul will retain the same subsistence, subjectivity, image of God, vocation, and transcendental relations that I have now, all of which belong to personhood as such. The separated soul also includes principles of persons, including form, *esse*, and value; I am not, and never will be, my soul, for I will always include other principles. If by "separated soul" is meant the whole immaterial entity that survives death, including its *esse*, accidents, and values, then that entity includes form but is not reducible to it.[107] Finally, God responds to the separated soul by punishing or rewarding it in part for how well the person's vocation has been fulfilled, and it would be unjust on God's part to do this to an entity distinct from the person. These survivalist claims raise two questions. The first is what defines human nature. Scholasticism has defined this as *rational animality*, but if we can exist without bodies, it is hard to see how we are essentially animals. The second is what individuates our nature. Thomism understood it to be matter; this must be revisited if our nature is entirely in the soul.

---

106. Cajetan, *In III ST*, v. 11, q.6, a.3, nn. 3, 98; Daniel De Haan and Brandom Dahm, "Thomas Aquinas on Separated Souls as Incomplete Human Persons," *The Thomist* 83, no. 4 (2019): 589–637; and De Haan and Dahm, "After Survivalism and Corruptionism," *Quaestiones Disputatae* 10, no. 1 (Fall 2020): 161–76.

107. De Haan and Dahm, "Thomas Aquinas on Separated Souls as Incomplete Human Persons" and "After Survivalism and Corruptionism."

Attempts at Defining Human Nature

A solution to the first question must reconcile the claims that human nature is entirely in the human soul, that the soul is the form of the body, that we have powers needed for our fulfillment that require the body, and that the body is not accidental to us and is required for our fulfillment. On most scholastic views, we belong to the genus *animal* (i.e., sensing, living, material substance), and *rationality* is the specific difference that sets us apart. Yet Aquinas also held that the human soul was both of the same genus as the angels or intelligences (or at least was potentially in this genus, a potentiality actualized at death) and can be called an animal inasmuch as it is an animal's form.[108] Renaissance Thomist Francis Sylvester of Ferrara held that our *esse* belongs to the soul properly, and only to the body insofar as it is elevated to share in spiritual life, a higher way of existing than properly belongs to material things.[109] A definition of human nature must capture our status as metaphysical "amphibians" occupying the "midpoint" between the material and the immaterial, without denying our evolutionary, genetic, microcosmic, and other relations to animals.[110] We are the site where the material gains access to a spiritual, conscious, self-conscious voice; where the spiritual gains access to full sensory expression; and where the whole cosmos gains access to itself as whole.[111]

A personalist definition of human nature, *incarnated* or *embodied spirit* or *intelligence*, captures these claims; to account for the possibility of existing apart from body, I suggest *incarnatable spirit*. We are primarily in the genus *spirit* or *intelligence* and have as our difference *being ordered to exist in and inform a body*.[112] It does not follow that we preexisted our bodies or that the body is accidental to us. Rather, the soul both is a spirit with a

---

108. Aquinas, *SCG* II, c. 68, 91; IV, c. 11; *ST* I, q.55, a.1, 2; q.87, a.1; q.88, a.2, ad 4; q.89, a.1; q.90, a.4, ad 2; III, q.8, a.4, ad 1; *In VII DDN*, lect. 4; *QDA*, a.1, ad 4; a.2, ad 10. Cf. Bonaventure, *QDSC*, a.2; *In II Sent.*, d.3, q.1, a.6, a.2. On Aquinas's view, once the soul is separated from the body, it takes on the condition of the angels, knowing material things through species infused by God; this is an aspect of our divinization, our becoming a "god." Separated souls could thereby take on the angels' stance toward the world, which is creative, and by which they stamp the world with their own character.
109. Francis Sylvester of Ferrara, *Commentary on Summa contra Gentiles*, in *Summa contra gentiles* (Rome: Leonine ed., 1918), c. 68, nn. 2.2, 442.
110. Stump, "Non-Cartesian Substance Dualism," 514.
111. Cf. Walsh, *Politics of the Person as the Politics of Being*, 102–4.
112. Clarke, *Person and Being*, 32–34, 40–41; James Lehrberger, "The Anthropology of Aquinas's '*De ente et essentia*,'" *Review of Metaphysics* 51, no. 4 (1998): 842–44; and Smith-Gilson, *The Metaphysical Presuppositions of Being-in-the-World*, 168–69. Cf. Anton Pegis, *At the Origins of the Thomistic Notion of Man* (New York: Macmillan, 1963), 34–58; Stein, *Finite and Eternal Being*, 296.

complete nature and is ordered to be the form of a body; when it informs and actualizes matter, the soul's existence and nature are communicated to the body, and the resulting composite is substantially, not accidentally, united. As Allison Thornton argues, we are normatively embodied, even if we can exist without bodies.[113] Death, on this view, is the loss of a part substantially united to me, a loss that resembles losing bodily limbs and organs. These are substantially united to me because they implement powers flowing from my essence, and because in them, my matter is divided into bodily parts. Losing body parts is not substantial change, in which a substance goes out of existence. One might object that it seems that my existence and nature could now be communicated to the part, were it reattached. But rather, when I take on new matter, I remain incommunicable, and the reattached (or new) matter is informed by my soul and so drawn into my incommunicable personhood. Parts communicate themselves to me, not vice versa. Likewise, my whole body's matter is drawn into sharing my soul's life, nature, and existence, and so into my personhood. Human death, the loss of all matter, is a *sui generis* change, neither substantial nor accidental, in which the soul ceases communicating human nature and *esse* to matter. This is an immense loss to the human substance—in Marco Stango's words, it is a "material kenosis," an emptying out of what we are, a "radical negation without annihilation," in which we are stripped to our roots (though not without some gain)—but it is not substantial corruption.[114]

The twelfth-century theologian Hugh of St. Victor proposes what I take to be the correct account of the relation between soul and body. He offers a philosophically insightful etymology of *persona* as *per se sonantem*, one who is speaking through him or herself, linked to the verb *personare*, to resound, chant, or speak forth. This property of self-disclosure fundamentally belongs to spirits and their powers and is only thence communicated to bodies. The body and animality are taken "from the earth" and joined "in person" to the soul, receiving actuality from the latter.[115] We do not result from property-less matter being joined to a soul. Rather, to synthesize Hugh's metaphysics with contemporary scientific findings, in the first humans, a fully evolved animal with its powers and tendencies was joined

113. Allison Thornton, "Disembodied Animals," *American Philosophical Quarterly* 56, no. 2 (2019): 203–17.

114. Marco Stango, "Death as Material Kenosis: A Thomistic Proposal," *The Heythrop Journal* 61, no. 2 (2020): 327–346.

115. Hugh of St. Victor, *De sacramentiis fidei Christianae*, in PL, v. 176 (Paris: Vivès, 1880), II, c. 11, 406–11.

hylomorphically and substantially to a newly created intelligence; in each new human being, the matter of sperm and egg with their tendencies is taken up into the life of a spirit, which is created by God in that moment to inform that body, as the actuality of that particular matter, such that one substance, with a single nature given by soul results. (How one substance can be taken up into another will be considered below.)

This view captures much that is obscured by the rational animal definition, though both definitions capture something true about what we are. While no definition can fully capture our *ousia*, both definitions express formalities in our essence. We are essentially animals in that we normatively have senses, we experience and perform acts in a bodily way, and, in virtue of our bodies, we have developed from and are akin to nonhuman sensing substances.[116] But since nonpersonal animals necessarily have actual physical senses, and we can survive the loss of those senses, we are animals only in a way analogous to other animals.[117] Our spirituality specifies and transforms our animality such that it exists only through our spiritual *ousia* and *esse*. Even the separated soul is an animal in that it has an *ousia* oriented to give rise to sensory powers when informing matter. But we are equally spirits modified and specified by animality or embodiment—that is, intelligences whose world-openness is specified by an orientation to incarnation in an animal body of a definite species.

One can make sense of the logic of this view of human nature in two ways; I prefer the second, though I do not endorse either view here. First, one could hold that, strictly speaking, we belong just to one genus (*spirit* or *animal*) and the other is said of us improperly or by analogy. Second, one could hold that there is not one single Porphyrian Tree that divides the category substance; rather, there are multiple, overlapping trees, according to the many formalities and transcendental relations in substances. Each tree actually carves nature at its joints, though there is not a single, hierarchical tree of genera and specific differences.[118]

---

116. Cf. Jason Eberl, *The Nature of Human Persons: Metaphysics and Bioethics* (Notre Dame, Ind.: University of Notre Dame Press, 2020), chap. 2.

117. For an argument that genus-terms like "animal" are analogous, see Armand Maurer, "St. Thomas and the Analogy of Genus," *New Scholasticism* 29, no. 2 (1955): 127–44.

118. This second view is partly inspired by the "promiscuous realism" of Louis Dupré (*Humans and Other Animals* [Oxford: Clarendon, 2006], 53–54) and the "rhizomatic" logic of Giles Deleuze and Felix Guattari, *A Thousand Plateaus*, trans. Brian Massumi (Minneapolis: University of Minnesota Press, 1987), 3–25.

Individuation of Human Nature

Locating human nature primarily in the soul brings us to the second question: how human natures are individuated. This is not the question of how persons or beings are unified, which has already been answered.[119] *Person* is distinct from *individual*.[120] A person is incommunicable, including and exceeding items at all levels of being, including individual natures. An individual is an item at the second level of being, a nature undivided from itself and able to be the source of acts and efficient causation. Unlike a universal, it is not applicable to many and is indivisible into instances. It is a determinate instance (or "this") of a specific, universalizable nature.[121] An individual is communicable, able (as in Christ's individualized human nature) to be assumed by another and needing completion by value, suppositality, and personhood. Some, like William of Ockham, think there is no problem of individuation, because all real items are individual of themselves.[122] However, there are real items, like Platonic Forms and common natures, that are not individual. Hence, we must ask what renders our natures individual. Aquinas contends that ontological actualities unreceived by some principle are infinite and unlimited.[123] I am asking what receives and limits our common nature. This is a metaphysical question about real principles, not an epistemic question about what allows us to know something as individual.[124] We can best answer it by considering various views of individuation in light of experience.

Our natures are first limited by matter. Since all humans are instances of the same specific kind, our natures must be limited by being received by something distinct from our common natures. While our natures can exist apart from matter, we are primarily given as located in matter and as coming to be through a material process. This is explained by our form

---

119. Some views, like that of Suárez (*DM*, d.5), in which beings are individuated by their own proper entity, conflate the questions.
120. Maritain, *The Person and the Common Good*, chap. 3; Balthasar, *Anthropology*, 103–5; Reginald Garrigou-Lagrange, *Beatitude*, trans. Patrick Cummins (St. Louis, Mo.: Herder, 1956), 75; and Berdyaev, *Slavery and Freedom*, 98, 133.
121. See Stein, *Finite and Eternal Being*, 481–82; Sharkey, *Thine Own Self*, 51, 117.
122. William of Ockham, *Scriptum in librum primum Sententiarum ordinatio*, v. 2 of *Opera theologica* (St. Bonaventure: Franciscan Institute, 1970), d.2, q.6, 196.
123. Aquinas, *SCG* II, c. 52; *ST* I, q.7, a.1; q.50, a.2. See John Wippel, "Thomas Aquinas and the Axiom That Unreceived Act Is Unlimited," in *Metaphysical Themes in Thomas Aquinas*, vol. 2 (Washington, D.C.: The Catholic University of America Press, 2007), 123–51.
124. Gracia, *Individuality*, 27–56.

and nature being intrinsically oriented to informing prime matter; our form and nature come into existence actualizing, and therefore limited by, this principle. However, prime matter as such cannot render me a determinate, concrete "this" because it has in itself no determination or concretion that it could confer, and nothing can give what it does not have. Yet by its resistance to form, it limits my form's impulse to communicate itself unlimitedly.

My soul is not only a form oriented to inform prime matter but also a concrete, determinate spiritual agent. Something in our souls themselves must render them (and our nature) determinate, limited, and concrete. A limiting principle of this sort is proposed by universal hylomorphism, on which all concrete creatures, even immaterial ones like human souls, have matter in the sense of something that resists, limits, is receptive, and is in potency to form. They do not have quantified, corporeal, or bodily matter, which localizes spatiotemporally, nor prime matter, that out of which material things are made, since the soul is created *ex nihilo*, not made out of any preexisting matter. Aquinas rightly rejects Solomon ibn Gabriol's version of universal hylomorphism on which corporeal and spiritual creatures are made out of the same kind of matter.[125] As we saw in chapter 3, prime and quantified matter are incompatible with intellectual receptivity, so our souls must lack them, but we must still posit in our souls something like matter that limits and concretizes the common human nature.[126] Aquinas recognizes the need for this, calling it "*yliatim*."[127] That the soul is in itself a composite of something like form and matter does not preclude it from also informing prime and quantified matter; by one formality, it is limited and determine, while by another, it is open to informing corporeal and prime matter.

While aspects of our nature's individuation are explained by prime matter and *yliatim*, our souls and natures are also oriented to quantified matter. According to Aquinas, our principle of individuation involves both matter and quantity.[128] (I shall not enter the controversy over Aquinas's exact view of the principle of individuation.) Since quantified matter just has probabilistic, quantum-mechanical properties, it lacks determinate quantifiable

---

125. Aquinas, *ST* I, q.50, a.2.
126. Cf. Stein, *Finite and Eternal Being*, 409–11; Nathan Jacobs, "Are Created Spirits Composed of Matter and Form? A Defense of Pneumatic Hylomorphism," *Philosophia Christi* 14, no. 1 (2012): 79–108.
127. Aquinas, *In LDC*, lect. 9.
128. Aquinas, *DEE*, 5.

properties, like definite location. Insofar as a being has this matter, there is some non-zero probability for it being in every place in the universe. Hence, this matter cannot entirely localize or determine our natures to be a concrete, determinate "this." Through quantified matter, my nature is still communicable to many batches of matter, though with a definite probability for being actually communicated to each.

Some Thomists distinguished a further aspect of matter: prior to substance, it has a transcendental relation (or mode) of being oriented to being determinately quantified.[129] This quantifiability distinguishes prime matter from the "spiritual matter" ("*yliatim*") in the soul. But, contrary to these Thomists, matter plus this relation also provides only a possibility for being a determinate, concretized this. This relation has no determinate uniqueness in itself, since it is only an orientation to determination, but not to any particular determinate quantity. Hence, it cannot confer determination.

In addition to having spiritual, prime, quantum-mechanical matter, and matter with an orientation to determinate quantity, I come to be (as we saw above) from formed matter, a union of particular sperm and egg, which has determinate, concretized individuality, and so can confer individuality upon me.[130] (Why fertilization is the moment of human origin will be considered below.) My form and nature are rendered a determinate, localized instance of human form and nature by being created as directed to inform this particular quantified batch of matter at this place and time. My continued individuation does not require that I thereafter continue to have my original, individuating matter; rather, having been once directed to that matter, my soul and nature are rendered limited and determinate, forever stamped by that initial limitation, which they have from then on as transcendental relations, regardless of new matter they later have.

These claims are evidence against two views of human nature, though not, I think, strong enough evidence to exclude these views altogether. First, they are evidence against views on which I could be reincarnated, insofar as such a view is understood as holding that this soul could inform another sperm-egg union after my death. My soul's unique identity was

---

129. See, for example, John of St. Thomas, *Cursus philosophicus thomisticus*, v. 3, p.2, q.9, a.3, 4, 48–68; Jorge Gracia and John Kronen, "John of St. Thomas," in *Individuation in Scholasticism: The Later Middle Ages and the Counter-Reformation*, ed. Jorge Gracia (Albany: State University of New York Press, 1994), 511–34.

130. Cf. Sharkey, *Thine Own Self*, 52.

fixed by the sperm-egg union from which I was made. Were it to inform a second such union, it would seem that it would take on a new unique identity, which sounds incoherent, or only some conceptions would give a person unique identity, which is contrary to how persons' identity is given experientially.

Second, they are evidence against views in which, at the resurrection, I must receive the same matter in which I died. I have no intrinsic, necessary, transcendental relation to that matter but only to the matter in which I came to be. Any matter that my soul informs is my matter. Hence, I can be resurrected in any matter. Still, it would be fitting for me to be resurrected with matter I had in my original life.

Each sort of matter surveyed here limits form in a distinct way, but I also have unique and positive (rather than purely limiting) characteristics of being this instance of human nature. Both being a this (given in all individuals) and the unique content or style of each individual (given in love or aesthetic cognition) are positive notions. Neither is the same as personal uniqueness or unrepeatability, for a concrete individualized human nature with a unique style can be assumed by another, as in the case of Christ's human nature. These positive characteristics of individuality, which Scotus and Stein call *thisness* (*haecceitas*) or the ultimate determination or reality of the form, are given as formalities within each human form.[131]

We can synthesize these accounts of individualization in the following way. Common human nature, which belongs primarily to my soul, is first (in the order of explanatory priority, not temporal priority) limited by being received in prime and quantum-mechanical matter. It is definitively individualized by being directed to the fully formed batch of matter that I received from my parents and from which I came to be, which has definite characteristics including genetic, structural, sexual, ethnic, and other physical, relational, and historical characteristics.[132] My form and nature have, from their origins, a transcendental relation of being oriented to this matter. My origins are essential to me: I could not have existed as this individual had not there been joined the particular sperm and egg from which I resulted, and in relation to which my soul and nature were created.[133] Indeed, since that sperm and egg would not have joined at that time and place if much of the prior history of the world had been different, I am

---

131. Scotus, *Ord.* II, d.3, q.6. Cf. Stein, *Finite and Eternal Being*, 486.
132. See Aquinas, *ST* I, q.85, a.7; *QQ* 7, q.1, a.3.
133. Cf. Saul Kripke, *Naming and Necessity* (Oxford: Blackwell, 1991), 111-14.

essentially transcendentally related to much of that history. My individuated nature is really identical to these transcendental relations. I cannot be reduced to a pure spirit contingently joined to a batch of matter; rather, I am thoroughly specified by being created with that matter, at that place and time, with its genetics, history, tradition, and culture.

But matter does not actively "confer" actuality on my nature or form. Rather, my form and nature are created by God with distinct essential content insofar as they actualize and are directed to this given batch of matter with these definite characteristics. In keeping with my metaphysics of generation, I also posit a Platonic Form as an ideal for each individual in which it participates and which is its exemplar.[134] My form's thisness or ultimate reality includes a pair of transcendental relations, one to my original matter and the other to my unique Platonic Form. Through these, I have an unchanging, given style, perceivable in all that I do.[135] While we cannot strictly define or conceptualize this essential individual content in each form, we can partially grasp it abstractly, as when we grasp the style of an artist, a person about whom we are writing a biography, or a beloved person.[136] While all human persons are members of the same species, each of us is also a kind unto ourselves, with an individual essence with distinct content. Matter is the occasioning principle of this positive individuation, while these formalities and relations in the soul are its actual principle— that is, the soul is the formal cause of these positive unique properties, but the soul has these properties because it is "terminated" by this matter with these definite properties. A form as such cannot explain why individualized nature is noninstantiable, since form in itself is unlimited; rather, this is explained by its *being directed to determinate matter and to a unique Platonic Form*. These relations are the soul's "spiritual matter," or "*yliatim*," limiting common human nature. These claims allow us to grasp what is correct in tripartite anthropologies that posit body, soul, and spirit in us: soul is our form's formality of directedness to matter, while spirit (or, in other versions of this view, the "spark of the soul" [*scintilla animae*]) is the formality of being directed to divine *energeiai* and Platonic Forms.[137]

---

134. Cf. Sharkey, *Thine Own Self*, 120.
135. Cf. Spaemann, *Persons*, 10–11.
136. Josef Seifert, "Personalism and Personalisms," in *Ethical Personalism*, ed. Cheikh Mbacke Gueye (Frankfurt: Ontos Verlag, 2011), 160–61.
137. Cf. Balthasar, *TD5*, 385–94, 434–44; Stein, *Finite and Eternal Being*, 370–78, 459–64.

Person and Individual as Part and Whole in Political Communities

Grasping the irreducible difference between personhood and individuality requires perceiving how, through each, we relate in distinct ways to communities. We are not entirely reducible to parts of any whole, as we are in some political reductionisms.[138] My discussion of this is inspired by a debate in twentieth-century Thomism between integralists like Charles de Koninck and personalists like Jacques Maritain.[139] I consider political issues here only insofar as they help us better grasp all irreducibilities in us; it is beyond the scope of this book to give particular political prescriptions, beyond some general claims about which sorts of politics fail to fit with irreducible persons.

Both sides of this debate take *person* to refer to a human being insofar as he or she has spiritual powers, and *individual* to refer to a human being purely as having matter and biological powers. They disagree as to how we are ordered to the ends of political communities like the state. Given their definitions of these terms, de Koninck rightly contends that the person-individual distinction is irrelevant to questions of our place in political society—we relate to and are ordered to the ends of political communities both as persons (in their sense of the word) and as material individuals. We have seen, however, that there is a better, philosophically and politically relevant distinction between person and individual. *Individual* refers to our entire nature, with its biological and spiritual powers, as individualized and concretized, at the first two levels of being. *Person* refers to each of us in our fullness, including all levels of being.

As an individualized nature and as acting through my natural potencies, I occupy a place within the ontological, cosmic hierarchy, and I am ordered teleologically to objective goods, especially God, who is the

---

138. Wojtyła, "Subjectivity and the Irreducible," 210–11; Karol Józef Wojtyła, "The Person: Subject and Community," in *Person and Community*, 238–41; Crosby, *The Selfhood of the Human Person*, 16–19; Mounier, *Personalism*, xii; Seifert, "Personalism and Personalisms," 175–77; and Gabriel Marcel, *Man Against Mass Society*, trans. G. S. Fraser (South Bend, Ind.: St. Augustine's Press, 2008).

139. On integralism, see De Koninck, *On the Primacy of the Common Good*, 36–94; Henri Grenier, *Moral Philosophy*, vol. 3 of *Thomistic Philosophy*, trans. J. P. E. O'Hanley (Charlottetown: St. Dunstan's University, 1949), 370–73; and Thomas Crean and Alan Fimister, *Integralism: A Manual of Political Philosophy* (Heusenstamm: Editiones Scholasticae, 2020). "Integralism" sometimes names the view of thinkers like de Lubac and Milbank, who hold that we are naturally ordered to grace; I do not use it in this sense. On personalism, see Maritain, *The Person and the Common Good*, 36–40, 49–70; Mounier, *Personalism*, 17–40; Berdyaev, *Slavery and Freedom*, 68–69, 201–2; and Balthasar, *TD2*, 282–84.

common good of the whole cosmos, the one who can be shared in by all creatures. The integralists contend that I am a part of the cosmos and of other communities (like the state), because I am, with other members of those communities, ordered to common goods that exceed us in perfection, around which these communities are organized, and as individual, this is true. As the integralists rightly contend, one source of our dignity is that we are ordered and subordinated to transcendent ends and common goods; through my spiritual powers, I am ordered to consciously seeking objective common goods like justice, knowledge, or God. As common goods, these can rightly be pursued only as sharable by many people and as worth pursuing for their own sake. I diminish in dignity as an individual by turning away from these ends and just pursuing my private good; I grow in dignity as an individual insofar as I act as an excellent part of societies pursuing these common goods.

On integralism, I am ordered by my natural potencies (and those obediential potencies, like the potency for grace, that order me to objective goods) to the common goods of a range of societies, including families, civic and economic groups like clubs, businesses, and universities, polities like nation, culture, and state, and ultimately the Church. Lower communities are ordered to the goods of the higher communities; for example, the family is ordered to, and only fully fulfilled in relation to, the nation and state, and by the common goods around which the latter are organized. (A *nation* is a community insofar as it pursues natural goods of culture, based on shared land, custom, and lifestyle; a *state* is a community insofar as it is organized in pursuit of natural political common goods like security and peace.[140]) Higher communities have a duty to practice subsidiarity, that is, to safeguard and foster lower ones. Each individual and community is ultimately ordered to God, integrating them as parts of the cosmos.

Personalists object that persons transcend goods (at least those other than God) and so we should pursue common goods for the sake of persons' fulfillment, rather than holding (as the integralists do) that we exist for the sake of common goods. I contend that insofar as we consider human beings just as individuals—that is, as ontological beings ordered to objective goods as ends—integralists are right: at that level, the personalist view confuses ends and means. We are ordered to ends, not the other way

---

140. Cf. Jacques Maritain, *Man and the State* (Washington, D.C.: The Catholic University of America Press, 1951), 1–19.

around; as individuals, we are parts of the communities that exist for the ends that are those common goods. To subordinate ends to individuals is potentially totalitarian, in that it makes the good of each individual a standard for all, resulting in a struggle for power among individuals pursuing their separate goods, such that the strong dominate others. As an individual, I am obliged to pursue the common goods of my communities, which may constrain me by law to pursue at least some of these goods. This is all true, however, only within limits: some common goods, like God, can only be authentically pursued by self-determination, and so it is illegitimate to use coercive force to move persons to pursue those goods.[141] I am, because of my rational nature (and my ordering thereby to universals), a political animal, able to flourish only in polities organized around pursuit of universal or common goods, like my state, the community of states, and the Church. In this sense, I am a part: at the level of individual nature, I have identity by participation in these communities.

But Maritain and other personalists rightly contend that I, as person, am not reducible to anything nonpersonal, which includes my individual nature and its teleology. So, I am not only a part of (or participant in) a whole; rather, I am a whole in myself. As a self-governing, self-possessing person, I am created by God for my own sake—not as a pure end (since I am further ordered to other ends) but as having value or importance in myself.[142] As person, I transcend nature, since I also have values and *energeiai*, and I act not only in a way directed to and motivated by ends and objective goods; as person, I include my individual nature's parthood in communities, but I also exceed it. The integralists are correct that common goods cannot be rightly pursued as a mere means to persons' fulfillment, but when achieved, common goods are encompassed by or included in the overall *Gestalt* that each person is—that is, those goods redound to each person's flourishing; they are not means to each person's flourishing but are aspects of that flourishing. In this way, common goods are for persons and persons are prior to all communities and goods. Flourishing as a part of a community (i.e., flourishing by achieving common goods) is just one aspect of each person's ultimate state; that state also includes responding to values for their own sake and living up to my own value, whereby I am

---

141. Cf. Vatican Council II, *Dignitatis humanae. Declaration on Religious Freedom*, December 7, 1965, n. 2–4.

142. Aquinas, *SCG* III, c. 111–13.

worthy to exist for my own sake. No common good can rightly be pursued at the expense of persons and their value and flourishing.

As John Paul II says, in what Michael Waldstein calls his "Carmelite Personalism," persons are not just teleologically ordered to ends but enter into relations of love and "mutual self-gift" with others.[143] While we are parts of communities (including the whole cosmos) and have private subjective lives, we are irreducible to these cosmological and anthropological aspects, for as persons we are open to others through love, self-gift, and *energeiai*.[144] We discover who we fundamentally are only through covenantal gift of self, which redounds to receiving others' self-gift. For example, I give myself to God in pursuing him as common good, but he also (both prior and subsequent to my self-gift) pours himself out to me in an excess of love—and I can pour myself out to him not just insofar as he is my objective good but insofar as he is valuable and personal, worth responding to for his own sake. This relation is modeled on the self-gift of the Trinitarian persons and is exemplified in the mutual self-gift proper to spouses, to friends, and to the ethical relation in which other persons call me to radical service. My ultimate state is one in which I achieve common goods as common (i.e., as overflowing into many persons including myself) but also one in which valuable goods (including other persons and God) give themselves to me and I give myself to them.

Fully flourishing communities of persons can be formed only through acts of creative, free self-gift, joining activities together in *sun-energeiai*, motivated by values and persons as such, rather than being formed just through ordering to common goods. Flourishing communities—exemplified by friendships, especially friendships between spouses—exhibit what Berdyaev and other Russian personalists call "togetherness" (*sobornost*): they are communities of free persons spontaneously and lovingly giving themselves to each other, acting together as a "we" community, and transcending themselves toward values, rather than only subordinating themselves to orders of law or authority.[145] Any community that impedes persons from engaging in the free solidarity of *sun-energeia*—say, by mak-

---

143. Michael Waldstein, introduction, in John Paul II, *Man and Woman He Created Them*, 29–34. Cf. Vatican Council II, *Gaudium et spes*, The Pastoral Constitution on the Church in the Modern World, December 7, 1965, n. 24.
144. Hans Urs von Balthasar, *Love Alone Is Credible*, trans. D. C. Schindler (San Francisco: Ignatius, 2004), chaps. 1–3.
145. Berdyaev, *Slavery and Freedom*, 68–69, 201–2; Berdyaev, *Spirit and Reality*, 38, 45. Cf. Gavrilyuk, *Georges Florovsky and the Russian Religious Renaissance*, 227–29.

ing most interactions among persons directed by a central authority or bureaucracy, or by allowing all interactions to be ruled by the interests of business or guided by techniques like marketing or propaganda—is reductionistic of the full range of relationships necessary for our ultimate fulfilling state. There is something properly *anarchical*—unable to be assumed into neat ordering to ends and guided by law—about communities guided by the immediate call of value and of persons as such, as seen in deep friendships, spontaneous religious communities, or the ethical relation of one person to another.[146] However, Berdyaev wrongly sees all law-based communities as enslaving. We are teleologically ordered to act within law-governed orders, and even spontaneous communities have a duty in justice to pursue common goods for all.[147] But we must also be able to transcend those orders in spontaneous, value-guided *per communionem* activity and mutual self-giving.

Two aspects of beauty are revealed in two aspects of community. Beauty involves what is proportioned, symmetrical, and ordered; this transcendental, ontological beauty is found in aspects of communities that are ordered to common goods. Beauty is also a value that can take new and unexpected forms, such as the surprising, ephemeral, amusing, ironic, funky, wild, carnivalesque, or playful; these beauties, which are crucial to perceive and instantiate for fully flourishing, intense human life, emerge through the spontaneous aspects of a community.[148]

In a flourishing community, each person is an encompassing whole in whose *energeiai* all others can participate. While as individuals no one is something common, as persons, each of us is a common good or end for all the others, one even worth dying for, for whom the whole political community should act.[149] Each person appears as having infinite beauty and value, and thereby, by super value-response, as an objective good for all others, too. Each person offers a unique space in which others can gain a distinctive perspective on the world. We see this, above all, in the communion of saints, where each saint's vocation is available to and helps

---

146. Levinas, *Otherwise Than Being or Beyond Essence*, 100–2. Cf. Dorothy Day, *The Long Loneliness* (New York: HarperOne, 1997), 169–235.
147. Levinas, *Otherwise Than Being or Beyond Essence*, 160.
148. Cf. Lingis, *The Imperative*, 3; Alphonso Lingis, *Foreign Bodies* (New York: Routledge, 1994), 162–63; Lingis, *The Community of Those Who Have Nothing in Common* (Bloomington: Indiana University Press, 1993); and Alexander Hooke, "Alphonso Lingis' We—A Collage, not a Collective," *Diacritics* 31, no. 4 (2001): 11–21.
149. Cf. de Saint-Exupéry, *Wind, Sand and Stars*, 190–92.

to actualize and enliven others, for example, through patronage, petition, intercession, and mediation of divine life. I perform activities in which others can share, such that together we bring about higher values. Persons participating in such a community (*koinonia*) are not entirely separated individuals, nor do they just become parts of a whole.[150] We are not only political animals or parts of polities in the sense described above: we are also wholes among wholes, each open to other wholes in our own unique way.[151] While we saw earlier that each person is a microcosm, each person is also a macrocosm, like a whole world unto him or herself, encompassing the whole material cosmos in his or her perspective.[152]

Insofar as states are ordered to natural ends while the Church is ordered to supernatural ends (which are more perfective than natural ends), states fully flourish only in being ordered to the ends of the Church. Each state, however, like every community, is also uniquely organized around values, including earthly and secular ones, like the values of land and tradition, free conversation and debate, family honor and nobility, justice and equality. Insofar as they are organized around and instantiate values, no community is teleologically subordinated to another. The integralist model captures human community insofar as we are motivated by objective goods; the personalist model adds motivation by value and persons.

By being ordered to common goods, communities avoid reductionistic politics like individualism (in which we are only organized as ordered to the end of individual, not personal, fulfillment), collectivism (in which individuals are ordered to the good of the community conceived of as an individual whose citizens are disposable organs), and any system in which we are ordered to or ruled by the good of some particular part of society, like businesses or other particular groups within society. By pursuing the free spontaneity of *per communionem* causality and *sun-energeia* motivated by value, however, communities avoid attempting to plan themselves in entirely rational, utility-oriented, or *per se*–caused ways, and are not reductionistic about crucial elements of human flourishing like custom and tradition. They also avoid the reductionisms risked by integralism,

---

150. Cf. John Zizioulas, *Being as Communion: Studies in Personhood and the Church* (Crestwood, N.Y.: St. Vladimir's Seminary Press, 1997), 164–65.

151. Walsh, *The Priority of the Person*, chap. 1.

152. Josef Soloveitchik, "The Community," *Tradition: A Journal of Orthodox Jewish Thought* 17, no. 2 (1978): 7–24, building on the Mishnah Sanhedrin; Nicodemos of the Holy Mountain, *A Handbook of Spiritual Counsel*, trans. Peter Chamberas (Mahwah, N.J.: Paulist Press, 1989), chap. 1. I am grateful to Rabbi Mark Gottlieb and Fr. James Brent, OP, for calling these texts to my attention.

especially the reduction of persons to being enslaved (in Berdyaev's sense) to the common good, law, or authority. These things are not inherently enslaving; rather, they are necessary for human flourishing, but they can become enslaving when they inhibit free self-determination and pursuit of value. Organizing communities around motivation by values and by persons also avoids reductionistic egalitarianisms that treat all persons in the same, levelling way, making us atoms of a mass society. Rather, a flourishing community will be organized around responding to the unique beauty of each person, even while it recognizes our radical equality as human individuals. Legitimate, obligation-bestowing authority belongs to a community through its directedness to common goods, values, and persons, not inherently to any class or role. A key challenge for a politics that recognizes the irreducibility of all features of human life is to organize around the value of meaningful traditions, especially religious ones, while rejecting aspects of traditionary life that prevent anyone from being fully self-determining and self-giving.

Given the many values around which communities can be organized, there will often be conflicts among even legitimate communities. In a fallen world, we cannot expect to integrate all values and objective goods together without being reductionistic about some of them; hence, both individual and communal history are often tragic, a mere rearranging of injustices even when justice is sought. The metaphysician of irreducibility recognizes values found in a range of political movements and communities and seeks to give each their due response, without expecting to adequately do so in every case, or to see how they all fit together, while hoping for these tragic features of human life to be ultimately taken up in a comic, reconciliatory order.[153]

On integralism, we have rights—moral guarantees that we should be treated a certain way—insofar as we have use of the right for the sake of the common good. I have a right to life (i.e., to not be murdered) because I have use of my life for the sake of the common good. In this view, rights, like persons, are subordinated to and explained by the common good.[154] German sociologist Hans Joas notes that personalism is part of a trend in contemporary thought that has "sacralized" the person, elucidating a further source of rights and dignity. We have rights not just in relation to

---

153. The hoped-for resolution to history through mercy is powerfully depicted in Shakespeare's *Measure for Measure*, *The Winter's Tale*, and *The Tempest*; see Balthasar, *TD1*, 465–78.
154. Crean and Fimister, *Integralism*, 38–39.

the common good but infinite value in ourselves. Integralists object that nothing about persons gives us infinite dignity in ourselves, but we have seen that this dignity is rooted in that unique beauty (or holiness) that each of us is as person, which is really identical to transcendental relations like our imaging of God. This beauty calls for, and so grounds rights to, due responses of protection, service, respect, reverence, love, and so forth. Joas contends that our life and personhood, and the dignity they ground, are not just givens continually received, but gifts delivered over to us, which we then have inalienably and intrinsically.[155]

To perceive our value is to grasp that we have rights to participation in common goods like political involvement, peace, traditional and cultural meaning-bestowing forms, knowledge, a flourishing natural world, and true religion. We also thereby have rights to individual goods necessary to such participation, like dignifying work, material goods sufficient for oneself and one's dependents, health care, and safety.[156] But a community in which persons flourish goes beyond just safeguarding these rights, in at least three ways. First, it recognizes that the beauty that grounds these rights, persons' status as wholes among wholes, and the fundamentally kenotic structure of being, makes it the case that each person places moral demands on all others. The citizens of a flourishing community do not emphasize their own rights but rather see themselves as one another's servants; as Fyodor Dostoyevsky says, "each of us is guilty before" and therefore responsible for "everyone, and I more than the others."[157] In other words, I must always recognize my failure to do as much as I could have done for others and allow that to drive my support for other persons and the community. Second, a flourishing community seeks to be a community of friends, sharing a common life, with all the merriment, festivity, and love that friendship involves.[158] Third, since the grounding for rights is our personal beauty and holiness, communities must be fundamentally oriented to increasing that beauty, producing great-souled or magnanimous persons, that is, saints, participants in divine life who intensely actualize what it is to be an irreducible person.[159]

---

155. Hans Joas, *The Sacredness of the Person: A New Genealogy of Human Rights*, trans. Alex Skinner (Washington, D.C.: Georgetown University Press, 2013), 140–41, 170.
156. See the United Nations' *Declaration of Human Rights*.
157. Fyodor Dostoyevsky, *The Brothers Karamazov*, quoted in Levinas, *Otherwise Than Being or Beyond Essence*, 146.
158. Cf. Aristotle, *NE*, VIII.9.
159. Cf. de Saint-Exupéry, *Wind, Sand and Stars*, 226–29.

Chapter 8 The Multiplicity of the Human Substance and the Principles of *Status*

Most of the foregoing chapters have focused on various sorts of unity in us, but we are not only unified beings and persons. We also include a multiplicity of items irreducible to any unity, and our beauty includes the self-manifestation of many irreducible substances, natures, and forms in us. The unity of persons is not the unity of an essence, the ontological unity of a substance, or the axiological unity of a community or an artifact but instead a kind of unity that uniquely encompasses and includes what is other than it, without annulling that otherness. In this chapter, I add to my portrait of the human person various irreducible multiplicities in us.

Experiences of Multiplicity and Fluidity

Scientific observations show that atoms, molecules, and other entities are regularly taken up into my body, such as during eating, drinking, and breathing.[1] Outside my body, these are substantial wholes with their own acts, teleology, and nature. In my body, they can be observed continuing to act in ways typical of their kinds and for their own ends. Aquinas holds that these "elements" are present in the body virtually or by power (*virtute*), not actually. On his view, their matter is incorporated into my body, informed by my one substantial form, and serves my human end.

---

1. This section builds on Mark K. Spencer, "Christologically Inspired, Empirically Motivated Hylomorphism," *Res Philosophica* 93, no. 1 (2016): 137–60, cowritten with Tim Pawl. I am grateful to conversations with Fr. Stephen Brock and Gary Atkinson that helped refine my position.

The substance that existed outside the body with its form, *esse*, and accidents ceases to exist. Powers and other accidents qualitatively identical to those that existed outside the body then begin to exist in the body. When I excrete water or breathe out carbon dioxide, a new form is educed from the matter of what I excrete, such that it becomes a substance of its own. According to this view, a batch of matter can exist and be unified substantially (*per se*) in only one way at a time. Were a batch of matter to have two substantial forms, it would be fundamentally two things at once; the contradictory result would be that it could be simultaneously living and nonliving, human and nonhuman, given that specific differences divide genera into contrary kinds.[2]

This view, however, does not adequately account for what is given in experience. We do not just incorporate matter and powers into ourselves. Rather, molecules can be tracked (for example, by radioactive tagging) in us; they appear as persisting wholes, with structure, acts, and teleology unaffected by their incorporation into our bodies, appearing just as those substances do outside the body.

Furthermore, as a human substance develops, it divides its matter into organs to serve as subjects for its powers and instruments for its acts. Aquinas contends that while these parts subsist and are the subjects of acts, they do not have complete natures, nor can they exist as wholes on their own. A severed hand and a functioning hand in a body are each called a "hand" only equivocally.[3] In organ transplantation, however, we remove organs from bodies such that they retain their function, teleology, and at least limited activity; when they are implanted in another body, they do not lose their own discrete functions, activities, and teleology, though they are caught up in that body's life, activity, unity, and teleology. Physiology, biochemistry, cell biology, and related disciplines have shown that body parts like organs, cells, organelles, and molecules can be understood well when treated as distinct entities. Thinking of them in this way guides us to perceive many aspects of them we would not perceive if we treated them only as parts of a larger whole. These experiences suggest that we are both unified substances and have multiple substances within us, all of which are included in us.[4]

Further consideration of human origins also reveals multiple substances

2. Aquinas, *In II DA*, lect. 8; *DME*; *In V Met.*, lect. 12.
3. Aquinas, *QDA*, a.1.
4. Cf. Stein, *Finite and Eternal Being*, 183–84, 195–98.

in us. On Aquinas's view, at a human body's origins, the molecules like DNA from which the body is made cease to actually exist. The new human substance comes to be just from prime matter, without genes from parents really being taken up into it. The molecules from which the body was made had powers, and new powers qualitatively but not numerically identical to those powers come to be in the new substance. Likewise, at the beginning of humanity, the first human body would have been created immediately by God; bodies would have evolved up to the point where God infused the first human soul into matter, but the numerically same body that evolved could not have been taken up by the first soul. However, this is contrary to the continuity displayed in speciation events and fertilization: in those events, genes and other molecular constituents are observed to be taken up into the new organism. This would be well explained by positing that we incorporate actual, preexisting substances into us.

A multiplicity of substances in our bodies is also given in experiences of fluidity in our bodies, emphasized by some feminist philosophers in the Thomistic tradition. Some of my parts are solid, with delimited spatial structure; others are liquid or gaseous, given as incapable of having precisely delimited, stable structure—and this mutability and lack of delimination (and concomitant multiplicity) renders them uniquely suited, as Stein says following phenomenologist Hedwig Conrad-Martius, to facilitate the changes involved in vital development.[5] We are not purely stable solid substances but are composed of many fluids that flow around and out of us, often uncontrollably, such as blood (including menstrual blood), breastmilk, amniotic fluid, lymph, saliva, sweat, semen, pus, bile, mucus, and tears.

In some experiences of fluidity, such as in some instances of sexual arousal and intercourse, my attention is drawn into the organs involved, such that I do not consciously aim at my human end but only at the ends of those organs and fluids.[6] Some organs aim at ends and facilitate experiences in a way only partially subordinated to my overall human end. In

---

5. Stein, *Finite and Eternal Being*, 198–200; Hedwig Conrad-Martius, "Realontologie," *Jahrbuch für Philosophie und phänomenologische Forschung* 6 (1923): 97–112. Cf. Beattie, *Theology after Postmodernity*, especially chaps. 13 and 19; Christina van Dyke, "Taking the 'Dis' out of Disability: Martyrs, Mystics, and Mothers in the Middle Ages," in *Disability in Medieval Christian Philosophy and Theology*, ed. Scott Williams (New York: Routledge, 2020), 203–32. Beattie builds on contemporary feminists like Luce Irigaray; both build on medieval mystics like Catherine of Siena.

6. Scruton, *Sexual Desire*, chap. 2; Dietrich von Hildebrand, *In Defense of Purity: An Analysis of the Catholic Ideals of Purity and Virginity* (Steubenville, Ohio: Hildebrand Press, 2017), chap. 1; and Gilles Deleuze, *Logic of Sense*, trans. Mark Lester (London: Athlone, 1990), 196–201.

experiences of fluidity having to do with pain, injury, and disease—like experiencing the flow of blood or pus—our attention is drawn, again, to how aspects of our bodies aim at their own ends and yield fragmented experiences that are distinctly mine but not clearly subordinated or directed to an overall human end. Experiences of the flow of amniotic fluid during childbirth or of milk from the breast during nursing draw attention to how the body forms instruments to accomplish its powers' ends that are easily detached from the body. Organs and fluids are oriented to kinds of self-gift—here, to children—in a way not up to the person whose body it is, and, again, not entirely subordinated to its end. Some of these experiences involve excessive pleasure (*jouissance*), pain, or other sorts of given infinitude; there is something like an image of God in these experiences, insofar as they reveal our participation in infinitude.[7]

Many experiences involving fluids involve an incarnate *sun-energeia*—that is, the activities of many substances join together in a way entirely occurring in bodies (*incarnated acts* will be considered further below). In sexual intercourse and in the nourishment of the prenatal or nursing child, exchange of fluids facilitates a *Gestalt*, a unified community of solidarity, among persons. These exchanges also manifest fluids' independence: they are oriented to leave one's body and join another. By them, I contribute to a *Gestalt* that is partly beyond my *per se* control. Likewise, in breathing air or drinking water, I experience my intertwining with my environment: these fluids flow through me, bearing the meaningful *energeiai* of other substances that have influenced them. Through them and through other intertwinings with the physical world, my whole natural environment flows through me. Their qualities affect my bodily powers, my phantasms, and thereby my thoughts and choices.[8] Yet, as Dean Dettloff, following Peter Sloterdijk, argues, the fluids I take in are also artifacts, with both sense-perceivable and scientifically graspable qualities affected (often negatively) by human activities on a global scale, in ways we cannot fully grasp.[9] Air, including polluted air, is a vast saturated phenomenon and *Gestalt* incarnating many *sun-energeiai*. I am, to use Charles Taylor's term again but in a more literal sense, "porous" to its influence, which is also

---

7. Beattie, *Theology After Postmodernity*; Jean-Luc Nancy, *Corpus II: Writings on Sexuality*, trans. Anne O'Byrne (New York: Fordham University Press, 2013), 94.

8. Abram, *The Spell of the Sensuous*, 225–39.

9. Dean Dettloff, "Catholic Air Conditioning," *The Heythrop Journal* 58, no. 6 (2017): 931–41, building on Peter Sloterdijk, *Terror from the Air*, trans. Amy Patton and Steve Corcoran (Los Angeles: Semiotext(e), 2009).

the influence of other persons, by an incarnate *sun-energeia* no one fully intends and that exceeds all that can be grasped and described. As person, I include, by my relations, this vast assemblage of fluids; my ultimate flourishing state requires flourishing intertwining with the environment that flows through me. Happiness requires receptivity to the enjoyment of water and wind, and to the meanings they convey, but I am ethically called by the saturated phenomenon they are to care for them.[10]

The Human Body: Multiple Substances and Forms, One Supposit and Person

We can account for these experiences by holding that bodily parts—those incorporated from without, those formed within us, solids, and fluids—are substances, subsistent composites of form and matter, subjects of acts, with their own nature and end. Substances can be parts of other substances without ceasing to be substances, but only the highest-order substance in a given batch of matter (for example, a human being) is a supposit. All substances have forms by which they give *ousia* and *esse* to matter, but supposits have modes whereby their essences are incommunicably their own and whereby they have *esse* proper to them, by which they exist in themselves rather than through another. A substance can persist without these modes. When one substance is a part of or assumed by another, the highest-order substance alone bestows *per se* unity and existence on its matter. Lower-order substances are completed by the higher-order substance's modes and *esse*; lower-order substances are rendered such that they belong to the supposit, not to themselves. Items belong to a supposit insofar as they are rendered concrete, completed, and able to act in the world through the supposit. Supposits "subsist in" the natures and other items within them; supposits exist and act in delimited ways through having those natures.

Christ, as understood by Aquinas, exemplifies these claims: the supposit who is the Son of God assumed an individual human nature, which thereby lacks modes of incommunicability and proper *esse* but exists through the divine supposit's *esse*. This does not make his human nature an accident. Accidents give *esse* to supposits whereby those supposits are rendered not *per se* existing and unified but unified and existing in some respect (*secundum quid*). Rather, Christ's human nature gives what Aqui-

---

10. Levinas, *Totality and Infinity*, 110–15.

nas calls *esse secundarium*. As John Froula explains, this is an ontological actuality in his humanity whereby he, the supposit, exists as substantially human. It is a kind of *esse* given by individualized natures and forms that belong to another. By this *esse*, a being is an existing, delimited being with a complete essence of some kind but is not thereby complete in the order of existence: it does not thereby have *per se* existence and unity.[11]

Something remotely similar happens when lower substances are incorporated in a supposit. (I say "remotely" similar because Christ's hypostatic union is ineffable and is the only case where a person has two substantial natures that characterize that person as a whole.) When a substance is not taken up into another, its form gives its supposit proper *esse* and essential incommunicability; when it is taken up into another, it gives *esse secundarium*. Matter actualized by multiple forms—such as in our bodies—is fundamentally characterized by the supposit's nature (in us, human nature) and secondarily by the part's nature (in us, the nature of, for example, an organ, cell, or molecule). Substantial parts are subordinate to, but not accidental to or inhering in, supposit wholes; a "part" in this context is what participates in a higher substance's *esse*. (Since *Gestalten* like communities are unified not by *esse* but by values, they are not substances of which we are parts.)

Contrary to the objection above, no essential property of one substance is contrary to the properties of another. For example, water's essence does not include the formality *nonliving* such that it would conflict with the human essence's formality *living*. Rather, water just does not include the formality *living*; it is indifferent to that formality. Genera are specified not by contrary properties but by positive specific differences, none of which excludes others. Matter can be multiply delimited—that is, given more than one substantial formal content—but it can receive only one *per se* existence and unity at a time.

This view resembles that of Scotus, on which we have multiple substances and forms in us, unified and coordinated by the highest-order form. In my view, however, forms inhere in matter; the supposit's form does not inhere in the substantial parts: such a view might suggest the false view that the parts primarily exist and that the supposit merely has accidental unity of order.[12] My view remotely resembles the views of scholastics

---

11. Aquinas, *ST* III, q.2, a.2; q.6, a.1; q.17, a.2; *QDUV*, a.4; John Froula, "*Esse Secundarium*: An Analogical Term Meaning that By Which Christ Is Human," *The Thomist* 78, no. 4 (2014): 557–80.

12. Scotus, *Ord*. IV, d.44, q.1; Thomas Ward, "Animals, Animal Parts, and Hylomorphism: John Duns Scotus' Pluralism about Substantial Form," *Journal of the History of Philosophy* 50, no. 4 (2012): 534.

Jacob Zabarella and Francisco Suárez, on which parts' forms combine in the total form of the whole. On my view, however, immaterial forms combine only in *Gestalten*.[13] My view captures what is right in William of Ockham's view that we have an intellectual soul, a sensitive soul, and a *forma corporeitatis*, which accounts for the body's physical structure and persists in the corpse.[14] While we have only one highest-level, unifying, spiritual form, we have sensitive animating principles in each of our organs' forms. We also have a *forma corporeitatis* in the unified appearance of the body, our perceivable *Gestalt* of sensible qualities and values, the "aesthetic essence" mentioned in chapter 5. This persists in the corpse and explains the reverence we ought to have for human corpses, relics, and organs.[15]

That my matter is *per se* unified by my human form and *esse* does not entail that it always acts in a unified way or serves my human end; experience shows it does not. My form confers powers on matter, efficiently causing new substantial parts like organs, cells, and fluids in me, to serve my ends, but those parts can then act in ways that aim at their own ends regardless of whether those acts serve my end. While my form does not perfectly unite everything in me considered as a supposit, all of this, even the conflicts among my parts, is united within me considered as a person, that is, within my unique beauty. Persons unite what is multiple such that multiplicity belongs to them without ceasing to be a multiplicity.

The Malleability and Evolution of the Human Body

Only persons, who primarily exist as indivisible immaterial spirits, are fully incommunicable, entirely unable to be taken up into another. Material substances are incommunicable only in the limited sense that they cannot be assumed or become part of another while remaining supposits. They are susceptible to becoming parts to different degrees; for example, adult higher animals are more indivisible, have greater uniqueness, and are taken up into another with more difficulty, compared with lower organisms.

All organisms, including our bodies, are highly malleable due to the multiplicity of substances in them. They can be disassembled and recom-

---

13. Pasnau, *Metaphysical Themes*, 577–81, 630–32. Cf. Gordon Barnes, "The Paradoxes of Hylomorphism," *Review of Metaphysics* 56, no. 3 (2003): 517–22.

14. Pasnau, *Metaphysical Themes*, 586.

15. Cf. Mathew Lu, "Explaining the Wrongness of Cannibalism," *American Catholic Philosophical Quarterly* 87, no. 3 (2013): 430–58; Balthasar, *TD3*, 245.

bined in many ways, as seen in scientific and technological experience like rewriting organisms' genetic codes, combining DNA and organs from multiple organisms, and extending organisms' powers using artifactual biological and inorganic parts.[16] (I here just consider what these acts reveal metaphysically; I am not assessing them ethically.) Aquinas recognized how easily divisible plants, worms, and other lower organisms are, contending that while they are actually one (with one soul or actuality), they are potentially many, and can become multiple substances by material division.[17] Some analytic philosophers like Derek Parfit have suggested that it is possible to transplant a brain from one adult human head to another, or half a brain into one head and the other half into a different head.[18] Since such processes are likely medically possible, all material substances, even our bodies, are potentially many substances. This is further reason to hold that all material bodies already contain many formally complete substances, each of which acts by its own principles.

Having recognized the malleability and multiplicity of human bodies, I must try to make the definition of human nature more precise. I am by nature necessarily a spiritual soul oriented to be the form of a body, and I am normatively an animal body (a form-matter composite) of a specific kind. An account of that body must enter any plausible definition of human nature.[19] We have mortal bodies, since our bodies' parts inherently tend to dissociate (even if this tendency can be blocked by, say, a preternatural or supernatural gift of immortality from God, which prelapsarian or resurrected bodies have, or even by medical anti-aging technologies).[20] Human bodies can fall only within a specifically delimited range of possible biological and genetic structures. Just as all organisms' form and matter fit together, so the human body is adapted to support its form's spiritual activity: for example, the brain facilitates intellectual activity, vocal and other organs are suited to expressing concepts, hands are suited to make anything designed by the intellect, and the body's upright posture is suited to free the hands to act and eyes and ears to perceive one's surroundings.[21]

Human bodies also are partly defined by a specific evolutionary de-

---

16. See, for example, Martin Jinek et al., "A Programmable Dual-RNA-Guided DNA Endonuclease in Adaptive Bacterial Immunity," *Science* 337, no. 6096 (2012): 816–21.
17. Aquinas, *In VII Met.*, lect. 16; *In II Sent.*, d.18, q.2, a.3.
18. Parfit, *Reasons and Persons*, 245–81.
19. Aquinas, *ST* I, q.75, a.4.
20. Aquinas, *ST* I, q.97, a.1.
21. Aquinas, *In I PH*, lect. 6; *ST* I, q.76, a.5, ad 2; q.91, a.3.

scent. Our animal ancestor species evolved until a body adapted to spiritual activity developed. Then God, because of his covenant with creation to produce persons when fitting conditions obtained, created a spiritual soul actualizing and informing its matter. At that point, the prepersonal organism and its soul ceased to exist as a distinct supposit, but its organs, cells, and molecules and their powers persisted in the new person.[22] Were material conditions for spiritual powers to obtain elsewhere—say, in a computer or in other organisms with a different evolutionary lineage, terrestrial or extraterrestrial—it seems reasonable that God would create a spiritual soul for that matter; the result would be a nonhuman but embodied person.

Kenneth Kemp has shown how this evolutionary view (on which, it is generally held, the original population of human organisms numbered in the thousands) is reconcilable with the biblical claim that there were two first human persons. On Kemp's proposal, God ensouled just two biological humans, but those persons could interbreed with their nonpersonal members of their biological species. All children of spiritual persons are spiritual persons, so all biological humans today are spiritual persons. The bodies of those first two human persons were elected for ensoulment perhaps because their bodies were especially suited to facilitate spiritual activity.[23]

But though human souls are created oriented to a body with this lineage, they could inform other sorts of matter. We could (though in many cases morally should not) alter our bodies, for example, by rewriting our genes or replacing our parts with functionally equivalent artifactual parts. Phenomenologist Claude Romano argues that we are the biological beings whose lives are most open to adaptation and responsiveness to the contingent; this physical openness and modifiability helps account for our vulnerability and fragility, and for the development of a wide range of cultures with many physical expressions and roles for human bodies.[24] Our biological openness is an expression of our openness as persons. As Anne O'Byrne notes, building on Jean-Luc Nancy, we are never purely finite or completed beings but, in our very embodiment, are always open to further ways of life.[25]

---

22. Cf. Karl Rahner, *Hominisation: The Evolutionary Origin of Man as a Theological Problem*, trans. W. J. O'Hara (New York: Herder and Herder, 1965), chap. 3; Teilhard de Chardin, *The Phenomenon of Man*, 164–80.

23. Kenneth Kemp, "Science, Theology, and Monogenesis," *American Catholic Philosophical Quarterly* 85, no. 2 (2011): 217–36.

24. Romano, *There Is*, 25.

25. O'Byrne, *Natality and Finitude*, 7–8.

Sexuality, Ethical Relations, and Disability

Our souls are directed to bodies that also have irreducible sexual and erotic aspects. Here, I synthesize a few metaphysics of sexual difference from the Catholic tradition; it is beyond the scope of this book to consider the morality that follows from this metaphysics. Aquinas regards sex as belonging to individuals because of properties in the matter from which human individuals come to be. One receives a reproductive tendency from one's genetics, and one's sex just is being such that one has that tendency. Males are oriented to beget children in another with that other's help, that is, they are oriented to fatherhood. Females are oriented to beget children within themselves with another's help, that is, they are oriented to motherhood. Both orientations are not only to the initial production of children but also to their whole formation as persons, and to the common life required for responsible parenthood.[26] Due to genetic or developmental variations, these tendencies can be had to different degrees. Stein, by contrast, holds that being male or female belongs to and colors all our activities, including spiritual acts; like each person's unique essence, it is explained by our souls, and men and women constitute, in a way, two species.[27]

Some Russian personalists like Berdyaev, building on Greek Fathers like Gregory of Nyssa, hold that sexual difference is a consequence of sin (or was given only to anticipate the fall) and that we are naturally "androgyne," uniting characteristics of both sexes.[28] Being male or female, on this view, enslaves the person to the species, making one an instrument in the propagation of children, who are born to replace those who have died: having a sex and exercising its potencies immerses us in mortality. But being in love (*eros*) is irreducible to having sexual difference or engaging in sexual activity; *eros* is a self-transcending, affective relation of in-love-ness unto death, like that between Tristan and Isolde in Wagner's opera, a creative force exercised among persons by which we develop our personalities, overcoming reduction to our biological features, including

---

26. Aquinas, *DEE*, c. 5. See *Supplement* q.44.
27. Stein, *Essays on Woman*, trans. Freda Mary Oban (Washington, D.C.: ICS Publications, 1987), especially 91–97. Cf. Burgos, *An Introduction to Personalism*, 230; Dietrich von Hildebrand, *Man and Woman: Love and the Meaning of Intimacy* (Manchester: Sophia Institute Press, 1992). I am grateful to Rob McNamara for discussing Stein's view with me.
28. Berdyaev, *Creative Act*, 172–97; Michael Martin, "Love, Sex, Beauty: Encountering Vladimir Solovyov on Eros and the Divine Sophia," *Logos* 49 (2009): 109–29; Nellas, *Deification in Christ*, 54; and Yannaras, *Variations on the Song of Songs*, trans. Norman Russell (Brookline: Holy Cross Orthodox Press, 2005), especially 33–35. Cf. Balthasar, *TD2*, 374–82.

attaining transcendence over death.[29] It is an intensely felt movement of one's whole person toward union with the beauty of the whole unique beloved, irreducible to their sex, which further multiplies beauty.

On the view that sexual difference is linked to the fall, most of our physical features—arousal, reproduction, eating, excretion, aging, sickness, death, exclusive tribal and familial allegiances, concern for survival, opposition among elements that constitute us, and subjection to physical necessity—are, unlike *eros* and corporeality as such, not part of our nature. Rather, they are the "garments of skin" with which God clothed us after the fall to punish us and as ascetical means to moral reform.[30] On some versions of this view, we first existed in a supra-worldly state and entered into an evolutionary state only because of the fall; all conflict, death, and corruption even among nonpersonal beings are results of the fall.[31]

This view, like the *Nouvelle théologie* view that reduces nature to grace, is opposed by the Thomistic tradition, according to which all these physical features are natural to us. Our bodies are of themselves sexual, animal bodies made of elements at odds with one another, and so are naturally mortal. Natural conflict and corruption are not results of the fall but necessary conditions for there to be many species of beings, each of which reveals God. (However, the Thomist could allow that, just as all angels stamp the world with their character, so fallen angels stamp the world with evil and devastating characteristics, so long as this does not lead to the view on which bodily difference and decay is evil in itself.) Some natural bodily tendencies, like sickness and death, were blocked by God's prelapsarian preternatural gifts; others, like sexual passion, arousal, and pleasure obeyed our practical reasoning and will, such that we could express them when we willed to have children, who do not merely overcome the loss of people to death but are valuable in themselves. Although sexual appetites as natural potencies aim at ends exceeding what fits with reason, they can participate as obediential potencies in intellect such that we desire only what we intellectually determine is good. The fall just led to a lack of fit and obedience between body and soul.[32]

---

29. For a powerful depiction of a model example of *eros*, see the relationship portrayed in Sheldon Vanauken, *A Severe Mercy* (New York: HarperCollins, 1977).

30. Genesis 3:21. Cf. Jude 23. See Nellas, *Deification in Christ*, 45–52, drawing on Gregory of Nyssa, *De anima et resurrection*, in PG, v. 46 (Paris: Vivès, 1863), 108A, 148C–149A; Zizioulas, *Communion*, 53. Cf. David Bentley Hart, "Spirits, Souls ... Tunics?" *Church Life Journal*, November 20, 2018, available at churchlifejournal.nd.edu/articles/spirits-souls-tunics.

31. Bulgakov, *Bride of the Lamb*, 112–14, 176–85. Cf. Paul Griffiths, *Christian Flesh* (Stanford, Calif.: Stanford University Press, 2018).

32. Aquinas, *ST* I, q.98.

The soul is united to the body substantially as its actuality, but it also has open-ended tendencies that are "completed," specified in a definite way, by characteristics of bodily matter. Prescinding from relations to matter, the soul is, as both Berdyaev and Aquinas suggest, prior to sexual distinction. Sexual distinction, I propose, arises as individuation does: I take on sexual characteristics from the genetics of the body to which my soul is originally directed. Just as the soul takes on a unique *haecceitas* because of its orientation to this matter, so likewise the soul takes on the formality of a sex. Each formality of the soul circumincessively affects all the others. As Stein suggests, my sex affects or colors all the other formalities and powers in my soul. Whether I have male or female sex affects how I experience and express my subjectivity, intellect, freedom, affectivity, and so forth.[33] Furthermore, sexual relations and activities are, by this circumincession, able to express spiritual features of the soul like intentionality, affectivity (especially *eros*), and the image of God.

Some Catholic thinkers, building on personalists like Stein or Hildebrand, allege that men are more active, independent, capable of abstract thought, while women are more receptive, relational, nurturing, or capable of emotion. But everyone knows persons who are counterexamples to these claims insofar as they flourish in their sex without these characteristics. There are certainly cultural trends in the behavior and roles of each sex. There are also anatomic, hormonal, neural, and other physical characteristics typically found in each sex, which can facilitate each sex's procreative orientation, but it would be reductionistic to take any of these to be essential or normative for being a man or a woman. Culturally defined roles and meanings associated with each sex can be meaningful *Gestalten*; the value of each should be perceived and given its due response, especially when they help us perceive the unique charm and mystery belonging to persons in their sexual nature. *Gestalten* of masculinity and femininity are primarily bearers of *aesthetic* values; they do not call each person to adopt them, though they do call for respect insofar as they represent the wisdom of one's tradition.[34] My orientation to this body at this time and place requires me to live out that orientation in culturally and traditionally devised ways, but ways of living must be opposed when they enslave us or restrict genuine flourishing. Contrary to Stein, it does not follow from sex

---

33. Cf. Merleau-Ponty, *Phenomenology of Perception*, chap. 5.
34. Cf. Russell Kirk, *The Conservative Mind* (Washington, D.C.: Regnery, 1985), 44–47, 499–500, building on Edmund Burke and G. K. Chesterton.

affecting all formalities that male and female constitute two fixed species or that there is a Platonic Form of each sex. Rather, arising as it does from each person's unique matter, having a sex belongs to each person's unique essence: we are each a member of our sex in our own way. Aside from procreative tendencies (which are also had in irreducibly personal ways), no characteristics belong to all and only men or women.[35]

The experience of *eros* reveals that it is indeed, as Berdyaev says, irreducible to relations involved in sex. *Eros* is a longing for ecstatic, self-transcending union with objective goods and values, especially the particular persons and their unique beauty. God can give a vocation to unite with some particular person and an ability to uniquely perceive that person's value, and this erotic directedness is irreducible to any sexual relation. But relations having to do with sex exceed and are irreducible to *eros*. *Eros* and sex affect one another; to oppose them, as Berdyaev does, is reductionistic. As John Paul II argues in his theology of the nuptial body, the very biological structure of sexual organs reveals our orientation as persons to complete self-gift. The personal, *sun-energeia* union of *eros* can be expressed in the union of flesh in sexual acts, a union which has its highest expression in a child, a new person produced through such acts. However, Berdyaev is experientially justified in claiming that *eros*, as a spiritual orientation, is of higher value than sexual or reproductive relations. To regard human sexual relations as aiming only at new persons, or to regard any human physical activity as only physical or biological, is enslaving and reductionistic. All aspects of the human body participate in and express our spiritual, personal nature. Human sexual acts express intentions, love, and value-perception, and constitute *Gestalten*, especially the common life (*sun-energeia*) of marriage, in which bodily and spiritual *energeiai* are joined; those acts' meaning is found in their orientation to ever-greater self-gift: to these *Gestalten*, to new persons, or to spiritual fruits, like those resulting from virginity for the sake of God.[36]

Sexual acts also reveal value in the weak, vulnerable, and dependent features of the body and their necessity for a flourishing human life; we have a value insofar as our bodies evolved from organisms that naturally engage in sexual reproduction, eat, age, die, and so forth. The garments of

---

35. I am grateful to Maria Fedoryka for discussing many of these points with me.
36. John Paul II, *Man and Woman He Created Them*, 167, 183–88, 211; Scruton, *Sexual Desire*, chaps. 2–4; Marion, *The Erotic Phenomenon*, 195–212; Hildebrand, *In Defense of Purity*, 10–11; and Aquinas, *ST* I-II, q.70, a.3, ad 2; II-II, q.152, a.5.

skin view is reductionistic of this value. Our bodies are fallen garments of skin only insofar as they now often fail to "incarnate" (in a sense to be explained below and in chapter 9) our spiritual acts, or, when they do, our incarnate spiritual acts are fragmented from each other or tend to be exercised excessively or deficiently. We must ascetically and penitentially accept that condition. However, the Christian, who through baptism participates in divinized, resurrected life, should recover aspects of our original corporeality, which will be explored in chapter 9.

Recognizing all these given features of bodily life also reveals the reductionism in Aquinas's contention that in the unfallen state we would have had rational and volitional control over all aspects of sexual relations. Sexual arousal and passion have an intentional structure in themselves, disclose aspects of personal uniquenesses, and allow new kinds of *Gestalten*, all of which would be obscured were they entirely controlled or directed rationally or volitionally. In being aroused and rendered sexually passionate by another, I experience my own uniqueness and that of the other: it is this person and no other that desires me here and now, and vice versa. I am oriented in my body's very moving—and not just in the experiences it involves—to a unique, embodied other; I receive these bodily events as gifts, just as spiritual affects are received as gifts. The proper stance toward them is not control but free and rational *Gelassenheit*. This welcoming of a gift would, when appropriate, have been our stance toward them in an unfallen state. In this receptivity, I am drawn by another into an experience of being embodied: by inflaming passion in me, I experience myself as one with and expressed in my body in a deeper way than usual. I experientially receive my sensing, enjoying flesh from the other and give this to the other; my body is *transfigured*, lifted from its everyday physical status, and rendered a gift for and from another, even in its feeling pleasure and its involuntary movements, such that it expresses and incarnates unique values. Both bodies engaged in sexual relations are joined in a *Gestalt* unified by subjective satisfaction, objective goods, and values of pleasure, vitality, beauty, and holiness, which are all experienced as incarnated.[37]

Sexual arousal is just one example of bodily movement expressing intentional, spiritual acts. Each such experience is ecstatic: I experientially transcend and stand outside (*ek-stasis*) an egocentric focus on myself. But,

---

37. Cf. Scruton, *Sexual Desire*, 26–30. Cf. Marion, *The Erotic Phenomenon*, 112–28, and Hildebrand, *In Defense of Purity*, 60.

contrary to some personalists like Berdyaev, this is never an ecstasy away from my nature, such that I leave it behind and have a purely personal experience. Rather, as Nikolaos Loudovikos says, it is an ecstasy of my whole nature.[38] It is an obediential raising of my nature to a new mode of being and acting. Another example of such an experience is found, as Levinas describes, when I am motivated to ethically serve another person as such. When I see another's suffering or when another speaks to me, I can feel bodily impelled to respond to the other, to give up my bodily goods to serve him or her, to suffer in his or her place. These are bodily experiences of being uniquely called by and rendered responsible to this other person. Like arousal, this is an experience had spontaneously, in receptivity to what the other evokes in me; I cannot produce it autonomously by rational decision.[39] In each case, I encounter the other's spirit expressed directly and immediately in the body. I do not just causally reason from bodily states to interior acts, or see the latter signified in the former. The body is not just causally related to the soul but directly manifests it.

Our bodies can also come into existence impaired or in atypical states (such as blindness, deafness, paralysis, and cognitive impairments), and they can take on such states during our lives. On many contemporary theories of disability, impairment is a lack, dysfunction, or atypical state of a subject that diminishes functioning relative to some norm, while disability is a loss of opportunity to take part in normal life, sometimes due to obstacles from society. Impairments need not be disabilities if society is structured to facilitate the full participation of those with impairments; for example, if a society has developed ways to make those unable to walk able to access buildings equally well as those who can walk, then being unable to walk ceases to be a disability. Apparent impairments can also lead to enhancements in other powers—for example, blind persons sometimes exercise other senses more acutely than seeing persons can—and this allows new cultures and ways of flourishing to form.[40]

Human powers can be specified in irreducibly distinct ways by different kinds of bodies, environments, cultures, and historical periods. Over the course of a life, we express powers differently at different ages. Each

---

38. Loudovikos, *Analogical Identities*, 259.
39. Cf. Levinas, *Otherwise Than Being or Beyond Essence*, 53–59.
40. Barbara Altman, "Disability: Definitions, Models, Classifications, and Applications," *Handbook of Disability Studies*, ed. Gary Albrecht et al. (Thousand Oaks, Calif.: Sage, 2001), 104–5; Ronald Berger, *Introducing Disability Studies* (Boulder, Colo.: Lynne Rienner, 2013), 25–50. I am grateful to Miguel Romero and Kevin Timpe for introducing these ideas to me.

power has a developmental history, existing in distinct states at different ages, and oriented to distinct sorts of acts based on those different states. This is also true of powers in atypical bodies. What are often taken, negatively, to be impairments can also be (especially if communal contexts are right) positive completions or specifications of human powers. Even traits of persons that seem to require high cognitive capacity, such as authentic self-determination, contemplation, or value response, can be lived in a range of irreducibly distinct ways by those who, for bodily reasons, lack such capacity. These ways of expressing, exercising, and completing human powers through diverse bodily structures instantiate unique values and allow formations of distinctive *Gestalten*. No person can actualize their powers in all ways available to human persons; there is an irreducible plurality of ways in which human powers are expressed in different kinds of bodies. It is beyond the scope of this book to explore, but an ethics rooted in irreducible persons must distinguish situations in which apparent impairments ought to be corrected medically from situations in which they are actually distinct forms of irreducible features of persons, allowing for distinct kinds of flourishing.

Minor Categories, Status, and En-Hypostasization

Human nature and personhood are specified not only in relation to bodily characteristics but also in relation to wider situations in which we live. We saw in chapter 6 that we take on modes when our open-ended tendencies for acting in the world are terminated, completed, directed, or specified by items around us. At the second level of being, these modes belong to the minor Aristotelian categories (*actio, passio, ubi, quando, situs, habitus*). At a higher level, they are included in *energeiai*. As a spiritual being with open-ended natural and obediential potencies, I can engage with the world in any way. To be in a place, to exist at a time, to wear clothes, or use tools all give definite, irreducible determinations to this open-ended stance, as do having a particular body or being in a certain culture.[41]

As explained in chapter 6, many Thomists understood the category *habitus* (which includes accidents like wearing a shirt or using a pencil) to include modes that belong to persons when we have artifacts around us.

---

41. Some of this material is from Spencer, "The Category of *Habitus*." See also Charles de Koninck, "Prolégomènes à la dixième catégorie," *Philosophia perennis* 3, no. 1 (1996): 5–23; Antonio Rubio, *Logica mexicana* (Lyon: Ioannes Pillehotte, 1625), 449–50.

My body has the soul's open-ended orientation to engage with the world, and taking up an artifact directs this open-ended stance in a definite way. This directedness modifies how thinking, willing, feeling, and acting are directed to the world. It also can modify how my beauty manifests itself, as when I wear clothes, jewelry, or other ornaments or decorations; cosmetics, the ways in which I adorn myself, reveal a distinctive way that I am ordered to the whole cosmos. Every aspect of the human body displays our spiritual openness, and so every aspect of the human body can be modified and directed by *habitus*. We can also modify nonhuman bodies with *habitus*, as when we put saddles on horses or leashes on dogs. They have an obediential openness to be actualized by us; when this potency is directed in a definite way, a *habitus* results.

Our openness to the world is also directed in irreducible ways by the places and times in which we exist. In most scholastic views, *ubi* was a category containing modes of being bounded or measured—given extrinsic, quantifiable limits—by one's physical surroundings, and the category *quando* contained modes of being measured by times. But times and places not only affect us in a formal, mathematically describable way but also complete us by their qualitative properties. We are irreducibly emplaced, historically situated beings. To be at a beloved home, at a sacred shrine, or at a soulless office bound us spatially in the same mathematically measurable sense, but each place carries values or disvalues that distinctively direct our powers and stance toward the world, as do each historical period and each period of a day or year.[42] Unlike animals that are born with the "tools," "clothing," places, and life states that they biologically need (such as claws, fur, or a niche in an ecosystem), we are, as Arnold Gehlen recognized, incomplete and anticipatory, requiring determination by the things we use and places and times we inhabit.[43] But even in being completed, we retain openness to further modes of completion and a partial alienation from any mode. In this life, we are always "pilgrims" or "wayfarers" (*viatores*), on the way to our ultimate state, and even that state is epektatic.[44]

By these modes (and the *energeiai* they constitute), I include artifacts, places, and times in my personhood. Like the enactive perception theorists

---

42. Cf. Joseph Owens, *An Elementary Christian Metaphysics* (Houston, Tex.: Center for Thomistic Studies, 1985), 208–9; Hildebrand, *Aesthetics*, vol. 1, 299–303.
43. Arnold Gehlen, *Man: His Nature and Place in the World*, trans. Clare McMillan and Karl Pillemer (New York: Columbia University Press, 1988), 24–25.
44. Pegis, *At the Origins of the Thomistic Notion of Man*, 40–43, 55.

mentioned in chapter 2, extended mind theorists describe how cognitive processes like reasoning and memory essentially include things like notepads or computers on which we write or work out arguments: thinking is not just an interior act but extends out into the world.[45] These acts include items that direct my openness to the world. While these items are supposits extrinsic to me at the second level of being, they enter into *sun-energeiai* with me, and so are included in me as person, without ceasing to be other than me.

Our world-openness is furthermore completed and directed by our roles and states.[46] For example, human persons and natures can exist in embodied or separated states; in states of grace, fallenness, integration among powers without grace, or pure nature; in states of being a beginner or perfect in the spiritual life; and in states like being a doctor, a judge, a farmer, and so forth. Ontologically, each state is a collection of accidents, but just as our activities are not reducible to accidents but are also *energeiai*, so a state is not reducible to accidents but is what Balthasar calls a total "way of existing" or "form of life"—what I call a *Gestalt* and what scholastics called, especially in confessional manuals, *status*. Each is a stable disposition of the whole person to exercise human nature and powers in a way specified by conditions under which the person lives.

Status originally meant physical standing, a property that is a member of the category *situs* (which includes bodily positions) and that is a way that one relates to one's surroundings. Jurisprudence applied the notion of *status* analogously to one's "standing" under civil, canon, natural, or divine law. My cultural, legal, and cosmic context make an irreducible metaphysical difference to who I am; they direct my personal openness and thereby confers an irreducible *status*. A *status* is a *Gestalt* of properties in relation to some context; it is irreducible to those properties, since it is a way that whole persons exist and act. For example, to be in the fallen state is to be under the law of sin. To be fallen is not to merely be under God's extrinsic judgment. Rather, it is a state in which my powers are at odds with one

---

45. Andy Clark and David Chalmers, "The Extended Mind," in *The Extended Mind*, ed. Richard Menary (Cambridge, Mass.: MIT Press, 2010), 27–39.

46. Many of the following ideas are from Spencer, "Grace, *Natura Pura*, and the Metaphysics of *Status*." See also *ST* I, q.94–102; I-II, q.109; II-II, q.183–89; Jean-Baptiste Gonet, *Clypeus theologiae thomisticae*, vol. 3 (Paris: Vivès, 1875), 303–95; Peter Maria Passerini, *De hominum statibus et officiis inspectiones morales* (Rome: Typis Nicolai Angeli Tinassii: 1663); Suárez, *De statibus*, Prolegomena 4; Homobono de Bonis, *De humanae vitae statibus* (Bononia: Ex Typographia Victorii Benatii, 1619); and Hans Urs von Balthasar, *The Christian State of Life*, trans. Mary Frances McCarthy (San Francisco: Ignatius Press, 1983).

another, and this disharmony is a deviation from a previous harmony. To be in the *status* of being embodied in a nonresurrected body is to be under physical laws. To be in the *status* of being a teacher is to have the duties of that role. In each *status*, I retain the same nature, powers, and end of flourishing, but I am directed as a whole person to exercise those powers and pursue that end in a distinctive way. These holistic forms of life come in many kinds, from stable *status* to easily changeable "grades" (like poverty or riches) or "dignities" (like a political position). They include "duties" (*offiicia*), whereby one is directed to the good of another (like kingship or motherhood), and "lives" (*vitae*), whereby one is directed to one's own good in a particular way (like contemplative or political lives). They also include sex, age, ethnicity, impairments, and so forth.

A soul's original directedness to a body is a permanent formality in that soul; these forms of life are not permanent, but like formalities, they affect all aspects of life, including how one expresses and experiences one's uniqueness and style. Like *energeiai*, they are variable features of personhood as such. Being a person involves having a role—hence, the historical use of terms for a theatrical mask or role, *prosopon* or *persona*, for denoting a person under law

The scholastic notion of *status* resembles Greek personalist John Zizioulas's patristically influenced notion of *hypostasis* and of persons being *en-hypostasized*. In Aquinas's sense, *hypostasis* denotes what has or bears a nature. In Zizioulas's sense, we take on *hypostases*—concrete, underlying identities—through conditions under which we exist. In the "biological *hypostasis*," a person exists under laws of necessity, subject to death, merely as an instance of a species. In the "ecclesial *hypostasis*," which comes about through baptism, one exists by participation in Christ, free from laws of necessity, as a member of the body of Christ, with one's identity oriented to eschatological life as revealed in the Eucharistic liturgy, already sharing in resurrected life. Each en-hypostasization gives a stable basis for acting and existing, though through the former we exist oriented toward death, while through the latter oriented toward eternal life.[47] Zizioulas shows how our openness can be holistically directed, but (as on the "garments of skin" view above) he reductionistically sees our biological lives as intrinsically fallen and he thinks there are only two possible en-hypostasizations of human nature. Rather, there are as many *hypostases* (in

---

47. Zizioulas, *Being as Communion*, 46–65.

Zizioulas's sense) as there are *status*. I cannot fully perceive a person if my perception is guided just by considerations of what persons are in general, for we only ever exist as en-hypostasized. To perceive a person, I must perceive his or her *status* or *hypostases*, and how they internally modify who he or she is as a person.

We can better perceive this irreducible layer of persons if we again consider the *status* of pure nature (already discussed in chapter 5), in which we would have been en-hypostasized as only exercising natural potencies and as directed only to natural ends. Grasping this possibility helps us perceive the contingency of every *status* that we can take on and how what is natural in us is irreducible to any role or supernatural actuality. As Falque describes, we fundamentally experience ourselves (at least in secular times) as a pure nature, as standing apart from any *status* or special orientation to God, with a core by which I experience just what I can achieve under my own effort in relation to other natural things.[48] Nevertheless, Christ and the Church reveal us to ourselves and direct us to our most perfect fulfillment, divinization. God desires all persons to reach union with him, and, in Christ, has made this possible for all. Because we live under these conditions, all human persons have the *status* of being concretely ordered to grace. David Braine argues that this orientation belongs to us as persons, rather than to our natures; it is not necessary to being a human person but is an additional gift.[49] All human persons in this actual, contingent history of the world have what Rahner calls a "supernatural existential," a determination of our personhood in a concrete direction by God's offer of self-gift to us.[50] This is a contingent *status* such that we are directed in a special way toward receiving grace, and this *status* affects all our formalities.

The debate over natural and supernatural ends develops an older problem from Aristotle, often called the "problem of the two lives."[51] Aristotle argues that our highest flourishing is in the life of contemplation, in which we participate in and perceive divine life and beauty; his term for flourishing, *eudaimonia*, refers etymologically to sharing in the life of

---

48. Falque, The *Metamorphosis of Finitude*, 15–19, 158–59.
49. David Braine, "The Debate between Henri de Lubac and His Critics," *Nova et Vetera* (English edition) 6, no. 3 (2008): 543–90.
50. Rahner, *Foundations of Christian Faith*, 120–28. Cf. Heidegger, *Being and Time*, 42.
51. Aristotle, *NE*, X.7–8; Lawrence Nannery, "The Problem of the Two Lives in Aristotle's Ethics: The Human Good and the Best Life for a Man," *International Philosophical Quarterly* 21, no. 3 (1981): 276–92. Some of these ideas are from Mark K. Spencer, "Full Human Flourishing: The Place of the Various Virtues in the Quest for Happiness in Aristotle's Ethics," *Proceedings of the American Catholic Philosophical Association* 81 (2007): 193–204.

transcendent persons, *daimones*. Yet this life is focused on acting intellectually as much as possible, and seems to abandon embodied activity, such as exercising moral virtues. Most people, in Aristotle's view, do not have the intellectual ability to contemplate and can only aim at the secondary flourishing of exercising political and moral virtue. This is still genuine flourishing because it perfects all of our powers, including our intellects insofar as they are oriented to rule our bodily activities.

One problem raised by these claims is that it is unclear how each life can fulfill us, given that each seems to downplay key personal activities. Another is that these claims suggest that we have two ultimate ends: political life fulfills us as embodied humans, and contemplative life fulfills us as beings able to share in divinity. These problems are solved by the notions of *status* and en-hypostasization. We are ordered by nature to God as common good and to ever-deepening exercise of our powers, especially spiritual powers in relation to God, but this end is specified by *status*: there are as many specified ends available to us as there are *status*. One can flourish as a doctor, an explorer, a politician, a dedicated contemplative, and so forth. In each *status*, our powers are perfected in distinct ways. *Status* and ends fit into a hierarchy, organized around value and objective goods; some ways we can achieve flourishing as human persons are better than others, absolutely speaking, though not best for each person, given each one's vocation. Yet each specification of our end requires all moral or political virtues—the perfection of our bodily powers under the rule of spiritual powers—and contemplation, understood as a loving, free, intellectual perception of and wonder at beings and their beauty, involving divinization or sharing in the life of transcendent persons, which is meant to be incarnated in our bodily stance toward the world. Contemplation can aid active life insofar as it allows grasping human nature, justice, and related forms in themselves, and moral virtue is necessary to contemplate, since one cannot do so if one's lower powers are not rightly ordered. In the many ways our end can be specified, we again perceive our irreducible openness. No human person ever is directed to or reaches the human end in every way that it can be reached; every human person is directed to that end in a unique way.

The Beginning and Conclusion of Embodied Human Life

Human nature is individualized in being directed to a body capable of spiritual life, and the nature of such a body just is human nature, communicated to it by the soul. Wherever we find a living human body—that is, a body, an organism of the same kind as me, which is directed to spiritual activity—we find a supposit with a spiritual nature, and so we find there a person. As we saw in considering impairments, typical ability to exercise one's powers is not a necessary condition for personhood. Likewise, many items in me are given as mine, including purely biological aspects, which are not subjectively available but are still included in me. Personhood is a *Gestalt* that transcends exercise of intellect, will, subjectivity, or other conscious formalities and powers; it is the unity that belongs to things that have spiritual natures.

A human body comes into existence at fertilization, when sperm and egg join in a new organism teleologically ordered to spiritual activity. Exceptions include twinning (when one human body buds off from another and a new soul is created to inform it), cloning (when a human body results from the joining of somatic genetic material and an egg), and certain kinds of activation of stem cells. At no later point in human development is there a clear break in growth, such that one substance is given as ceasing to be and another as beginning. Hence, at no later point than this does individuated human nature or personhood begin.[52] Since it is a human body, the embryo is not just potentially a person, but actually a person, though with many unactualized potentialities. The human organism, from its beginnings, is oriented to developing organs that serve and express spiritual life. Even if these organs never develop, such an organism is oriented to that mode of life. What develops from fertilization onward is a being that is, by nature, subjective, free, intellectual, affective, and has that unique beauty by which one is due love and respect. Human beings who are incapable of exercising spiritual powers are persons since they are of the same nature as persons capable of spiritual activity. Any definition of personhood that focuses on consciousness or rationality so as to exclude them from personhood fails to grasp how personhood consists in a beautiful unity, rather than in those properties.[53]

---

52. Patrick Lee and Robert George, *Body-Self Dualism in Contemporary Ethics and Politics* (Cambridge: Cambridge University Press, 2008), chap. 4.

53. Cf. Miguel Romero, "The Happiness of "Those Who Lack the Use of Reason,"" *The Thomist* 80,

Since the soul is intrinsically and normatively oriented to formally causing, actualizing, and unifying the body, a person's embodied *status* ceases only when the body cannot be unified by the soul, when human unity entirely breaks down and exercise of powers ceases. If the body retains some human powers and unity and its activities have their meaning as aspects of a larger whole and as directed to the human end, human nature and personhood remain. Even human organisms who are "brain dead," lacking brain function and sustained only by artificial means, are persons as long as their bodies have formal unity and some powers remain. Human identity over time requires only that human nature (*ousia*) be present, not that one engage in any particular sort of activity (*energeia*). Even if some activities are efficiently caused by life-support machines, human nature and personhood can remain, so long as some bodily unity remains. The soul strives to implement its powers in the body as long as possible. Death occurs when implementation of human *ousia* and *energeiai* in matter entirely and irreversibly ceases.[54]

Dependencies involved in the beginning and conclusion of embodied life reveal further features of the including relation and ways that one person can participate in another. Pregnancy involves multiple persons, one or more located within another. The baby is not included in the mother's personhood as her organs are included, since it is a distinct person and suppost, with its own *ousiai* and *energeiai*, yet they are deeply included in one another's personhood. A person includes not only parts and principles but also others in the sense of being world-open to them, such that a person can act with them by *sun-energeia*. In pregnancy, mother and child constantly act together (and so have *sun-energeiai*) in sustaining the child's life. While other communities (such as those constituted by friendship, being in love, or holiness) involve greater intertwining of spiritual *energeiai*, and while other communities (like those brought about by sexual intercourse) involve incarnate *sun-energeia*, no other physical coacting involves closer *sun-energeia* than pregnancy. The entire development of the person who is the baby is a *sun-energeia*, a joint activity with another. Insofar as this is the development of a spiritual person, this is a spiritual *sun-energeia*,

---

no. 1 (2016): 49–96; Scott Williams, "When Personhood Goes Wrong in Ethics and Philosophical Theology," in *The Lost Sheep in the Philosophy of Religions: New Perspectives on Disability, Gender, Race, and Animals*, ed. Blake Hereth and Kevin Timpe (Oxford: Routledge, 2019), 264–90.

54. For background on these claims, see Mark K. Spencer, "A Reexamination of the Hylomorphic Theory of Death," *The Review of Metaphysics* 63, no. 4 (2010): 843–70.

as well. This community is continued, albeit with a lower degree of inclusion, in the nursing relationship. In the prenatal *status*, the child cannot be perceived except as included in the mother; while pregnant, the mother cannot be fully perceived except as ordered to sustaining this child.[55] The two form a *Gestalt*, which calls for a value-response of special care.

Setting aside the possibility of future persons being born from artificial wombs, each human person has a transcendental relation of having been born from a mother. Natality or having been born, which befalls us prior to the full awakening of subjectivity but not prior to the beginning of personhood, permanently marks the soul, specifying how one is a gifted one. We have seen that Balthasar describes how subjectivity ideally awakens through the gaze of the mother (or another loving caregiver). This is not a purely experiential event but an incarnate one, which occurs insofar as human persons are open to one another primarily corporeally, exposed to each other "skin to skin."[56] The spiritual awakening of the child by the other occurs, ideally, through the tenderness of touch and fluidity of milk.

Setting aside the possibility of future persons being cloned or developed from adult stem cells, each human person also has a transcendental relation of having been generated by a father. Fatherhood lacks the incarnate *sun-energeia* of motherhood: the father does not experience the child developing within him. Rather, fatherhood is an ordering to taking up responsibility for the child, to a vow of fidelity to the child and of hope in the child's future beyond the father's own life. This "creative vow" is incarnated, like motherhood, in self-sacrifice for the child.[57]

Pregnancy and life-sustaining technologies, in which our acts are efficiently caused by beings extrinsic to us, highlight our dependency on others. Unless both particular things (like other persons and artifacts) and large-scale conditions (like the gravitational pull of the earth, the pressure of the atmosphere, and so forth) continually acted efficiently on us, we would die. Our relation to the natural and artifactual world, and even to the sustaining influence of God, is analogous to the relation of a prenatal child to his or her mother. Likewise, various substances are included in each of us, not as our organs and cells are included but in a more distant fashion. Artifacts like prostheses and cybernetic implants are not part of my substance, yet they engage in *sun-energeia* with me and are *included*

---

55. I am grateful to Barb Dugan for suggesting several of these points to me.
56. O'Byrne, *Natality and Finitude*, 13, drawing on Jean-Luc Nancy.
57. Marcel, *Homo Viator*, 62–117; Marion, *Negative Certainties*, 99–103.

in my personhood, in the total *Gestalt* of my life. Similar are the natural "prostheses" of bacteria and fungi in and on my body (and even in my very cells), with which I am in symbiosis (or *sun-energeia*), and which are necessary for my body's biological functioning (such as my digestive and immune functions) and thereby for embodied subjective and spiritual life. Each bacterium or fungus is an organism and supposit with its own life and ends (which I partly serve), yet like those cells that are parts of me, each is also directed to facilitating my pursuit of my end, revealing the porous boundaries of supposits and persons. In considering the way in which we are entire ecosystems of irreducible organisms, and yet are also irreducible persons, we perhaps see most clearly how personhood includes both irreducible unity and irreducible multiplicity.[58]

---

58. Cf. Merlin Sheldrake, *Entangled Life: How Fungi Make Our Worlds, Change Our Minds, Shape Our Futures* (New York: Random House, 2020).

Chapter 9 The Incarnation of Souls and Persons and the Principle of *Prosopon*

Soul and body are both included in the person, and they are substantially and ontologically united: soul relates to body as formal, efficient, and final cause, while the body signifies, participates in, and is obedient to the soul. Yet, as related in these ways, some acts are in the body and some are in the soul alone. Although the body shares in and is caused by the spiritual soul, and so is always spiritualized, raised above the physical mode of being found in nonpersonal beings, the body is also (as we saw in the last chapter) an aggregate of physical substances with their own natures. Our bodies are irreducible both to having a purely material mode of being like other bodies and to entirely flowing from and manifesting the soul's spiritual mode of being. In this final chapter, I explore how insofar as we normatively are (or are oriented to) bodies like this, we are irreducible to being nothing but souls.

More importantly, I consider here how, as we saw in the cases of sexual passion and ethical relating, activities of body and soul can be joined more holistically than just being connected in the ways explored so far. A view on which soul and body relate only by causality, signification, participation, or obedience is reductionistic of other ways that they relate. Such a view does not adequately guide us to perceive the single holistic beauty that a human person is, or the beautiful liturgical activity which is our ultimate state. As contemporary Greek theologian Panayiotis Nellas says, a human person is not a body or soul alone—or, I add, a combination of soul and matter where these are completely distinct principles—but a "single form of beauty constituted from combination of soul and body."[1] I turn now to experiences that reveal further ways in which they are joined, so as to train us to perceive each person as a single beauty. By introducing ideas that guide us to a complete perception of this beauty, I will have accomplished my goal in painting this metaphysical portrait of the human person.

Layers of Experience

In chapter 1, I described how phenomenological bracketing focuses attention on layers of experience, kinds of experience (and of nonconscious events) that are related such that some of them condition others. For example, subjectivity presupposes and is conditioned by receiving subjectivity as a gift: since they are related in this way, the latter is a deeper layer than the former. I now distinguish layers of experiences of relations between soul and body. In distinguishing these layers, I draw on many phenomenologists' descriptions of experiences, though I set aside their claims that some particular layer is "transcendental," the one condition for the possibility of all other experience. Any such claim is reductionistic. Rather, what conditions and underlies all experiences—what is "transcendental" in the Kantian or Husserlian sense—is the complete structure of the person and of reality. While transcendental subjectivity unites those aspects of soul and body that can be regarded through intentional acts, deeper unity is provided by the substantial soul and by personhood.

Juan Manuel Burgos describes how personalists avoid dualisms that completely separate soul and body by positing three layers of experience.[2] First, entirely intentional, meaningful, self-conscious experiences belong to the spiritual layer. Spiritual experiences like intellectual, volitional, affective, social, and spiritual perceptive acts belong just to the soul, but spiritual acts located in the body will be considered below. Second, the somatic layer includes nonintentional feelings like hunger and pain and biological events, all of which actualize the body's powers. At this layer, the soul operates as the body's formal, efficient, and final cause. Third, the psychological layer—what was called psyche in chapter 1—bridges the gap between the first two layers. It includes acts of imagination (and other in-

---

1. Nellas, *Deification in Christ*, 46.
2. Burgos, *An Introduction to Personalism*, 224.

ternal senses), appetite, association among ideas, dreams, and unconscious mental processes, which are not just caused by the soul, but can participate in, facilitate, affect, and can be obedient to spiritual acts. To make random associations among ideas is not in itself a self-consciously meaningful act but a purely causal event in which one act of imagination causes another. But it presupposes that we can meaningfully—that is, spiritually—grasp the meaning of those ideas. Psychological acts reveal how bodily events are raised above the somatic mode to share in spiritual acts.

Further layers can be distinguished within the somatic layer posited by the personalists. My body can be given as a physical thing that is an object of intentional acts, which Scheler calls a body-object (*Körper*). My body is given as a purely physical object, for example, in some medical or surgical examinations. As such, my body is given as formally structured by my soul, but subjective, self-sensing bodily experiences are bracketed. When those experiences are not bracketed, the body is given as "lived body" (*Leib*), the body as experienced subjectively from within.[3] Within the layer of *Leib*, at least three further layers can be distinguished.

First, I can experience my body simultaneously as object and subject. For example, as Hildebrand says, I can experience a bodily pain both subjectively from within and as an object located at a particular point on my body. Nonintentional sensations, as when a harsh noise assaults my ears or a delightful scene caresses my eyes, can also be given in both ways.[4] In chapter 1, I related Merleau-Ponty's description of how the body's subjective and objective aspects are intertwined, two sides of a fleshly unity, as grasped, for example, in touching my hands to one another. In focusing on that sort of experience, my body is given simultaneously as an experiencing subject and as a sensed object. Similarly, physical things distinct from me are given as simultaneously objects of my intentional acts and as similar to subjects in manifesting themselves. I sense myself in sensing the world, and the world gives itself to my senses; the world at this layer appears as a communion between subjective and objective aspects, each tending toward the other, each an aspect of more fundamental unity. Merleau-Ponty calls this layer *wild being*; its wildness appears in how different beings' subjectivity and objectivity are given as inseparably unified and as tending toward an uncontrollable, self-unfolding communion rather than as entirely distinct

---

3. Scheler, *Formalism in Ethics and Non-Formal Ethics of Values*, 398–415.
4. Hildebrand, *Aesthetics*, vol. 1, 23–24, 114–15.

bodies.⁵ This experience of wildness also reveals our need to encounter the world as uncontrollable and beautifully self-manifesting in this bodily way. Human persons are not only political animals in need of stable communities but also animals in need of bodily immersion in wilderness, the uncontrolled natural world. Fully grasping our irreducibility as persons requires, once again, perceiving and preserving the irreducibility of natural substances and of the whole natural world as an intertwined whole.⁶

Second, I experience my body as a subjective whole. This differs from the first *Leib* layer because it is an experience of the body as a holistic unity entirely from within, without any consideration of discrete experiences on or parts of that body, and without any consideration of the body as object. For example, I can experience my body unified by vitality, an overall sense of health or strength, when hiking in nature and feeling my life caught up in the surging vitality around me, or when caught up in dancing or athletic activity.⁷ Once again, I fully grasp this layer of my vitality in experiencing myself interconnected with all living things, feeling their life and health in itself and as it affects me.⁸ Grasping the irreducible meaning of the human body requires an ecological context. We can grasp this layer through Scheler's "Dionysian reduction" described in chapter 4 or through Michel Henry's reduction, described in chapter 1. This layer is, strangely, a "disembodied" kind of bodily experience, since it includes no awareness of the body as an object or as located in space.⁹ It is purely an experience of my bodily self-sensing, immanent to itself, though it is awakened by immersion in the wider stream of natural life. This layer includes the "Freudian" or bodily unconsciousness, the unconscious aspects of the body that continually affect subjectivity.¹⁰

Third, I experience myself as a subject belonging to the world as a body. As Claude Romano describes it, I experience myself as a distinct body occupying a particular location in the world, reciprocally affecting and being affected by the things around me.¹¹ In experiences at this lay-

---

5. Merleau-Ponty, *The Visible and Invisible*, chap. 4. There is an analogue of wild being given at the psychological layer: I simultaneously express others and myself, and they press upon me to express them.

6. Abram, *The Spell of the Sensuous*, 261–74.

7. Scheler, *Formalism in Ethics and Non-Formal Ethics of Values*, 106–7, 277–80, 336, 585–88.

8. Cf. John Muir, *My First Summer in the Sierra*, in *Nature Writings*, ed. William Cronon (New York: Library of America, 1997).

9. Joseph Rivera, *The Contemplative Self After Michel Henry* (Notre Dame, Ind.: University of Notre Dame Press, 2015), 192–201.

10. Maritain, *Creative Intuition in Poetry and Art*, chap. 3; Desmond, *The Gift of Beauty and the Passion of Being*, chap. 1.

11. Romano, *There Is*, xiii, 170–71.

er, I do not distinguish subjective or objective aspects of myself; rather, I experience myself as a "spread-out body" or (in Gilles Deleuze's term) as "meat" (*Fleisch*)—that is, I experience my material and biological aspects just as subjective, without distinguishing between them and my subjectivity: I am given as a physical object in the world that is conscious as physical. This is how our bodies are given in everyday experience, when we do not reflectively distinguish their subjective and objective sides. My lived body here is, in Falque's terms, a "chaos" (*tohu-bohu*), a mishmash of bodily and animal events, sensations, feelings, desires, pleasures, and pains. Not all of these come to full conscious awareness, but all impact my consciousness. We have seen how matter is a chaotic mixture of indefinite properties in the account of sublimity in chapter 2, in the quantum picture of matter in chapter 3, and in accounts of the multiplicity of the body in chapter 8.[12]

When reasoned about in a metaphysical, effect to cause way, these layers presuppose that my body's matter has been formally structured as a human body with human powers by the soul. They also reveal that my body as a whole shares in my subjectivity, which is a spiritual formality in my soul. We see the body's spiritual mode of being in that I can, though the spiritual act of a phenomenological reduction, come to awareness of my body's layers from the interior, subjective point of view. This would not be possible unless my spiritual subjectivity were present in my body.

Expressive and Hylomorphically Related Acts of Soul and Body

While human vegetative and sensitive acts are partly explained by the soul's causality and flow from the soul's spiritual nature, they are not generally caused by the soul's spiritual acts, nor do they always participate in or obey those acts. But many locomotive acts, like walking or raising my hand, are performed under the command of intellect and will. Here, experientially and ontologically distinct bodily and spiritual acts are related by efficient causation, and the soul rules the body "despotically": I make a choice in my soul, and my body immediately follows that choice. The body's natural

---

12. Emmanuel Falque, *The Wedding Feast of the Lamb: Eros, the Body, and the Eucharist*, trans. George Hughes (New York: Fordham University Press, 2016), 6–15, 41–43; Gilles Deleuze, *Francis Bacon: The Logic of Sensation*, trans. Daniel W. Smith (London: Continuum, 2005). Cf. the twelfth-century scholastic Bernard Silvestris, *Cosmographia*, in *Poetic Works*, ed. Winthrop Wetherbee (Cambridge, Mass.: Harvard University Press, 2015).

potencies are actualized by the soul's acts, without obedientially sharing in a spiritual mode of acting or being.

By contrast, in bodily acts in the psychological layer, like acts involved in habituation and exercise of moral virtue, bodily acts participate in spiritual acts. When I exercise a virtue, I have feelings that are in accord with my intellectual and volitional aims. In these acts, my bodily powers' obediential potencies for acting in accord with intellect, will, and spiritual affectivity are actualized. Here, the soul's powers rule the body "politically," allowing the body to contribute to virtue-formation and exercise.[13] Similarly, when I have happiness in will and affectivity, this can overflow into my sensitive appetites, so that I have bodily pleasure, too. In these cases, there are two accidents and *energeiai*, one in the soul and one in the body, but the body's act participates in and is extrinsically formally caused (or given meaning) by the soul's act.

In a closer conjoining of bodily and spiritual acts, we can perform spiritual acts in the body—that is, a numerically single act can be performed in soul and body together. Husserl describes how my body can be given as a physical object and as a thing that can be moved by will, but also as the direct appearance of spirit in the natural world.[14] Many of the "basic powers" described in chapter 6, such as powers to write, play a musical instrument, and perform athletic acts, are single powers that join bodily and spiritual powers. As we have seen, an act is *spiritual* when it is fully self-conscious, intentional, meaningfully motivated, and performed with a power whereby one is open to all beings or to acting under a formal object that is a property of being. When I dance or play the clarinet, my act has these characteristics; it aims, for example, at the transcendental beauty. My bodily movements express my spiritual intentions; others can perceive the latter by observing the former. When I see another playing an instrument well, I do not observe this bodily act and then reason to or find my attention conveyed to a distinct, underlying volitional, intentional, or affective act. The proficient musician does not first think about how to move his or her fingers, and then command the fingers to obey those thoughts. Rather, he or she acts on the basis of a single power present in both soul and body; the act of playing is a single act inhering simultaneously in soul and body. This act should be understood as a *sun-energeia* between powers of soul

---

13. See Aquinas, *ST* I, q.81, a.3, ad 2.
14. Husserl, *Ideas Pertaining to a Pure Phenomenology*, vol. 2, 297–98.

and body, and, ontologically, as hylomorphically structured such that a bodily act is related to the act of soul as matter to form. Although a bodily act is a union of form and matter, it can, because of the body's obediential relation to the soul, take on further identity by participating in acts of the soul as a new intrinsic formal cause—as that which directly gives kindhood and numerical identity to the act.[15]

In attending to acts of sense perception, I experience the latter to be intrinsically, self-consciously meaningful. Here, too, an act of soul (attention, discussed in chapter 6) is related to acts of body (sense perception) as form to matter; the bodily act is obedientially raised above its natural, physical mode of being such that it is exercised in an intrinsically meaningful, spiritual manner. While I can exercise sense perception in a merely animal way, as when I do so automatically, without subjectively and willfully attending to what I am sensing, I can also exercise sense perception in a spiritual, attentive, fully awakened and alert way. Since the body is related by obedience to the spiritual soul, our corporeal matter can be spiritualized, so that its acts are not just an instrument, sign, or effect of spiritual activity but an expression of spiritual activity, a site where spiritual activity takes place. Similarly, in aesthetic perception, when we are aware of a being's intelligible beauty in the act of sensing it—what Maritain calls "intellectualized" sense—a single act is performed, where act of soul is related to act of body as form to matter.[16]

Furthermore, while we can perform intellectual acts, such as intuitive cognition and insights into Platonic Forms, apart from expressing them linguistically or corporeally, we normally think in language or other sensible media. This is not due, as Aquinas argues, to the weakness of our intellects.[17] Rather, it is a way in which we live out our role as microcosms, as the linchpin of the cosmos tying together the spiritual and the material, and so thinking in language belongs to our perfection.[18] As Hegel describes, we normally must externalize or objectify our intellectual acts in speech or writing to fully understand them.[19] We can use language to express or aid already formed conceptual thoughts, but, normally, thinking itself takes place in (i.e., is mediated by) words or images, not just concepts.

---

15. See Spencer, "What Is It Like to Be an Embodied Person? What Is It Like to Be a Separated Soul?"
16. Maritain, *Art and Scholasticism*, 162. See Spencer, "Beauty, First and Last of all the Transcendentals."
17. Aquinas, ST I, q.76, a.5; q.84, a.3, ad 1.
18. Cf. Loudovikos, *Analogical Identities*, 352.
19. Hegel, *Encyclopedia of the Philosophical Sciences*, §381–83, 425–26.

I often think by trying out different combinations of words and seeing what makes sense; here again, the intellectual act (say, the act of intending essences) is related to the linguistic act in the brain or vocal organs as form to matter, such that they constitute one act. I also do this when I write or read for the sheer pleasure of the words: reading, too, can be an act of the whole body-soul composite.[20]

Similarly, one can think in many other media: the dancer or athlete "thinks in" bodily movements, the sculptor in masses and volumes of bronze or marble. Members of nonliterary cultures and those who are close to the natural world (as David Abram—and Owen Barfield, as seen in chapter 2—describes) often think in terms of animals, plants, landforms, and other elements of their surroundings. They do so through myth, symbol, and actual physical interaction with nonpersonal beings. As in the extended mind view, in this "magical" or participatory thinking, human thought extends into the natural world and engages holistically with non-human substances.[21] Once again, a proper understanding of the relation between soul and body reveals how we are not just at home in the *polis* but require the wild, the whole cosmos, as well; human spiritual life can only flourish in an ecologically flourishing context. In the Christian Hermetic and Sophiological traditions, one learns to think in terms of sensory symbols or *arcana* and in terms of *mysteries* or life-changing liturgical (and, so, sensory) events. Symbols and liturgies include an intellectually graspable content greater than what can be expressed abstractly. This content acts as a "ferment" in the mind, leading, if good, to greater spiritual vitality.[22]

In each of these examples, one's intentional, meaningful, transcendentally open grasp on and fit with the world is facilitated not by a concept or intelligible species but by these material items. At these times, one reasons following a logic dictated not by relations among concepts or propositions but by relations among, for example, images or sounds.[23] Understanding and interpreting various phenomena requires grasping the logic according to which they were made. For example, grasping many artworks is not a matter of abstractly grasping conceptual content but of interpreting how intelligibility is incarnated there.[24]

---

20. Cf. Leclercq, *The Love of Learning and the Desire for God*, 18–20.
21. Abram, *The Spell of the Sensuous*.
22. Valentin Tomberg, *Meditations on the Tarot: A Journey into Christian Hermeticism* (Shaftesbury: Element, 1985), 4. Cf. Martin, *The Submerged Reality*, 192–201.
23. Cf. Calasso, *Ardor*, chap. 9.
24. Cf. Patrick O'Brien, *Pablo Ruiz Picasso* (New York: Norton, 1976), 142.

Similar to the intertwining that Merleau-Ponty describes, expressive bodily acts include, as Hildebrand explains, an aspect that is experienced subjectively and an aspect that can be observed from without.[25] As I described in chapter 1, we often directly see a person's interior states on their faces. Similarly, in a body's whole bearing, we can see persons' body-feeling, the way that they feel in and relate to their body—for example, their noble or pure, immodest or embarrassed relation to their body.[26] One side of my act is better grasped by others than by me. We learn something distinctive about acts like writing or dancing not just by doing them but by reading about them or watching others do them; we observe not a sign of an interior act but a spiritual act present in the body. My perception can be trained, joined hylomorphically to my intellect, so that I directly perceive the intellectualized structure of another's bodily acts.

In each case, spiritual acts actualize the entirety of a bodily act, including its physiological aspects. Neurological events and cells, for example, can obedientially actualized by my soul's acts. Eleonore Stump emphasizes how mirror neurons, a neurological system that is activated both when one performs some act and when one observes another perform that kind of act, are necessary for acts of joint attention or for perceiving another's psychological state.[27] This neurological event is only fully understood if we grasp that it is actualized by a spiritual act. Likewise, other physiological features of acts can be entirely taken up into and informed by spiritual acts. Human persons can just eat like other animals, but eating, with all its aspects, can also be informed by spiritual acts, like intending to carry out customs and rituals, such that it is transformed into dining or feasting. Likewise, mating can be transformed into making love.[28]

My spiritual acts can also relate in all these ways to nonpersonal beings.[29] First, we can relate to material things despotically, efficiently acting on them (as when we act upon matter in making artifacts or killing animals) or using them as the sensory basis for abstractive activity—though this carries the moral danger of using them without concern for their objective good or value.[30] Second, we can relate to them politically, training

---

25. Hildebrand, *The Nature of Love*, 11–13.
26. Hildebrand, *Aesthetics*, vol. 2, 188–89.
27. Stump, *Wandering in Darkness*, 67–80.
28. Leon Kass, *The Hungry Soul: Eating and the Perfecting of Our Nature* (Chicago: University of Chicago Press, 1999), 163–64.
29. Cf. Daniel Horan, *All God's Creatures: A Theology of Creation* (Lanham, Md.: Lexington Books, 2018).
30. Aquinas, *ST* I, q.96, a.2.

and elevating them to share in spiritual activity by *sun-energeia*, as when we domesticate, farm, or train animals, cultivate crops, or when we contemplate, articulate, and offer the world as stewards or priests (as described above). Third, nonpersonal beings can participate in our personhood by *sun-energeia*, so that they express spiritual being, as when an artist thinks with and expresses him or herself in paint or marble. Following my priestly role, I can also express a stance of *Gelassenheit* in my bodily acts, when I allow the world of nature to develop and manifest itself on its own terms. We do this when we safeguard wilderness areas, admire natural landscapes, and wonder at deep space or prehuman natural history.[31] This stance is motivated by recognizing that while the spiritual is ontologically superior to the material, the material bears vital, aesthetic, and religious values that exceed many values belonging to persons.[32] Fulfilling our intrinsic relations to the cosmos requires us to appreciate how nonhuman beings relate to one another and to God in ways unmediated by, unordered to, and unaffected by our spiritual acts. Perceiving the distinct beauty of the natural world in these ways gives us, as John Muir says, a deep sense of peace and vitality, and so an increase in our own beauty.[33] In each of these ways of acting toward nonpersonal beings, our fundamental stance is one of treating the world as an offering or sacrifice, either to ourselves, to itself, or to God.[34]

Incarnated Spiritual Acts

Philosophers in the broadly Catholic tradition have also described acts and experiences in which soul and body are even more closely joined than anything described so far.[35] Spiritual acts can be incarnated in the body and bodily acts can immediately manifest spiritual activity. If we consider what these acts must be to appear as they do, we find that they require

---

31. Cf. Christopher Thompson, *The Joyful Mystery: Field Notes Towards a Green Thomism* (Steubenville, Ohio: Emmaus Road, 2017), chap. 5. However, protecting wilderness can also be motivated by reductionisms about persons, like racism, as when areas are designated as wilderness when they were actually previously inhabited and shaped by native populations. This is not to deny that human persons require wilderness for our flourishing, or that we ought to have a stance of *Gelassenheit* toward the purely natural, but just to say that we can wrongly believe we are doing these things when we are not, due to reductionistic attitudes.

32. See the reading of Robinson Jeffers's poetry in William Everson, *The Excesses of God: Robinson Jeffers as a Religious Figure* (Stanford, Calif.: Stanford University Press, 1988).

33. Muir, *My First Summer in the Sierra*, 180, 212. Cf. Harman, *Guerilla Metaphysics*, 163–64, 174.

34. Cf. Roberto Calasso, *The Celestial Hunter*, trans. Richard Dixon (New York: Farrar, Straus and Giroux, 2020).

35. I am grateful to Maria Fedoryka for discussing some of these points with me.

positing new, irreducible aspects of soul-body relations and of persons. We have already considered some such experiences, like the bodily experiences of being ethically called and of some cases of sexual arousal. In the latter, a physiological response— like changes in one's sexual organs—has an intrinsic intentional meaning. This bodily event, in itself and apart from thoughts or feelings about the person stimulating one, aims meaningfully at that particular person, where that meaning is due to the dramatic or narrative order of events that have transpired with that person. Like aesthetic perception, this experience epistemically "individuates" its object—that is, it gives an awareness of the other person as someone particular, where one is aroused and attracted by him or her.[36] This is, by the criteria already considered, a spiritual act: it is not explicable just by automatic, physical causality, but is meaningfully motivated and intentional or object-directed. Even so, it is an entirely bodily act. It is true, as John Paul II argues, that sexual acts should express love—that is, the spiritual affect of love should relate to these physiological events as form to matter.[37] Nevertheless, sexual responses in themselves, apart from expressing love, have a spiritual structure. Hildebrand describes these experiences as involving the spirit being "pulled" into the body and rendered its "prisoner."[38] Marion describes them as an opening of one person to another entirely through the body, in which the body is "glorified," rendered entirely a manifestation of the unique, self-transcending person.[39] Whether it is rightly described as the descent of the spirit into the body or the transfigured ascent of the body into the spirit, a "materialization of spirit" or a "spiritualization of matter" (to use Vladimir Soloviev's phrases), the result is the same: an incarnated spiritual act, an act that is not a joining of acts of soul and body but a bodily act that has a spiritual structure.[40]

Something similar happens in laughter and in tears. Being able to laugh (*risibilis*) and to express sorrow through weeping (*flebilis*) were taken by the scholastics to be proper accidents (*propria*) of human beings, following from our being both rational (and hence able to grasp the comical or sorrowful) and animal (and hence having the organs necessary for laugh-

---

36. Scruton, *Sexual Desire*, 96–109.
37. John Paul II, *Man and Woman He Created Them*, 183–88.
38. Hildebrand, *In Defense of Purity*, 60.
39. Marion, *The Erotic Phenomenon*, 126–27.
40. Vladimir Soloviev, *God, Man and the Church: The Spiritual Foundations of Life*, trans. Donald Attwater (London: James Clarke, 1938) 134, cited in Finlan, "The Comedy of Divinization in Soloviev," 171. Cf. Balthasar, *GL3*, 279–325.

ter or tears).⁴¹ In many cases, one first intellectually grasps something as comical, and then this grasp is expressed in laughter, as when we laugh at someone. Some laughter is a purely physiological response, as when we are tickled. However, Hildebrand contends that in other cases, when we are moved by something comical, we are meaningfully affected and respond in laughter itself: that bodily event just is the meaningful affective response to the value of the comical.⁴² Here again, we have a bodily act that is entirely spiritual. Something similar can happen in the case of the "gift of tears," recognized by the Christian spiritual tradition (in supplication for which there is even a Votive Mass in the Roman Missal), where one is moved to tears as an act of repentance.⁴³

Another such experience is meaningful or redemptive suffering. Frequently, suffering, especially bodily and psychological pain, is experientially given as a meaningless physical event with which a person is freighted, which imprisons attention and impedes achievement of any human or divine end or objective good. But we can also experience suffering to be meaningful when we grasp it through an intellectual act, seeing it, for example, as furthering some end, as a punishment, or as a necessary consequence of the laws of nature. However, as Levinas points out, most such attempts to render suffering meaningful fail: many instances of suffering are given as exceeding any attempt to render them intelligible, remaining given as terrible mysteries. Suffering can become entirely meaningful, however, when it is lived in itself as a sacrifice, as undergone for the sake of others, including (as we see in the lives of many saints) as participation in Christ's sufferings and abandonment for others.⁴⁴ In some such cases, suffering expresses an act of the soul, but in many cases, bodily suffering is itself a response to and a sharing in others' sufferings. The entire body then takes on a spiritual disposition.

Such experiences are related to the points about en-hypostasization above. I can be en-hypostasized in such a way that my whole life, including all my bodily acts, are ordered toward death: that ultimate cessation

---

41. See, for example, Suárez, *In DA*, d.2, q.4, n. 8.
42. Hildebrand, *Aesthetics*, vol. 2, 418–22.
43. See, for example, Evagrios the Solitary, "On Prayer: 153 Texts," in *The Philokalia*, vol. 1, ed. Nikodimos of the Holy Mountain and Makarios of Corinth, trans. G. E. H. Palmer et al. (New York: Farrar, Straus and Giroux, 1979). 58
44. Cf. Balthasar, *TL2*, 245–59; Levinas, *Otherwise Than Being or Beyond Essence*, 77–90; Richard Cohen, *Out of Control: Confrontations between Spinoza and Levinas* (Albany: State University of New York Press, 2016), 99.

of life is given as the context of all my acts, rendering them ultimately meaningless. I can even be en-hypostasized such that the extinction of the human race or the heat death of the universe is the context in which I live my acts, such that I see all events, not just those of my life, as ultimately meaningless and valueless.[45] But I can also live, in the "ecclesial *hypostasis*" described by Zizioulas, such that I live toward eternal life in hope. As Balthasar describes, Christ reveals how even physical death and separation from God can be modes of the highest life and love: a loving, hopeful adherence to God can be incarnated in every act, even my death.[46] Even sleeping can be meaningfully performed by making one's whole bodily disposition an obediential offering to God.[47] (Sleep is in itself a perfecting and regenerating act or mode of our powers; since it is analogous to various impairments, it should lead us to see them not just as privations, but as positive ways to live human powers.[48])

Similarly, Hannah Arendt describes the experience of the laboring body, the body engaged in repetitive, often rhythmic, movements aiming at procuring or consuming necessities of life. She also describes what she calls "action," the decisive, irreversible, unrepeatable speaking of noble words and performance of great bodily deeds that are meaningful in themselves. When laboring—say, by harvesting a field, digging a ditch, working on an assembly line, or exercising—one often engages in work, the production of some product. But the experience of laboring itself (and of "action"), prescinding from production, is an experience of bodily movement that aims at continuing to live. In labor, one responds to one's surroundings in a meaningful, intentional way in the very movements of one's body.[49] (Something similar is true of the labor of childbirth.[50]) The laboring body as such—like the lived body as such—stands in a meaningful, and so spiritual, relationship to its surroundings. Many acts often called "animalistic"—including sexual acts, bodily laboring, and feelings of "Dionysian" vitality—are really spiritual , though they often tend to be performed viciously or in a way not in harmony with each other.

The structure of incarnated acts is further seen in play, as described by

---

45. Ray Brassier, *Nihil Unbound: Enlightenment and Extinction* (New York: Palgrave Macmillan, 2007).
46. Balthasar, *E*, 117–23.
47. Merton, *No Man Is an Island*, 85.
48. See Aristotle, *OS*.
49. Hannah Arendt, *The Human Condition* (Chicago: University of Chicago Press, 1998), 79–93.
50. Simone de Beauvoir, *The Second Sex*, trans. Constance Borde and Sheila Malovany-Chevallier (New York: Vintage, 2011), 92–93.

Johan Huizinga, following Romantics like Friedrich Schiller.[51] In games, performances, acts of artistic creativity, rituals, and liturgy, human beings step out of the ordinary course of life and perform spontaneous, enchanting, mirthful bodily acts. Acts in a game have meaning within the game but are not done, at least primarily, to secure necessities of life or for any end extrinsic to the game. Play involves skilled bodily acts, which are often done through basic powers that join powers of body and soul. Schiller describes play (and sensory beauty) as joining interior, meaningful form to exterior, sensible matter. Play is a meaningful disposition of the whole body as it responds by its movements to other movements in the game. Just as the whole person, in en-hypostasization, takes on holistic *status* toward the world, so the body can take on such stances. Since it is included in a person with a spiritual soul and is completed by that soul, the human body can be spiritualized or transfigured, making it an equal partner with the soul. Furthermore, insofar as artifacts (especially fine artworks) are used and produced through playful acts, matter outside human persons can incarnate a spiritual, intrinsically meaningful stance toward the world and participate in the whole beautiful *Gestalt* of the human person.

As I said in the introduction, this book is meant to lead us to perceive persons in the manner of one attending a religious festival. Attitudes of festivity, including attitudes of solemn joy and merry-making, are examples of play in Huizinga's sense and so are examples of incarnated spiritual acts.[52] One does not properly attend and celebrate festivals as a means to some further end. Rather, festive celebrations—and, with them, all incarnated spiritual acts—are given as meaningful in themselves, acts of bodily response to value, to other persons, to the glory and beauty of being itself, and, above all, to God. They take us out of the ordinary workaday world. They are ecstatic: in them, we are caught up in what transcends us, such as a beloved person, a vision of beauty, an artistic inspiration, or God. Plato calls many such acts "madness" (*mania*) to indicate that in them we are not entirely under our own volitional, intellectual control, just as in mental illness. In many instances of *mania*, we are enabled to act in ways that are *better* than our ordinary, controlled actions.[53]

---

51. Johann Huizinga, *Homo ludens: A Study of the Play Element of Culture* (Boston: Beacon Press, 1955), 1–13; Friedrich Schiller, *On the Aesthetic Education of Man*, trans. Reginald Snell (Mineola: Dover, 2004), Letters 14–15.

52. Cf. Joseph Ratzinger, *The Spirit of the Liturgy*, trans. John Saward (San Francisco: Ignatius Press, 2000), 13–23.

53. Plato, *Phaedrus*, 244a–245b. Cf. Hildebrand, *The Heart*, 30.

Most important among festive acts are liturgical acts and the liturgical disposition of the body.⁵⁴ To walk in a procession or to go on a pilgrimage is not just to express my intellectual movement toward God in my bodily walking; rather, it is to move toward God with my body, such that the bodily movement itself has that meaning, regardless of whether acts of thinking, feeling, or attending accompany it. Kneeling is not just a bodily symbol of interior reverence or a reminder to myself that I should adopt that attitude; rather, it can be intrinsically meaningful, a bodily *confessio* or self-sacrifice. To praise God, as described by Hildebrand, to exalt him in one's speech.⁵⁵ The body can display liturgical receptivity, creative obedience, *confessio*, and sacrifice. Our very breathing can be a prayer, and our spiritual attention can be present as bodily wakefulness, as the Greek *hesychast* tradition recognized.⁵⁶ Just as sexual passion can be joined to feelings of love such that the two become hylomorphically one, so interior religious acts can be hylomorphically joined to bodily liturgical acts. But just as sexual passion is intrinsically meaningful and spiritual, so are bodily liturgical acts.

The Greek Fathers (building on Neoplatonists like Iamblichus and their notion of *theurgy*, liturgical rites by which one conforms one's bodily acts to the structure of the cosmos and, by participating in or imitating the gods' giving of the cosmos, helps make transcendent persons present) further describe how the bodily senses can be transformed into spiritual senses by participating in divine *energeiai*.⁵⁷ Our senses not only facilitate spiritual activity and receive overflows of joy from the soul but can participate directly in God's *energeiai*. We can perceive God's activities with our bodily senses, as Greek Fathers like Maximus and Palamas contend the Apostles did in seeing the light emanating from Jesus' body at his Transfiguration. We have seen that all positive ontological features of the world are participations in divine *energeiai*, and that among the transcendental properties of being are something like sensible qualities. For these reasons, God has *energeiai* corresponding to sensible qualities and is spiritually sensible in himself.⁵⁸ By having our body's direct obedience to God actualized, our senses can be raised above their natural level of acting to grasp those

---

54. Much of following content is from Spencer, "Perceiving the Image of God." Cf. Martin Mosebach, *The Heresy of Formlessness*, trans. Graham Harrison (San Francisco: Ignatius, 2006), chap. 7; John Paul II, *Man and Woman He Created Them*, 614.
55. Hildebrand, *Liturgy and Personality*, 13–14.
56. Loudovikos, *Analogical Identities*, 107–26, building on Symeon the New Theologian.
57. See Bradshaw, *Aristotle East and West*, 207–20; Marcus Plested, *Orthodox Readings of Aquinas* (Oxford: Oxford University Press, 2012), 78–84. Cf. Shaw, *Theurgy and the Soul*
58. Carnes, *Beauty*, 107–08, explaining the position of Gregory of Nyssa.

divine *energeiai* whereby the sensory world exists. Conversely, our minds can "descend into our hearts"—that is, our mental acts and wakefulness can be experientially centered in our physical hearts, not just understood as organs that pump blood but felt as the site where our affective and sensing selves are centered. Through this prayerful descent, we relate to God in an entirely bodily, felt, sensory, yet fully spiritual, way, facilitated by bodily acts like receiving the Eucharist.[59] The human body—and the whole material world—is constituted such that it can be transfigured, rendered directly participatory in and incarnating of God's activities. This transfiguration is anticipated in the natural incarnational acts described above, in which the body takes on, and is transfigured by, a spiritual mode of being.

The Incarnate Image of God and the Face (or Prosopon) of Human Persons

Spiritual acts incarnated in the body are not entirely explained by the soul's formal causality on the body or by *sun-energeia* between spiritual and physical acts, for they are acts with a structure that normally only belongs to immaterial substances but are here entirely in the body. Explaining these acts metaphysically requires grasping a central aspect of human personhood, the *face* or *prosopon*, and seeing how the image of God is present in our bodies.

We have seen that we image God in our souls and as whole persons, but Aquinas also describes how our bodies include "secondary" images of God: the child comes from and images the parent, and the two share human nature, just as the Son is begotten of and images the Father, and both have divine nature; the soul is in the body as its ruler as God is in the world as its ruler.[60] These are loose analogies to God, resembling the "traces" of the Trinitarian God in all things, more than the images of God in soul and person that signify God's triunity more properly. But I contend that just as my *ousia* and *energeiai* belong to my soul but are communicated to my body, so the proper images of God in soul and person are communicated to my body.

As person, I image God by receiving myself from him, subsisting in my-

---

59. Gregory Palamas, *The Triads*, 35–43. I am grateful to Fr. James Brent, OP, for calling the importance of this point to my attention.

60. Aquinas, *In I Sent*, d.3, q.3, a.1, ad 4; *ST* I, q.91, a.1; q.93, a.3; I-II, q.17, a.8, ad 2.

self, and being ordered to self-manifestation, self-gift, and self-expression. This dynamic structure, John Paul II explains, is expressed in the body's structure: it is received from the soul, the body subsists in itself, and the body is oriented to communions with and self-gift to others. Just as the soul better images God the more we know and love him, so the body better images God the more we give ourselves; both soul and body are oriented, by the image they bear, to divinization.[61]

As Stein explains, the image of God in my soul—my remembering, thinking, and loving self and God—arises only on the basis of bodily self-awareness and self-affection. Bodily self-sensing and self-feeling is a key aspect of my memory of self and God. The body is structured by the soul, and through the connections between soul and body, spiritual activity arises—just as the Son proceeds from the Father, and through their relations, the Spirit proceeds.[62] In liturgical acts, the memory, knowledge, and love of God that image God in the soul are incarnated in the body. As Donald Keefe observes, we remember self and God primarily through bodily engagement with liturgy, sacraments, and concrete narrative memorials, on the basis of which we understand the intelligible order of reality, including God and our fallen selves who are in need of repentance, from which love for God arises.[63] Complete, concrete acts of faith, hope, love, and other supernatural dispositions, of which the image of God in us mostly consists, are bodily, liturgical acts.[64] In the disposition and activity of the liturgical body—and, in a lesser sense, in any incarnate spiritual act—we see the whole image of the infinite in the body and its acts.

Some might object that these claims about incarnate spiritual acts are inconsistent with my earlier claim that spiritual properties cannot exist in matter, a claim that was part of my argument for immateriality of the soul. I claimed earlier in the book that matter's natural potency is just for individual forms and effects, and that matter is present to itself only by one batch of matter being spatially juxtaposed to another, while spirit is open to universal forms and is fully, reflexively self-present. By now contending that spiritual acts can occur in matter, I seem to be undermining my arguments defending the irreducibility of the spiritual soul to the body.

---

61. John Paul II, *Man and Woman He Created Them*, 152, 162–65, 176, 179–81, 214, 239–44, 257, 353, 391–93.

62. Stein, *Finite and Eternal Being*, 449–63.

63. Keefe, *Covenantal Theology*, vol. 2, 280–314. See Spencer, "Covenantal Metaphysics and Cosmological Metaphysics."

64. Cf. Loudovikos, *Analogical Identities*, 32–41.

Corporeal and prime matter are in natural potency only to individual forms, and material bodies cannot naturally be fully self-present and grasp or aim at meanings as such. Experiences to which I appealed in earlier chapters are evidence for there being kinds of matter that are not spiritual, and for human persons having an immaterial, subsistent, spiritual soul and performing spiritual acts that transcend all matter. However, the experience of incarnated spiritual acts requires positing an obediential potency in matter. These acts are not explained by the body or matter as such but by the participation of the body in what transcends the body. We have seen how in acts of divinization (as in receiving and acting through the gifts of the Holy Spirit), we act not by our own proper *energeiai* but by God's, though this involves taking on an accident of participation in God's *energeiai*. Likewise, in incarnated spiritual acts, the material body acts not by its own *energeiai* but by the soul's, though this involves taking on a bodily accident, an actualization of the obediential potency for participating in the soul. In incarnated spiritual acts, such as sexual arousal, play, or liturgy, the body still aims only at particulars. The body does not become fully self-present (i.e., self-conscious in the reflexive manner proper to spiritual acts), nor does it become transcendentally open or capable of grasping universals. These bodily acts are spiritual in that they are intentional, meaningfully motivated, and aimed at their objects through a transcendental formal object.

Phenomenologists have described this phenomenon using an ancient dramatological, metaphysical, and Christological concept, the *face* or *prosopon*. This is an item of experience, a metaphysical item in us, a new image of God in us, and what is needed to explain incarnated spiritual acts. Hildebrand introduces the notion of the face as a feature of all beings and values. Animals, landscapes, moral virtues like justice, and the unique value of each person are all described as having not just particular manifestations—what I call *energeiai*—but also a unique, holistic self-manifestation or beauty whereby they fully manifest, announce, and give themselves as the unique supposits or principles that they are.[65] No being or value just statically or impassively calls for a response but enters instead into dramatic interrelations with other beings and values. Hildebrand names this holistic, dynamic self-manifestation by analogy to the human face, where,

---

65. Hildebrand, *Aesthetics*, vol. 1, 85–88, 297, 315; Hildebrand, *What Is Philosophy?* 99–101; and Hildebrand, *Ethics*, 6.

especially in the look of another's eyes, the sound of his or her voice, and the variability of his or her facial movements, the other is disclosed as a person, in a way not ordinarily paralleled in other parts of the body. No being can exist without *energeiai*, but a being could exist without a face, without a distinctive, definitive self-manifestation, were it damaged or obscured in certain ways.

Levinas focuses on the distinct sense in which embodied persons (rather than beings and values in general) have faces: in seeing another's eyes or hearing another's voice, I experience his or her untotalizable holiness and otherness, which exert a unique ethical, divine call to protect and serve this other, both for his or her own sake and for the sake of God, who calls me in the look of the other's face.[66] Levinas resists talking about the face in aesthetic terms: in his view, we see another's face as such (and the image of God in him or her) not when we admire its beauty but when we feel ourselves bodily called, in an absolute (and so divine) way, to respond ethically with service, protection, and kindness.

Hildebrand shows how these ethical and aesthetic aspects of the face are joined. We have seen that, considered holistically, each person is a unique beauty. Experientially, the beauty that each person is appears especially in his or her face, which simultaneously invites aesthetic admiration and ethical response. Similarly, Marion argues that another's face can call for ethical, aesthetic, and cognitive responses.[67] Certain spiritual or transfigured states render another's body "all face"; Marion gives as examples a loving, sexually passionate person or a nursing mother, while the film director Robert Bresson gives the example of a model or actor in a successfully directed film.[68] Whereas ordinarily another's eyes and voice primarily disclose his or her personhood, in incarnated spiritual acts, his or her whole body becomes like a face, holistically disclosing his or her personhood and spiritual mode of being. The sensing and vegetative body fits its surroundings only in a potentially intelligible way; the spiritualized body is intrinsically and actually intelligible, responding to its surroundings in a meaningfully motivated way and appearing as such. We have seen how all material things are actually intelligible insofar as they are beautiful, but in the face—and the body rendered all face—we find a higher mode of

---

66. Levinas, *Totality and Infinity*, 194ff.
67. Marion, *In Excess*, 118.
68. Marion, *The Erotic Phenomenon*, 125–27; Robert Bresson, *Notes on the Cinematograph*, trans. Jonathan Griffin (New York: New York Review Books Classics, 1986), 22, building on Michel de Montaigne.

beauty, matter rendered spiritual, meaningfully motivated and uniquely, intentionally related to things.

Phenomenologist Richard Kearney arrives at the notion of the face or *prosopon* by his version of the phenomenological method.[69] Husserl brackets consideration of beings as real, so as to arrive at their essential structure; Heidegger brackets consideration of individual essences and beings, so as to arrive at Being itself; Marion brackets consideration of Being, so as to arrive at givenness. Kearney proposes a fourth, "eschatological" or "prosopological," reduction. After having performed those other reductions, and without denying what they each reveal, we bracket these rarified focuses on essence, being, and gift, and the misleading impression they can give of showing transcendental conditions for all other experiences. We focus instead on the "everyday," the "accidental and the anecdotal," the ephemeral, flesh-and-blood features of other persons whereby they reveal themselves and we come to encounter them face-to-face. We thereby seek to perceive each concrete person (*prosopon*) as an "epiphany" or "eschaton," as the incarnate presence of the divine and as called to a greater revelation and reception of themselves. Underlying essences, being, and the given is their gracious possibility; in encountering real people and things, but with our perception trained by the phenomenological reductions, we can see the gratuity that allows them to be given, to be, and to be intentionally grasped. They appear as called to and capable of living up to their divine *Logos* or pure form, to which God calls them. This reduction involves taking up a stance of open and welcoming "hospitality" to all the possibilities that are offered to us in persons, considered in their fullness. The full, unique face (*prosopon*) of the other is their uniqueness thoroughly incarnated and made manifest, an entirely bodily image (or "micro-epiphany") of God.[70]

In a similar method, phenomenologist Samuel Rocha also helps us grasp others' faces in this full sense. Even more fundamental than being given, things *offer themselves*. To be given implies some completion of the act of giving; to be offered is a first stage of giving, an appearance that need not be completed. Some things, like the offer of a gift, do not involve any

---

69. The content of this paragraph and the next are from Spencer, "The Many Phenomenological Reductions."
70. Richard Kearney, "Epiphanies of the Everyday: Toward a Micro-Eschatology," in *After God: Richard Kearny and the Religious Turn in Continental Philosophy*, ed. John Panteleimon Manoussakis (New York: Fordham University Press, 2006), 4–8. Cf. Loudovikos, *Analogical Identities*, 269.

givenness, nor are they a being or object whose meaning is constituted by me. Of course, when someone offers me something without being able to give it, the offer *qua* offer is given to me, but what is offered is not given to me—yet it appears in the offering. Since the offering does not even need to be completed to appear, it is entirely untotalizable. If we bracket persons as given, we can see their initial self-offering, their hospitality and opening to being hospitably received, which is displayed in the expressions of their face or in their utterances of their voice, whether those are fully given or not. The offering or sacrifice again appears at the foundation of reality.[71]

The face or *prosopon* is a fundamental metaphysical feature of persons. Both in its ordinary placement around the eyes and mouth and in its extension to the whole spiritualized body, the face is a privileged, perceptible manifestation of our personhood, unique beauty, and imaging of God. In the face, a person's infinitude—participation in God, openness to spiritual acts, and openness to be hospitably participated in by others—is sensible. In perceiving another's face, we see, hear, and touch (and even, as parents and lovers know, smell and taste) his or her uniqueness and irreducibility to anything nonpersonal. But as Levinas's ethical analysis shows, although it manifests itself, the face is never fully given to the perceiver, such that it is at the perceiver's disposal; rather, a person's face, in Rocha's language, offers itself to perception and calls for a response, without being totally given and graspable. In seeing another's face, I see both how I can act with that other, but also how that other is real, radically extramental, separated and independent from me and all others, never fully given over to me. More than *energeiai*, a face or a privileged site of self-offering belongs to and shows best our personhood.

Introducing this new metaphysical aspect of the person allows us to more fully grasp the possible irreducible *status* under which human nature could exist. Cajetan holds that the greatest *status* under which human nature can exist is in Christ, as united in *hypostasis* or in person to a divine person, such that it wholly characterizes and is exercised by that person.[72] The highest *status* under which most other human natures can

---

71. Samuel Rocha, *Folk Phenomenology: Education, Study, and the Human Person* (Eugene, Ore.: Pickwick, 2015), 4–8; Rocha "Folk Phenomenology and the Offering of Teaching," *Journal of Curriculum and Pedagogy* 13, no. 2 (2016): 124–30; and Samuel Rocha and Adi Burton, "A Phenomenology of Utterance and Prophetic Teaching in the Threshold," *Journal for Continental Philosophy of Religion* 3 (2021): 144–63.

72. Cajetan, *In I-II ST*, v. 7, q.109, a.2, 292.

exist is being united to God in *energeiai*, such that we wholly act with God. But as Maximillian Kolbe points out, there is a way of being united to God intermediate between these: one can have the same *face* or *prosopon* as a divine person—that is, a human person and a divine person have the same privileged site of appearance and self-offering, such that the two not only always act together (as we should) but also always appear as one. Kolbe sees this *status* in Mary, who he understands to be the quasi-incarnation of, or one in *prosopon* with, the Holy Spirit.[73] Similar is the view on which Mary is the privileged revelation of divine wisdom (*Sophia, Sapientia*) or beauty, God's humble but definitive creaturely self-revelation, his face in a created person.[74] Regardless of whether one affirms these Mariological claims as such, they illustrate the difference between *prosopon* and *energeia* in human persons.

The face is also where the person can be most obscured: it can reveal the truth about the person, but in its looks, speaking, and so forth, it can also lie, masking who the person is (even from him or herself), or dissemble, inauthentically displaying some truth. Heidegger explains inauthenticity as "everydayness": that is, to act solely on the basis of influence from others or on the basis of routine, as we often do in everyday life.[75] But in genuine perception of faces, and in allowing my body to become a face and incarnate spiritual acts, we see another sense of everydayness, in which ordinary life, freely lived, becomes a site for manifestation of the full unique value and holiness of persons. To perceive the ordinary faces of human persons in this sense is to return from all our metaphysical and phenomenological wanderings and abstractions to see ordinary people in ordinary life, as if for the first time, in all their glory.[76]

Liturgical Divinization

With the notion of the face, my portrait of the irreducible human person is nearly complete. I have unpacked different perceptions of the human person in various principles, drawn from the Catholic tradition, which

---

73. See H. M. Manteau-Bonamy, *Immaculate Conception and the Holy Spirit: The Marian Teaching of St. Maximillian Kolbe* (Libertyville, Ill.: Marytown Press, 2008). Cf. Bulgakov, *Bride of the Lamb*, 91, 97.

74. Cf. Charles de Koninck, *Ego Sapientia: The Wisdom That Is Mary*, in *The Writings of Charles de Koninck*, vol. 2, trans. Ralph McInerny (Notre Dame, Ind.: University of Notre Dame Press, 2009).

75. Heidegger, *Being and Time*, 41ff.

76. Cf. Adam G. Cooper, *Naturally Human, Supernaturally God: Deification in Post-Conciliar Catholicism* (Minneapolis, Minn.: Fortress Press, 2014), chap. 8.

culminated in this account of the face. Guided by all these principles, we can perceive that the most concrete and everyday personal feature, one's own face, is the privileged revelation of one's irreducibility and beauty.

What remains is to draw some last conclusions about the ultimate, best state of human persons. I make these claims on the basis of my analysis throughout this book of the structure of our powers and other aspects. While our ultimate state transcends anything that we can fully now conceive, we can determine some parameters into which such a state would have to fit in order to be fulfilling to us. At the very least, such a state must fit with all my aspects; did it not, it could not be fulfilling to me as the kind of being I am. We have seen that we are ordered to God as our final end and to the ever-deepening exercise of our spiritual powers in relation to him, in a way open to creatively willing further goods, especially to other persons. Our ultimate state includes but is not reducible to our natural or supernatural end of God and of lovingly perceiving him, though our ultimate state has to do with God in all respects. In our ultimate state, we are motivated not just by objective goods and ends but also by values and persons in themselves. In addition to reaching God as our end, our ultimate state also includes making affective responses to God for his own sake.

It also includes making due response to other valuable beings, especially other persons. Our powers for social acts and spiritual perception would also be fulfilled in our ultimate state. I will experience my ultimate state in a way distinctive to me, based on my unique essence, style, and *status*. Since others can participate in my personhood, I can hospitably open to them the possibility of sharing in my unique mode of happiness, just as by loving another person in this life I can share in his or her way of being open to the world. My happiness will be enhanced by receiving and sharing in that of others; it will be an essentially interpersonal state. I cannot be fulfilled alone but only as a member of a perfected community, an integrated part and a whole among wholes in the body of Christ, the Kingdom of God.

We have seen how our natural and supernatural end of lovingly contemplating God and intimately sharing in his *energeiai* can be attained just through powers in my soul. When matter is rejoined to my soul in the resurrection, happiness will overflow into the resulting body—that is, my intellect and will shall efficiently cause sensitive pleasure. But my analysis of expressed and incarnated spiritual acts requires a further account of the role of the body in our ultimate state: the body can be fulfilled and rendered happy in further ways than just by receiving the soul's overflow; it can also share in divine *energeiai*. In such a state, the beauty to which the human person is identical would be revealed definitively in the body rendered all face. Our ultimate state is the state of divinization where we live entirely, body and soul, in a liturgical way, contemplating and acting in relation to God, as holistic beauties receiving beauty from God, who is beauty itself. In such a state, we would have not just moments of being all face but would permanently have faces, that is, we would be permanently and entirely in that spiritualized bodily condition, with all our incarnate spiritual acts performed harmoniously in a divinized way.[77]

On most scholastic views, the resurrection of the body is needed to complete human nature and personhood. While the separated soul, without the body, can achieve all that is essential to the end of a loving beatific experience of God, it is not, on those views, a complete person or human being since it lacks matter, which is regarded as essential to human nature. On some scholastic views, the soul is impeded from being fully happy because it lacks something essential to its nature and so cannot enjoy its happiness as fully as it would were it whole; on other views, the soul longs to govern the body, and so, even while achieving its end, has an unfulfilled desire.[78]

But I have argued that the separated soul does constitute a person and contains the whole human *ousia*. One might worry that I have removed a key motivation to hold that the resurrection is necessary or important for our happiness. However, while I have removed some scholastic motivations for this claim, I retain a strong motivation to affirm that the resurrection is desirable and important for human persons. Insofar as they are oriented to intentional acts, the spiritual powers of the soul are fulfilled (or reach their end) by achieving their objects; the intellect, insofar as it is oriented to grasping being, is fulfilled by the vision of God. But our spiritual powers are also oriented to express themselves in bodily acts, to hylomorphically bestow their identity on bodily acts, such that a single act is performed in body and soul. The intellect does not just overflow happiness into the body, causing distinct acts of happiness there; it also expresses itself in the body such that our bodily perceptual and appetitive powers

---

77. C. S. Lewis, *Till We Have Faces: A Myth Retold* (New York: HarperCollins, 1984), 335.
78. Aquinas, *ST* I-II, q.4, a.5, 6; Bonaventure, *In III Sent.*, d.5, a.2, q.3, 136–37; Matthew of Aquasparta, *Quaestiones disputatae de anima beata*, q.2, 209–23.

share in acts of seeing and loving God, as part of the essence of those acts. In performing spiritual acts in the soul, I ideally take on the motivation in which, out of a fullness of bliss, I long to give that bliss to others and especially to my own body. More importantly, the soul is ordered to raising matter to share in its spiritual mode of being and to incarnate itself in matter. We are not in our best state until these things have occurred—that is, until our beauty reveals itself in every way pertaining to human persons. That requires a body, and so, the resurrection is necessary for our ultimate flourishing state.

The scholastics claim that the resurrected or spiritualized body will have various gifts, for example, it will be able to fly and move very quickly, be unable to be harmed, and be transparent and shining with light.[79] I need not assess whether these claims are plausible; I do not exclude them as possibilities. What I do claim is that in the ultimate state of the human person, the body is all face, entirely and permanently acting in a spiritual way, a privileged site of the revelation of our own unique beauty and the beauty that is God. It is not only rendered entirely subject to the soul's efficient causality or control, as on many scholastic views. Rather, it is rendered an incarnation of the soul and of our personhood, in ways anticipated by current incarnate spiritual acts. Among scholastics, Bernardine of Siena comes close to this view. He holds that the body's happiness is not just accidental to the soul's happiness (as many other scholastics claim); the body does not just contribute to the "well-being" (*bene esse*) or "ornamentation" of the soul's happiness, that is, it is not just a welcome addition to a happiness that already has all that is essential to it apart from the body. Rather, according to Bernardine, the body's happiness is "consubstantial" with the soul's happiness.[80] In my terms, the happiness essentially in the soul becomes present in the body by expression and incarnation. The separated soul has no face in the sense proper to human persons; while the person is present there and can engage with others, he or she cannot engage in the definitive self-revelation of persons, nor can he or she fully manifest the image of the infinite God. For all this, the body as face is needed.

In incarnated spiritual acts, we see definitively how we are made ac-

---

79. See, for example, Aquinas, *SCG* IV, c. 86; *In IV Sent.*, d.49.
80. Franco Mormando, "What Happens to Us When We Die? Bernardine of Siena on the Four Last Things," in *Death and Dying in the Middle Ages*, eds. Edelgard DuBruck and Barbara Gusick (New York: Peter Lang, 1999), 126–29. I am grateful to Fr. Steven McMichael, OFM, for calling my attention to Bernardine's views.

cording to the image of God (*ad imaginem Dei*)—that is, made following the paradigm of the true image of God, Jesus Christ, in whom the spiritual and the material are perfectly and covenantally joined.[81] Maximus tells us that Christ did human things, like suffering, in a divine manner and divine things, like miracles, in a human manner.[82] Likewise, when our spiritual mode of being is fully incarnate in the body, we will do all bodily things in a spiritual manner, and spiritual things, like contemplating and spiritually loving God, in a bodily manner. We will be holistically divinized, acting entirely by conscious, freely assumed participation in divine *energeiai*. We will be as beautiful as we can be at any moment and enabled to epektatically become ever more beautiful. Then, we will fully participate in the Son of God, and will, in him, be entirely children of God. We will be entirely bodily responsive to God's bodily presence to us and so will rightly be called the spouse and friend of God.

The human soul and person are oriented to humility, both to recognizing their own intrinsic lack of being and need to receive being as a gift, and to the humble *kenosis* or self-sacrifice that is a transcendental property of all being. This is obscured by pride, by which we seek only our own higher beauty and to seize beauty that properly belongs to what is greater than us rather than consenting to receive beauty along with others. It is also obscured by concupiscence, by which we seek only to seize beauty from what is ontologically lower than us for our enjoyment rather than receiving that beauty as a gift. Human persons and souls are oriented to humbly receiving beauty from God through what is ontologically lower than us, as in the sacraments of the Church and as when we experience God sacramentally in the corporeal world. We can and must receive beauty in these ways because we have, and normatively are, bodies. Matter in us is not just instrumental (for example, facilitating intellectual activity) but is crucially required for us to reach our highest value, humble holiness, and so become definitively beautiful as human persons. It is the beauty of human persons that can unite all the other beauties in the universe, without ever annulling their distinctive beauty and its value. The body is most necessary to live the properly human life, the holy life of incarnated, humble, everyday spiritual activity—as elaborated, for example, in the Little Way of St. Thérèse of Lisieux.[83] In the human body standing in obedience to the soul, such that

---

81. Genesis 1:27. Cf. Keefe, *Covenantal Theology*, vol. 1, 318.
82. Maximus, *The Ambigua*, 26–27.
83. Thérèse of Lisieux, *The Story of a Soul*. Cf. Ulrich, *Homo Abyssus*, 41.

spiritual acts are incarnated there, material, spiritual, and divine *energeiai* all intersect in the transfigured finite body, and the fullest revelation of beauty can occur.[84] We see this in Christ's incarnate life, in his sacrificial self-offering upon the cross, and in his resurrected and Eucharistic flesh. Given these orientations of the person to God through what is lower than him or her, our ultimate state must be a bodily state. This does not negate my earlier conclusions that it involves intellectual contemplation and other spiritual acts, but these will be not only present in the soul but also incarnated and expressed in the body.

Our ultimate state is best anticipated by the full liturgical life centered on the Eucharist, the ongoing covenantal joining of God and humanity.[85] (Even if one thinks that Catholic liturgical theology is false, one can still take this account as a hypothetical model for our ultimate state, revealing the sorts of acts we would have to perform in order to be completely fulfilled, given the various aspects of personhood.) In liturgy, when properly performed, we perform the highest acts of contemplation and love, including through bodily acts that express and incarnate worshipping God and entering into communion with other human persons, without denying the importance of solitary acts and aspects of persons.[86] We have already seen how liturgical acts like processing and kneeling are incarnate acts of worshipping God, but in the Eucharistic liturgy, even our very physiological acts of eating and digesting become incarnate acts of worship, of offering and giving ourselves to God and receiving his self-offering and self-giving. Liturgy is focused on the cycle of official ecclesial rites (such as the Mass, Divine Liturgy, or Divine Office). But in engaging in liturgy in this life, we are so disposed toward God as whole persons that all aspects of our lives become oriented around to him in a liturgical way. For the person who incarnates a liturgical disposition, liturgy includes things like freely and creatively performed ritual devotions, parish festivals, acts of spousal love, merry conversation, meditations upon nature or art, *Gelassenheit* toward nonpersonal beings, hikes in the wilderness and swims in the ocean, acts of kindness and alleviation of suffering, experiences of suffering offered in sacrifice, mourning for the brokenness of the world and for one's own

---

84. Cf. Luke Timothy Johnson, *The Revelatory Body: Theology as Inductive Art* (Grand Rapids, Mich.: Eerdmans, 2015); Falque, *The Metamorphosis of Finitude*.

85. Keefe, *Covenantal Theology*; Russell, *The Doctrine of Deification in the Greek Patristic Tradition*, chap. 8, summarizing Dionysius and Maximus.

86. Cf. Loudovikos, *Analogical Identities*, 110, following Symeon the New Theologian.

sinfulness, everyday labor done in pursuit of the highest goods and values, and so forth. This disposition includes and incarnates feelings of solemnity, merriness, festivity, contrition, compassion, mourning, celebration, excitement, awe, and spontaneous bestowals of kindness and mercy upon others, which Levinas calls "the little humanity that adorns the world."[87]

Liturgy involves cycles—basically the same feasts each year, the same offices each day, the same readings each year, similar daily activities of labor and love, the same seasonal and astronomical events. But it also involves a sense of things deepening: the feasts and seasons mean something new to us as they come around each year, our daily labors become greater bearers of value, new feasts are added as all things are taken up into service of God. The liturgical life is *epektatic*, never static or entirely cyclically repeating, and this continual deepening of liturgical activity is not a process in pursuit of a further end but an incarnated act that is valuable in itself.[88] A remarkable feature of liturgy is that all things can be taken up and celebrated in it—even including aspects of reality that seem to do violence to it; hence, there are even liturgies that celebrate battles, like that of the feast of Our Lady of Victory. The ultimate state is not one in which struggle (*agon*) is entirely left behind; in the numinousness of God and sacrificial rites, there is a place even for the beauty of the horrifying and sublime. We are trained by liturgy to perceive beauty supremely in what might ordinarily be thought the most shameful and ugly of all spectacles, the Crucifixion of the Son of God. Through liturgy, we come to see how beauty is found not only in what shines forth pleasantly, holistically, or awe-inspiringly, or in what is formed and ordered; beauty can appear unexpectedly: its full depths and range of possible manifestations can never be entirely anticipated. In the mystery of the cross, revealed to us in the liturgy, we see the form of Christ's loving descent into and embrace of formlessness and suffering. We see how even feelings of horror, anxiety, and abandonment, felt in the spirit and expressed in the body, can be joined with divine *energeiai* and take their place in the beauty of sacrificial love. The very brokenness and multiplicity of the human body incarnates and shows Christ's sacrificial offering of himself to us and to the Father.[89] The fundamental notes of beauty, found, above all, in self-gift and self-offering, are present supremely in the darkest of dramatic spectacles. Not only can suffering express and

---

87. Levinas, *Otherwise Than Being or Beyond Essence*, 185.
88. *Contra* Griffiths, *Decreation*.
89. Balthasar, *GL1*, 451–511; *GL7*, 211–38.

incarnate spirit, but it can incarnate the structure of beauty in an entirely unexpected and unique way. This teaches us that there very well could be ways that beauty can be revealed in the body that we cannot now anticipate, and that will hopefully be perceived in the resurrected body.

The total liturgical life allows us to perceive all things as beautiful, and it thereby makes us entirely beautiful—and so, since persons fundamentally are beauties, it entirely fulfills us as persons. In the Eucharistic liturgy, we experience beauty with our whole person, even with our taste, touch, and nutritive acts. The liturgy renders all material things sharers in face, able to be grasped and enjoyed as intrinsically self-manifesting, uniquely valuable, and manifestive of God by directly sharing in and being transfigured by his *energeiai*, such they do not just signify God, but directly reveal him and make him present.

Although our ultimate state entirely transcends our current life, that life can already participate in resurrected life. Even on the natural level, the body can be spiritualized, obeying the soul's nature, as seen in the face and in its extensions to the aroused, laboring, worshipping, playing, or suffering body. It is even more spiritualized for those living the life of supernatural grace. Even now, all aspects of human bodily life, down to our vegetative acts, can be taken up into incarnate spiritual or liturgical life, either naturally or supernaturally, when one seeks to perceive and perform all actualizations as meaningfully motivated.[90] The multiplicity and temporality of the human body are not left behind in our ultimate state, nor are the many substances, fluids, quantified matter, and so forth in us absorbed or annulled in some overarching spiritual unity. Rather, when the body is all face, each and every aspect of the body, in its own proper nature, will be spiritualized, obedientially rendered fully meaningful. We aim at an ultimate state in which we are perfected as whole persons, with all our irreducible aspects, rather than at an ultimate state in which some aspects of human life are done away with for the sake of those that are higher. For this reason, the metaphysician of irreducibility must affirm that material, vital, vegetative, and animal processes, experiences, and acts continue and are perfected in the resurrected body, but all rendered spiritual in some

---

90. An example of this is the life of Jewish *halakha*, in which all aspects of life are lived in light of divine law; see Josef Soloveitchik, *Halakhic Man* (New York: Jewish Publication Society, 1983). For phenomenological analyses of how all aspects of the body can be taken up in meaningful bodily action, see Maurice Merleau-Ponty, *The Primacy of Perception*, trans. William Cobb (Evanston, Ill.: Northwestern University Press, 1964).

currently not fully conceivable way. When the Kingdom of God, the new heavens and the new earth, is likened to a feast or a marriage, to a life of farming or of going up mountains, these are in some sense literally true.

We have already seen how, by participating in other human persons, we can enjoy God and other valuable items, including those persons themselves, in ways to which only they can open us. We have seen how in our epektatic state we must creatively do good to others. Hence, my ultimate state essentially must include other created persons and incarnated relations to them. Because of my intrinsic relations to nonpersonal creatures, there will have to be other creatures in the world to come, like animals, plants, mountains, artworks, and so forth. My ultimate state is centered on God as my end and as most valuable, and it is thereby a state in which I am ontologically perfected, but that state also requires my relations to other creatures be fulfilled. Our liturgical consummation is a continual sacrifice: it involves receiving the world from God in love, letting it be free through a stance of *Gelassenheit*, and offering it back to God, and it involves receiving love from God and bestowing it in compassion on others. Furthermore, our beauty, to which we are identical, includes our intrinsic relations to other creatures; we will not appear as beautifully as we can without them.

It is beyond the scope of this book to determine whether the organisms that live now will be preserved and resurrected, or whether there will be new ones there. In either case, liturgy both in this life and in our ultimate state requires an "integral ecology," a stance that gives a proper, interconnected place to all things.[91] On the one hand, creatures around us are transitory. Perceiving their beauty requires grasping them as transitory, for there is a unique beauty, like that of the *wabi-sabi*, that belongs to the ephemeral and even the decaying, and manifests their being. If current creatures were preserved and resurrected, it would render the way in which they are currently given somewhat deceptive. But on the other hand, each human person is intrinsically, transcendentally, analogically related to every other creature. We would not be as fulfilled as possible if all creatures were not present with us in the resurrected state. Since our fulfillment is ever-deepening, and no one can be fulfilled in every possible way, none of this is a reason to affirm that all creatures (or even all persons) will be present in our ultimate state. Nor is the presence of these

---

91. Pope Francis, *Laudato Si',* Encyclical Letter (May 24, 2015), chap. 4.

other creatures required for us to reach our natural or supernatural ends; their presence would fulfill relational aspects of our personhood, not our teleologically ordered nature. However, there is something deeply beautiful about an image of resurrected human persons in a state where all things and persons are recapitulated and taken up into the universal, epektatic, liturgical worship and manifestation of God; hence, it must be possible.

With this image of human persons taking their place in the total irreducible glory of all created beings transfigured by God, I close this book. My goal has been to paint a picture of the irreducible human person, drawing on many strands of the Catholic and other traditions, so that, guided by that picture, we can better perceive human persons in all their beauty. I have sought to display us so that, like ones who attend a religious festival, we could celebrate and honor human persons. May the images I have provided in this book guide many people to better perceive and celebrate the irreducible beauty of each unique person.

Bibliography

Abelard, Peter. *Logica 'Ingredientibus.'* In *Beiträge zur Geschichte der Philosophie des Mittelalters*. Vol. 21, Heft 1. Edited by Bernhard Geyer. Münster: Verlag der Aschendorffschen Verlagsbuchhandlung, 1919
Abram, David. *The Spell of the Sensuous: Perception and Language in a More-Than-Human World*. New York: Vintage, 1996.
Adams, Robert. "Idealism Vindicated." In *Persons: Human and Divine*, edited by Peter van Inwagen and Dean Zimmerman, 35–54. Oxford: Oxford University Press, 2007.
Aertsen, Jan. *Medieval Philosophy as Transcendental Thought: From Philip the Chancellor (ca. 1225) to Francisco Suárez*. Leiden: Brill, 2012.
Albert the Great. *Commentarii in I Sententiarum*. Vol. 25 of *Opera omnia*. Paris: Vivès, 1893.
———. *De homine*. Vol. 27.2 of *Opera omnia*. Aschendorff: Monasterii Westfalorum, 2008.
Alexander of Hales. *Glossa in IV Libros Sententiarum*. Quaracchi: Collegium S. Bonaventura, 1957.
Alston, William. *Perceiving God: The Epistemology of Religious Experience*. Ithaca, N.Y.: Cornell University Press, 1991.
Altman, Barbara. "Disability: Definitions, Models, Classifications, and Applications." In *Handbook of Disability Studies*, edited by Gary Albrecht et al., 97–122. Thousand Oaks, Calif.: Sage, 2001.
Anatolios, Khaled. *Deification through the Cross: An Eastern Christian Theology of Salvation*. Grand Rapids, Mich.: Eerdmans, 2020.
Anscombe, G. E. M. *Intention*. Cambridge, Mass.: Harvard University Press, 2000.
Arendt, Hannah. *The Human Condition*. Chicago: University of Chicago Press, 1998.
Aristotle. *The Complete Works of Aristotle*. 2 Vols. Edited by Jonathan Barnes. Princeton, N.J.: Princeton University Press, 1984.
———. *Metaphysics*. Translated by Joe Sachs. Santa Fe, N.M.: Green Lion Press, 1999.
Auerbach, Erich. *Mimesis: The Representation of Reality in Western Literatures*. Translated by Willard R. Trask. Princeton, N.J.: Princeton University Press, 2003.
Augustine. *On the Trinity*. Translated by Gareth Matthews. Cambridge: Cambridge University Press, 2002.

———. *Confessions*. Translated by Henry Chadwick. Oxford: Oxford University Press, 2009.

Austriaco, Nicanor. "Defending Adam after Darwin." *American Catholic Philosophical Quarterly* 92, no. 2 (2018): 332–52.

———. "Plants Too Have Sensitive Souls." Presentation at 2019 Annual Meeting of the American Catholic Philosophical Association. November 23, 2019.

Bachelard, Gaston. *Intuition of the Instant*. Translated by Eileen Rizo-Patron. Evanston, Ill.: Northwestern University Press, 2013.

———. *The Poetics of Space*. Translated by Maria Jolas. New York: Penguin, 2014.

Bañez, Domingo. *Scholastica commentaria in primam partem*. Salamanaca: S. Stephanum, 1585.

Barfield, Owen. *Poetic Diction: A Study in Meaning*. Middletown, Conn.: Wesleyan University Press, 1973.

———. *Saving the Appearances: A Study in Idolatry*. Middletown, Conn.: Wesleyan University Press, 1988.

Barnes, Gordon. "The Paradoxes of Hylomorphism." *Review of Metaphysics* 56, no. 3 (2003): 501–23.

Barral, Mary Rose. "Thomas Aquinas and Merleau-Ponty." *Philosophy Today* 26, no. 3 (1982): 204–16.

Beattie, Tina. *Theology after Postmodernity: Divining the Void—A Lacanian Reading of Thomas Aquinas*. Oxford: Oxford University Press, 2013.

Beaudoin, John. "The World's Continuance: Divine Conservation or Existential Inertia?" *International Journal for Philosophy of Religion* 61, no. 2 (2007): 83–98.

Berdyaev, Nicolas. *Freedom and the Spirit*. Translated by Oliver Fielding Clarke. New York: Charles Scribner's Sons, 1935.

———. *Spirit and Reality*. Translated by George Reavey. New York: Scribner's, 1939.

———. *Slavery and Freedom*. Translated by R. M. French. New York: Charles Scribner's Sons, 1944.

———. *The Meaning of the Creative Act*. Translated by Donald Lowrie. New York: Collier, 1962.

Berger, Ronald. *Introducing Disability Studies*. Boulder, Colo.: Lynne Rienner, 2013.

Bergson, Henri. *Time and Free Will: An Essay on the Immediate Data of Consciousness*. Translated by L. Pogson. Mineola, N.Y.: Dover, 2001.

———. "An Introduction to Metaphysics." In *The Creative Mind: An Introduction to Metaphysics*. Translated by T. E. Hulme. Mineola, N.Y.: Dover, 2010.

Bernard of Trilia. *Quaestiones de cognition animae separatae a corpore*. Edited by Stuart Martin. Toronto: Pontifical Institute of Medieval Studies, 1965.

Bernard Silvestris. *Cosmographia*. In *Poetic Works*, edited by Winthrop Wetherbee. Cambridge, Mass.: Harvard University Press, 2015.

Billot, Louis. *De verbo incarnato*. Rome: Propaganda Fide, 1895.

Blanchette, Oliva. *Philosophy of Being: A Reconstructive Essay in Metaphysics*. Washington, D.C.: The Catholic University of America Press, 2003.

Blondel, Maurice. *Action (1893): Essay on a Critique of Life and a Science of Practice*. Translated by Oliva Blanchette. Notre Dame, Ind.: University of Notre Dame Press, 1984.

Boethius. *Contra Eutychen.* http://individual.utoronto.ca/ pking/resources/oethius/ Contra_Eutychen.txt.

Bonaventure. *Commentaria in quatuor libros Sententiarum.* Vols. 1–4 of *Opera omnia.* Quarracchi: Collegium S. Bonaventurae, 1882–1889.

———. *Quaestiones disputatae de scientia Christi.* In *Opera omnia.* Vol. 5. Quarracchi: Collegium S. Bonaventura, 1891.

———. *Reductione atrium ad theologiam.* In *Opera omnia.* Vol. 5. Quarracchi: Collegium S. Bonaventura, 1891.

Bradshaw, David. *Aristotle East and West: Metaphysics and the Division of Christendom.* Cambridge: Cambridge University Press, 2007.

Braine, David. *The Human Person: Animal and Spirit.* Notre Dame, Ind.: University of Notre Dame Press, 1992.

———. "The Debate Between Henri de Lubac and His Critics." *Nova et Vetera* (English edition) 6, no. 3 (2008): 543–90.

Brassier, Ray. *Nihil Unbound: Enlightenment and Extinction.* New York: Palgrave Macmillan, 2007.

Brock, Stephen. "Is Uniqueness at the Root of Personal Dignity? John Crosby and Thomas Aquinas." *The Thomist* 69, no. 2 (2005): 173–201.

Brown, Christopher. "Souls, Ships, and Substances: A Reply to Toner." *American Catholic Philosophical Quarterly* 81, no. 4 (2007): 655–68.

———. *St. Thomas on God and Perfect Human Happiness: Philosophical Problems, Thomistic Solutions.* Washington, D.C.: The Catholic University of America Press, 2021.

Brown, Montague. *Reason, Revelation, and Metaphysics: The Transcendental Analogies.* Washington, D.C.: The Catholic University of America Press, 2020.

Brown, Peter. *Augustine of Hippo: A Biography.* Berkeley: University of California Press, 2000.

Buber, Martin. *I and Thou.* Translated by Walter Kaufmann. New York: Touchstone, 1970.

Bulgakov, Sergius. *The Bride of the Lamb.* Translated by Boris Jakim. Grand Rapids, Mich.: Eerdmans, 2002.

Buras, Todd, and Trent Dougherty. "Parrying Parity." In *Idealism: New Essays in Metaphysics,* edited by Tyron Goldschmidt and Kenneth Pearce, 1–16. Oxford: Oxford University Press, 2017.

Burgos, Juan Manuel. *An Introduction to Personalism.* Translated by R. T. Allen. Washington, D.C.: The Catholic University of America Press, 2018.

Butler, Edward P. "Bhakti and Henadology." *Journal of Dharma Studies* 1 (2018): 147–61.

Bychkov, Oleg. *Aesthetic Revelation: Reading Ancient and Medieval Texts after Hans Urs von Balthasar.* Washington, D.C.: The Catholic University of America Press, 2010.

Cajetan, Thomas de Vio. *De nominium analogia.* In *Opuscula omnia.* Lyon: Apud haeredes Iacobi Iuntae, 1558.

———. *Commentaria in summa theologiae.* Rome: S. C. de Propaganda Fide, 1888–1906.

Calasso, Roberto. *The Marriage of Cadmus and Harmony*. Translated by Tim Parks. New York: Knopf, 1993.

———. *Ardor*. Translated by Richard Dixon. New York: Farrar, Straus and Giroux, 2014.

———. *The Celestial Hunter*. Translated by Richard Dixon. New York: Farrar, Straus and Giroux, 2020.

———. *The Book of All Books*. Translated by Tim Parks. New York: Farrar, Straus and Giroux, 2021.

Camus, Albert. *The Myth of Sisyphus*. Translated by Justin O'Brien. New York: Random House, 1955.

Capreolus, John. *Defensiones theologiae divi Thomae Aquinatis*. Turin: Alfred Cattier, 1900.

Carlo, William. *The Ultimate Reducibility of Essence to Existence in Existential Metaphysics*. The Hague: Martinus Nijhoff, 1966.

Carnes, Natalie. *Beauty: A Theological Engagement with Gregory of Nyssa*. Eugene, Ore.: Cascade Books, 2014.

Casey, Edward S. *Getting Back into Place: Toward a Renewed Understanding of the Place-World*. 2nd ed. Bloomington: Indiana University Press, 2009.

Chenu, Marie-Dominique. *Nature, Man, and Society in the Twelfth Century: Essays on New Theological Perspectives in the Latin West*. Translated by Jerome Taylor and Lester Little. Chicago: University of Chicago Press, 1957.

Chrétien, Jean-Louis. *The Ark of Speech*. Translated by Andrew Brown. New York: Routledge, 2004.

Clark, Andy, and David Chalmers. "The Extended Mind." In *The Extended Mind*, edited by Richard Menary, 27–39. Cambridge, Mass.: MIT Press, 2010.

Clarke, Norris. "Person, Being, and St. Thomas." *Communio* 19, no. 4 (1992): 601–18.

———. *Person and Being*. Milwaukee, Wisc.: Marquette University Press, 1993.

———. "Action as the Self-Revelation of Being." In *Explorations in Metaphysics: Being-God-Person*, 45–64. Notre Dame: Ind.: University of Notre Dame Press, 1994.

———. "A New Look at the Immutability of God." In *Explorations in Metaphysics: Being-God-Person*, 183–210. Notre Dame: Ind.: University of Notre Dame Press, 1994.

———. "System: A New Category of Being?" In *The Creative Retrieval of St. Thomas Aquinas: Essays in Thomistic Philosophy, New and Old*, 39–47. New York: Fordham University Press, 2009.

Chaberek, Michael. *Aquinas and Evolution*. The Chartwell Press, 2020.

Chalmers, David. *The Conscious Mind: In Search of a Fundamental Theory*. Oxford: Oxford University Press, 1997.

Churchland, Paul. *Matter and Consciousness*. Cambridge, Mass.: MIT Press, 1988.

Cohen, Richard. *Out of Control: Confrontations between Spinoza and Levinas*. Albany: State University of New York Press, 2016.

Conrad-Martius, Hedwig. "Realontologie." *Jahrbuch für Philosophie und phänomenologische Forschung* 6 (1923): 97–112.

———. *Die "Seele" der Pflanze: Biologisch-ontologische Betrachtungen*. Breslau: 1934.

Bibliography

Cooper, Adam G. *Naturally Human, Supernaturally God: Deification in Post-Conciliar Catholicism*. Minneapolis, Minn.: Fortress Press, 2014.
Cory, Therese Scarpelli. *Aquinas on Human Self-Knowledge*. Cambridge: Cambridge University Press, 2014.
———. "Rethinking Abstractionism: Aquinas' Intellectual Light and Some Arabic Sources." *Journal of the History of Philosophy* 53, no. 4 (2015): 607–46.
———. "Knowing as Being? A Metaphysical Reading of the Identity of Intellect and Intelligible in Aquinas." *American Catholic Philosophical Quarterly* 91, no. 3 (2017): 333–51.
Crean, Thomas, and Alan Fimister. *Integralism: A Manual of Political Philosophy*. Heusenstamm: Editiones Scholasticae, 2020.
Crosby, John F. "The Idea of Value and the Reform of the Traditional Metaphysics of Bonum." *Aletheia* 1, no. 2 (1977): 231–338.
———. *The Selfhood of the Human Person*. Washington, D.C.: The Catholic University of America Press, 1996.
———. "Is All Evil Really Only Privation?" *Proceedings of the American Catholic Philosophical Association* 75 (2001): 197–210.
———. "A Neglected Source of the Dignity of Persons." In *Personalist Papers*, 3–32. Washington, D.C.: The Catholic University of America Press, 2004.
———. "Doubts about the privation theory that will not go away." *American Catholic Philosophical Quarterly* 81, no. 3 (2007): 489–505.
Cross, Richard. "Aquinas and the Mind-Body Problem." In *Mind, Metaphysics, and Value in the Thomistic and Analytic Traditions*, edited by John Haldane, 36–53. Notre Dame, Ind.: University of Notre Dame Press, 2002.
———. *Duns Scotus on God*. Aldershot: Ashgate, 2005.
Dahm, Brandon. "The Acquired Virtues are Real Virtues: A Response to Stump." *Faith and Philosophy* 32, no. 4 (2015): 453–70.
———. "Distinguishing Desire and Parts of Happiness: A Response to Grisez." *American Catholic Philosophical Quarterly* 89, no. 1 (2015): 97–114.
Dawson, Christopher. *Progress and Religion: An Historical Inquiry*. Washington, D.C.: The Catholic University of America Press, 2001.
Day, Dorothy. *The Long Loneliness*. New York: HarperOne, 1997.
de Beauvoir, Simone. *The Second Sex*. Translated by Constance Borde and Sheila Malovany-Chevallier. New York: Vintage, 2011.
de Finance, Joseph. *Être et agir dans la philosophie de Saint Thomas*. Rome: Presses de l'Université Grégorienne, 1965.
De Haan, Daniel. "Perception and the *Vis Cogitativa*: A Thomistic Analysis of Aspectual, Actional, and Affectional Percepts." *American Catholic Philosophical Quarterly* 88, no. 3 (2014): 397–437.
———. "Simon and Maritain on the Vocation of *Species in Medio*." In *Redeeming Philosophy: From Metaphysics to Aesthetics*, edited by John Conley, 54–82. Washington, D.C.: American Maritain Association, 2014.
———. "Hylomorphic Animalism, Emergentism, and the Challenge of the New Mechanist Philosophy of Neuroscience." *Scientia et Fides* 5, no. 2 (2017): 9–38.

———. "The Interaction of Noetic and Psychosomatic Operations in a Thomist Hylomorphic Personalism." *Scientia et Fides* 6, no. 2 (2018): 1–29.

De Haan, Daniel, and Brandom Dahm. "Thomas Aquinas on Separated Souls as Incomplete Human Persons." *The Thomist* 83, no. 4 (2019): 589–637.

———. "After Survivalism and Corruptionism: Separated Souls as Incomplete Human Persons." *Quaestiones Disputatae* 10, no. 1 (2020): 161–76.

de Koninck, Charles. "Prolégomènes à la dixième catégorie." *Philosophia perennis* 3, no 1. (1996): 5–23.

———. *On the Primacy of the Common Good: Against the Personalists*. Translated by Sean Collins. Reprinted in *The Aquinas Review* 4 (1997): 1–100.

———. *The Writings of Charles de Koninck*. Vol. 1. Translated by Ralph McInerny. Notre Dame, Ind.: University of Notre Dame Press, 2008.

———. *The Writings of Charles de Koninck*. Vol. 2. Translated by Ralph McInerny. Notre Dame, Ind.: University of Notre Dame Press, 2009.

de Lubac, Henri. *Surnaturel: Études Historiques* Paris: Aubier, 1946.

———. *The Mystery of the Supernatural*. Translated by Rosemary Sheed. New York: Crossroad, 1998.

de Saint-Exupéry, Antoine. *Wind, Sand and Stars*. Translated by Lewis Galantiére. Orlando, Fla.: Harcourt, 1992.

de Sales, Francis. *Treatise on the Love of God*. Translated by Henry Benedict de Mackey. Rockford: Tan, 1997.

de Unamuno, Miguel. *Tragic Sense of Life*. Translated by J. E. Crawford Flitch. New York: Dover, 1954.

Deeley, John. "The Immateriality of the Intentional as Such." *New Scholasticism* 42, no. 2 (1968): 293–306.

———. *Semiotic Animal: A Postmodern Definition of "Human Being" Transcending Patriarchy and Feminism*. South Bend, Ind.: St. Augustine's Press, 2010.

Deleuze, Gilles. *Nietzsche and Philosophy*. Translated by Hugh Tomlinson. New York: Columbia University Press, 1985.

———. *Logic of Sense*. Translated by Mark Lester. London: Athlone, 1990.

———. *Francis Bacon: The Logic of Sensation*. Translated by Daniel W. Smith. London: Continuum, 2005.

Deleuze, Giles, and Felix Guattari. *A Thousand Plateaus*. Translated by Brian Massumi. Minneapolis: University of Minnesota Press, 1987.

Demetracopoulos, John. "Palamas Transformed. Palamite Interpretations of the Distinction between God's 'Essence' and 'Energies' in Late Byzantium." In *Greeks, Latins, and Intellectual History 1204–1500*, edited by Martin Hinterberger and Chris Schabel, 263–372. Leuven: Peeters, 2011.

Dennett, Daniel. "Quining Qualia." In *Consciousness in Contemporary Science*, edited by A. J. Marcel and E. Bisiach, 42–77. Oxford: Clarendon, 1988.

———. *Consciousness Explained*. Boston: Little, Brown, and Company, 1991.

Denzinger, Heinrich. *Enchiridion symbolorum: A Compendium of Creeds, Definitions, and Declarations of the Catholic Church*. Edited by Peter Hünermann. San Francisco: Ignatius Press, 2012.

Bibliography 397

Derrida, Jacques. *Given Time: I. Counterfeit Money.* Translated by Peggy Kamuf. Chicago: University of Chicago Press, 1992.

Descartes, Rene. *Meditations on First Philosophy.* In *Selected Philosophical Writings.* Translated by John Cottingham et al. Cambridge: Cambridge University Press, 1988.

Desmond, William. *The Intimate Strangeness of Being: Metaphysics After Dialectic.* Washington, D.C.: The Catholic University of America Press, 2012.

———. *The Gift of Beauty and the Passion of Being: On the Threshold between the Aesthetic and the Religious.* Eugene, Ore.: Cascade Books, 2018.

———. *The Voiding of Being: The Doing and Undoing of Metaphysics in Modernity.* Washington, D.C.: The Catholic University of America Press, 2020.

Dettloff, Dean. "Catholic Air Conditioning: *Laudato Si'* and the Overcoming of Phenomenology." *The Heythrop Journal* 58, no. 6 (2017): 931–41.

Dewan, Lawrence, "Is Truth a Transcendental for St. Thomas Aquinas?" *Nova et Vetera* (English edition) 2, no. 1 (2004): 1–20.

———. *St. Thomas and Form as Something Divine in Things.* Milwaukee, Wisc.: Marquette University Press, 2007.

Dillard, Annie. *Pilgrim at Tinker Creek.* New York: Harper & Row, 1974.

Doolan, Gregory. *Aquinas on the Divine Ideas as Exemplar Causes.* Washington, D.C.: The Catholic University of America Press, 2008.

Doyle, John P. *On the Borders of Being and Knowing: Late Scholastic Theory of Supertranscendental Being.* Edited by Victor M. Salas. Leuven: Leuven University Press, 2012.

Dreyfus, Hubert, and Sean Dorrance Kelly. *All Things Shining: Reading the Western Classics to Find Meaning in a Secular Age.* New York: Free Press, 2011.

Dudai, Yadin, and Micah Edelson. "Personal memory: Is it personal, is it memory?" *Memory Studies* 9, no. 3 (2016): 275–83.

Dumont, Stephen. "Duns Scotus' Parisian Question on the Formal Distinction." *Vivarium* 43, no. 1 (2005): 7–62.

Dupré, Louis. *Humans and Other Animals.* Oxford: Clarendon, 2006.

Eberl, Jason. "Do Humans Persist between Death and Resurrection?" In *Metaphysics and God: Essays in Honor of Eleonore Stump,* edited by Kevin Timpe, 188–205. New York: Routledge, 2009.

———. *The Nature of Human Persons: Metaphysics and Bioethics.* Notre Dame, Ind.: University of Notre Dame Press, 2020.

Eccles, John. *How the Self Controls Its Brain.* Berlin: Springer, 1994.

Eliade, Mircea. *The Sacred and the Profane: The Nature of Religion.* Translated by Willard R. Trask. Orlando, Fla.: Harcourt, 1987.

Emery, Gilles. *The Trinitarian Theology of St. Thomas Aquinas.* Translated by Francesca Aran Murphy. Oxford: Oxford University Press, 2010.

Emonet, Pierre-Marie. *The Dearest Freshness Deep Down Things: An Introduction to the Philosophy of Being.* Translated by Robert Barr. New York: Crossroad, 1999.

Evagrios the Solitary. "On Prayer: 153 Texts." In *The Philokalia.* Vol. 1. Edited by Nikodimos of the Holy Mountain and Makarios of Corinth. Translated by G. E. H. Palmer et al., 55–71. New York: Farrar, Straus and Giroux, 1979.

Everson, William. *The Excesses of God: Robinson Jeffers as a Religious Figure*. Stanford, Calif.: Stanford University Press, 1988.

Fabro, Cornelio. *La nozione metafisica di partecipazione secondo S. Tommaso d'Aquin*. Turin: Società edittice internazionale, 1950.

———. *Participation et causalité selon S. Thomas d'Aquin*. Paris: Editions Béatrice-Nauwelaerts, 1961.

———. "The Intensive Hermeneutics of Thomistic Philosophy: The Notion of Participation." In *Selected Works of Cornelio Fabro*. Vol. 1. Edited by Nathaniel Dreyer, 65–104. Chillum, Md.: IVE Press, 2016.

Falque, Emmanuel. *The Metamorphosis of Finitude: An Essay on Birth and Resurrection*. Translated by George Hughes. New York: Fordham University Press, 2012.

———. *The Wedding Feast of the Lamb: Eros, the Body, and the Eucharist*. Translated by George Hughes. New York: Fordham University Press, 2016.

Farges, Albert. *Mystical Phenomena*. Translated by S. P. Jacques. New York: Benzinger, 1926.

Feingold, Lawrence. *The Natural Desire to See God According to St. Thomas and His Interpreters*. Naples, Fla.: Sapientia Press, 2010.

———. "Heavenly Beatitude According to Thomas Aquinas." In *Eschatology: Proceedings of the 37– Annual Convention of the Fellowship of Catholic Scholars, September 26–27, 2014*, edited by Elizabeth Shaw, 123–52. Notre Dame, Ind.: Fellowship of Catholic Scholars, 2015.

Feser, Edward. *Philosophy of Mind*. Oxford: Oneworld, 2005.

———. *Scholastic Metaphysics: A Contemporary Introduction*. Heusenstamm: Editiones Scholasticae, 2014.

Feynman, Richard. *Six Easy Pieces: Essentials of Physics as Explained by Its Most Brilliant Teacher*. Reading, Mass.: Addison-Wesley, 1995.

Fink, Eugen. *Sixth Cartesian Meditation: The Idea of a Transcendental Theory of Method*. Translated by Ronald Bruzina. Bloomington: Indiana University Press, 1995.

Finlan, Stephen. "The Comedy of Divinization in Soloviev." In *Theosis: Deification in Christian Theology*, edited by Stephen Finlan and Vladimir Kharlamov, 168–83. Cambridge: The Lutterworth Press, 2006.

Finnis, John, Germain Grisez, and Joseph Boyle. "Practical Principles, Moral Truth, and Ultimate Ends." *American Journal of Jurisprudence* 32 (1987): 99–151.

Fischer, John Martin. "Stories and the Meaning of Life." *Philosophic Exchange* 39, no. 1. https://digitalcommons.brockport.edu/phil_ex/vol39/iss1/4.

Florovsky, Georges. "Creation and Creaturehood." In *The Collected Works of Georges Florovsky*. Vol. 3, *Creation and Redemption*, 43–78. Belmont, Mass.: Norland, 1976.

Fodor, Jerry. "Materialism." In *Materialism and the Mind-Body Problem*, edited by David Rosenthal, 128–49. Indianapolis, Ind.: Hackett, 2000.

Francis. *Laudato Si.'* Encyclical Letter. May 24, 2015.

Freddoso, Alfred. "God's General Concurrence with Secondary Causes: Pitfalls and Prospects." *American Catholic Philosophical Quarterly* 68, no. 2 (1994): 131–56.

Fritz, Peter Joseph. *Karl Rahner's Theological Aesthetics*. Washington, D.C.: The Catholic University of America Press, 2014.

Frost, Gloria. "Peter Olivi's Rejection of God's Concurrence with Created Causes." *British Journal for the History of Philosophy* 22, no. 4 (2014): 655–79.
——. "Scotus on How God Causes the Created Will's Volitions." In *Interpreting Duns Scotus: Critical Essays*, edited by Giorgio Pini. Cambridge: Cambridge University Press, 2021.
Froula, John. "*Esse Secundarium*: An Analogical Term Meaning that By Which Christ Is Human." *The Thomist* 78, no. 4 (2014): 557–80.
Gadamer, Hans-Georg. *Truth and Method*. Translated by Joel Weinsheimer and Donald G. Marshall. London: Continuum, 2004.
García-Norro, Juan J., and Rogelio Rovira. "A New Look at A Priori Knowledge and Hildebrand's Discovery of Different Kinds of Unities." *American Catholic Philosophical Quarterly* 91, no. 4 (2017): 567–88.
Garrigou-Lagrange, Reginald. *Predestination*. Translated by Bede Rose. St. Louis: Herder, 1946.
——. *Beatitude*. Translated by Patrick Cummins. St. Louis: Herder, 1956.
Gavrilyuk, Paul L. *Georges Florovsky and the Russian Religious Renaissance*. Oxford: Oxford University Press, 2014.
Gavrilyuk, Paul L., and Sarah Coakley, eds. *The Spiritual Senses: Perceiving God in Western Christianity*. Cambridge: Cambridge University Press, 2012.
Geach, Peter. "Identity." *Review of Metaphysics*, 21, no. 1 (1967): 3–12.
——. *God and the Soul*. London: Routledge, 1969.
Gehlen, Arnold. *Man: His Nature and Place in the World*. Translated by Clare McMillan and Karl Pillemer. New York: Columbia University Press, 1988.
Geiger, Louis-Bertrand. *La participation dans la philosophie de S. Thomas d'Aquin*. Paris: Vrin, 1942.
George, Marie I. "Aquinas's Teachings on Concepts and Words in His Commentary on John contra Nicanor Austriaco, OP." *American Catholic Philosophical Quarterly* 94, no. 3 (2020): 357–78.
Gerson, Lloyd P. *Aristotle and Other Platonists*. Ithaca, N.Y.: Cornell University Press, 2006.
Gibson, James. *The Senses Considered as Perceptual Systems*. Boston: Houghton Mifflin, 1966.
——. *The Ecological Approach to Visual Perception*. Hillsdale, N.J.: Erlbaum, 1986.
Gill, Eric. *Beauty Looks After Herself*. Freeport, N.Y.: Books for Libraries Press, 1933.
Gilson, Etienne. *Being and Some Philosophers*. Toronto: Pontifical Institute of Medieval Studies, 1952.
——. *Painting and Reality*. New York: Pantheon, 1957.
Girard, René. *Things Hidden Since the Foundation of the World*. Translated by Stephen Barr and Michael Metteer. Stanford, Calif.: Stanford University Press, 1987.
Girgis, Sherif. "Subjectivity without Subjectivism: Revisiting the Is/Ought Gap." In *Subjectivity: Ancient and Modern*, edited by R. J. Snell and Steven F. McGuire, 63–88. Lanham, Md.: Lexington Books, 2016.
Goetz, Stewart, and Charles Taliaferro. *Naturalism*. Grand Rapids, Mich.: Eerdmans, 2008.
Gonet, Jean-Baptiste. *Clypeus theologiae thomisticae*. Paris: Vivès, 1875.

Gould, Stephen Jay. *Wonderful Life: The Burgess Shale and the Nature of History.* New York: Norton, 1989.

———. *The Structure of Evolutionary Theory.* Cambridge, Mass.: Harvard University Press, 2002.

Goth, Sebastian. "Venus Anadyomene: The Birth of Art." In *Venus as Muse: From Lucretius to Michel Serres,* edited by Hanjo Berressem et al., 15–40. Leiden: Brill, 2015.

Gracia, Jorge J. E. *Individuality: An Essay on the Foundations of Metaphysics.* Albany: State University of New York Press, 1988.

———. *Metaphysics and Its Task: The Search for the Categorial Foundation of Knowledge.* Albany: State University of New York Press, 1999.

Gracia, Jorge J. E., and John Kronen. "John of St. Thomas." In *Individuation in Scholasticism: The Later Middle Ages and the Counter-Reformation, 1150–1650,* edited by Jorge Gracia, 511–34. Albany: State University of New York Press, 1994.

Grant, W. Matthews. "Aquinas on How God Causes the Act of Sin without Causing Sin Itself," *The Thomist* 73, no. 3 (2009): 455–96.

———. "Can a Libertarian Hold that Our Free Acts are Caused by God?" *Faith and Philosophy* 27, no. 1 (2010): 22–44.

———. *Free Will and God's Universal Causality: The Dual Sources Account.* London: Bloomsbury, 2019.

Greco, John. "Perception as Interpretation." *Proceedings of the American Catholic Philosophical Association* 72 (1999): 229–37.

Gregory of Nyssa. *De hominis opificio.* In PG. Vol. 44. Paris: J.-P. Migne, 1863.

———. *In Hexaemeron explicatio apologetica.* In PG. Vol. 44. Paris: J.-P. Migne, 1863.

———. *Contra Eunomium.* In PG. Vol. 45. Paris: J.-P. Migne, 1863.

———. *De anima et resurrection.* In PG. Vol. 46. Paris: J.-P. Migne, 1863.

Gregory Palamas. *The Triads.* Translated by Nicholas Gendle. Mahwah, N.J.: Paulist Press, 1983.

———. "Topics of Natural and Theological Science and on the Moral and Aesthetic Life: 150 Texts." In *The Philokalia.* Vol. 4. Edited by Nikodimos of the Holy Mountain and Makarios of Corinth. Translated by G. E. H. Palmer et al. London: Faber and Faber, 1995.

———. *Dialogue between an Orthodox and a Barlaamite.* Translated by Rein Ferwerda. Binghamton: Episteme, 1999.

Grenier, Henri. *Moral Philosophy.* Vol. 3 of *Thomistic Philosophy.* Translated by J. P. E. O'Hanley. Charlottetown: St. Dunstan's University, 1949.

Gricoski, Thomas. *Being Unfolded: Edith Stein on the Meaning of Being.* Washington, D.C.: The Catholic University of America Press, 2020.

Griffiths, Paul. *Decreation: The Last Things of All Creatures.* Waco, Tex.: Baylor University Press, 2014.

———. *Christian Flesh.* Stanford, Calif.: Stanford University Press, 2018.

Grisez, Germain. "Sketch of A Future Metaphysics." *New Scholasticism* 38, no. 3 (1964): 310–40.

———. "The First Principle of Practical Reason: A Commentary on the *Summa theologiae,* Question 94, Article 2." *Natural Law Forum* 10, no. 1 (1965): 168–201.

Geschwandtner, Christina. *Degrees of Givenness: On Saturation in Jean-Luc Marion.* Bloomington: Indiana University Press, 2014.
Guardini, Romano. *The Lord.* Translated by Elinor Castendyk Briefs. South Bend, Ind.: Gateway, 1954.
———. *The World and the Person.* Translated by Stella Lange. Chicago: Regnery, 1965.
Hacker, Peter. *Appearance and Reality: A Philosophical Investigation into Perception and Perceptual Qualities.* Oxford: Blackwell, 1987.
Hadot, Pierre. *The Present Alone Is Our Happiness: Conversations with Jeannie Carlier and Arnold I. Davidson.* Translated by Marc Djaballah. Stanford, Calif.: Stanford University Press, 2009.
Haldane, John. "Insight, Inference and Intellection." *Proceedings of the American Catholic Philosophical Association* 73 (1999): 32–46.
———. "The Breakdown of Contemporary Philosophy of Mind." In *Mind, Metaphysics, and Value in the Thomistic and Analytic Traditions,* edited by John Haldane, 54–72. Notre Dame, Ind.: University of Notre Dame Press, 2002.
Han, Byung-Chul. *Saving Beauty.* Translated by Daniel Steuer. Cambridge: Polity, 2018.
Hankey, Wayne. *God in Himself: Aquinas' Doctrine of God as Expounded in the* Summa Theologiae. Oxford: Oxford University Press, 2000.
Hart, David Bentley. *The Beauty of the Infinite: The Aesthetics of Christian Truth.* Grand Rapids, Mich.: Eerdmans, 2003.
———. "Spirits, Souls ... Tunics?" *Church Life Journal,* November 20, 2018. churchlifejournal.nd.edu/articles/spirits-souls-tunics.
———. *That All Shall Be Saved: Heaven, Hell, and Universal Salvation.* New Haven, Conn.: Yale University Press, 2019.
Hartmann, Nicolai. *Zum Problem der Realitätsgegebenheit.* Berlin: Pan-Verlagsgesellschaf, 1931.
Harman, Graham. *Guerilla Metaphysics: Phenomenology and the Carpentry of Things.* Chicago: Open Court, 2005.
Hayek, F. A. "The Results of Human Action but Not of Human Design." In *Studies in Philosophy, Politics, and Economics.* Chicago: University of Chicago Press, 1967.
Hegel, G. W. F. *The Phenomenology of Mind.* Translated by J. B. Baillie. New York: Harper & Row, 1967.
———. *Encyclopedia of the Philosophical Sciences in Basic Outline.* Translated by William Wallace. www.marxists.org/reference/archive/hegel/li_hegel.htm.
Heidegger, Martin. "Building Dwelling Thinking." In *Poetry, Language, Thought,* translated by Albert Hofstadter, 141–60. New York: Harper & Row, 1971.
———. "Science and Reflection" In *the Question Concerning Technology and Other Essays,* translated by William Lovitt, 155–82. New York: Harper and Row, 1977.
———. *Aristotle's Metaphysics* Θ *1–3: On the Essence and Actuality of Force.* Translated by Walter Brogan and Peter Warnek. Bloomington: Indiana University Press, 1995.
———. *Being and Time.* Translated by Joan Stambaugh. Albany: State University of New York Press, 1996.
———. "The Onto-Theo-Logical Conception of Metaphysics." In *Identity and Differ-*

ence, translated by Joan Stambaugh, 42–74. Chicago: University of Chicago Press, 2002.

———. *Country Path Conversations.* Translated by Bret Davis. Bloomington: Indiana University Press, 2010.

———. *Introduction to Metaphysics.* Translated by Gregory Fried and Richard Polt. New Haven: Yale University Press, 2014.

Heider, Daniel. "Abstraction, Intentionality, and Moderate Realism: Suárez and Poinsot." In *Hircocervi and Other Metaphysical Wonders: Essays in Honor of John Doyle*, edited by Victor Salas, 177–211. Milwaukee, Wisc.: Marquette University Press, 2013.

Henninger, Mark G. *Relations: Medieval Theories 1250–1325.* Oxford: Oxford University Press, 1989.

Henry, Michel. *The Essence of Manifestation.* Translated by Girard Etzkorn. The Hague: Martinus Nijhoff, 1973.

———. *Philosophy and Phenomenology of the Body.* Translated by Girard Etzkorn. The Hague: Martinus Nijhoff, 1975.

———. *I Am the Truth: Toward a Philosophy of Christianity.* Translated by Susan Emmanuel. Stanford, Calif.: Stanford University Press, 2006.

———. *Material Phenomenology.* Translated by Scott Davidson. New York: Fordham University Press, 2008.

Henry of Ghent. *Quodlibet I.* Vol. 5 of *Opera omnia.* Edited by Raymond Macken. Leuven: Leuven University Press, 1979.

Hershenov, David. "Shoemaker's Problem of Too Many Thinkers." *Proceedings of the American Catholic Philosophical Association* 80 (2007): 225–36.

———. "Soulless Organisms? Hylomorphism vs. Animalism." *American Catholic Philosophical Quarterly* 85, no. 3 (2011): 465–82.

Hesychios the Priest. "On Watchfulness and Holiness." In *The Philokalia.* Vol. 1. Edited by Nikodimos of the Holy Mountain and Makarios of Corinth. Translated by G. E. H. Palmer et al., 162–198. New York: Farrar, Straus and Giroux, 1979.

Hibbs, Thomas. *Aquinas, Ethics, and Philosophy of Religion: Metaphysics and Practice.* Bloomington: Indiana University Press, 2007.

Hilary of Poitiers. *De Trinitate.* Translated by E. W. Watson and L. Pullan. In *Nicene and Post-Nicene Fathers, Second Series.* Vol. 9. Edited by Philip Schaff and Henry Wace. Buffalo: Christian Literature Publishing Co., 1899. www.newadvent.org/fathers/3302.htm.

Hipp, Stephen. *The Doctrine of Personal Subsistence: Historical and Systematic Synthesis.* Fribourg: Studia Friburgensia, 2012.

Hochschild, Joshua. *The Semantics of Analogy: Rereading Cajetan's De Nominium Analogia.* Notre Dame, Ind.: University of Notre Dame Press, 2010.

Hoel, Erik. "When the Map Is Better than the Territory." *Entropy* 19, no. 5 (2017). doi:10.3390/e19050188.

Hoffman, Tobias. "Freedom Beyond Practical Reason: Duns Scotus on Will-Dependent Relations." *British Journal for the History of Philosophy* 21, no. 6 (2013): 1071–90.

Hoffmann, Tobias, and Cyrille Michon. "Aquinas on Free Will and Intellectual Determinism." *Philosopher's Imprint* 17, no. 10 (2017): 1–36.

Homobono de Bonis. *De humanae vitae statibus*. Bononia: Ex Typographia Victorii Benatii, 1619.

Hooke, Alexander. "Alphonso Lingis' We—A Collage, not a Collective." *Diacritics* 31, no. 4 (2001): 11–21.

Hopkins, Gerard Manley. *The Major Works*. Edited by Catherine Phillips. Oxford: Oxford University Press, 1986.

Horan, Daniel. *All God's Creatures: A Theology of Creation*. Lanham, Md.: Lexington Books, 2018.

Hughes, Margaret I. "Does Taste Matter for Thomists?" *The Thomist* 81, no. 1 (2017): 107–23.

Hugh of St. Victor. *De sacramentiis fidei Christianae*. In PL. Vol. 176. Paris: Vivès, 1880.

Huizinga, Johann. *Homo ludens: A Study of the Play Element of Culture*. Boston: Beacon Press, 1955.

Husserl, Edmund. *The Crisis of European Sciences and Transcendental Phenomenology: An Introduction to Phenomenological Philosophy*. Translated by David Carr. Evanston, Ill.: Northwestern University Press, 1970.

———. *Cartesian Meditations: An Introduction to Phenomenology*. Translated by Dorion Cairns. The Hague: Martinus Nijhoff, 1973.

———. "Foundational Investigations of the Phenomenological Origins of the Spatiality of Nature." Translated by Fred Kersten. In *Husserl: Shorter Works*, edited by Peter McCormick and Frederick Elliston, 222–33. Brighton: Harvester, 1981.

———. *Ideas Pertaining to a Pure Phenomenology and to a Phenomenological Philosophy*. Vol. 1, *General Introduction to a Pure Phenomenology*. Translated by Fred Kersten. The Hague: Martinus Nijhoff, 1983.

———. *Ideas Pertaining to a Pure Phenomenology and to a Phenomenological Philosophy*. Vol. 2, *Studies in the Phenomenology of Constitution*. Translated by Richard Rojcewicz and André Schuwer. Dordrecht: Kluwer Academic, 1989.

———. *On the Phenomenology of the Consciousness of Internal Time*. Translated by John Barnett Brough. Dordrecht: Kluwer, 1991.

———. "Phenomenology and Anthropology." In *Psychological and Transcendental Phenomenology and the Confrontation with Heidegger (1927-1931)*, edited by Thomas Sheehan and Richard Palmer, 485–500. Dordrecht: Kluwer Academic, 1997.

———. *Analyses Concerning Passive and Active Synthesis: Lectures on Transcendental Logic*. Translated by Anthony Steinbock. Dordrecht: Kluwer, 2001.

———. *Logical Investigations*. 2 vols. Translated by J. N. Findlay. London: Routledge, 2001.

———. *Grenzprobleme der Phänomenologie: Analyzsen des Unbewusstseins un der Instinkte, Metaphysik, Späte Ethik: Texte aus dem Nachlass (1908-1937)*. Vol. 42 of *Gesammelte Werke Husserliana*. Edited by Rochus Sowa and Thomas Vongehr. Dordrecht: Springer, 2014.

Ingarden, Roman. *The Literary Work of Art*. Translated by George G. Grabowicz. Evanston, Ill.: Northwestern University Press, 1973.

———. *On the Motives which led Edmund Husserl to Transcendental Idealism*. Translated by Arnor Hannibalsson. The Hague: Martinus Nijhoff, 1975.

Ingham, Mary Beth. "Symphonic Grandeur: Moral Beauty and the Judgment of Harmony in John Duns Scotus." In *Beauty and the Good: Recovering the Classical Tradition from Plato to Duns Scotus*, edited by Alice Ramos, 319–46. Washington, D.C.: The Catholic University of America Press, 2020.

Irigaray, Luce. *Speculum of the Other Woman*. Translated by Gillian Gill. Ithaca, N.Y.: Cornell University Press, 1985.

Jackson, Frank. "Epiphenomenal Qualia." *Philosophical Quarterly* 32, no. 127 (1982): 127–36.

Jacobs, Nathan. "Are Created Spirits Composed of Matter and Form? A Defense of Pneumatic Hylomorphism." *Philosophia Christi* 14, no. 1 (2012): 79–108.

James, William. *Some Problems of Philosophy*. Cambridge, Mass.: Harvard University Press, 1979.

Jaroszyński, Piotr. *Metaphysics and Art*. Translated by Hugh McDonald. New York: Peter Lang, 2002.

———. *Beauty and Being: Thomistic Perspectives*. Translated by Hugh MacDonald. Toronto: Pontifical Institute of Medieval Studies, 2011.

Jaspers, Karl. *Philosophy of Existence*. Translated by Richard Grabau. Philadelphia: University of Pennsylvania Press, 1971.

Jaynes, Julian. *The Origin of Consciousness in the Breakdown of the Bicameral Mind*. New York: Mariner Books, 2000.

Jeffers, Robinson. *The Selected Poetry of Robinson Jeffers*. Edited by Tim Hunt. Stanford, Calif.: Stanford University Press, 2002.

Jensen, Steven. *Good and Evil Actions: A Journey through St. Thomas Aquinas*. Washington, D.C.: The Catholic University of America Press, 2010.

———. *Knowing the Natural Law: From Precepts and Inclinations to Deriving Oughts*. Washington, D.C.: The Catholic University of America Press, 2015.

Jinek, Martin et al. "A Programmable Dual-RNA–Guided DNA Endonuclease in Adaptive Bacterial Immunity." *Science* 337, no. 6096 (2012): 816–21.

Joas, Hans. *The Sacredness of the Person: A New Genealogy of Human Rights*. Translated by Alex Skinner. Washington, D.C.: Georgetown University Press, 2013.

John Damascene. *An Exposition of the Orthodox Faith*. Translated by E. W. Watson and L. Pullan. In *Nicene and Post-Nicene Fathers*. Vol. 9. Edited by Philip Schaff and Henry Wace. http://newadvent.org/fathers/3304.htm.

John Duns Scotus. *Reportata Parisiensia*. Vols. 22–24 of *Opera omnia*. Paris: Vivès, 1894.

———. *Quaestiones super libros metaphysicorum*. Vol. 4 of *Opera philosophica*. Edited by Girard Etzkorn, Robert Andrews, Bernardo Bazàn, and Mechthild Dreyer. St. Bonaventure: Franciscan Institute. 1997.

———. *Ordinatio*. Vols. 1–14 of *Opera omnia*. Vatican City: Typis Vaticanis, 2013.

John of St. Thomas. *Cursus theologici in primam partem divi Thomae*. Vol. 2. Lugundi: Petrus Prost, 1642.

———. *Cursus theologicus*. Vol. 1. Cologne: Wilhelm Metternich, 1711.

———. *Cursus philosophicus thomisticus*. 3 Vols. Paris: Vivès, 1883.

John of the Cross. *Collected Works of St. John of the Cross*. Translated by Kieran Kavanaugh and Otilio Rodriguez. Washington, D.C.: ICS Publications, 1991.

John Paul II. See Karol Wojtyła.
Johnson, Luke Timothy. *The Revelatory Body: Theology as Inductive Art*. Grand Rapids, Mich.: Eerdmans, 2015.
Johnston, William. *The Still Point: Reflections on Zen and Christian Mysticism*. New York: Fordham University Press, 1970.
Jordan, Mark D. "The Evidence of the Transcendentals and the Place of Beauty in Thomas Aquinas." *International Philosophical Quarterly* 29, no. 4 (1989): 393–407.
Josephson-Storm, Jason. *The Myth of Disenchantment: Magic, Modernity, and the Birth of the Human Sciences*. Chicago: University of Chicago Press, 2017.
Kant, Immanuel. *Critique of Judgment*. Translated by Werner Pluhar. Indianapolis, Ind.: Hackett, 1987.
———. *Grounding for the Metaphysics of Morals*. Translated by James Ellington. Indianapolis, Ind.: Hackett, 1993.
———. *Critique of Pure Reason*. Translated by Paul Guyer and Allen Wood. Cambridge: Cambridge University Press, 1999.
———. *Critique of Practical Reason*. Translated by Mary Gregor. Cambridge: Cambridge University Press, 2015.
Kass, Leon. *The Hungry Soul: Eating and the Perfecting of our Nature*. Chicago: University of Chicago Press, 1999.
Kearney, Richard. "Epiphanies of the Everyday: Toward a Micro-Eschatology." In *After God: Richard Kearney and the Religious Turn in Continental Philosophy*, edited by John Panteleimon Manoussakis, 3–20. New York: Fordham University Press, 2006.
Keefe, Donald J. *Covenantal Theology: The Eucharistic Order of History*. 2 vols. Lanham, Md.: University Press of America, 1991.
Keiser, Kevin. "The Moral Act in St. Thomas: A Fresh Look." *The Thomist* 74, no. 2 (2010): 237–82.
———. *The Natural Desire to See God as an Innate Appetite of the Intellect and its Implications for the Moral Life and the Relationship between the Natural and Supernatural Orders*. PhD diss., Pontifical University of St. Thomas, 2018.
Kemp, Kenneth. "Science, Theology, and Monogenesis." *American Catholic Philosophical Quarterly* 85, no. 2 (2011): 217–36.
Kierkegaard, Søren. *The Sickness unto Death: A Christian Psychological Exposition for Upbuilding and Awakening*. Translated by Howard V. and Edna H. Hong. Princeton, N.J.: Princeton University Press, 1983.
Kilby, Karen. *Balthasar: A (Very) Critical Introduction*. Grand Rapids, Mich.: Eerdmans, 2012.
Kirk, Russell. *The Conservative Mind: From Burke to Eliot*. Washington, D.C.: Regnery, 1985.
Knasas, John F. X. *Being and Some 20th Century Thomists*. New York: Fordham University Press, 2003.
Kohák, Erazim. *The Embers and the Stars: A Philosophical Inquiry into the Moral Sense of Nature*. Chicago: Chicago University Press, 1987.
Koons, Robert. "Staunch vs. Faint-Hearted Hylomorphism: Toward an Aristotelian Account of Composition," *Res Philosophica* 91, no. 2 (2014): 151–77.

———. "Hylomorphic Escalation: A Hylomorphic Interpretation of Quantum Thermodynamics and Chemistry." *American Catholic Philosophical Quarterly* 92, no. 1 (2018): 159–78.

Koons, Robert, and Matthew O'Brien. "Objects of Intention: A Hylomorphic Critique of the New Natural Law Theory." *American Catholic Philosophical Quarterly* 86, no. 4 (2012): 655–703.

Koren, Leonard. *Wabi-Sabi for Artists, Designers, Poets, and Philosophers*. Point Reyes, Calif.: Imperfect Publishing, 2008.

Koslicki, Kathrin. *The Structure of Objects*. Oxford: Oxford University Press, 2008.

Krąpiec, Mieczysław. *I-Man: An Outline of Philosophical Anthropology*. Translated by Marie Lescoe et al. New Britain, Conn.: Mariel Publications, 1983.

———. *Metaphysics: An Outline of the History of Being*. Translated by Theresa Sandok. New York: Peter Lang, 1991.

Kripke, Saul. *Naming and Necessity*. Oxford: Blackwell, 1991.

Lakoff, George, and Mark Johnson. *Philosophy in the Flesh: The Embodied Mind and its Challenge to Western Thought*. New York: Basic Books, 1999.

Leclercq, Jean. *The Love of Learning and the Desire for God: A Study of Monastic Culture*. Translated by Catharine Misrahi. New York: Fordham University Press, 1961.

Leask, Ian. *Being Reconfigured*. Newcastle-upon-Tyne: Cambridge Scholars, 2011.

Lee, Patrick. "The Goodness of Creation, Evil, and Christian Teaching." *The Thomist* 64, no. 2 (2000): 239–70.

———. "Evil as Such Is a Privation." *American Catholic Philosophical Quarterly* 81, no. 3 (2007): 469–88.

Lee, Patrick, and Robert George. *Body-Self Dualism in Contemporary Ethics and Politics*. Cambridge: Cambridge University Press, 2008.

Leftow, Brian. "Souls Dipped in Dust." In *Soul, Body, and Survival: Essays on the Metaphysics of Human Persons*, edited by Kevin Corcoran, 120–38. Ithaca, N.Y.: Cornell University Press, 2001.

Leibniz, G. W. "Discourse on Metaphysics." In *Philosophical Essays*, translated by Roger Ariew and Daniel Garber. Indianapolis, Ind.: Hackett, 1989.

———. "The Principles of Philosophy, or, the Monadology." In *Philosophical Essays*, translated by Roger Ariew and Daniel Garber. Indianapolis, Ind.: Hackett, 1989.

Lehrberger, James. "The Anthropology of Aquinas's '*De ente et essentia*.'" *Review of Metaphysics* 51, no. 4 (1998): 829–47.

Levering, Matthew. *Mary's Bodily Assumption*. Notre Dame, Ind.: University of Notre Dame Press, 2016.

Levinas, Emmanuel. *Totality and Infinity: An Essay on Exteriority*. Translated by Alphonso Lingis. Pittsburgh: Duquesne University Press, 1969.

———. *Existence and Existents*. Translated by Alphonso Lingis. The Hague: Martinus Nijhoff, 1978.

———. *Time and the Other*. Translated by Richard Cohen. Pittsburgh: Duquesne University Press, 1987.

———. *Difficult Freedom: Essays on Judaism*. Translated by Seán Hand. Baltimore: The Johns Hopkins University Press, 1997.

———. *Entre Nous: On Thinking-of-the-Other*. Translated by Michael Smith and Barbara Harshav. New York: Columbia University Press, 1998.

———. "God and Philosophy." In *Collected Philosophical Papers*, translated by Alphonso Lingis, 153–74. Pittsburgh: Duquesne University Press, 1998.

———. *Otherwise than Being or Beyond Essence*. Translated by Alphonso Lingis. Pittsburgh: Duquesne University Press, 1998.

———. "Reality and Its Shadow." In *Collected Philosophical Papers*, translated by Alphonso Lingis, 1–14. Pittsburgh: Duquesne University Press, 1998.

———. *On Escape: De l'évasion*. Translated by Bettina Bergo. Stanford, Calif.: Stanford University Press, 2003.

Levine, Joseph. "Materialism and Qualia: The Explanatory Gap." *Pacific Philosophical Quarterly* 64, no. 4 (1983): 354–61.

Lewis, C. S. *The Four Loves*. London: Fontana Books, 1960.

———. *The Discarded Image: An Introduction to Medieval and Renaissance Literature*. Cambridge: Cambridge University Press, 1964.

———. *Till We Have Faces: A Myth Retold*. New York: HarperCollins, 1984.

Lewis, V. Bradley. "Personalism and Common Good: Thomistic Political Philosophy and the Turn to Subjectivity." In *Subjectivity: Ancient and Modern*, edited by R. J. Snell and Steven F. McGuire, 175–96. Lanham, Md.: Lexington Books, 2016.

Lingis, Alphonso. *The Community of Those Who Have Nothing in Common*. Bloomington: Indiana University Press, 1993.

———. *Foreign Bodies*. New York: Routledge, 1994.

———. *The Imperative*. Bloomington: Indiana University Press, 1998.

———. *Dangerous Emotions*. Berkeley: University of California Press, 2000.

Little, Joyce. *Toward a Thomistic Methodology*. Lewiston, N.Y.: The Edwin Mellen Press, 1988.

Locke, John. *An Essay Concerning Human Understanding*. New York: Penguin, 1997.

Lonergan, Bernard. "The Natural Desire to See God." In *Collection: Papers by Bernard Lonergan, SJ*, edited by Frederick Crowe and Robert Doran, 81–91. New York: Herder and Herder, 1967.

———. *Verbum: Word and Idea in Aquinas*. Notre Dame, Ind.: University of Notre Dame Press, 1967.

———. *Insight: A Study of Human Understanding*. Toronto: University of Toronto Press, 1992.

Long, Steven. *The Teleological Grammar of the Moral Act*. Naples, Fla.: Sapientia Press, 2007.

———. *Natura Pura: On the Recovery of Nature in the Doctrine of Grace*. New York: Fordham University Press, 2010.

———. "Fundamental Errors of the New Natural Law Theory." *National Catholic Bioethics Quarterly* 13, no. 1 (2013): 105–31.

Loudovikos, Nikolaos. *Analogical Identities: The Creation of the Christian Self*. Turnhout: Brepols, 2019.

Lowe, E. J. *A Survey of Metaphysics*. Oxford: Oxford University Press, 2002.

———. *Personal Agency: The Metaphysics of Mind and Action*. Oxford: Oxford University Press, 2008.

Lu, Mathew. "Explaining the Wrongness of Cannibalism." *American Catholic Philosophical Quarterly* 87, no. 3 (2013): 430–58.

———. "*Hexis* within Aristotelian Virtue Ethics." *Proceedings of the American Catholic Philosophical Association* 88 (2015): 197–206.

Luis de Molina, *Liberi arbitrii cum gratiae donis, divina praescientia, providentia, praedestinatione, et reprobatione concordia*. Antwerp: Ex officina typographica Ioachimi Trognaesii, 1595.

MacIntyre, Alasdair. *After Virtue*. Notre Dame, Ind.: University of Notre Dame Press, 1984.

———. *Dependent Rational Animals: Why Human Beings Need the Virtues*. Chicago: Open Court, 1999.

MacMurray, John. *Persons in Relation*. New York: Harpers and Brothers, 1961.

Madden, James D. *Mind, Matter, and Nature: A Thomistic Proposal for the Philosophy of Mind*. Washington, D.C.: The Catholic University of America Press, 2013.

Mallory, J. P., and D. Q. Adams. *The Oxford Introduction to Proto-Indo-European and the Proto-Indo-European World*. Oxford: Oxford University Press, 2006.

Manoussakis, John Panteleimon. "The Time of the Body: Sex, Liturgy, Eschatology." In *On Time: Philosophical, Theological, and Literary Accounts*, edited by Marina Marren, 31–46. Newcastle-upon-Tyne: Cambridge Scholars, 2016.

Manteau-Bonamy, H. M. *Immaculate Conception and the Holy Spirit: The Marian Teaching of St. Maximillian Kolbe*. Libertyville, Ill.: Marytown Press, 2008.

Marcel, Gabriel. *Being and Having*. Translated by Katherine Ferrer. Westminster: Dacre Press, 1949.

———. *The Philosophy of Existentialism*. New York: Citadel, 1984.

———. *Man Against Mass Society*. Translated by G. S. Fraser. South Bend, Ind.: St. Augustine's Press, 2008.

———. *Homo Viator: Introduction to the Metaphysic of Hope*. Translated by Emma Craufurd and Paul Seaton. South Bend, Ind.: St. Augustine Press, 2010.

Marías, Julián. *Anthropologia metafisica*. Madrid: Alianza, 1970.

Marion, Jean-Luc. *God Without Being: Hors-Texte*. Translated by Thomas Carlson. Chicago: University of Chicago Press, 1995.

———. *Reduction and Givenness: Investigations of Husserl, Heidegger, and Phenomenology*. Translated by Thomas Carlson. Evanston, Ill.: Northwestern University Press, 1998.

———. *Being Given: Toward a Phenomenology of Givenness*. Translated by Jeffrey Kosky. Stanford, Calif.: Stanford University Press, 2002.

———. *Prolegomena to Charity*. Translated by Stephen Lewis. New York: Fordham University Press, 2002.

———. *In Excess: Studies of Saturated Phenomena*. Translated by Robyn Horner and Vincent Berraud, New York: Fordham University Press, 2004.

———. *The Erotic Phenomenon*. Translated by Stephen Lewis. Chicago: University of Chicago Press, 2008.

———. *The Reason of the Gift*. Translated by Stephen Lewis. Charlottesville: University of Virginia Press, 2011.

———. *In the Self's Place: The Approach of Saint Augustine*. Translated by Jeffrey Kosky. Stanford, Calif.: Stanford University Press, 2012.

———. *Negative Certainties*. Translated by Stephen Lewis. Chicago: University of Chicago Press, 2015.

———. *Believing in Order to See: On the Rationality of Revelation and the Irrationality of Some Believers*. Translated by Christina M. Gschwandtner. New York: Fordham University Press, 2017.

Maritain, Jacques. *Three Reformers: Luther—Descartes—Rousseau*. New York: Charles Scribner's Sons, 1929.

———. *Art and Scholasticism*. Translated by J. F. Scanlan. New York: Charles Scribner's Sons, 1930.

———. *Man and the State*. Washington, D.C.: The Catholic University of America Press, 1951.

———. *Creative Intuition in Poetry and Art*. New York: Pantheon, 1953.

———. *Bergsonian Philosophy and Thomism*. Translated by Mabelle Andison. New York: Philosophical Library, 1955.

———. *An Essay on Christian Philosophy*. Translated by Edward Flannery. New York: Philosophical Library, 1955.

———. *The Peasant of the Garonne: An Old Layman Questions Himself about the Present Time*. Translated by Michael Cuddihy and Elizabeth Hughes. New York: Holt Reinhardt, 1966.

———. *Untrammeled Approaches*. Translated by Bernard Doering. Notre Dame, Ind.: University of Notre Dame Press, 1977.

———. *The Person and the Common Good*, Translated by John Fitzgerald. Notre Dame, Ind.: University of Notre Dame Press, 1994.

———. *The Degrees of Knowledge*. Translated by Gerald B. Phelan. Notre Dame, Ind.: University of Notre Dame Press, 1995.

Martin, Michael. "Love, Sex, Beauty: Encountering Vladimir Solovyov on Eros and the Divine Sophia." *Logos* 49 (2009): 109–29.

———. *The Submerged Reality: Sophiology and the Turn to a Poetic Metaphysics*. Kettering, Ohio: Angelico Press, 2015.

Matthew of Aquasparta. *Quaestiones disputatae de anima separata, de anima beata, de ieiunio et de legibus*. Quaracchi: Collegium S. Bonaventura, 1959.

Maurer, Armand. "St. Thomas and the Analogy of Genus." *New Scholasticism* 29, no. 2 (1955): 127–44.

Mauro, Sylvester. *Opus theologicum*. Rome: Nicolai Angeli Tinassii, 1687.

Maximus the Confessor. *On Difficulties in the Church Fathers: The Ambigua*. Translated by Nicholas Constas. Cambridge, Mass.: Harvard University Press, 2014.

Mazur, Piotr, Barbara Kiereś, Ryszard Skrzyniarz, and Agata Płazińska. *Jacek Woroniecki*. Krakow: Ignatianum University Press, 2019.

McCool, Gerard. *The Neo-Thomists*. Milwaukee, Wisc.: Marquette University Press, 1994.

McDaniel, Kris. *The Fragmentation of Being*. Oxford: Oxford University Press, 2017.

McDowell, John. *Mind and World*. Cambridge, Mass.: Harvard University Press, 1996.

McGinn, Colin. "Can We Solve the Mind-Body Problem?" *Mind* 98, no. 391 (1989): 349–66.

McInroy, Mark. *Balthasar on the Spiritual Senses: Perceiving Splendor*. Oxford: Oxford University Press, 2014.

McNeill, William. *The Glance of the Eye: Heidegger, Aristotle, and the Ends of Theory*. Albany: State University of New York Press, 1999.

McTaggart, J. M. E. "The Unreality of Time." *Mind* 17, no. 68 (1908): 457–73.

Meconi, David Vincent. *The One Christ: St. Augustine's Theology of Deification*. Washington, D.C.: The Catholic University of America Press, 2018.

Meillassoux, Quentin. *After Finitude: An Essay on the Necessity of Contingency*. Translated by Ray Brassier. London: Continuum, 2010.

Merleau-Ponty, Maurice. *The Primacy of Perception*. Translated by William Cobb. Evanston, Ill.: Northwestern University Press, 1964.

———. *The Visible and the Invisible*. Translated by Alphonso Lingis. Evanston, Ill.: Northwestern University Press, 1969.

———. *Structure of Behavior*. Translated by Alden Fischer. Pittsburgh: Duquesne University Press, 1983.

———. *Phenomenology of Perception*. Translated by Colin Smith. London: Routledge, 2002.

Merton, Thomas. *No Man Is an Island*. New York: Image Books, 1955.

———. *The New Man*. New York: Farrar, Straus and Giroux, 1961.

———. *New Seeds of Contemplation*. New York: New Directions, 1961.

———. *Zen and the Birds of Appetite*. New York: New Directions, 1968.

———. "Marxism and Monastic Perspectives." In *The Asian Journal of Thomas Merton*, 32–43. New York: New Directions, 1975.

Milbank, John. "Can a Gift Be Given? Prolegomena to a Future Trinitarian Metaphysics." *Modern Theology* 11, no. 1 (1995): 119–61.

———. "The Soul of Reciprocity Part One: Reciprocity Refused," *Modern Theology* 17, no. 3 (2001): 335–91.

———. "The Soul of Reciprocity Part Two: Reciprocity Regained," Modern Theology 17, no. 4 (2001): 485–507.

———. *The Suspended Middle: Henri de Lubac and the Debate Concerning the Supernatural*. Grand Rapids, Mich.: Eerdmans, 2005.

———. *Theology and Social Theory: Beyond Secular Reason*. Oxford: Blackwell, 2006.

———. *Beyond Secular Order: The Representation of Being and the Representation of the People*. Oxford: Wiley-Blackwell, 2013.

———. "Christianity and Platonism in East and West." In *Divine Essence and Divine Energies: Ecumenical Reflections on the Presence of God*, edited by C. Athanasopouls and C. Schneider, 158–209. Cambridge: Clarke, 2013.

Miller, Joshua. *On whether or not Merleau-Ponty's phenomenology of lived body experience can enrich St. Thomas Aquinas's integral anthropology*. PhD diss., Duquesne University, 2009.

Milton, John. *Paradise Lost and Paradise Regained*. New York: New American Library, 2001.

Minerd, Matthew. "Beyond Non-Being: Thomistic Metaphysics on Second Intentions,

Ens morale, and *Ens artificiale*." *American Catholic Philosophical Quarterly* 91, no. 3 (2017): 353–79.

Moore, G. E. "The Refutation of Idealism." *Mind* 12, no. 48 (1903): 433–53.

Montgomery, Marion. *Making: The Proper Habit of Our Being*. South Bend, Ill.: St. Augustine, 2000.

Mormando, Franco. "What Happens to Us When We Die? Bernardine of Siena on the Four Last Things." In *Death and Dying in the Middle Ages*, edited by Edelgard DuBruck and Barbara Gusick, 109–42. New York: Peter Lang, 1999.

Mosebach, Martin. *The Heresy of Formlessness*. Translated by Graham Harrison. San Francisco: Ignatius, 2006.

Mounier, Emmanuel. *Personalism*. Translated by Philip Mairet. London: Routledge, 1952.

Muir, John. *My First Summer in the Sierra*. In *Nature Writings*, edited by William Cronon. New York: Library of America, 1997.

Nagel, Thomas. *The View from Nowhere*. Oxford: Oxford University Press, 1986.

Nancy, Jean-Luc. *Corpus II: Writings on Sexuality*. Translated by Anne O'Byrne. New York: Fordham University Press, 2013.

Nannery, Lawrence. "The Problem of the Two Lives in Aristotle's Ethics: The Human Good and the Best Life for a Man." *International Philosophical Quarterly* 21, no. 3 (1981): 276–92.

Narcisse, Gilbert. *Les Raisons de Dieu: Argument de Convenance Et Esthétique Théologique Selon Saint Thomas d'Aquin Et Hans Urs von Balthasar*. Fribourg: Editions Universitaires Fribourg Suisse, 1997.

Nellas, Panayiotis. *Deification in Christ: Orthodox Perspectives on the Nature of the Human Person*. Translated by Norman Russell. Crestwood, N.Y.: St. Vladimir's Seminary Press, 1987.

Nevitt, Turner. "Aquinas on the Death of Christ: A New Argument for Corruptionism." *American Catholic Philosophical Quarterly* 90, no. 1 (2016): 77–99.

———. "What Has Aquinas Got Against Platonic Forms?" *Proceedings of the Society for Medieval Logic and Metaphysics* 15 (2018): 67–79.

Newman, John Henry. *Discussion and Arguments on Various Subjects*. London: Longmans, Green, and Co., 1907.

———. *An Essay in Aid of a Grammar of Assent*. New York: Image, 1955.

Nicholas of Cusa. *On Learned Ignorance*. Translated by Jasper Hopkins. Minneapolis, Minn.: Benning, 1981.

Nicodemos of the Holy Mountain. *A Handbook of Spiritual Counsel*. Translated by Peter Chamberas. Mahwah, N.J.: Paulist Press, 1989.

Nietzsche, Friedrich. *The Birth of Tragedy*. Translated by Francis Golffing. New York: Doubleday, 1956.

———. *Thus Spake Zarathustra*. In *The Portable Nietzsche*, translated by Walter Kaufmann. New York: Penguin, 1977.

———. *Twilight of the Idols*. In *The Portable Nietzsche*, translated by Walter Kaufmann. New York: Penguin, 1977.

———. *On the Genealogy of Morality*. Translated by Maudemarie Clark and Alan Swensen. Indianapolis, Ind.: Hackett, 1998.

Noë, Alva. *Action in Perception*. Cambridge, Mass.: MIT Press, 2004.
Novotný, Daniel. *Beings of Reason: A Study in the Scholasticism of the Baroque Era*. PhD diss., University at Buffalo, 2008.
———. *Ens rationis from Suárez to Caramuel: A Study in Scholasticism of the Baroque Era*. New York: Fordham University Press, 2013.
Nussbaum, Martha, and Hilary Putnam. "Changing Aristotle's Mind." In *Essays on Aristotle's De Anima*, edited by Amelie Rorty, 27–56. Oxford: Clarendon, 1992.
O'Brien, Patrick. *Pablo Ruiz Picasso: A Biography*. New York: Norton, 1976.
O'Byrne, Anne. *Natality and Finitude*. Bloomington: Indiana University Press, 2010.
Oderberg, David. *Real Essentialism*. New York: Routledge, 2007.
Oliva, Mirela. "The Challenge of the Thomistic *Sensus Communis*: A Hermeneutic View." In *Thomas Aquinas: Teacher of Humanity*, edited by John Hittinger, 255–70. Newcastle-upon-Tyne: Cambridge Scholars, 2015.
———. "Hermeneutics and the Meaning of Life." *Epoché* 22, no. 2 (2018): 523–39.
Olson, Eric. *What Are We? A Study in Personal Ontology*. Oxford: Oxford University Press, 2007.
Oord, Thomas Jay. *The Uncontrolling Love of God: An Open and Relational Account of Providence*. Downers Grove, Ill.: IVP Academic, 2015.
Ortega y Gasset, José. *What Is Philosophy?* Translated by Mildred Adams. New York: Norton, 1960.
Osborne, Thomas. *Human Action in Thomas Aquinas, John Duns Scotus, and William of Ockham*. Washington, D.C.: The Catholic University of America Press, 2014.
Otto, Rudolf. *The Idea of the Holy*. Translated by John Harvey. Oxford: Oxford University Press, 1958.
Owens, Joseph. "Aquinas on Knowing Existence." *Review of Metaphysics* 29, no. 4 (1976): 670–90.
———. *An Elementary Christian Metaphysics*. Houston: Center for Thomistic Studies, 1985.
Pabst, Adrian. *Metaphysics: The Creation of Hierarchy*. Grand Rapids, Mich.: Eerdmans, 2012.
Parfit, Derek, *Reasons and Persons*. Oxford: Oxford University Press, 1986.
Pasnau, Robert. *Theories of Cognition in the Later Middle Ages*. Cambridge: Cambridge University Press, 1997.
———. *Thomas Aquinas on Human Nature*. Cambridge: Cambridge University Press, 2002.
Passerini, Peter Maria. *De hominum statibus et officiis inspectiones morales*. Rome: Typis Nicolai Angeli Tinassii: 1663.
Patočka, Jan. *Plato and Europe*. Translated by Petr Lom. Stanford, Calif.: Stanford University Press, 2002.
Pedro da Fonseca. *In libros metaphysicorum Aristotelis Stagirita*. Frankfurt: Schanuertteri, 1599.
Pegis, Anton. *At the Origins of the Thomistic Notion of Man*. New York: Macmillan, 1963.
Penrose, Roger. *The Road to Reality: A Complete Guide to the Laws of the Universe*. New York: Knopf, 2005.

Percy, Walker. *Lost in the Cosmos: The Last Self-Help Book*. New York: Washington Square Press, 1983.
Pereira, José. *Suárez: Between Scholasticism and Modernity*. Milwaukee, Wisc.: Marquette University Press, 2007.
Perl, Eric. *Thinking Being: Introduction to Metaphysics in the Classical Tradition*. Leiden: Brill, 2014.
Petavius, Dionysius. *Opus de theologicis dogmatibus*. Venice: Ex Typographia Remondiniana, 1757.
Petcu, Liviu. "The Doctrine of Epektasis: One of the Major Contributions of Saint Gregory of Nyssa to the History of Thinking." *Revista Portuguesa de Filosofia* 73, no. 2 (2017): 771–82.
Peter Auriol. *Commentariorum in secundum librum Sententiarum*. Rome: Zannetti, 1595.
Peter John Olivi. *Quaestiones in secundum librum Sententiarum*. Quaracchi: Collegium S. Bonaventura, 1926.
Phelan, Gerard. "The Being of Creatures." *Proceedings of the American Catholic Philosophical Association* 31 (1957): 118–27.
———. "The Esse of Accidents." *New Scholasticism* 43, no. 1 (1969): 143–48.
Philip of the Trinity. *Summa theologiae mysticae*. Lyon: Borde, Arnaud, and Rigaud, 1656.
Pickstock, Catherine. *After Writing: On the Liturgical Consummation of Philosophy*. Oxford: Blackwell, 1998.
———. *Repetition and Identity*. Oxford: Oxford University Press, 2013.
Pico della Mirandola, Giovanni. *Oration on the Dignity of Man*. Translated by Elizabeth Forbes. In *Renaissance Philosophy of Man*, edited by Ernst Cassirer et al. Chicago: University of Chicago Press, 1948.
Pinckaers, Servais. *The Sources of Christian Ethics*. Translated by Mary Thomas Noble. Washington, D.C.: The Catholic University of America Press, 1995.
Pieper, Josef. *Leisure the Basis of Culture*. Translated by Alexander Dru. New York: New American Library, 1963.
———. *In Tune with the World: A Theory of Festivity*. Translated by Richard and Clara Winston. South Bend, Ind.: St. Augustine's Press, 1999.
Pierce, C. S. *Collected Papers*. Cambridge, Mass.: Harvard University Press, 1965.
Pinsent, Andrew. *The Second-Person Perspective in Aquinas' Ethics: Virtues and Gifts*. London: Routledge, 2013.
Plato. *Complete Works*. Edited by John Cooper. Indianapolis, Ind.: Hackett, 1997.
Plested, Marcus. *Orthodox Readings of Aquinas*. Oxford: Oxford University Press, 2012.
Polanyi, Michael. *The Tacit Dimension*. Chicago: University of Chicago Press, 2009.
Proclus. *The Elements of Theology*. Translated by E. R. Dodds. Oxford: Clarendon, 1992.
Przywara, Erich. *Analogia Entis: Metaphysics: Original Structure and Universal Rhythm*. Translated by John Betz and David Bentley Hart. Grand Rapids, Mich.: Eerdmans, 2014.
Quine, Willard V. "On What There Is." *The Review of Metaphysics* 2, no. 5 (1948): 21–38.

Radhakrishnan, Sarvepalli, and Charles A. Moore, eds. *A Sourcebook in Indian Philosophy*. Princeton, N.J.: Princeton University Press, 2014.

Rahner, Karl. "Concerning the Relationship between Nature and Grace." In *Theological Investigations*. Vol. 1. Translated by Cornelius Ernst, 297–318. Baltimore: Helicon Press, 1961.

———. *Hominisation: The Evolutionary Origin of Man as a Theological Problem*. Translated by W. J. O'Hara. New York: Herder and Herder, 1965.

———. "The Concept of Mystery in Catholic Theology." In *Theological Investigations*. Vol. 4. Translated by Kevin Smyth, 36–73. Baltimore: Helicon Press, 1966.

———. "Theology of Freedom." In *Theological Investigations*. Vol. 6. Translated by Karl-H. and Boniface Kruger, 178–96. New York: Seabury, 1974.

———. *Spirit in the World*. Translated by William Dych. New York: Continuum, 1994.

———. *Foundations of Christian Faith*. Translated by William Dych. New York: Crossroad, 1999.

Ramos, Alice. "Beauty and the Perfection of Being." *Proceedings of the American Catholic Philosophical Association* 71 (1997): 255–68.

Ratzinger, Joseph. *The Spirit of the Liturgy*. Translated by John Saward. San Francisco: Ignatius Press, 2000.

———. "The Feeling of Things, the Contemplation of Beauty." Message to the Communion and Liberation Meeting at Rimini, August 24–30, 2002. http://www.vatican.va/ roman_ curia/congregations/ cfaith/documents/ rc_con_cfaith_doc_20020824_ratzinger-cl-rimini_en.html.

Reimers, Adrian. *The Soul of the Person: A Contemporary Philosophical Psychology*. Washington, D.C.: The Catholic University of America Press, 2014.

Reinach, Adolf. "The A Priori Foundations of Civil Law." Translated by John Crosby. *Aletheia* 3 (1983): 1–142.

Rhonheimer, Martin. *The Perspective of the Acting Person: Essays in the Renewal of Thomistic Moral Philosophy*. Washington, D.C.: The Catholic University of America Press, 2008.

Richard of St. Victor. *De Trinitate*. In PL. Vol. 196. Paris: J.-P. Migne, 1855.

Richards, Amy. "Response to Christopher Tollefsen." In *Subjectivity: Ancient and Modern*, edited by R. J. Snell and Steven F. McGuire, 11–24. Lanham, Md.: Lexington Books, 2016.

Rilke, Rainer Maria. *The Poetry of Rilke*. Edited by Edward Snow. New York: North Point Press, 2009.

Rivera, Joseph. *The Contemplative Self After Michel Henry*. Notre Dame, Ind.: University of Notre Dame Press, 2015.

Rocha, Samuel D. *Folk Phenomenology: Education, Study, and the Human Person*. Eugene, Ore.: Pickwick, 2015.

———. "Folk phenomenology and the offering of teaching." *Journal of Curriculum and Pedagogy* 13, no. 2 (2016): 121–35.

Rocha, Samuel, and Adi Burton. "A Phenomenology of Utterance and Prophetic Teaching in the Threshold." *Journal for Continental Philosophy of Religion* 3 (2021): 144–63.

Rolnick, Philip. *Person, Grace, and God*. Grand Rapids, Mich.: Eerdmans, 2007.

Romano, Claude. *At the Heart of Reason*. Translated by Michael Smith and Claude Romano. Evanston, Ill.: Northwestern University Press, 2015.

———. *There Is: The Event and the Finitude of Appearing*. Translated by Michael Smith. New York: Fordham University Press, 2015.

Romero Carrasquillo, Francisco J. "The Role of *Gloria* in Aquinas' Philosophy of Religion." *Acta Philosophica* 23 (2014): 311–32.

Romero, Miguel. "The Happiness of 'Those Who Lack the Use of Reason.'" *The Thomist* 80, no. 1 (2016): 49–96.

Rubin, Michael. "Aquinas on Bodily or Sensible Beauty." *Proceedings of the American Catholic Philosophical Association* 94 (2020): forthcoming.

Rubio, Antonio. *Logica mexicana*. Lyon: Ioannes Pillehotte, 1625.

Russell, Norman. *The Doctrine of Deification in the Greek Patristic Tradition*. Oxford: Oxford University Press, 2004.

Sacred Congregation of Studies. *24 Thomistic Theses*. Rome, 1914.

Sadler, Gregory. *Reason Fulfilled by Revelation: The 1930s Christian Philosophy Debates in France*. Washington, D.C.: The Catholic University of America Press, 2003.

Salmanticenses. *De beatitudine*. In *Cursus theologicus*. Vol. 5. Paris: Victor Palmé, 1878.

Samajdar, Saunak. "Intimacy, Hospitality and Jouissance: A 'Feminine' Knowing of Difference." *Michigan Feminist Studies* 20 (2006–07). http://hdl.handle.net/2027/spo.ark5583.0020.004.

Sartre, Jean-Paul. *Nausea*. Translated by Lloyd Alexander. New York: New Directions, 1964.

———. *Being and Nothingness*. Translated by Hazel Barnes. New York: Washington Square Press, 1984.

Schaefer, Donovan. "Do Animals Have Religion? Interdisciplinary Perspectives on Religion and Embodiment." *Anthrozoös* 25 (2012): S173–89.

Schaeffer, Matthew. "Thick-*Esse*/Thin-Essence in Thomistic Personalism." *American Catholic Philosophical Quarterly* 89, no. 2 (2015): 223–51.

Scheeben, Matthias. *The Mysteries of Christianity*. Translated by Cyril Vollert. New York: Crossroad, 2006.

Scheler, Max. *On the Eternal in Man*. Translated by Bernard Noble. New York: Harper, 1960.

———. *Man's Place in Nature*. Translated by Hans Meyerhoff. New York: Farrar, Straus and Giroux, 1962.

———. *The Nature of Sympathy*. Translated by Peter Heath. Hamden, Conn.: Archon Books, 1970.

———. *Formalism in Ethics and Non-Formal Ethics of Values: A New Attempt Toward the Foundation of an Ethical Personalism*. Translated by Manfred Frings and Roger Funk. Evanston, Ill.: Northwestern University Press, 1973.

———. "Idealism and Realism." In *Selected Philosophical Essays*, translated by David Lachterman, 288–356. Evanston, Ill.: Northwestern University Press, 1973.

———. "*Ordo Amoris*." In *Selected Philosophical Essays*, translated by David Lachterman, 98–135. Evanston, Ill.: Northwestern University Press, 1973.

———. "Phenomenology and the Theory of Cognition." In *Selected Philosophical*

Essays, translated by David Lachterman, 136–201. Evanston, Ill.: Northwestern University Press, 1973.

———. "The Theory of the Three Facts." In *Selected Philosophical Essays*, translated by David Lachterman, 202–87. Evanston, Ill.: Northwestern University Press, 1973.

———. *Ressentiment*. Translated by Lewis Coser. Milwaukee, Wisc.: Marquette University Press, 1994.

———. *The Constitution of the Human Being*. Translated by John Cutting. Milwaukee, Wisc.: Marquette University Press, 2008.

Schiller, Friedrich. *On the Aesthetic Education of Man*. Translated by Reginald Snell. Mineola: Dover, 2004.

Schindler, D. C. "What's the Difference? On the Metaphysics of Participation in a Christian Context." *The Saint Anselm Journal* 3, no. 1 (2005): 1–27.

———. *Freedom from Reality: The Diabolical Character of Modern Liberty*. Notre Dame, Ind.: University of Notre Dame Press, 2019.

Schindler, David L. "Norris Clarke on Person, Being, and St. Thomas." *Communio* 20 (1993): 580–92.

———. *Heart of the World, Center of the Church: Communio Ecclesiology, Liberalism, and Liberation*. Grand Rapids, Mich.: Eerdmans, 1996.

Schmitz, Kenneth L. *The Gift: Creation*. Milwaukee, Wisc.: Marquette University Press, 1982.

———. "Substance Is Not Enough. Hegel's Slogan: From Substance to Subject." *Proceedings of the American Catholic Philosophical Association* 61 (1987): 52–68.

Schneider, Susan. "Idealism, or Something Near Enough." In *Idealism: New Essays in Metaphysics*, edited by Tyron Goldschmidt and Kenneth Pearce, 275–90. Oxford: Oxford University Press, 2017.

Schweitzer, Othmar. *Person und hypostatische Union bei Thomas von Aquin*. Freiburg: Universitätsverlag, 1957.

Scruton, Roger. *Sexual Desire: A Philosophical Investigation*. London: Continuum, 2006.

———. "Confessions of a Skeptical Francophile." *Philosophy* 87 (2012): 477–95.

———. *How to Think Seriously About the Planet: The Case for an Environmental Conservatism*. Oxford: Oxford University Press, 2012.

Searle, John. *Speech Acts: An Essay in the Philosophy of Language*. Cambridge: Cambridge University Press, 1970.

———. *The Rediscovery of the Mind*. Cambridge, Mass.: MIT Press, 1992.

———. *The Construction of Social Reality*. New York: Free Press, 1995.

———. *Mind, Language, and Society: Philosophy in the Real World*. New York: Basic Books, 1999.

Seifert, Josef. "Die Verschiedenen Bedeutungen von 'Sein'–Dietrich von Hildebrand als Metaphysiker und Martin Heideggers Vorwurf der Seinsvergessenheit." In *Warheit, Wert und Sein: Festgabe für Dietrich von Hildebrand zum 80. Geburtstag*, edited by Balduin Schwartz, 301–32. Regensburg: Habbel, 1972.

———. *Was ist und was motiviert eine sittliche Handlung?* Regensburg: Pustet, 1976.

———. "*Essence and Existence*: A New Foundation of Classical Metaphysics on the Basis of "Phenomenological Realism" and a Critical Investigation of "Existentialist Thomism." *Aletheia* 1, nos. 1 and 2 (1977): 17–157, 371–459.

―――. *Back to 'Things in Themselves': A Phenomenological Foundation for Classical Realism*. New York: Routledge and Kegan Paul, 1987.

―――. *Essere e persona: Verso una fondazione fenomenologica di una metafisica classica e personalistica*. Rome: Vita e pensiero, 1989.

―――. "Personalism and Personalisms." In *Ethical Personalism*, edited by Cheikh Mbacke Gueye, 155–85. Frankfurt: Ontos Verlag, 2011.

Sevier, Christopher Scott. *Aquinas on Beauty*. Lanham, Md.: Lexington Press, 2015.

Sharkey, Sarah Borden. *Thine Own Self: Individuality in Edith Stein's Later Writings*. Washington, D.C.: The Catholic University of America Press, 2012.

Shaw, Gregory. *Theurgy and the Soul: The Neoplatonism of Iamblichus*. University Park: Pennsylvania State University Press, 1995.

Sheldrake, Merlin. *Entangled Life: How Fungi Make our Worlds, Change our Minds, and Shape our Futures*. New York: Random House, 2020.

Sherman, Jacob Holsinger. *Partakers of the Divine: Contemplation and the Practice of Philosophy*. Minneapolis, Minn.: Fortress Press, 2014.

Shoemaker, Sydney. "Self, Body, and Coincidence." Supplement to the *Proceedings of the Aristotelian Society* 73, no. 1 (1999): 287–306.

Sider, Theodore. *Four-Dimensionalism: An Ontology of Persistence and Time*. Oxford: Oxford University Press, 2002.

Simon, Yves. *An Introduction to Metaphysics of Knowledge*. Translated by Vukan Kric and Richard Thompson. New York: Fordham University Press, 1934.

Sloterdijk, Peter. *Terror from the Air*. Translated by Amy Patton and Steve Corcoran. Los Angeles: Semiotext(e), 2009.

Smart, J. J. C. "Sensations and Brain Processes." *Philosophical Review* 68, no. 2 (1959): 141–56.

Smith, Wolfgang. *The Quantum Enigma: Finding the Hidden Key*. San Rafael, Calif.: Sophia Perennis, 2005.

Smith-Gilson, Caitlin. *The Metaphysical Presuppositions of Being-in-the-World: A Confrontation between St. Thomas Aquinas and Martin Heidegger*. New York: Continuum, 2010.

Soccorsi, Philippus. *Quaestiones scientificae cum philosophia coniunctae de physica quantica*. Rome: Gregorian and Biblical Press, 1956.

Sokolowski, Robert. *Husserlian Meditations: How Words Present Things*. Evanston, Ill.: Northwestern University Press, 1974.

―――. *Phenomenology of the Human Person*. Cambridge: Cambridge University Press, 2008.

―――. "Hildebrand's Defense of the Philosophical Life." Introduction. In *What Is Philosophy?* Steubenville, Ohio: Hildebrand Press, 2020.

Soloveitchik, Josef. "The Community." *Tradition: A Journal of Orthodox Jewish Thought* 17, no. 2 (1978): 7–24.

―――. *Halakhic Man*. New York: Jewish Publication Society, 1983.

Soloviev, Vladimir. *God, Man and the Church: The Spiritual Foundations of Life*. Translated by Donald Attwater. London: James Clarke, 1938.

―――. *Lectures on Divine Humanity*. Translated by Boris Jakim. Hudson, N.Y.: Lindisfarne, 1995.

Spaemann, Robert. *Persons: The Difference between 'Someone' and 'Something.'* Translated by Oliver O'Donovan. Oxford: Oxford University Press, 2006.
Spencer, Mark K. "Full Human Flourishing: The Place of the Various Virtues in the Quest for Happiness in Aristotle's Ethics." *Proceedings of the American Catholic Philosophical Association* 81 (2007): 193–204.
———. "A Reexamination of the Hylomorphic Theory of Death." *The Review of Metaphysics* 63, no. 4 (2010): 843–70.
———. "Ethical Subjectivity in Levinas and Thomas Aquinas: Common Ground?" *The Heythrop Journal* 53, no. 1 (2012): 137–47.
———. *Thomistic Hylomorphism and the Phenomenology of Self-Sensing*. PhD diss., University at Buffalo, 2012.
———. "Transcendental Order in Suárez." *Studia Neoaristotelica* 10, no. 2 (2013): 157–95.
———. "Habits, Potencies, and Obedience: Experiential Evidence for Thomistic Hylomorphism." *Proceedings of the American Catholic Philosophical Association* 88 (2014): 165–80.
———. The Personhood of the Separated Soul." *Nova et Vetera* (English edition) 12, no. 3 (2014): 863–912.
———. "Aristotelian Substance and Personalistic Subjectivity." *International Philosophical Quarterly* 55, no. 2 (2015): 145–64.
———. "The Category of *Habitus*: Artifacts, Accidents, and Human Nature." *The Thomist* 79, no. 1 (2015): 113–54.
———. "Created Persons Are Subsistent Relations: A Scholastic-Phenomenological Synthesis." *Proceedings of the American Catholic Philosophical Association* 89 (2015): 225–43.
———. "Divine Causality and Created Freedom: A Thomistic Personalist View." *Nova et Vetera* (English edition) 14, no. 3 (2016): 375–419.
———. "Quantum Randomness, Hylomorphism, and Classical Theism." *Journal of Analytic Theology* 4 (2016): 147–70.
———. "What Is It Like to Be an Embodied Person? What Is It Like to Be a Separated Soul?" *Angelicum* 93 (2016): 219–46.
———. "The Flexibility of Divine Simplicity: Aquinas, Scotus, Palamas." *International Philosophical Quarterly* 57, no. 2 (2017): 123–39.
———. "Grace, Natura Pura, and the Metaphysics of *Status*: Personalism and Thomism on the Historicity of the Human Person and the Genealogy of Modernity." *Proceedings of the American Catholic Philosophical Association* 91 (2017): 127–43.
———. "The Many Powers of the Human Soul: Von Hildebrand's Contribution to Scholastic Philosophical Anthropology," *American Catholic Philosophical Quarterly* 91, no. 4 (2017): 719–35.
———. "Beauty, First and Last of All the Transcendentals: Givenness and Aesthetic, Spiritual Perception in Thomism and Jean-Luc Marion." *The Thomist* 82, no. 2 (2018): 157–87.
———. "Perceiving the Image of God in the Whole Human Person." *The Saint Anselm Journal* 13, no. 2 (2018): 1–18.
———. "Beauty and Being in von Hildebrand and the Aristotelian Tradition." *Review of Metaphysics* 73, no. 2 (2019): 311–34.

———. "Beauty and the Intellectual Virtues in Aristotle." In *Beauty and the Good: Recovering the Classical Tradition from Plato to Duns Scotus*, edited by Alice Ramos, 93–114. Washington, D.C.: The Catholic University of America Press, 2020.

———. "Covenantal Metaphysics and Cosmological Metaphysics: An Aesthetic Critique and an Aesthetic Synthesis." *The Saint Anselm Journal* 15, no. 2 (2020): 19–38.

———. "The Metaphysics of Justice: The Category of Artifacts and Free Cooperative Causality." *The Heythrop Journal* 61, no. 2 (2020): 241–52.

———. "The Separated Soul: Disability in the Intermediate State," in *Disability in Medieval Christian Philosophy and Theology*, edited by Scott Williams, 235–57. New York: Routledge, 2020.

———. "The Many Phenomenological Reductions and Catholic Metaphysical Anti-Reductionism." *American Catholic Philosophical Quarterly* 95, no. 3 (2021): 367–88.

Spencer, Mark K., and W. Matthews Grant. "Activity, Identity, and God: A Tension in Aquinas and His Interpreters." *Studia Neoaristotelica* 12 (2015): 5–61.

Spencer, Mark K., and Tim Pawl. "Christologically Inspired, Empirically Motivated Hylomorphism." *Res Philosophica* 93, no. 1 (2016): 137–60.

Spiering, Jamie. "What Is Freedom? An Instance of the Silence of St. Thomas." *American Catholic Philosophical Quarterly* 89, no. 1 (2015): 27–46.

Staniloae, Dumitru. *The Experience of God*. Vol. 1. Translated by Ioan Ionita and Robert Barringer. Brookline, Mass.: Holy Cross Orthodox Press, 1994.

Stango, Marco. "Death as Material Kenosis: A Thomistic Proposal." *The Heythrop Journal* 61, no. 2 (2020): 327–46.

Stein, Edith. *Essays on Woman*. Translated by Freda Mary Oban. Washington, D.C.: ICS Publications, 1987.

———. *Finite and Eternal Being*. Translated by Kurt Reinhardt. Washington, D.C.: ICS Publications, 2002.

———. *The Science of the Cross*. Translated by Josephine Koeppel. Washington, D.C.: ICS Publications, 2003.

———. *On the Problem of Empathy*. Translated by Waltraut Stein. Washington, D.C.: ICS Publications, 2016.

Strawson, Galen. "Realistic Monism: Why Physicalism Entails Panpsychism." *Journal of Consciousness Studies* 13 (2006): 3–31.

Strawson, P. F. *Individuals: An Essay in Descriptive Metaphysics*. London: Routledge, 1990.

Stump, Eleonore. "Non-Cartesian Substance Dualism and Materialism Without Reductionism." *Faith and Philosophy* 12, no. 4 (1995): 505–31.

———. "Aquinas' Account of Freedom: Intellect and Will." *The Monist* 80, no. 4 (1997): 576–97.

———. *Aquinas*. London: Routledge, 2005.

———. *Wandering in Darkness: Narrative and the Problem of Suffering*. Oxford: Oxford University Press, 2010.

———. "The Non-Aristotelian Character of Aquinas' Ethics: Aquinas on the Passions." *Faith and Philosophy* 28, no. 1 (2011): 29–43.

Suarez, Antoine. "Free Will and Nonlocality at Detection as Basic Principles of Quantum Physics." In *Is Science Compatible with Free Will? Exploring Free Will and Consciousness in the Light of Quantum Physics and Neuroscience*, edited by Peter Adams and Antoine Suarez, 63–79. Dordrecht: Springer, 2013.

Suárez, Francisco. *De concursu, motione, et auxilio Dei.* In *Opera omnia.* Vol. 11. Paris: Vivès, 1858.

———. *De scientia Dei futurorum contingentium.* In *Opera omnia.* Vol. 11. Paris: Vivès, 1858.

———. *De statibus humanae naturae.* In *Opera omnia.* Vol. 7. Paris: Vivès, 1859.

———. *Disputationes metaphysicae.* Vols. 25–26 of *Opera omnia.* Paris: Vivès, 1861.

———. *Commentaria una cum quaestionibus in libros Aristotelis De anima.* Edited by Salvador Castellote. Madrid: 1978–1992. www.salvadorcastellote.com/investigacion.htm.

Sylvester of Ferrara, Francis. *Commentary on Summa contra Gentiles.* In *Summa contra gentiles.* Rome: S.C. de Propaganda Fide, 1918.

Tanizaki, Jun'ichiro. *In Praise of Shadows.* Translated by Thomas Harper and Edward Seidensticker. New Haven, Conn.: Leete's Island Books, 1977.

Taylor, Charles. *The Ethics of Authenticity.* Cambridge, Mass.: Harvard University Press, 1991.

———. *A Secular Age.* Cambridge, Mass.: Harvard University Press, 2007.

Teilhard de Chardin, Pierre. *The Phenomenon of Man.* Translated by Julian Huxley. New York: Harper and Row, 1965.

Teresa of Avila. *Interior Castle.* Translated by E. Allison Peers. New York: Image, 1989.

Theodore the Studite. *On the Holy Icons.* Translated by Catherine Roth. Crestwood, N.Y.: St. Vladimir's Seminary Press, 1981.

Thérèse of Lisieux. *The Story of a Soul.* Translated by Robert J. Edmondson. Brewster, Mass.: Paraclete Press, 2006.

Thomas Aquinas. Navarre: Fundación Tomás de Aquino, 2011. All citations drawn from www.corpusthomisticum.org.

———. *Scriptum super Sententiis.* Parma: Petrus Fiaccadori, 1856.

———. *Super psalmos Davidis expositio* (*Reportatio Reginaldi de Piperno*). Parma: Petrus Fiaccadori, 1863.

———. *Expositio libri Posteriorum Analyticorum.* Rome: S. C. de Propaganda Fide, 1882.

———. *In libros Aristotelis De caelo et mundo exposition.* Rome: S. C. de Propaganda Fide, 1886.

———. *Summa theologiae.* Rome: S. C. de Propaganda Fide, 1888–1906.

———. *De ente et essentia.* Münster: L. Baur edition, 1933.

———. *Sentencia libri De memoria et reminiscencia.* Taurini: Marietti, 1949.

———. *Sentencia libri De sensu et sensato.* Taurini: Marietti, 1949.

———. *In librum Beati Dionysii De divinis nominibus expositio.* Taurini: Marietti, 1950.

———. *Sententia libri Metaphysicae.* Taurini: Marietti, 1950.

———. *Super Evangelium Sancti Ioannis lectura.* Taurini: Marietti, 1952.

———. *Quaestio disputata de anima.* Taurini: Marietti, 1953.

———. *Quaestio disputata de spiritualibus creaturis.* Taurini: Marietti, 1953.

———. *Quaestio disputata de unione Verbi incarnata.* Taurini: Marietti, 1953.

———. *Quaestiones disputatae de potentia Dei*. Taurini: Marietti, 1953.
———. *Super Epistolam Beati Pauli ad Colossenses lectura*. Taurini: Marietti, 1953.
——— *Super Epistolam Beati Pauli ad Galatas lectura*. Taurini: Marietti, 1953.
———. *Commentaria in octo libros Physicorum*. Taurini: Marietti, 1954.
———. *Compendium theologiae*. Taurini: Marietti, 1954.
———. *Expositio in Symbolum Apostolorum*, Taurini: Marietti, 1954.
———. *Expositio libri Boetii De hebdomadibus*. Taurini: Marietti, 1954.
———. *Super Librum de causis exposition*. Fribourg: 1954.
———. *Expositio libri Peri hermeneias*. Taurini: Marietti, 1955.
———. *Quaestiones de quolibet*. Taurini: Marietti, 1956.
———. *Sentencia libri De anima*. Taurini: Marietti, 1959.
———. *Super Boetium De Trinitate*. Leiden, 1959.
———. *Summa contra gentiles*. Taurini: Marietti, 1961.
———. *De substantiis separatis*. Rome: Commissio Leonina, 1968.
———. *Expositio super Isaiam ad litteram*. Rome: Commissio Leonina, 1969.
———. *Sententia libri Ethicorum*. Rome: Commissio Leonina, 1969.
———. *Super I Epistolam Beati Pauli ad Corinthios lectura* (*Reportatio Reginaldi de Piperno*). Rome: Commissio Leonina, 1969.
———. *Quaestiones disputatae de veritate*. Rome: Commissio Leonina, 1970.
———. *De motu cordis*. Rome: Commissio Leonina, 1972.
———. *De operantibus occultis naturae ad quondam militem ultramontanum*. Rome: Commissio Leonina, 1972.
———. *De principiis naturae*. Rome: Commissio Leonina, 1972.
———. *De mixtione elementorum ad magistrum Philippum de Castro Caeli*. Rome: Commissio Leonina, 1976.
Thompson, Christopher. *The Joyful Mystery: Field Notes Towards a Green Thomism*. Steubenville, Ohio: Emmaus Road, 2017.
Thornton, Allison. "Disembodied Animals." *American Philosophical Quarterly* 56, no. 2 (2019): 203–17.
Tolkien, J. R. R. *The Fellowship of the Ring*. Boston: Houghton Mifflin, 1994.
———. "On Fairy Stories." In *Tales from the Perilous Realm*, 315–400. New York: HarperCollins, 2008.
———. *The Silmarillion*. New York: Del Rey, 1999.
Tollefsen, Christopher. "First- and Third-Person Standpoints in the New Natural Law Theory." In *Subjectivity: Ancient and Modern*, edited R. J. Snell and Steven F. McGuire, 95–114. Lanham, Md.: Lexington Books, 2016.
Tomberg, Valentin. *Meditations on the Tarot: A Journey into Christian Hermeticism*. Shaftesbury: Element, 1985.
Toner, Patrick. "St. Thomas on Death and the Separated Soul." *Pacific Philosophical Quarterly* 91, no. 4 (2010): 587–99.
Torre, Michael. *God's Permission of Sin: Negative or Conditioned Decree? A Defense of the Doctrine of Francisco Marin-Sola, O. P., based on the Principles of Thomas Aquinas*. Fribourg: Studia Friburgensia, 2009.
Tracy, David. *The Analogical Imagination: Christian Theology and the Culture of Pluralism*. New York: Crossroad, 1981.

Treanor, Brian, and Richard Kearney. "Introduction: Carnal Hermeneutics from Head to Foot." In *Carnal Hermeneutics*, edited by Brian Treanor and Richard Kearney, 1–11. New York: Fordham University Press, 2015.

Tullius, William. "A Critical Evaluation of Edith Stein's Critique of Husserl's Idealism." Presentation at 2015 meeting of the North American Society of Early Phenomenology.

———. "Renewal and Tradition: Phenomenology as "Faith Seeking Understanding" in the Work of Edmund Husserl," *American Catholic Philosophical Quarterly* 89, no. 1 (2015): 1–26.

United Nations. *Universal Declaration of Human Rights*. Paris, 1948.

Vatican II. *Dignitatis humanae*. Declaration on Religious Freedom. December 7, 1965.

———. *Gaudium et Spes*. The Pastoral Constitution on the Church in the Modern World. December 7, 1965.

Vanauken, Sheldon. *A Severe Mercy*. New York: HarperCollins, 1977.

Van Dyke, Christina. "Not Properly a Person: The Rational Soul and Thomistic Substance Dualism." *Faith and Philosophy* 26, no. 2 (2009): 186–204.

———. "Taking the 'Dis' out of Disability: Martyrs, Mystics, and Mothers in the Middle Ages." In *Disability in Medieval Christian Philosophy and Theology*, edited by Scott Williams, 203–32. New York: Routledge, 2020.

van Inwagen, Peter. "The Possibility of Resurrection." *International Journal for Philosophy of Religion* 9, no. 2 (1978): 114–121.

———. *Material Beings*. Ithaca, N.Y.: Cornell University Press, 1990.

———. "The Place of Chance in a World Sustained by God." In *God, Knowledge, and Mystery: Essays in Philosophical Theology*, 42–65. Ithaca, N.Y.: Cornell University Press, 1995.

———. "Being, Existence, and Ontological Commitment." In *Metametaphysics: New Essays on the Foundations of Ontology*, edited by David Chalmers et al., 472–506. Oxford: Clarendon, 2009.

———. "God and Other Uncreated Things." In *Metaphysics and God: Essays in Honor of Eleonore Stump*, edited by Kevin Timpe, 3–20. New York: Routledge, 2009.

Velleman, J. David. "A Right of Self-Termination?" *Ethics* 109, no. 3 (1999): 606–28.

Viladesau, Richard. *Theological Aesthetics: God in Imagination, Art, and Beauty*. Oxford: Oxford University Press, 1999.

von Balthasar, Hans Urs. *A Theological Anthropology*. New York: Sheed and Ward, 1967.

———. *The Christian State of Life*. Translated by Mary Frances McCarthy. San Francisco: Ignatius Press, 1983.

———. *The Glory of the Lord: A Theological Aesthetics*. Vol. 2, *Studies in Theological Style: Clerical Styles*. Translated by Andrew Louth et al. San Francisco: Ignatius Press, 1984.

———. "Transcendentality and *Gestalt*," *Communio* 11, no. 1 (1984): 4–12.

———. *The Glory of the Lord: A Theological Aesthetics*. Vol. 3, *Studies in Theological Style: Lay Styles*. Translated by Andrew Louth et al. San Francisco: Ignatius Press, 1986.

———. *Truth Is Symphonic: Aspects of Christian Pluralism*. Translated by Graham Harrison. San Francisco: Ignatius Press, 1987.

———. *Theo-Drama: Theological-Dramatic Theory*. Vol 1, *Prolegomena*. Translated by Graham Harrison. San Francisco: Ignatius Press, 1988.
———. *The Glory of the Lord: A Theological Aesthetics*. Vol. 4, *The Realm of Metaphysics in Antiquity*. Translated by Brian McNeil et al. San Francisco: Ignatius Press, 1989.
———. *The Glory of the Lord: A Theological Aesthetics*. Vol. 7, *Theology: The New Covenant*. Translated by Brian McNeil. San Francisco: Ignatius Press, 1989.
———. *Theo-Drama: Theological Dramatic Theory*. Vol. 2, *The Dramatis Personae: Man in God*. Translated by Graham Harrison. San Francisco: Ignatius Press, 1990.
———. *The Glory of the Lord: A Theological Aesthetics*. Vol. 5, *The Realm of Metaphysics in the Modern Age*. Translated by Oliver Davies et al. San Francisco: Ignatius Press, 1991.
———. *The Glory of the Lord: A Theological Aesthetics*. Vol. 6, *Theology: The Old Covenant*. Translated by Brian McNeil and Erasmo Leiva-Merikakis. San Francisco: Ignatius Press, 1991.
———. *Theo-Drama: Theological Dramatic Theory*. Vol. 3, *The Dramatis Personae: The Person in Christ*. Translated by Graham Harrison. San Francisco: Ignatius Press, 1992.
———. *The Theology of Karl Barth*. Translated by Edward Oakes. San Francisco: Ignatius, 1992.
———. *Theo-Drama: Theological Dramatic Theory*. Vol. 4, *The Action*. Translated by Graham Harrison. San Francisco: Ignatius Press, 1994.
———. *Theo-Drama: Theological Dramatic Theory*. Vol. 5, *The Last Act*. Translated by Graham Harrison. San Francisco: Ignatius Press, 1998.
———. *Theo-Logic: Theological Logical Theory*. Vol. 1, *Truth of the World*. Translated by Adrian J. Walker. San Francisco: Ignatius Press, 2000.
———. *Epilogue*. Translated by Edward Oakes. San Francisco: Ignatius, 2004.
———. *Love Alone is Credible*. Translated by D. C. Schindler. San Francisco: Ignatius, 2004.
———. *Theo-Logic: Theological Logical Theory*. Vol. 2, *Truth of God*. Translated by Adrian J. Walker. San Francisco: Ignatius Press, 2004.
———. *Theo-Logic: Theological Logical Theory*. Vol. 3, *The Spirit of Truth*. Translated by Graham Harrison. San Francisco: Ignatius Press, 2005.
———. *The Glory of the Lord: A Theological Aesthetics*. Vol. 1, *Seeing the Form*. 2nd ed. Translated by Erasmo Leiva-Merikakis. San Francisco: Ignatius Press, 2009.
von Hildebrand, Dietrich. "The Modes of Participation in Value." *International Philosophical Quarterly* 1, no. 1 (1961): 58–84.
———. *Trojan Horse in the City of God*. Chicago: Franciscan Herald Press, 1967.
———. *Metaphysik der Gemeinschaft: Untersuchungen über Wesen und Wert der Gemeinschaft*. Vol. 4 of *Gesammelte Werke*. Regensburg: Verlag Josef Habbel, 1975.
———. *Moralia*. Vol. 9 of *Gesammelte Werke*. Regensburg: Verlag Josef Habbel, 1980.
———. *Sittlichkeit und ethische Werterkenntnis*. Paris: Vallendar-Schönstatt, 1982.
———. *Transformation in Christ*. Manchester, N.H.: Sophia Institute Press, 1990.
———. *Man and Woman: Love and the Meaning of Intimacy*. Manchester, N.H.: Sophia Institute Press, 1992.

———. *The Heart: An Analysis of Human and Divine Affectivity*. South Bend, Ind.: St. Augustine's Press, 2007.

———. *The Nature of Love*. Translated by John F. Crosby. South Bend, Ind.: St. Augustine's Press, 2009.

———. *Aesthetics*. Vol. 1. Translated by Brian McNeil. Steubenville, Ohio: Hildebrand Press, 2016.

———. *Liturgy and Personality*. Steubenville, Ohio: Hildebrand Press, 2016.

———. *In Defense of Purity: An Analysis of the Catholic Ideals of Purity and Virginity*. Steubenville, Ohio: Hildebrand Press, 2017.

———. *Aesthetics*. Vol. 2. Translated by John F. Crosby et al. Steubenville, Ohio: Hildebrand Press, 2018.

———. *Ethics*. Steubenville, Ohio: Hildebrand Press, 2020.

———. *What Is Philosophy?* Steubenville, Ohio: Hildebrand Press, 2021.

von Hildebrand, Dietrich, and Alice. *Graven Images: Substitutes for True Morality*. Steubenville, Ohio: Hildebrand Press, 2019.

———. *The Art of Living*. Steubenville, Ohio: Hildebrand Press, 2017.

Waldstein, Michael. "Dietrich von Hildebrand and St. Thomas Aquinas on Goodness and Happiness." *Nova et Vetera* (English edition) 1, no. 2 (2003): 403–64.

———. Introduction, in John Paul II, *Man and Woman He Created Them: A Theology of the Body*. Boston: Pauline Books and Media, 2006.

Wallenfang, Donald. *Human and Divine Being: A Study on the Theological Anthropology of Edith Stein*. Eugene, Ore.: Cascade Books, 2017.

Walsh, David. *Politics of the Person as the Politics of Being*. Notre Dame, Ind.: University of Notre Dame Press, 2016.

———. *The Priority of the Person: Political, Philosophical, and Historical Discoveries*. Notre Dame, Ind.: University of Notre Dame Press, 2020.

Walter, Henrik. "Contributions of Neuroscience to the Free Will Debate: From Random Movement to Intelligible Action." In *The Oxford Handbook of Free Will*, edited by Robert Kane, 515–29. Oxford: Oxford University Press, 2011.

Walz, Matthew. "What Is a Power of the Soul? Aquinas' Answer." *Sapientia* 60, no. 218 (2006): 319–48.

Wang, Connie X. et al. "Transduction of the Geomagnetic Field as Evidenced from Alpha-band Activity in the Human Brain." *eNeuro* 6, no. 2 (2019). https://doi.org/10.1523/ENEURO.0483-18.2019.

Wang, Stephen. *Aquinas and Sartre: On Freedom, Personal Identity, and the Possibility of Happiness*. Washington, D.C.: The Catholic University of America Press, 2009.

Ward, Michael. *Planet Narnia: The Seven Heavens in the Imagination of C. S. Lewis*. Oxford: Oxford University Press, 2008.

Ward, Thomas. "Animals, Animal Parts, and Hylomorphism: John Duns Scotus' Pluralism about Substantial Form." *Journal of the History of Philosophy* 50, no. 4 (2012): 531–57.

Watkin, E. I. *A Philosophy of Form*. New York: Sheed and Ward, 1935.

Weber, Max. "Science as a Vocation." In *From Max Weber: Essays on Sociology*, edited by H. H. Gerth and C. Wright Mills, 129–56. New York: Routledge, 2009.

Whitman, Walt. "Song of Myself." In *American Poetry and Prose*, edited by Norman Foerster, 854–92. Boston: Houghton Mifflin, 1947.

Wippel, John. *The Metaphysical Thought of Thomas Aquinas: From Finite Being to Uncreated Being*, Washington, D.C.: The Catholic University of America Press, 2000.

———. "Thomas Aquinas and the Axiom that Unreceived Act is Unlimited" In *Metaphysical Themes in Thomas Aquinas*, vol. 2, 123–51. Washington, D.C.: The Catholic University of America Press, 2007.

Wilhelmsen, Frederick. *The Metaphysics of Love*. New York: Sheed and Ward, 1962.

———. *The Paradoxical Structure of Existence*. New Brunswick, N.J.: Transaction, 2014.

William of Ockham. *Scriptum in librum primum Sententiarum ordinatio*. Vol. 2 of *Opera theologica*. St. Bonaventure: Franciscan Institute, 1970.

———. *Quaestiones in librum secundum Sententiarum (Reportatio)*. Vol. 5 of *Opera theologica.*. St. Bonaventure: Franciscan Institute, 1981.

———. *Quaestiones in librum quartum Sententiarum (Reportatio)*. Vol. 7 of *Opera theologica*. St. Bonaventure: Franciscan Institute, 1984.

Williams, Bernard. "The Makropulos case: reflections on the tedium of immortality." In *Problems of the Self: Philosophical Papers 1956–1972*, 82–100. Cambridge: Cambridge University Press, 1973.

Williams, Charles. *Descent into Hell*. Grand Rapids, Mich.: Eerdmans, 1966.

Williams, Scott. "Persons in Patristic and Medieval Christian Theology." In *Persons: A History*, edited by Antonia LoLordo, 52–86. Oxford: Oxford University Press, 2019.

———. "When Personhood Goes Wrong in Ethics and Philosophical Theology: Disability, Ableism, and (Modern) Personhood." In *The Lost Sheep in the Philosophy of Religion: New Perspectives on Disability, Gender, Race, and Animals*, edited by Blake Hereth and Kevin Timpe, 264–90. New York: Routledge, 2019.

Wilshire, Bruce. *The Much-at-Once: Music, Science, Ecstasy, the Body*. New York: Fordham University Press, 2016.

Winckelmans de Cléty, Charles. *The World of Persons*. New York: Sheed and Ward, 1967.

Wink, Walter. *Unmasking the Powers: The Invisible Forces that Determine Human Existence*. Minneapolis, Minn.: Fortress Press, 1986.

Wittgenstein, Ludwig. *Philosophical Investigations*. Translated by G. E. M. Anscombe. Malden: Blackwell, 2001.

Wohlleben, Peter. *The Hidden Life of Trees: What They Feel, How They Communicate—Discoveries from a Secret World*. Translated by Jane Billinghurst. Vancouver: Greystone, 2016.

Wojtyła, Karol. (John Paul II). *The Acting Person*. Translated by Anna-Teresa Tymieniecka. Dordrecht: Riedel, 1979.

———. *Redemptor hominis*. Encyclical Letter. March 4, 1979.

———. *Love and Responsibility*. Translated by H. T. Willets. San Francisco: Ignatius Press, 1981.

———. *Reconciliatio et Paenitentia*. Post-Synodal Exhortation. December 2, 1984.

———. "The Person: Subject and Community." In *Person and Community: Selected Essays*, translated by Theresa Sandok, 219–61. New York: Peter Lang, 1993.

———. "Subjectivity and the Irreducible in the Human Being." In *Person and Community: Selected Essays*, translated by Theresa Sandok, 209–17. New York: Peter Lang, 1993.

———. *Man and Woman He Created Them: A Theology of the Body*. Translated by Michael Waldstein. Boston: Pauline Books and Media, 2006.

Wood, Jordan Daniel. "Creation is Incarnation: The Metaphysical Peculiarity of the *Logoi* in Maximus the Confessor." *Modern Theology* 34, no. 1 (2018): 82–102.

Woznicki, Andrew N. *Being and Order: The Metaphysics of Thomas Aquinas in Historical Perspective*. New York: Peter Lang, 1990.

———. *Metaphysical Animal: Divine and Human in Man*. New York: Peter Lang, 1996.

Ulrich, Ferdinand. *Homo Abyssus: The Drama of the Question of Being*. Translated by D. C. Schindler. Washington, D.C.: Humanum Academic Press, 2018.

Yadav, Sameer. *The Problem of Perception and The Experience of God: Toward a Theological Empiricism*. Minneapolis, Minn.: Fortress Press, 2016.

Yannaras, Christos. *Variations on the Song of Songs*. Translated by Norman Russell. Brookline, Mass.: Holy Cross Orthodox Press, 2005.

———. *Person and Eros*. Translated by Norman Russell. Brookline, Mass.: Holy Cross Orthodox Press, 2007.

Viñas, Miguel. *Philosophia Scholastica*. Genoa: Antonii Casamarae, 1709.

Zizioulas, John. *Being as Communion: Studies in Personhood and the Church*. Crestwood, N.Y.: St. Vladimir's Seminary Press, 1997.

Zubiri, Xavier. *On Essence*. Translated by A. Robert Caponigri. Washington, D.C.: The Catholic University of America Press, 1980.

——— *Dynamic Structure of Reality*. Translated by Nelson Orringer. Champaign: University of Illinois Press, 2003.

Index

Abelard, Peter, 141n93
Abram, David, 57n39, 91n46, 96n60, 97n63, 100n77, 103n87, 104n92, 337n8, 363n6, 366
abortion, 19
abstraction, 3, 16, 25–26, 33, 34–35, 43, 48, 53, 63, 67, 112–16, 118–20, 133–34, 136, 138, 140–46, 150, 155, 157–58, 168–69, 172, 174, 188, 203–4, 216, 233–34, 245, 295, 299, 302–3, 305, 366–67, 380
absurdity, 159, 175, 187
abundance (or interior fullness or surplus), 197–98, 203–5, 285–86, 383. *See also* excess
accidents, 48–49, 51, 64, 81, 83, 130, 136, 143, 147, 149, 173, 206, 209–13, 215–16, 252, 257–58, 262–67, 271, 273, 279, 300, 303–4, 308, 317–18, 335, 338–39, 351, 364, 376, 378, 383; proper accidents (*propria*), 241, 369
acquaintance (*notitia*), 125
action or performing great deeds, 371
activities, 64–65, 104, 111, 157, 184, 189, 214, 231, 257, 263–65, 301, 335, 351, 356. *See also energeia*
act of existence (*actus essendi*). *See* existence
act (or actuality) and potency, 18, 33–34, 43, 49–54, 58, 62–64, 67–68, 74, 76–79, 83, 88–89, 92, 105, 110, 113–17, 120, 122–23, 125–26, 132, 141–43, 147–51, 155, 157, 169–70, 173–74, 176, 180, 183–84, 192–93, 196–98, 206, 208–10, 227, 233–36, 242, 248–50, 253, 256–58, 262–64, 273–75, 279–81, 291, 300, 303–4, 312, 319, 321–25, 333, 334–35, 339, 341–42, 345, 356, 359, 367, 387; acting

(transcendental), 93; *agere sequitur esse*, 207–8, 291–92; category *actio*, 209, 349; free or surplus actuality, 197–98, 242, 275, 277–81; natural potency, 116, 143, 158, 169, 179, 197, 200, 205, 219, 230, 232, 235–37, 248, 258, 326–27, 344, 349, 353, 364, 375–76; obediential potency, 116, 120, 129, 143, 158, 179–80, 192–93, 197–98, 200, 205, 232–37, 244, 248, 251, 258, 271, 304, 309, 314, 327, 344, 348–50, 364, 367, 373, 376; ontological and axiological acts, 206–7; superactual attitudes, 251–52
Adams, D. Q., 19n44, 100n44
Adams, Robert, 91n44
Aertsen, Jan, 143n102
aesthetic cognition. *See* intuition
aestheticism, 230
aesthetic method. *See* methods.
affectivity: *affectio commodi* and *affectio iustitiae*, 179–80, 235; affective cognition, 191, 243; affective language, 35; being affected or moved, 218–20, 228–31, 233–34, 249; emotional infection or contagion, 72, 267; general feelings located in the body, 363–64; heart or spiritual affectivity, 199, 218–21, 232–34, 236, 241–42, 244, 249, 252, 254, 292, 295, 301, 305, 343–45, 347, 350, 355, 360, 364, 373–74; and interpretation, 216; natural and obediential, 232–35; non-intentional feeling, 221, 360–61; passions, 218–19, 228, 347, 359; and porosity, 238–40; powers of, 8, 36–37, 99, 106, 110, 199; preference and placing after, 222, 224–25;

427

Index

affectivity: (cont.)
  relation to value or other modes of importance, 59–61, 200; in the soul, 226; value-feeling or value-perception, 216, 221, 224–25, 227–28, 233–35, 246, 283, 296–97, 333, 346. *See also* appetite; responses
affirmation, 117, 148, 150, 193, 203–4, 216, 226, 229–32, 240; by others, 307; self-affirming or self-positing, 182, 194–95. *See also* responses
aging, 62, 69, 182, 344, 346
Albert the Great, 166n3, 190–91, 296n19, 297n22
Alexander of Hales, 248n21, 295n16
alienation, 26, 159, 196, 239, 261, 350. *See also* restlessness
aliquid or something (transcendental), 92, 314
Alston, William, 246n18
Altman, Barbara, 348n40
altruism (or selflessness), 200, 203–4
analogy, 49–51, 58, 77, 91, 97, 127, 130–33, 143–44, 175–76, 192, 226, 272, 278, 301–2, 307, 309, 320, 357, 374, 376, 388; of attribution, 130, 313; iconic or qualitative or correspondence, 131–33, 219, 247; of proportionality, 130–31, 313
anarchy, 330
Anatolios, Khaled, 269n77, 314
angels. *See* gods
Angelus Silesius, 158n160
animals (and animality), 99, 105, 117, 140–42, 217, 256, 260, 278–80, 286, 295, 303–4, 309, 311, 317–20, 340–42, 344, 350, 363, 366, 367–70, 376, 387–89; animalism, 66; animalistic acts, 371; domesticating of, 368; killing of, 367
anonymity, 82–83
Anscombe, Elizabeth, 243
anxiety, 47, 109, 219, 253, 386
apatheia. See Gelassenheit
Aphrodite, 98. *See also* Venus
Apollo, 178
apophaticism. *See* God; perception
appetite, 92, 104, 107–11, 176, 200, 206, 233, 252, 361, 382–83; concupiscible and irascible, 108–9; intellectual appetite, 165, 196

a priori conditions. *See* transcendental conditions
Arendt, Hannah, 371
Aristotle: Aristotelianism, 6, 34, 56, 75, 87; Aristotelian science, 14, 19, 59n44, 237; Aristotelian Way, 33; on art, 187n75; on beauty, 19, 86n27, 106n100, 160, 177n35, 202n12; on categories, 215; on *causa sui*, 194n99; on contemplation, 18n43, 157n158; on *energeia*, 257; on form, 260n52; on friendship, 268n71, 333n158; on gods, 282n116; on hylomorphism, 63; on place, 89; on the problem of the two lives, 353–54; on saving the appearances, 35–36; on sleep, 371n48; on the soul, 304; on virtue, 177n34
artifacts (and tools), 80, 140, 156, 163–64, 169, 187, 200, 211–12, 216, 231, 256, 264–65, 334, 337, 341, 349–51, 356–57, 367, 372; persons as, 298; replacing body parts with, 341–42
artist (and artistry), 72, 80, 94, 120, 139, 157, 213–14, 225, 268–70, 325, 368, 372
artwork, 54, 65, 72, 120, 187, 210, 214, 216, 269–70, 305, 366, 372, 385, 388
asceticism, 26
aspect, definition of, 34
Atkinson, Gary, 334n1
Atman, 261
atomism, 66
attention, 115, 117, 216, 249–52, 254, 308, 337, 365, 373; joint attention, 267, 367
attraction, 107
attunement, 89, 97, 105, 109, 176–77, 297. *See also* fittingness
Auerbach, Erich, 150n128
Augustine, 60, 61n48, 101, 111n121, 126–27, 138, 218n59, 250, 261n55, 308; Augustinian Way, 33
Austriaco, Nicanor, 99n72, 150n129, 280n108
authenticity, 62, 191–94, 225, 229–30, 237, 328, 349, 380
authority, 239, 329, 332
auto-affection. *See* self-sensing
autonomy, 161, 193–95, 227, 307
Averroism, 113
Avicennianism, 113

Bachelard, Gaston, 24n55, 104n93, 120, 219n60
bacteria, 99, 358
Bañez, Domingo, 275
bare particular, 53
Barfield, Owen, 95, 100, 106, 366
Barnes, Gordon, 340n13
Barral, Mary Rose, 65n59
beatific vision (or union with God), 126–27, 166, 180, 190, 194–95, 198, 235–36, 242, 247, 270–72, 382–83
Beattie, Tina, 72, 336n5, 337n7
Beaudoin, John, 282n114
beauty, 4–5, 10–11, 15, 17–19, 30, 37, 60, 69, 86, 88, 92–94, 97–98, 101, 106–9, 112, 117–22, 132, 135, 153–54, 158, 160, 175–77, 180, 184–86, 190, 201–3, 207, 210–13, 216–17, 220–21, 225, 229, 233–34, 239, 248–49, 255–56, 262–63, 277, 282–85, 287, 291, 295, 298, 301–2, 305–9, 311–16, 330, 333, 334, 347, 350, 354, 362, 364–65, 368, 372, 377–78, 380, 382–84, 386–89; beauty of the second power, 211, 222–23, 282–85; *bonum honestum*, 5, 200; and elegance, 283; *Gesamtschönheit* or unique beauty of persons, 202–3, 211, 222, 224, 226, 228, 246, 254, 263, 296–97, 300, 302–3, 330, 332–33, 340, 344, 346, 355, 359–60, 379, 383, 389; negative beauty, 284
Beethoven, Ludwig van, 210
being: adding to God's being, 285; and affirmation, 203–4; beyond being, 145, 159; contingent, 52, 132, 135, 147, 153, 155, 159, 175, 183–84, 223, 261–63, 307, 311; definition of real being, 61–62; *ens* (or existent or real being), 11, 23, 29, 34, 49–53, 61–62, 78, 92–93, 107, 110, 112–14, 118–19, 121–23, 129–30, 132–34, 136–37, 141, 143–44, 148, 151–56, 162, 177, 206–7, 220, 222, 301, 305–6, 339, 378–79; exceeds thought, 152, 231, 255, 260, 272, 300; experiential, 55; face of, 376–77; formal object of intellect, 147, 248, 301; as gift or given, 180, 315–16, 384; hierarchy of, 99–100, 233, 256, 295–96, 309, 320, 326, 384; idiocy of, 158–59; modes (or ways or kinds) of, 86–87, 90, 102, 115–16, 118, 125, 131–32, 153, 242, 246, 258, 300–301, 308, 314, 348, 351, 359, 363–65, 374, 377, 383–84; nuptial bond with, 145–46; and ontophany, 256; power of, 154; question of, 59; of reason, 28, 138–39, 164, 231, 269; relation to *ousia*, 260; and sacrifice, 285; and security, 253; stable or unstable, 311, 313, 315; structure of, 208, 245, 258, 260, 262–63, 265, 267; thick and thin conceptions of, 144, 151, 153; universal being or being in itself (*ens commune*), 124–25, 132–33, 144, 153n141, 195, 256; univocal sense, 143–44, 153. *See also* analogy; existence; layers; transcendentals; unity; value

Berdyaev, Nicolas, 120, 191–93, 195, 298, 311n82, 321n120, 326n139, 329–30, 332, 343, 345–48
Berger, Ronald, 348n40
Bergson, Henri, 188
Bernardine of Siena, 383
Bernard of Clairvaux, 218n59
Bernard of Trilia, 316n104
Bernard Silvestris, 363n12
bias, 137–38
Bible, 34, 99, 185, 245, 267, 342; Colossians, 308; Galatians, 268n73; Genesis, 308, 310, 344n30, 384n81; Jude, 344n30; Luke, 259, 293n9; Proverbs, 97n65; Psalms, 314n96; Song of Songs, 97n65; Wisdom, 102n84
Billot, Louis, 300
birth (and conception or fertilization), 47, 315, 323–24, 336, 355–57, 371; and natality, 357; and other kinds of human origins, 355, 357
Blanchette, Oliva, 93n49
bliss, 201, 203–4, 226, 285, 383. *See also* end; pleasure
Blondel, Maurice, 127, 139n85, 189n79, 193n92, 230, 240, 278n103
blood, 107n103, 248, 314, 336–37
body, 8, 10, 31, 37, 45, 54–58, 64–66, 69–74, 78, 85, 91, 99, 102–3, 105, 107–10, 125–26, 133, 138, 143, 149, 162, 165, 169–70, 174–75, 181, 193–96, 216–19, 221, 235, 248, 251, 254–56, 260, 284, 291–92, 294, 305, 309, 316–20, 334–50, 352, 354–58, 359, 360–67, 374–76, 383; adaptation to spiritual activity or spiritualization of, 342–43, 359, 361, 377–79, 382–83, 387–88; bodily abilities, 182; body-feeling, 367; body-schema, 103;

Index

body (*cont.*)
  category *situs* or posture, 209, 264, 341, 349, 351; disembodied experience of, 362; embodiment or incarnate acts, 291, 294, 319–20, 337–38, 342, 347, 351–52, 354, 357–58, 366, 368–87; expressing spiritual acts, 345–49, 365–70, 381–83, 385–87; face of, 377; *Fleisch*, meat, or spread-out body, 363; *Körper* and *Leib*, 361–62; as prison, 182, 369; resurrected, 381–89; and somatic layer, 360–63; technological modification of, 341, 357. *See also* face; life; resurrection; sense
Boethius, 299, 301–2
Bonaventure, 67n67, 79–80, 138, 190–91, 295n16, 296n19, 297n22, 382n78
boredom, 230, 253, 293
Boyle, Joseph, 160n167
bracketing. *See* reduction, phenomenological
Bradshaw, David, 259n47, 259n48, 373n57
brain (and neurology), 25, 56–57, 64, 68, 85, 102n86, 103–5, 115, 124, 169, 235, 250, 341, 345, 366–67; brain death, 356; brain division and transplant cases, 341; and mirror neurons, 367
Braine, David, 7n18, 65, 69n77, 137n35, 353
Brassier, Ray, 371n45
breathing (and breath), 100, 213, 308, 334–35, 337, 373
Brent, Fr. James, 331n152, 373n59
Bresson, Robert, 377
Brock, Stephen, 296n17, 334n1
Brown, Christopher, 190n83, 294n14
Browning, Robert, 187n72
Brown, Montague, 127n54
Brown, Peter, 193n94s
Buber, Martin, 245, 306n57
Buddhism, 253, 272n89, 311
Bulgakov, Sergius, 101–2, 182, 195, 261n56, 277n99, 281n113, 302, 308, 344n31, 380n73
Buras, Todd, 91n44
bureaucracy, 330
Burgos, Juan Manuel, 30n71, 194n97, 199n2, 300, 343n27, 360
Burke, Edmund, 345n34
Burton, Adi, 379n71
Butler, Edward P., 303n44
Bychkov, Oleg, 5n10

Cajetan, Thomas de Vio, 67n67, 115, 130n57, 274n92, 299, 317n106, 379
Calasso, Roberto, 94n56, 101n79, 158n160, 185n67, 186n71, 197n108, 219n60, 261n53, 366n23, 368n34
Camus, Albert, 97n64, 195
Capreolus, John, 147
caress, 83, 98
Carlo, William, 14n33, 23, 151, 154, 304
Carmelite tradition, 329. *See also* names of particular Carmelites
Carnes, Natalie, 4n9, 18n43, 190n84, 285n124, 310n78, 373n58
Casey, Edward, 89
categories (or senses of being), 31, 50–51, 67, 99, 105, 140, 173, 209–10, 215–16, 263–64, 320, 349. *See also* names of particular categories
Catherine of Siena, 336n5
causality: and abstract or concrete being, 277; and activity or being at work, 257; creaturely, 256, 276; definition, 35; divine, 26, 183, 261, 313; and enslavement, 192; essentially ordered, 274–75, 282; as explanation, 25; first cause, 273–75; and fittingness, 48, 65; four causes, 33, 56, 63; free versus unfree, 175; and meaning, 112, 150, 219, 252–53, 361, 369; new causal chains, 168, 175; as objective principle, 18, 151; *per communionem*, 214, 267, 269, 276, 278–79, 310, 330–31; *per se* and *per accidens*, 213–14, 255, 266–69, 276–79, 285–86, 310, 331, 337; and phenomenological constitution, 42; and phenomenological reduction, 27; primary and secondary, 275, 281–83; and real being, 62–63; and self-manifestation, 79; and sense, 90, 95; of spiritual soul, 284, 365; and subjectivity, 55–56, 61–62, 167; sufficient reason or cause, 174, 196–98; total, 275; and value, 210, 213, 282–83; what is in effect comes from cause, 50, 58, 196, 261. *See also* effect-to-cause reasoning; efficient cause; end; form; matter
Chaberek, Michael, 279n106
Chalmers, David, 58n41, 351n45
change and persistence, 63–66, 178, 279, 319, 356; in experience versus in actuality, 123, 273–74

Index   431

chaos. *See* matter
charism, 268
Chenu, Marie-Dominique, 280n109
Chesterton, G. K., 345n34
Chrétien, Jean-Louis, 311n81
children, 71, 78, 180, 255, 285, 337, 342–44, 346, 355–57, 374; of God, 25, 270–71, 308, 384
choice, 162, 165, 167, 169, 172, 181–82, 191, 194, 196–97, 205, 222, 240, 286, 363. *See also* freedom
Christian philosophy, 7–8. *See also* Jesus Christ
Church, 233, 268, 287, 327, 331, 352–53, 381
Churchland, Paul, 56n34
circumincession (or *perichoresis*), 143, 345
Clark, Andy, 351n45
Clarke, Norris, 8n22, 93n49, 123, 151, 215n49, 233n94, 274n91, 318n112
classic texts, 6
Claudel, Paul, 139n84
clothing, 264–65, 349
Coakley, Sarah, 16n40, 246n18, 248n21
cogitative power, 105–6, 156, 227
cogito, 31, 47; tacit *cogito*, 70, 103
cognitive science, 106n99
Cohen, Richard, 370n44
coherentism, 92
coinhering, 268–69
collapse, quantum state. *See* reduction, quantum state
collectivism, 239, 331
color (sensible quality), 27, 67, 82–84, 87–88, 94, 103–4, 113, 264, 305
comedy, 223, 225–26, 369–70; and reconciliation, 332
common law, 214
common sense, 103–4, 106–8, 111, 148, 251. *See also* senses
communicability, 53, 70–71, 93, 163, 292, 297, 299, 319, 321–23, 355, 374. *See also* incommunicability
community or society, 150, 163, 179, 191, 200, 211–17, 227, 245, 267–69, 310, 326–33, 334, 337, 339, 348, 356–57, 362, 381; collective guilt and merit, 214, 269, 333; communion, 214, 233, 267–69, 283, 361–62, 375, 385; *koinonia*, 331

compatibilism, 167
concepts (and conceptualization), 10–11, 15–16, 18–19, 34, 41–42, 48, 63–64, 82, 92–93, 96–97, 99, 105–6, 112–15, 117–22, 130, 133–34, 136, 139–40, 144–48, 151–54, 156–58, 210, 216, 231, 244–45, 247, 250, 258, 260, 325, 365–66; functionalization of, 16, 302. *See also* object
concupiscence, 235, 298, 384
concurrentism, 183–86, 255, 273–76, 286
confessio, 314–15, 373
connaturality, 36, 89, 108, 126, 177, 203, 216, 246, 270–71
Conrad-Martius, Hedwig, 101, 336
consent. *See* freedom
conservatism, 239
conscience, 167, 226–27
consciousness. *See* subjectivity
consciousness-world gap problem, 31
conservation of energy problem, 170, 174
constitution (metaphysical), 64, 193, 291, 294, 298–300, 307, 316, 350, 360, 382
constitution (phenomenological), 18, 42, 46, 54, 61–62, 106, 119, 124, 134, 136, 138, 145–46, 313, 379
consubstantiality, 307
consumerism, 19, 25, 200, 239
contact, 170
contemplation, 18, 111, 140, 157–58, 163, 177, 189–90, 246, 249, 254, 257, 261, 264, 296, 310–11, 349, 352–54, 368, 381–82, 384–85
conveniens. *See* fittingness
conversation, 71, 114, 212, 214, 245, 266, 331, 385
conversion, 252
Coolman, Boyd Taylor, 248n21
Cooper, Adam G., 380n76
corruptionism, 294–95
Cory, Therese Scarpelli, 34n85, 102n85, 115, 125n46
Councils: Chalcedon, 307; Second Council of Nicaea, 259n49; Second Vatican Council, 328n141, 329n143; Third Council of Constantinople, 259n49
covenant, 267–69, 271, 276, 278, 281–82, 284–87, 329, 342, 383, 385
Crean, Thomas, 326n139, 332n154
creation. *See* God

creativity, 100–101, 120, 139, 150, 152, 160–61, 164, 187, 189–91, 193, 216–17, 231, 239, 255–56, 268, 281, 287, 293, 310, 314, 318n108, 329, 343, 373, 385, 388; creative fidelity, 357; self-creation, 182, 189, 191–93, 195, 197, 225, 237; subcreation, 139, 187
Crosby, John, 33n80, 61n48, 62, 69n77, 187n74, 206–8, 210n35, 221n63, 227, 249n26, 296, 297n23, 303n48, 326n138
cross (and crucifixion), 285, 386
Cross, Richard, 79n11, 140n91
culture and tradition, 95, 137, 140, 149–50, 216–17, 239, 267–68, 283, 325, 327, 331–32, 342, 345, 348–49, 351, 366
custom, 106, 214, 327, 331, 367

Dahm, Brandon, 190n84, 251n33, 317n106, 317n107
dance, 182, 243, 362, 364, 366–67
dark night of the soul, 201n5, 248, 272
Davidson, Donald, 92n47
Dawson, Christopher, 150
Day, Dorothy, 330n146
death, 47, 285–86, 291–92, 294–95, 315–17, 319, 323, 343–44, 346, 352, 356–57, 370–71; and corpses, 340; heat death of the universe, 371; persons as worth dying for, 330
de auxiliis controversy, 7, 182
de Beauvoir, Simone, 371n50
Debussy, Claude, 225
decoration or ornament, 218, 350, 383
deconstruction, 227, 240, 281n110
Deeley, John, 84n21, 137n75
de Finance, Joseph, 93n49, 306n57
De Haan, Daniel, 77n4, 84n22, 105n98, 169, 174–75, 317n106, 317n107
deification. *See* divinization
de Koninck, Charles, 172n22, 279n107, 281n112, 296n17, 326, 348n41, 380n74
Deleuze, Gilles, 139n84, 203n13, 231n89, 320n118, 336n6, 363
de Lubac, Henri, 126–29, 236n98, 326n139
Demetracopoulos, John, 259n47
de Molina, Luis, 187–88
de Montaigne, Michel, 377n68
Dennett, Daniel, 13n32, 59n43
Denzinger, Heinrich, 259n49
dependence, 193–94, 204, 346–47, 356–57

depth. *See* surface and depth
Derrida, Jacques, 315
de Saint-Exupéry, Antoine, 187n75, 330n149, 333n159
Descartes, Rene, 28, 31–32, 47
desire, 79–80, 97, 109–10, 113, 180, 190, 200, 202–3, 205–6, 224, 253–54, 292–93, 363; desire to see God, 112, 126–29, 166, 190, 193, 195, 235, 254, 347, 353; ethical desire (or motivation by persons), 204–5, 329–33, 348, 369, 377, 381; of the heart, 245
Desmond, William, 5, 21n48, 30, 69, 94, 97n64, 97n65, 121, 131n58, 131n59, 155n149, 158–59, 227n80, 238–39, 249n24, 307n63, 307n64, 362n10
despair, 97, 108, 155, 159, 196, 226
determinism, 168–69, 171, 175, 192
Detloff, Dean, 337
de Unamuno, Miguel, 6
deus. See God
development, 109, 315, 335, 348–49, 355–57
Dewan, Lawrence, 23, 133n62, 282n115
dignity, 186–87, 192, 195, 198, 207, 210, 263, 295–96, 327, 332–33
Dillard, Annie, 97n65
Dilthey, Wilhelm, 91n46
Dionysius (the Areopagite), 385n85
Dionysius (the god), 176–78, 371
disability or impairment, 192n89, 348–49, 352, 355, 371
disponabilité. See Gelassenheit
distinctions: between being and act of existence, 52, 132, 147, 151–56, 304; conceptual or rational, 52, 141–42, 155–56, 262; formal, 141–43, 242, 156, 193, 262–63; modal, 264; *ousia-energeia*, 262–63; real, 52, 141–42, 155, 241, 262–63; subject-object, 253
distraction, 62, 219, 234, 241–42, 249–50
divinization, 7, 8, 19, 232–33, 236, 270–73, 285–87, 308, 314–15, 318n108, 330–31, 333, 347, 352–54, 374–76, 382–89
Docetism, 286
Don Quixote, 285
Doolan, Gregory, 276n98
Dostoyevsky, Fyodor, 285, 333
Dougherty, Trent, 91n44
Doyle, John P., 143n102

drama, 145, 177, 180, 187, 216–17, 231, 285, 298, 332n153, 352, 369, 376–77, 386
dreams, 24, 104, 178, 361
Dreyfus, Hubert, 57n39, 101n79
dualism, 7, 14, 31, 41, 44, 170, 360
Dudai, Yadin, 105n95
Dugan, Barb, 357n55
Dumont, Stephen, 140n91
Dupré, Louis, 320n118

eating, 89, 334–35, 344, 346, 385; and feasting, 367, 388
Eberl, Jason, 294n14, 320n116
Eccles, John, 174n25
ecology, 362, 366; integral ecology, 388. *See also* nature
ecstasy, 94, 108–9, 229n85, 254, 272, 346–48, 372; from nature or of nature, 348
Edelson, Micah, 105n95
eduction, 79–82, 120, 147, 163, 281, 335
effect-to-cause reasoning, 3, 33, 35–36, 62, 65, 74, 122, 147, 178, 184, 259, 283, 348
efficient cause, 56, 63, 68, 79–81, 93–94, 102n86, 136, 169–70, 173–74, 176, 181, 209, 215, 235, 241–42, 255, 276–77, 280, 284, 313, 321, 340, 356–57, 360, 363, 367–68, 383
egalitarianism, 332
egoism (or eudaimonism), 200
Eigenleben (or what most concerns me), 194, 249, 312
Eliade, Mircea, 309n76
eliminative materialism, 56
elements, 99, 334–35, 344
embryos, 355. *See also* birth
emergentism, 57, 66, 79, 102n86, 123, 217–18, 256
Emery, Gilles, 314n92
Emonet, Pierre-Marie, 80n15
emotion. *See* affectivity
empathy, 69, 224. *See also* sympathy
empiricism, 24
enchantment and disenchantment, 238–40, 372
end (or final cause or fulfillment or ultimate state): accidental and consubstantial with happiness, 383; of artifacts, 163–64; of communities, 326–29; enslavement and teleology, 192, 331; entelechial and transentelechial acts, 205n21; final cause in general, 56, 63, 81, 206, 209, 275, 278, 292; and games, 372; happiness as a gift, 201–2; of human persons, parts, and powers, 19, 73, 81, 127, 132, 158, 160–63, 166–67, 169–70, 175, 179–81, 189–91, 193–98, 200–205, 219, 229n85, 235–38, 243, 246, 251, 253–54, 261, 269, 275, 287, 292–93, 296, 306, 310, 312, 314, 318, 326–33, 334–38, 340, 344, 346–47, 349–54, 358, 359–60, 366, 370, 375, 381–89; and modes, 264; of moral objects, 162; of natures, 128, 160–63; of nonpersonal beings, 311, 334–35, 337–38, 358; persons as ends, 61, 167, 195, 198, 328–29; and pure form, 81–82, 161, 378; supernatural, 182, 189, 235–37, 271–72, 287, 331, 353, 381, 389; ultimate state or consummation, 286, 381–89; and value, 210–13, 216, 221. *See also* beatific vision; goodness
energeia: definition and kinds, 257–58; distinction from *kinesis*, 157, 189–90, 214–15, 257; and *erga*, 269–71, 277; in general, 37, 63, 111, 241, 285, 356; in the Palamite sense, 257–74, 276–87, 291, 298, 303, 309, 315, 317, 325, 328–30, 337, 349–52, 364, 373–74, 376–77, 379–82, 384–85, 387. *See also* actuality; activities; *sun-energeia*
energy (physical), 170, 174–75, 257n46
enjoyment. *See* joy
ens. *See* being
enslavement (or bad faith), 191–95, 231, 237, 239, 249, 283, 330, 332, 343, 345–46
environment, 77, 83, 85, 191, 303, 337–38, 348, 357–58. *See also* nature
epektasis, 189–90, 194–95, 202–3, 231, 254, 261, 271, 273, 312, 350, 381, 384, 386, 388–89
epochē. *See* reduction, phenomenological
equality, 201, 331–32
esse. *See* existence
esse intelligibile. *See* being
esse naturale. *See* being
esse sensibile. *See* being
essence: aesthetic, 217; as delimiting beings, 154–55, 339; dependent on God, 256; essential content or properties, 26–28, 34, 51, 98, 130, 134, 140–42, 154–55, 281, 339, 378;

essence: (cont.)
  ideal essence or Platonic Form, 52, 81, 98–99, 112, 134–39, 141–42, 153, 155, 161, 164, 208, 210, 219, 234, 246, 255, 265–66, 276–85, 313, 316, 321, 325, 346, 365; knowledge of, 30, 33, 76, 105, 114, 117–18, 136, 138, 140, 154, 157, 206, 246; as limitation or relative nonbeing, 151, 154; of moral acts, 162; order of *esse essentiae*, 147, 155; as principle, 53, 66, 78, 81, 92, 112, 115, 122, 125, 141, 144, 147, 151–52, 154, 206, 208–10, 212, 214–15, 241, 258, 260, 262–63, 266, 297, 299–304, 306–8, 319–20, 338; relation to *ousia*, 260; Thomistic and Palamite views of, 271–72; unique essence, see *haecceitas*. See also nature; *ousia*
essentiality of origins, 324–25
ethics (or morality), 19, 60, 144–45, 160–63, 178–80, 185, 195–96, 201–5, 222, 227, 239–40, 252, 281–83, 293, 296, 309–10, 315, 329–30, 332–33, 338, 341, 343, 348–49, 377, 379; casuistry and *halakha*, 205, 387n90
Eucharist, 284, 314, 352, 374, 385–87. See also liturgy
eudaimonia, 353–54. See also end
Evagrios the Solitary, 370n43
events, 11, 72, 121, 150, 168, 170–72, 175, 181, 213, 215, 217, 256, 278–80, 293, 298, 336, 357, 360, 370; occasional events, 215; persons as, 315; transcendental events, 208
Everson, William, 368n32
everydayness, 378, 380
evil, 161, 180, 184–85, 188, 203–8, 223, 230, 255, 282–84, 295, 344
evolution (and evolutionary speciation events), 81, 175, 255–56, 279–81, 318–20, 336, 341–42, 344, 346
excess, 61, 94, 96, 101–2, 116–22, 125, 128–29, 136, 145, 154–56, 195, 203, 205, 214, 217, 232–33, 236, 255–56, 260, 263, 280, 300, 313, 321, 328–29, 337–38, 347, 368, 370. See also abundance
excretion, 78n8, 335, 344
existence: as actuality (*esse*), 49, 52–53, 75, 80–81, 92–93, 112, 122, 125, 130, 132, 144, 146–56, 206, 208–10, 255, 257–58, 260, 262–63, 265–66, 277, 281–82, 285, 292, 296–97, 300–301, 303–5, 307, 315, 317–20, 335, 338–39; *de suyo* or *sui iuris* or in its own right, 260, 272, 297–98, 300, 303; *esse commune* or finite being as such, 153, 209, 266, 282, 292, 311–12, 378; *esse secundarium*, 339; existential quantifier, 53, 144, 153, 209; factual, 53, 148, 151; as gift, 47, 52–53, 152, 159, 183, 187, 193, 256; kinds of, 153–54, 318; knowledge of, 23, 25, 29–30, 146, 149, 152–54, 157, 159, 177–78, 206, 246; in oneself or through another, 297, 300, 338–39; order of *esse existentiae*, 147, 155, 300, 339; received and exercised, 300, 317; subjective mode, 31n77, 125; of unities of value, 208; value of, 19, 222. See also being; essence; thereness; unity
exitus-reditus, 16
experience, definition of, 2, 105. See also layers; *qualia*; structure of experience
extended mind theory, 351, 366
extinction, 371
extramentality, 29, 61, 91, 135, 146–47, 152, 154, 255, 272, 282, 300, 379

Fabro, Cornelio, 23, 52n23, 154n144, 265–66
face, 69, 144, 179–80, 204, 233, 244, 291, 293, 374, 376–83, 387; body as all face, 377, 382–83. See also *prosopon*
faith, 116, 247, 252, 375
fallenness, 189, 191, 235–36, 285, 332, 343–44, 347, 351–52
Falque, Emmanuel, 236, 309n75, 353, 363, 385n84
family, 327, 331, 344. See also fatherhood; motherhood
Farges, Albert, 247n20
fatherhood (and fathers), 343, 357
fathers of the church, 34, 37, 241, 258–59, 266, 343, 373
fear, 107–9, 221, 228
feature, definition of, 34
Fedoryka, Maria, 346n35, 368n35
feeling. See affectivity
Feingold, Lawrence, 113n4, 116n16, 117n17, 126n50, 129n56, 161n168, 235n97
feminist tradition, 72, 336
Feser, Edward, 7n18, 142n97
festival (and festivity), 18–19, 109, 225, 267, 285, 316, 372–73, 385–86, 389

Feynman, Richard, 172n21
Fichte, Johann Gottlieb, 179n42, 182n58
fictions, 134, 138–39, 164, 280
Fimister, Alan, 326n139, 332n154
finitude, 47, 101, 121, 124, 127, 129, 132, 155, 185, 194, 196–98, 210, 253, 266, 270, 276, 285, 309, 311–12, 322, 337, 385; metamorphosis of, 309. *See also* essence
Fink, Eugen, 33n82, 145n109
Finlan, Stephen, 93n52, 369n40
Finnis, John, 160n167
Fiorenza, Francis, 124n43
first-person. *See* subjectivity
Fischer, John Martin, 149n125
fittingness (or fit), 5, 15, 25–26, 47–48, 50, 65, 68, 77, 83, 87–89, 92, 107, 109, 115, 117–19, 121, 126–27, 146, 149, 158–60, 176–77, 181, 199–200, 220, 232, 243, 295, 324, 332, 342, 344, 366, 381
flesh. *See* body; intertwining; world
Florovsky, Georges, 187, 193n92
flourishing. *See* end
flowing. *See* overflow
fluids, 304, 336–38, 340, 357, 387
Fodor, Jerry, 57n36
forces, 76, 177–78; coercive force, 328; normative force, *see* importance
formalities or empty forms, 141–45, 154, 208–9, 242, 250–52, 254, 260, 266, 277, 295, 297, 299–301, 303, 307, 311, 316, 320, 322, 325, 339, 345, 352, 354–55
form (*morphē*): acts of soul to acts of body, 169–70; Aristotelian and Platonic, 137; and beauty, 121; cause or principle of being, 41–43, 45, 56, 63–66, 68, 78–82, 120–22, 125, 143, 147, 155, 163–64, 173–75, 177–78, 206, 209, 255, 257, 260, 263, 266, 280–81, 284, 295, 297, 315, 317–25, 334–35, 338–42, 356, 360–61, 363–67, 369, 372, 374, 376; *forma corporeitatis*, 340; and God, 272, 282, 308; intentional and moral, 163–64, 214; knowledge of, 30, 115, 136, 176; of life, *see* states; and sense, 84, 96, 110; in structure of experience, 42–43, 51, 56, 73–74; and value, 210–14, 216. *See also* end; essence; Gestalt
frailty, 47
Francis de Sales, 108

Francis of Assisi, 225, 268
Francis, Pope, 388n91
Freddoso, Alfred, 183n61
freedom, 31n77, 36, 60, 83, 104, 117, 127–29, 149, 161, 165–67, 171–72, 174–76, 179–98, 200, 226, 230, 237–40, 242, 249, 255–57, 261, 268, 273–76, 278, 281–82, 284, 297–98, 308, 310, 329, 331–32, 345, 384–85, 388; conditionals of, 188; for excellence and of indifference, 196; for-itself not in-itself, 194; free center, 249; quasi-freedom, 174, 255, 276, 278. *See also* actuality; autonomy; creation; self-determination
Freud, Sigmund, 119n22, 150n126, 362
friendship, 180, 203, 267–68, 329–30, 333, 356; with God, 384
Fritz, Peter Joseph, 156n150, 256n43, 312n86
Frost, Gloria, 183n60, 183n61, 274n93, 275n94
Froula, John, 339
four-dimensionalism, 66, 215
full content, 51, 66, 132
functionalism, 57, 157n156
fungi, 99, 358

Gadamer, Hans-Georg, 18n43, 21n48, 103n90, 212, 214, 215n47, 217, 218n55, 270n80
Gallus, Thomas, 248n21
games, 214, 372
Garcia-Norro, Juan, 30n74
garments of skin, 344, 346–47, 352
Garrigou-Lagrange, Reginald, 183n60, 185n66, 275n95, 321n120
Gavrilyuk, Paul, 16n40, 187n73, 246n18, 248n21, 277n101, 329n145
Geach, Peter, 142
Gehlen, Arnold, 350
Geiger, Louis-Bertrand, 266
Gelassenheit (or *apatheia* or *disponabilité* or *indifferencia* or letting things be or quiescence), 230–31, 239–40, 310, 347, 368, 385, 388
genetics (and genes), 81, 279, 318, 324–25, 336, 341, 343, 345
George, Marie, 150n129
George, Robert, 355n52
Gerson, Lloyd, 137n74

Gestalt, 5, 12, 18, 21, 43, 65–66, 69, 73–74, 77, 81, 85, 102–4, 191, 212–17, 237, 239, 245, 249, 252, 255, 265–70, 278–79, 286–87, 298, 300, 303, 312, 328, 337, 339–40, 345–46, 349, 351, 355, 357–58, 372; coming to presentation, 214–17

Gibson, James, 103n89

gift, 47, 52–53, 119, 126, 129, 152, 159, 180, 186, 193, 201, 228–30, 285–86, 306, 311, 313–15, 333, 347, 353, 360, 370, 378–79, 384; gifts of the Holy Spirit, 231–32, 247, 265, 270, 376; gifts of the resurrected body, 383; mutual self-gift, 329–30; preternatural and supernatural, 247, 341, 344; problem of the gift, 315; self-gift, 86, 93, 154, 186, 189, 206, 213, 220–21, 229–30, 255–58, 262–63, 267–68, 278, 283, 303–4, 307, 311–12, 315–16, 329, 332, 337, 346, 375, 385–87. *See also* given; existence; *l'adonné*

Gill, Eric, 122n33

Gilson, Étienne, 23, 80, 146–48, 151, 154, 164n171, 214

Giotto, 225

Girard, René, 314n95

Girgis, Sherif, 160n167

given (and givenness), 2–3, 10–12, 25–26, 29, 31–32, 42, 53–54, 61, 92, 95, 108, 119, 121, 147, 152, 155, 158, 168, 171, 182, 186, 191–92, 194–96, 198, 200, 208, 210–11, 217, 219, 237–39, 251, 256, 262–63, 304, 306, 310, 312–16, 333, 335, 364, 376, 378–79; pregivenness, 89–90, 113

God: absolute call of infinite goodness, 204, 227; as Atman, 261; and beauty, 97n64, 101–2, 185–86, 254, 256, 302, 311–13, 372, 382–83; and being, 132–33, 152–54, 192, 208–9, 271–73, 285, 313, 315–16; bodily responses to, 372–73; creation and providence, 28n67, 100–102, 128, 161, 175, 182, 184, 197, 223, 255–56, 261, 270, 274–86, 306, 315, 320, 325, 328, 336, 342, 344, 357; as common good, 326–29, 354; and con-creation, 277, 281; darkness or unknowability, 259, 271–73; and deception, 294; divine ideas and knowledge, 135–36, 184, 188, 273–77, 286; divine illumination, 138, 316; divine impassibility, 233, 256; divine judgment, 185–86, 193; divine power, 68, 139; divine simplicity, 184, 256, 273–74; *energeiai*, 259, 270, 311, 325, 373–74, 376, 380–82, 384–85, 387; and faces, 377–78, 387; and free perfections, 274n92; and gifts, 231–32, 235, 247, 261–62, 312–16, 329, 353; holiness of, 201, 223, 225, 237, 254; humans partner with, 187, 285–87, 316; as incomprehensible, 312–13; innermost in us, 46n9, 261; interaction with creaturely acts, 82, 165, 182–88, 230, 238, 255–56, 265, 269–87; intimacy with, 312; invisible, 313; and love, 285–86; making self an offering to, 371, 385; as Mercy itself, 316; and nonpersonal beings, 311; and obediential potency, 116, 129, 232, 310, 373; object of desire and knowledge, 18–19, 124, 126–28, 133, 160, 163, 166, 180–81, 190–91, 196, 198, 200–201, 229n85, 236, 244, 246, 251, 253–54, 295, 353, 375, 381–89; object of liturgical praise, 314–15, 382, 385; participated by creatures, 265–66, 368; persons of the Trinity, 8, 139, 143, 149, 204, 231–33, 259n49, 260, 270–71, 285–87, 297, 307–8, 313–15, 329, 338–39, 374–75, 379–80, 386; phenomenon of *deus*, 100n77; problem of divine causality, 175, 182–88, 208, 223, 241, 254–57, 273–84; and restful activity, 189–90, 273; and sensible qualities, 100–101, 259, 373; and value, 208, 223, 228, 237, 249, 283, 329; and vocation, 346; and vulnerability, 186, 286

gods (or angels, or *henads*, or intelligences, or separate substances, or transcendent persons), 19, 82, 98–102, 108, 120–21, 131, 186, 214, 219, 223, 227–28, 238, 246, 268, 281, 283, 301–3, 309, 318, 344, 353–54, 373

Goethe, J. W. von, 98n66

Goetz, Stewart, 168n13

Gonet, Jean-Baptiste, 351n46

goodness (and goods), 19, 92–93, 100, 127, 154, 158–59, 161, 176–77, 179–81, 184–85, 187, 190–91, 193, 195–98, 200–203, 206, 210, 218–20, 230, 235–36, 253, 269, 285, 293, 295–96, 301n40, 302–3, 306, 308–9, 311, 315, 344, 388; basic goods, 160–62; common good, 163, 200, 268–69, 327–33, 354; as formal object of will, 166, 179–80, 205; hierarchy of, 162–63; objective goods

for persons, 200–205, 221, 224, 227, 232, 267, 326–33, 346–47, 354, 381, 386
Goth, Sebastian, 121n28
Gottlieb, Rabbi Mark, 331n152
Gould, Stephen Jay, 175n27, 279n105
glory, 270–71, 285, 314, 369, 372, 380, 389
grace, 7, 116, 121n31, 126–29, 180, 182, 185, 195, 198, 230, 233, 235–37, 247, 284–85, 291, 310, 327, 344, 351, 353, 387; created and uncreated grace, 270–71; gracefulness, 222; gracious possibility, 378
Gracia, Jorge J. E., 1n1, 156, 199, 321n124, 323n129
Grant, W. Matthews, 184, 257n44
gratitude, 155, 194, 221, 315
Greco, John, 16n40, 246n18
Gregory of Nyssa, 6, 178n40, 189–90, 308n71, 310, 312–13, 343, 344n30, 373n58
Gregory Palamas, 6, 241, 259–60, 262, 265–66, 373–74; Palamism, 263, 270–72. *See also* energeia
Grenier, Henri, 326n139
Griffiths, Paul, 8n23, 189n80, 190n83, 229n85, 315n98, 344n31, 386n88
Grisez, Germain, 160n167
growth, 78, 80, 315, 355
Gschwandtner, Christina, 47n10
Guardini, Romano, 201n7, 296, 297n23
Guattari, Felix, 320n118

habitus: background to acts, 251; category, 209, 264–65, 349–50; cognitive, 226–27; definition, 176, 243; and dispositions, 243–44, 251, 351; habitual self-understanding, 125, 250; habitual sense and appetite, 106, 109; habituation of body, 364; of inclinations, 195; of will, 167. *See also* vice; virtue
Hacker, Peter, 93n53
haecceitas (or thisness or unique essence), 321–25, 343, 345–46, 381
Haldane, John, 65
Han, Byung-Chul, 190
Hankey, Wayne, 16n37
happiness. *See* end
Harman, Graham, 255n42, 260n51
Hart, David Bentley, 14–17, 121n30, 196n107, 249n24, 344n30

Hartmann, Nicolai, 177n36
hatred, 107–8, 127, 219, 226, 231, 252n34
Hayek, F. A., 214
health care, 19, 333
hearing, 82, 361
heart (organ), 78, 248–49, 374
heart (power for feeling). *See* affectivity
heavenly bodies, 82n17, 99–100
Hegel, G. W. F., 67n68, 151–52, 179n42, 185, 365
Heidegger, Martin, 14n33, 18n43, 21n48, 25n59, 28n67, 59n45, 62n50, 89, 98n66, 109n115, 124n42, 133n63, 152, 153n141, 178, 231, 253, 295n11, 303n48, 306n60, 311, 353n50, 378, 380
Heider, Daniel, 115n9
hell, 198
henads. *See* gods
Henniger, Mark, 122n35
Henry, Michel, 45–47, 53–54, 103n90, 121n111, 182n52, 272n89, 308n72, 362
Henry of Ghent, 147, 155
Heraclitus, 63, 155
Hermetic tradition, 366
Hershenov, David, 304–5
Hesychios the Priest, 249n25
heteronomy, 227, 307
Hibbs, Thomas, 108
Hilary of Poitiers, 308n71
Hipp, Stephen, 299n32
history, 149–50, 175, 184, 187, 191, 214, 224, 226, 255, 281, 285–86, 324–25, 348, 350, 354, 368; as rearrangement of injustices, 332. *See also* time
Hochschild, Joshua, 130n57
Hoel, Eric, 66n65
Hoffmann, Tobias, 166n4, 167n10, 180n48
holiness, 60, 128, 185, 193, 201, 203–4, 221–23, 225, 232, 237–39, 247, 254, 256, 269, 271, 282, 296, 301, 311, 333, 347, 356, 377, 380; holy fool, 285, 315–16
home. *See* rootedness
Homobono de Bonis, 351n46
Hooke, Alexander, 330n148
hope, 108–10, 231, 332n153, 357, 371, 375
Hopkins, Gerard Manley, 55n27, 86n26, 297n25
Horan, Daniel, 367n29

horizon, 87, 124, 216, 254; merging of horizons, 217
hormones, 107
horror, 83, 97, 121, 159, 175, 223, 255, 311, 386
hospitality, 245–46, 268, 378–79, 381
Hughes, Margaret, 216n50
Hugh of St. Victor, 319
Huizinga, Johan, 372
human nature, 3, 37, 53, 116, 126, 140, 160–61, 191, 193–96, 205, 208, 233, 235, 237, 241, 260, 286, 291, 296, 306, 314, 317–26, 328, 338, 349, 351–52, 354–56, 374, 379–80, 382; animals in need of wilderness, 362, 366; incarnatable spirit, 318–19; metaphysical amphibians, 318; political animality, 328, 331, 362, 366; possible definitions of, 311, 317–20, 341–42; proper accidents of, 369–70; rational animality, 318, 320. *See also* nature; person, definitions; states
humility, 109, 187, 195, 284–85, 309, 316, 380, 384
Husserl, Edmund, 3n5, 24–28, 31–32, 41–48, 61, 67n69, 73, 88, 91, 106n99, 107n101, 111n121, 119, 125, 142n95, 146–48, 152, 360, 364, 378
hylomorphism, 35, 41–45, 47, 63–66, 73–74, 76–77, 79, 90, 105, 150, 170, 172, 178, 304, 320, 365, 367, 373, 382; universal hylomorphism, 322
hypostasis (and hypostasization), 286–87, 296, 302–3, 308, 313, 339, 352–53, 379; biological and ecclesial *hypostases*, 352, 371; en-hypostasization, 352–54, 370–72

Iamblichus, 120n27, 137n74, 373
icons, 131, 133, 144, 183, 270, 302, 309, 313–14
idealism, 3, 7, 14, 24, 41, 59n42, 88, 91–92, 124–26, 140, 144–45, 151–52, 277, 304
identity. *See* distinctions; multiplicity; unity
idolatry, 101
illness, 252n35, 372
illumination, 112–15, 122, 118, 138, 255–56, 259, 278, 316
image of cosmos. *See* microcosm
image of God, 7, 8, 18, 269, 285, 291, 307–13, 315, 317, 333, 337, 345, 374–77, 379, 383–84
imagination, 95–96, 104, 106, 123–24, 360–61
"I," meaning of. *See* subjectivity

Imgrund, Owen, 57n36
immateriality, 74, 75, 78, 82, 87, 90, 103–4, 110–11, 115–16, 125, 132, 141, 166, 174, 206, 218–19, 233, 258, 262, 264, 284, 292, 322, 340, 375–76. *See also* matter
immortality, 235–36, 292–95, 308, 341
impairment. *See* disability
importance: conferred by persons, 192, 296; end of spiritual powers, 310; modes of, 101, 181, 199–205, 219–20, 249, 282, 292; normative force, 161–63, 200–201, 204. *See also* goodness; subjectively satisfying; value
incarnate acts and events. *See* body
including. *See* relations
incommensurability, 132, 162, 296
incommunicability, 297–301, 312, 317, 319, 321, 338–40. *See also* communicability
Indian philosophy, 261, 298n28. *See also* Buddhism
indifferencia. See Gelassenheit
individualism, 239, 331
individuals (and individuality), 1, 64, 94, 98, 101, 114, 124, 135–37, 156–59, 227, 296–97, 299, 303, 321–23, 375–76; distinction from personhood, 321, 326–31; epistemic individuation, 369; principle of individuation, 156, 291, 317, 321–25, 345
Indo-European, 19n44, 100n77
Indra, 98
Ingarden, Roman, 27n66, 139n82
Ingham, Mary Beth, 176n33
inscape and instress, 297n25
insight. *See* intuition
inspiration, 118, 120, 372
instruments, 78, 84, 99, 103, 242–43, 335, 337, 343, 365, 384
integralism, 7, 326–33
intellect (or intelligence), 8, 11, 19, 34–36, 60, 82, 92, 99, 105, 112–19, 122–30, 133–34, 137, 156–57, 160, 164, 166–67, 169, 171, 176–77, 179–82, 189, 193, 195–98, 206, 216, 227, 233, 236, 239, 241, 243–47, 249–50, 253–54, 264, 272, 274, 292–93, 295, 299, 301, 308, 322, 341, 345, 350, 354–55, 360, 363–67, 369–70, 372, 375, 381–82, 384–85; agent intellect, 113, 115–16, 118, 120, 122, 124–25, 138; and cognitive impairment, 348–49;

Index

possible intellect, 118, 122–23; practical and productive reasoning, 112, 156, 159–64, 167, 179–81, 191, 240, 344; reasoning as such, 12–17, 140, 147, 151–52, 154, 157–58, 246, 301, 348, 351; taking cognizance, 148; unfolds into other powers, 148, 220
intellectualism (view on freedom), 167, 196, 254. *See also* idealism
intelligences. *See* gods
intelligible properties, 34, 92, 94, 115, 119, 178, 220, 242, 311; actual and potential intelligibility, 113, 115, 117, 122, 377
intelligible species, 114–15, 117, 123, 133, 138, 145–47, 157–58, 234, 247, 250, 273–74, 366
intensity, 19, 25, 51–52, 78, 119, 190, 202, 219, 330, 333, 344
intention (act of will), 160–63, 167–69, 267, 346; *intentio benevolentiae* and *intentio unionis*, 202
intentionality (object-directedness), 18, 27–30, 32, 41–43, 46, 50–51, 54–56, 58, 61, 67, 77, 107, 110, 123, 134, 136, 142, 145–46, 148, 157, 219–21, 228–29, 234, 251, 258, 272–74, 304, 338, 345, 347, 360–61, 364, 366, 369, 371, 376–78; counter-intentionality, 145, 313; intentional forms, 163, 200, 211–12, 229; intentional properties, 84; particular intentions, 105; second intentions, 134n68. *See also* relations
interaction problem, 170
interior castle, 55n27
interpretation, 21, 70, 84–86, 95–96, 104–5, 216–17, 224, 297, 366
intersubjectivity, 54, 114, 145, 150, 179, 193, 244, 381; being with or *Mitsein*, 306; coacting or joint activity, 245, 265–70, 280, 356, 380; coexperiencing, 72, 267; interpersonal space or social reality, 138–40, 162, 164, 245, 268, 285, 330; second-person, 163, 243–45
intertwining, 73, 85, 89, 103, 107, 110, 150, 246, 267–69, 337–38, 356, 361–62
intrinsic, definition of, 262
intuition (or insight): aesthetic cognition or poetic intuition, 117–20, 122–23, 133, 145, 157–58, 233, 235, 246, 253, 263, 301, 324, 365, 369; cointuition, 138; conditions for, 123, 157; as direct perception of phenomena, 30, 25; fontal knowledge, 118; of God, 126; intuition of being, 156–58, 177, 210, 235, 246, 258, 274, 316; intuitive cognition, 35–36, 99, 112, 115, 159, 177, 301, 365; intuitive contemplation, 158; of Platonic Forms, 134–35, 137, 278, 294, 365; sense as intuitive, 90; and spiritual perception, 246; sympathetic, 188–89; value-perception as intuitive, 221
Irigaray, Luce, 253, 336n5
irreducibility, definitions and kinds, 1, 56–57. *See also* reductionisms
isomorphism of mind and world, 36, 135–36, 142
item, definition of, 10

Jackson, Frank, 58n41
Jacobs, Nathan, 322n126
James, William, 94n56
Japanese aesthetics, 175
Jaroszyński, Piotr, 5, 117
Jaspers, Karl, 304
Jaynes, Julian, 57n39
Jeffers, Robinson, 97n64, 368n32
Jensen, Steven, 161n168
Jesus Christ, 5, 7, 18, 19, 21, 259n49, 260, 270, 285–87, 297, 300, 307–9, 321, 324, 352–53, 370–71, 373, 379–81, 383–85; Christology, 8, 286–87, 338–39, 376
Jinek, Martin, 341n16
Joas, Hans, 332–33
John Damascene, 78, 308n71
John Duns Scotus, 36, 123, 126n52, 138n78, 140–44, 153n141, 156–57, 176n33, 179–81, 183, 197n109, 218n58, 242, 243n8, 250, 253–54, 255n41, 259; Scotism, 2, 6, 24, 248, 263, 275, 293n6, 299, 312, 324, 339–40
John of St. Thomas (John Poinsot), 23, 67n67, 84n22, 117n17, 139, 150–51, 154, 157n156, 264–65, 306, 323n129
John of the Cross, 201n5, 272
John Paul II. *See* Wojtyła, Karol
Johnson, Luke Timothy, 385n84
Johnson, Mark, 106n99
Johnston, William, 253n38, 272n89
Jordan, Mark D., 86n27, 122n33
Josephson-Storm, Jason, 238n102

joy (or enjoyment), 19, 51–52, 61, 91, 94, 97–98, 108–11, 117, 135, 190, 201, 203–4, 218, 228, 234, 253, 259, 267, 338, 372–73; *jouissance*, 253, 337

judgment, 27, 34, 81, 84, 86, 103–4, 118, 126, 146–49, 151, 158, 163, 167, 177, 184–85, 193, 206, 209–10, 216, 227–28, 255, 314, 351–52. See also responses

Jupiter, 98

justice, 185, 201, 210, 225, 234, 269, 316–17, 330–32, 354, 376

kalon, 5, 86n27, 160

Kant, Immanuel, 28, 31–32, 61n48, 87, 103n90, 121–22, 124n42, 195, 200, 293, 360

Kass, Leon, 367n28

Kearney, Richard, 85, 378

Keefe, Donald, 267, 375, 384n81, 385n85

Keiser, Kevin, 126n50, 126n52, 161n168, 176n31

Kelly, Sean, 57n39, 101n79

Kemp, Ken, 342

kenosis, 93, 152, 283–85, 333, 384; material kenosis, 319. See also sacrifice

Kierkegaard, Søren, 139n84, 196, 306n59

Kilby, Karen, 20, 22

Kirk, Russell, 345n34

Kohák, Erazim, 16, 33–34, 60n46, 99n70, 159, 168, 177n36, 223n67, 301n40, 311n83

Kolbe, Maximillian, 380

Koons, Robert, 64n54, 161n168, 170n20, 243n5

Koren, Leonard, 175n27

Koslicki, Kathrin, 64n54

Knasas, John, 150n130

Krąpiec, Mieczysław, 33n80, 117n18, 149, 297n21

Kripke, Saul, 324n133

Kronen, John, 323n129

labor, 192, 371, 386–87

l'adonne, 47, 306, 313–15; and natality, 357. See also gift

Lakoff, George, 106n99

land, 150, 239, 327, 331, 366; landscapes, 210–11, 213, 217, 229, 278, 368, 376

language and linguistic ability, 99, 114, 150, 214, 216, 365–66

laughter, 72, 369–70

layers (or levels): of acts, 248–49, 257–58, 373–74; of being and unity, 206, 208–12, 215, 217, 233, 244, 255, 257–58, 285, 291, 298, 300, 321, 326, 330, 334, 349, 351; of bodily or somatic experience, 361–63; of experience, 27, 46–47, 55, 58, 62, 360–63; of freedom, 191; of sensible qualities, 95; of world, 91. See also being

Leask, Ian, 47n11

Leclercq, Jean, 36n88, 218n59, 366n20

Lee, Patrick, 207n26, 355n52

Leftow, Brian, 79n11

legitimacy (political), 268–69, 328, 332

Lehrberger, James, 318n112

Leibniz, G. W., 224n70, 261

Leontius of Byzantium, 299n33

Levering, Matthew, 294n12

Levinas, Emmanuel, 14n33, 62n50, 83, 98, 144–45, 147–48, 152, 159, 163, 178–79, 186n70, 195, 197n111, 204, 295n11, 302, 309, 315n97, 316, 330n146, 330n147, 333n157, 338n10, 348, 370, 377, 379, 386

Levine, Joseph, 58n41

Lewis, C. S., 100n75, 186, 382n77

Lewis, V. Bradley, 192–93

liberalism, 237, 239

libertarianism (view on free will), 167

libertarianism (view on politics), 239

Libet, Benjamin, 169

life: after death, 295; beginning of embodied life, 291, 355, 357; biological, 83, 303, 326, 335–36, 340–44, 346, 352, 355, 358, 363; caught up in, 335; definition of nonliving, 76; end or termination of embodied life, 356–57; formalities of living and nonliving, 339; form of, *see* states; life history, 149, 214, 298, 348–49; lived body (*Leib*), 361–63, 371; lived experience, 50, 70, 103, 361–63; living in my acts, 44–46, 54, 104, 188, 229; living with a *Gestalt*, 216; living up to my value, 328–29; nature of, 75–78, 175, 184; necessities of, 371–72; problem of two lives, 353–54; right to, 332–33; vitality, 60, 78, 84, 94, 119, 176–78, 182, 201, 203, 219, 221–22, 347, 362, 368, 371; world-soul or Platonic Form of life, 280–81. See also birth; death

Index   441

life-world (*Lebenswelt*), 32, 91, 95
light, 67, 82, 96, 99, 113, 116, 122, 247, 259, 270
likeness, 79, 81, 266. *See also* representation; sign
Lingis, Alphonso, 89, 97n65, 330n148
Little, Joyce, 36n88, 95n59, 150n130, 266n66, 267n69
liturgy (or worship), 7, 19, 37, 101, 105, 177–78, 189, 201, 229, 267, 291, 314–15, 352, 359, 366, 372–73, 375–76, 382, 385–89; Mass or Divine Liturgy, 314, 370, 385–87
Locke, John, 299
locomotion, 104, 109–11, 348, 363–64, 366, 371–72
logical laws, 10–11, 24, 48, 53, 142–43, 159, 201, 240; and Porphyrian tree, 320; and rhizomatic logic, 320n118; of sense, 366
Logos and *logoi*, 260–61, 276–77, 280, 286, 308, 378; words about being, 148, 228–29, 231
Lonergan, Bernard, 5, 33n80, 36n88, 113n2, 113n4, 115, 126n52, 138n78, 146
Long, Steven, 129n56, 161n168
Loudovikos, Nikolaos, 196n105, 270n78, 283n117, 286n126, 298n27, 307, 348, 365n118, 373n56, 375n64, 378n70, 385n86
love: *agape*, 204, 285; as appetite, 107–8; and beauty, 93, 97, 177, 202–3; charity or love of God, 180, 272, 285, 375, 384–85, 388; divine, 127, 154, 180, 200–201, 237, 256, 271–72, 286, 307, 329, 388; *ens amans*, 225; *eros*, 97–98, 203, 343–46; and evolution, 279; falling or being in love, 10, 18, 88, 219, 227, 252, 343–46, 356, 379; and fire, 71–72, 219; guiding perception, 17, 60, 108, 202–3, 210, 261, 263, 296–97, 324–25, 381; imaging God, 308, 310, 314n92, 375; lavished on others, 285; and melting, 229n83; as metaphysical attitude, 109; and mutual indwelling, 272; of nonpersonal beings, 301; as openness to all value, 225–26, 231, 252n34; *ordo amoris*, 60, 224, 245, 252n34; response to persons, 19, 60, 202–3, 244–45, 296, 329, 333, 355; sexual expression of, 346, 369, 373, 377; as transcendental, 93, 152; as value-response, 202–3, 220, 228–29, 249, 252; and will, 165, 180, 218, 226

Lovecraft, H. P., 122n32, 178n37
Lowe, E. J., 5n12, 66n63, 105n98, 168n13
Lu, Mathew, 176n32, 340n15

MacIntyre, Alasdair, 105n97, 193n92, 238
MacLeish, Archibald, 158n160
MacMurray, John, 244n10, 306n57
Madden, James, 7n18, 56n33, 57n37, 59n43, 124n41, 168n13, 170n19
magic, 366
magnanimity, 333
Mallory, J. P., 19n44, 100n77
mania (or madness), 372
Manicheanism, 183–84, 208
Manoussakis, John Panteleimon, 251n32
Manteau-Bonamy, H. M., 380n73
Marcel, Gabriel, 55, 109n115, 142, 145–46, 186, 326n138, 357n57
Marias, Julián, 300
Marion, Jean-Luc, 3n6, 5, 6, 8n23, 11, 13n30, 14n33, 21n48, 29, 46–47, 61, 88, 101n81, 119, 122, 131n58, 145, 152, 195n100, 215n47, 245, 250, 253, 272, 283n118, 293, 313–16, 346n36, 347n37, 357n57, 369, 377–78
Maritain, Jacques, 3n7, 8n20, 23, 27n66, 29, 36n90, 86n28, 104n91, 117n18, 119n22, 120, 130n57, 134n65, 156–57, 158n160, 177n34, 189n80, 203n14, 272, 297n23, 321n120, 326–28, 362n10, 365
marriage, 203, 329, 346, 385; image for the Kingdom of God, 388; spiritual marriage, 247, 384; and virginity, 346
Martin, Michael, 98n66, 102n84, 281n113, 343n28, 366n22
Marx, Karl, 150n126
Mary (and Mariology), 287, 380
masks, 8, 97, 227, 298–99, 312, 352, 380
mass society, 239, 332
materialisms, 7, 14, 44, 56–60, 92, 128, 172, 224, 284
matter (*hulē*): cause or principle, 41–43, 56, 63–64, 77–80, 82, 84, 115, 117, 120, 123, 133, 147, 149, 156, 164, 165, 174, 178, 206, 209, 218, 235, 243, 263, 266, 269, 286, 291, 295, 297, 304, 319, 321, 326, 334–35, 338–42, 356, 359, 363, 365–69, 372, 375; and chaos or *tohu-bohu*, 121, 208, 363; as conscious, 58–59, 363, 382; cooperating with form, 214;

matter (*hulē*): (*cont.*)
corporeal, 56–58, 79, 87, 90, 105, 111, 114, 173, 175, 319, 322, 344–46, 376; and desire, 79–80; as disposed to have properties, 281, 323; as force, 178; irreducibility of persons to, 35, 44, 56–58, 167, 169; knowledge of, 30, 35, 177; of organs, 68, 74, 319; original, 323–25; phases of, 336; prime, 79, 173–74, 178, 322–24, 376; quantified, 173–75, 292, 322–23, 387; quantum, 170–74, 255, 278, 322–24, 363; sacramental, 384; and speciation events, 279, 320; of sperm and egg, 320, 323–24, 336, 343, 355; spiritual, 322–23, 325; spiritualization of, 369, 372, 377–79, 383–84; in structure of experience, 42–43, 56, 73–74; *yliatim*, 322–23, 325

Matthew of Aquasparta, 316, 382n78

Maurer, Armand, 320n117

Mauro, Sylvester, 143n102

Maximus the Confessor, 197, 259n47, 260, 272n84, 286n127, 310n80, 373, 384

Mazur, Piotr, 110n118, 176n32, 192n88, 197n108

McCool, Gerard, 150n130

McDaniel, Kris, 153

McDowell, John, 2n3, 92n47

McGinn, Colin, 59n43

McInroy, Mark, 246n18, 270n80

McMichael, Steven, 383n80

McNamara, Rob, 343n27

McNeill, William, 18n43, 97n65

McTaggart, J. M. E., 188

meaning (and meaningfulness), 18, 24–26, 28, 31–32, 42, 46–48, 64, 77, 91–92, 95, 100, 106, 112–13, 115, 117–18, 121–22, 125, 128–29, 133, 146, 154–56, 158–59, 163, 169, 178, 191, 196, 200, 211–12, 214, 216–17, 219–20, 228, 239–40, 249, 251, 256, 267, 269, 281, 286, 291, 310, 313, 337–38, 345–46, 360–61, 364–66, 369–73, 376–79, 387; of life, 149, 307

means, 61, 160, 163, 167, 181, 189, 205, 222n65, 327–29, 372. *See also* utility

mechanistic explanations, 58, 60, 77, 159, 169

Meconi, David Vincent, 268n74

medium, 67, 83–87, 96, 102, 112, 366

Meillassoux, Quentin, 152n138, 255

Meister Eckhart, 231, 308n72

memory, 104–5, 149, 241, 250–52, 254, 260–61, 299, 303, 308, 351, 375

mercy, 316, 332, 386

mere conservationism, 183, 274–75

merit, 185, 190n83, 214, 269

Merleau-Ponty, Maurice, 25, 65, 69n77, 70, 73, 77, 82–83, 85, 88, 103, 181–82, 243n7, 345n33, 361–62, 367, 387n90

Merton, Thomas, 232n92, 261n54, 272n89, 312n89, 371n47

metaphor, 35, 71–72, 177, 248

metaphysics, 5–6, 12, 14–15, 27–28, 31–33, 36n88, 41, 57–58, 61, 107–8, 120, 138, 153, 192, 200, 209, 217–18, 237, 250, 263, 341, 376, 380; definition of metaphysician of irreducibility, 32; metaphysical attitudes, 108, 159; and parsimony, 217–18

metaxu (or suspended middle), 155, 307

methods: aesthetic, 4–5, 12, 14–21, 30, 32, 36, 43; circularities in, 19–21; dialectical and rhetorical, 14–16, 138; focused on experience, 2–4, 9–18, 140; focused on objective principles, 2–4, 9–18, 35, 63; metaxological, 21n51, 155; phenomenological, 18, 24–36, 41–47, 54, 76, 79, 119, 125, 136, 199, 378; scholastic, 18, 33, 34–36, 48, 53–54, 62–63, 76, 79, 125, 199; symphonic, 21

Michon, Cyrille, 167n11

microcosm, 8, 74, 309–10, 318, 331, 365. *See also* world

Milbank, John, 14–17, 65, 127n54, 139n85, 144n104, 155n149, 178n41, 189n79, 236n98, 259n48, 262n58, 307n64, 315–16, 326n139

Miller, Joshua, 65n59

Milton, John, 180

mind-body problem, 68

mind-brain identity theory, 56

Minerd, Matthew, 163n170

mine, what is, 55, 126, 186, 242, 292, 299–300, 337, 355

Mishnah Sanhedrin, 331n152

misogyny, 19

mission, 270–71, 307

modernity, 159, 236–38

modes, 263–64, 299, 301n37, 323, 338, 349–50

Montgomery, Marion, 139n86

moods, 62, 251–53

Moore, Charles A., 261n56, 298n28

Moore, G. E., 123n36
Mormando, Franco, 383n80
Mosebach, Martin, 373n54
motherhood (and mothers), 71, 180, 244, 343, 356–57. *See also* nursing; pregnancy
motion, 76–78, 103, 109–10, 166, 206, 236, 347; premotion, 183, 275
motivation, 59–60, 101, 112, 117, 199–206, 210, 219, 221, 228, 235, 249, 285, 291, 328–29, 364, 369, 376–78, 381, 383, 387. *See also* desire; importance
Mounier, Emmanuel, 306n57, 326n139
Mozart, W. A., 65
Muir, John, 362n8, 368
multiplicity, 37, 63–64, 100–101, 320, 334–40, 358, 363, 386–87; of aggregate or heap, 207–8, 213, 359; transcendental multitude, 314
muses, 120
music, 65, 72, 92, 158, 210, 214, 243, 364
mystery, 68, 154–56, 190, 197, 201, 260, 271, 312, 345, 370; and *arcana*, 366
myth, 35, 91, 95, 120, 158, 177, 238, 366

Nagel, Thomas, 138n77
Nancy, Jean-Luc, 337n7, 342, 357n56
Nannery, Lawrence, 353n51
narrative, 105, 149–50, 157, 163, 182, 285, 298, 315, 369, 375
nation, 327
natural attitude, 25–26
naturalism, 58, 236
natural law, 112, 160, 192, 195, 200–201, 204, 227, 240; traditional and new natural law theories, 7, 160–63, 190
nature: animal, 295; assumable, 297, 299–300, 321, 324, 338, 340; care for natural environment, 19, 180, 310–11, 337–38, 362, 366; Christ's two natures, 307, 339; common nature, 141, 321–22, 324–25; complete and incomplete, 335; and conversion, 252; dominion over, 310; and ecosystems, 213, 217, 278–79, 350, 358; ecstasy of, 348; and enslavement, 191–93; freely appropriated, 298; and grace, 7, 116, 128–29; and *hypostasis*, 352; individualized, 296–97, 299, 303, 305, 317, 321, 325–26, 338–39, 355; of moral acts, 162; multiplicity of, 334;

Natura naturans or *Sophia*, 281; nature absolutely considered, 114, 134, 136, 215, 234; nonpersonal, 97, 159, 217, 239, 255, 276, 279–81, 284, 298, 310–11, 320, 344, 350, 357–58, 361–62, 366–68, 385; philosophy of, 5, 77; relation to *ousia*, 260; relations to supposits, 338; and suffering, 370. *See also* essence; human nature; *ousia*; natural law; states
Nellas, Panayiotis, 294n11, 309n75, 310n80, 343n28, 344n30, 359–60
neurology. *See* brain
Nevitt, Turner, 135n71, 294n13
Newman, John Henry, 226–27, 229n83
new natural law theory. *See* natural law
Nicholas of Cusa, 272
Nicodemos of the Holy Mountain, 331n152
Nietzsche, Friedrich, 26n60, 150n126, 178, 187n72, 203n13, 283n117, 309n74, 316n103
nihilism, 26, 35, 286
Noë, Alva, 57n38, 103
nominalism, 105n98
nothingness, 11, 132, 143n102, 152, 240, 253, 322; and nihilation, 194
Nouvelle théologie, 6, 126–29, 236–38, 344
Novotný, Daniel, 9n25, 138n80
numinous, 121, 201, 386
nursing (or breastfeeding), 336–37, 357, 377
Nussbaum, Martha, 57n37

obedience, 116, 118–21, 128, 133, 137–38, 140, 152, 161, 164, 179–80, 187, 191–93, 195–97, 225, 231, 234–35, 237, 247, 287, 296, 310, 314, 359, 363–65, 373, 384, 387. *See also* act and potency
objectification (and commodification), 192
objectivity (and object), 2, 14, 17, 30, 44, 50–51, 55–60, 67–74, 162, 250, 361–64, 379; *conceptus formalis* and *obiectivus*, 134; formal object, 67, 116–17, 129, 148, 165, 219, 244–45, 248, 251, 304, 364, 376; moral object, 162; objectless acts, 252–53, 361
O'Brien, Matthew, 161n168, 243n5
O'Brien, Patrick, 366n24
O'Byrne, Anne, 281n110, 342, 357n56
occasionalism, 183
oceanic experiences, 253n38
Oderberg, David, 8n21, 294n14

Oetinger, Friedrich Christoph, 103n90
offering, 311, 315, 368, 371, 378–80, 385, 388;
   self-offering, 379–80, 385–86. *See also*
   sacrifice
oil drop, 77
Oliva, Mirela, 48n14, 103n90, 149n125
Olson, Eric, 66n62, 304–5
one (*unum*). *See* unity
Oord, Thomas Jay, 276n97
openness, 90, 109, 113, 118–19, 125–26, 128–29, 133, 161–62, 167, 169, 179–80, 189, 191, 193, 197, 204, 220, 224, 230, 236–37, 241, 245–46, 248, 254, 264, 278, 286, 292, 301, 303–4, 307–8, 349–54, 364, 366, 376, 378–79, 381, 388; biological, 342, 346; corporeal, 357, 369; uncontrolling openness, 276, 283; world-openness, 303–4, 320, 350–51, 356
open theism, 184, 276
orders of being and knowing, 36
organisms, 64, 76, 80–81, 99–100, 140–41, 175, 279–81, 340–41, 355–56, 358, 362, 388
organs. *See* brain; matter; parts; physiology
Ortega y Gasset, José, 204n16, 298n26
Osborne, Thomas, 240n106
others (and otherness), 62, 69, 84–87, 125, 131, 144–45, 147, 149, 160, 163, 167, 179–80, 185, 193–95, 202–5, 229n85, 232–33, 244–45, 252, 254, 261, 264–65, 268, 272, 285, 293–94, 297, 303–4, 307, 309, 312, 315, 329–33, 334, 347–48, 351, 356, 370, 377, 379–81, 388–89; as members of a "we," 245, 329; Thou, 180, 245, 301. *See also* intersubjectivity; relations
Otto, Rudolf, 185n65, 201n6
ousia, 241, 259n49, 260–63, 265–67, 271–73, 277, 285–86, 291–92, 298–99, 312, 317, 320, 338, 356, 374, 382. *See also* essence; nature
overflow (or flowing), 181, 200–202, 205, 242, 258, 261, 265, 274, 285, 329, 359, 364, 373, 381–82
Owens, Joseph, 146, 151, 350n42

Pabst, Adrian, 52n23
pain. *See* suffering
painting, 65, 72, 92, 119, 305, 368
panpsychism (or panprotoexperientialism), 58–59, 76
pantheism, 46n9
panzoism, 76
paradox, 151–53
Parfit, Derek, 311n85, 341n18
Parmenides, 63, 152, 155
Parsifal, 285
participation, 52–54, 78, 81–86, 90, 99–103, 111, 114–17, 122, 128–29, 131–33, 135–38, 141–42, 151, 153–54, 157, 166, 181, 183–84, 189–90, 195, 197, 208–9, 231, 233–34, 246–47, 254–55, 258, 265–73, 275, 277–83, 285, 292, 300, 303, 305, 307, 309, 311, 313, 325, 328, 330–31, 333, 337, 339, 346, 348, 352, 354, 359, 361, 363–66, 368, 370, 372–74, 376, 379, 381, 384, 387–88; kinds of, 265–66; participable and imparticipable, 266, 276–77
particles (and atoms and molecules), 66, 76, 78–79, 95, 334–36, 342
parts, 26, 34, 64, 73, 78, 94, 107, 109, 142, 163, 170, 184, 273, 279, 295, 297, 300, 319, 326–33, 334–40, 356; conflicts among, 340, 344
Pasnau, Robert, 34n85, 90, 115, 178, 250n27, 340n13, 340n14
Passerini, Peter Maria, 351n46
Patočka, Jan, 62
pausing at the irreducible, 3, 26, 50
Pawl, Timothy, 334n1
peace, 15, 97, 121–22, 163, 190, 203, 368
Pedro da Fonseca, 123n36, 273–74
Pegis, Anton, 318n112, 350n44
Péguy, Charles, 268n75
Pelagianism, 193
Penrose, Roger, 170n20
perception: action-based or enactive philosophies of, 103–4, 110, 350–51; as activity, 257; by apophatic awe or learned ignorance, 272; apperception, 42, 106, 251; being perceived by others, 245–46; of beings as irreducible, 258, 262; and concepts, 10, 16, 63, 67, 96–97, 130, 217; by connaturality, 36, 176–77, 216, 246; definition, 2–3; of faces, 378–81; fecundating, 145; foundation of reasoning, 15, 34, 60, 63; and the given as such, 29; of God, 183, 283; and interpretation, 216; and intuition or insight, 30, 140; and judgment, 27; and language, 70; and love, 17, 202–3; and meaningful appear-

ance, 26, 73–74, 95, 131; of microcosms, 309; of others' intentions, subjectivity, or uniqueness, 69–74, 144, 168, 172, 202–4, 224, 227–28, 246, 299, 302, 312–13, 333, 346, 353, 364, 367, 389; perceptual order, 92; phenomenological analysis of, 41, 73–74; of real beings, 29; sense perception, 34, 82–106, 365, 382–83; spiritual, see senses; tacit, 216; and value, 60–61, 207–8, 212–13, 216, 224; what is directly perceived is something in itself, 12, 44, 57–58, 108. See also affectivity

Percy, Walker, 25n59, 58n40, 137n75
Pereira, José, 152n139
perfectum, definition of, 295
performatives, 150
Perl, Eric, 137n74, 266n67
per se nota. See propositions
personalism, 2, 6, 7, 24, 30, 99, 120, 154, 199, 206, 209, 218, 220, 297, 318, 326–33, 345, 348, 352, 360–61; Carmelite personalism, 329; Russian personalism, 329–30
personality, 55, 191–94, 225, 231, 249, 252, 299, 343–44; personalence, 192n88; and stable identity, 194–95, 311, 313
personal value-essence, 224–25, 227, 268. See also vocation
person, definitions and indefinability of, 1, 8, 22, 37, 97–102, 209, 263, 286, 291, 295–302, 311–17, 319–21, 342, 355, 359–60, 362. See also human nature
personhood, principle or formal constituent of, 298–302, 321
person, nonhuman embodied, 342
person, portrait of, 8, 10, 14–15, 17, 22, 36, 55, 75, 79–80, 99, 102, 120, 131, 172, 206, 217, 252n35, 256, 259, 291, 299, 313, 360
perspective, 14–15, 17–18, 27, 86, 95, 104, 133, 137–38, 155, 161, 188, 216–17, 224, 330–31
Petavius, Dionysius, 259n48
Petcu, Liviu, 190n83
Peter Auriol, 274
Peter John Olivi, 183n61, 250, 274
phantasms, 104–6, 113–5, 118, 122–23, 133, 138, 149, 156, 198, 234–35, 250, 337
Phelan, Gerard, 151
phenomenology, 2, 6, 7, 10–14, 18, 24–34, 41–46, 53, 57n37, 74, 88, 163, 200, 237, 242, 247, 360, 376, 378, 380, 387n90; phenomenological language, 71; realist phenomenology, 28–30, 33, 35, 54, 61, 88, 135–36, 140, 204, 244
Philip of the Trinity, 246n17
physiology, 68–69, 110, 334–36, 367, 369–70, 385
Picasso, Pablo, 366n24
Pickstock, Catherine, 8n23, 139n84, 315–16
Pico della Mirandola, Giovanni, 310
Pieper, Josef, 18n43, 303n48
Pierce, C. S., 178n38
piety, 194–95, 239
pilgrims. See wayfarers
Pinckaers, Servais, 17n41, 117–18, 189n92, 196
Pinsent, Andrew, 244n9, 251n33
place (or location), 89, 110, 114, 117, 132, 171, 174, 270, 321–23, 345, 350, 362–63; category *ubi*, 209, 264, 349–50. See also land; rootedness
plants, 97, 99, 101, 217, 279, 309, 341, 366, 388; cultivating of, 368
Plato: on beauty, 86n27, 97–98, 101n80, 217n52; on the body, 182n54; on gods and *daimones*, 100, 227; on the Good, 203n15, 315n97; on iconicity, 131n58, 270n80; on inspiration and myth, 120; on intuition, 35–36; on *mania*, 372; Platonic experiences, 98, 137, 141; Platonic Forms, see essence; Platonism, 6, 16, 34, 100, 135, 137, 302, 310, 373; on powers, 108–9, 218; on the really real, 277
play, 214, 286, 303, 330, 371–72, 376, 387
pleasure, 60, 83, 107–9, 111, 117, 122, 158, 166, 177, 182, 189, 200, 210, 222, 253, 257, 293, 337, 347, 363–64, 366, 381–82, 386. See also joy
pleonexia, 191
Plested, Marcus, 373n57
Plotinus, 261
pneuma, 100
poetry, 71–72, 91, 97, 120, 157–58, 177, 216, 223. See also intuition
Polanyi, Michael, 216n51
poles of personhood, 306
politics, 196, 237, 239–40, 268–69, 326–33, 351–52, 354
pornography, 19, 192

portrait. *See* person, portrait of
possession by transcendent person, 186
potentiality (or potency). *See* act
powers, 35–37, 45, 67–74, 75, 77, 83, 85, 99–100, 107, 111, 115, 118, 125, 143, 148, 161–63, 173, 183, 191, 200, 219–20, 226, 233, 238, 241–46, 248–50, 252, 254, 258, 264, 274–75, 292, 295, 303–5, 308, 310, 319, 335–37, 340, 351–52, 354–56, 363–64, 371–72, 381; active and passive potencies, 116, 118; basic, 243, 364; of being, 154; combining powers, 181, 242, 250, 254, 265, 287; distinction of powers of body or soul, 165; higher and lower powers, 218, 247; and impairment and enhancement, 348–49, 355; natural, 243–44; unfolding from unified power of soul, 220, 242, 254. *See also names of particular powers*
practices, 109, 162, 239
praise, 101, 167, 210, 221, 254, 272, 314, 373; persons as doxological beings, 314
prayer, 181, 259, 314, 316, 373–74
preapprehension (*Vorgriff*), 124, 128–29, 133
prediction, 59–60, 66
pregnancy, 356–57. *See also* mother; nursing
presence and absence, 251, 258, 261, 274. *See also* self-presence
pride, 195, 201n7, 219, 252, 384
priesthood, 311, 368
primary and secondary qualities, 90–91
Prince Mishkin, 285
private language, 69–70
probabilistic states, 171–74, 278, 322–23
processes, 110–11, 168, 189–90, 264. *See also energeia*
Proclus, 100n76, 266n67, 302–3
promiscuous realism, 320n118
promising, 244, 267
properties of being. *See* transcendentals
proportion. *See* analogy; fittingness
propositions, 92, 105, 140, 146–47, 157–58, 209, 255, 366; self-evident propositions, 10–11, 240
proprioception, 103
prosopon (or *persona*), 291, 352, 374, 376–80. *See also* face
prostheses, 356–57
providence. *See* God

Przywara, Erich, 33n80, 154–55, 307n64, 308
psyche (or psychological layer), 54–55, 58, 360–61, 362n5, 364, 370; psychic feelings, 110
psychologism, 24
pulchrum, 5. *See also* beauty
pure form. *See* end
purusa, 298n28
Putnam, Hilary, 57n37

qualia (or what it's like), 58, 71, 82, 86, 106, 229n85
quality (category), 209
quantity (and quantitative properties), 56, 79, 84, 87, 90–91, 94, 102, 114, 131, 173–74, 178, 188, 209, 322–23, 350
quantum mechanics, 170–74, 237, 255, 278, 322–23
quiescence. *See Gelassenheit*
quietism, 286
Quine, Willard V., 53n24

race or ethnicity, 324, 352; racism, 19, 201, 226, 269, 368n31
Radhakrishnan, Sarvepalli, 261n56, 298n28
Rahner, Karl, 33n80, 59n45, 83n20, 87–90, 124, 126, 132, 156, 187, 294, 342n22, 353
Ramos, Alice, 86n27, 122n33
Rati, 98
rationalism. *See* idealism
Ratzinger, Joseph, 18, 372n52
reading, 57, 216, 243, 366–67
receptivity, 95, 104, 148, 157, 183–84, 186–87, 193, 195, 219–20, 231, 233, 242, 245, 266, 268, 306, 312–16, 321–22, 333, 338, 347–48, 360, 373–75, 378–79, 384, 388; category *passio*, 209, 233, 263–64, 349; *passio essendi* and *conatus essendi*, 238–39, 307
recollection, 249–50, 261
reductionisms, 1, 6–7, 13–14, 22, 26, 32, 41, 45–46, 56–61, 66, 217, 226, 230, 237, 284, 315; axiologically reducible, 199; causally reducible, 57; ontologically reducible, 56, 199; political reductionisms, 326; theological reductionism, 254, 284
reduction, phenomenological, 24–31, 34, 41–46, 54–55, 61, 65, 71, 88, 125, 158, 168,

360–63, 378–79; Dionysian reduction, 176–78, 362
reduction, quantum state, 171, 173–74, 255
Reimers, Adrian, 137n75, 140n88, 178n38
Reinach, Adolf, 244
reincarnation, 323–24
relations: bearing or carrying, 296–97, 303, 314, 352; being created, 306, 325; being given, 313; beings, persons, or principles as intrinsically relational, 132, 141, 143, 306–14, 368, 388; empty to filled, 142–43, 215; and *energeiai*, 265; *esse ab*, *esse in*, and *esse ad*, 306, 308; ethical, 144–45, 330, 369; to extrinsics, 209, 264, 349–50; founding, 27, 208; having, 45, 55, 292, 296–97; incarnated, 388; including or encompassing, 257–58, 296–98, 300, 303–5, 307, 313, 321, 328, 334, 338, 350–51, 356–58, 372; intentional or experiential, 123, 157, 233–34, 258, 273–74; opposed, 141–42, 262; of order, 208; participation, 271; pedestal, 211; real, 122–23, 258, 273; of reason, 122–23, 273; species to genus, 266, 302, 318, 320, 335, 339; subsistent, 307; transcendental, 143, 193, 306, 309, 317, 320, 323–25, 333, 357, 388; transitive and nontransitive, 266. *See also* termination
religion (and religious acts and values), 133, 217, 222–23, 230, 236–40, 252, 303, 330, 332, 368, 372, 389. *See also* liturgy
Rembrandt van Rijn, 65
repetition, 139, 314. *See also* uniqueness
representation, 90, 104; political, 268–69. *See also* likeness; sign
reproduction (or procreation), 78, 80, 162, 164, 255, 278–80, 284, 343–47. *See also* sexuality
resistance, 177–80, 182, 246, 322
respect, 61, 190, 210, 296, 301, 333, 345, 355
responses, 148, 150, 218; affective, 228, 230, 370, 381; due, 206, 210, 220–23, 228, 231, 233–34, 332, 345, 355, 381; free or volitional, 191, 193, 228, 230–31; to grace, 230; as social act, 244; super value-response, 202, 330; theoretical, 148; value-response, 201–2, 205, 220–26, 228, 254, 328–29, 349, 357, 372
responsibility, 31n77, 141, 145, 167, 179–80, 190–91, 195, 293, 302, 314, 333, 343, 348
restlessness, 126–27, 129, 190, 195, 203, 231, 271, 273. *See also* God
resurrection, 270, 276, 291, 295, 324, 341, 347, 352, 381–85, 387–89
revelation, 7, 100, 116, 127, 129, 132, 138, 149, 187, 228, 255, 270, 286, 291, 309, 311, 313, 378, 380–81, 387; and concealment or veiling, 190, 312. *See also* self-manifestation
reverence, 101, 109, 190, 210, 219, 229, 252, 263, 270, 296, 333, 340
Rhonheimer, Martin, 160n167
Richard of St. Victor, 301–2, 314n92
Richards, Amy, 163
rights, 214, 297, 332–33
Rilke, Rainer Maria, 4n8, 122n32
Rivera, Joseph, 362n9
Rocha, Samuel, 378–79
Rococo, 218
roles. *See* states
Rolnick, Philip, 315n100
Roman jurisprudence, 297–98, 351
Romano, Claude, 27n66, 92n47, 175, 342, 362–63
Romanticism, 372
Romero Carrasquillo, Francisco J., 270n80
Romero, Miguel, 348n40, 355n53
rootedness (or being at home), 89, 103, 196, 239, 350, 366. *See also* land; place
Rovira, Rogelio, 30n74
Rubin, Michael, 94n55
Rubio, Antonio, 349n41
Russell, Norman, 7n19, 186n69, 232n91, 385n85
Rusticus the Deacon, 299n33

sacralization of persons, 332–33
sacrament, 133, 246–47, 255, 270, 282, 284, 311, 375, 384
Sacred Congregation of Studies, 181n50
Sachs, Joe, 257n45
sacrifice, 93, 163, 189, 191, 221, 285, 298n28, 311, 314–15, 357, 368, 370, 373, 379, 385–86. *See also* self-renunciation
Sadler, Gregory, 8n20
saint, 131–32, 221, 225, 247, 268, 330–31, 333, 370; communion of, 330–31
Salmanticenses, 248n21
Samajdar, 253n38

Sanford, J. J., 213n41
Sartre, Jean-Paul, 159, 187n72, 194–95, 316n103
Satan (or demons or fallen angels), 180, 283, 344
saturated phenomena, 119–21, 128, 215–16, 255, 293, 313, 337–38
Schaefer, Donovan, 303n49
Schaeffer, Matthew, 151n133
Scheeben, Matthias, 284n121, 314n93
Scheler, Max, 3n5, 16, 25–28, 45, 55n28, 59–61, 72n83, 94n56, 108, 141n94, 176–78, 181, 201n6, 203n14, 214n42, 218, 222, 224–26, 227n78, 232n93, 242, 252n34, 267n70, 303, 312n88, 361–62
Schelling, F. W. J., 182n58
Schiller, Friedrich, 372
Schindler, David L., 306, 308
Schindler, D. C., 153n140, 181n49
Schmitz, Kenneth, 33n80, 51, 144n103, 186–87, 233n94, 306n58, 309n74, 316n104
Schneider, Susan, 59n42
scholasticism, 11, 13, 14, 18, 24, 33, 34–36, 42, 45, 51–53, 62–63, 65, 78, 88, 95, 100, 116, 148, 163, 200, 205, 209, 235, 241, 263, 295, 297, 299–300, 304, 315, 317, 339–40, 382–83; Baroque Jesuit tradition, 123, 187–88, 273; and confessional manuals, 351; Franciscan tradition, 138, 140, 156, 250, 274–75, 316
Schwarz, Balduin, 30n74
Schweitzer, Othmar, 299n31
science (and scientific properties), 56–60, 66, 75–77, 88, 91, 95–96, 105, 158, 168–74, 255, 319, 335, 337, 341. *See also* Aristotle
Scruton, Roger, 3n7, 5, 27n66, 45n6, 69n77, 95, 179n42, 239n104, 249n24, 336n6, 346n36, 347n37, 369n36
Searle, John, 2n4, 57n38, 140n87, 150n127
secularity, 236–40, 316, 353
security, 25, 47, 109, 190, 253
sedaka (transcendental), 245
seduction, 97, 121, 190, 223, 284
Seifert, Josef, 3n5, 27n63, 29–30, 153n143, 154–55, 167n10, 179n43, 202n8, 205n21, 206, 208–10, 298, 325n136, 326n138
self-awareness or self-consciousness. *See* subjectivity
self-determination, 180, 187–97, 206, 219, 230, 237, 239, 262, 298, 307, 331–32, 349. *See also* freedom
self-manifestation (or self-communication or self-expression or self-revelation), 18, 68–74, 76–77, 79–80, 84, 86, 92–94, 99, 118, 120–22, 139, 144, 149, 154–55, 157–58, 177, 190, 201, 206, 216, 231, 233, 241, 257–68, 283, 300, 302–3, 305, 309, 344, 350, 361, 369, 375–77, 380, 383, 387; self-declaration or self-disclosure or self-saying, 149, 319. *See also* gift
self-motion. *See* life; motion
self-positing. *See* affirmation
self-possession (and self-governing), 296–98, 300, 303, 312, 328
self-presence, 74, 78, 82, 84–85, 125, 132, 166, 206, 218, 261, 297, 376
self-renunciation (or self-sacrifice), 193–94, 225, 298n28, 357, 373, 384. *See also* sacrifice
self-sensing (or auto-affection or self-feeling), 10, 46, 54–55, 73–74, 79, 85, 103, 109, 111n121, 181–82, 188, 250–51, 347, 361–63
self-transcendence, 8, 29, 54, 68, 86, 88, 99–100, 109, 113, 144–45, 155, 158, 191, 194, 201–2, 204–5, 221, 228, 233, 239, 249, 251, 261, 271, 281, 291, 298, 303–4, 306, 310, 314, 327–29, 343–44, 346–48, 372
Sellars, Wilfrid, 92n47
seminal reasons, 280
semi-person or incomplete person, 317
senses: bodily in general, 34, 67, 73–74, 99, 107, 110, 112, 123–24, 137, 234–35, 238, 245–48, 251, 316, 320, 348–49, 361, 363, 373, 377; exterior, 82–102, 115, 148; illative, 226–27; impairments of, 348–49; intellectualized, 365; interior, 102–6, 117, 360–61; spiritual, 16, 36, 89, 241, 246–48, 254, 259, 265, 301, 360, 373, 381. *See also* names of particular senses
sensible properties or qualities, 36, 82–84, 86, 88–100, 104, 108, 112–14, 120, 135, 177–78, 214, 217, 247, 278, 305, 340; analogous spiritual qualities as transcendentals, 248, 373; as messages from God or gods, 97, 100, 131, 210; *per se* and *per accidens*, 102–3
sensible species, 83–88, 90, 95–96, 99, 104, 106, 109, 114, 266, 316

Index   449

separate substances. *See* gods
separation, 186, 197–98, 261, 285, 312–13, 316, 371, 379
Sevier, Christopher Scott, 86n27
sexuality: acts and experiences, 107n104, 191–92, 247, 284, 336–37, 344, 346–47, 356, 359, 369, 371; androgyny, 343; arousal or sexual passion, 110, 218, 336, 344, 347–48, 369, 373, 376–77, 387; colors other aspects of persons, 343, 345–46; definition of male and female, 343, 345; and *eros*, 343–46; mating and making love, 367; sexual difference, 343–46; sexual properties, 324, 336–37, 343–46
sickness (and disease), 292, 337, 344; and immune system, 358
Sider, Theodore, 5
sides of single unities, 68–72, 77, 80, 85, 367
signs (and signification), 91, 139, 171, 313, 348, 359, 365, 367, 387. *See also* likeness; representation
Simeon the New Theologian, 310n80
Simon, Yves, 84n22
sin (or wrongdoing), 166, 183, 185, 191, 193, 205, 214, 228, 252n35, 298, 314–15; original sin, 235, 269, 351–52, 386
Sharkey, Sarah Borden, 33n81, 321n121, 323n130, 325n134
Shakespeare, William, 332n153
Shaw, Gregory, 120n27, 137n74, 373n57
Sheldrake, Merlin, 358n58
Sherman, Jacob Holsinger, 131n58
Shewmon, Alan, 78n9
Shoemaker, Sydney, 305n53
skepticism, 31
skin, 73, 94, 357
sleep, 62, 371. *See* dreams
Sloterdijk, Peter, 337
Smart, J. J. C., 56n35
Smith-Gilson, Caitlin, 231n90, 318n112
Smith, Wolfgang, 170n20
sobornost (or togetherness), 329–30
Soccorsi, Philippus, 170n20
social acts, 241, 244–46, 248, 267, 292, 301, 316, 360, 381
Sokolowski, Robert, 3n5, 13, 30n71, 71, 103n89, 114, 123–23, 149, 150n129, 251n32
solidarity, 53, 127, 129, 141, 265, 304, 329, 337

solitude, 312–13, 316, 385
Solomon ibn Gabriol, 322
Soloveitchik, Josef, 331n152, 387n90
Soloviev, Vladimir, 93, 343n28, 369
sons of God. *See* children
Sophia, 102, 277, 287, 302, 308, 380; Sophiology, 93, 98n66, 101–2, 120, 261, 281, 302, 313–14, 366
soul, 8, 37, 45, 76–77, 87, 125, 143, 165, 197, 219–20, 226, 240, 248–50, 252, 254, 258, 260, 284, 291–95, 299, 304, 308, 317–25, 336, 340–45, 355, 360, 370, 372, 374–76, 381–83, 387; despotic and political rule, 363–64, 367–68; kinds of relation to body, 348, 350–52, 356, 359–60, 363–70, 376, 382–83; separated soul, 7, 8, 37, 291, 294–95, 316–17, 318n108, 351, 382–83; spark of, 325; world-soul, 280–81
space, 27, 54, 87–90, 112, 170–71, 362, 368. *See also* intersubjectivity; place
Spaemann, Robert, 33n80, 89n40, 297, 325n135
speaking, 244–45, 272, 319, 348, 365–66, 373; and voice, 110, 162, 318, 341, 376, 379
species. *See* essence; intelligible species; nature; sensible species
speculative realism, 152n138
Speiring, Jaime, 166n3
Spencer, Mark K., 24n52, 24n53, 50n20, 65n60, 109n112, 117n17, 117n18, 123n36, 143n102, 148n121, 170n20, 180n45, 211n38, 235n97, 243n5, 246n18, 257n44, 263n60, 265n62, 267n68, 267n69, 275n95, 291n1, 299n33, 306n54, 334n1, 349n41, 351n45, 353n51, 356n54, 365n15, 373n54, 375n63, 378n69
spheres of acts, 55, 312
spiritual acts and powers (and spirit), 45, 55, 100, 111, 118, 165, 167, 214, 224, 235, 237, 242, 246, 252, 291–92, 301, 304, 308–10, 312–13, 318–20, 322, 325–27, 340–42, 346–49, 354–57, 360–61, 363–83, 385; definition of, 112; materialization of spirit, 369, 385
spiritual perception. *See* senses
spiritual senses. *See* senses
spite, 180, 205, 207
splendor, 4, 86, 94, 106, 109, 131, 158, 263, 283
Stango, Marco, 319

Index

Staniloae, Dumitru, 314n93
state (political), 326–33
states (*status*), 235–37, 291, 351–54, 356, 372, 379–81; and ages, 349, 352; fallen, 235–36, 351–52; and grades, dignities, duties, and lives, 352; original state of grace, 235; of pure nature, 235–37, 291, 316, 351, 353
Stein, Edith, 8n20, 33, 41–52, 55–56, 58, 61–62, 65–66, 69, 76, 80–81, 101, 103n90, 135, 136n72; 137n73, 139n81, 140–41, 147, 208, 215n47, 218, 224–25, 242, 250, 252–53, 261, 272, 297n20, 303, 318n112, 321n121, 322n126, 324, 325n137, 335n4, 336, 343, 345–46, 375
Stoicism, 34
Strawson, Galen, 59n42
Strawson, P. F., 36n88
structure of experience, 24, 27–28, 35–36, 47
Stump, Eleonore, 8n21, 36n90, 79n11, 115, 166n7, 230, 244n9, 245n12, 251n33, 294n14, 318n110, 367
style, 65–66, 68, 74, 77, 139, 191, 212–14, 217, 225, 267–68, 270, 297, 299, 324–25, 352, 381
Suárez, Antoine, 170n20
Suárez, Francisco, 67n67, 87n31, 87n32, 89n40, 116n16, 123n36, 134, 143n102, 152, 173, 178n39, 187–88, 207n27, 218n58, 235n97, 243n8, 273–74, 321n119, 340, 351n46, 370n41; Suárezianism, 6
subjective: definition, 2
subjectively satisfying, 200, 204–5, 222n65, 223, 232, 234, 313, 347. *See also* joy
subjectivism. *See* idealism
subjectivity (or pure subject or self-consciousness), 10, 24, 28–32, 36, 41, 43–45, 49–62, 68–74, 76, 91, 97, 112, 125–26, 131–32, 148–49, 156, 160–62, 166–67, 175–76, 186, 219–20, 226, 228, 232, 235, 237, 242–43, 249, 252, 261, 267, 274, 291, 298–99, 305, 312, 315, 317–18, 329, 345, 355, 357, 360–65, 367, 376; core self and empirical self, 261; frontal and lateral self-consciousness, 229–31, 312; loss of subject-object distinction, 253, 272–73, 361–63; no self, 311; porous and buffered self, 238–40, 337–38, 358; therapeutic "I," 238. *See also* Eigenleben; personality
sublimity, 97, 121–22, 128, 363, 386

subsistence, 291, 296–97, 299n33, 305, 307, 312, 317, 338, 374–76
substance, 28–29, 31, 37, 44, 51, 64–68, 77, 80, 94, 99, 102, 118, 136–37, 140, 149, 173–75, 209, 211–16, 226, 242–43, 252, 255, 258, 260, 262, 266, 274–75, 277–78, 291–92, 296–300, 305, 308, 319–20, 334–41, 345, 355, 359, 387; moral substances, 163–64
suffering (or pain), 62, 70–71, 107, 110, 180, 182, 195, 204, 220, 268, 294, 309, 336–37, 348, 360–61, 363, 385–87; redemptive, 370
sun-energeia, 266–67, 269–71, 276, 279, 287, 304, 306, 310, 329, 331, 351, 356–58, 364, 368; incarnate *sun-energeia*, 337–38, 346, 356–57, 374
supernatural existential, 353
supposit (and suppositality), 296, 299–301, 305, 321, 338–40, 342, 355, 357–58, 376
surface and depth, 95–96, 170, 248–54, 261, 263
survivalism, 294–95, 316–17
Sylvester of Ferrara, Francis, 318
symbol, 72, 119, 181n49, 305, 309, 366, 373
Symeon the New Theologian, 385n86
sympathy, 72, 177–78, 188, 267
syncretism, 22–23
synderesis, 240
systole and diastole, 78

Taliaferro, Charles, 168n13
Tanizaki, Jun'ichiro, 175n27
taste (aesthetic), 15, 17, 19, 86, 216, 297
Taylor, Charles, 195n104, 238, 337–38
tears, 72, 336, 369–70; gift of, 370
technology, 189, 341, 355–57
Teilhard de Chardin, Pierre, 311n81, 342n22
teleology. *See* end
Terence, 8
Teresa of Avila, 55n27
termination (or completion) of acts, 157, 264–65, 270, 274, 299, 325, 345, 348–51, 372
terror (or the terrible, terrifying, or threatening), 97–98, 121–22, 159, 190, 221
Thales of Miletus, 282
Theodore the Studite, 131n58, 270n80
theology, 8, 284; process theology, 184; theology of the body, 310n79, 312n88, 329, 346, 369, 375

theonomy, 227, 307
theophany, 256
theoria. See contemplation
theoros, 18–19, 22
theos. See God; gods
theosis. See divinization.
thereness, 83, 156–59
Thérèse of Lisieux, 8, 203n15, 225, 268, 384
theurgy, 120, 373
thing (transcendental), 92
third-person. *See* object; objectivity
Thomas Aquinas: on analogy, 130–31, 133; on appetite, 107–11, 219n60; on being and its principles and properties, 11, 34, 49–50, 63–66, 74, 92–94, 99–100, 122, 126, 135, 141–42, 147, 152, 153n141, 173, 206, 209–10, 282, 314, 321–22, 338–39, 341; on bodily parts and properties, 324n132, 334–36, 338–39, 341, 343, 346n36, 364n13; on categories, 264–65; on causality, 55n31, 56, 79, 80, 170, 213, 276; on Christ: 307n61, 339; on connaturality, 36, 177; on conscience, 226n75; in dialogue with Eastern Christianity, 259, 270–71; on divine and human action, 183; on divinization, 270–72; on the fall, 344; on gifts of the Holy Spirit, 232n91, 247; on glory, 270n80; on God, 46n9, 126, 143n101, 183, 247, 271–72, 276, 277n102; on goodness, 200; on image of God, 308–9, 374; on intellect, 16, 34–36, 112–17, 123, 125, 133–34, 136–38, 140, 156–57, 166–67, 176, 240, 244, 250, 253, 301, 365; interpretations of, 22–23, 130; on justice and mercy, 316; on life, 75–77; on love, 180, 202n11, 218, 229n83; on metaphysics, 5; methodology, 34–36; on nonpersonal beings, 367n30; on personhood, 1, 254, 295–97, 300, 352; on powers, 241–42, 250; on principle of noncontradiction, 10–11; on relations to God, 306; on resurrection, 382n78, 383n79; on senses, 67–68, 82–84, 86–88, 91, 99, 102–8, 110–11; on the soul, 284n120, 292, 294–95, 304, 316n104, 317, 322, 345, 364n13; on spiritual senses, 36, 247–48; on states of life, 351n46; on taste, 19; on temporality, 189n81; on vegetative powers, 78–79; on virtue, 182, 364n13; on will, 166–67, 176, 179n43, 205; on writing, 270n79

Thomism, 2, 6, 23–24, 36, 48, 131, 136, 142, 146–47, 152, 240, 248, 300; analytic, 69–70, 142, 220, 230, 243, 264–66, 270–72, 275–78, 294–95, 317, 323, 326–33, 336, 344; Baroque, 150; existential, 151, 304; Lublin, 117, 149, 193; Renaissance, 318; traditional, 127–29; transcendental, 87, 124, 129. *See also names of particular Thomists*
Thompson, Christopher, 368n31
Thornton, Allison, 319
thrownness, 311
thumos, 108–9
time, 47, 74, 87–90, 103–4, 110–11, 112, 114, 117, 132, 151, 171, 188–89, 194, 215, 251, 270, 293, 345, 350, 387; aeviternity, 189; category *quando*, 209, 264, 349–50; distension, 47, 315; duration, 188–89, 204, 251; eternity, 111, 128, 184, 222–23; *kairos*, 224; retention and protension, 111, 251, 315; and waiting, 193. *See also* history
Timpe, Kevin, 348n40
Tolkien, J. R. R., 97n65, 139n86, 187, 281n112
Tollefsen, Christopher, 160n167
Tomberg, Valentin, 366n22
Toner, Patrick, 294n13
too many thinkers problem, 303–4
Torre, Michael, 274n91
totalizing, 144–47, 179, 202, 245, 304–5, 377, 379; totalitarianism, 239, 328
touch, 67–68, 82, 103, 247, 357, 361, 379, 387; case of two hands touching, 73–74, 85, 361
traces, 147–49, 204, 374
Tracy, David, 6n17
tradition. *See* culture and tradition
tragedy, 203, 332
transcendental conditions, 31, 45–47, 87–88, 111, 124, 232–33, 360, 378. *See also* subjectivity
transcendentals (or properties of being), 34, 92–93, 114, 121, 151, 158, 161, 183, 206, 210, 219, 245, 248, 258, 260, 267, 300, 302, 364, 373, 376, 384; supertranscendentals, 143n102. *See also names of individual transcendentals*
transcendent causes, 59, 82, 108, 116, 193, 238–39. *See also* God; gods
transcendent persons. *See* God; gods

transfiguration, 259, 347, 369, 372–74, 377, 385, 387, 389
Treanor, Brian, 85
tripartite anthropology, 325
Tristan and Isolde, 343
truth, 19, 60, 92–93, 113, 158, 160, 177, 191, 244, 301n40
Tullius, William, 26n62, 28n67

Ulrich, Ferdinand, 93n51, 152–53, 186n70, 194n96, 206n22, 231, 384n83
unconsciousness (or subconsciousness), 106n99, 118–20, 169, 193, 249, 252n35, 261, 361–62
uniqueness (or irreplaceability or unrepeatability), 3, 46, 65, 100, 131–32, 149, 159, 171, 191–92, 202–3, 207, 210, 217, 224, 227, 245, 296–97, 299–300, 302–3, 323–25, 331–33, 340, 347–48, 352, 354, 369, 371, 376–79, 381, 387, 389
United Nations, 333n156
unity: accidental, 206, 210, 213, 319; of acts in soul and body, 364–80, 382, 384; actual unity and potential multiplicity, 341; aesthetic, 97, 217, 269; with all things, 311; with another, 83, 86–87; axiological or of value, 207, 210–16; bodily, 335, 356; of essence, 51, 81, 114, 141, 147, 208, 299–300, 334; of existence, 147–48, 152, 154, 208–9, 300, 334; of fictional content, 139; and form, 42, 63–66, 74, 110, 137, 295; of henads, 302–3; holistic, 1, 4–5, 11–12, 14, 18, 36–37, 43, 60, 66, 73, 77–78, 82, 86, 92, 94, 103, 107, 117–20, 122, 157, 210, 220, 231, 249, 257–58, 262–64, 279, 295–97, 302–3, 305, 362, 376–77, 382, 386; identity over time, 356; irreducibility to, 334; of material and spiritual acts or phenomena, 100, 106, 169–70, 382, 384–85; and memory, 250; necessary and morphic, 135; one in being, 263; of order, 207, 212–15, 233, 339; *per se* or *secundum quid*, 338–40; of persons, 100, 296–98, 300, 302, 321, 326, 334, 340, 355, 360; and powers, 77–78, 82, 86; real identity, 184, 307; self-identity, 11, 74, 76, 237, 252, 299, 305, 311; of sense and intellect, 120, 137, 363–64; of spontaneous order, 214; strict identity, 142–43, 263, 304–5; of subjective and objective, 68–74, 77, 85, 107, 361–62; substantial, 319–20, 334–35, 359; the transcendental one or *unum*, 92; of transcendentals, 92; of world, 101–2. *See also* existence; *Gestalt*; layer; multiplicity; value
universals, 26, 34, 63, 105–6, 114, 124, 130, 134–36, 163, 227, 240, 244–45, 296–97, 302, 321, 328, 376
Upanishads, 261n56
utilitarianism, 200
utility (or use), 60–61, 117, 128, 136, 167, 171, 179, 192, 222, 224, 331–33

value: and aesthetic essence, 217, 340; of all things, 310, 387; blindness, 60, 224, 234–35; call of, 191–92, 195, 221, 224, 227, 234, 249, 330, 357, 376; caused by creatures, 283; disvalue, 207–8, 223, 232, 255, 281–83; earthly, 128, 188, 223, 226, 255–56, 278, 282–83, 331; and enslavement, 332; evokes being affected, 228, 230; of experience, 230, 239; face of, 376–77; and form, 64; hierarchy and kinds, 60, 128, 132, 193, 222–26, 233, 249, 296, 354, 368; of life, 149, 195, 198, 307; in life-world, 91; as message, 95–97, 100, 222–23, 255, 282; as motivation, 59–60, 101, 199, 201–5, 235, 237, 329–31, 346, 381, 386; and neutrality, 17, 60, 95; of nonpersonal nature, 255, 301, 310–11; of places and times, 350, 386; of powers, 253–54; relation to affectivity, 36–37, 59–60, 88, 108, 220; relation to bearers, 210–11; of responses, 148; sense of valuelessness, 371; in sensible qualities, 89, 105; of sexes and *eros*, 345–47; and structure of being, 93, 95, 159, 206–8, 210, 212–13, 233, 263, 267, 282–83, 297, 300, 303, 305, 317, 321, 328; unifying power of, 211–16, 231, 268–70, 278, 283, 331, 334, 339–40; of unique persons, 202–4, 232, 237, 310, 328, 330, 332–33, 344, 349, 376, 380; of weakness, 346–47. *See also* affectivity; beauty; importance
Vanauken, Sheldon, 344n29
Van Dyke, Christina, 294n13, 336n5
van Inwagen, Peter, 53n24, 66n64, 277n100, 279n104, 294n10
vegetative acts and powers, 75, 78–80, 85, 94, 101, 110, 145, 363, 377, 387

Velleman, J. David, 192n90
Venus, 121. *See also* Aphrodite
vice, 108, 176–77, 195, 231, 243, 251–52, 269, 347, 371
Vico, Giambattista, 103n90
view from nowhere, 14, 138, 188
Viladesau, Richard, 72n82, 109n115, 124n42
Viñas, Miguel, 143n102
violence, 97, 121, 311, 386; and *agon*, 386; battle, 215, 386
virtual presence, 334–35
virtue: acquired and infused, 176, 180, 251–52; moral, 30, 59–60, 109, 176–77, 182, 193–95, 220, 224, 229, 231, 243, 354, 364, 376; particularist virtue ethics, 227; prudence (or practical wisdom), 226; social, 269
vision, 67, 82, 103, 130, 248–49, 361
vitalism, 77n2
vitality (and vital power and vital acts). *See* life
vocation, 62, 185, 225, 231, 268, 307, 312, 317, 330–31, 346, 354
voice. *See* speaking
volitional power. *See* will
voluntarism, 167, 254
Vorgriff. *See* preapprehension
von Balthasar, Hans Urs, 5, 17–21, 33n80, 71, 87, 91n46, 92–93, 126, 139n84, 141n94, 143n101, 145n111, 149, 152, 155, 176n30, 177n35, 180, 191n87, 217n52, 233n94, 236n98, 244–46, 259n48, 267n69, 268, 272n85, 284–85, 297n23, 297n25, 301n37, 303n46, 307, 310n79, 311, 312n88, 321n120, 325n137, 326n139, 329n144, 332n153, 340n15, 343n28, 351, 357, 370n44, 371, 386n89
von Hildebrand, Alice, 109n115, 221n64, 222n66
von Hildebrand, Dietrich, 3n5, 3n6, 5, 8n22, 10, 25n57, 30, 61n49, 62n52, 68n73, 69n75, 69n77, 71–72, 83n20, 87, 89n40, 93, 95–101, 103n90, 109n115, 110, 118, 120n27, 125–26, 127n53, 128n55, 131n58, 134–35, 145, 148, 163n170, 170, 192n88, 194, 200–207, 210–12, 215n47, 217–24, 227n78, 228, 229n84, 230n86, 231, 234, 244, 249, 251–52, 260, 263n59, 297n24, 303n46, 303n47, 336n6, 343n27, 345, 346n36, 347n37, 350n42, 361, 367, 369–70, 372n53, 373, 376–77

von Uexküll, Jakob, 303n48
vulnerability, 47, 175, 186, 190, 193, 195, 206, 233, 286, 309, 342, 346

wabi-sabi, 175, 282, 311, 388
Wagner, Richard, 343
wakefulness (or watchfulness or *hesychia*), 62, 233, 249, 365, 373–74
Waldstein, Michael, 3n7, 329
Wallenfang, Donald, 33n81
Walsh, David, 179n42, 270, 302, 318n111, 330n151
Walter, Henrik, 169n15
Wang, Connie X., 248n22
Wang, Stephen, 194n96
Ward, Michael, 100n75
Ward, Thomas, 339n12
Walz, Matthew, 67n66
Watkin, E. I., 102n85, 157n158
wayfarers (*viatores*) or pilgrims, 350, 373
Weber, Max, 238n102
Wenisch, Fritz, 30n74
what it's like. *See* qualia
Whitman, Walt, 310n77
wholeness. *See* unity
wildness and wilderness, 55n27, 255, 285, 316, 330, 361–62, 366, 368, 385
Wilhelmsen, Frederick, 23, 151–54, 204n16
will, 8, 36, 92, 127, 139, 164, 165–70, 174–82, 184–91, 193–98, 202, 205–6, 216, 218–20, 226, 228–31, 236, 238–40, 241, 244, 246, 249, 253–54, 277, 287, 292, 295, 301, 305, 308, 344, 347, 350, 355, 360, 363–64, 372, 381; gnomic and natural, 197; sanction and disavowal of feeling, 220–21, 230, 239–40; will to power or *libido dominandi*, 203, 249
William of Ockham, 156–57, 242, 321, 340
Williams, Bernard, 293n5
Williams, Charles, 268n73
Williams, Scott, 299n33, 355n53
Wilshire, Bruce, 94n56
Winckelmans de Cléty, Charles, 281n112
Wippel, John, 23, 34n84, 151, 154, 265n63, 321n123
Wittgenstein, Ludwig, 69–71
Wohlleben, Peter, 99n71
Wojtyła, Karol (John Paul II), 3, 6, 25n57, 26n61, 30, 33n80, 50–51, 53, 61n48, 182,

Wojtyła, Karol (John Paul II) (*cont.*) 193n92, 228, 269n76, 297n23, 303n47, 310n79, 312n88, 326n138, 329, 346, 369, 373n54, 375
wonder, 17–19, 25, 89, 94, 101, 109, 113, 129, 133, 155, 157, 217, 229, 263
Wood, Jordan Daniel, 286n127
work, 333
world (or cosmos), 30–32, 83, 91, 101–2, 193, 245, 252, 258, 264, 303–4, 310–11, 318, 329, 350–51, 361–63, 366, 368, 373–74; being in the world, 89–90; human aspect of the world, 95–96, 246; human person as little world, *see* microcosm; human person as macrocosm, 331. *See also* openness

Woroniecki, Jacek, 110, 176n32, 192n88, 197n108
worship. *See* liturgy
Woznicki, Andrew, 66n61, 193
writing, 57, 90, 114, 164, 270, 364–67

Yadav, Sameer, 2n3, 92n47, 246n18
Yannaras, Christos, 131, 144n105, 178, 236n98, 259n47, 259n48, 304n52, 343n28
Yosemite Valley, 210–11

Zabarella, Jacob, 340
Zizioulas, John, 330n150, 344n30, 352–53, 371
Zubiri, Xavier, 204n16, 260

The Irreducibility of the Human Person: A Catholic Synthesis was designed in Minion and composed by Kachergis Book Design of Pittsboro, North Carolina. It was printed on 55-pound Natural Offset and bound by Maple Press of York, Pennsylvania.

www.ingramcontent.com/pod-product-compliance
Lightning Source LLC
Chambersburg PA
CBHW020313010526
44107CB00054B/1818